T0345019

# FUNDAMENTALS OF PERFORMANCE EVALUATION OF COMPUTER AND TELECOMMUNICATION SYSTEMS

# FUNDAMENTALS OF PERFORMANCE EVALUATION OF COMPUTER AND TELECOMMUNICATION SYSTEMS

**MOHAMMAD S. OBAIDAT**

**NOUREDDINE A. BOUDRIGA**

A JOHN WILEY & SONS, INC., PUBLICATION

Published by John Wiley & Sons, Inc., Hoboken, New Jersey
Published simultaneously in Canada

For general information on our other products and services or for technical support, please contact
our Customer Care Department within the United States at (800) 762-2974, outside the United
States at (317) 572-3993 or fax (317) 572-4002.

Wiley also publishes its books in a variety of electronic formats. Some content that appears in print
may not be available in electronic formats. For information about Wiley products, visit our web site
at www.wiley.com.

*Library of Congress Cataloging-in-Publication Data:*

Obaidat, Mohammad S. (Mohammad Salameh), 1952-
    Fundamentals of performance evaluation of computer and telecommunication systems /
Mohammad S. Obaidat, Noureddine A. Boudriga.
        p. cm.
    Includes bibliographical references and index.
    ISBN 978-0-471-26983-0 (cloth)
    1.  Computer systems—Evaluation. 2.  Computer systems—Simulation methods.
    3.  Telecommunication systems—Evaluation. 4.  Telecommunication systems—Simulation
    methods I.  Boudriga, Noureddine. II.  Title.
    QA76.9.E94O23 2009
    004.2–dc22

                                                                    2009028766

Printed in the United States of America

10  9  8  7  6  5  4  3  2  1

To Our Families

Mohammad Salameh Obaidat
Noureddine A. Boudriga

# CONTENTS

# PREFACE

Performance evaluation of computer and telecommunication systems has become an important subject in recent days because of the widespread use and general pervasiveness of these systems in our daily life. Evaluating the performance of these systems is needed at every stage in their life cycle. There is no point in designing and implementing a new system that does not have competitive performance and cost. Performance evaluation of an existing system is also essential as it assists in determining out how well it is performing and whether any improvements are needed to enhance the performance or meet future demands.

The performance of computer and telecommunication systems can be assessed by measurement/real testing, analytic modeling, and simulation techniques. After a system has been built and is running, its performance can be evaluated using the measurement technique. To evaluate the performance of a component or a subsystem that cannot be measured, for example, during the design and development stages it is necessary to use analytic or/and simulation modeling.

The objective of this book is to provide an up-to-date treatment of the fundamental techniques, theories, and applications of performance evaluation of computer and telecommunication systems. It consists of 12 chapters that cover three main techniques of performance evaluation of computer and telecommunication systems along with their applications and case studies.

Chapter 1 introduces the fundamental concepts and viewpoints of performance evaluation of computer and telecommunication systems. It sheds light on objectives, challenges, and application of performance evaluation. It also deals with techniques that can be used, performance metrics, workload characterization, and benchmarking.

Chapter 2 reviews the basic concepts in probability theory that are needed for a better understanding of all topics related to performance analysis. It presents the basic theories in probability theory including conditional probability, sampling, and reasoning with less precise data. In addition, it investigates the fundamental properties of random variables, both discrete and continuous. Regression models and their analysis are discussed along with Markov chains.

In Chapter 3, we focus on the fundamental concepts of the measurement technique, tracing, tools, monitors and monitoring techniques, program optimizers, accounting logs, and traffic issues and solutions.

Chapter 4 discusses the issues related to benchmarking and capacity planning along with the problems, associated with them. The types of benchmarking programs and common mistakes in benchmarking are given. A separate section has been dedicated to capacity planning for Web service, which addresses the scalability, architecture, and network capacity along with server overloading issues for improving the performance of Web servers.

Chapter 5 deals with data representation, graphical representation, ratio game, program profiling, state machine models, finite-state machine (FSM) validation, queuing Petri nets, Petri net-based validation, and advanced topic in validation molding.

Chapter 6 reviews the basics of queueing theory and models along with their applications to performance evaluation of computer and telecommunication systems. Queue parameters and queueing theory notation are examined. Little's law, priority management in queues, common queues such as M/M/m, M/G/1, M/E$_r$/1, M/G/1, and queueing models with insensitive length distribution are all analyzed and examples are given.

Chapter 7 studies the fundamentals properties of queueing networks including major classes of queueing networks, such as open queueing networks, closed queueing networks, Jackson networks, Jackson's Theorem, BCMP networks, Baskett, Chandy, Muntz and Palacios (BCMP) theorem, analysis using flow-equivalent servers, and the product form networks, along with related examples.

Chapter 8 reviews the fundamentals of operational laws, mean value analysis (MVA) technique, approximate MVA technique, the bounding analysis scheme, bottleneck analysis method, Chandy-Neuse Linearizer algorithms, Zahorjan-Eager-Sweillam aggregate queue length algorithm, Asymptotic bounds, and the balanced systems bounds.

Chapter 9 introduces the fundamental concepts of simulation as a performance evaluation technique for computer and telecommunication systems. The principles and basics of simulation technique, simulation terminology, and random-number generation techniques, such as linear congruential, mixed, Tausworthe, and Extended Fibonici schemes, are also studied. It also reviews The state-of-the-art schemes to generate random variates, including Inverse transformation, rejection, characterization, and composition techniques. The testing of random numbers and random variates is also investigated.

Chapter 10 is devoted to a review of the main characteristics of the commonly used distributions in modeling and simulation of computer and telecommunication systems. Some of these distributions are continuous, whereas the others are discrete. Among the major probability distributions that are investigated are the exponential, Poisson distribution, uniform, normal, Weibull, Pareto, geometric, beta, binomial, Gamma, Erlang, chi-square, inverse chi-distribution, F distribution, and student's t-distribution.

In Chapter 11, we study the various techniques used for verifying and validating a simulation model. The chapter deals with both the functional and structural verification processes. Major schemes in verification and validation are investigated and discussed along with examples. We also investigate various techniques that are used in transient removal and simulation stopping.

Finally, Chapter 12 discusses the alternatives for selecting software tools to develop simulation models. A comparison of the simulation languages with the general purpose programming languages is provided to evaluate which language is better suited for simulation and what makes one language better than another. A survey of commonly used simulation packages/tools for modeling computer and telecommunication systems is given.

The book contains numerous examples and case studies along with exercises and problems for possible use as homework and programming assignments. The authors will provide an instructor manual that contains solutions for exercises and problems in the book as well as a set of power point viewgraphs that will be available to instructors who adopt the book for their courses.

The book is an ideal text for a graduate or senior undergraduate course in performance evaluation of computer and telecommunication systems, performance evaluation of communication networks, performance analysis of computer and communication systems, modeling and simulation of computer and telecommunication systems, and performance analysis of computer and telecommunication systems. It can also serve as an excellent reference for practitioners and researchers in performance evaluation as well as for system administrators, computer, electrical, system, and software engineers; and computer and operation research scientists.

We would like to thank the reviewers of the original book proposal for their helpful suggestions and input. Also we are grateful to our students for some of the feedback that we received while class testing the manuscript. Many thanks go to the editors and editorial assistants of John Wiley & Sons for their kind cooperation and fine work.

MOHAMMAD S. OBAIDAT
NOUREDDINE A. BOUDRIGA

# CHAPTER 1

# INTRODUCTION AND BASIC CONCEPTS

Performance evaluation of computer and telecommunication systems has become an increasingly important issue given their general pervasiveness. An evaluation of these systems is needed at every stage in their life. There is no point in designing and implementing a new system that does not have competitive performance/cost ratio. Performance evaluation of an existing system is also essential because it helps to determine how well it is performing and whether any improvements are needed to enhance the performance.

Computer and telecommunication systems performance can be evaluated using the measurement, analytic modeling, and simulation techniques. Once a system has been built and is running, its performance can be evaluated using the measurement technique. To evaluate the performance of a component or a subsystem that cannot be measured, for example, during the design and development phases, it is necessary to use analytic or simulation modeling so as to predict the performance [1–15].

The objective of this book is to provide an up-to-date treatment of the fundamental techniques and applications of performance evaluation of computer and telecommunication systems.

*Fundamentals of Performance Evaluation of Computer and Telecommunication Systems,*
By Mohammad S. Obaidat and Noureddine A. Boudriga
Copyright © 2010 John Wiley & Sons, Inc.

## 1.1  BACKGROUND

Performance evaluation aims at predicting a system's behavior in a quantitative manner. When a new computer and telecommunication system is to be built or an existing system has to be tuned, reconfigured, or adapted, a performance evaluation can be employed to forecast the impact of architectural or implementation modifications on the overall system performance.

Today's computer and telecommunication systems are more complex, more rapidly evolving, and more pervasive and essential to numerous parties that range from individual users to corporations. This results in an increasing interest to find new effective tools and techniques to assist in understanding the behavior and performance of existing systems as well as to predict the performance of the ones that are being designed. Such an understanding can help in providing quantitative answers to questions that arise during the life cycles of the system under study, such as during initial design stages and implementation, during sizing and acquisition, and during evolution and fine tuning.

To evaluate the performance of a system, we can use the measurement technique if the system exists and it is possible to conduct the required experiments and testing on it. However, when the system does not exist or conducting the measurements is expensive or catastrophic, then we rely on simulation and analytic modeling techniques. The last two techniques try to answer important questions related to the design or tuning of the system under study, where the term "system" refers to a collection of hardware, software, and firmware components that make a computer or telecommunication system. It could be a hardware component such as an Asynchronous Transfer Mode (ATM) switch and a central processing unit (CPU); a software system, such as a database system; or a network of several processors, such as a multiprocessor computer system or a local area network (LAN) [1–21].

Examples of the type of predictions that can be made from performance analysis studies include [1–21]:

- The number of stations that can be connected to a LAN and still maintain a reasonable average frame delay and throughput
- The fraction of cells that can be discarded from an ATM system during overload
- The number of sources that can be supported in an Available Bit Rate (ABR) voice service over ATM networks so that a specific cell loss ratio (CLR) threshold is not exceeded
- The fraction of calls that are blocked on outgoing lines of a company's telephone system and how much improvement we can get if an extra line is added
- The improvement in speedup and latency that we can achieve if we add a processor or two to a multiprocessor system
- The best switch architecture for a specific application

- The improvement in mean response time of a network if the copper wires are replaced by optical fiber

All such questions and more can be answered using the three main techniques of performance evaluation. The results from one or more of these techniques can be used to validate the results obtained by the other. For example, we can use analytic results to validate simulation results or vice versa. We can also use the analytic results from a prototype version of the system, which can be designed to validate simulation results and so on.

It is worth mentioning here that validation and versification (V&V) are important procedures that should be performed for any simulation model. Also, validation is needed for analytic models. These subjects are important for performance evaluation, and many conferences and journals have dedicated tracks/section for them [1, 2, 14, 15]. We will deal with V&V in Chapter 11.

## 1.2  PERFORMANCE EVALUATION VIEWPOINTS AND CONCEPTS

All engineering systems should be designed and operated with specific performance requirements in mind. It is essential that all performance requirements of any system to be designed should be stated at the outset and before investing time and money in the final design stages, which include testing and implementation. The work conducted by Erlang in 1909 on telephone exchange is considered the beginning of performance evaluation as a new discipline. Even though the range of performance evaluation is now wide, the fundamentals are the same.

It is desirable to evaluate the performance of a system make sure that it is suitable for the intended applications and that it is cost effective to build it, or if it exists physically, it can be operated and tuned to provide optimum performance under given resource constraints and operating conditions. The best performance metrics and desired operational requirements of a system under study depend on the nature of applications, constraints, and environments. For example, the metrics to be considered for a LAN or a computer system that are operating in a manned space shuttle may be different from those on a campus of a company or college.

Experimentation with the real system or a prototype version of it is usually expensive, laborious, inflexible, and prohibitive. Moreover, it gives accurate information about the system under special cases or a specific set of assumptions. However, analytic modeling and simulation are flexible, inexpensive, and usually provide fast results.

In the context of modeling, we can define a model as an abstraction of the system or subsystem under study. A model can be envisioned as a description of a system by symbolic language or theory to be viewed as a system with which the world of objects can be communicated. Shannon defined a model as " the process of designing a computerized model of a system (or a process) and conducting experiments with this model for the purpose of either understanding the behavior of the system or of evaluating various strategies for the operation of the system" [1, 2].

In the context of performance evaluation, we can provide three possible definitions for the term "system" [1, 2, 14]:

- An assemblage of objects so combined by nature or human as to form an integral unit
- A regularly interacting or interdependent group of objects forming a unified whole [*Webster's Dictionary*]
- A combination of components/objects that act together to perform a function not possible with any of the individual parts [*IEEE Standard Dictionary of Electrical and Electronic Terms*]
- A set of objects with certain interactions between them

From the above definitions, we observe two major features in these definitions:

1. A system consists of interacting objects/components.
2. A system is associated with a function/work that it performs.

It is important to mention here that a system should not always be coupled with physical objects and natural laws as a set of equations that defines a function is considered a system.

Systems can be divided into the following three types:

- Continuous systems: Here the state changes continuously over time.
- Discrete systems: In this type, the state varies in fixed quanta.
- Hybrid systems: Here, the system state variables may change continuously in response to some events, whereas others may vary discretely.

We can also classify systems into stochastic and deterministic types. The stochastic systems contain a certain amount of randomness in their transitions from one state to another. A stochastic system can enter more than one possible state in response to a stimulus. Clearly, a stochastic system is nondeterministic because the next state cannot be unequivocally predicted if the current state and the stimulus are known. In the deterministic systems, the new state of the system is completely determined by the previous state and by the stimulus.

Modeling and simulation is considered one of the best instruments to predict performance as they roll data into knowledge and knowledge into experience. It is also flexible, cost effective, and risk free. In modeling and simulation, we need three types of entities: (1) real system, (2) model, and (3) simulator. These entities have to be understood as well as their interrelation to one another. The real system, if either it exists physically or its design is available, is a supply of raw data, whereas the model is a set of instructions for data generating. The simulator (simulation program) is a tool to implement the model and carry out its instructions [1, 2, 6, 14, 15].

Moreover, systems can be divided into open and closed systems. In a closed system, all state changes are prompted by internal activities, whereas in an open system, state change occurs in response to both internal and external activities.

## 1.3  GOALS OF PERFORMANCE EVALUATION

The objectives of any performance evaluation study depend mainly on the interest, applications, skills, and capabilities of the analysts. Nevertheless, common goals in any performance evaluation study are typical for computer and telecommunication systems [1, 2, 4]. The major ones are briefly described below.

1. **Compare alternative system designs.** Here, the goal is to compare the performance of different systems or component designs for a specific application. Examples include deciding the best ATM switch for a specific application or the type of buffering used in it. Other examples include choosing the optimum number of processors in a parallel processing system, the type of interconnection network, size and number of disk drives, and type of compiler or operating system. The objective of performance analysis in this case is to find quantitatively the best configuration under the considered operating environments.

2. **Procurement.** In this case, the goal is to find the most cost-effective system for a specific application. It is essential to weigh out the benefit of choosing an expensive system that provides a little performance enhancement when compared with a less expensive system.

3. **Capacity planning.** This is of great interest to system administrators and managers of data processing installations. This is done to make sure that adequate resources will be available to meet future demands in a cost-effective manner without jeopardizing performance objectives. In some literature, capacity management, which is used to ensure that the available resources are used to provide the optimum performance, is included under capacity planning. In general, capacity planning is performed using the following main steps: (a) instrument the system, (b) observe it, (c) select the workload, (d) forecast the performance under different configurations and alternatives, and (e) select the best cost-effective configuration alternative.

4. **System tuning.** The objective in this case is to find the set of parameter values that produce the best system performance. For example, disk and network buffer sizes can impact the overall performance. Finding the set of best parameters for these resources is a challenge but is important to have the best performance.

5. **Performance debugging**. In some applications, you may come to a situation where the application or control software of the system is working, but it is slow. Therefore, it is essential to discover through performance analysis why the program is not meeting the performance expectation. Once the cause of the problem is identified, the problem can be corrected.

6. **Set expectation**. This is meant to enable system users to set the appropriate expectations for what a system actually can do. This is imperative for the future planning of new generations of routers, switches, and processors.

7. **Recognize relative performance**. The objective in this circumstance is to quantify the change in performance relative to past experience and previous system generations. It can also be to quantify the performance relative to the customer's expectations or to competing systems.

## 1.4   APPLICATIONS OF PERFORMANCE EVALUATION

The performance evaluation of computer and telecommunication systems is needed for a variety of applications; the major ones are described below [1–3, 5–7]:

- **Design of systems**. It is important that before implementing any system, we conduct a performance evaluation analysis to select the best and most cost-effective design. In general, before designing any new system, one typically has in mind specific architectures, configurations, and performance objectives. Then, all related parameters are chosen to reach the goals. This process entails constructing a model of the system or subsystem at an appropriate level of detail, and this model is evaluated using either analytic modeling or simulation to estimate its performance. It is worth pointing out that analytic modeling may give quick rough results to eliminate inadequate and bad designs; however, simulation would be an effective tool for conducting experiments that can help in making detailed design decisions and avoiding mistakes. Analytic modeling can be used to validate simulation results. In some cases, a prototype version of the system to be designed can be built to make special case validation to simulation and analytic results.

- **System upgrade and tuning**. This process is needed to upgrade or tune the performance of the system or components of the system by either replacing some components with new ones that have better capabilities or by replacing the entire system or subsystem with one depending on the required performance and capacities. The cost, performance, and compatibility dictate the chosen type of system, subsystem, or component, as well as the vendor. In such a case, analytic modeling is used; however, for large and complex systems, simulation is a must. Furthermore, this process may

entail changing resource management policies, such as the buffer allocation scheme, scheduling mechanism, and so on. In applications like these,
direct testing and measurement is the best to use; however, it may not be
feasible in many situations. Analytic techniques may be attractive, but we
may not be able to change the aspects easily. This means that simulation
analysis may be the best in such cases, especially if direct experimentation
is not possible. Nevertheless, if the goal is just to get a rough estimate or to
track the change in output in response to some changes in input
parameters, then analytic modeling is a viable option.

- **Procurement.** In this application, the objective is to select the best system
  from a group of other competing systems. The main criteria are usually the
  cost, availability, compatibility, and reliability. Direct testing may be
  the best for such an application, but it may not be practical. Therefore,
  decisions can be made on some available data with simple modeling.

- **System analysis**. When the system is not performing as it is expected, a
  performance analysis is conducted to find the bottleneck device or cause of
  sluggish behavior. The reason for such a poor performance could be either
  inadequate hardware devices or system management. This means there is a
  need to identify and locate the problem. If the problem is caused by an
  inadequate hardware device, then the system has to be upgraded, and if it
  is caused by poor management, then the system has to be tuned up. In
  general, the system has to be monitored using hardware, software, or
  hybrid monitors to examine the behavior of various management schemes
  under different operating environments and conditions. A measurement
  technique is usually used in such cases to locate the hardware components
  or code in question. However, in some cases, simulation and analytic
  analysis are used, especially if the system is complex.

## 1.5  TECHNIQUES

Three methods can be used to characterize the performance of computer and
telecommunication systems. These are (a) analytic modeling, (b) simulation, and
(c) measurement and testing. These alternatives are arranged here in increasing
order of cost and accuracy. Analytic models are always approximate: This price
must be paid for tractability and obtaining closed-form solution expressions of
the performance metrics in terms of design parameters and variables. However,
they are usually computationally inexpensive, and expressions can be obtained
in a fast manner. Simulations require considerable investment of time in
deriving the model, designing and coding the simulator, and verifying and
validating the model, but they are more flexible, accurate, and credible. Real
measurements and experiments on a variation of a prototype or on the actual
system are the most expensive of all and require considerable engineering
efforts; however, these measurements are the most accurate. It is important to

note that these three methods complement one another and are used in different phases of the development process of the system [1, 5, 6]. Some of them can be used to validate the results obtained by the others.

In the early stage of the design, when the system designer/architect is searching to find the optimum system configuration, it is impossible to carry out experiments on prototype, and it is time consuming to conduct detailed simulation experiments. During this early stage of the design, the designer is interested in basic performance tradeoffs and in narrowing the range of parameters to be considered. Conducting real-time measurement on a prototype or constructing detailed simulation experiments may be tedious and not cost effective. All that is required at this early stage is approximate calculations to indicate the performance tradeoffs. Analytic performance models provide such an approximate initial quick and rough analysis. It is important to keep in mind that almost all analytic models are approximate. Also, there is often no way to bound tightly the accuracy of such models. That is, one cannot guarantee that the real performance measure is within x% of that predicted by the analytic model, for some finite y%. In most cases, the only way to assess the accuracy of the model is to conduct a few simulation runs and compare the simulation results with the analytic results. Although analytic models are approximate, they are accepted because these models themselves might be used to explore design alternatives, and it is sufficient to have approximate estimates of the expected behavior and performance. If a more accurate performance characterization is required, then the designer must turn to the simulation or measurement on a prototype version of the system, which is more expensive. It is worth noting that the accuracy of an analytic model depends on the quality of input data and on the appropriateness of the chosen performance measure. Regardless of how good the analytic model may be, it cannot give accurate results if the input data are inaccurate or not representative of the workload that the system will be subjected to in the real world. That is to say, collecting representative workload data is crucial for accurate performance modeling [1–7].

## 1.6 METRICS OF PERFORMANCE

The selection of performance metrics is essential in performance evaluation. These metrics or measures should be selected with the type of application and service in mind, as a performance metric for one application may not be of interest to another application. A good performance metric should have the following characteristics: (a) the performance metric should allow an unambiguous comparison to be made between systems, (b) it should be possible to develop models to estimate the metric, (c) it should be relevant or meaningful, and (d) the model used to estimate the metric should not be difficult to estimate.

In general, performance evaluation analysts are typically interested in the: (a) frequency of occurrence of a specific event, (b) duration of specific time intervals, and (c) size of some parameter [4, 5–7]. In other words, the interest is in count, time, and size measures.

If the system performs the intended service correctly, its performance can be measured by the rate at which the service is performed, the time needed to perform the service, and the resources consumed while performing the service. These are often called productivity, responsiveness, and usage metric/measures, respectively. The productivity of a multiprocessor computer system is measured by its throughput (number of packets or requests processed per unit time) or speedup (how fast the system compared with a single processor system). The responsiveness of the same system is measured by the mean packet delay, which is the mean time needed to process a packet. The utilization metric gives a measure of the percentage of time the resources of the multiprocessor system are busy for a given load level. The resource [usually a processor, but can be a memory or an input/output (I/O) device] with the highest use is called the bottleneck device [1–4].

Performance evaluation metrics of a computer and telecommunication systems can be classified into the following chief categories [1–2]:

- Higher better metrics (HB). In this category, the higher the value of the metric, the better it is. Productivity comes under this category.
- Lower better metrics (LB). Here, the lower the value of the metric, the better it is. Responsiveness is an example of this type.
- Nominal better metrics (NB). In this class, the performance metric should not be too high or too low. A value of usage between 0.5 and 0.75 is desired. Utilization is an example on such metrics.

Other performance measures that are becoming of great interest to performance analysts are availability and reliability. Availability is quantified by two known measures: (a) mean time to failure (MTTF) and (b) mean time between failures (MTBT) [1–3]. Reliability is defined as the probability that the system survives until some time $t$. If $X$ is time to failure of the system, where $X$ is assumed to be a random variable, then reliability, $R(t)$, can be expressed as $R(t) = P(X > t) = 1 - F(t)$, where $F(t)$ is the distribution function of the system lifetime $X$ [1, 4, 8].

It is important to point out that performance of computer and telecommunication systems from the viewpoint of performance tends to be optimistic as it usually ignores the failure-repair behavior of the system. A new trend these days is to consider the performance, availability, and capacity together. This process is important because in a computer communication network, the failure of a link or router causes partial outage of the network, namely, the decrease in network's capacity that affects the system's quality of service (QoS) as well as its performance [5–8].

## 1.7   WORKLOAD CHARACTERIZATION AND BENCHMARKING

Regardless of which performance evaluation technique is used, we need to provide input to the model or real system under study. Many new computer and network applications and programming paradigms are constantly emerging. Understanding the characteristics of today's emerging workloads is essential to design efficient and cost-effective architectures for them. It is important to characterize web servers, database systems, transaction processing systems, multimedia, networks, ATM switches, and scientific workloads. It is also useful to design models for workloads. An accurate characterization of application and operation system behavior leads to improved architectures and designs. Analytical modeling of workloads is a challenge and needs to be performed carefully. This is because it takes significant amounts of time to perform trace-driven or execution-driven simulations due to the increased complexity of the processor, memory subsystem, and the workload domain. Quantitative characterization of workloads can help significantly in the creation and validation of analytic models. They can capture the essential features of systems and workloads, which can be helpful in providing early predication about the design. Moreover, quantitative and analytical characterization of workloads is important in understanding and exploiting their interesting features [10–12]. Figure 1.1 depicts an overall block diagram of workload characterization process.

In this context, there are two types of relevant inputs: (a) parameters that can be controlled by the system designer, such as resource allocation buffering technique and scheduling schemes, and (b) input generated by the environments in which the system under study is used such as interarrival times. Such inputs are used to drive the real system if the measurement technique or the simulation model is used. They also can be used to determine adequate distributions for the analytic and simulation models. In the published literature, such inputs are often called workloads.

Workload characterization is considered an important issue in performance evaluation, as it is not always clear what (a) level of detail the workload should have (b) aspects of the workload are significant, and (c) method to be used to represent the workload. In workload characterization, the term "user" may or

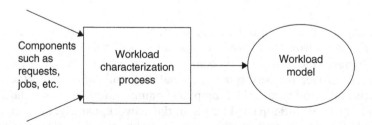

**FIGURE 1.1.** Overall workload characterization process.

may not be a human being. In most related literature, the term "workload component" or "workload unit" is used instead of user. This means that workload characterization attempts to characterize a typical component. Examples of workload components include (a) applications such as website, e-mail service, or program development (b) sites such as several sites for the same company, and (c) user sessions such as monitoring complete sessions from user login and logout and applications that can be run during such sessions. Measured quantities, requests, and resource demands used to characterize the workload are called parameters. Transaction types include (a) packet sizes, (b) source and destination of packets, and (c) instructions. In general, workload parameters are preferable over system parameters for the characterization of workloads. The parameters of significant impact are included, whereas those of minor impact are usually excluded. Among the techniques that can be used to specify workload are (a) averaging, (b) single-parameter histogram, (c) multiparameter histogram, (d) Markov models. (e) clustering, (f) use of dispersion measures such as coefficient of variation (COV), and (g) principal-component analysis [10–12].

The averaging is the simplest scheme. It relies on presenting a single number that summarizes the parameter values observed, such as arithmetic mean, median/mode/geometric or harmonic means. The arithmetic means may not be appropriate for certain applications. In such cases, the median, mode, geometric means, and harmonic means are used. For example, in the case of addresses in a network, the mean or median is meaningless, therefore, the mode is often chosen.

In the single-parameter histogram scheme, we use histograms to show the relative frequencies of various values of the parameter under consideration. The drawback of using this scheme is that when using individual-parameter histograms, these histograms ignore the correlation among various parameters. To avoid the problem of correlation among different parameters in the single-parameter scheme, the multiparameter scheme is often used. In the latter scheme, a $k$-dimensional histogram is constructed to describe the distribution of $k$ workload parameters. The difficulty with the same technique is that it is not easy to construct joint histograms for more than two parameters.

Markov models are used in cases when the next request is dependant only on the last request. In general, we can say that if the next state of the system under study depends only on the current state, then the overall systems is behavior follows the Markov model. Markov models are often used in queuing analysis. We can illustrate the model by a transition matrix that gives the values of the probabilities of the next state given present state. Figure 1.2 shows the transition probability matrix for a job's transition in a multiprocessor computer system. Any node in the system can be in one of three possible states: (a) active state where the node (computer) is executing a program (code) using its own cache memory, (b) wait (queued) state where the node waits to access the main memory to read/write data, and (c) access state where the node's request to access the main memory has been granted. The probabilities of going from

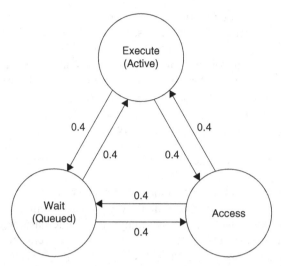

**FIGURE 1.2.** State transition diagram for the Markov model of the multiprocessor system.

one state to the other make what is called the transition matrix [16]; see Figure 1.2.

The clustering scheme is used when the measured workload is made of a huge number of components. In such a case, these huge components are categorized into a small number of clusters/tiers such that the components in one cluster are as akin to each other as possible. This is almost similar to what is used in clustering in pattern recognition. One class member may be selected from each cluster to be its representative and to conduct the needed study to find out what system design decisions are needed for that cluster/group.

Figure 1.3 shows the number of cells delivered to node A and the numbers delivered to node B in a computer network. As shown in Figure 1.3, the cells can be classified into six groups (clusters) that represent the six different links that they arrive on. Therefore, instead of using 60 cells for each specific analysis, we can use only 6 cells.

The use of dispersion measure can give better information about the variability of the data, as the mean scheme alone is insufficient in cases where the variability in the data set is large. The variability can be quantified using the variance, standard deviation or the COV. In a data set, the variance is given by:

$$\text{Variance} = s^2 = 1/(n-1) \sum_{i=1}^{n} (x_i - x')'$$

and COV $= s/x'$

where $x'$ is the sample mean with size $n$. A high COV means high variance, which means in such a case, the mean is not sufficient. A zero COV means that

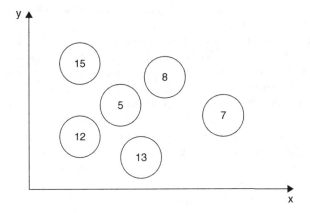

**FIGURE 1.3.** An example of 60 cells in 6 groups (clusters).

the variance is zero, and in such a case, the mean value gives the same information as the complete data set.

The principal-component analysis is used to categorize workload components using the weighted sum of their parameter values. If $d_i$ is the weight for the $i^{th}$ parameter $x_i$, then the weighted sum $W$ is as follows:

$$W = \sum_{i=1}^{k} \alpha_i x_i$$

The last expression can be used to group the components into clusters such as low, medium, and high-demand classes [2, 14].

The weights to be used in such cases can be determined using the principal-component analysis that permits finding the weights $w_j$'s such that $W_i$'s provide the maximum discrimination when compared with other components. The value of $W_i$ is called the principal factor or principal component. In general, if we are given a set of $k$ parameters, such as $x1, x2,...., xn$, then the principal-component analysis produces a set of factors and $W1, W2, .......,  Wk$, such that: (a) the $W$'s are linear combinations of $x$'s, (b) the $W$'s form an orthogonal set, which means that their inner product is zero:

Inner Product $= \Sigma W_j \cdot W_j = 0$, and the $W$'s form an ordered set so that $W1$ describes the highest percent of the variance in resource demands, $W2$ describes a lower highest percent, and so forth.

If the system under study is to be used for a specific application, such as airline reservation, online banking, or stock market trade, then representative application programs from these applications or a representative subset of functions for these applications should be used during the performance evaluation study. Usually, benchmark programs are described in terms of the functions to be performed, and they exercise all resources in the system such as peripherals, databases, networks, and so on.

The term "benchmark" is often used to mean workload or kernel. Benchmarks are usually run by vendors or third parties for typical configurations and workloads. This process should be done with care as it may leave room for misinterpretation and misuse of the measures. Clearly, it is essential to perform this task accurately. A benchmark program is used as a standard reference for comparing performance results using different hardware or different software tools. It is supposed to capture processing and data movement characteristics of a category of application. Benchmarks are meant to measure and predict the performance of systems under study and to reveal their design weakness and strong aspects. A benchmark suite is basically a set of benchmark programs together with a set of specific rules that govern the test conditions and methods such as testbed platform environment, input data, output results, and evaluation metrics (measures). A benchmark family is a set of benchmark suites.

In computer systems, benchmarks can be classified based on the application, such as commercial applications, scientific computing, network services, signal processing, scientific computing, and image processing. Moreover, we can classify benchmarks into microbenchmarks, macrobenchmarks, synthetic benchmark programs, program kernels, and application benchmark programs [9, 13].

A microbenchmark tends to be a synthetic kernel. Microbenchmarks measure a specific portion of the computer system, such as the CPU speed, memory speed, I/O speed, interconnection network, and so on. A small program can be used to test only the processor-memory interface, or the floating-point unit, independent of other components of the system. In general, microbenchmarks are used to characterize the maximum possible performance that could be obtained if the overall system's performance were limited by that single component. Examples on microbenchmarks include [9]:

- LINPAC: This suite measures numerical computing, and it is a collection of Fortran subroutines that analyzes and solves linear equations and linear least-square problems.
- LMBENCH: This suite measures system calls and data movement operation. It is portable and used to measure the operating system overheads and capability of data transfer among the processor, cache, main memory, network, a disk or various Unix platforms.
- STREAM: This simple synthetic benchmark measures sustainable bandwidth of memory and the corresponding computation rate.

A macrobenchmark measures the performance of the system as a whole. Basically, it compares different systems when running a specific application on them. This is of great interest to the system buyer. Keep in mind that this class of benchmarks does not reveal why the system performs well or bad.

Usually, this class of benchmarks is used for parallel computer systems. Examples on macrobenchmark programs include [9, 16–21] the following:

- NPB suite: The Numerical Aerodynamic Simulation (NAS) Parallel Benchmark (NPB) was developed by the (NAS) program at National Aeronautics and Space Administration (NASA) at Ames for performance evaluation of supercomputers. It consists of five kernels: Embarrassing Pascal (EP), multigrid method (MG), conjugate gradient method (CG), fast fourier-based method for solving a three-dimensional (3D) partial differential equation (FT), and Integer Sorting (IS), as well as the simulated applications block lower triangular, block upper triangular (LU), scalar penta-diagonal (SP) and block tri-diagonal (BT) programs.

- PARKBENCH: This was called after the Parallel Kernel and Benchmarks committee. The current benchmarks are for distributed memory multi-computers, coded using Fortran 77 plus Parallel Virtual Machine (PVM) or Message Passing Interface (MPI) for message passing.

- STAP: The Space-Time Adaptive Processing (STAP) benchmark suite is basically a set of real-time, radar signal processing programs originally developed at MIT Lincoln Laboratory. The suite consists of computational-intensive programs that require one to perform $10^{10}$-$10^{14}$ FLOPS.

- TPC: This was developed by the Transaction Processing Performance Council. TPC has released five benchmarks: TPC-A, TPC-B, TBC-C, TPC-D, and TPC-E. The first two released benchmarks became obsolete in 1995.

- SPEC: This suite was developed by Standard Performance Evaluation Corporation (SPEC), which is a nonprofit corporation that is made of major vendors. It is becoming the most popular benchmark suite worldwide. SPEC started with benchmarks that measure CPU performance, but now it has suites that measure client-server systems, commercial applications, I/O subsystems, and so on. Among the suites, there are SPECT95, SPEChpc96, SPECweb96, SFS, SDM, GPC, SPEC SFS97, SPECjAp, and SPECjAppServer2001, which is a client/server benchmark for measuring SPEC HPC2002, and SPECviewperf 7.1. SPEC periodically publishes performance results of various systems, both in hard copy and on their website (http://www.spec.org).

  In 2003, SPECapc (SPEC application, performance, characterization) releases the new Solid Edge V12 benchmark, and SPECviewperf 7.1. SPECapc for Solid Edge Version 12 is an updated benchmark based on new features in the software's latest version. The new version increases the graphics and CPU workloads without requiring additional memory. The CPU tests now include a recompute calculation for a part with 500 features and a mass property calculation of the assembly. SPECviewperf 7.1 inserts a small amount of variation at regular intervals within its application-based test files, called viewsets. This ensures that the test system examines and processes each frame individually, as it would in typical real-world applications. For more updated information, visit SPEC website [17].

Despite the problems involved in using the instruction mix to evaluate performance of computer systems, there is still interest in them. An instruction mix is attractive for some analysts in that it abstracts many details of real application programs. An instruction mix is a specification of different instructions coupled with their usage frequency. Examples of an instruction mix include the Gibson mix, which was originally developed by Jack C. Gibson for the IBM 704 system [1, 2].

The program kernel is a generalization of the instruction mix. It is used to characterize the main portion of a specific type of application program. The Kernel benchmark is usually a small program that has been extracted from a large application program. Because the kernel is small, including a dozen lines of code, it should be easy to port it to many different systems. Evaluating the performance of different systems by running such a small kernel can provide an insight into the relative performance of these systems. Because kernels do not exercise memory hierarchy, which is a major bottleneck in most systems, they are of limited value to make a conclusive overall performance comparison or prediction of system performance. Examples of kernels include Puzzle, Tree Searching, Ackermann's Function, and Application benchmark programs are often used when the computer system under evaluation is meant to be used for a specific application, such as an airline reservation or scientific computing. These benchmarks are usually described in terms of the functions to be performed and make use of almost all resources of the system. Keep in mind that application benchmarks are real and complete programs that produce useful results. Collection of such programs is often made on emphasizing one application. To reduce the time needed to run the entire set of programs, they usually use artificial small input data sets, which may limit the application's ability to model memory behavior and I/O requirement accurately? They are considered effective in giving good results. Examples of such benchmark programs include the Debit-Credit benchmark, which is used to compare transaction processing systems [9, 17–21].

Network quality benchmarking services is designed to provide independent examination of network quality and performance. QoS is measured externally based on drive tests, whereas performance is measured internally based on network management system data. Quality benchmarking services for a network is-useful for performance target setting and instant comparison. It is also useful for long-term monitoring. Its main benefits include (a) objective evaluation of network quality, (b) end-user point of view (c) comparison with competitors, and (d) good for long-term network planning.

### 1.7.1  Case Study: Website Characterization

The phenomenal growth of the World-Wide Web (WWW), in both the volume of information on it and the numbers of users desiring access to it, is dramatically increasing the performance requirements for large-scale information servers.

WWW server performance is a central issue in providing ubiquitous, reliable, and efficient information access [10–12].

It is important that the WWW traffic workload be understood as it is crucial in the analysis of a server's performance. Capturing the main characteristics of such systems, such as the distributions of file sizes and buffering schemes, is vital to provide a quantitative measure of the aggregate overall advantage of a particular server system's optimization. Workload generators that can be used for such systems include SpecWeb96, WebStone, and SURGE [10–12].

In the characterization of a web server, we need to choose parameters that best describe the characteristics of the workload of the servers and system software used, monitor the systems to obtain some raw performance data, analyze performance data, and finally construct a workload model of the system under investigation. Workload characterization allows us to understand the current state of the system under investigation. Characterizing workload is also essential to the design of new system components [11, 12].

In Arlitt and Jin [10] from Hewlett-Packard (HP) have conducted a workload characterization of the of the 1998 World Cup website. Measurements from the World Cup website were collected over a 3-month period, and during this time, the site received 1.35 billion requests, which is considered large, and if not the largest Web workload analyzed to date, it is definitely one of the largest. The authors determined how Web server workloads are evolving. They found that improvement in the caching architecture of the World-Wide Web are changing the workloads of Web servers and that major improvements to that architecture are still necessary.

World Cup 1998 was held in France from June 10 through July 12, 1998. It was commonly called, France '98, and it is considered the most widely covered media event in history. The estimated cumulative television audience is about 40 billion who watched the 64 matches, more than twice the cumulative television audience of the 1996 Summer Olympic Games in Atlanta, Georgia. The URL of France '98 was as follows: www.france98.com. It received more than 1 billion client requests during the tournament [10].

The World Cup tournament is held once every 4 years to determine the best soccer (called football outside the United States) team in the world. This tournament is open to all countries worldwide. Because of the number of participating teams, a qualifying round is usually used to select the teams that will play in the World Cup tournament. The qualifying round for France '98 was held between March 1996 at November 1997 and out of the 172 countries that participated only 30 were selected to compete in France '98, along with the host country, France, and the reigning champions, Brazil. Each match lasted for 90 minutes in length and was played in two 45-minute halves. The website of the 1998 World Cup provided current scores of the matches in real time. Moreover, fans were able to access previous match results; player statistics, player info such as there biographies, ages, and so on; team backgrounds;

information in English and French about stadiums; and local attractions; a wide range of photos and sound clips from the game; and some interviews with players and coaches. Fans were able to download free software, such as World Cup screensavers and wallpapers from the France '98 website [22]. Several companies cooperated to establish the website, which includes: France Telecom, EDS, Hewlett-Packard, and Sybase. Thirty servers were used, and were distributed across four locations: 4 servers in Paris, 10 servers in Herndon, Virginia; 10 servers in Plano, Texas; and 6 servers in Santa Clara, California. The creation and updating of all web pages were done in France. A Cisco Distributed Director was used to distributed client requests across the four locations where various load balancers were used to distribute the incoming requests among the available servers.

Arlitt and Williamson in [10] observed the following main characteristics in the web of the World Cup workload and the performance implications of these characteristics, which include the following:

1. HTTP/1.1 clients that have become more common, accounting for 21% of all requests. Widespread deployment of HTTP/1.1 compliant clients and servers is necessary for the functionality of HTTP/1.1 to be fully exploited.
2. About 88% of all requests were for image files; an additional 10% were for HTML files, signifying that most users interests were in cacheable files.
3. About 19% of all responses were "Not Modified," signifying that cache consistency traffic had a greater impact in the World Cup workload than in previous Web server workloads [11].
4. The workload was rather bursty.
5. For timeouts of 100 seconds or less, many users' sessions contained only a single request and a single response. Arlitt and Wiliamson [10] believed that this is due to improved Web caching architecture that now exists, which has potential implications on both server and protocol design.
6. During periods of peak user interest in World Cup site, the volume of cache consistency traffic increased noticeably.

## 1.8 SUMMARY

Performance evaluation can be considered both an art and science. This discipline has become more and more important because of the complexity and widespread applications of both computer and telecommunication systems. This chapter aimed to provides an introduction and background information to performance evaluation. We discussed the viewpoint and chief concepts as well as the objectives of performance evaluation. Then we reviewed the main application areas and techniques. Workload characterization and benchmarking were addressed along with examples.

# REFERENCES

[1] M. S. Obaidat, and G. I. Papadimitriou (Eds.), "Applied System Simulation: Methodologies and Applications," Springer, New York; 2003.

[2] R. Jain, "The Art of Computer Systems Performance Analysis," Wiley, New York, 1991.

[3] K. Kant, "Introduction to Computer System Performance Evaluation," McGraw-Hill, New York, 1992.

[4] D. J. Lilja, "Measuring Computer Performance," Cambridge University Press, Cambridge, UK, 2000.

[5] M. S. Obaidat, "Advances in Performance Evaluation of Computer and Telecommunications Networking," Computer Communication Journal, Vol. 25, Nos. 11–12, pp. 993–996, 2002.

[6] M. S. Obaidat, "ATM Systems and Networks: Basics Issues, and Performance Modeling and Simulation," Simulation: Transactions of the Society for Modeling and Simulation International, Vol. 78, No. 3, pp. 127–138, 2003.

[7] M. S. Obaidat, "Performance Evaluation of Telecommunication Systems: Models Issues and Applications," Computer Communications Journal, Vol. 34, No. 9, pp. 753–756, 2003.

[8] M. C. Ghanbari, J. Hughes, M. C. Sinclair, and J. P. Eade, "A Principles of Performance Engineering for Telecommunication and Information Systems," IEE, Herts, UK, 1997.

[9] K. Hwang, and Z. Xu, "Scalable Parallel Computing," McGraw-Hill, New York, 1998.

[10] M. Arlitt, and T. Jin, "Workload Characterization of the 1998 World Cup Website," HP Technical Report 1999–35R1, Hewlett-Packard, 1999.

[11] M. Arlitt, and C. Williamson, "Internet Web Servers: Workload Characterization and Performance Implications," Transactions on Networking, Vol. 5, No. 5, pp. 631–645, 1997.

[12] L. John, and A. Maynard, (Eds.), "Workload Characterization of Emerging Applications," Springer, New York, 2003.

[13] J. L. Hennessy, and D. A. Patterson, "Computer Architecture: A Quantitative Approach," Morgan, Kaufmann, 3rd edition, 2003.

[14] J. Banks, J. S. Crason II, B. L. Nelson, and D. Nicol, "Discrete-Event System Simulation," 3rd edition, Prentice Hall, Upper Saddle River, NJ, 2001.

[15] S. M. Ross, "Simulation," 2nd edition, Harcourt Academic Press, San Diego, 1997.

[16] M. S. Obaidat, "Performance Evaluation of the IMPS Multiprocessor System," Journal of Computers and Electric Engineering, Vol. 15, No. 4, pp. 121–130, 1989.

[17] The Standard Performance Evaluation Corporation: http://www.spec.org

[18] http://imls.lib.utexas.edu/redesign/slideshow/tsld009.html

[19] NAS Parallel Benchmarks: http://science.nas.nasa.gov/software/npb/

[20] Parkbench Parallel Benchmarks: http://www.netlib.org/parbench/

[21] Transaction Processing Council (TPC) Benchmarks: http://www.tpc.org/

[22] www.france98.com

## EXERCISES

1. Compare and contrast the possible techniques to evaluate a computer or a network system.

2. Visit the website of SPEC and write a report on the new benchmark programs that have been released recently and their applications.

3. For each of the following computer and telecommunications systems, give two performance metrics that can used to assess its performance:

   a. A web sever

   b. WiMax network

   c. A Wi-Fi wireless LAN

   d. A cross-bar–based multiprocessor computer system

   e. An airline reservation system

4. Describe what you think would be the most effective way to evaluate each of the following systems:

   a. A 1000-processor massively parallel computer system

   b. The performance of an ATM-based LAN system

   c. A battlefield-communication system

   d. A cellular network in a large city

5. Explain the role of empirical experimental studies and trace-driven simulation analysis in the performance evaluation of computer and telecommunication systems.

6. To estimate the performance of a multiplexer, the packet arrival should be modeled accurately. Recent empirical studies have shown that the Poisson process is an inaccurate model for the packet arrival process. The statistical structure of the packet arrival process is more complex than assuming it to follow a Poisson process or a finite source models that are often used for modeling call arrivals.

   Explain why this statement is correct. What is the process that is used nowadays to accurately model such an arrival process? Give examples from published literature.

# CHAPTER 2

# PROBABILITY THEORY REVIEW

Probability is a numerical measure of the likelihood of an event. It is a number, from 0 to 1, that is attached to an event. Probabilities are generally hard to measure. However, it is easy to measure probabilities of events that are extremely rare. In addition, one can observe that when a sequence of experiments forms an independent trials process, the possible outcomes for each experiment are the same and occur with the same probability, which means that the outcomes of the previous experiments do not influence the predictions for the outcomes of the next experiment.

Probability theory also allows the study of chance processes for which prediction for future experiments is dependent on the knowledge of previous outcomes. In fact, when we observe a sequence of likelihood experiments, all the past outcomes could influence the predictions for the next experiment. In particular, the study of a special type of likelihood processes, called Markov chain, where the outcome of a given experiment can influence the outcome of the next experiment, has been extensively studied in the literature. The Markov chains have observed a large range of application in communication networks and computer systems.

In this chapter, we introduce the essential concepts in probability theory needed for a better understanding of the following chapters in this book. To this end, we present the basic concepts including conditional probability, sampling, and reasoning with less precise data. In a second step, we study the basic properties of random variables, discrete and continuous. Then, we introduce the

*Fundamentals of Performance Evaluation of Computer and Telecommunication Systems,*
By Mohammad S. Obaidat and Noureddine A. Boudriga
Copyright © 2010 John Wiley & Sons, Inc.

regression models and their analysis and discuss the basic ideas behind the distribution functions. Finally, we develop a study of the Markov chains.

## 2.1 BASIC CONCEPTS ON PROBABILITY THEORY

To introduce the probability theory, let us consider a random experiment of which all possible results are included in a nonempty set, denoted by $\Omega$, which is usually called the sample space. An element $\omega \in \Omega$ is often called a sample point of the experiment. An event of a random experiment is specified as a subset of $\Omega$, An event $\alpha$ is called true if the simple point $\omega \in \Omega$ has been chosen with $\omega \in \alpha$. Otherwise, it is called false. A set $A$ of events in $\Omega$ is called algebra if the following statements are satisfied [1, 2]:

- $\Omega \in A$
- If $\alpha, \beta \in A$, then $\alpha \cup \beta \in A$ and $\alpha \cap \beta \in A$
- if $\alpha \in A$ and $\bar{\alpha}$ is the complementary subset of $\alpha$, then $\bar{\alpha} \in A$

**Example.** Let $\Omega = [0, 1] \times [0, 1]$ be the unit square and $\sigma$ be the set of all sets of the form $A \times B$, where $A$ and $B$ are interval. Thus, the smallest algebra $\Delta(\sigma)$ containing $\sigma$ is the set containing the empty set and the objects of the form $\bigcup_{i \in I} \sigma_i$, where $I$ is a finite set of integers. To show this, one can easily observe that: a) $\Omega \in \Delta(\sigma)$; b) the empty set is an element of $\Omega$; c) the union and intersection of elements of $\Delta(\sigma)$ are also elements of $\Delta(\sigma)$; and d) any other algebra containing $\sigma$ contains $\Delta(\sigma)$. The algebra $\Delta(\sigma)$ is called the algebra generated by (or the closure of) $\sigma$.

Now, let $A$ be an algebra, a function $\pi : A \to R^+$ is called a measure on $A$ if, for every pair of disjoint sets of events $\alpha, \beta \in A$, we have $\pi(\alpha \cup \beta) = \pi(\alpha) + \pi(\beta)$. We say that a measure $\pi$ is a probability measure on $A$ if $\pi$ takes its values in [0, 1] and $\pi(\Omega) = 1$. Obviously, a measure satisfies the following properties [3]:

- $\pi(Emptyset) = 0$
- $\pi(\bigcup_{i=1}^{n} \alpha_i) = \sum_{i=1}^{n} \pi(\alpha_i)$ for any finite set of pairwise disjoint events $\alpha_1, .., \alpha_n \in A$
- $\pi(\alpha \cup \beta) = \pi(\alpha) + \pi(\beta) - \pi(\alpha \cap \beta)$ for all pair $\alpha, \beta \in A$

More generally, let $\alpha_1, .., \alpha_n \in A$ ; then the Probability $\Pr(\bigcup_{i=1}^{n} \alpha_i)$ can be computed recursively as follows:

$$\Pr\left(\bigcup_{i=1}^{n} \alpha_i\right) = \sum_{k=1}^{n} (-1)^{k+1} \sum_{i_1 < .. < i_k} \Pr\left(\bigcap_{j=1}^{k} \alpha_{ij}\right)$$

For the special case where $n = 2$, we obtain:

$$\Pr(\alpha_1 \cup \alpha_2) = \pi(\alpha_1) + \pi(\alpha_2) - \pi(\alpha_1 \cap \alpha_2)$$

Special cases of inequalities, referred to as Boole's inequalities, can be deduced from the preceding equation. They are as follows:

$$\sum_{k=1}^{n} \Pr(\alpha_i) \geq \Pr\left(\bigcup_{i=1}^{n} \alpha_i\right) \geq \sum_{k=1}^{n} \Pr(\alpha_i) - \sum_{1 \leq i < j \leq n} \Pr(\alpha_i \cap \alpha_j)$$

Finally, let us define the probability of an event $\alpha$ to be true, with respect to a probability measure $\pi$, as $\pi(\alpha)$. The 3-tuple $(\Omega, A, \pi)$ will be called *probability space* if, and only if, $A$ is an algebra in $\Omega$ and $\pi$ is a probability measure.

**Example.** Assume that $n$ packets need to be placed in $n$ buffers in a switch belonging to a communication network. Each packet is placed in a buffer that is chosen randomly, independently, and uniformly. Then let us compute (a) the probability that a given buffer contains at least $k$ packets and show that $\frac{1}{2}$ is an upper bound for the probability of having $k$ packets in a buffer and (b) a lower bound for the probability of having at least one packet at a buffer. To do this, let $\alpha_{i,k}$, $1 \leq i \leq n$, be the event that buffer $i$ contains $k$ packets and $E_k$ be the event that there exists a buffer with at least $k$ packets. Then $E_k = \bigcup_{i=1}^{n} \alpha_{i,k}$ and the Boole's inequality shows that

$$P(E_k) \leq \sum_{k=1}^{n} \Pr(\alpha_{i,k})$$

The computation of $\Pr(\alpha_{i,k})$ can be performed using events $\alpha_{i,F}$, where $F \subseteq \{1, .., n\}$ and $i \in \{1, ..., n\}$. Event $\alpha_{i,F}$ states that the packets in buffer $i$ are characterized by $F$. Obviously, we have $\alpha_{i,k} = \bigcup_{F: |F|=k} \alpha_{i,F}$ and

$$P(\alpha_{i,k}) \leq \sum_{F: [F]=k} \Pr(\alpha_{i,F})$$

The number of subsets $F \subseteq \{1, .., n\}$, $|F| = k$ is equal to $\binom{n}{k}$, and the probability $\Pr(\alpha_{i,F})$ is equal to $\frac{1}{n^{|F|}} = \frac{1}{n^k}$. Therefore,

$$\Pr(E_k) \leq n \binom{n}{k} \frac{1}{n^k}$$

A classic computation shows that

$$n\binom{n}{k}\frac{1}{n^k} \leq n.2^{-\log n-1} \leq \frac{1}{2}$$

This proves (a). To compute the second bound, let $\beta_i$ be the event that exactly $k$ packets are placed in buffer 1 and $\beta$ be the event of having at least one packet at buffer 1. Then $\beta = \bigcup_{1\leq i\leq n} \beta_i$. The Boole's equation gives:

$$\Pr(\beta) = \Pr(\bigcup_{i=1}^{n} \beta_i) \geq \sum_{k=1}^{n} \Pr(\beta_i) - \sum_{1\leq i<j\leq n} \Pr(\beta_i \cap \beta_j)$$

$$= \sum_{i=1}^{n}\frac{1}{n} - \sum_{1\leq i<j\leq n}\frac{1}{n^2} = 1 - \binom{n}{2}\frac{1}{n^2}$$

$$\geq 1 - \tfrac{1}{2} = \tfrac{1}{2}$$

**Example.** Three optical packets $A$, $B$, and $C$, are contending for an output port, in a switch node. We assume that one and only one packet can get through the port. The sample space may be taken as the 3-element set $\Omega = \{A,B,C\}$, where each element corresponds to the outcome of that candidate's getting into the output port. Suppose that $A$ and $B$ have the same chance of winning, and that $C$ has only $1/2$ the chance of $A$ or $B$. Thus, we assign the following elementary probabilities:

$$p(A) = p(B) = 2p(C)$$

Since $p(A) + p(B) + p(C) = 1$, we deduce that

$$2p(C) + 2p(C) + p(C) = 1$$

which implies that $5p(C) = 1$. Hence,

$$p(A) = \frac{2}{5}, \ p(B) = \frac{2}{5}, \ p(C) = \frac{1}{5}$$

Let $E$ be the event that either packet $A$ or $C$ gets to the output port. Then $E = \{A,C\}$ and

$$p(E) = p(A) + p(C) = \frac{3}{5}$$

### 2.1.1  Conditional Probability

The conditional probability of event $\beta$ assuming an event $\alpha$, such that $\Pr(\alpha) > 0$ is denoted by $\Pr(\beta|\alpha)$ and defined as follows:

$$Pr(\beta|\alpha) = \frac{Pr(\alpha \cap \beta)}{Pr(\alpha)}$$

This can be generalized as follows: If $\alpha_1, .., \alpha_n$ are events satisfying $Pr(\bigcap_{1 \le i \le n-1} \alpha_i) \ne 0$, then:

$$Pr(\bigcap_{1 \le i \le n} \alpha_i) = \prod_{j=1}^{n} Pr(\alpha_i \Big| \bigcap_{k=1}^{j-1} \alpha_k)$$

Using the particular cases of this formula, when $n = 2$, we obtain two equalities:

$$Pr(\beta|\alpha) \cdot Pr(\alpha) = Pr(\alpha \cap \beta) = Pr(\alpha|\beta) \cdot Pr(\beta)$$

which are valid when $Pr(\alpha) > 0$ and $Pr(\beta) > 0$. This gives the so-called Bayes's formula:

$$Pr(\alpha|\beta) = \frac{Pr(\alpha) \cdot Pr(\beta|\alpha)}{Pr(\beta)}$$

This allows the following definition: Two events $\alpha$ and $\beta$ are called *independent* if, and only if, $Pr(\alpha|\beta) = Pr(\alpha)$, or equivalently $Pr(\beta|\alpha) = Pr(\beta)$. In the opposite, if $Pr(\alpha|\beta) \ne Pr(\alpha)$, then the two events are called *correlated*. Two disjoint events $\alpha$ and $\beta$ with nonzero probabilities cannot be independent because the $Pr(\beta|\alpha) = \frac{Pr(\alpha \cap \beta)}{Pr(\alpha)} = 0$ implies that $Pr(\beta|\alpha) = 0$. On the one hand, because $Pr(\beta) \ne 0$, we deduce that $Pr(\beta|\alpha) \ne Pr(\beta)$. On the other hand, one can show in this case that:

$$Pr(\alpha \cup \beta) = Pr(\alpha) + Pr(\beta)$$

**Example.** Consider in a switch the problem of $n$ packets to be placed in $n$ buffers randomly, independently, and uniformly as discussed earlier. Let $\alpha$ be the event that buffer 1 has no packets, and let $\beta$ the event that some buffer $i$, for fixed $i$, has no packets. Then, for n = 3

$$Pr(\beta|\alpha) = \frac{1}{8}, \ Pr(\beta) = \frac{8}{27}$$

This shows that the two events are correlated.

## 2.2  ELEMENTARY SAMPLING

It is important to realize how much of probability theory can be derived from no more than the conditional probability formulas that we have established in the previous section. Many important results that are often thought to lie beyond the domain of probability theory can be derived. The applications of the theory given in this section are rather simple compared with the serious scientific inference that we hope to achieve later in the following sections. Nevertheless, our reason for considering them in close detail is not only of simple pedagogical form. Failure to understand the logic of these concepts can have serious consequences [4, 5].

### 2.2.1  Sampling Without Replacement

Let us consider a traditional problem that we present using a simple example in communication. A buffer in a switch contains $N$ packets, which are identical in their structure and header except that they carry sequence numbers $1, 2, ..., N$. The packets are assumed to belong to two different flows. The first flow, say $R$, has $M$ packets; and the second flow, say $W$, has the remaining $(N - M)$ packets. The switch takes a packet from the buffer randomly, serves it and records its flow type, drops it, and repeats the process until $n$ packets have been dropped, $0 \leq n \leq N$.

Let $\alpha_i$ and $\beta_i$ be the events that "*the packet serviced at the ith extraction belongs to flow R*" and the "*packet serviced at the ith extraction belongs to flow W*," respectively. Since only packets from flows R and W can be extracted, we have $\Pr(\alpha_i) + \Pr(\beta_i) = 1$ , which leads to saying that the events are related by negation; i.e., $\overline{\alpha_i} = \beta_i$ . We also have, for $i = 1$,

$$\Pr(\alpha_1) = \tfrac{M}{N} \quad \text{and} \quad \Pr(\beta_1) = \tfrac{N-M}{N}$$

These equalities represent a description of the state of knowledge of the switch prior to the drawing of the first packet. Changes in the switch's state of knowledge (in terms of the number of packets of types $R$ and $W$) appear when we attempt to compute the probabilities referring to the second packet service. For example, what is the probability for having a packet from $R$ in the first two extractions? From the product rule, this is:

$$\Pr(\alpha_1 \wedge \alpha_2) = \Pr(\alpha_1).\Pr(\alpha_2|\alpha_1) = \frac{M(M - 1)}{N(N - 1)}$$

This result can be easily extended to the computation of $\Pr(\alpha_1 \wedge \alpha_2 \wedge ... \wedge \alpha_k)$. The following formula holds:

$$\Pr(\alpha_1 \wedge \alpha_2 \wedge ... \wedge \alpha_k) = \prod_{i=0}^{k-1} \frac{M-i}{N-i} = \frac{\binom{M}{k}}{\binom{N}{k}} \quad \text{for} \quad r \leq M$$

Then, the probability of having the event $\alpha_1 \wedge \alpha_2 \wedge ... \wedge \alpha_k \wedge \beta_{k=1} \wedge ... \wedge \beta_n$ is given by:

$$\Pr(\beta_{k+1} \wedge ... \wedge \beta_n | \alpha_1 \wedge \alpha_2 \wedge ... \wedge \alpha_k) = \frac{M!(N-M)!(N-n)}{N!(M-k)!(N-M-(n-k))!}$$

$$= \frac{\binom{M}{k}\binom{N-M}{n-k}}{\binom{N}{K}\binom{N-K}{r}}$$

This result was derived for a particular order of packets of type $R$ and $W$. However, the probability of serving $k$ packets of type $R$ and $l-k$ packets of type $W$ in any specified order is the same. Let $\gamma$ be the event of having $k$ packets served within $n$ packets in any order. Then, it holds that

$$\Pr(\gamma) = \binom{n}{k} \Pr(\beta_{k+1} \wedge ... \wedge \beta_n | \alpha_1 \wedge \alpha_2 \wedge ... \wedge \alpha_k)$$

Let $h(k|N, M, n)$. (Here we abbreviate by $h(k)$ this expression.) Then,

$$h(k|N, M, n) = \frac{\binom{M}{k}\binom{N-M}{n-k}}{\binom{N}{n-k}}$$

Obviously, $h$ satisfies the following:

$$h(k|N, M, n) = h(k|N, n, M) = h(n-k|N, N-M, n)$$

The most probable value of $k$ can be obtained by solving $h(k) = h(k-1)$. This gives: $k_0 = \frac{(n+1)(M+1)}{N+2}$ and $\frac{k_0}{n+1} = \frac{M+1}{N+2}$. If $k_0$ is not an integer, the next integer below $k_0$ is the most probable. Thus, the most probable fraction $f = k_0/r$ of packet served from $R$ (or in the sample) is approximately equal to the fraction $M/N$, as one can expect it.

Until this point, we have considered only the case where we sample without replacement (i.e., packet are dropped after service). It may be appropriate for many real situations that the sample can be made with replacement. For example, in a quality-control application, one may need to have to sample objects and get them back to their places. This case of sampling with replacement may be complicated conceptually, but with some assumptions usually made, it ends up being simpler mathematically than sampling without replacement. For the sake of simplicity, let us go back to discuss the aforementioned subject, but we assume now that we sample packets from the buffer, and after recording the type of traffic (i.e., type $R$ or $W$) of each packet, we replace it in the buffer before taking the next packet. For this, we still have an equation like:

$$\Pr(\alpha_1 \wedge \alpha_2) = \Pr(\alpha_1) . \Pr(\alpha_2 | \alpha_1)$$

But this probability equals $(\frac{M}{N})^2$, which also leads us to write the probability of having exactly $k$ packets from traffic type $R$ within a sample of $n$ served packets, regardless of the order, as shown below:

$$\binom{n}{r} . \left(\frac{M}{N}\right)^r \left(\frac{N-M}{N}\right)^{n-1}$$

### 2.2.2   Reasoning with Less Precise Data

Assume now that after $k$ extractions of packets, the system knows that packets of type $R$ will be found at least once in later extractions, but it does not know which extraction or extractions will occur. Such an event, denoted by $\alpha_{Futur}$, can be formally written as follows:

$$\alpha_{Futur} = \alpha_{k+1} \vee \alpha_{k+2} \vee ... \vee \alpha_n$$

where $\alpha_i$ is the event "the packet serviced at the ith extraction belongs to flow $R$. To compute $P(\alpha_{Futur})$, let us consider its complementary event, which represents the statements that all packets serviced after the $k + 1$ extractions are of type W.

$$\bar{\alpha}_{Futur} = \beta_{k+1} \wedge \beta_{k+2} \wedge ... \wedge \beta_n$$

Using the exchangeability rule previously discussed, the probability $P(\bar{\alpha}_{Futur})$ is the same as the probability serving packets of type $W$ at the first $(n-k)$ extractions, regardless of what can happen after that. Therefore, we have:

$$\Pr(\bar{\alpha}_{Futur}) = \binom{N-M}{n-k} \binom{N}{n-k}^{-1}$$

In a similar way, the probability $P(\bar{\alpha}_{Futur})$ is the same as in the case containing $(N-1)$ packets, $(M-1)$ of which are of type $W$:

$$\Pr(\bar{\alpha}_{Futur}|\alpha_k) = \binom{N-M}{n-k}\binom{N-1}{n-k}^{-1}$$

This gives the probability $P(\alpha_{Futur})$. Now, let us go to $P(\alpha_k|\alpha_{Futur})$, where we have:

$$P(\alpha_k\alpha_{Futur}) = P(\alpha_k|\alpha_{Futur})P(\alpha_{Futur}) = P(\alpha_{Futur}|\alpha_k)P(\alpha_k)$$

Thus, we can deduce that:

$$P(\alpha_k|\alpha_{Futur}) = P(\alpha_k)\frac{P(\alpha_{Futur}|\alpha_k)}{P(\alpha_{Futur})}$$

Using (2.6), this equality becomes:

$$P(\alpha_k|\alpha_{Futur}) = \frac{M}{N-n+k} \cdot \frac{\binom{N-1}{n-k} - \binom{N-M}{n-k}}{\binom{N}{n-k} - \binom{N-M}{n-k}}$$

**Example.** Let us apply this result to the simple case, where $N = 4$, $M = 2$, $n = 3$, $k = 1$, and let us compute $P(\alpha_k|\alpha_2)$. We have:

$$\alpha_{Futur} = \alpha_2 \vee \alpha_3, \quad P(\alpha_1|\alpha_{Futur}) = \frac{2}{4-3+1} \cdot \frac{\binom{3}{2} - \binom{2}{2}}{\binom{4}{2} - \binom{2}{2}} = \frac{3-1}{6-1} = \frac{2}{5}$$

and $P(\alpha_1|\alpha_2) = \frac{1}{3}$

This shows the following interesting result:

$$P(\alpha_1|\alpha_{Futur}) > P(\alpha_1|\alpha_2)$$

## 2.3  RANDOM VARIABLES

Let $R$ be the probability space obtained by considering the algebra generated by the set of subsets $\{x\}$, $x \in R$. A numerical function $X : \Omega \rightarrow R$ defined on a probability space (or sample space) $\Omega$ is called a random variable if, for every real $x$, $X(k)$, $k \in R$ is measurable. Thus, $X$ assigns a real value to every element of the sample space. This process enables statistics to be conveniently computed over a probability space. In the sequel, we will consider only real-valued random variables: $X : \Omega \rightarrow R$. Three types of random variables can be considered: discrete, continuous, and mixed variables. A discrete random variable takes only isolated values with nonzero probabilities. The number of values it is allowed to take may be infinite, but they should be countable. That is, it must be possible to arrange its values in a sequence so that the $r^{th}$ number is identifiable for any integer $r$. A continuous random variable $X$ is a variable satisfying the following integral for the computation of the probability of the event $\{X \le x\} = \{\omega \,|\, X(\omega) \le x\}$ using a function, called probability density function of $X$:

$$\Pr(X \le x) = \int_{-\infty}^{x} p_x(t)dt$$

A random variable is called mixed if it has both discrete and continuous parts.

### 2.3.1 Discrete Variable

A discrete random variable $X$ is called non-negative if $X(\omega) \ge 0$ for all $\omega \in \Omega$. It is called a *binary* or *Bernoulli* random variable if it takes its values in $\{0, 1\}$. A binary random variable $X$ is called an indicator of event $\alpha$ (and can be denoted by $\chi_\alpha$) if $X(\omega) = 1$ if, and only if, $\omega \in \alpha$.

For a discrete random variable, taking its values into an increasing sequence $\{x_x\}_{1 \le k}$, and a real number $x$, we have

$$\Pr(X \le x) = \sum_{k:\, x_k \le k} \Pr(X = x_k), \quad \Pr(X \ge x) = \sum_{k:\, x_k \ge k} \Pr(X = x_k)$$

For the sake of simplicity, we will assume that the values of a discrete variable $X$ are integers. The function $p_X : N \rightarrow R$, defined by $p_X(k) = \Pr(X = k)$, is called the probability distribution of $X$ (probability mass function, (PMF)), and the function $G_X(k) = \Pr(X \le k)$ is called the cumulative distribution function (CDF) of $X$. Finally, the function $H_X(k) = \Pr(X \ge k)$ is called the survival distribution function.

The most important measures used in combination with random variables are called expectation (also called the expected value) and variance. The following definition specifies these metrics [6, 7].

**Definition 1.** Let $(\Omega, A, \pi)$ denote a probability space and $X : \Omega \rightarrow R$ be an arbitrary discrete random variable. Then the expectation (also called expected value or mean) $E(X)$ of $X$ is defined as follows:

$$E(X) = \sum_{k \in \text{Im}(X)} k \Pr(X = k)$$

where $\text{Im}(X)$ represents the set of values of $X$ (assumed to be in $N$). The $n$th moment of $X$, $n > 1$, is equal to expectation $E(X^n)$ of the of random variable $X^n$.

The following statements describe the basic features of the expected value of a discrete variable $X$:

- If $X$ is non-negative, then $E(X) \geq 0$
- $E(|X|) = |E(X)|$
- $E(\lambda X) = \lambda E(X)$, for all real $\lambda$
- $E(X + Y) = E(X) + E(Y)$

Consider now two discrete random variables. They are called independent if for all real numbers $x$ and $y$:

$$\Pr(X = x | Y = y) = \Pr(X = x)$$

Then, $X$ and $Y$ have the following property:

$$E(X \cdot Y) = E(X) \cdot E(Y)$$

A proof of this statement is given as follows. For all real number $a$ and $b$, consider the events $\alpha$ and $\beta$ defined as follows:

$$\alpha_a = \{X = a\} \quad \text{and} \quad \beta_b = \{X = b\}$$

Using the fact that $X$ and $Y$ are independent, we have $\Pr(\alpha \cap \beta) = \Pr(\alpha) \cdot \Pr(\beta)$. Using the indicator variables $\chi_a$, $a \in R$, which are defined by $\chi_a(x) = 1$ if and only if $a = x$, we rewrite $X \cdot Y$ as follows:

$$X \cdot Y = \left( \sum_{a \in R} a \chi_a \right) \cdot \left( \sum_{a \in R} b \chi_b \right) = \sum_{a,b \in R} a \cdot b \chi_{\alpha_a \cap \beta_b}$$

The expectation (expected value) of $X.Y$ can be computed as follows:

$$E(X \cdot Y) = E\left(\sum_{a,b \in R} a \cdot b\chi_{\alpha_a \cap \beta_b}\right) = \sum_{a,b \in R} a \cdot b \Pr(\alpha_a \cap \beta_b)$$

$$= \sum_{a,b \in R} a \cdot b \Pr(\alpha_a) \cdot \Pr(\beta_b)$$

$$= \left(\sum_{a,b \in R} a \Pr(\alpha_a)\right) \cdot \left(\sum_{a,b \in R} b \Pr(\beta_b)\right)$$

$$= E(X) \cdot E(Y)$$

**Example.** Let $X1$, $X2$, and $X3$ be three random variables defined on the unit square in the Euclidean space by:

$$X_1(\varpi_1, \varpi_2) = \varpi_1^2, \quad X_2(\varpi_1, \varpi_2) = \varpi_2^2, X_3(\varpi_1, \varpi_2) = \varpi_1 + \varpi_2$$

We need to show that $X1$ and $X2$ are independent, and that $X1$ and $X3$ are not independent.

Let us consider the functions:

$$F_{jk}(r, t) = P(X_j \le r, X_k \le t), \quad j \ne k \in \{1, 2, 3\}; F_s(r) = P(X_1 \le r,), \quad s = 1, 2, 3$$

An easy computation shows that $F_s(r) = \sqrt{r}$, $s = 1, 2$, and

$$F_{12}(r, t) = P(\varpi_1 \le \sqrt{r}, \varpi_2 \le \sqrt{t}) = \sqrt{r.t} = F_1(r)F_2(t)$$

However, for $r = 1/4$ and $t = 1$, we have:

$$F_{13}\left(\frac{1}{4}, 1\right) = P\left(\varpi_1 \le \frac{1}{2}, \varpi_1 + \varpi_2 \le 1\right) = Area(E_1) = \frac{1}{2} - \frac{1}{8} = \frac{3}{8}$$

Area $E_1$ is depicted in Figure 2.1. A computation of $F_3$ shows that:

$$F_3(t) = \begin{cases} 0, & \text{if } t < 0 \\ \frac{t^2}{2}, & \text{if } 0 \le t \le 1 \\ 1 - \frac{(2-t)^2}{2}, & \text{if } 1 \le t \le 2 \\ 1, & \text{if } 2 < t \end{cases}$$

and that $X1$ and $X3$ are not independent random variables.

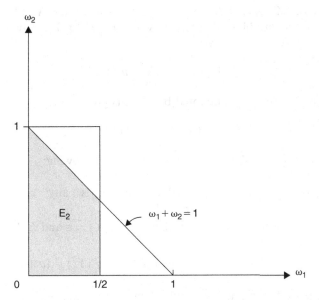

**FIGURE 2.1.** The spaces $E$ and $E_1$.

The conditional expectation of a discrete random variable $X$ with respect to an event $\alpha$ is defined by:

$$E(X \mid \alpha) = \sum_{a \in R} a \cdot \Pr(X = a \mid \alpha)$$

This formula allows the definition of random variable $E(X|Y)$ by setting $E(X|Y)(y) = E(X|Y = y)$. Therefore, $E(X|Y)$ is a discrete random variable for which the equality $E(Y.X) = E(Y)E(X|Y)$ does not hold, in general. The expectation of the random variable given that another variable $Y$ takes the value $Y = y$ is

$$E(X \mid Y = y) = \sum_{a \in R} a \cdot \Pr(X = a \mid Y = y)$$

$E(X|Y = y)$ is a function of $y$. By applying this function on the values of the random variable $Y$, one obtains a random variable $E(X|Y)$ called the conditional expectation. The properties of $E(X|Y)$ include the following:

- $E(X|Y) = E(X)$ if X and Y are independent
- $E(\lambda X|Y) = \lambda E(X|Y)$ for all real $\lambda$
- $E(X + Z|Y) = E(X|Y) + E(Z|Y)$ for any variable Z
- $E(g(Y)X|Y) = g(Y)E(X|Y)$ for any function g on R.

**Definition 2.** Let $(\Omega, A, \pi)$ denote a probability space and $X : \Omega \rightarrow R$ be an arbitrary random variable with expected value $\mu = E(X)$. Then the variance of $X$ denoted by $V(X)$ is as follows:

$$V(X) = E((X - \mu)^2)$$

The *standard deviation* of $X$, denoted by $\sigma(X)$, is given by

$$\sigma(X) = \sqrt{V(X)}$$

Among the features of $V(X)$, one can mention the following:

- If $X$ is any random variable and $c$ is any constant, then $V(cX) = c^2 V(X)$ and $V(X + c) = V(X)$.
- If $X$ and $Y$ are two random variables and $E(X) = a$ and $E(Y) = b$, then

$$V(X + Y) = E(X^2) + 2E(X)E(Y) + E(Y^2) - (a + b)^2$$

**Example.** A packet is selected at random among $n$ packets $p_1, p_2, \ldots, p_n$. Let $X$ be the index of the selected packet. Then we can easily show that $E(X) = (n + 1)/2$ since $E(X) = \sum_{i=1}^{n} i/n$. In addition, we can show that: $V(X) = (n - 1)(n + 1)/12$ using the following equality:

$$1^2 + 2^2 + \ldots + n^2 = n(n + 1)(2n + 1)/6$$

### 2.3.2 Examples of Discrete Random Variables

The followings are some examples of discrete random variables that are important to the subsequent chapters. Chapter 10 discusses in detail the properties of these variables in addition to other variables.

- *Bernoulli discrete random variable*: Consider a random experiment that has two outcomes 0 and 1. The probability distribution of random variable $X$ is given by:

$$p = P(X = 1) \text{ and } (1 - p) = P(X = 0)$$

- *Binomial discrete random variable*: An experiment with only two outcomes, say 1 and 0, is considered $n$ times where successive tests are assumed independent. The random variable $X$ counts now the number of times the outcome 1 occurs. The probability distribution of $X$ is given by:

$$P(X = k) = \binom{n}{k} p^k (1 - p)^{n-k}$$

- where $p \in [0,1]$ and $k \in \{1, 2, .., n\}$. It is clear that $p = P(X = 1)$.
- *Geometric random variable*: Here, the experiment with two possible outcomes is carried out several times. The random variable represents the number of trials it takes for the outcome 1 to occur. The probability distribution of $X$ is given by:

$$P(X = k) = p(1 - p)^{k-1}$$

- *Poisson random variable*: A Poisson variable $X$ is defined by the probability distribution:

$$P(X = k) = \frac{\alpha^k}{k!} e^{-\alpha} \quad \text{for} \quad 0 \le k \text{ and } \alpha > 0$$

The main parameters of the aforementioned variables can be derived from the probability distribution functions for the aforementioned discrete random variables. In particular, the expected value, the $n$th moments, and the $n$th central moment can be easily determined.

- *Expected value*: It is given by $E(X) = \sum_{all\,k} k \Pr(X = k)$
- *The nth moment*: This is given by $E(X^n) = \sum_{all\,k} k^n \Pr(X = k)$
- *The nth central moment*: This is given by $E[(X\text{-}E(X))^n]$

Let us, for example, compute $E(X)$ for a geometric random variable. Then

$$E(X) = \sum_{k \ge 0} kp(1 - p)^{k-1} = p \sum_{k \ge 0} k(1 - p)^{k-1}$$

To compute this, assume $|x| < 1$ and then the sum $\sum_{k \ge 0} x^k = \frac{1}{1-x}$. By differentiating this expression, we obtain:

$$\sum_{k \ge 1} kx^{k-1} = \frac{1}{(1 - x)^2} \quad \text{So,} \quad E(X) = \frac{p}{(1 - (1 - p))^2} = \frac{p}{p^2} = \frac{1}{p}$$

Now, let $X$ be a random variable with expected value $\mu = E(X)$. Then, the variance and standard deviation $X$, denoted by $V(X)$ and $\sigma(X)$, respectively, are defined by:

$$V(X) = E((X - \mu)^2), \quad \sigma(X) = \sqrt{V(X)}$$

A useful alternative form for computing the variance is given by $V(X) = E(X^2) - \mu^2$. This can be obtained as shown below:

$$V(X) = E((X - \mu)^2) = E(X^2 - 2\mu X + \mu^2)$$
$$= E(X^2) - 2\mu E(X) + \mu^2 = E(X^2) - \mu^2$$

Several properties can be established for the variance. Some of these properties are special and different from those characterizing the expectation. For instance, if $\lambda$ is a real number, we have:

$$V(\lambda X) = \lambda^2 V(X), V(\lambda + X) = V(X)$$

For the first assertion, for example, let $\mu = E(X)$. Then $\mu\lambda = E(\lambda X)$ and

$$V(\lambda X) = E((\lambda X - \lambda\mu)^2) = \lambda^2 E((X - \mu)^2) = \lambda^2 V(X)$$

On the other hand, let $X_1, .., X_n$ be $n$ random variables with $E(X_i) = \mu$ and $V(X_i) = \sigma$, for all $i$. Let $S_n$ be the sum $\sum_{i=1}^{n} X_i$ and $A_n = \frac{S_n}{n}$. Then, the following statements can be easily established:

$$V(S_n) = n\sigma^2, \quad V(A_n) = \frac{\sigma^2}{n}$$

In fact, the statement is trivial for $n = 1$. The general case is deduced from $S_n = S_{n-1} + X_n$

### 2.3.3 Continuous Random Variables

In this subsection, we consider the basic properties of the expected value and the standard deviation of continuous variables. The definition of these mathematical entities is basically similar to that for discrete random variables. The expected value of a real-valued random variable $X$ with density function (also called probability density function) $f$ is given by:

$$\mu = E(X) = \int_{-\infty}^{+\infty} xf(x)dx$$

The variance $V$ (also denoted by $\sigma^2$) of $X$ is defined by:

$$\sigma^2 = \int_{-\infty}^{+\infty} (x - \mu)^2 f(x)dx \quad \text{where } E(X) = \mu$$

Assume that $X$ and $Y$ are real-valued random variables and that $f$ and $g$ are their continuous probability distribution functions. Then the following results are true:

1. $E(XY) = E(X)E(Y)$ provided that $E(|X|)$ and $E(|X|)$ exist
2. $E(aX + bY) = aE(X) + bE(Y)$ for all real numbers $a$ and $b$

Because statement two is obvious, we check only the first statement. The proof is performed in two steps. The first step proves the result in the case where the ranges of $X$ and $Y$ are contained in intervals $[a, b]$ and $[c, d]$, respectively. The second step uses the hypotheses to extend this result for the case where the ranges are general. Let $f$ and $g$ be the density functions of $X$ and $Y$, respectively, and the density function of $XY$ is $fg$. Thus, we have

$$E(XY) = \int_a^b \int_c^d xyf(x)g(y)dxdy$$

$$= \int_a^b xf(x)dx \int_c^d yg(y)dy = E(X)E(Y)$$

The extension is feasible knowing that, because of the hypotheses, one can say that, for all $\varepsilon > 0$, there are four real values $a, b, c,$ and $d$ such that:

$$\left| E(X) - \int_a^b xf(x)dx \right| < \varepsilon \text{ and } \left| E(Y) - \int_c^d yg(y)dy \right| < \varepsilon$$

and so that $E(XY)$ and $E(X) E(Y)$ are close to $\int_a^b \int_c^d xyf(x)g(y)dxdy$, and $\int_a^b xf(x)dx \int_c^d yg(y)dy$, respectively.

In addition to the aforementioned properties, the following relations are valid for the variance/standard deviation:

- $\sigma^2(X) = E(X^2) - E(X)^2$
- $\sigma(cX) = c\sigma(X)$, for all $c$
- $\sigma^2(X+c) = \sigma^2(X)$ for all $c$

where $c$ is a constant.

**Example 1.** Let $X$ be a distributed continuous random variable with the density function $f$ given by:

$$f(t) = \begin{cases} \lambda e^{-\lambda t}, & t \geq 0, \lambda > 0 \\ 0, & \text{elsewhere} \end{cases}$$

An easy computation of $E(X)$ and $\sigma(X)$ gives:

$$E(X) = \int_0^\infty t\lambda e^{-\lambda t}dt = \frac{1}{\lambda}, \text{ and } \sigma^2(X) = \int_0^\infty t^2\lambda e^{-\lambda t}dt - \frac{1}{\lambda^2} = \frac{1}{\lambda^2}$$

The above distribution is an exponential distribution. It is clear that for the exponential distribution, the variance is the equal to the square of the mean.

## 2.4   SUMS OF VARIABLES

In this section, we discuss the important problem of determining the distribution of a sum of independent random variables in terms of the distributions of the individual variables. We will distinguish between the case of discrete random variables and the case of continuous variables. For the first case, the variables are assumed to be defined for all integers and to have the value 0 where they are not defined.

### 2.4.1   Sums of Discrete Variables

Assume that $X_i, i \in \{1,2\}$ are two independent discrete random variables and $f_1$ and $f_2$ are their probability density functions. Let $Y = X_1 + X_2$ and $f_3$ be its probability density function. To determine the distribution $f_3$, we determine the probability that $Y$ takes an arbitrary value $y$. Assume that $X_1 = k$ and then $Y = y$ if and only if $X_2 = y - k$. Thus, the event $\{Y = y\}$ is the union of events $A_k$ defined by

$$A_k = \{X_1 = k\} \wedge \{X_2 = y - k\}, \ k \in Z$$

The probability of event $\{Y = y\}$ therefore is given by

$$P(Y = y) = \sum_{k=-\infty}^{\infty} P(X_1 = k) \cdot P(X_2 = y - k)$$

Hence, we conclude that the probability distribution $f_3$ is given by the convolution product of $f_1$ and $f_1$

$$f_3(k) = \sum_{k=-\infty}^{\infty} f_1(j) f_2(k - j), j \in Z$$

This result can be extended to the sum $S_n$ of $n$ independent random variables $X_i, i \in \{1,2,..,n\}$ with density probability $f_i, i \in \{1,2,..,n\}$. For this to be established, we can use the following sequence of sums:

$$S_n = S_{n-1} + X_n, n \geq 2, \ S_1 = X_1$$

Therefore, we can find the distribution function of $S_n$ by induction. The density function

$$f_{S_n}(k) = f_1^* f_2^* ...^* f_n \cdot (k)$$

**Example.** A die is rolled three times. Let $X_i, i = 1, 2, 3$ be the outcomes, and let $S_3$ be the sum of these outcomes, $S_3 = X_1 + X_2 + X_3$. The random variables $X_i, i = 1, 2, 3$ have a common distribution $m$ defined by $m(i) = \frac{1}{6}, i \in \{1,..6\}$. The distribution function of $S_3$ is then the convolution of this distribution with the distribution of $S_2$. Thus,

$$\Pr(S_3 = 3) = m(1)^3 = \frac{1}{216}$$

$$\Pr(S_3 = 4) = m(1)\Pr(S_2 = 3) + m(2)\Pr(S_2 = 2)$$

$$= m(1)(m(1)m(2) + m(2)m(1)) + m(2)m(1)^2 = \frac{3}{216}$$

The computation of $\Pr(S_3 = i)$, $18 \geq i \geq 5$, can be done in a similar way.

### 2.4.2  Sums of Continuous Random Variables

We now consider the case of two independent continuous random variables and study the distribution of their sum. Let $X$ and $Y$ be the two random variables and assume that their density functions are denoted by $f$ and $g$, respectively. Assume also that $f$ and $g$ are defined for all real numbers. Then the convolution, denoted $f * g$, of $f$ and $g$ is the function given by

$$f * g(z) = \int_{-\infty}^{\infty} f(z - y)g(y)dy = \int_{-\infty}^{\infty} g(z - y)g(y)dy$$

The definition of the convolution is similar to the definition provided in the discrete case. Therefore, it should not be surprising that if $X$ and $Y$ are independent, then the density of their sum is the convolution of their densities. This fact is stated as follows. The sum $X + Y$ is a continuous variable with density function $h$ equal to the convolution $f^* g$.

**Example.** Let $X$ and $Y$ be two continuous random variables and $f$ and $g$ their probability density functions. Assume that $f$ and $g$ are given by

$$f(x) = g(x) = \begin{cases} e^{-\lambda x}, & x \geq 0 \\ 0, & \text{otherwise} \end{cases}$$

Using the equalities

$$\int_{-\infty}^{\infty} f(z - x)g(x)dx = \int_{0}^{z} e^{-\lambda(z-x)}e^{-\lambda x}dx = \int_{0}^{z} e^{-\lambda z}dx = ze^{-\lambda z}$$

the density function $h$ of the random variable $X + Y$ can be computed by

$$h(z) = \begin{cases} ze^{-\lambda z}, & z \geq 0 \\ 0, & \text{otherwise} \end{cases}$$

## 2.5 REGRESSION MODELS

A regression model is a system of the form:

$$Y_i = f(X_i, \gamma) + \epsilon_i$$

where $\gamma = (\gamma_0,..,\gamma_{p-1})$ is a vector of $p$ parameters; $X_i = (X_{i,1},..,X_{i,p})$ is a known constant vector, called predictor variable; and $\varepsilon_i$, $i \geq 1$ are independent random variables, called the random error term with mean $E(\varepsilon_i) = 0$ and variance $\sigma^2(\varepsilon_i) = \sigma^2$ [8, 9]. They are assumed uncorrelated so that their covariance is zero, meaning that $\text{Cov}(\varepsilon_i, \varepsilon_j) = 0$, $\forall i, j : i \neq j$. Note here that if $X$ and $Y$ are any two random variables, then the covariance of $X$ and $Y$ is defined by:

$$\text{Cov}(X, Y) = E[(X - E(X))(Y - E(Y))]$$

Obviously, one can show that the covariance satisfies three main statements:(a) $\text{Cov}(X,X) = 0$; (b) $\text{Cov}(X,Y) = 0$ if $X$ and $Y$ are independent; and (c) one can have $\text{Cov}(X,Y) = 0$ and $X$ and $Y$ not independent.

The regression model is said to be simple if it has only one predictor variable. It is said to be linear in the parameters if no parameter appears as an exponent, multiplied or divided by another parameter. It is linear in the predictor variable if the predictor variable appears only in the first power. A model that is linear in the parameters and in the predictor variable is also called a first-order model. For the sake of simplicity, the regression model is called simple, multilinear, and nonlinear if it has the following forms:

- $Y_i = \gamma_0 + \gamma_1 X_i + \varepsilon_i$
- $Y_i = \gamma_0 + \gamma_1 X_{i,1} + .. + \gamma_{p-1} X_{i,p-1} + \varepsilon_i$
- $Y_i = f(X_i, \gamma) + \varepsilon_i$, where $f$ is not linear in $X_i$

Two examples of classes of nonlinear regression models are of special importance and are widely used. They are the exponential regression models and the logistic regression models. The first class uses functions under the form $Y_i = \gamma_0 + \gamma_1 e^{\gamma_2 X_i} + \varepsilon_i$. It is commonly used in growth studies, where the rate of growth at a given time is proportional to the amount of growth as time increases. In this case, parameter $\gamma_0$ represents the maximum growth value. The second class uses models of the form $Y_i = \frac{\gamma_0}{1+\gamma_1 e^{\gamma_2 X}} + \varepsilon_i$ . This model has been largely used in population studies to relate, for example, the number of types ($Y$) to time ($X$). Figure 2.2 shows the two functions with specific values of the parameters.

Regression models are widely used in business, communication, and many other disciplines. A few examples of applications are as follows:

- The child's height will increase with his age up to a certain age. The growth pattern may be different from one child to another.

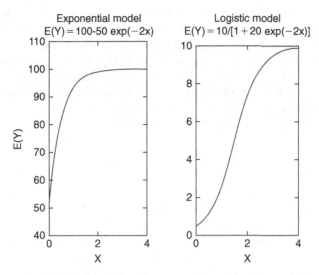

**FIGURE 2.2.** Examples of exponential and logistic models.

The overall growth pattern can be predicted by using the relationship among the growth pattern, the number of children, and the heights at different ages.

- The performance of an employee on a given job can be predicted by using the relationship between performance and a series of aptitude tests.
- The length of hospital stay of a surgical patient can be predicted by using the relationship between the time in the hospital and the severity of the operation.

## 2.5.1 Linear Regression Models

For the sake of simplicity, we consider in the following linear regression models of the form:

$$Y_i = \beta_0 + \beta_1 X_i + \varepsilon_i$$

where $\gamma_i$ is the value of the response variable in the $i$th trial, $\beta_0$ and $\beta_i$ are parameters, $X_i$ is a known constant called the predictor variable of the $i$th trial, and $\varepsilon_i$ is a random error term with mean $E(\varepsilon_i) = 0$ and variance $\sigma^2(\varepsilon_i) = \sigma^2$. In addition, the variables are assumed uncorrelated. The results we will set in this subsection can be extended to more general linear models. The important features of the model include the following:

- $E(Y_i) = E(\beta_0 + \beta_1 X_i) + E(\varepsilon_i) = E(\beta_0 + \beta_1 X_i) = \beta_0 + \beta_1 E(X_i)$
- $\sigma^2(Y_i) = \sigma^2(\beta_0 + \beta_1 X_i + \varepsilon_i) \, \sigma^2(\varepsilon_i) = \sigma^2$

The observational data to be used for estimating the parameters of the regression function consist of observations on the predictor variable $X$ and the corresponding observations on the response variable $Y$. For each trial, there is an $X$ observation and a $Y$ observation. We denote the $(X, Y)$ observations for the $i$th trial as $(X_i, Y_i)$, with $i = 1,...,n$. To find efficient estimators of the regression parameters $\beta_0$ and $\beta_1$, we can use the method of least squares, which requires that we consider the sum of the $n$ squared deviations. This criterion is denoted by the following sum $Q$ and is defined by:

$$Q = \sum_{i=1}^{n} (Y_i - \beta_0 + \beta_1 X_i)^2$$

According to the method of least squares, the estimators of $\beta_0$ and $\beta_1$ are those values $b_0$ and $b_1$, respectively, that minimize the $Q$ value for the given sample observations $(X_i, Y_i)$, where $i = 1,...,n$. The estimators $b_0$ and $b_1$ that satisfy the least squares criterion can be found following two ways:

1. Numerical search procedures can be used to evaluate in a systematic fashion the least squares criterion Q for different estimates $b_0$ and $b_1$ until the ones that minimize Q are found.
2. Analytical procedures can often be used to find the values of $b_0$ and $b_1$ that minimize Q. The analytical approach is feasible when the regression model is not mathematically complex.

Using the analytical approach, it can be shown for regression model that the values $b_0$ and $b_1$ that minimize $Q$ for any particular set of sample data are given by the following equations:

$$\sum_{1 \leq i \leq n} Y_i = nb_0 + b_1 \sum_{1 \leq i \leq n} X_i \text{ and } \sum_{1 \leq i \leq n} X_i Y_i = b_0 \sum_{1 \leq i \leq n} X_i + b_1 \sum_{1 \leq i \leq n} X_i^2$$

These equations can be derived from the partial derivatives as follows:

$$\frac{\partial Q}{\partial \beta_0} = -2 \sum_{1 \leq i \leq n} (Y_i - \beta_0 - \beta_1 X_i)$$

$$\frac{\partial Q}{\partial \beta_0} = -2 \sum_{1 \leq i \leq n} X_i (Y_i - \beta_0 - \beta_1 X_i)$$

We can write

$$E(Y) = nb_0 + b_1 E(X) \text{ and } E(YX) = b_0 E(X) + b_1 E(X^2)$$

Equations (7.15) can be solved for $b_0$ and $b_1$. This gives:

$$b_1 = \frac{E(X)E(Y) - nE(XY)}{E(X)^2 - nE(X^2)} \text{ and } b_0 = E(Y) - b_1 E(X)$$

Given sample estimators $b_0$ and $b_1$ of the parameters in the regression function, we estimate the regression function at level $X$ as follows: $\hat{Y} = b_0 + b_1 X$ where $\hat{Y}$ is the value of the estimated regression function at the level $X$ of the predictor variable. We call a value of the response variable a response and $E\{Y\}$ the mean response. Thus, the mean response stands for the mean of the probability distribution of $Y$ corresponding to the level $X$ of the predictor variable. $\hat{Y}$ is referred to as a *point estimator* of the mean response when the level of the predictor variable is $X$.

### 2.5.2 NonLinear Regression models

In a nonlinear regression model of the form $Y_i = f(X_i, \gamma) + \varepsilon_i$, the function $f$ is referred to as the *response function* [10]. Nonlinear response functions that can be linearized by a transformation are often called intrinsically linear response functions. For example, the exponential response function:

$$f(X_i, \gamma) = \gamma_1 e^{\gamma_2 X_i}$$

can be linearized using the logarithm function and be transformed to:

$$\log_e f(X_i, \gamma) = \log_e(\gamma_1) + \gamma_2 X$$

and be used to determine some characteristics of the response function $f$.

Typically, the estimation of the parameters of a nonlinear regression model is performed by the method of least squares or the method of maximum likelihood. This is similar to what is done by the linear regression models. In addition, both of these methods of estimation yield the same parameter estimates when the error terms in nonlinear regression model are independent and normally distributed with constant variance. Unlike linear regression, it is usually not possible to find analytical expressions for the least squares and maximum likelihood estimators for nonlinear regression models. Instead, numerical procedures have been developed with these estimation procedures, requiring intensive computations. The analysis of nonlinear regression models is therefore realized by using standard computer software programs.

One can recognize that the method of maximum likelihood leads to the same criterion here when the error terms $\varepsilon_i$ are independent and normally distributed with constant variance by considering the likelihood function. To obtain the normal equations for a nonlinear regression model:

$$Y_i = f(X_i, \gamma) + \varepsilon_i$$

It may be useful to minimize the least squares criterion $Q$:

$$Q = \sum_{i=1}^{n} (Y_i - f(X_i, \gamma))^2$$

with respect to $\gamma_0,..,\gamma_{p-1}$. Computing the partial derivative with respect to $\gamma_i$ gives

$$\frac{\partial Q}{\partial \gamma_k} = \sum_{i=1}^{n} -2(Y_i - f(X_i, \gamma)) \left[ \frac{\partial f(X_i, \gamma)}{\partial \gamma_k} \right]$$

When the partial derivatives are all set to 0, say $\frac{\partial Q}{\partial \gamma_k} = 0$, and the parameters are replaced by the least squares estimates, we obtain the following $p$ equations:

$$\sum_{i=1}^{n} Y_i \left[ \frac{\partial f(X_i, \gamma)}{\partial \gamma_k} \right] = \sum_{i=1}^{n} f(X_i, \gamma)) \left[ \frac{\partial f(X_i, \gamma)}{\partial \gamma_k} \right], \quad k = 0, 1, 2, .., p-1$$

The solution of these equations gives the vector solutions: $g = (g_0,...,g_{p-1})$. The resolution of such systems is often difficult to perform. Numerical search procedures need to be set to obtain a solution $g$ recursively. In particular, when $f$ is the response function of the exponential model is given by:

$$f(X_i, \gamma) = \gamma_0 e^{\gamma_1 X_i}$$

The preceding equations obtained by partial derivative computation gives the following the main equation:

$$\sum_{i=1}^{n} Y_i e^{\gamma_1 X_i} = \gamma_0 \sum_{i=1}^{n} e^{2\gamma_1 X_i} \text{ and } \sum_{i=1}^{n} X_i Y_i e^{\gamma_1 X_i} = \gamma_0 \sum_{i=1}^{n} e^{2\gamma_1 X_i}$$

These equations are not linear in $\gamma_0$ and $\gamma_1$ and are difficult to solve. A numerical approach can be used.

The Gauss-Newton method, which is also called the linearization method, can be applied to approximate the nonlinear regression model with linear terms. It uses a Taylor series expansion and employs ordinary least squares to estimate the parameters. Generally, the Gauss-Newton method begins with initial values for the regression parameters $\gamma_0,..,\gamma_{p-1}$. We denote these initial values by $\gamma_0^{(0)}, .., \gamma_{p-1}^{(0)}$. Typically, the initial values may be collected from earlier, similar cases or theoretical estimations. The values $\gamma_k^{(j)}$ obtained at the $j$th iteration are obtained from $\gamma_k^{(j-1)}$ using the following approach and approximating the mean response $f(X_i, \gamma)$ for the $n$ cases by the linear terms in the Taylor series close to $\gamma_k^{(j-1)}$. It holds that:

$$f(X_i, \gamma) \approx f(X_i, \gamma^{(j-1)}) + \sum_{i=1}^{p-1} \left[ \frac{\partial f(X_i, \gamma)}{\partial \gamma_k} \right]_{\gamma = \gamma^{(j-1)}} (\gamma_k - \gamma_k^{(j-1)})$$

Introducing new variables and constants by stating that:

$$f_i^{(j-1)} = f(X_i, \gamma^{(j-1)}), \quad \beta_k^{j-1} = \gamma_k - \gamma_k^{(j-1)}, \quad D_{ik}^{(j-1)} = \left[\frac{\partial f(X_i, \gamma)}{\partial \gamma_k}\right]_{\gamma = \gamma^{(j-1)}},$$

and

$$Y_k^{(j-1)} = Y_k - f_i^{(j-1)}$$

Replacing them in previous main equation leads to the following linear regression model:

$$Y_k^{(j-1)} = \sum_{k=0}^{p-1} D_{ik}^{(j-1)} \beta_k^{(j-1)} + \varepsilon_i$$

This regression model has the form $Y_i = \sum_{k=1}^{p-1} \beta_k X_k + \varepsilon_i$, where $X_k = D_{ik}^{(j-1)}$. The responses $y_k^{(j-1)}$ are residuals and represent the deviations of the observations around the nonlinear regression function $f$, and the X variables observations are the partial derivatives of the mean response evaluated for each case $i$ of the $n$ cases. Because model described by previous main equation is linear, we can estimate the parameters $\beta^{(j-1)}$ by ordinary least squares and obtain the vector of least squares estimated regression coefficients $\mathbf{b}^{(j-1)}$. The iteration is engaged by setting:

$$\gamma_k^{(j)} = \gamma_k^{(j-1)} + b_k^{(j-1)}$$

It has been shown that the revised regression coefficients represent the adjustments in the right direction using the criteria $Q = \sum_{i=1}^{n} (Y_i - f(X_i, \gamma))^2$ and showing that:

$$\sum_{i=1}^{n} (Y_i - f(X_i, \gamma^{(j-1)}))^2 = \sum_{i=1}^{n} (Y_i - f_i^{(j-1)})^2 > \sum_{i=1}^{n} (Y_i - f_i^{(j)})^2$$

$$= \sum_{i=1}^{n} (Y_i - f(X_i, \gamma^{(j)}))^2$$

For the sake of space, we will not prove this property.

As a first step, we take up regression analysis when a single predictor variable is used for predicting the response or outcome variable of interest. In the following, we will consider the construction of regression modeling and analysis when two or more variables are used for making predictions, and we discuss the estimation of the parameters of regression models containing a single predictor variable and the case of nonlinear regression.

### 2.5.3   Regression Analysis

Real problems must be reduced to manageable proportions whenever models are constructed for the problem resolution. Only a limited number of explanatory or predictor variables can—or should—be included in a regression model for any situation of interest. Building a regression model follows the following three steps:

*Selection of Predictor Variables.* A central problem in building a regression model is that of choosing a finite set of predictor variables that is efficient in some meaning for the objectives of the analysis. A major concern in making this choice is the extent to which a selected variable contributes to reducing the remaining part of the regression model. Other considerations include the extent to which observations on the variable can be obtained more accurately, quickly, or economically than on competing variables, as well as the degree to which the variable can be controlled.

*Regression Relation.* The choice of the functional form of the regression relation depends on the choice of the predictor variables. Typically, the basic form of the regression relation is not known in advance and must be decided empirically after the data have been collected. Polynomial regression functions (e.g., linear or quadratic) can be considered satisfactory approximations to regression functions of unknown form or when the known form is highly complex but can be reasonably approximated by a linear or quadratic regression function.

*Scope of Model.* In formulating a regression model, the model designer often needs to restrict the coverage of the model to some domain of values of the predictor variable(s). The scope is determined either by the design of the investigation or by the range of data at hand. For instance, a telecommunications operator studying the effect of communication minute price on the volume on communications sold can investigate certain price levels, ranging in different intervals. The shape of the regression function substantially outside this range would be in serious doubt because the investigation provided no evidence as to the nature of the relation outside the regions.

Generally, the model designer does not know the values of the regression parameters involved in the regression model (such as $\beta_i$, in the linear regression models), and these values must be estimated from relevant data. Frequently, the designed model does not have acceptable *a priori* knowledge of the appropriate predictor variables and of the functional form of the regression relation (e.g., linear or nonlinear), and the designer must rely on an analysis of the data for developing a suitable regression model.

Data for regression analysis may be observational as obtained from nonexperimental or experimental studies. Observational data do not control the predictor (or explanatory) variable(s) of interest. For example, assume that the company managers wish to study the relation between age of employee ($X$) and number of days of illness in a given year (e.g., last year) ($Y$). The needed data for use in the regression analysis can be collected from personnel records. Such data are observational data because the predictor variable (i.e., age) is not controlled. A major limitation of observational data is that they often do not provide adequate information about cause-and-effect relationships.

Nevertheless, it is possible to perform a controlled experiment to provide data from which the regression parameters can be estimated. The data obtained will be experimental data because control is exercised over the explanatory variable. When control over the explanatory variable(s) is exercised through random assignments, the resulting experimental data provide better information about cause-and-effect relationships than do observational data. The reason is that randomization tends to hide the effects of any other variables that might affect the response variable, such as the effect of aptitude of the employee on productivity.

## 2.6  IMPORTANT DENSITY AND DISTRIBUTION FUNCTIONS

In this section, we discuss the definition and some properties of some important discrete probability distributions and continuous probability densities that we encounter most often in the analysis of experiments. A more detailed review will be provided in Chapter 10.

### 2.6.1  Distribution Functions

Three important discrete probabilities are discussed. They are the binomial, Poisson, and geometric distributions.

**Binomial Distribution.**  This distribution is characterized by three parameters $n$, $p$, and $k$. Typically, it is the distribution of the random variable $X$, which counts the number of heads occurring when a coin is thrown $n$ times, assuming that on any one toss, the probability that a head occurs is $p$.The distribution function $b(-)$ is given by the formula

$$b(n, p, k) = \binom{n}{k} p^k (1 - p)^{n-k}$$

Random variable $X$ can be written as the sum $X = X_1 + \ldots + X_n$ of $n$ independent variables $X_j$, taking the value 1 with probability $p$.

**Poisson Distribution.**  Suppose that we have a situation in which a certain type of occurrences (such as phone calls) happen at random over a period of time. We want to model this situation so that we can consider the probabilities of events such as there are more than $n$ occurrences in a time interval. To compute such probabilities, we can assume that the average rate, i.e., the average number of occurrences per time unit, is constant. This rate is denoted by $\lambda$. Let us consider the random variable $X$ to be the number of occurrences in a given time interval. We want to calculate the distribution of X. For the sake of simplicity, we assume that the time interval is of length 1. If this interval is divided into $n$ equal subintervals, then the probability of occurrence of an event in a subinterval is equal to $p = \frac{\lambda}{n}$ .

We then can deduce that $P(X = 0) = (1 - p)^n = b(n, p, 0) = (1 - \frac{\lambda}{n})^n$. For large $n$, this is approximated by $e^{-\lambda}$. More generally, we can prove that $P(X = k) \approx \frac{\lambda^k}{k!} e^{-\lambda}$ using the recursive formula:

$$\frac{b(n, p, k)}{b(n, p, k-1)} = \frac{\lambda - (k-1)p}{k(1-p)}$$

**Geometric Distribution.** Consider a Bernoulli trials process continued for an infinite number of trials. An example is a station sharing a communication medium with other stations. The station can keep sending a packet until it is received. A packet is assumed to have a probability $p$ to get in collision with other packets. We can compute the distribution for any discrete random variable $X$ related to the Bernoulli trials process, provided that, for any $k$, the probability $P(X = k)$ can be determined using a finite number of elements. For example, let $X$ be the number of packet transmission until a success. Then

$$P(X = 1) = p, P(X = 2) = p(1 - p), P(X = k) = p(1 - p)^{k-1}, k \geq 1$$

Obviously, the sum $\sum_{k \geq 1} P(X = k)$ is equal to

$$\sum_{k \geq 1} p(1 - p)^{k-1} = p \sum_{k \geq 0} (1 - p)^k = 1$$

### 2.6.2 Probability Density Functions

We consider in this subsection three of the most used density functions also called probability density functions (pdf): the gamma, and exponential, normal densities.

**Exponential Density.** The exponential probability density function is defined by

$$f(x) = \begin{cases} \lambda e^{-\lambda x}, & x \geq 0 \\ 0, & \text{otherwise} \end{cases}$$

where $\lambda$ is a positive real number dependent on the experiment. The cumulative distribution function (CDF) of the exponential density can be determined easily. For this, let $X$ be an exponentially random variable with parameter $\lambda$.

Then, the cumulative distribution function $F$ is given, at x $\geq$ 0, by:

$$F(x) = P(X \leq x) = \int_0^x \lambda e^{-\lambda u} du = 1 - e^{-\lambda x}$$

In addition, one can prove that $P(X > x + r | X > r) = P(X > x)$. This is called the *memoryless* property.

**Gamma Density.** The gamma probability density function, with parameters $\lambda$ and $n$, is defined by:

$$g_n(x) = \begin{cases} \lambda \frac{(\lambda x)^{n-1}}{(n-1)!} e^{-\lambda x}, & x \geq 0 \\ 0, & \text{otherwise} \end{cases}$$

One can easily show iteratively that the cumulative distribution function (CDF) related to $g_n$ is given by:

$$G_n(x) = \begin{cases} 1 - e^{-\lambda x} \sum_{k=1}^{n} \frac{(\lambda x)^{k-1}}{(k-1)!}, & x \geq 0 \\ 0, & \text{otherwise} \end{cases}$$

**Normal Density.** The normal probability density function with parameters $\mu$ and $\sigma$ is defined by:

$$f(x) = \frac{1}{\sqrt{2\pi}\sigma} e^{-(x-\mu)^2/2\sigma^2}$$

It is shown that parameter $\mu$ represents the expected value of the density function and the parameter $\sigma$ represents its standard deviation. Because the cumulative function associated with the normal density cannot be written in terms of usual function, its computation is made numerically and special tables are used for it. A special transformation of the form $X = \sigma Y + \mu$ transforms a normal random variable $X$ with parameter $\mu$ and $\sigma$ into a normal random variable $Y$ with parameter 0 and 1. Now, assume that we need to compute the cumulative function $F_X(x)$, at $x > 0$, then we can write

$$F_X(x) = P(X \leq x) = P(Y \leq \frac{x-\mu}{\sigma}) = F_Y(\frac{x-\mu}{\sigma})$$

The rightmost term in the last equation can be found in a table of values of the cumulative distribution function $F_Y(-)$ [11].

### 2.6.3 Multivariate Distributions

Random variables that are vector valued are called multidimensional variables. They can be treated in a similar way as the simple valued random variables. The following definitions represent a natural extension [12, 13].

**Definition 3.** The multidimensional distribution function of a random vector $X = (X_1, \dots, X_n)$ is defined as

$$F_X(x) = F_{(X_1, \dots, X_n)}(x_1, \dots, x_n) = P(X_1 \leq t_1, \dots, X_n \leq t_n)$$

The expectation $E(X)$ of $X$ is the vector $(E(X_1), \dots, E(X_n))$. When the random variable is continuous, a density $f_X(s)$ is used to define $F_X(x)$ as follows:

$$F_X(x) = \int_{-\infty}^{x_1} \int_{-\infty}^{x_2} \dots \int_{-\infty}^{x_n} f(s_1, \dots, s_n) ds_1 \dots ds_n$$

**Definition 4.** Let $X = (X_1, \dots, X_n)$ be a random vector and $v = (v_1, \dots, v_n)$ a real vector having integer components, the $n^{\text{th}}$ moment of $X$, denoted by $\mu_n(X)$ is equal to:

$$\mu_n(X) = E(X^n) = E(X^{v_1} X^{v_2} \dots X^{v_n})$$

If $X$ is continuous with density function $f$, the $v$th moment is given by:

$$\mu_v(X) = \int_{-\infty}^{\infty} \int_{-\infty}^{\infty} \dots \int_{-\infty}^{\infty} s_1^{v_1} \dots s_1^{v_n} f(s_1, \dots, s_n) ds_1 \dots ds_n$$

**Example.** The random vector $X = (x^2, y^3, z^4)$ on the unit cube $\Omega = [0, 1]^3$ with Lebesgue measure; then $E(X) = (1/3, 1/4, 1/5)$. If $v = (2, 3, 2)$, then

$$\mu_v(X) = \int_0^1 \int_0^1 \int_0^1 x^4 y^9 z^8 dx dy dz = \frac{1}{450}$$

### 2.7 MARKOV PROCESSES

A Markov process can be defined by a family of random variables $X = \{X_t | t \in T\}$, where $T$ is a set that can be any subset of the real numbers such that for integer $n$, any increasing sequence of $n + 1$ indexes in $T$, say $0 = t_0 < t_1 < \dots < t_n < t_{n+1}$, and $n + 1$ values $x_j$, the conditional distribution function (CDF [14]):

$$\text{CDF}_X(t, s) = P(X_{t_n} \leq s_n | X_{t_{n-1}} = s_{n-1}, \dots, X_{t_1} = s_1, X_{t_0} = s_0)$$

depends only on the last previous value of $X_{t_{n-1}}$ [1]. This means that

$$\text{CDF}_X(t, s) = P(X_{t_n} \leq s_n | X_{t_{n-1}} = s_{n-1})$$

### 2.7.1  Discrete-Time Markov Chain

The Markov process is called discrete or continuous if its random variable, $X_t$, is discrete or continuous, respectively. A discrete-time Markov chain (DTMC) $X$ is a discrete Markov process satisfying the following relation for every integer $n$, time $t$, and state $s$:

$$\text{CDF}_X(t, s) = P(X_{t_n} = s_n \mid X_{t_{n-1}} = s_{n-1})$$

Starting from state $s_0$, a DTMC evolves, step by step, over time using one-step probability transitions. To explain this, assume for the sake of simplicity that the state space $S$ of $X$ is reduced to the set of integers. Let the probability $\pi_{i,j}(n)$ be given by $\pi_{i,j}(n) = P(X_{n+1} = s_{n+1} = j \mid X_n = s_n = i)$. Then the following holds:

$$\pi_{i,j}(n) = P(X_{n+1} = j \mid X_n = i)$$

$$= P(X_1 = j \mid X_0 = i)$$

Then, starting from a state $i$, the DTMC can move to some state $j$ with probability $\pi_{i,j}(n)$, such that $\Sigma \, \pi_{i,j}(n) = 1$. Probabilities $\pi_{i,j} = \pi_{i,j}(n)$ form a nonnegative matrix called the stochastic transition matrix $P$ defined by:

$$\begin{pmatrix} \pi_{0,0} & \pi_{0,1} & \cdots \\ \pi_{1,0} & \pi_{1,1} & \cdots \\ \cdots & \cdots & \cdots \end{pmatrix}$$

The DTMC can be graphically represented as a state transition diagram, where state $i$ is depicted by a vertex, and a one-step transition from state $i$ to state $j$ is depicted by an edge labeled with the probability $\pi_{i,j}$. The following figure depicts an example of DTMC.

Now let $\pi_{i,j}^s(t, t')$ be given the probability that the DTMC moves from state $i$, at time $t$, to state $j$, at time $t'$. $\pi_{i,j}^s(t, t')$ is called the $s$-step transition probability. We have:

$$\pi_{i,j}^s(t, t') = P(X_{t'} = j \mid X_t = i), \ 0 \le t \le t', \ s = t' - t$$

Then, the following statements hold:

- $\sum_j \pi_{i,j}^s(t, t') = 1, \ 0 \le t \le t', \ s = t' - t$
- $\pi_{i,j}^{t'-t}(t, t') = \pi_{i,j}^{t'-t}(t, t') = \pi_{i,j}^{t'-t}(t, t') =$
- The matrix $P^{(s)}$ of $s$-step transition probabilities is given by $P^{(s)} = P \cdot P^{(s-1)}$ $= P^s$

**Example.** The one-step transition probability matrix of a DTMC $X$ having a two state space $\{0, 1\}$ is given by:

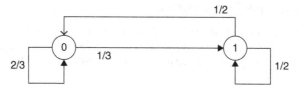

**FIGURE 2.3.** Example of DTMC.

$$P = \begin{pmatrix} \frac{2}{3} & \frac{1}{3} \\ \frac{1}{2} & \frac{1}{2} \end{pmatrix}$$

A transition of the DTMC from state 0 to 1 is made with probability 0.75, where as the DTMC remains in state 0 with probability 0.25. Figure 2.3 depicts the two-state DTMC.

Two types of state can be of interest for a DTMC, the reachable states and the absorbing states. A state $j$ is called reachable from any other state $i$ if there is an integer $n$ such that the $n$-step transition probability $\pi_{i,j}^{t'-t}(t, t')$ is nonnull. State $j$ is called absorbing for the DTMC if no other state can be reachable from $j$. Finally, let us notice that the time between two state changes plays an important role in the dynamics of a DTMC. At every instant, the probability of leaving a state is given by:

$$\pi_i = 1 - p_{i,i} = \sum_{i \neq j} p_{i,j}$$

Applying this many times would define a random variable $X_i$ equal to the sojourn time at state $i$. Variable $X_i$ satisfies the following:

$$P(X_i = k) = (1 - p_{i,j})p_{i,j}^{k-1}, \text{ for all } k > 0$$

$$E(X_i) = \frac{1}{1 - p_{i,i}}, \quad \sigma(X_i) = \frac{\sqrt{p_{i,i}}}{1 - p_{i,i}}$$

### 2.7.2  Continuous-Time Markov Chain

Like DTMC, a continuous-time Markov chain (CMTC) provides modeling tools. The following equation is referred to as the transition probability:

$$P(X_{t_n} = s_{n+1}|X_{t_n} = s_n, .., X_{t_1} = s_1, X_{t_0} = s_0) = P(X_{t_n} = s_{n+1}|X_{t_n} = s_n)$$

The transition probability defined by:

$$p_{i,j}(s,t) = \begin{cases} P(X_s = j | X_t = i), & s \neq t \\ 1 & , \quad s = t, \ i = j \\ 0 & , \quad \text{otherwise} \end{cases}$$

When $s = t$, the transition probability is defined by

$$p_{i,j}(s,s) = \begin{cases} 1, & i = j \\ 0, & i \neq j \end{cases}$$

If the transition probabilities $p_{i,\,j}$ $(s,\ t)$ depend only on the time difference $t - s$, and on the values of $s$ and $t$, then the CTMC is called time-homogeneous and the following holds:

$$p_{i,j}(t) = p_{i,j}(s,t) = P(X_{s+t} = j | X_s = i) = p(X_t = j | X_0 = i), \ \forall u$$

Like the discrete-time case, the transition probability $P_{i.j}(s,t)$ is related to any time $w$ in $[s,\ t]$ by the following:

$$p_{i,j}(s,t) = \sum_{k \in S} p_{i,k}(s,w) \cdot p_{k,j}(w,t), \ 0 \leq s \leq w < t$$

But unlike the DTMCs, this equation is difficult to solve and used to deduce the state probabilities. This will require establishing a partial differential equation as follows.

Consider the period of time $[t,\ t + \Delta t]$ for a small $\Delta t$. Assume that the following limits exist:

$$q_{i,j}(t) = \lim_{\Delta t \to 0} \frac{p_{i,j}(t, t + \Delta t)}{\Delta t}, \ i \neq j$$

$$q_{i,i}(t) = \lim_{\Delta t \to 0} \frac{p_{i,i}(t, t + \Delta t) - 1}{\Delta t}, \ i = j$$

Then the aforementioned equation can be written in $(t,\ t + \Delta t)$ as follows:

$$p_{i,j}(s, t + \Delta t) - p_{i,j}(s,t) = \sum_{k \in S} p_{i,k}(s,w)(p_{k,j}(w, t + \Delta t) - p_{k,j}(w,t))$$

This allows the establishment of the following equation:

$$\frac{\partial p_{i,j}(s,t)}{\partial t} = \sum_{k \in S} p_{i,k}(s,t) q_{k,j}(t), \ 0 \leq s < t$$

If the CTMC is homogeneous, then the rates $q_{i,j}$ are time independent and the following differential equation can be deduced and solved:

$$\frac{dp_{i,j}(t)}{dt} = \frac{dp_{i,j}(0,t)}{dt} = \sum_{k \in S} p_{i,k}(t) q_{k,j}, \quad 0 < t$$

In this case, the unconditional state probabilities $\pi_i(t)$ at time $t$ can be written as follows:

$$\frac{d\pi_j(t)}{dt} = \frac{\partial \sum_{k \in S} p_{i,k}(s,t)\pi_k(s)}{\partial t}$$

$$= \sum_{k \in S} q_{k,j}\pi_k(t)$$

## 2.8  LIMITS

### 2.8.1  Chebychev-Markov Inequality

Let $X$ be a random variable; the next theorem provides a lower bound for $\Pr(X \geq k)$.

**Theorem** (Chebichev-Markov inequality). Let $X$ be an arbitrary random variable that is non-negative and $h: R \to R$ be a positive function. Suppose that $h(X)$ is integrable. Then, the next result is obtained.

$$h(k)\Pr(X \geq k) \leq E(h(X)) \quad \text{for all } k \ R \ (2.2)$$

**Proof.** Let $\chi_{X \geq k}$ be the characteristic function of the subset $\{X \geq k\}$ (i.e., $\chi_{X \geq k}$ $(\omega) = 1 \Leftrightarrow X(\omega) \geq k$). Integrating the inequality gives us:

$$h(c)\chi_{X \geq k} \leq h(X)$$

Using the monotonicity and linearity of the expectation would lead to the required result.

Two cases are found of interest: (a) $h(x) = x$ and (b) $h(x) = x^2$. The first case provides a simple probability bound by stating:

$$\Pr(X \geq k) \leq \frac{E(X)}{k}$$

The second case considers the Chebychev-Markov inequality applied to $X - E(X)$. The following inequality can be easily deduced:

$$\Pr(|X - E(X)| \leq a) \leq \frac{\sigma^2(X)}{a^2} \quad \text{for all real } a$$

### 2.8.2 Laws of Large Deviation

Consider a sequence $X_n$, $n \geq 1$, of random variables on a probability space ($\Omega$, $A$, $P$) Let us consider now the sum $S_n = X_1 + .. + X_n$ and study the asymptotic behavior and convergence of $S_n$ for $n \to \infty$. The following theorem holds [15, 16].

**Theorem.** Assume a large number of random variables $X_i$, $i \leq n$, having common expectation $E(X_i) = m < \infty$, and satisfying $\sup_n \frac{1}{n} \sum_{i=1}^{n} \sigma^2(X_j) < \infty$. If $X_i$, $i \leq n$, are pairwise uncorrelated, then:

$$\lim_{n \to \infty} \frac{S_n}{n} = m; \ i \leq n \text{ in probability.}$$

The result provided by the theorem states that, for all $\varepsilon > 0$,

$$\lim_{n \to \infty} P(\left|\frac{S_n}{n} - m\right| \geq \varepsilon) = 0.$$

**Proof.** Using the fact that $\sigma^2(X + Y) = \sigma^2(X) + \sigma^2(Y) + 2\text{cov}(X, Y)$ and that $X_i$, $i \leq n$, are pairwise uncorrelated, we can deduce that $\sigma^2(X_j + X_k) = \sigma^2(X_j) + \sigma^2(X_k)$. Because the expectation is linear, we can deduce the following two statements:

- $E(\frac{S_n}{n}) = m$
- $\sigma^2\left(\frac{S_n}{n}\right) = E\left(\frac{S_n^2}{n^2}\right) - \frac{E(S_n)^2}{n^2} = \frac{\sigma^2(S_n)}{n^2} = \frac{1}{n^2} \sum_{k=1}^{n} \sigma^2(X_k)$

Obviously, $\lim_{n \to \infty} (\frac{1}{n^2} \sum_{k=1}^{n} \sigma^2(X_k)) = 0$. Using the Chebytchev-Markov (2.9) inequality obtained for $h(x) = x^2$, we deduce that

$$P(\left|\frac{S_n}{n} - m\right| \geq \varepsilon) \leq \frac{\sigma^2\left(\frac{S_n}{n}\right)}{\varepsilon^2}$$

### 2.8.3 Central Limit Theory (CLT)

The central limit theorem of probability is one of the major theorems used with random variables. It states that if $S_n$ is the sum of $n$ mutually independent random variables, then the distribution function of $S_n$ is well approximated by a function $f_{\mu,\sigma}$ known as a normal density function given by [17]:

$$f_{\mu,\sigma} = \frac{1}{\sqrt{2\pi}\sigma} e^{-(x-\mu)^2/2\sigma^2}$$

In this subsection, we will discuss the applications of the CLT in the case where random variables are identically distributed; knowing that the theorem can apply for more general cases. For this, let φ denote the function $f_{0,1}$. We have $\phi(x) = \frac{1}{\sqrt{2\pi}} e^{-x^2/2}$.

**CLT for continuous independent variables.** Let $S_n = X_1 + .. + X_n$ be the sum of $n$ independent continuous random variables with common density function $f$, having expected value $\mu$ and standard deviation $\sigma$. Let $S_n^* = \frac{S_n - n\mu}{\sqrt{n}\sigma}$. Then the CLT states that:

$$\lim_{n \to \infty} P(a < S_n^* < b) = \frac{1}{\sqrt{2\pi}} \int_a^b e^{-x^2/2} dx$$

A proof of this assertion is out of the scope of this chapter. A complete proof can be found in many references [2, 18]. A proof can be sketched as follows. Each variable $X_i$ has the same moment generating function $g(t)$. Function $g(t)$ is defined by $g(t) = \sum_{k=0}^{\infty} \frac{\mu_k t^k}{k!} = \int_{-\infty}^{\infty} e^{tx} f(x) dx$, where $f$ is the density function of $X_i$. The sum $S_n$ has moment generating function $g_n(t) = (g(t))^n$, and the standard sum $S_n^*$ has moment generating function $g_n^*(t) = (g(\frac{t}{\sqrt{n}}))^n$ . Then, using the unicity of the moment generation function, one can show that $\lim_{n \to \infty} g_n^*(t) = e^{t^2/2}$ and that $e^{t^2/2}$ is the moment generating function of $\phi(x) = \frac{1}{\sqrt{2\pi}} e^{-x^2/2}$. Finally, the distribution functions $G_n^*(x)$ of the sum $S_n^*$ are shown to be convergent to the distribution function of $F_{Norm}^*$ of the normal variable *Norm,* which means that

$$F_{Norm}^*(a) = P(S_n^* \leq a) \xrightarrow[n \to \infty]{} \frac{1}{\sqrt{2\pi}} \int_{-\infty}^0 e^{-x^2/2} dx$$

In addition, the density $f_n^*(x)$ of $S_n^*$ is shown to converge to $\phi(x) = \frac{1}{\sqrt{2\pi}} e^{-x^2/2}$.

**CLT for discrete independent variables.** Let $S_n = X_1 + .. + X_n$ be the sum of $n$ independent discrete random variables with common distribution having expected value $\mu$ and standard deviation $\sigma$. Then the CLT states that

$$\lim_{n \to \infty} P(a < \frac{S_n - n\mu}{\sqrt{n}\sigma} < b) = \frac{1}{\sqrt{2\pi}} \int_a^b e^{-x^2/2} dx$$

A proof of this statement can be made in the same way used for the case of continuous variables.

## 2.9  COMPARING SYSTEMS USING SAMPLE DATA

### 2.9.1  Confidence Interval

A *confidence interval* (CI) for a population parameter is an interval of real number of the form [a, b] along with an associated probability $p$, which is generated from a random sample of the population, such that whenever the sampling is repeated and the confidence interval recalculated from the used sample using the same method, a proportion $p$ of the confidence intervals would contain the population parameter.

If $X$ and $Y$ are observable random variables whose probability distribution depends on some unobservable parameter $\Theta$ and $x$ is a real in [0, 1] such that:

$$\Pr(X < \Theta < Y) = x$$

then the random interval $(X, Y)$ is a called the $100 \cdot x\%$ confidence interval for $\Theta$. The number $x$ (or $100 \cdot x\%$) is called the confidence level. The selection of a confidence level for an interval determines the probability that the confidence interval produced will contain the true parameter value. Often, confidence intervals are stated at the confidence level of 0.90, 0.95, and 0.99. In the case of normal density, for example, a 95% confidence interval covers 95%, the probability of observing a value outside of this area is less than 0.05. For a confidence interval with level $C$, the value $p$ is equal to $(1 - C)/2$. As shown in Figure 2.4, three areas can be distinguished when the confidence level $c$ is fixed: the central area and the areas in each tail of the curve. These areas equal to $c$, $\frac{1-c}{2}$, and $\frac{1-c}{2}$, respectively. The confidence interval $[X, Y]$ with level $c$ can be deduced as follows.

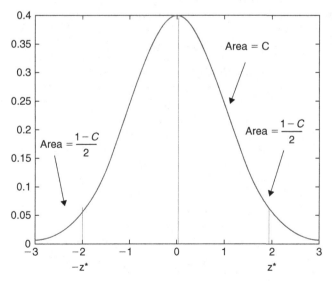

**FIGURE 2.4.** Example of confidence levels.

The value $Y$ representing the point on the standard normal density curve such that the probability of observing a value greater than $Y$ is equal to $p$ is known as the upper $p$ critical value of the standard normal distribution. For example, if $p = 0.025$, then:

$$P(Z > Y) = 0.025, \quad \text{or} \quad P(Z \leq Y) = 0.975, \text{ implies that } Y = 1.96.$$

A 95% confidence interval for the standard normal distribution is the interval $[-1.96, 1.96]$, since 95% of the area under the curve falls within this interval.

**Example.** Suppose that we are measuring the delay observed for the transmission of a packet in an optical fiber and observing the readings (in s) on six different samples:

$$x_1 = 102.5, x_2 = 101.7, x_3 = 103.1, x_4 = 100.9, x_5 = 100.5, \text{ and } x_6 = 102.2$$

We then calculate the sample mean to be 101.82. If one knows that the standard deviation for this procedure is 1.2 $\mu$s, then the confidence interval for the population mean at a confidence level c, is used to estimate the true mean delay of the fiber using the results of the aforementioned measurements.

If the measurements follow a normal distribution, then the sample mean will have the distribution $N(\mu, \frac{\sigma}{\sqrt{n}})$. By standardizing we get a random variable:

$$Z = \frac{\bar{X} - \mu}{\sigma/\sqrt{n}} = \frac{\bar{X} - \mu}{0.49}$$

dependent on $\mu$, but with a standard normal distribution independent of the parameter $\mu$ to be estimated. Hence it is possible to find numbers $-z$ and $z$, independent of $\mu$, where $Z$ lies in between with probability 12 $\alpha$, a measure of how confident we want to be. We take $1 - \alpha = 0.95$. So we have: $P(-z \leq Z \leq z) = 1 - \alpha = 0.95$. The number $z$ follows from:

$$\Phi(z) = P(Z \leq z) = 1 - \alpha/2 = 0.975$$

$$z = \Phi^{-1}(\Phi(z)) = \Phi^{-1}(0.975) = 1.96$$

and we get

$$0.95 = 1 - \alpha = P(-z \leq Z \leq z) = P(-1.96 \leq \frac{\bar{X} - \mu}{\sigma/\sqrt{n}} \leq 1.96)$$

$$= P(\bar{X} - 1.96\frac{\sigma}{\sqrt{n}} \leq \mu \leq \bar{X} + 1.96\frac{\sigma}{\sqrt{n}})$$

$$= P(\bar{X} - 1.96 \times 0.49 \leq \mu \leq \bar{X} + 1.96 \times 0.49)$$

$$= P(\bar{X} - 0.98 \leq \mu \leq \bar{X} + 0.98)$$

This might be interpreted as follows. With probability 0.95, one will find the parameter $\mu$ between the stochastic end points. The use of confidence intervals occurs in two different cases:

*Confidence Intervals for Unknown Mean and Known Standard Deviation.* For a population with unknown mean $\mu$ and known standard deviation $\sigma$, a confidence interval for the population mean, based on a simple random sample of size $n$, is $\bar{X} \pm z \times \frac{\sigma}{\sqrt{n}}$, where $z$ is the upper $(1-c)/2$ critical value for the standard normal distribution. Therefore, an increase in sample size will decrease the length of the confidence interval without reducing the level of confidence. This is because the standard deviation decreases as $n$ increases.

*Confidence Intervals for Unknown Mean and Unknown Standard Deviation.* In most practical cases, the standard deviation for the population of interest is not known. In this case, it is replaced by the estimated standard deviation $\sigma$, which is also known as the *standard error*. Because the standard error is an estimate for the true value of the standard deviation, the distribution of the sample mean $\bar{x}$ is no longer normal with mean $\mu$ and standard deviation $\frac{\sigma}{\sqrt{n}}$. Instead, the sample mean follows the *t distribution* with mean $\mu$ and standard deviation $\frac{\sigma}{\sqrt{n}}$. The $t$ distribution is also described by its *degrees of freedom*. For a sample of size $n$, the $t$ distribution will have $n - 1$ degrees of freedom. The notation for a $t$ distribution with $k$ degrees of freedom is $t(k)$. As the sample size $n$ increases, the $t$ distribution becomes closer to the normal distribution, because the standard error approaches the true standard deviation $\sigma$ for large $n$.

For a population with unknown mean $\mu$ and unknown standard deviation, a confidence interval for the population mean, based on a simple random sample of size $n$, is $\bar{X} \pm t \times \frac{\sigma}{\sqrt{n}}$, where $t$ is the upper $(1 - c)/2$ critical value for the $t$ distribution with $n - 1$ degrees of freedom, $t(n - 1)$.

## 2.9.2 Hypothesis Test

A *statistical hypothesis* is a statement about the distribution of the data variable $X$. The hypothesis specifies a *set* of possible distributions of $X$. *Hypothesis testing* aims at checking whether there is a sufficient statistical evidence available to reject a presumed *null hypothesis*, say $H_0$, in favor of a conjectured *alternative hypothesis*, denoted by $H_1$, [7, 19]. Thus, a hypothesis test is a *statistical decision*; the conclusion will either be to *reject* the null hypothesis or *fail to reject* it. The decision must be based on variable $X$ and aims at finding a subset $R$ of the sample space $\Omega$ and reject $H_0$ if and only if $X$ in $R$. The set $R$ is known as the *rejection region*. Usually, the critical region is defined in terms of a statistic $W(X)$, which is known as a *test statistic* [20, 21].

In a hypothesis test, a type I error occurs when the null hypothesis is rejected when it is in fact true; that is, $H_0$ is wrongly rejected. The ultimate decision may be correct or may be in error. There are two types of errors, depending on which of the hypotheses is actually true:

- A type 1 error is rejecting the null hypothesis when it is true.
- A type 2 error is failing to reject the null hypothesis when it is false.

If $H_0$ is true (that is, the distribution of $X$ is specified by $H_0$), then $P(X \in R)$ is the probability of a type 1 error for this distribution. If $H_1$ is true (that is, the distribution of $X$ is specified by $H_1$), then $P(X \in \overline{R})$ is the probability of a type 2 error for this distribution. If $H_1$ is true (that is, the distribution of $X$ is specified by $H_1$), then $P(X \in R)$, the probability of rejecting $H_0$ (and thus making a correct decision), is known as the *power* of the test for the distribution.

**Tests of the Mean in the Normal Model.** Suppose that $X_1, X_2, \ldots, X_n$ is a random sample from the normal distribution with mean $\mu$ and standard deviation $\sigma$. To construct hypothesis tests for $\mu$, the test procedure is different, depending on whether $\sigma$ is known or unknown. For this reason, $\sigma$ is called a *nuisance parameter* for the problem of testing $\mu$. The key elements in the construction of the tests are the sample mean $\bar{X} = \dfrac{1}{n} \sum_{i=1}^{n} X_i$ and sample variance $\sigma = \sqrt{\dfrac{1}{n} \sum_{i=1}^{n} (X_i - \bar{X})^2}$, and the properties of these statistics when the sampling distribution is normal.

Suppose first that the standard deviation $\sigma$ is known. Thus, the parameter space is $\{\mu: \mu \text{ in } R\}$, and a hypothesis can be any subset of this space. The basic test statistic that we used is as follows:

$$Z_0 = \frac{(M - \mu_0)}{\sigma / \sqrt{n}}$$

Note that $Z_0$ gives the directed distance from the sample mean to $\mu_0$ in units of standard deviations. Thus, $Z_0$ should give good information about competing hypotheses with $\mu_0$ on the boundary. It has the normal distribution and standard deviation given by [21]:

$$E(Z_0) = \frac{(\mu - \mu_0)}{\sigma / \sqrt{n}}, \quad (Z_0 = 1)$$

In particular, if $\mu = \mu_0$, then $Z_0$ is the standard normal distribution. The following tests have significance level $r$:

- Reject $H_0$: $\mu = \mu_0$ versus $H_1$: $\mu \neq \mu_0$ if and only if $Z_0 > z_{1-r/2}$ or $Z_0 < -z_{1-r/2}$.
- Reject $H_0$: $\mu \leq \mu_0$ versus $H_1$: $\mu > \mu_0$ if and only if $Z_0 > z_{1-r}$.
- Reject $H_0$: $\mu \geq \mu_0$ versus $H_1$: $\mu < \mu_0$ if and only if $Z_0 < -z_{1-r}$.

Knowing that the *power function* for a test of $\mu$ is $Q(\mu) = P(\text{Reject } H_0 \mid \mu)$, we can compute the power function explicitly in terms of the standard normal distribution function $G$, in the following tests:

$$H_0 : \mu \le \mu_0 \text{ versus } H_1 : \mu > \mu_0 \quad \text{at significance level } a, \text{s}$$

We can easily show that:

$$Q(z) = G\left(-z_{1-r} + \frac{\mu - \mu_0}{\sigma/\sqrt{n}}\right), \quad \text{and} \quad Q(\mu_0) = r$$

Consider now the more realistic statement that $\sigma$ and $\mu$ are unknown. In this case, the parameter space is $\{(\mu, d): \mu \text{ in } R, d > 0\}$ and the hypotheses are defined by subsets of this space. The basic test statistic that can be used for tests about $\mu$ is $T_0 = \frac{M - \mu_0}{S/\sqrt{n}}$. $T_0$ is called the Student's $t$-distribution with $n - 1$ degrees of freedom. It will be studied later in chapter 3. When $\mu \ne \mu_0$, the distribution of $T_0$ is known as the *non-central t-distribution*. Let us denote by $t_{k,p}$ the order $p$ for the $t$-distribution $T_0$. It can be shown that the following tests have significance level $r$:

- Reject $H_0$: $\mu = \mu_0$ versus $H_1$: $\mu \ne \mu_0$ if and only if $T_0 > t_{n-1, 1-r/2}$ or $T_0 < t_{n-1, 1-r/2}$.
- Reject $H_0$: $\mu \le \mu_0$ versus $H_1$: $\mu > \mu_0$ if and only if $T_0 > t_{n-1,1-r}$.

**Tests in the Bernoulli Model.** Suppose that $X_1, X_2, \ldots, X_n$ is a random sample from the Bernoulli distribution with unknown parameter $p$ in $]0, 1[$. They are independent indicator variables taking the values 1 and 0 with probabilities $p$ and $1-p$, respectively. To build hypothesis tests for the parameter $p$, the parameter space selected is $\{p: 0 < p < 1\}$, whereas the hypotheses are defined by any subset of this space. Recall that $N = X_1 + \ldots + X_n$ has the binomial distribution with parameters $n$ and $p$. It has a mean and variance equal to $np$ and $np(1 - p)$, respectively.

For $r$ in $]0, 1[$, let $b(r, n, p)$ denote the quantile of order $r$ for the binomial distribution with parameters $n$ and $p$. Because the binomial distribution is discrete, only certain quantiles are possible. The following tests have significance level $r$:

- Reject $H_0$: $p = p_0$ versus $H_1$: $p \ne p_0$ if and only if $N < b(r/2, n, p_0)$ or $N > b(1 - r/2, n, p_0)$.
- Reject $H_0$: $p < p_0$ versus $H_1$: $p > p_0$ if and only if $N > b(1 - r, n, p_0)$.

When $n$ is large, the distribution of $N$ is approximately normal according to the central limit theorem.

Thus, an approximate normal test can be constructed using the test statistic:

$$Z_0 = \frac{N - np_0}{\sqrt{np_0(1 - p_{\dot{a}})}}$$

Obviously, $Z_0$ is the standard score of $N$, under the null hypothesis. If $n$ is large, then the following tests have approximate significance level $r$:

Reject $H_0: p = p_0$ versus $H_1: p \neq p_0$ if and only if $Z_0 > -z_{1-r/2}$ or $Z_0 < -z_{1-r/2}$.

## 2.10 SUMMARY

This chapter has studied the basic properties of the probability theory, regression models, random processes, and Markov chains. The chapter gives also some examples where these entities have been used to study the behavior and features of computer and communication systems. The comparison of systems using sample data has also been addressed, and some methods for hypothesis testing and confidence interval definition have been presented. The chapter contains different examples to illustrate the presented concepts.

## REFERENCES

[1] A. Allen, "Probability, Statistics, and Queueing Theory with Computer Science Applications," 2$^{nd}$ Edition, Academic Press, New York, 1990.

[2] H. P. Shu, Probability, Random Variables and Random Processes. McGraw-Hill, New York, 1997.

[3] G. Bolch, S. Greiner, H. de Meer, and K.S. Trivedi, Queueing Networks and Markov Chains, John Wiley, New York, 1998.

[4] R. L. Chambers and C. J. Skinner (Eds.), "Analysis of Survey Data," Wiley, New York, 2003.

[5] W.G. Cochran, "Sampling Techniques," Wiley, New York 1977.

[6] F. Daly, D. L. Hand, M. C. Jones, A. D. Lunn, and K. J. McConway, "Elements of Statistics," Addison-Wesley, Boston, MA, 1995.

[7] E. L. Lehmann, "Testing Statistical Hypotheses," 2$^{nd}$ Edition, Springer, New York, 1997.

[8] J. S. Long, "Regression Models for Categorical and Limited Dependent Variables," Sage Publishers, Thousand Oaks, CA, 1997.

[9] Ch. A. Charalambides, M. V. Koutras, and N. Balakrishnan, "Probability and Statistical Models with Application," CRC Press, Boca Raton IL, 2001.

[10] G. A. F. Seber, and C. J. Wild., "Nonlinear Regression". John Wiley, New York, 1989.

[11] H. L. Harter, and D. B. Owen, "Selected Tables in Mathematical Statistics," Vol. 3, Institute of Mathematical Statistics, American Math Society, Providence, RI, 1975.

[12] N. L. Johnson, S. Kotz, and N. Balakrishnan, "Discrete Multivariate Distributions," John Wiley, New York, 1997.

[13] S. Kotz, N. Balakrishnan, and N. L. Johnson, "Continuous Multivariate Distributions, Volume 1: Models and Applications," 2nd Edition, John Wiley, New York, 2000.

[14] O. C. Ibe, Markov, "Processes for Stochastic Modeling," Academic Press, New York, 2008.

[15] A. Dembo, and O. Zeitouni, "Large Deviation and Applications," 2nd Edition, Springer, New York, 1998.

[16] A. Weiss, An Introduction to Large Deviations for Communication Network, Journal on Selected Areas in Communications Vol. 13, pp. 928–952, 1995.

[17] M. Rosenblatt, "A Central Limit Theorem and a Strong Mixing Condition," Proceedings of the National Academy of Science USA, Vol. 42, No. 1, pp. 43–47, 1956.

[18] H. Tijms, "Understanding Probability: Chance Rules in Everyday Life," Cambridge University Press, Cambridge, UK, 2004.

[19] D. R. Anderson, K. P. Burnham, and W. L. Thompson, "Null Hypothesis Testing: Problems, Prevalence, and an Alternative," Journal of Wildlife Management Vol. 64, pp. 912–923. 2000.

[20] E. L. Lehmann, Testing Statistical Hypotheses, 3rd Edition, Springer, New York, 2005.

[21] M. S. Obaidat, and G. I. Papadimitriou (Eds.)," Applied Systems Simulation: Methodologies and Applications," Springer, New York, 2003.

## EXERCISES

1. Assume that an urn contains $n = \sum_{i=1}^{k} n_i$ balls, partitioned into $k$ colors, and assume that the urn contains $n_j$ balls of color $j$. A user draws $m$ balls without replacement.

   a. What is the probability that the user has at least one ball of each color?

   b. Assume $k = 5$ and $n_j = 8$ for all $j$. Define how many balls does the user need to draw to have at least 0.8 probability of getting a full set.

   c. Suppose now $k$ is initially unknown and that $n = 60$. Drawing out 24 balls, the user finds three different colors. i) Show that $k$ satisfies: $3 \leq k \leq 33$; ii) Is there a narrower interval $k_1 \leq k \leq k_2$ that can be stated?

2. Let $X$ be a random variable with distribution function $f_X(*)$ defined by
   $f_X(-1) = 1/5; f_X(0) = 1/5; f_X(1) = 2/5; f_X(2) = 1/5$

   a. Let $Y$ be the random variable defined by the equation $Y = X + n$. Find the distribution function $f_Y(*)$ of $Y$.

   b. Let $Z$ be the random variable defined by the equation $Z = X^n$, for $n > 0$. Find the distribution function $Z$.

3. Let $\Omega$ be the sample space $\Omega = \{0,1,2,3,....\}$ and define the following function $f$:

$$f(j) = (1 - \gamma)^j \gamma$$

For some fixed real value $\gamma$, $0 < \gamma < 1$, and for 0,1,2,3, ..

    a. Show that $f$ is a distribution for $\Omega$.

    b. Assume that the probability that a packet arriving to a switch node with error is equal to $r$ and that an erroneous packet is immediately resent to that node. Compute the probability that a packet arrives correct at the $j$th transmission. Compute also the average number of packet retransmission.

4. Let $X1$, $X2$, and $X3$ be independent random variables with common distribution $f$.

    a. Find the expression using $f$ of distribution of the sum $S3 = X1 + X2 + X3$.

    b. If the distribution $f$ is given by:

$$f = \begin{pmatrix} 0 & 1 & 2 & 3 \\ \frac{1}{4} & \frac{1}{2} & \frac{1}{8} & \frac{1}{8} \end{pmatrix}$$

    c. Find the distribution of the sum $S3$.

5. The price of a stock on a given trading day changes according to the distribution $g$ given by

$$g = \begin{pmatrix} -1 & 0 & 1 & 2 \\ \frac{1}{4} & \frac{1}{2} & \frac{1}{8} & \frac{1}{8} \end{pmatrix}$$

Find the distribution for the change in stock price after three (independent) trading days.

6. Corporation A sells an imported copier on a franchise basis and performs preventive maintenance and repair service on this copier. The data below have been collected from 45 recent calls on users to perform routine preventive maintenance service; for each call, $X$ is the number of copiers serviced and $Y$ is the total number of minutes spent by the service person. Assume that simple regression model is appropriate.

| 1 : | 1 | 2 | 3 | $\cdots$ | 43 | 44 | 45 |
|---|---|---|---|---|---|---|---|
| $X_{1:}$ | 2 | 4 | 3 | $\cdots$ | 2 | 4 | 5 |
| $Y_{1:}$ | 20 | 60 | 46 | $\cdots$ | 27 | 61 | 77 |

    a. Obtain the estimated regression function.

    b. Plot the estimated regression function and the data. How well does the estimated regression function fit the data?

    c. Interpret $b_0$ in your estimated regression function. Does $b_0$ provide any relevant information here? Explain.

    d. Obtain a point estimate of the mean service time when $X = 5$ copiers are serviced.

7. Consider the simple linear regression model $Y = \beta_0 + \beta_1 X + \varepsilon$, where the intercept $\beta_0$ is known.

   a. Find the least squares estimator of 1 for this model. Does this answer seem reasonable?

   b. What is Var($\hat{\beta}_1$ ,) for the least squares estimator $\hat{\beta}_1$ found in the previous question?

   c. Compare this estimator with the one found for the case where both slope $\beta_1$ and intercept $\beta_0$ are unknown?

8. Consider the *power function* for a test of $\mu$ is $Q(\mu) = P(\text{Reject } H_0 \mid \mu)$. For the test
   $H_0: \mu = \mu_0$ versus $H_1: \mu \neq \mu_0$ at significance level $r$, associated with a normal distribution with mean $\mu_0$, show the following results for the function $Q$:

   a. $Q(\mu) = G[-z_{1-r/2} + (\mu - \mu_0)/(d/n^{1/2})] + G[-z_{1-r/2} - (\mu - \mu_0)/(d/n^{1/2})]$

   b. $Q(\mu)$ is symmetric about $\mu_0$.

   c. $Q(\mu)$ decreases for $\mu < \mu_0$ and increases for $\mu > \mu_0$.

   d. $Q(\mu_0) = r$.

   e. $\lim_{\mu \to \infty} Q(\mu) = 1$ and $\lim_{\mu \to -\infty} Q(\mu) = 1$.

9. Suppose we choose independently 30 numbers at random (uniform density) from the interval $[0; 24]$.

   a. Find the normal densities that approximate the densities of their sum $S_{36}$, their standardized sum $S_{36}^*$ ,and their average $A_{36}$.

   b. Let $N$ be the normal approximation of $A_{36}$, $F(x) = P(|A_{36} - 12| \geq x), f(x) = P(|N - 12| \geq x)$, and $g(x) = \frac{4}{3x^2}$. Compare how $f(x)$ and $g(x)$ are as estimates for $F(x)$.

10. A die is rolled 36 times. Use the central limit theorem to estimate the probability that:

    a. The sum is greater than 90.

    b. The sum is equal to 90.

11. Given a two-state DTMC having the following transition probability matrix:

$$P = \begin{pmatrix} 1-a & a \\ b & 1-b \end{pmatrix}, \quad 0 \leq a,b \leq 1, \quad |1-a-b| < 1$$

   a. Show that $n$-step transition probability matrix $P(n)$ is given by

$$P(n) = \frac{1}{a+b} \begin{pmatrix} b+a(1-a-b)^n & a-a(1-a-b)^n \\ b-b(1-a-b)^n & a+b(1-a-b)^n \end{pmatrix}$$

   b. Compute the limit of $P(n)$ when $a = \frac{1}{4}$, $b = \frac{1}{2}$, and $n \to \infty$.

12. Consider the CMTC with the transition diagram shown below. Identify all the 3-tuples (a, b, c) in $R_+^3$ that make the CTMC reversible.

# CHAPTER 3

# MEASUREMENT/TESTING TECHNIQUE

The measurement technique of performance evaluation of computer and telecommunication systems is considered the most credible technique; however, it is the most expensive. The measurement or testing technique can be implemented on the real system or the prototype version of the system intended to be built. System performance measurement involves monitoring the system under study while it is being subjected to a particular set of workload or benchmark application programs. It is vital that the system performance analyst understand the following concepts before invoking the task of performance measurements: (a) system application, (b) performance metrics (measures) of interest to the analyst, (c) method of system instrumentation and how the system under study is monitored, (d) representative of workload to real applications, (e) methods of presenting performance results, and (e) techniques to design measurement monitors [1–21].

This chapter focuses on the fundamental concepts of the measurement technique, tracing, tools, as well as issues and solutions.

## 3.1 MEASUREMENT STRATEGIES

In the measurement technique, different kinds of performance metrics are usually needed depending on the nature of the system under test and application.

*Fundamentals of Performance Evaluation of Computer and Telecommunication Systems,*
By Mohammad S. Obaidat and Noureddine A. Boudriga
Copyright © 2010 John Wiley & Sons, Inc.

From the viewpoint of event type, these metrics can be categorized into the following classes [1–3, 7]:

- **Event-count metrics.** This class includes metrics that are simply counts of the number of times a specific event takes place, such as the number of packets that arrive with noise, number of cells discarded because of congestion or deadlock, and number of cache misses.
- **Profiles.** In computer systems, a profile represents an aggregate metric for characterizing the overall behavior of a program or a whole system. For example, degree of parallelism (DOP) represents the total number of active processors in a parallel computer system at each instant of time during the execution of a specific application program.
- **Auxiliary-event metrics.** Auxiliary metrics note the values of secondary system parameters when a specific event happens.

The strategy used to measure the performance metric of interest can be decided based on the event type classification discussed above. The chief strategies are as follows [2, 6, 17–21]:

- **Event-driven strategy.** This scheme records the needed information to calculate the metric whenever the events of interest occur. For instance, the desired metric may be the number of cells lost in a computer network's or the number of cache miss in a computer system. To find this number, the analyst should provide a way to record these events whenever they occur and update the appropriate counter. At the end of the session, a mechanism should be provided to dump the content of the counter. This strategy has the advantage that the overhead needed to monitor the event of interest is spent only when the event happens. However, this characteristic is considered as a drawback when the event occurs frequently.
- **Tracing strategy.** This scheme relies on recording more data than only a single event. This means that we need more storage space for this strategy compared with the event-driven scheme.
- **Indirect.** This scheme is used when the performance measure (metric) of interest cannot be measured directly. In such a case, the analyst should look for a metric that can be measured directly and from which the required metric can be derived.
- **Sampling.** This strategy relies on recording the system's state needed to find out the performance metric of interest. Clearly, the sampling frequency here determines the measurement overhead. The latter is determined by the resolution needed to sample the required events.

## 3.2  EVENT TRACING

In general, a trace consists of an ordered list of events and their related variables.

Such captured information is gathered using profiling tools, and it provides a summary representation of the overall execution of a task. The events of a trace can be a time-ordered list of all instructions executed by a program, sequence of cache addresses by a program, sequence of disk blocks referenced by a file system, and so on. Events may be represented at several levels of details, such as variable trace, procedure trace, or event trace. It is worth mentioning that tracing adds additional processing overhead. Thus, it is important to provide switches to enable or disable tracing as needed.

The traces can be investigated and analyzed to characterize the behavior of a program or a system. In simulation tasks such as cache memory simulation and communication network simulation, traces can be used to drive the simulation programs. Other examples include paging algorithms, central processing units (CPUs) scheduling schemes, and deadlock avoidance algorithms in parallel and distributed systems, among others. Because the size of such traces is usually large, trace compression is often used in such cases to expedite the process of simulation.

Traces are also often used to verify simulation models and to analyze and tune resource management algorithms. However, it is worth pointing out here that trace-driven simulation has many advantages, including [1–10]: (a) better credibility, (b) fair comparison of alternative schemes; (c) less randomness and more close to real operating conditions; (d) more detailed, which helps to find the best trade off alternative; and (e) easier to validate.

The main drawbacks of trace-driven simulation include (a) single point validation, because traces give only one point of validation; (b) unnecessary high-level details as traces are generally long; (c) trace-driven simulation is complex as it requires a more detailed simulation of the system; (d) finiteness characteristic as a detailed trace of a minute or so may fill an entire disk and a simulation result based on such a few minutes may not represent the behavior of the system under study; and (e) poor representation, as traces may become obsolete faster than other forms of workload types.

Any tracing system consists of three key parts (a) the application program being traced that generates the traces; (b) the trace consumer, which is the program that uses the information (e.g., simulator); and (c) the disk file to store the traces. The latter may not be needed in cases where the traces are too large to fit in a disk. In such a case, the traces are used online. Figure 3.1 shows a simplified block diagram of a tracing system.

Traces can be generated using several techniques. These are as follows:

- **Software exception**. Some microprocessors have a mode of operation called the trace mode. A special control bit called the trace bit is used, and when it is enabled, tracing is performed. This is a sort of software exception, which slows down the program being executed.
- **Modification of source code**. In this technique, the source program to be traced is modified so that when it is compiled and executed, extra statements are executed to generate the required traces. This scheme

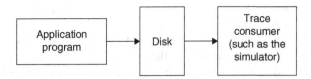

**FIGURE 3.1.** A simplified block diagram of a tracing system.

allows the performance analyst to trace specific events, which reduces the need to store a huge volume of traces. The main drawback of this scheme is that inserting the trace points is prone to error as it is a manual process.

- **Modification of microcode.** This approach was used when microprocessors were used to execute their instruction sets using interpretation. In such processors, it was possible to modify the microcode to generate traces of each executed instruction. However, in today's state-of-the-art micropro-cessors, there is no microcode, which limits the applicability of this scheme.
- **Emulation.** In this scheme, the emulation program is modified to trace the execution of the application program. Keep in mind that emulation enables us to execute a program by emulating a processor's instruction sent.
- **Modification of the executable code produced by the compiler.** In the technique, we add supplementary instructions at the beginning of each block in order to mark when the block is inserted.

One major concern when generating traces is the large volume of data produced in a very short time. This prompted performance analysts to devise schemes to compress the traces without affecting the degree of representation. The major techniques that can be used to reduce the size of information produced by tracing are as follows [2]:

- **Data compression.** This technique relies on applying data compression techniques to reduce the size of traces. It has the potential to reduce the size of traces by a factor of 25% of the original size. The tradeoff in using this scheme is the additional time needed to compress and uncompress the traces when traces are generated and consumed, respectively.
- **Compression of traces online.** The idea here is to consume the traces online as generated without the need to store them for later use. This saves the need to have a large disk system to store the traces; however, there is a possible problem in multitask environments. There is no guarantee that the next time the program is traced, the same succession of events will occur because system events happen asynchronously with respect to a traced program. Clearly, this is of great concern when repeatability in generating traces is needed.
- **Sampling of traces.** The main idea here is to save only a relatively small part of the trace sequences scattered throughout the collected or generated

trace data. Because such samples are considered statistically representative of the entire trace data, they can be used to drive the simulator. This has the advantage of storing a small part of the trace data. It is worth mentioning here that there is no theoretical basis to help the performance analysts decide on the size of each sample as well as the sampling rate. This technique has been used in the simulation of cache memory systems.

- **Abstract execution**. This scheme separates traces into the following two stages: (a) compiler analysis of the program to be traced to identify a small part of the entire trace that can be used later on to reproduce the entire trace and (b) execution of special trace-generation procedures to convert this small part of the trace data into the full trace data. Empirical studies have shown that this tracing scheme slows down the execution of the program being traced by an average factor of 6, which is not higher than other tracing schemes. Moreover, because this scheme records information only about the changes that actually occur during run time, it can reduce the volume of trace data stored by a factor of several hundreds.\

## 3.3  MONITORS

Monitors are defined as tools that are used to observe and record the activities of a system under testing and analysis. The main functions of a monitor used in performance evaluation are to: (a) observe the performance of the system, (b) collect performance statistics, (c) analyze the data collected, and (d) display the results if possible. Hardware monitors have gone through several generations of developments. State-of-the art hardware monitors are intelligent and have programmable devices as well as smart components such as processors and needed peripherals. Almost all monitors when embedded in the system under test cause overhead. It is desired to reduce the monitor overhead [1–5].

Monitors can be categorized based on the implementation level, trigger mechanism, and display capability. From point of view of the levels at which monitors are implemented, we have the following types of monitors: (a) hardware monitors, (b) software monitors, and (c) hybrid or firmware monitors. A brief description of each of them is given below.

### 3.3.1  Hardware Monitors

A hardware monitor is a device that consists of several components. It is attached to the system to be monitored and analyzed to collect information related to events of specific interest. Probes are usually used to connect the components of the hardware monitor to the system under test. In general, a hardware monitor consumes no system resources, and it has a lower overhead as compared with to a software monitor. Hardware monitors are usually faster than software monitors. The basic building blocks of a hardware monitor are as follows:

- **Probes.** These are used to connect the monitor to the circuit or hardware points of interest of the system under test. A probe in general has high impedance.
- **Logic gates.** These components are needed to construct various functional units that help to indicate events that may increment counters or test conditions.
- **Counters.** These devices are needed to increment or decrement the occurrence of events of interest.
- **Timers.** These are needed for time stamping or triggering a sampling operation.
- **Comparators.** Such components are used to compare contents of counters and to test for specific conditions.
- **Storage device.** Almost all hardware monitors have built-in storage devices, such as tapes or compact disk (CD) drivers, to store observed data.

### 3.3.2 Software Monitors

These types of monitors are basically computer programs that are embedded in the operating system. They are meant to observe events in the operating system and higher level software, such as in databases and networks. It is essential to have the operating rate of the monitor high enough so that it can observe the needed events and collect the needed data properly. Also, the overhead should be small.

In general, software monitors have lower input rates, lower resolution, and higher overhead when compared with hardware monitors. However, they have higher input width and recording capacities than hardware monitors. Also, they are less expensive and easier to implement than hardware monitors. Because software monitors have high overhead, they should be designed so that their function can be easily disabled when needed using a simple flag.

In designing any software monitor, several issues should be considered. Among these are the following:

1. **Buffer size.** The size of the buffer memory should be optimal. This means that it should be large enough so that the rate of writing to the auxiliary storage is reduced, and at the same time, it should be small so that the time lost per writing operation is not too large.
2. **Number of buffers.** The minimum number of buffers should be two. This is because if there is only one buffer, then the monitoring (filling of buffer) and recording (emptying) processes cannot be performed simultaneously.

3. **Method of activation**. This refers to the way by which the software monitor's data collection procedure is triggered. Among these methods that are used in microprocessor systems are: (a) trace mode, (b) trap instruction(s), and (c) timer interrupt.

The trace mode is available in most microprocessors. In this scheme, the execution of instructions is interrupted after each instruction, and control is passed on to a special procedure to collect data. This technique suffers from a high overhead.

The trap instruction-based scheme relies on using a trap instruction in the middle of the code where it is inserted at selected points. When the trap instruction is executed, program execution is transferred to a special data collection procedure.

The timer interrupt-based scheme is provided by the operating system to transfer control of execution to a special data collection procedure at fixed intervals. One interesting characteristic of this scheme is that it has low overhead because the overhead is independent of the event rate.

4. **Enable/Disable.** Because of the overhead incurred when the software monitor is enabled, it is desired to disable the software monitor easily when monitoring is no longer needed. Moreover, such an on/off capability permits debugging of the code.

5. **Overflow management**. There is always a possibility that the monitor's buffer reaches the overflow state. To avoid losing traces, designers of software monitors should provide a mechanism by which the monitoring process is stopped whenever the buffer overflows. The choice between overwriting the buffer or not depends on the application and needs of the analyst. The goal here is to detect the occurrence of buffer overflow.

6. **Programming language**. To reduce overhead and latency, it is desired to write the monitor code in low-level languages such as assembly language. However, because the monitor is embedded in the system software, therefore, it is better to have both written in the same programming language.

7. **Monitor priority**. To minimize the effect of the monitor's on system's operation, it should be given a low priority, especially if the monitor is run asynchronously. However, if it is required to observe important timely observations, then the monitor should be given a high priority.

### 3.3.3 Hybrid Monitors

This type of monitors is also called by other authors as firmware monitors. These monitors are often used for applications where speed and timing consideration prevent the use of software monitors, and difficulty of accessing probe points prevents the use of hardware monitors. They are popular to monitor networks where existing interfaces can be easily microprogrammed to monitor the flow of traffic. Furthermore, they can be used to generate address profiles of microcode, which are used to optimize the code to improve the speed of execution.

Hybrid monitor use software and hardware means for their operation. When implemented properly, hybrid monitors have the potential of providing the high-resolution characteristics of hardware monitors and the data reduction capabilities of software monitors.

It is worth mentioning in this context the distributed-system monitors that are used to monitor distributed and parallel systems. In such a case, the monitor itself must be distributed and should be made of several components that are supposed to work concurrently. The main functions of a distributed and parallel-system monitor are:

1. Gathering of data from individual system's components.
2. Collection of data from different observers.
3. Analysis of data collected using special statistical routines that summarize the data characteristics.
4. Preparation of performance reports.
5. Interpretation of performance reports using either human experience or expert systems.
6. Based on result's interpretation, a special entity is supposed to make decisions to set or change system parameters or configurations. The component that performs this task is often called the manager, and it is implemented in advanced monitors with automated monitoring and control features [1–4].

## 3.4 PROGRAM OPTIMIZERS

Program execution monitors or program execution analyzers (program optimizers) are of great interest to performance evaluation analysts. Monitoring the execution of a computer program is needed for the following reasons:

1. To locate the execution path of a code
2. To determine the time spent in various sections of a program
3. To locate the most frequent or most time-consuming segment of the program
4. To test the relationship between the variables and parameters of a program
5. To establish the adequacy of a test run of the program

In general, programs to be monitored are chosen depending on the following criteria: (a) frequency of use, (b) time criticality, and (c) resource demand.

The chief issues in designing a program execution (optimizer) monitor are pretty much similar to these for software monitors. In addition there are several issues that are specific to the optimizer monitors, including [1, 4] the following:

1. **Frequency and time histogram.** Almost all program monitors produce an execution profile with different levels of hierarchy, such as summaries by modules, for each module by procedures, and for each procedure by statement. Monitors have the capability to scale up or down the amount of detail.

2. **Measurement units.** An execution program divides the program into smaller units called modules, procedures, high-level language statements, or machine instructions. Data associated with each unit are noted and shown in the final report. Lower level reports such as machine instruction profiles may be too comprehensive for certain applications.

3. **Measurement methods.** We can have two basic measurement schemes: sampling and tracing. The sampling scheme makes use of the system's timer convenience, and it records states at cyclic intervals. If the elapsed time sampling approach is used, then the program may be in a wait state, until an input/output (I/O) operation or some other event is completed. The tracing scheme uses either explicit loops or the trace mode of a microprocessor.

4. **Instrumentation means.** In this scheme, instrumentation can be added before compilation, during compilation, before linking (after compilation), or during run time. To instrument a source code, a high-level routine call statement is added at a strategic location in the program. This call statement transfers control to the monitor procedure that it is supposed to collect data [2].

## 3.5   ACCOUNTING LOGS

Accounting logs provide interesting useful information about the usage and performance of the system; therefore, many analysts consider them software monitors. It is recommended that before creating a monitor, the analyst should benefit from the data provided by accounting logs.

Accounting logs can be used without extra efforts as they are built into the system. Data collected using accounting logs are accurate as they represent real operation with little overhead. However, accounting log analysis programs are not generally provided. For a more accurate analysis, a system analyst should develop additional analysis programs, including statistical analysis programs.

In general, the precision of accounting logs is not high, and most of them contain no system-level information including device utilization, queueing time, or queue length. In addition to the queueing time, the elapsed time includes the service time of resources. Moreover, almost all accounting logs do not record the time spent waiting for user inputs; therefore, this time cannot be distinguished from the queueing time. The typical information provided by an accounting log include the program name, program start time, program end time, CPU time used by the program, number of disk reads and writes, number of terminal reads and writes, and so on.

The main usages of accounting logs are to know: (a) usage of resources, (b) programs that users should be trained to use more efficiently, (c) programs that need better code optimization, (d) which application programs are I/O bound, (e) programs that have poor locality of reference, (f) number of jobs that can be run at the same time without performance degradation, and (g) programs that provide the best opportunity for better human interface [1, 2, 4].

## 3.6  SUMMARY

This chapter presented the main aspects of the measurement/testing technique of performance evaluation of computer and telecommunication systems. In particular, we studied the strategies to be followed when invoking into a measurement task, which include the event-driven, tracing, and sampling strategies. We also studied the main performance metrics that depend on the applications and objectives of the performance evaluation study. Then we studied event tracing and its significance, drawbacks, applications, approaches, components, and methods of trace compression. Software, hardware, and hybrid monitors have been investigated along with their functions, types, and design issues. We also have shed some light on program optimizers or program execution analyzers. In particular, we reviewed the main issues in their design such as frequency and time histogram, measurement unit and methods, and instrumentation means. The last section covered in this chapter is accounting logs. Although accounting logs are not accurate, they provide a rough estimate of the performance of resources, especially their use. Accounting logs provide interesting useful information about the usage and performance of the system; therefore, many analysts consider them software monitors. It is recommended that before creating a monitor, the analyst should benefit from the data provided by accounting logs. Also, we addressed the main applications and characteristics of accounting logs.

## REFERENCES

[1] M. S. Obaidat, and G. I. Papdimitriou (Eds.), "Applied System Simulation: Methodologies and Applications," Springer, New York, 2003.

[2] R. Jain, "The Art of Computer Systems Performance Analysis," Wiley, New York, 1991.

[3] K. Kant, "Introduction to Computer System Performance Evaluation," McGraw-Hill, New York, 1992.

[4] D. J. Lilja, "Measuring Computer Performance," Cambridge University Press, Cambridge, UK, 2000.

[5] M. S. Obaidat, "Advances in Performance Evaluation of Computer and Tele-communications Networking," *Computer Communication Journal* Vol. 25, No. 11–12, pp. 993–996, 2002.

[6] M.S. Obaidat, "ATM Systems and Networks: Basics Issues, and Performance Modeling and simulation," Simulation: Transactions of the Society for Modeling and Simulation International, Vol. 78, No. 3, pp. 127–138, 2003.

[7] M.S. Obaidat, "Performance Evaluation of Telecommunication Systems: Models Issues and Applications," Computer Communications Journal, Vol. 34, No. 9, pp. 753–756, 2001.

[8] M. Ghanbari, C. J. Hughes, M. C. Sinclair, and J. P. Eade, "Principles of Performance Engineering for Telecommunication and Information Systems," IEE, Herts, UK, 1997.

[9] K. Hwang, and Z. Xu, "Scalable Parallel Computing," McGraw-Hill, New York, 1998.

[10] M. Arlitt, and T. Jin, "Workload Characterization of the 1998 World Cup Web Site," HP Technical Report 1999-35R1, Hewlett-Packard, 1999.

[11] M. Arlitt, and C. Williamson, "Internet Web Servers: Workload Characterization and Performance Implications," IEEE/ACM Transactions on Networking, Vol. 5, No. 5, pp. 631–645, 1997.

[12] L. K. John, and A. M. G. Maynard, (Eds.)" Workload Characterization of Emerging Applications," Kluwer Academic Publisher, Dordrecnt, The Netherlands, 2001.

[13] J. L. Hennessy, and D. A. Patterson, "Computer Architecture: A Quantitative Approach," 3rd edition Morgan Kaufmann, New York, 2003.

[14] J. Banks, J. S. Crason II, B. L. Nelson, and D. Nicol, "Discrete-Event System Simulation," 3rd edition, Prentice Hall, Upper Saddle River, 2001.

[15] S. M. Ross, "Simulation," 2nd edition, Harcourt Academic Press, San Diego, CA, 1997.

[16] M. S. Obaidat, "Performance Evaluation of the IMPS Multiprocessor System," Journal of Computer and Electrical Engineering, Vol. 15, No. 4, pp. 121–130, 1989.

[17] The Standard Performance Evaluation Corporation: http://www.spec.org.

[18] http://imls.lib.utexas.edu/redesign/slideshow/tsld009.html.

[19] NAS Parallel Benchmarks: http://science.nas.nasa.gov/software/npb/.

[20] Parkbench Parallel Benchmarks: http://www.netlib.org/parbench/.

[21] Transaction Processing Council (TPC) Benchmarks: http://www.tpc.org/.

## EXERCISES

1. What are the strategies that can be used for the measurement technique of performance evaluation?

2. Compare and contrast hardware and software monitors.

3. What are the main applications of accounting logs?

4. Which programs must be chosen for I/O optimization? Explain.

5. Choose an IEEE 802.11 wireless local area network (WLAN), review published articles related to its performance evaluation, and make a list of the benchmarks used in these articles.

6. Choose a multiprocessor computer system architecture. Review the related published articles on its performance evaluation, and make a list of the used performance metrics.

7. Select a measurement study of the performance evaluation of a computer system or a communication network in which hardware monitors are used in the study. Explain how useful such monitors are for providing accurate and real measurement about the behavior of the system. Discuss whether you can replace the hardware monitor by a software monitor, and give the advantages and disadvantages for doing so.

8. A workstation uses a 500-MHz processor with a claimed 100-MIPS rating to execute a given program mix. Assume a one-cycle delay for each memory access.

   a. What is the effective cycle per instruction (CPI) of this machine?

   b. Suppose that the processor is being upgraded with a 1000-MHz clock. However, the speed of the memory subsystem remains unchanged, and consequently, two clock cycles are needed per memory access. If 30% of the instructions require one memory access and another 5% require two memory accesses per instruction, what is the performance of the upgraded processor with a compatible instruction set and equal instruction counts in the given program mix?

9. A linear pipeline processor has eight stages. It is required to execute a task that has 600 operands. Find the speedup factor, $S_k$, assuming that the CPU runs at 1.5 GHz. Note that the speedup factor of a liner pipeline processor is defined by the following expression: Sk = speedup = (time needed by a one-stage pipeline processor to do a task)/(time needed by $k$-stage processor to do the same task) = $T_1/T_k$.

10. Devise an experiment to find out the performance metrics for an IEEE 802.3 local area network (LAN)

   a. The throughput of the network as a function of the number of nodes in the LAN.

   b. The average packet delay as a function of the number of nodes in the LAN.

   c. The throughput-delay relationship.

# CHAPTER 4

# BENCHMARKING AND CAPACITY PLANNING

This chapter deals with benchmarking and capacity planning of performance evaluation for computer and telecommunication systems. We will address types of benchmark programs and common mistakes in benchmarking. Examples of popular benchmark programs will be surveyed. The main procedures for capacity planning and tuning as well as the problems encountered in such a task will be studied as well. Benchmarks are designed for particular types of environments, and hence, we need to select the specific benchmark that suits the system under study. Most often, benchmarks evaluate the systems only by calculating the performance of the application services and the load by undermining the architecture and the underlying protocols on which the application is based. Moreover, it is difficult to estimate the performance characteristics of a system accurately with the help of a benchmark, as it may not address all the properties of the system. To enable the system, server, or network to provide high performance, we must optimize the load on the network and servers, as well as optimize the use of input/output (I/O) resources. This can be handled with the help of capacity planning. The chapter discusses the issues related to capacity planning along with the problems associated with it. We dedicated a section that deals with the capacity planning for providing efficient Web service. This section addresses the scalability, architecture, and network capacity along with server overloading issues for

*Fundamentals of Performance Evaluation of Computer and Telecommunication Systems,*
By Mohammad S. Obaidat and Noureddine A. Boudriga
Copyright © 2010 John Wiley & Sons, Inc.

improving the performance of Web servers. A summary of the main points reviewed in this chapter will be given at the end.

## 4.1  INTRODUCTION

The best computer programs that should be used to evaluate the performance and behavior of a computer system or network are the ones that are often used by the user/application. However, this is not usually feasible or cost effective as it often requires a substantial amount of time and effort to port the application programs to the system under test, especially if the aim is to find the performance of a new system when such an application is run on it. Clearly, because of such difficulties in running the user's application programs on the systems being evaluated, surrogate programs called benchmark programs are used. The hope is that such benchmark programs can characterize the behavior of the intended applications. The results of running such benchmark programs can be used to predict the performance and behavior of the system for the intended application. The accuracy of these predictions when validated with real applications can determine the quality of such benchmarks.

Benchmarking can be defined as the process of running a particular program or workload on a specific system and measuring the resulting performance. This process provides an accurate assessment of the performance of the system under study for that considered workload. Benchmark programs can be either whole applications, kernels (most executed parts of a program), or synthetic programs.

Benchmarking is an important scheme to compare the performance of two or more systems for various purposes, including procurement, capacity planning, and tuning. Because different application areas have different execution characteristics and behavior, a spectrum of benchmark programs have been developed to address these different domains and environments. For example, designers of processors use (at the early stages of the design) small benchmarks that can aid in estimating performance using simulation. However, for procurement, the analysts use more complex benchmarks because decisions to purchase such expensive systems are based on such measurements. Benchmark programs should be easy to use, port to different systems, and execute [1–47].

It is interesting to point out that there is no complete agreement within the system performance evaluation community on what makes a good benchmark program. The strategies that can be followed to measure a system's performance are as follows [1–29]:

1. **Fixed computation technique.** Here, the total time needed to execute the specific computation task of the benchmark is used as a metric.
2. **Fixed time.** Here, we fix the amount of time the system is allowed to execute the benchmark program and use the total amount of computation it completes in this time as a metric.

3. **A combination of execution time and amount of computation completed within this time is used as a performance metric**. Example on this includes the quality of improvements per second (QUIPS) that is used in the HINT benchmark.

Capacity planning can be defined as the process by which we ensure that adequate system resources will be available to meet future demands in a cost-effective way without violating performance objectives. Another process that is related to capacity planning is called capacity management. This process deals with making sure that present resources are used efficiently to provide the utmost performance.

In general, benchmarking consists of a set of programs, that are used for performance evaluation purposes. It can even be used to compare the performance of other systems over different architectures. The performance evaluation results obtained by benchmarking are often not easy to draw up conclusions about the system performance. Benchmarks rarely evaluate the system on the basis of the mixed workloads, which is a similar comparison with that of the real workload. Also, they do not evaluate the I/O resource usage and memory accesses in the system. With the evolution of new types of networks, such as grids and cluster environment, some workloads that are used for evaluation are grid friendly, whereas others are not. Most of the time benchmarks evaluate quality of service (QoS) on the basis of the system's raw performance. Moreover, benchmarks evaluate the performance of the system on the basis of application services and loads at the system and network by ignoring the underlying architecture and the protocols used by the system. Benchmarks are not developed on the basis of standards, but they are developed with respect to a particular type of computer system or an environment.

## 4.2  TYPES OF BENCHMARK PROGRAMS

A benchmark is a performance testing program that is meant to catch processing and data movement characteristics of a group of applications. Benchmark programs are used to measure and forecast the performance of systems and reveal their behavior as well as strong and weak aspects. Also, we define a benchmark suite as a set of benchmark programs jointly with a set of well-defined rules governing test conditions and procedures, including platform environment, input and output data, and performance measures.

Benchmark programs (benchmarks) can be categorized into macro and micro benchmarks. Micro benchmarks measure a specific aspect of a system, such as memory or I/O speed, processor speed, network throughput or latency, and so on. However, macro benchmarks measure the performance of a system in its entirety. The latter is important for applications that require comparing competitive systems or designs, and that is why it is often used to compare different systems with respect to a certain application category, especially for procurement purposes.

Others classify benchmarks based on application types, such as network services, business applications, interactive applications like airline reservation and financial applications, scientific computing, multimedia and signal processing, and so on. Moreover, benchmarks can be full-fledged applications or kernels. The latter types are usually much smaller and simpler programs taken out from applications while upholding the main characteristics. A benchmark can be a real program that performs a real application or a synthetic one that is usually designed specifically to exercise certain functional units or subunits at various working conditions.

In general, benchmarks used for comparing the system's performance can be broadly categorized into the following major types:

1. Addition instruction: When computers were introduced initially, the most expensive component of the system was the processor. Hence, the system's performance was measured as the performance of the processor [1, 16–23]. Few instructions were supported initially, and the addition instruction was most frequently used. The system used to compute these addition instructions at a faster rate was supposed to perform better. Hence, the performance metric used for measuring the systems performance was the time used for executing the addition instruction.

2. Instruction mixes: With the advancement in the design of processors, the number of instructions supported by the CPU also increased. Hence, calculating the time required for executing the addition instruction was no longer sufficient for evaluating the performance of the computer system. Hence, the frequencies of different instructions used on the real system were to be measured so as to use them as a weighing factor for performance evaluation [1–4, 8–15]. Thus, an instruction mix can be defined as the description of various instructions with their frequencies. By using the above information, the computational time required for executing the instructions on each of the processors can be calculated and can be compared with the performance of the other competing processors. Several such instruction mixes exist. Among those available in the computer industry is the Gibson mix. In the Gibson mix, the instructions are classified into 13 different categories, which contain the execution time for each of these instructions. The weights for these instructions are based on the relative frequencies of the operations [1, 2]. Certainly, some disadvantages are associated with these instruction mixes. With the innovation in computer technology, the instructions nowadays are more complex and these changes are not reflected in the instruction mixes. These changes are not reflected in the mixes provided for some processors. Normally, the execution time is calculated in terms of millions instructions per second (MIPS) and millions floating-point operations

per second (MFLOPS). Moreover, the instruction mixes only calculate the processor speed. Keep in mind that the system performance depends not only on the processor speed but also on the other components, which are not addressed in the instruction mixes.

3. Kernels: Because of the introduction of new mechanisms, such as various addressing schemes, caching and pipelining, and prefetching, the execution time of the instruction is highly variable. Hence, it is more important to find the execution time of a function or service provided by the processor that comprises a set of instructions rather than evaluating the execution time for single instruction [2, 16–29]. Most kernels defined in the literature do not consider the input and output devices, and they characterize the systems performance only on the basis of the processor performance. Hence, these are also referred to as processing kernels. Kernels can be defined as instruction mix generalizations. We can identify several applications and then compare the performance of the processor based on the kernel performance. Most disadvantages that apply to the instruction mixes also apply to the kernels [2–10]. A major disadvantage of using the kernels is that they do not make use of I/O devices for calculating the system's performance. Hence, the performance of the kernel will not visualize the performance of the system as a whole.

4. Synthetic programs: The kernels that are used for evaluating the system's performance do not use the services offered by the operating system or the input and output devices. Most applications designed these days are not only used for processing but also cater to a lot of input/output operations with the help of external devices. Hence, these have become an integral part of the workload, which needs to be considered for evaluating the system's performance in the real world [3, 23–29]. The performance of the input/output is measured by using the exerciser loops, which make the input/output requests. These loops help in calculating the average amount of time required for executing a single service call or an input/output request. These loops are termed "synthetic programs" and are usually written in high-level languages. The loops that are defined can be controlled with the help of control parameters so as to ensure that they make a limited number of input/output requests. Apart from calculating the amount of time required for executing input/output requests, the exerciser loops can also be used for measuring the services provided by the operating system, such as creating the process, forking the child processes, and allocating the memory requirements. A major advantage of the exerciser loops is that they can be developed quickly. Apart from this, they can be easily modified so that they can be executed on different platforms [1–4]; they are also easily portable. Moreover, these loops have measurement capabilities, which are built in. Thus, the process of measurement is automated, which can be used to run these loops several times on the system so as to measure the performance gain and losses of

the system. The major drawback of these exerciser loops is that they are too small. Mechanisms such as page faults and disk cache are not generally addressed. More precisely, these are not well suited for multiuser environments.

5. Application benchmarks: Application benchmarks are mainly used to evaluate the performance of systems, which are used for a particular application, such as airline reservation, banking, sorting, weather forecasting, and so on [1–4, 16–23]. For such applications, benchmarks are defined as a collective group of functions, which make use of all the resources of the system.

## 4.3 BENCHMARK EXAMPLES

This section sheds some light on most known benchmark programs.

- **WebTP:** This benchmark is mainly used for evaluating the Web system's performance and in particular the order management system. This system is basically used on the web for purchasing the services and the goods over the Internet [2–4, 30]. It is also considered as one of the most important electronic applications. An integrated order management system may include modules such as product information, vendors, purchasing, and receiving; marketing (catalogs, promotions, pricing, etc.), customers, and prospects; order entry and customer service, including returns and refunds; financial processing; order processing such as selection, printing, picking, packing, shipping, data analysis, and reporting; and financial matters, such as accounts payable and accounts receivable. The order management system is an integral application of e-commerce, and therefore, WebTP has applicability to all types of e-businesses applications.

  The Web application performance depends on the technology on which it is developed, and this is supported by different versions of WebTP. The transactions supported by such Web-based systems are specified in the TPC-C benchmark, which is used by the WebTP [2, 3, 30]. The TPC-C benchmark supports five types of transactions, such as new order, payment, order status, delivery, and stock-level transactions.

  The Transaction Processing Council (TPC) was established with the goal of developing benchmark programs for systems that perform online transaction processing (OLTP). The latter application includes airline reservation systems, automatic teller machine (ATM) systems, credit card verification systems, and inventory control systems. In such systems, it is important to perform the transaction within a given response time limit, maintain a consistent data flow, and be available essentially all the time.

  The TPC devised several benchmark programs, including the TPC-A, which was based on an early Debit-Credit benchmark that was intended to stimulate kinds of transactions that would be likely to occur in an ATM system environment. In this benchmark the actual program to be executed is not specified; instead a high-level function is specified. The main performance requirement was that 90% of the transactions must complete in less than 2 s. The performance metric used was transactions per minute. There are other versions of TPC including the TPC-D, which deals with decision-support systems, and TPC-W, which focuses on e-commerce applications.

The benchmark programs that are used to characterize the performance of client-server systems are typically run on the clients, which send a stream of files-access commands or other types of requests to the server. Common performance metrics that are often used for such an environment are the number of requests that can be completed per unit time and the average time needed to react to the requests.

An example on such benchmark programs is the SFS/LADDIS 1.1 benchmark that was designed to measure the throughput of UNIX-based servers, which run the Network File System (NFS) protocol. Others call this program as LADDIS, which is the acronym of the companies that cooperated to develop it, namely, Legato, Auspex, Digital, Data General, Interphase, and Sun. The SFS 2.0 is a new version of SFS that was released in 1997 and is an improved version of SFS 1.1. SFS 2.0 has many improvements including larger and more recent workloads that reflect the mix of operations observed in more than 1,000 NFS application environment and it can support TPC and UDP network transmission protocols.

The Standard Performance Evaluation Corportion (SPEC) developed a benchmark program in order to measure the throughput rates of Web servers. This was called the SPECweb benchmark and it was developed on the framework of SFS/LADDIS benchmark. The SPECweb benchmark programs continuously send HTTP requests to a Web server system at a rate that is progressively increased until the server can no longer reply within the predefined upper limit response time. The value of the rate at which requests can be served before the server's response time starts to decrease is considered the reported performance metric for the system under study [18–20, 42].

- **Probing**. Probing stands for purchaser-oriented benchmarking. Most of the benchmarks look for services, but probing mainly concentrates on the activity [1–30]. The process of benchmarking is performed in four stages in the case of probing, which are as listed below:
  1. Planning: In this stage, we need to: (a) identify the subject for the benchmark, (b) identify the partner for the benchmark, and (c) identify the method for collecting the data.
  2. Analysis: This stage involves identifying: (a) the competitive gap and (b) future performance of the project.
  3. Integration: This deals with communications and functional goal establishment.

4. Action: This stage includes: (a) creating the action plans, (b) deploying the plans and then monitoring the results obtained, and (c) recalibrating benchmarks.

    Each of the single item is identified is benchmarked during the planning phase of probing. Based on the information obtained during the analysis phase, it can be directly used in the next steps of the benchmarking.

- **NpBench**. NpBench is a benchmarking tool that is mainly used for networking applications. In this benchmark, all the applications are classified into three functional groups [31–33, 46]. These are traffic management and QoS group (TQG), security and media group (SMG), and packet processing group (PPG).

    Most of the benchmarks designed for network applications addressed only data plane applications, whereas NpBench is designed to address both data plane and control plane applications [3–7, 23, 46]. NpBench supports 12 different types of workloads and more; see Figure 4.1. Multiple processing engines are encapsulated in the architecture of the NpBench. Often, these processing elements are arranged either in a pipelined or in a parallel manner. To increase the performance of the processing elements, multithreading is deployed in the architecture. This helps in making the context switch faster between the applications.

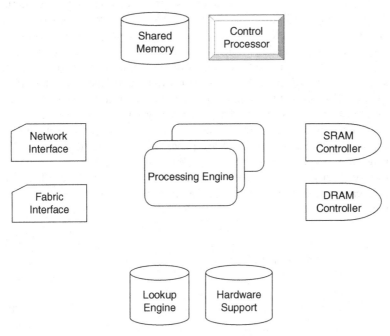

**FIGURE 4.1.** NpBench architecture.

The processing of the control functions are supported by the user interface [3–7, 46]. The workloads are categorized as data workload and control workload. Network applications are classified as data plane and control plane applications. The processing requirements are more complex in case of control functions when compared with that of data functions. The functions in the NpBench benchmark are broadly categorized as data plane functions and control plane functions.

- **Grey Relation Analysis (GRA).** The performance of a system can be evaluated with the help of performance metrics/indicators. For the process of evaluation, if all the performance indicators are used, then the process of collecting the data will become highly difficult [24]. Also, this leads to wasted resources. To reduce the number of indicators used, benchmarking is used for identifying the relevant performance indicator so as to reduce the overall complexity. The main purpose of using the GRA is to identify the relevant performance indicators and to reduce the overall indicators used for evaluating the performance. The selection of these performance indicators can be based on clustering. The performance indicators are then selected only when the amount of data collected is large enough so as to ensure that the data distribution is normal [24]. However, most often the data collection is incomplete. Hence, these incomplete data are referred to as grey elements.

- **NetBench.** NetBench is a benchmarking tool that is mainly used for the performance evaluation of the network processors. There are nine applications in the NetBench benchmark, which are similar to that of the applications supported by the network processors [25]. For these applications, packet processing is supported at all levels. The NetBench suite is composed of benchmarking applications, which are divided into three levels. These include the low level or the microlevel routines, Internet Protocol(IP)-level programs, and the application level programs. The microlevel routines are used for processing the simpler tasks, which act as a component for the complex tasks. The applications which are supported at the routing level are processed with the help of the IP-level programs. Programs that need to make some wise decisions based on the information in the data packets are processed with the help of the application-level benchmarks. These applications are highly time consuming, as the requirements consume a lot of processing time.

- **Sieve kernel.** The performance of microprocessors and the personal computers can be compared and evaluated with the help of the Sieve kernel. The design of the Sieve kernel revolves around an algorithm called the Eratosthenes Sieve algorithm. This algorithm is mainly used for computing the list of all of the given prime numbers that are less than "$n$". The algorithm works as follows. First, we write the list of all the numbers up to "$n$" from 1 [26–27]. Then, we try to cancel out all the multiples of $k$, where $k$ equals 2 to square root ($n$). For example, if we want to know the list of prime numbers between 1 and 20, then the steps are as follows:

1. List all numbers between 1 and 20 and consider all the numbers as prime.
2. From the given list of primes, try removing all multiples of 2.
3. Repeat the above step by removing multiples of 3.
4. Because the next number from the sequence is 5 and because its square is greater than 20, the rest of the list is considered to be prime numbers.

- **Ackermann's function**. The performance evaluation of the procedure-oriented languages such as ALGOL is done with the help of this kernel. The kernel is a function that supports two parameters that are recursively defined. Systems are compared based on the following criteria: (a) the average time of execution per call, (b) the number of instructions executed for each such call, and (c) the amount of space occupied for each of such function calls [26, 27]. This kernel is designed by using the SIMULA programming language. It is worth mentioning that SIMULA is considered one of the earliest object-oriented languages, and some people consider it the earliest. It was designed in the early 1960s to facilitate simulation analysis. It has been used in a wide range of applications, such as simulating algorithms, protocols, graphics, and very large-scale integration (VLSI) designs. SIMULA influenced all other later widely used object-oriented languages such as C++.

- **Whetstone**. The Whetstone kernel consists of 11 modules, which have been designed to match the frequency of the operations in the ALGOL programs. All the operations of the processor such as addressing of arrays, arithmetic using fixed and floating point, subroutine calls, and passing the parameters using referencing are addressed. These modules can be translated into other programming languages such as Fortran. The performance assessment in Whetstone is measured in KWIPS, which stands for Kilo Whetstone Instructions Per Second [25–27]. Because different permutations of this kernel exist, we need to make sure that the source code is the same before evaluating it on different systems. Even though it supports a mixture of operations, it is often considered a floating point benchmark. This benchmark is mainly used for evaluating the scientific and engineering applications, which are relatively small. The design of the modules in Whetstone is such that it reduces the compiler optimizations.

- **Dhrystone**. Dhrystone is a kernel whose source code consists mainly of several function calls that are used to represent the programming environment of the system. This kernel was implemented in programming languages known such as C, Ada, Fortran, and Pascal. Among all these implementations, the C implementation is popular. The performance assessment is represented as DIPS, which stands for dhrystone instructions per second. The function calls in Dhrystone usually have a lower depth of nesting. For each function call defined, the number of instructions executed is usually low [25–27]. Also, most of the execution time is spent in copying the strings and in characters and in comparing them. This benchmarking is famous for evaluating the integer performance and does not support the floating point and processing of input and output. It does not focus on issues related to compiler optimization. Dhrystone attempts to represent the result more eloquently than MIPS, because MIPS cannot be used across different instruction sets (i.e., CISC vs RISC) for the same computation requirement from users. Hence, the main grade is just Dhrystone loops per second. Others use another representation of the Dhrystone benchmark that is called the Dhrystone MIPS, (DMIPS), obtained by dividing the Dhrystone score by 1757, which is the number of Dhrystones per second obtained on the VAX 11/780 computer machine.

- **Lawrence Livermore loops**. The workload in this benchmark consists of 24 distinct tests that are mainly focused on the scientific calculations. This benchmark can be executed on a laptop computer as well as on a supercomputer. It is usually difficult to interpret the results obtained from this benchmark, as they are too complex to understand. The unit of performance measurement in this benchmark is MFLOPS [27]. The results display the arithmetic, geometric, and harmonic means along with the minimum and maximum performance levels. Most often, (say about 60% of the time) scientific applications are consumed in calculating the floating point operations. These kernels are developed using the Fortran programming language. They are used as a standard for evaluating the performance of the computational systems. This kernel highly resists vectorization and does evaluate the performance of single-precision and double-precision floating-point calculations.

- **Debit-Credit Benchmark**. This benchmark is used as a standard for comparing the performance of the processing systems that are based on transactions. A banking network which is distributed is represented by this benchmark [26, 27]. The performance is evaluated in terms of transactions per second (TPS) such that more than 90% of the transactions have a response time less than 1 s. The response time in these systems is measured as the time required for sending the last bit on the communication line and the arrival of the first bit. The comparison of the performance of different transaction systems is based on the price-performance ratio [26, 27]. The workload supports four record types, which are teller, account, history, and branch. The benchmark is written in the COBOL programming language.

The Debit-Credit benchmark was devised in the 1970s to test the performance of computer systems that run a fledgling online teller network at the Bank of America. This benchmark represents the transaction processing load of a supposed bank with one or more branches and many tellers. The transactions are made of the debits and credits to customers accounts with the system maintaining track of customers account, the balance of each teller and branch, and a history of the banks up to date transactions.

- **NAS Parallel Benchmarks**. The NAS Parallel Benchmarks (NPBs) are a set of programs designed to assist and evaluate the performance of parallel computers. They are derived from computational fluid dynamics (CFD) applications. NAB benchmark programs consist of five kernels and three pseudoapplications. They come in several types. NPB is a benchmark suite that is mainly used for evaluating the parallel computer systems. This benchmark comprises of eight programs, which deal with several relevant issues of parallel systems [27]. Apart from these programs, it also has three pseudo applications and five kernels. The output derived from the kernel consists of the data that represent the execution time along with Mega operation per second. NPB consists of three versions NPB1, NPB2, and NPB3. For benchmarking the grid applications, GridNPB3 is used. These benchmarks are implemented in FORTRAN and Java programming languages. The source code for the programs is implemented using the message passing interface (MPI) mechanisms. NAS seeks NPB 1 results from all sources, especially computer vendors. Such results are assembled in a tabular manner in periodic reports posted on the Web by NASA.

- **PARKBENCH**. The Parallel Kernels and Benchmarks committee (PARK-BENCH) was established in 1992 by professionals who were interested in benchmarking for parallel processing. The committee established a set of performance measures and notations. The main objectives of the PARK-BENCH group are as follows [39]:

  1. To establish a comprehensive set of parallel benchmarks that is generally accepted by both users and vendors of parallel systems
  2. To provide a focus for parallel benchmark activities and avoid duplication of effort and proliferation of benchmarks
  3. To set standards for benchmarking methodology
  4. To make the benchmarks and results freely available to the public.

     The initial interest of the parallel benchmarks is the new generation of scalable distributed memory message-passing architectures for which there is a notable lack of existing benchmarks. That is why the initial benchmark release focuses on Fortran77 message-passing codes using the widely-available Parallel Virtual Machine (PVM) MPI for portability. Release 2.0 of the benchmark suite adopted the MPI. It is expected that future releases will include Fortran90 and High-Performance Fortran (HPF) versions of the benchmark [30, 40].

     The PARKBENCH committee makes a benchmarking suite used for parallel computer systems. This suite consists of three application sets, which are low-level benchmarks, kernel benchmarks, and compact application benchmarks [4, 39]. The parameters on which the architecture of a parallel system is based are measured with the help of a low-level benchmark. The kernel benchmarks are used to evaluate the parallel systems over a wide range of applications, which are intensively computational. Some of the source code for these benchmarks is taken from NAS, Genesis, and so on which are also the parallel benchmark suites. Compact application benchmarks are mainly used for evaluating the parallel systems for research-based applications. These applications differ from the kernel applications in that they produce results that are scientifically useful.

- **LINPACK**. The LINPACK is basically a collection of Fortran subroutines, which analyze and solve linear equations and linear least-squares problems. The matrices involved can be general, banded, symmetric indefinite, symmetric positive definite, triangular, and tridiagonal square. LINPACK was created by Jack Dongarra at the University of Tennessee. In general, this benchmark is easy to use and can give a good indication about the numerical computing capability of the system under study. The LINPACK benchmark is mainly designed for evaluating supercomputers. This benchmark is written in the Fortran programming language. It is composed of a single application that is used to solve the linear algebraic problems. It evaluates the performance based on Gaussian elimination [27]. The results are represented as MFlops. It is available in three flavors: (100*100), (1000*1000), and variable size. To measure the performance of large-scale distributed systems, we use high-performance LINPACK (HPL). The matrix sizes are varied and for each size the benchmark is run so as to check as to which matrix size the benchmark performance increases.

- LMBENCH. The LMBENCH is another example on microbenchmarks that is maintained by Larry McVoy. It was designed to measure the overheads of operating systems and capability of data transfer among the processor, cache, main memory, network, and disk on various UNIX platforms. This benchmark is useful for finding bottlenecks in the design and for design optimization. The results of LMBENCH are available for major computer vendors, including SUN, IBM, HP, and SGI [32, 47].

- STREAM. The STREAM benchmark is synthetic. It was created by John McCalpin while he was at the University of Delaware. The motivation for the creation of this benchmark is to study the effect of limited memory bandwidth on system's performance, as these days processors are becoming fast, and application programs are limited by the memory bandwidth, not by processor's speed. The main operations performed by STREAM are copy, scale, sum (addition), and triad. The latter is often called after the operation of the form: $A(i) = B(i) + k \times C(i)$. STREAM measures real-world bandwidth sustainable from normal user programs [33].

- **HINT**. HINT is a benchmarking tool that stands for hierarchical integration. This tool was developed at the Scalable Computing Laboratory, which is funded by the U.S. Department of Energy. The hierarchical integration tool is neither used to fix the problem size nor the time required for calculation [27]. It is used to measure the system performance using a new measure called QUIPS. This enables the hierarchical integration tool to present the machine speed for a given specification of the machine and the size of the problem. The change in speed while accessing the main memory and the disk memory is clearly displayed by the hierarchical integration tool. This tool is highly scalable and portable. It can be scaled down to an extent that it can be run on a calculator, and it can also be scaled up to run on a supercomputer.

- **SPLASH.** The Stanford Parallel Applications for Shared Memory (SPLASH) is a benchmark that is used for the performance evaluation of parallel systems. The benchmark is written in the C programming language except for one application, which is written in Fortran language. These applications use the fork/join models for supporting the parallelism [4, 27]. The benchmark consists of two parts known as kernels and applications. These two components are used for performance evaluation of the systems. The latest version of benchmark available in SPLASH is SPLASH-2. The performance of the system is measured in MIPS.

- **COMSS.** COMSS is a low-level benchmark that is used for evaluating the performance of parallel systems. The three variants of this benchmark are known as COMMS1, COMMS2, and COMMS3. COMMS1 evaluates the communication system performance by transmitting messages of variable length among various nodes [27]. Another name for the COMMS1 benchmark is ping pong benchmark. COMMS2 also functions the same way as that of COMMS1 except that the exchange of messages between the nodes is simultaneous. COMMS3 evaluates the parallel systems performance by incrementally varying message lengths between nodes. The total bandwidth available to the communication link is estimated by transmitting the messages. Every process in the system sends a message to all nodes and then waits to receive all the sent messages [27–29]. The length of the messages is incrementally increased until the saturation of the bandwidth. At the end, the benchmark displays available total bandwidth and the bandwidth that can be allocated to each processor.

- **Bit to the User.** Bit to the User (BTU) is a benchmark that is used for evaluating the performance of the system over a network [28]. The BTU benchmark was developed to take into consideration both concurrent activities within a workstation and concurrent activities on the network. The BTU benchmark can produce results at various levels of abstraction that range from a single number that exemplifies average performance to a report of how all the individual test suite components performed. It deals with the specification of the source code along with the test bed for duplicating the results. The performance is represented by calculating a BTU number, which indicates the workstations' communication performance. Along with the BTU number it also specifies the penalty factor, which indicates the degradation of the performance. Not only are BTU numbers used for representing workstation communication performance, but also they can be used for assessing the performance of any individual application along with its respective penalty factors [28]. The performance data are compiled for independent components of the benchmark test. If the test result is abnormal, then for such type of results, BTU provides the results with a TCP time sequence chart, which can be used for analyzing the results in depth.

- **TinyBench.** TinyBench is a benchmark which is used for evaluating the performance of wireless-based sensor network devices [29]. TinyBench is a single-node benchmark suite. This benchmark simplifies the process of code development and function development across multiple platforms. Four classes of benchmarks are related to sensor network nodes: (a) level microlevel benchmarks for components of hardware, (b) stressmarks at node level, (c) real applications at the node level, and (d) real applications at the network level. TinyBench measures the performance of the applications at the node level and the stressmarks at the node level. Based on the class of the application, the characteristics of the hardware differ [30]. Apart from evaluating the performance of the systems, it also shows the amount of power consumed for each operation performed.

- **Express.** This is a benchmark used for evaluating the performance of parallel systems. The type of programming model used in Express is host-node model, where host represents the master and node the worker [30]. It uses a host-free programming model to avoid writing programs to the host, which is known as Cubix. The design of Express follows a layered approach. The implementation consists of three layers as follows:

  1. The layer at the lowest level contains the utilities that are mainly used for controlling hardware that includes processor allocation and program loading, among others.
  2. The layer at the medium level provides the support for partitioning the problem. Apart from this it also allows the communication between the nodes and also between the control processor and the node.
  3. The layer at the highest level consists of the facilities that are used by the programs in the node for performing the input output operations. Also, it consists of utilities that can be used for accessing the operating system at the host.

    Because of the layered approach design, the tool is portable. The design follows a top-down approach.

- **Parallel Virtual Machine.** The Parallel Virtual Machine (PVM) is used for assessing the performance of parallel systems that consist of heterogeneous computers. This benchmark is portable similar to that of the Express. PVM contains the functions that can be used for starting the tasks automatically on the virtual machine. It also allows the tasks to interact with each other by communicating and allows them to synchronize. Tasks are basically units of the computation. Apart from evaluating the performance of the heterogeneous computers in the parallel systems, heterogeneous applications can also be evaluated. Routines are provided by PVM, which helps in creating and transmitting the messages between tasks. It can evaluate both synchronous and asynchronous transmissions. Apart from this it also models the fault tolerance in the parallel system [30, 40]. It can even detect the dynamic addition and removal of hosts to the parallel system.

- **GENESIS.** This benchmark is used for evaluating the distributed and parallel systems [31]. The GENESIS benchmarks are written in the FORTRAN programming language. Each GENESIS benchmark has a sequential and a parallel version. The sequential benchmark is used for defining the problem and also provides the algorithm that needs to be used for solving the problem [31, 32]. The parallel version of the GENESIS benchmark uses message passing for defining the programming model. In all 16 codes are supported by GENESIS for measuring the machine parameters related to synchronization and communication. The design of the GENESIS benchmark follows a hierarchical structure approach. The application kernels in GENESIS are used for evaluating the applications for the distributed and parallel systems. It also performs code optimizations for improving the performance of the parallel systems [32].

- **Space-Time Adaptive Processing.** The Parallel Space-Time Adaptive Processing (STAP) suite benchmark suite is basically a set of real-time, radar signal processing programs developed at Massachusetts Institute of Technology (MIT) Lincoln Laboratory [33]. STAP is a computationally demanding technique for mitigating clutter as viewed by airborne radar. Delivered processing power on-major STAP kernel computations is of major importance because of the real-time nature of radar processing systems. Because algorithm requirements for STAP systems are under continuous development, the scalability of processing power both in terms of machine and problem size is of great interest. Such an increased interest has led us to consider Single Instruction, Multiple Data (SIMAD) streams parallel architectures as possible candidates for a STAP processor. The original version of STAP that was developed at Lincoln Laboratory was sequential. STAP has been converted to a parallel STAP at the University of Southern California to evaluate massively parallel systems (MPPs) by Hwang and his group. The STAP benchmarks are considered computation-intensive as they require in the order of $10^{10}$ to $10^{14}$ floating point operations over 100 to 10,000 MB of data in a fraction of a second. The STAP consists of five programs [4, 33] as follows:
  - The Adaptive Processing Testbed **(APT)** performs a Householder Transform to generate a triangle learning, which is used in a later step called beamforming to null the jammers and clutter.

- The High-Order Post-Doppler **(HO-PD)** has two adaptive beamforming steps that are combined into one step.
- The Beam Space PRI-Staggered Post Doppler **(BM-Stag)** is similar to HO-PD; however, it uses a staggered interference training algorithm in the beam space.
- The Element Space PRI-Staggered Post Doppler **(EL-Stag)** is also similar to the HO-PD; however, it uses a staggered interference training algorithm in the element space.
- General **(GEN)** consists of four independent component programs to perform sorting (SORT), Fast Fourier Transform (FFT), Vector multiplication (VEC), and Linear Algebra (LA).

The first four benchmark programs start with a Doppler Processing step, where the program performs a large number of one-dimensional FFT operations. All of these four programs end with a Target Detection step.

- **PERFECT**. The Performance Evaluation of Cost-Effective Transformation (PERFECT) club benchmark suite consists of a set of 13 Fortran application programs drawn to characterize the range of applications that need to be run using high performance computing systems. Such programs characterize computational fluid dynamics, physical and chemical modeling, signal processing and engineering design applications. The main goal of this benchmark was to evaluate the effectiveness of compiler transformations for automatically converting serial programs to parallel form so as to execute them on parallel systems [4].
- **SPEC**. There is a popular benchmark family called SPEC, which has been developed by a nonprofit organization called Standard Performance Evaluation Corporation (SPEC). The latter stresses developing real applications benchmarks and SPEC suites are updated every few years in order to reflect new applications. SPEC started with benchmarks that measure the performance of processors (CPUs), but now it has benchmarks that evaluate client/server platforms, I/O subsystems, commercial applications, WWW applications, and so on. For more updated information, suites, and news, visit www.spec.org.

  SPEC was founded in 1988 by Apollo/Hewlett-Packard, Digital Equipment, MIPS, and Sun Microsystems. The goal was to provide a standard set of application programs and standard methodology for running the programs and reporting results to have a fair comparison. The first SPEC benchmark program, SPEC89, had four programs written in C and six programs written in Fortran. Every few years, SPEC provides a new version of its benchmarks [4, 18–20, 42]. SPEC has expanded recently to include Open System Group (OSG), High-Performance Group (HPG), and Graphics Performance Characterization Group (GPCG).

SPEC scheme is based on providing the benchmarker with a standardized suite of source code relied on current applications that have already been moved to a wide variety of platforms by its users. The evaluator then takes this source code, compiles it for the system under consideration and then can tune the system in order to obtain the best results. Using an already accepted and ported code can greatly reduce unfair performance comparison among systems manufacturing and avoid problems that may occur such as the game ratio.

SPEC started with a group of workstations vendors aiming at devising CPU metrics. Now, SPEC has grown into a big organization that includes three main groups: OSG, HPG, and Graphics and Workstation Performance Group (GWPG). A brief description of each is given below:

1. Open System Group. This group is basically the founding group of SPEC. It concentrates on benchmarks for high-end workstations, desktop systems, and servers running open systems environments. OSG includes several subcommittees:
   - CPU subcommittee. This includes all persons who devised SPEC-marks and the other CPU benchmarks such as SPECint, SPECfp, and SPECrates.
   - JAVA subcommittee. This includes those who devised JVM98, JBB2000, and JBB2005; the Java client and server-side benchmarks; and the jAppServer Java Enterprise application server benchmarks.
   - MAIL subcommittee. It includes persons who devised SPEC-mail2001, the consumer Internet Service Provider (ISP) mail server benchmark.
   - POWER AND PERFORMANCE subcommittee. This subcommittee started the development of the first-generation SPEC benchmark for evaluating the energy efficiency for server class computers.
   - SFS subcommittee. It is the subcommittee who developed the SFS93 (LADDIS), SFS97, and SFS97_R1. It is also working now on other file server benchmarks.
   - SIP subcommittee. This subcommittee started the development of the first-generation SPEC benchmark for comparing performance for servers using the Session Initiation Protocol (SIP).
   - Virtualization subcommittee. This subcommittee started the first generation SPEC benchmark for comparing virtualization performance for data center servers.
   - WEB subcommittee. It is the subcommittee who developed the WEB96, WEB99, WEB99_SSL, WEB2005, and the web server benchmarks.
2. High Performance Group HPG. The HPG is involved in establishing, maintaining, and endorsing a suite of benchmarks that characterize high-performance computing applications for standardized and

cross-platform performance evaluation. Such benchmark programs are aimed at high-performance system architectures, including symmetric multiprocessor computer systems, clusters of workstations, parallel systems with distributed memory, and conventional vector parallel computers.

3. Graphics and Workstation Performance Group. This group includes groups that build reliable and well-known graphics and workstation performance benchmarks and reporting procedures. The main GWPG project groups are the SPECapc and SPECgpc.

   - SPECAPC group. The Application Performance Characterization (SPECapcSM) group was established in 1997 to provide a broad-ranging set of standardized benchmarks for graphics and workstation applications. Its present benchmarks cover popular CAD/CAM, visualization, and digital content creation applications.
   - SPECgpc group. This group started its work in 1993. Basically, it establishes performance benchmarks for graphics systems running under OpenGL and other application programming interfaces (APIs). One of its popular benchmark is SPECviewperf(r), which is meant to be used for evaluating performance based on popular graphics applications [42].

**Other Benchmarks**. Other examples of benchmark programs include:

- Winbench and WinStone from Ziff-Davis, which are used for Windows PC applications and Windows PC graphics and disks.
- AIM benchmark from AIM Technology, which is used for UNIX workstations and server systems evaluation.
- NetBench from Ziff-Davis, which was developed for PC file server applications.
- SYSmarks from BAPC0, which was developed for retail PC software packages.
- MacBench from Ziff-Davis, which was developed for general Apple Macintosh computer performance measurement.
- Business Benchmark, which was developed by Nelson and Associates to benchmark Unix server throughput.
- MediaStones, which was developed by Providenza and Boekelheide for PC file server benchmarking.

## 4.4   FREQUENT MISTAKES AND GAMES IN BENCHMARKING

There are frequent mistakes that many performance analysts fall in because of inexperience or lack of awareness of fundamental concepts. Also, tricks are played by experienced analysts to fool customers and to promote their products unethically. Let us start with the following main frequent mistakes [1, 38]:

1. **Misalignment.** This deals with selecting a benchmarking area that is not aligned with the general policy and objectives of the business. Benchmarking has to be overseen by a leader at the strategic level to make sure that it is in line with what is going on in the business.

2. **Only mean behavior is represented in the benchmark program.** In this case, the workload ignores the variance and only average behavior is represented in the workload.

3. **The process is too large and multifaceted to be manageable.** It is recommended to avoid trying to benchmark a whole system as it will be enormously costly and difficult to remain focused. The approach is to select one or a few processes that form a part of the total system, work with it in the beginning, and then move on to the next part of the system.

4. **Using device utilizations for performance comparisons.** Utilizations of the devices are also used for comparing the performance measurements of the systems. In such situations, lower utilization is considered. But in certain environments, such measurements seem to be meaningless. For example, if we have two systems where one of the system has a faster response time, then in such a case the number of requests generated is higher, thereby increasing the device use. The second system is a bit slower, and hence, the device utilization is less in the second case compared with the first one [1–4]. This does not mean that the second system is better. Here, the right way to compare the performance is to measure it in terms of throughput with respect to the requests generated per second. One more mistake here is validating the models based on these device utilizations. The predicted utilization of the model if matched with the model in the real time environment does not ensure the validity of the model.

5. **Inadequate buffer size.** If the buffer size considered in a performance study is insufficient, then it will affect the performance measures. Keep in mind that the size and number of buffers are important parameters, and their values in performance measurement and testing should represent reasonable values similar to real-world systems.

6. **Uneven distribution of I/O request.** Many performance studies assume that I/O requests are evenly distributed among all peripherals. However, practically, this is not always the case. Such inaccurate assumption may lead to inaccuracy in predicting the response time of computer and network systems.

7. **Ignoring the cache effect.** In state-of-the art systems, such as Web systems, caching has become a de-facto standard. However, most benchmark programs do not represent the behavior of caching accurately, specifically the fact that cache memory is sensitive to the order of requests. Such order is lost in almost all workload characterization studies.

8. **Ignoring monitoring overhead.** In almost all measurement performance studies, hardware, software, or hybrid monitors are often used to collect data about the system's resources performance. Ignoring the monitor overhead may lead to erroneous results and conclusions.

9. **Ignoring validation of measurement results.** Performance results obtained through testing or measurement on real systems should be validated. The analyst should not assume always that measurement results are accurate, because any misplacing of a probe or a device may lead to error in the measurement.

10. **Disregarding sensitivity analysis.** If the performance results are sensitive to the initial conditions or input parameters, then more factors should be added to the benchmark program model. Moreover, in such a case, a more thorough sensitivity analysis should be conducted.

11. **Ignoring transient performance.** Some systems are most often in transient, moving from one state to another. Therefore, analyzing their performance under steady-state conditions does not really represent the real system's performance. Of course, this applies to measurement and simulation models as well as testing/measurement settings.

12. **Collecting too much data, but not much data analysis.** In many studies, you will find the team collecting a huge volume of data results, but little analysis is performed with such data. It is important to analyze the data using statistical techniques. Hence, it is important to have the needed expertise in the performance analysis team, especially someone who has a good knowledge of statistical analysis and inference, in addition to a system engineer, statistician/mathematician, programmer, and a good technical writer.

13. **Skewness of device demand is ignored.** The basic assumption is that the requests for the input/output are evenly distributed among all the resources that accept these input/output requests [1–7]. However, this is not the case in a real environment. All the requests for the input/output follow to a single device that serves these requests, which leads to queuing of these requests and higher delays. This strategy is not represented in the test workload, and hence, ignoring this will show the bottlenecks that are created to the devices in the real-time environments.

14. **Loading level is controlled inappropriately.** Several parameters are used in the test workload for increasing the level of the load on the system. For example, the number of users using the system could be increased, the resource demand for each user could be increased, and also the users think time can be decreased. The results for all the above options are not the same. A more realistic approach of increasing the number of users is by increasing the number of resources. To do this, the other two alternatives can be used [1–4]. One possibility is changing the users think time, but this is not equivalent to the first option, as this alternative would not change the order of arrival of requests to the

various devices. Because of this reason, the number of misses in the cache is less when compared with the system with more users. The workload is changed significantly by the second alternative, and hence, it could not be a correct representation of the real environment.

15. **Not ensuring the same initial conditions.** Whenever a benchmark is run, the system state is changed. This change in the state of the system could be caused by a change in disk space or change in the contents of the records. Hence, we need to make sure that all the initial conditions are reset [1–9]. This could be possibly done by removing the files created while executing the benchmark and by retaining the changed contents of the records to its original state. Another approach could be determining the results of sensitivity during the phenomena. The workload should be added with more factors provided the sensitivity of the results is higher with respect to the initial conditions.

16. **Only mean behavior is represented in test workload.** The test workload is designed so as to represent the real workload. The resource demands that are required during the test workload are designed by the analysts so as to represent the resource demand similar to that of a real-time environment. Here, only the average behavior of the environment is represented by ignoring the variance. For example, in certain scenarios, the average number of resource requests in the test workload may be similar to that of the resource demand in the real environment. However, if the arrival of requests for the resource takes an exponential, Poisson, Weibull, or other distributions, then in such a case we may have to represent the resource demand in the form of variance or a much detailed representation must be used.

As for the games that are played by experienced performance analysts to boost unethically the reputation of their systems or products, following is a list of these games that result in a benchmarking study that is disingenuous or unfair:

1. **Compilers are arranged in a way to optimize workload.** In such a case, the compiler is set up in a way to completely do away with the main loop in a synthetic benchmark program, thus giving better performance results than competing systems.

2. **Small benchmark sizes.** Using a small benchmark may mean 100% cache hit, thus, ignoring the effect of overhead of I/O and memory units. Undoubtedly, it is important to use several workloads in any performance analysis study rather than relying on a small benchmark program.

3. **Biased test specifications.** It is important to have the test specifications more general rather than biased to specific system or network.

4. **Manual optimizing of benchmarks.** In such a case, obtained performance measures depend on the capability of translator rather than the system under study.

5. **Running benchmarks on two systems with different configurations**. In this case, you will find that the benchmarks are being run in two systems with different memory and I/O configurations.

## 4.5 PROCEDURES OF CAPACITY PLANNING AND RELATED MAIN PROBLEMS

Capacity planning is considered an important process in any performance analysis study as it ensures that sufficient computing resources are available to meet future workload demands in a cost-effective method while meeting overall performance goals. The term performance tuning is related to capacity planning and is defined as the procedure to modify system parameters to optimize performance. Another process related to capacity planning is capacity management, which deals with current systems, while capacity planning deals with future systems and settings [1–40].

To invoke into a capacity planning process, the analyst should follow the following steps:

1. Implement the system under study.
2. Observer system usage.
3. Describe workload.
4. Forecast performance under different configurations and environments.
5. Select the most cost-effective alternative.

In the first phase, we should make sure that there are proper device setup for the process, such as suitable counters, monitors, and hooks in the system to record current usage. Accounting log facility that is usually built-in in any operating system can be used as well. In the second phase, the usage of the system is monitored to collect needed data about the behavior of the operation of the system. Then, the workload is characterized and data are collected for some time. Such data are analyzed and summarized in a way so that it can be input to a system model to carry out performance prediction/estimation and analysis. Different configurations and future workloads are input to a model of the system to perform the needed model experimentation. If the goal is to conduct a capacity management rather than a capacity planning study, then the current configurations and workloads are input into a tuning model, usually a simulation model that gives what changes in the system parameter settings should be made to meet the needed objectives.

In the process of capacity planning, we usually start by predicting the workload based on monitoring the system under test for a long period of time. Next, various configurations and potential workloads/benchmarks are entered to a model to forecast performance. In this context, we call the process of choosing equipment "sizing." Many performance analysts employ analytic modeling for the sizing process [1–6, 15–30].

Performance analysts who work on capacity planning experience many problems, including lack of unique standard for terminology, difficulty in measuring model input in many cases, and difficulty to model distributed environments, among others. A brief description of these difficulties is given below.

Currently, there is no standard definition of the term "capacity"; some define it in terms of maximum throughput, and others define it in terms of maximum number of users that the system can provide for while meeting a specified performance goal. Also, it seems that each vendor makes capacity planning tools with goals and functions in mind that are different from what the analysts need. For example, some vendors integrate capacity planning and management and call the technique a capacity planning tool. There are not many vendor-independent workloads; most of the available benchmarks are vendor dependent. Each system has three different types of capacities. These include the knee capacity, nominal capacity, and usable capacity. Nominal capacity for a system can be defined as the maximum throughput that can be achieved by the system when the workload conditions are ideal. In case of computer networks, bandwidth is defined as the nominal capacity. This is represented in terms of bits per second [1–5, 12]. Usable capacity can be defined as the maximum throughput that can be achieved within the specified response time that is fixed. In most applications, the optimal operating point is considered the knee of the response-time curve or the knee of the throughput. The throughput at knee is termed as the systems knee capacity; see Figure 4.2.

In capacity planning, we plan for the expected future workload; however, expectations are not always accurate. For example, mainframe computers are no longer around as they have been replaced by more cost-effective workstations. This means that the predictions that mainframe computers will stay around us were wrong.

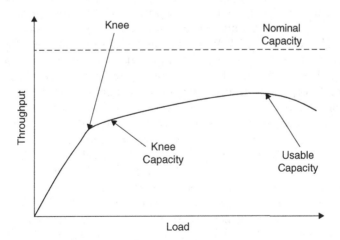

**FIGURE 4.2.** System capacity representation.

Some inputs used in analytic and simulation models are not exactly quantifiable, such as the think time used in analytic models. In almost all analytic models, this does not consider interruptions caused by tea or coffee breaks, for example.

The validation of projected operation is not an easy task; although validation on current system configuration is not difficult, projection validation is difficult as it requires changing workloads and configurations, as well as confirming that the model output matches the changed real system's performance. It is hard to manage workload configurations on a real system.

It is important to point out here that performance is one part of capacity planning; cost is crucial as well. When we talk about cost in this context, not only do we mean the cost of hardware, but also we should include the cost of software, maintenance, personnel, power, humidity control, and so on.

In today's computing systems, distributed systems are pretty much common. This means focusing too much on capacity planning on individual device is no longer vital. However, such systems are not easy to model. These days, you can find special commercial tools for capacity planning with built-in models for specific systems as well as workload analyzers and monitors that recognize the accounting logs of such systems.

## 4.6   CAPACITY PLANNING FOR WEB SERVICES

Capacity planning for Web services is considered unique because: (a) Web servers rely on large-scale systems of computers, networks, programs, and users; (b) they are complex; and (c) they are used by a large number of users who request service at random. The latter aspect makes management and planning of such systems complicated and challenging. Web systems are characterized by being dynamic, requiring high quality of service (QoS) and high performance, and needing to integrate with different systems, such as databases, scheduling, planning, management, and tracking systems [34–37].

The World Wide Web (WWW) is an evolving information technology system that grows at an impressive exponential rate. It has experienced extraordinary growth and has become the dominant application in both the public Internet and internal corporate intranet environments. Some recent research studies have found out that over 75% of the traffic on the Internet backbone is Hypertext Transfer Protocol HTTP-based [4, 24–40]. Many applications such as e-commerce, including mobile commerce (m-commerce), e-government, e-services, digital libraries, distance learning, and video-on-demand, are all based on the Web infrastructure. Moreover, such applications have even become more and more widely used because of the proliferation of wireless networks and devices. Popular websites such e-government, and digital library sites get millions of requests per day, which increase the average response time of such sites. Clearly, this has become an important issue for website administrators and IT managers of all kinds of organizations. Identifying the bottlenecks, forecast future capacities, and finding out the best cost-effective approach to upgrade the system to cope with the expected increase in the workload are essential for any proper web service. In web services, it is important to support the increase in load without sacrificing the response time. Capacity planning is vital for web services as it: (a) guarantees customer satisfaction, (b) prevents potential money losses, (c) protects the image of the organization/company, and (d) provides proper plans for future expansion.

Most websites these days can fall in the following main categories: (a) interaction as used for registration in conferences, booking in hotels, airline reservation, and so on, (b) informational as used for online newspapers, magazines, and books; (c) web portals, such as electronic shopping malls, search engines, and webmail services; (d) shared environment as in collaborative design tools; (e) transactional, as in online banking and stock trading; (f) workflow, as in online scheduling and inventory systems; (g) news groups, as in online discussion groups; and (h) online auction [4, 37].

A web server is basically a mixture of hardware devices, operating systems, and application software/contents that cooperate and collaborate to provide satisfactory service. The characteristics of these components and the way they interact/connect with each other influence the overall performance of the Web servers and intranets.

The major performance metrics for any web system are: (a) end-to-end response time and site response time, (b) throughput in request/sec or/and in Mbps, (c) visitors per day, (d) hit value, (e) errors per second, (f) startup latency, and (g) jitter. The latter two metrics are important for streaming services. The QoS of Web services is crucial to keep current customers and attract new ones. The QoS metrics of Web services should represent response time, availability, reliability, predictability, security, and cost [4, 37].

The main components of a Web system are the browser, network, and server. The user usually clicks on a hyperlink to request a document. Then, the client browser tries to find the needed document in the local cache; if it is found, then we say we have a hit. Otherwise, we say that we have a miss, and in such a case, the browser asks the Domain Name System DNS service to map the server hostname to an IP address. Then, the client opens a Transmission Control Protocol (TCP) connection to the server defined by the URL of the link and sends an HTTP request to the server, which provides a response. Next, the browser formats and displays the document and provides the needed document. The latter is stored in the browser's cache.

The network enforces delays to bring information from the client to the server and back from the server to the client. Such delays are a function of the different components located between the client and server including modems, routers, communication links, bridges, and so on.

When the request arrives from the client, the server parses it according to the operation of the HTTP protocol. Then, the server executes the requested method, such as GET, HEAD, and so on. If the method, for example, is a GET, then the server looks up the file in its document tree using the file system where the file can be in the cache or on disks. Then, the server reads the file and writes it to the network port. Now, when the file is totally sent, the server closes the connection. As the number of clients and servers increases, end user performance is usually constrained by the performance of components such as bridges, routers, networks, and servers along the path from client to server. Obviously, identifying the device/component that limits the performance is essential. Such a device/component is called the bottleneck device.

Among the techniques that can be used to improve the performance in terms of reducing the mean access time and the bandwidth needed to transfer the document and security of Web systems are: (a) proxy, (b) cache, and (c) mirror. The proxy server is used to act as both a server and client. Figure 4.3 shows an overall organization of a Web proxy server.

As shown in Figure 4.3, a proxy accepts requests from clients and forwards them to Web servers. The proxy in turns passes responses from remote servers to the clients. Proxy servers can also be configured so that they can cache relayed responses and become a cache proxy. Caching reduces the mean access time by bringing the data as close to the users in need of it as possible. In addition, caching reduces the overall server load and improves the availability of the Web system by replicating documents among servers. In caching, we need to: (a) decide for how long to keep the document and (b) make sure that the updated version of the document is in the cache.

The main metrics used to evaluate caching are as follows:

- Hit ratio: This is defined as the ratio of number of requests satisfied by the cache to the total number of requests. The miss ratio, which is (1-hit ratio), is also used in this context.
- Byte hit ratio: It is used instead of the traditional hit ratio because there is a high variability of web document sizes. Basically, this is hit ratio weighted by the document size.
- Data transferred: This metric represents the total number of bytes transferred between the cache and outside environment during an operational session.

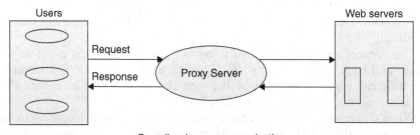

Overall web proxy organaization

**FIGURE 4.3.** Overall Web proxy organization.

The growth of Internet usage during the last several years has increased in an exponential manner. Different applications over the Web have different requirements. To provide the quality of service guarantees we need to identify and separate the services with different service characteristics. Also, we should focus on managing the load on the Web servers to provide efficient service [34]. Hence, we need to deal with the challenges posed by the network as well as by the Web servers. That is, we should scale up the capacity of the server by keeping in mind the network capacity available for providing a service.

Below is a brief description of what needs to be addressed for scaling the Web services so as to meet the needed quality of service guarantees:

1. **Improving the LAN speed**. To support a server throughput of 1 Gb/s, it is not sufficient to have the Gigabit Ethernet. This is because the server may not be able to provide the required throughput due to several drawbacks in the protocols, chip-set, and operating system. To overcome these issues and to support the required server throughput, we need to have at least 10-G Ethernet [34–35]. Also, this could not be the only possible solution; rather, we also need to look into several issues that caused the performance bottlenecks. Moreover, to meet the increasing performance demand, we need to have a layered server architecture for the server that is distributed. It is important to avoid the bottleneck caused by the operating system and should support the user-level I/O.

2. **Handling the dynamic content**. Using the intercache protocols for communication, push and pull proxies have reduced the latency for getting the information and have reduced a lot of load on the server [35]. However, the major challenge that needs to be addressed is the dynamic content of the Web, which is constantly increasing. To solve this, we need to track the dynamic Web pages for the individual components and define a structure for these pages. This not only allows caching but also allows the functionality such as inserting the dynamic content at different hierarchy levels of the Web server. The main advantage of this structure is that it helps in pushing the content to the servers at the edge. The proxies, which do the transformation of the content, support both the wireless and wired applications [36]. To support this, we need to enhance the Internet-based protocols. To reduce the overhead created by the dynamic content, novel management techniques are used.

3. **Web server scaling to store large content and increase hit rates**. Scaling the Web servers using a traditional approach performs the balancing of the load on the server with the help of a load distributor at the front end. Looking in depth, this solution is not a scalable one, because if the operation of the front end takes place at the transport layer, then there will be a problem with the scalability because of content duplication in the cache of the servers. However, there will be a bottleneck with the

load distributor itself if the amount of work exceeds what is expected [35–36]. To resolve this issue, we need to address on-demand requests with the help of service control points. We can use clustered servers instead of independent servers for improving the scalability. Scalability can be increased by implementing the lightweight communication protocols for the clustered environment.

4. **Internet service distribution**. The Internet model that is used currently more or less is a centralized model that stores all the information in a single repository. Such a model is not scalable. To increase the scalability, the current model needs to be shifted to a distributed environment. This has several security and access issues that need to be addressed. To overcome this, the infrastructure for the Internet is viewed as a collection of servers where each server holds the data. Moreover, the efficiency of the Internet is measured not by the method used for accessing the required data, but rather by how the services are supported efficiently [34–37]. To implement the distributed services efficiently, there is a need to modify the existing protocols to address the related issues.

5. **Large servers engineering and management.** The operation support system and capacity planning procedures are used to support telecommunication systems. Web servers lack such a kind of support. With the increase in volume and complexity of the traffic in the Web servers, there is a need for developing efficient engineering practices that support the characterization of the traffic at the Web servers. It becomes complicated because of the bursty nature of the traffic, nonstationary nature over small intervals, and the complexity in estimating the requirements for the dynamic content of the web pages [35, 36]. With server pool supporting thousands of servers, the issue of managing these servers efficiently by considering the performance, recovery, replication and high availability becomes difficult. The challenge here is to find a viable solution for managing the increase in the number of the servers.

6. **Issues pertaining to I/O and architecture**. Usually the performance of the Web servers are measured only in terms of application services and the underlying protocols that support them by neglecting the influence of the operating system and the hardware [34–36]. With the increase in the I/O and the processing requirements, the issues relating to architecture are important as they prevent scalability. One such example is improper event recognition techniques, which could lead to bottlenecks. Most of the multiprocessor systems performance degrades because of the spinning on locks by the processor for the shared resources. Most I/O operations require copying of data from one memory to another, which reduces the performance. Also, most often, processing of the protocols is not cache friendly. Because cache hits are becoming less and that the increase in demand on the servers would increase cache misses, the server's performance would degrade. With the increase in audio and video streaming,

the servers must be able to support an excess of 10,000 streams or so. To provide this, the cache hits should be high and the number of I/O should be less. As the bandwidth for the local area network (LAN)/wide area network (WAN) is increasing rapidly, the amount of data sent per request is almost unrelated when compared with the I/O requests.

7. **Issues pertaining to QoS.** With the evolution of different networks, the types of traffic supported by these networks are also increased [35, 36]. All these traffic types should be provided with quality service at the server level and also at the network level. Examples of the traffic types include discrete data traffic, continuous data traffic, variable data traffic, real-time data traffic, non-real-time data traffic, and so on. Hence, all these traffic types should be differentiated, and the service parameters for each should be served. One such possibility is negotiating with the network if the network has the necessary characteristics to support the traffic across it. If it addresses all the quality of service (QoS) parameters, then the service is provided. But this is addressing only QoS at the network and not at the server, which should also be looked at. If this issue is not addressed at the server, then it could lead to bringing the traffic from the network and dropping at the server.

8. **Issues related to performance and scaling for back-end systems.** Usually, the focus of the Internet servers has been on the front-end servers, but because of the evolution of e-commerce and e-business applications, the focus needs to shift to the system as a whole [35, 36]. The issues for scaling are difficult with respect to the back-end systems at the web server. This is because inherent dependencies exist when accessing the data. Hence to avoid this problem it is better to use databases at the clustered or distributed environment.

9. **Controlling the overload at the Internet server.** The Internet server performance is measured by the server throughput and the response time for serving a client request. The server throughput enhances up to a certain level known as the threshold; thereafter, it decreases because of overload. This threshold is termed as the overloading point. Because of overload, the response time also increases to a larger extent. To control the load on the Web server, we use efficient mechanisms for overload control [34–37]. These mechanisms do not allow the load on the Web server to exceed the overload point. To implement the overload control efficiently, the data packets need to be classified at the lowest level of the protocol stack. Overload control is nonexistent for the Web servers [38]. Hence, a need exists to design schemes for overload control and denial of service scenarios.

10. **Secure transaction performance issues.** Using the Secure Socket Layer (SSL) protocol for e-commerce applications takes a high processing time because of the overhead incurred. This leads to a slow response from the Web server. However, SSL provides the most secure e-commerce

transactions however it has a bottleneck because of excessive overhead. The security feature provided by the IPSec introduces these issues at the network stack lower level [38]. Also, we need to consider the type of transactions the server handles (i.e., whether the transactions are secure or nonsecure). If dedicated servers are used to handle SSL, then the overload needs to be addressed. Also, we need to devise mechanisms that tradeoff caching as caching conflicts with the security.

11. **Data repository for server performance**. The performance of the server is logged in HTTP logs. To address the issues on performance caused by architecture, we need more detailed information [35–38]. We should have standard encoding schemes for HTTP, and traces obtained from the bus should secure the information. This information is recorded from the sites when they are extremely busy with no impact on the performance of these sites. Even the log stored by the HTTP does not characterize the traffic. Apart from this, the total size of the requested web page and the time taken to process the request needs to be logged into the logs [34–38].

It is worth mentioning that Web traffic is bursty, which means that data are transmitted randomly with peak rates exceeding the mean rates by a high factor that usually ranges between 9 and 10. The term burtness is defined as the peak rate divided by the mean rate. The bursty behavior of Web systems makes it difficult to size the server's capacity and bandwidth demand created by load spikes/burtness. The effect of peak spikes on performance of the website is critical.

## 4.7   SUMMARY

Benchmarking and capacity planning are essential procedures in the performance evaluation of most computer systems and networks ranging from single computer systems, multiprocessor computer systems, distributed and parallel systems, local area networks, metropolitan area networks, wide area networks, wireless networks, client-server systems, and web systems.

Because of changes in the traffic and in the architecture of the various systems, new techniques need to be designed for evaluating computer systems and networks. Most benchmarks used for grid and cluster performance assessment use the Message Passing Interface (MPI) for evaluating these environments. Apart from these, computer system benchmarks have also been developed for evaluating the websites' performance. The performance of the Web server is evaluated on the basis of the server load and the network load. Each benchmark used has different mechanisms for representing the performance evaluation results. To improve the performance of the websites, we need to optimize the load on the Web server' which requires capacity planning strategies. Different applications over the Web have different requirements, and to provide the required quality of service we need to identify and separate the resources with different service characteristics and also should focus on managing the load on the web servers so that it does not exceed the overloading point. This helps in optimizing the load and providing efficient service. Also, the resource use for I/O should be optimized.

Experimentation is often used instead of analytic analysis that uses approximate queueing and other mathematical models. It is essential to implement the needed experiments properly to have confidence in all performed tests under various operating conditions and environments. Of course, such an arrangement should be done in a cost-effective manner without affecting the credibility of the obtained results and conclusions. It is expected to get some variations in the results obtained from the experiments because of all types of errors or noncontrolled variables; however, such errors should be taken into account when the results are analyzed. Constructing the confidence intervals is an important analyzing step to determine the integrity of the chosen workloads and benchmarks. Finally, it is essential that the performance analyst avoids the common mistakes and myths that many performance analysts fall into in order to have a credible analysis and results.

## REFERENCES

[1] R. Jain," The Art of Computer System Performance Analysis: Techniques for Experimental Design, Measurement, Simulation and Modeling," John Wiley, New York, 2001.

[2] D. A. Menascé, V. A. F. Almeida, and L. W. Dowdy, "Performance by Design: Computer Capacity Planning by Example," Prentice Hall, Upper Saddle River, NJ, 2004.

[3] D. A. Menascé, and V. A. F. Almeida, "Capacity Planning for Web Services: Metrics, Models, and Methods," Prentice Hall, Upper Saddle River, NJ, 2001.

[4] D. J. Lilja, " Measuring Computer Performance: A Practitioner's Guide," Cambridge University Press, Cambridge, UK, 2000.

[5] K. Hwang, and Z. Xu, " Scalable Parallel Computing: Technology, Architecture and Programming," MCGraw-Hill, New York, 1998.

[6] J. Ward, "Space-Time Adaptive Processing for Airborne Radar," MIT Lincoln Laboratory Technical Report 1015.

[7] W. L. Melvin, "Space-Time Adaptive Processing and Adaptive Arrays: Special Collection of Papers," IEEE Transactions on Aerospace and Electronic Systems, Vol. 36, No. 2, pp. 508–510 2000.

[8] A. Choudhary, W-K Liao, D. Weiner, P. Varshney, R. Linderman, and R. Brown, "Design, Implementation and Evaluation of Parallel Pipelined STAP on Parallel Computers," IEEE Transactions on Aerospace and Electronic Systems, Vol. 36, No. 2, pp. 528–548, 2000.

[9] K. Hwang, Z. Xu, and M. M. Arakawa, "Benchmark Evaluation of the IBM SP2 for Parallel Signal Processing", Vol. 13, No. 4, pp. 50–66, 1996.

[10] C. J. Wang, C.-L., Wang, and K. Hwang, " STAP Benchmark Evaluation of the T3D, SP2, and Paragon," Proceedings of the 1997 Intl. Conference on Parallel and Distributed Computing Systems, New Orleans, CA, October, 1997.

[11] J. L. Hennessy, and D. A. Patterson, "Computer Architecture: A Quantitative Approach, 3rd Edition" Morgan Kaufmann, San Francisco, CA, 2003.

[12] D. A. Menascé, and V. A. F. Almeida, "Scaling for E-Business: Technologies, Models, Performance, and Capacity Planning," Prentice Hall, Upper Saddle River, NJ, 2000.

[13] D. A. Menascé, V. A. F. Almeida, and L. W. Dowdy, "Capacity Planning and Performance Modeling: from Mainframes to Client-Server Systems," Prentice Hall, Upper Saddle River, NJ, 1994.

[14] C. Milsap, "Optimizing Oracle Performance: A Practitioner's Guide to Optimizing Response Time" O'Reilly, Sebastopol, CA, 2003.

[15] B. Wong, "Configuration and Capacity Planning for Solaris Servers," Prentice Hall, Upper Saddle River, NJ, 1997.

[16] A. Cockcroft and R. Pettit," Sun Performance and Tuning," 2nd Edition, Prentice Hall, Upper Saddle River, NJ, 1998.

[17] P. Nicopolitidis, M. S. Obaidat, G. Papadimitriou, and A. S. Pomportsis, "Wireless Networks," Wiley, New York, 2003.

[18] M. S. Obaidat, and G. Papadimitriou, "Applied System Simulation: Methodologies and Applications," Kluwer, Doidvecht, The Netherland, 2003.

[19] M. S. Obaidat, H. Khalid, and K. Sadiq, "A Methodology for Evaluating the Performance of CISC Computer Systems Under Single and Two-level Cache Environments," Microprocessing and Microprogramming: The Euromicro Journal, Vol. 40, No. 6, pp. 411–426, 1994.

[20] M. S. Obaidat, and H. Khalid, "Estimating Neural Networks-Based Algorithm for Adaptive Cache Replacement," IEEE Transactions on Systems, Man and Cybernetics, Part B: Cybernetics, Vol. 28, No. 4, pp. 602–611, 1998.

[21] H. Khalid and M. S. Obaidat, "KORA: A New Cache Replacement Scheme," Journal of Computers & EE, Vol. 26, No. 3–4, pp. 187–206, 2000.

[22] H. Khalid, and M. S. Obaidat, "Application of Neural Networks to Cache Replacement," Neural Computing & Applications Journal, Vol. 8, pp. 246–256, 1999.

[23] K. Khalil, J. C. Hand, and M. S. Obaidat, "Methodologies for Characterizing Traffic in Wide Area Networks: Analysis and Benchmarking," International Journal of Communication Systems, Vol. 8, No. 2, pp. 117–127, 1995.

[24] B. Lee, and L. John, "NpBench: A Benchmark Suite for Control Plane and Data Plane Applications for Network Processors," Proceedings of the 21st International Conference on Computer Design, Vol. 3, 125–132, 2003.

[25] C. Ho, and Y-S Wu, "Benchmarking Performance Indicators for Banks," Benchmarking: An International Journal, Vol. 13, No. ½, pp. 147–159, 2006.

[26] G. Memik, W. H. M. Smith, and W. Hu, "NetBench: A Benchmarking Suite for Network Processors," Proceedings of the 2001 International Conference on Computer Aided design, pp. 39–42 2001.

[27] R.W. Hockney, "The Science of Computer Benchmarking (Software, Environment and Tools)," SIAM Books, Philadelphia, PA, 1995.

[28] G. Alfonsi and L. Muttoni, "Performance Evaluation of a Windows NT Based PC Cluster for High Performance Computing," Journal of Systems Architecture, pp. 345–359 2004.

[29] K. Maly, A. Gupta, and S. Mynam, "BTU: A Host Communication Benchmark," Computer, Vol. 31, No. 5, pp. 66–74, 1998.

[30] M. Hempstead, M. Welsh, and D. Brooks, "TinyBench: The Case for a Standardized Benchmark Suite for Tiny OS based Wireless Sensor Network Devices," Proceedings of the 29th Annual IEEE International Conference on Local Area Networks, pp. 12–13, 2004.

[31] I. Ahmad, "Express Versus PVM: A Performance Comparison," Journal of Parallel Computing, pp. 783–812, 1997.

[32] B. K. Szymanski, Y. Liu and R. Gupta, "Parallel Network Simulation under Distributed Genesis", Proceedings of the 17th Workshop on Parallel and Distributed Simulation, pp. 212–219, June 2003.

[33] V. S. Getov, A. J. G. Hey, R. W. Hockney, and I. C. Wolton, "The GENESIS Benchmark Suite: Current State and Results," Proceedings of Workshop on Performance Evaluation of Parallel Systems, pp. 182–190, 1993.

[34] K. Hwang, C. Wang, C. L. Wang, and Z. Xu, "Resource Scaling Effects on MPP Performance: The STAP Benchmark Implications," IEEE Transactions on Parallel and Distributed Systems, Vol. 10, No. 5, pp. 509–527, 1999.

[35] N. Boudriga, and M. S. Obaidat, "Intelligent Agents on the Web: A Review," IEEE Journal of Computing in Science and Engineering, pp. 35–42, 2004.

[36] K. Kant, and P. Mohapatra, "Scalable Internet Servers: Issues and Challenges," ACM SIGMETRICS Performance Evaluation Review, Vol. 28, No. 2, pp. 5–8, 2000.

[37] D. Ardagna, and C. Francalanci, "A Cost Oriented Methodology for the Design of Web Based IT Architectures," Proceedings of the 2002 ACM Symposium on Applied Computing, pp. 1127–1133, March 2002.

[38] M. Arlitt, D. Krishnamurthy, and J. Rolia, "Characterizing the Scalability of a Large Web Based Shopping System," ACM Transactions on Internet Technology, Vol. 1, No. 1, pp. 44–69, 2001.

[39] A. Eucens, "Avoid these Ten Benchmarking mistakes." Available at: http://www.benchmarkingplus.com.au/mistakes.htm.

[40] http://www.netlib.org/parkbench/html/.

[41] "Index for PVM3 Library," Available at: http://www.netlib.org/pvm3/.

[42] "The Message Passing Interface (MPI) standard," Available at: http://www-unix.mcs.anl.gov/mpi/index.html.

[43] "Standard Performance Evaluation Corporation," Available at: http://www.spec.org/.

[44] "Benchmark programs and Reports," Available at: http://www.netlib.org/benchmark/.

[45] "Benchmark Applications" Active Hardware, Available at: http://active-hardware.com/english/benchmarks/benchmarks.htm.

[46] "Web TP," Available at: http://webtp.eecs.berkeley.edu/.

[47] "NP Bench," Available at: http://projects.ece.utexas.edu/ece/lca/npbench/.

[48] "LM bench – Tools for performance analysis" Available at: http://www.bitmovera.com/lmbench/.

## EXERCISES

1. Search the literature and review a few recently published articles on benchmarking and capacity planning. Investigate whether the studies have any mistakes.
2. What are the aims of capacity planning of a computer system or network?
3. Go to the Standard Performance Evaluation Corporation, SPEC, website (http://www.spec.org/), and write a report on its recent benchmarks.
4. What are the advantages and disadvantages of synthetic benchmarks?
5. List good performance measures for a multiprocessor computer system and a local area network. Discuss commonalities and differences.
6. Explain the difference, if any exists, between the capacity planning of a computer systems and a local area computer network.
7. State and compare some of the potential measures of computation in a computer system.
8. Amdahl's law pointed at the inherent limitations in trying to improve computer system performance by using multiple processors. Express mathematically the speedup formula and discuss what sort of limitations we have in this regard.
9. An 800-MHz processor was used to execute a benchmark program with the following instruction mix and clock cycle counts:

| Instruction Type | Instruction Count | Clock Cycle Count |
|---|---|---|
| Integer Arithmetic | 450,000 | 1 |
| Data Transfer | 320,000 | 2 |
| Floating Point | 15,000 | 2 |
| Control Transfer | 8,000 | 2 |

Determine the effective cycle per instruction (CPI) rate, MIPS rate, and execution time for this program.

# CHAPTER 5

# DATA REPRESENTATION AND ADVANCED TOPICS ON VALIDATION MODELING

Modeling a computer system assumes the availability of techniques, models, and methodologies to handle data structures, activities, practices, tools, and deliverables applied at every phase of the system's life cycle. This ensures that the system will be designed, implemented, and operated to meet various functional and nonfunctional requirements defined for the systems. The major models to achieve these objectives include the following:

- The representation of data occurring in the exchanged messages, input and outputs of the major components of the systems, and properties that the system needs to fulfill.
- The performance modeling of the system based on the measurable variables that characterize the quality of service it can provide and that can be used to plan, dimension, and operate it.
- The specification model of the protocols that describe a set of standard rules for data representation, signaling, authentication, and error detection required to send information over the entities of the system. The behavioral modeling reproduces the required behavior of the original analyzed system, in a way that there is a one-to-one correspondence between the behavior of the real system and the model representing

*Fundamentals of Performance Evaluation of Computer and Telecommunication Systems,*
By Mohammad S. Obaidat and Noureddine A. Boudriga
Copyright © 2010 John Wiley & Sons, Inc.

the system. This implies, in particular, that the model uniquely predicts future system states from its past system states.

- The verification and validation models aim at checking that the system meets its specifications and that it fulfills its intended purpose. Although a validation technique establishes documented evidence that provides a high degree of assurance that the system accomplishes its intended requirements, the verification is a quality process that is used to evaluate whether the system complies with a specification or conditions imposed at the start of a development phase.

- The simulation modeling that is represented by a mathematical model and a computer program whose role is to represent and simulate the behavior of the communication system.

All the aforementioned techniques and models have become a useful part of any mathematical and experimental model of many systems. Moreover, they are part of the process of engineering new technologies to achieve insight into the operation of those systems or to better observe their behavior.

A validation process can generally be categorized into the following two classes:

- *Prospective validation*: This class includes the tasks conducted before new items are released to make sure that the characteristics of the items are functioning properly and meet the standards.

- *Proactive validation*: This class includes the tasks conducted after items are set up to make sure that the characteristics of the items are functional and meet the specifications after these specifications have been modified.

Although the performance modeling and simulation modeling have been largely studied in the other chapters of this book, the models needed to understand data representation, measurements, errors measurements, and program profiling have not been discussed. In addition, little has been done for the study of systems behavior and validation models on a formal basis. The objective in this chapter is to address these two issues.


## 5.1   DATA REPRESENTATION

In the near future, larger volumes of data need to be collected and analyzed than ever before for different needs of analysis, engineering, and management of communication networks and computer systems. The complexity of the data will grow rapidly, because communication nodes are increasing tremendously their capabilities of performing computations, exchanging messages, and displaying structured data. This process will achieve ways that were literally unreachable only several years ago. It also will have a great impact on the design, modeling, and analysis of the systems themselves. An essential component of the design will be data collection, data modeling, and data analysis to predict/determine the system performance.

As more and more data are gathered for design and analysis, iterations may need to be carried out to achieve better granularity and description. It is therefore essential that the data be structured at the beginning of the data collection, storage, and display. This structure can be referred to as a *representation model*. All these models should be easy to translate into analytic or simulation models, which may be needed to be performed at any time in the life cycle of the communication and computer system. The translation process can be particularly used during initial design, development, manufacturing, system operations, and system maintenance. Analytic models can help in getting accurate performance evaluation of the system for which the collection data process has been performed. However, simulation models provide useful and effective tools to direct analytical evaluation of system performance.

Typically, the output data from a network modeling or simulation is presented in a table, or a matrix, showing how data were impacted by the changes in the simulation parameters. However, it can be easily noted that some trends could quickly be better perceived by examining graphs or even moving images generated from the data. For example, the prediction of some complex events can be better deduced from observing a moving chart faster than scanning tables of related parameters.

## 5.1.1  Graphical Representation

Among the most used representation models, one can find the graphic charts. A graphical chart provides a visual display of numerical information that otherwise would be presented in a table. Ideally, a chart conveys ideas about the data that would not be readily visible if they were displayed in a table or as text. Graphic charts such as line charts, pie charts, and histogram charts are used for different reasons including the easiness they provide to look at the figure they produce to deduce quickly the major features of the system under study. Graphic charts also can help simplifying the study of a particular property.

Designing good charts, however, presents more challenges than the tabular display as they draw on the talents of both the scientist and the artist. Indeed, the designer has to know and understand the data and needs a good sense of how the reader will visualize the chart's graphical elements. Such graphical displays, which go beyond the set of numbers and formulas, sometimes lead to output that lacks coordinate grid or omitted timestamps, as if straying too far from numeric data displays. Our main objective in this chapter is to describe the known technique for data representation and measurement errors.

Graphical representation allows the display of qualitative and quantitative variables. As opposed to a quantitative variable, a graphical chart provides a visual display of numerical information that otherwise would be presented in a table. Preferably, a chart expresses special features about the data that would not be readily apparent if they were displayed in a table or as part of a text. The design of good charts, therefore, presents more challenges than tabular display as it requires the talents of both the scientist and the artist. One has to know and understand the data, but he also needs a good sense of how the reader will visualize the chart's graphical elements.

Two features are important for a graphical chart: the *efficient display* of meaningful and *unambiguous data*. In fact, it is essential for the charting process to choose meaningful data, to define clearly what the variables represent, and to present the data in a manner that allows the reader to comprehend quickly what the data mean. In addition, it is worth noticing that data ambiguity in charts originates from the failure to define exactly what the data represent. Two problems may also arise in charting. First, poor choices in graphic design can provide a distorted picture of the numbers and the relationships they represent. Second, hiding what the data might tell or allowing a design that distracts the chart reader from quickly finding the meaning of the evidence presented in the chart may induce unacceptable errors in the analysis of the systems under display.

Three basic components are shared by most charts. They are the textual labels, the chart's graphical elements, and the X- and Y-axes. Figure 5.1 depicts the components of a generic graphic chart. The textual labels define the numbers and are represented in the chart including the chart's title, axes titles, axes labels, legends, and notes. The chart's graphical elements represent the magnitudes of the numbers and include, but are limited to, bars, pie slices, and lines. The X- and Y-axes define the scale of the numbers represented in the chart.

Charts can be classified into four basic categories: pie charts, bar charts, time series charts, and scatterplots. Choosing the category of chart depends mainly on

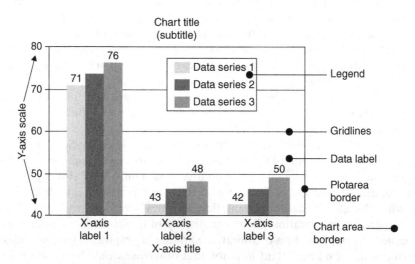

**FIGURE 5.1.** Components of a chart.

the characteristics of the data and the relationships to be displayed. Pie charts are used to represent the distribution of the categorical components of a single variable. One can notice here that this feature induces the fact that pie charts should be rarely used, because multivariate comparisons provide for more meaningful analysis than do single-variable distributions. However, bar charts typically display the relationship between one or more categorical variables with one or more quantitative variables represented by the length of the bars. The categorical variables are usually defined by the categories displayed on the X-axis.

The time series chart is one of the most efficient means of displaying a large amount of data, whereas the two-dimensional scatterplot is the most efficient medium for the graphical display of data. A simple scatterplot will relay better information about the relationship between two interval-level variables than any other method of presenting such data.

The title, which is depicted in Figure 5.1, is typically used to define the data series, without imposing any data interpretation on the reader. The magnitude of the graphical elements of a chart is defined by the axis scale and the individual data labels. If it seems necessary to label every value in a chart, then consider that a table is probably a more efficient way of presenting the data. Legends are used when a chart has more than one data series. They are typically needed for bar charts. With time series charts, labeling usually works better than a separate legend, and sometimes it can eliminate the need to distinguish the lines with additional markers. If legends are used, then they should be ordered to correspond to the ordering of the graphical elements they represent.

### 5.1.2  Proper Results Plotting

Various guidelines have been provided to enhance the graphical representations of modeling results. Among the important guidelines, one can consider the following:

- The representation of results should require a minimum effort from the reader of the chart. In fact, the level of effort required from the reader to understand the chart can be an efficient metric to measure the goodness of the graphic chart. Individual curves should be, in particular, individually labeled, and the units of measurement well indicated.
- The graphic chart should be self-sufficient: The chart should contain sufficient information to achieve this goal. In particular, the labels should be as informative as possible, and appropriate key words can be used instead of symbols. In particular, the title of the chart should be self-explanatory and concise.
- The graphic chart should maximize the information-to-ink ratio; unnecessary information should be avoided. In particular, the grid lines used in the chart should be kept hidden unless they are needed to provide the value of a parameter accurately. In addition, the number of curves should be reasonably small.

- Commonly accepted practices should be used and ambiguity should be avoided when drawing a graphic chart. Common practices include representing causes on the X-axis and plotting the effects on the Y-axis, for example. Ambiguity can be avoided, in particular, by applying simple rules such as showing axes, scales, and origin. In addition, the minimum and maximum ranges should be shown on the axes.

In additions, one should avoid many mistakes that have been frequently seen in the graphic charts reporting performance results. Among those mistakes, one can mention the following:

- Presenting too many alternatives on a single graphic chart: In fact, it has been noticed that the average reader cannot take hold of more than a few messages at a time. Thus, a chart containing too many curves should be avoided.
- Presenting too many Y-variables on a single chart: Plotting a large number of Y-variables saves space; but it can leave the task of associating the curves with the appropriate scale to the reader. Limiting the number of different graphs would allow the chart to be clear and unambiguous.
- Using symbols instead of clear text: A chart with unknown symbols would be difficult to read and comprehend. It may require from the reader an extra effort to search for the meaning of these symbols. In such a case, the messages conveyed by the graphic chart may be lost.
- Selecting scale ranges improperly: It is often necessary to override manually the automatic rules that select and specify the ranges of scales to be shown for one or more parameters. In that case, a particular care has to be provided in the selection of ranges.
- Using the line chart in place of the column chart and vice versa: Typically, the line chart and the column chart are used to convey different messages. Whereas the former allows the interpolation of intermediate values using the lines joining successive points, the latter reports on some features related to the partition of a set. Thus, it seems clear that the chart should be appropriately selected.
- Plotting random values without showing the confidence interval: In this case, the measurement of random parameters would not give the same results, and the variance would be high when they are repeated. To handle this, it is necessary to repeat the measurement many times, plot the average value, and provide the confidence interval.

## 5.2  MEASUREMENTS

Physical variables cannot be measured with perfect certainty because there are always errors in any measurement. This means that measuring a physical quantity and then repeating the measurement will almost certainly provide two different values. However, when taking greater care measuring and applying more refined experimental methods, one can reduce the errors and, thereby, gain greater confidence that the measurements approximate more closely the true value. The notion of measurement is closely related to data representation. Two concepts are frequently related to the meaning of measurement error. They are *precision* and *accuracy*. The concept of precision refers to the reproducibility of a measurement. It measures how closely two or more measurements agree with each other. It is sometimes referred to as repeatability or reproducibility because a measurement that is highly reproducible tends to give values that are close to each other. Accuracy is a measure of the nearness to true value. It measures how close a measured value is to the true value or accepted value.

A common belief considers that no measurement is meaningful unless it is accompanied by an estimate of its uncertainty or error, no measurement can be considered exact, and an error is always associated with an experimental measurement. In fact, the experimental equipment and measuring instruments have limitations that prevent a user from determining a measurement with sufficient accuracy. Because a true or accepted value for a physical quantity may be unknown, it is sometimes not possible to determine the accuracy of a measurement. All experiments, no matter how thoroughly they are planned and executed, have some level of uncertainty. In computer and communication systems, one should be able to know how to identify, correct, or evaluate sources of an error in an experiment and how to express the accuracy and precision of measurements operated when collecting data or reporting values about a system.

### 5.2.1 Measurement Errors

Three general types of errors occur in measuring communication and computer systems: random errors, systematic errors, and gross errors. Random errors are caused by uncontrollable variations and unpredictable changes in the values of variables that affect experimental results. Changes may occur in the measuring instruments or in the environmental conditions. Examples of causes of random errors are as follows:

- An electronic noise in the circuit of an electrical instrument
- Irregular changes in the temperature collector because of changes in the system environment

Random errors often have a Gaussian normal distribution. In such cases, statistical methods may be used to analyze the data. The mean $\mu$ of several measurements of the same quantity is a good estimate of that quantity, and the standard deviation $\sigma$ of the measurements shows the accuracy of the estimate. The standard error of the estimate $\mu$ is $\frac{\sigma}{\sqrt{n}}$, where $n$ is the number of measurements. The estimated standard deviation is typically reported with measurements because random errors are difficult to eliminate.

Systematic errors are errors that affect the accuracy of a measurement. They can be instrumental, methodological, or caused by personal mistakes producing irregular data, which is consistently deviated from the exact value. The accuracy of measurements subject to systematic errors cannot be improved by repeating those measurements. In addition, systematic errors cannot easily be analyzed by statistical analysis. They can be difficult to detect; but once detected, they can be reduced only by refining the measurement technique. Examples of systematic errors include the instrumental error results, such as spectrometer deviations away from its calibrated settings or a personal error that can occur when an experimenter records only even numbers. Systematic errors can be identified and eliminated after careful inspection of the experimental methods, cross-calibration of instruments, or assessment of techniques. Finally, gross errors are caused by experimenter's carelessness or equipment failure.

**Precision of a set of measurements.** A data set of repetitive measurements is often expressed as a single representative number called the mean or average. The mean $\mu$ is the sum of individual measurements ($x_i$) divided by the number of measurements ($n$). Precision $\sigma$ is indicated by the deviation from the mean $\mu$,

$$\mu = \frac{1}{n} \sum_{i=0}^{n} x_i, \quad \sigma^2 = \frac{1}{n^2} \sum_{i=0}^{n} (\mu - x_i)^2$$

Widely scattered data results in a large average deviation indicating poor precision. A small average deviation indicates that data points are clustered closely around the mean and good precision.

Percent error (or fractional difference) measures the accuracy of a measurement by the difference between a measured value $M$ and a true or accepted value $R$. The percent error, denoted by %Error, is calculated from the following equation:

$$\%\text{Error} = \frac{M - R}{R} \times 100$$

The *relative average deviation* is the average deviation divided by the average of the measurements. Relative average deviation shows how significant the average deviation is in proportion to the measured value. The relative average deviation is commonly expressed as a percent:

$$\text{Percent relative average deviation} = 100 \left( \frac{\text{Average Deviation}}{\text{Average}} \right)$$

**Example.** An engineer made four independent measurements of the number of packets of a constant bit rate traffic on a communication link. He obtained the

values 1541 packets/s, 1567 packets/s, 1575 packets/s, and 1505 packets/s. The average deviation of this set of measurements can be computed as follows:
The average is

$$\mu = \frac{1541 + 1567 + 1575 + 1505}{4} = 1547 \text{ packets/s}$$

The deviation of each of these measurements from the average is:
$1541 - 1547 = -6$
$1567 - 1547 = 20$
$1580 - 1547 = 33$
$1505 - 1547 = -42$
The average deviation of this set of measurements is:

$$\frac{-6 + 20 + 33 - 42}{4} \approx 1.25$$

The relative average deviation is:

$$\frac{1.25}{1547} \times 100 = 0.08\%$$

**Accuracy of a result.** The accuracy of a measured result can be measured by computing the percent error, which is only found if the true value is known. The percent error is usually expressed as an absolute value; however, it can be given a negative or positive sign to indicate the direction of error with respect to its true value.

Rejection of measurements can be decided on the deviations they may have with respect to the true values. The $Q$-test, which can be used for rejecting data, determine whether an individual measurement should be rejected or retained. For this, the quantity $Q$ is the absolute difference between the measurements (denoted by $x_s$) under study and the next closest measurement (denoted by $x_n$) divided by the spread ($\omega$), which is the difference between the largest and smallest measurement of the entire set of measurements:

$$Q = \frac{x_s - x_n}{\omega}$$

If $Q$ is greater than a particular confidence level, then the measurement should be rejected. If $Q$ is less than this value, the measurement should be retained. It is worth noticing that, although a set of measurements may have a high precision (characterized by small standard deviations), the measured results can be inaccurate because of systematic error, for example. However, experimental measurements with poor precision (with large standard deviations) from random errors can still give an average result close to true value.

## 5.2.2 Ratio Game

Ratios have a numerator and a denominator, which is referred to as the base of the ratio. Two ratios with different bases are not comparable in general. The techniques of using ratios with incomparable bases and combining them are called the *ratio game*. Ratios games can be applied even when more than two communication or computer systems (or metrics) are involved. A particular form where the ratio games are used is by selecting a suitable performance metric that is computed as the average of two different metrics. The following example shows a simple example of the use of the ratio game.

**Example.** Let A and B be two nodes linked by links, S1 and S2, having 622 Mbps and 155 Mbps capacity, respectively. Assume that during the time period $[t, t + a[$ link S1 usage ratio is 65% and that during the time period $[t, t + b[$, where $b < a$, link S2 usage is 25%. Then, three ways can be selected to average the utilization of the connection from S1 to S2:

- Take the average of the two ratios: This gives a ratio equal to 45% for the period $[t, t + a[$.
- Compute the whole capacity (= 777 Mbps) and the sum of the traffic sizes $(0.65 \times 622 + 0.25 \times 155)$, per second, and deduce the ratio. This gives about 57% (= $(404.3 + 38.75)/777$)
- Apply the second method for the two periods of time $[t, t + b[$ and $[t + b, t + a[$. This gives the ratio 57% for the first interval and 52% for the second interval.

The simplest way to use ratios is by presenting the performance of $n$ systems on various workloads and then using the average ratio to show that one's proposed system is better than the others. Therefore, it can be shown that by appropriately choosing the base system, one can easily reverse the conclusion of the performance evaluation under discussion.

Several practical approaches have been introduced to provide the conditions under which the conclusions related to the performance evaluation of a communicating system can be reversed by changing the base in a ratio game. These approaches have highlighted the following guidelines. If one system is better on all metrics, then contradicting the conclusions cannot be achieved. Contradicting the conclusions means that one system can be shown to be better performing than the second one on some base, and the other is performing better on other bases. Thus, if a system is performing better on some benchmark and worse on others, then contradicting conclusions is easy to achieve.

Consider now the case of two systems S1 and S2 with two benchmarks B1 and B2. Assume that the performance of S1 on B1 and B2 is $\alpha$ and $\beta$, respectively, and the performance of S2 on B1 and B2 is $x$ and $y$, respectively.

Using these data, one can say that system S1 is performing better than S2 if, and only if, the following inequality stands:

$$y < -\frac{\alpha}{\beta}x + \frac{\alpha + \beta}{\beta}$$

The analysis of this inequality shows the following. On the one hand, if system S1 is used as a base, then it will be considered better if and only if:

$$\frac{x+y}{2} < 1 \ (\text{or } y < 2 - x)$$

On the other hand, if system S2 is used as a base, then system S1 will be considered better if and only if:

$$\frac{1}{x} + \frac{2}{y} > 2 \left( \text{or } y < \frac{x}{-1+2x} \right)$$

## 5.3 PROGRAM PROFILING AND OUTLINING

Profiling is a well-known technique for recording program behavior and measuring program performance. It is commonly used to measure instruction set use, estimate program execution times for code optimization, and identify program bottlenecks. Typically, program profiling involves counting specific events of interest, such as entering a basic block or taking a particular control flow edge. Events are counted each time they happen during the execution of a program. These data are written out at the end of the program's execution. Profile programming typically involves two steps: During the first step, the program is rewritten to insert additional code, called the *profiling code*, which records the runtime events of interest as they occur. During the second step, the modified program is executed with the same input; it generates the output data of the original program, denoted by *data-gen*, and writes the profile data, denoted by *program-counts* [1].

On the one hand, to obtain execution counts for each basic block (or a straight-line sequence of instructions) in a program, one can insert specific code into each basic block of the program to increment a block-specific counter each time that block is used. On the other hand, more sophisticated profiles, including path profiles, require more complex processing, but the general scheme remains the same. Profilers may also use more sophisticated profiling logic to reduce runtime overheads.

It is worthy to notice that two independent types of errors can be added in the profiling process. The first type includes instrumentation errors that occur when rewriting the program to insert the profiling code (or instrument). The second type includes profiling code errors that appear when a bug in the code records runtime events. The instrumentation errors produce incorrect profile data regardless of the type of profiling code that is inserted. In particular, when we consider the case of the basic block profile, one can induce an error in the rewriting process, for example, that does not update branches correctly and causes the profiling code to be skipped in some occasion. If the profiling code has an error, such as using a block-specific counter that is too small, it is possible to overflow the counter. In both cases, the result of the profile data does not match the actual execution of the program.

On the other hand, in addition to inserting profiling code for the need of counting and recording profiling events in a program, a profiler may require allocation of memory space for the profile counters he or she has inserted. The number of counters and the size of the memory space can be determined statically by examining the program, in simple cases such as the basic block profiles; however, for more complex profiles, it may not be possible to determine statically how many counters and memory space are required. In this situation, the counters may have to be dynamically allocated during execution. In both cases, data addresses in the original program would change and the errors in the profile data that result can be thought of as profiling errors.

Therefore, the act of inserting profiling codes into a program can slightly modify its behavior. Thus, in implementing a profile checker, the profiler can avoid the program being profiled to help identify profiling errors. The checker observes the runtime behavior of a program the same way a human uses a debugger to debug a program: by single stepping, setting breakpoints, running until breakpoints are reached, and examining the memory space of the program. In the process, the checker counts the profiling events as they appear and checks whether the resulting counts match those generated by the profiler. The checker also controls the execution of the original program on the original input file and takes the event counts data as an input and produces diagnostics and verification output as appropriate.

Various techniques can be used to provide program profiling. To explain the typical steps in these techniques, let us first discuss some basics of graph theory.

A control-flow graph (CFG) is a rooted directed graph, say $G = (V, E)$, that corresponds to a procedure in a program such that each vertex in $V$ represents a basic block of instructions (or a straight-line sequence of instructions) and each edge in $E$ represents the transfer of control from one basic block to another. In addition, the CFG includes a special vertex *EXIT* that corresponds to procedure *exit*, and the root vertex represents the first basic block in the procedure. Finally, a directed path from the root to every vertex and a directed path from every vertex to *EXIT* are assumed to exist in the CFG.

A weighting $W$ of a CFG $G$ is a function that assigns a non negative value (an integer or a real) to every edge and that satisfies the Kirchoff's flow law, in the sense that, for each vertex $v$, the sum of the weights of the incoming edges to $v$ must be equal to the sum of the weights of the outgoing edges from $v$. The *weight* of a vertex is the sum of the weights of its incoming (or outgoing) edges. The *cost* of a set of edges and/or vertices is the sum of the weights of the edges and/or vertices in the set. An *execution* of a procedure is represented by a directed path $EX$ in the CFG that begins at the root vertex (procedure entry) and ends at $EXIT$. The *frequency* of a vertex $v$ or edge $e$ in an execution $EX$ is the number of times that $v$ or $e$ appears in $EX$. If a vertex or edge does not appear in $EX$, its frequency is zero.

A *spanning tree* of a directed graph $G = (V, E)$ is a subgraph $H = (V, T)$, where $T \leq E$, such that every pair of vertices in $V$ is connected by a unique path (i.e., $H$ connects all the vertices in $V$ and there are no cycles in $H$). A *maximum* spanning tree of a weighted graph is a spanning presenting a maximal cost of the tree edges. The maximum spanning tree for a graph can be computed efficiently using a variety of algorithms.

Now let us get back to program profiling. To determine the number of executions of each basic block in a program, counting code can be inserted to the program at every basic block. However, some drawbacks to such an approach can be observed, including the fact that many counters may be unnecessarily added.

Program profiling can be solved by addressing the *vertex profiling* problem, denoted by $Vprof(cnt)$, or the *edge profiling* problem, which is denoted by $Eprof(cnt)$. The first problem aims at determining a placement of counters $cnt$ (a set of edges and/or vertices) in program CFG such that the frequency of each vertex in any execution of $G$ can be deduced exclusively from the graph and the measured frequencies of edges and vertices in $cnt$. In addition, on the one hand, to reduce the cost of profiling, the set $cnt$ should minimize cost for a weighting map $W$. On the other hand, $Eprof(cnt)$ aims at determining a placement of counters in $cnt$ in CFG $G$ such that the frequency of each edge in any execution of $G$ can be deduced from the CFG $G$ and the measured frequencies of edges and vertices in $cnt$. Let us finally notice that a solution to the edge frequency problem obviously implies a solution to the vertex frequency problem by summing the frequencies of incoming or outgoing edges of each vertex.

Knowing that one can place counters on vertices or edges, a counter placement can be classified into three forms: a set of edges ($Ecnt$), a set of vertices ($Vcnt$), and a mixture of edges and vertices ($Mcnt$). Mixed placements are of some interest because of two reasons: (a) placing counters on vertices rather than on edges would remove the need to insert unconditional jumps and (b) the fact that a vertex is executed more frequently than any of its outgoing edges implies that it might be valuable to add code at some outgoing edges rather than the vertex.

Various profiling problems can be solved by providing an optimal solution, including the following three problems [2]: the Vertex Profiling with Vertex Counters [$Vprof(Vcnt)$], the Edge Profiling with Edge Counters [$Eprof(Ecnt)$], and the Vertex Profiling with Edge Counters [$Vprof(Ecnt)$]. For the sake of space, let us focus only on how to solve $Eprof[Ecnt]$ .

To see how a placement is done, consider a CFG denoted by $G$ and a set $Ecnt$ such that $E - Ecnt$ is a spanning tree of $G$. Assume that each edge $e \in Ecnt$ has an associated counter that is initially set to 0 and is incremented once every time edge $e$ *is* executed. If vertex $v$ is a leaf in the spanning tree (i.e., only one tree edge is incident to $v$ in the spanning tree), then all remaining edges incident to $v$ are in *Ecnt*. Because the edge frequencies for an execution satisfy Kirchoff's law, the unmeasured edge's frequency is uniquely determined by the flow equation for $v$ and the known frequencies of the other incoming and outgoing edges of $v$. The remaining edges with unknown frequency still form a tree, so this process can be repeated until the frequencies of all edges in $E - Ecnt$ are uniquely computed. If $E - Ecnt$ contains no cycles, but is not a spanning tree, then $E - Ecnt$ is a forest of trees. The above approach can be applied to each tree separately to determine the frequencies for the edges in $E - Ecnt$.

**Example.** Consider the following simple program P. Figure 5.2 shows a weighting CFG graph (which includes six vertexes associated with simple blocks in P), its maximum spanning tree, and a solution for the *Eprof* (*Ecnt*) problem. *Eprof* (*Ecnt*) has been solved by placing a counter on the outgoing edges of each vertex having at least two outgoing edges. However, it can be shown that this placement uses more counters than necessary (Six counters, as represented by dots on the related edges).

    **Program P**
       While P do
           if Q then A else B
           if R then break
           C
      end

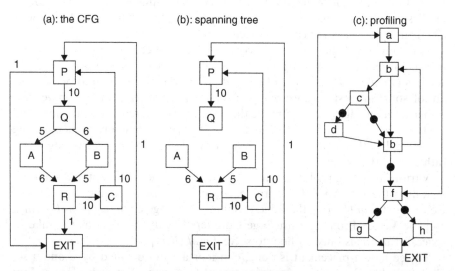

**FIGURE 5.2.** A CFG with a weighting, its maximum spanning tree, and a profiling solution.

## 5.4 STATE MACHINE MODELS

State machine models are ubiquitous models for specifying, setting up, and verifying different aspects of computing and telecommunication systems. The idea behind a state machine is simple: A computer or communication system is characterized by a set of states (or values of the variables constituting the system activity) that it handles. The system receives a series of inputs that may cause the machine to produce an output and/or move to a different state, depending on its current state. A finite state machine is a state machine that can be in only one of a limited number of states. More powerful and complex state machine models allow a larger and possibly infinite number of states.

An example of finite state machines is given by a simplified state diagram of a telephone activity, for which the states can be reduced to belong to the finite set {idle, dial tone, dialing, ringing, talking}; the events that cause the system to go from one state to another include the following:

- Lifting the handset: This event causes a move from state "idle" to state "dial tone."
- Touching a digit: This event causes a move from "idle tone" to "dialing," or from "dialing" to "dialing."
- Answering: The answering event causes the shift from "ringing" to "answering."
- Hanging up: The event leads the machine from state "answering" to state "idle."

Figure 5.3 depicts the finite-state machine (FSM) characterizing the aforementioned telephone activity.

The concept of the state machine as a model of computing applications was set up a long time ago. It has been demonstrated that such a machine could serve as a general-purpose computer and communication system. In both academia and industry, related models were proposed and studied during several decades, resulting in a definitive paper demonstrating the tractability of limited models [3]. This work enabled the finite state machine to reach maturity as a theoretical model.

Nowadays, it is well understood that the design of correct communication protocols is a non trivial task. The application of the formal methods to the analysis of such protocols resulted in many improvements in the accuracy of the protocols, including special protocols such as the security protocols. In particular, the recent two decades have viewed considerable progress in the field of formal analysis of security protocols, which has generated a large number of methods and tools for protocol verification [4]. Similarly, the last several years have observed progress in the field of system verification. Many approaches have emerged for the need of specifying and checking many interesting properties of communication systems using state machines.

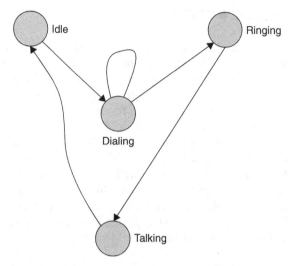

**FIGURE 5.3.** Example of state machine.

Formally, a finite state machine is defined as a 5-tuple, $(Q, S, T, q_0, F)$, where $Q$ is finite set of states, S is a finite set of input events, $T$ is a transition function $T: Q \times S \rightarrow Q$, $q_0$ ($q_0 \in Q$) is a an *initial* state, and $F$ is a set of states distinguished as *accepting* (or *final*) *states* ($F \subseteq Q$). When the transition function has its images in the power set of Q, say $T: Q \times S \rightarrow P(Q)$, the FSM is called nondeterministic, which means that, for any input event, the next state is not uniquely determined but may be any one of several possible states selected by $T$.

However, a communicating FSM can be defined as a nondeterministic FSM $(Q, M, T, q0, F)$, where $Q$ is a finite, nonempty set of states, $q0$ is an element of $Q$, the *initial state*, as defined above, $M$ is a set of message queues, and $T$ is a state transition relation. Communicating FSMs can be managed through two major operations: the execution of machines and the minimization of machines.

Consider a system of $n$ communication state machines, with possibly overlapping sets of messages, and let $q_0^j$, $j \leq n$, the initial state of the $j^{th}$ machine and M the set of all messages. An execution of the communicating finite state machines is a sequence of states $(q_0, q_1,...,q_n)$ by applying the following rules, where the elements related to the $i^{th}$ finite state machine are referred to with a superscript $i$:

$$\forall i : \exists j, q_i - q_0^j \vee \left( \exists e, k : (k < i), q_i \in T^i(q_k, e) \right)$$

The set of all executions can be obtained by the application of the following three-step algorithm:

**Step 1.** Set all machines in their initial state, and initialize all message queues to empty.

**Step 2**. Select an arbitrary machine $i$ and an arbitrary transition function $T^i$ with $T^i(q,e^i)$ not empty and execute it; meaning that a new state in $T^i(q, e^i)$ is selected as the new state of the $i^{th}$ machine.

**Step 3**. If no executable transition functions remain, then the algorithm terminates.

However, the optimization is based on the concept of *equivalent machines*. Two machines are said to be equivalent if they can output the same sequence of actions when they are offered the same sequence of input actions. When the communication FSMs are nondeterministic, two equal machines can behave differently when offered the same input symbols. Thus, the rule for equivalence is that the machines must have equivalent choices to be in equivalent states. Two states within a machine are said to be equivalent if the machine can be started in any one of these states and generate the same set of possible sequences of outputs when offered any given test sequence of inputs.

Using the equivalence concept, the set of states of a communicating finite-state machine can be minimized, without changing the external behavior of the machine, by replacing every set of equivalent states with a single state.

### 5.4.1 FSM Validation

FSM validation is the problem of verifying the logical consistency of the FSM. Most automated validation systems are based on exhaustive reachability analysis, which attempts to generate and look over all the states of a distributed system that are reachable from a given initial state. Implicitly, the approach constructs all possible execution sequences. To establish the observance of state invariants, then, it suffices to verify their correctness with a simple Boolean test for each state that is reachable from a given initial system state.

The three main approaches of reachability analysis are the full search, the controlled partial search, and the random simulation. The full search is a simple procedure. It performs the most thorough analysis of the search algorithms; however, it can only analyze a reduced class of protocols. The controlled partial search tries to optimize the quality of the reachability analysis specifically for those cases where a full search is infeasible. It attempts the analysis by selecting an optimal portion of the full state space that can be searched using given constraints of memory and time. Finally, the random simulation techniques are specifically meant for the validation of systems of large complexity.

***Full search.*** An exhaustive reachability analysis tries to determine which states are reachable and which are not. Every reachable state and every sequence of reachable states can be checked for a given set of correctness criteria. These criteria can be general conditions that must hold for any protocol, such as the absence of deadlocks or buffer overruns, or they can be protocol-specific requirements, such as a temporal claim about the proper working of a message retransmission discipline. In many cases, protocol-specific requirements can be formalized as state invariants, the correctness of which can be verified with a simple Boolean test in every reachable system state.

The reachability analysis process typically handles two sets, a set of states that have been analyzed, called A, and a working set of system states to be analyzed, called B. When the reachability analysis terminates, it should have examined all the reachable system states. The order in which states are retrieved from working set B and moved seems irrelevant at a first look; however, it turns out to be an important control point. In fact, if the states are stored in set B in *first-in–last-out* order, the algorithm applies a depth-first search of the state space tree. If the states are stored and removed in a *first-in– first-out* order, the algorithm will perform a breadth-first search

A breadth-first search has the advantage to find the shortest error sequences first, whereas a depth-first search presents the advantage to require a smaller work set B. The depth of the search tree depends on the maximum length of the execution sequences. The width of the tree, however, is defined by the maximum number of distinct execution sequences, which is usually a much larger number.

**Controlled partial search.** If the state space is large (in the sense that the available memory cannot accommodate, the aforementioned exhaustive search effectively), then the methods are performed to implement a partial search that guarantees, in some sense, that the most important parts of the space of states are inspected. This new class of algorithms, which specifically try to exploit the benefits of a partial search, is based on the assumption that, in most realistic cases, the maximum number of states that can be analyzed, $A$ is only a fraction of the total number of reachable states $R$. A controlled partial search, then, has the following objective: to select the set of states $A$ in such a way that the probability of finding any given error is better than the coverage $A/R$.

An algorithm implementing the partial search should be similar to the full search algorithm, with only one difference: Not all successor states are analyzed. However, it adds some rules to select the next states to analyze. The selection can also be based on a heuristic that supports executions that are likely to reveal design errors. Many different ways of organizing a controlled partial search have been developed. Among the most important selection methods, one can mention the probabilistic searches, the depth-bounds, and the partial orders.

In a probabilistic search, the next states are explored in decreasing order of their probability of occurrence. All transitions in the FSM are labeled, minimally with a value that defines probability of occurrence; these labels are used as the selection criteria. The depth-bounds search is a simple partial search technique that places a bound on the length of the execution sequences that are analyzed. It limits the search to a useful subset of behaviors, eliminating degenerate cases of multiple overlapping executions. Such a search allows us to restrict the maximum size of the set B.

The partial orders aims at avoiding the state space explosion problem by reducing number of possible interleavings of concurrent events and make use of the fact that not all interleavings are necessarily relevant in the search for error states. To do so, a method can use one among the following heuristics: the *fair progress* state exploration and the *maximum progress* state exploration. Both heuristics implement a search priority to the processes. In particular, the number of transitions that are inspected during the search can be limited, with a preference assigned to the transitions that belong to higher priority processes.

**Random simulation.** This technique is independent of the size and complexity of the network being modeled by the FSM and can be applied when the size is infinite. A random simulation discards sets A and B from the partial search algorithm and explores the state space using the random walk approach. The algorithm does not terminate but outputs a message any time an error state is found. However, an exhaustive coverage can be guaranteed, for finite state spaces, provided that a sufficient amount of time is allowed for the simulation.

### 5.4.2   FSM-Based Conformance Testing Validation

A conformance test of a communication system aims at checking whether the external behavior of a given implementation of a communication system is equivalent to its formal specification. In particular, a FSM specifying a communication would be based on the conformance test of the system. Finite state machines, thus, can be used to validate a communication protocol and detect the anomalous behavior in the traffic, flowing under the control of this protocol, by describing the progression of a connection through all the states, which result from events based on header content of the flowing packets.

Assume now that we are given a known reference specification in FSM format, and an unknown implementation, which is considered as a black box that can be executed on a finite set of inputs and for each input it is able to generate an output. Assume also that the only task that can be performed with the black box is to provide it with sequences of input actions (or messages) and examine the resulting outputs. The conformance of the implementation to test, referred to as the IT, is stated if all observed outputs match those prescribed by the FSM. In that case, the set of input sequences that is used to examine the conformance of the IT is called a conformance test suite (CTS). The CTS is derived from the reference specification, ideally by a mechanical procedure.

The first attempt to build an effective CTS has two main goals:

- To prove that the IT implements all the functions required by the FSM, over the full range of parameter values
- To demonstrate that the IT properly rejects erroneous inputs in a way that is consistent with the FSM

The conformance testing typical scheme operates through a three-step procedure that is applied for all combinations of a state $i$ and an input signal $j$.

First, a *reset* message is used to take the IT to the initial state, and then use a *set* a message to move the IT to state $i$. Second, the signal $j$ is submitted to the IT and the output received is checked if it matches the output required by the FSM. Third, a *status* message is used to interrogate the IT about its final state and the final state is checked whether it matches the one required by the FSM.

Conformance testing schemes have become a challenging issue when the administrators of a (public or private) data networks have to assess the adequacy of commercial solution that can be acquired and used on their networks. The test verifies that the solution can correctly perform all state transitions in the FSM. Moreover, the CST should include specific messages such as the *set*, *reset*, and *status*. If the assessment passes positively, the implementation can reproduce the behavior of the FSM; however, it remains unknown whether the solution is capable of any other behavior. In particular, if the solution to assess is faulty, then it may violate the fact the solution implements a finite-state machine with a known maximum number of states and with a known input and output vocabulary. The acceptance of an input signal that is outside the official input vocabulary may then cause a transition of the faulty solution into a set of states that produces erroneous behavior. The cost of the test can be expressed using the length of the test suite, that is, as the total number of messages that is sent to the IT. Assume that the FSM contains $n$ states and has an input vocabulary of $v$ distinct messages, including the *set*, *reset*, and *status* messages. Then the cost is equal to $4nv$.

### 5.4.3 FSM-Based Validation of TCP

To study the use of finite-state machines, we consider the Transmission Control Protocol (TCP). To do so, let us recall some features of TCP, which is a reliable protocol whose behavior follows a pattern that is predictable to some extent. TCP is based on a three-step process: The first step is a three-way handshake. The second step is the data exchange, and the final step is a closing procedure. The content of the TCP header expresses the commands that carry a connection through these stages. A TCP packet has a header, which includes source and destination Internet Protocols (IPs) and ports, sequence numbers, acknowledgement number and some flags that carry information important to the progression of the connection. TCP connection anomalies can impart information that is important to the network management functions, such as unresponsive hosts and behaviors that lead to resource consumption, and problems in network security [5].

A TCP connection is negotiated by the user and the server via TCP three-way handshake. For this, the user requests the establishment of a connection by sending a packet with a SYN flag (denoted by S). The server agrees to open a connection by transmitting it using a packet (denoted by SA or SYN acknowledgement). Whenever a packet is sent, the receiver must acknowledge receipt by transmitting a packet with the ACK flag set so that the sender knows that the packet was received. These acknowledgments are usually piggybacked on other packets to reduce network charge. A packet acknowledging SA completes the handshake and data transfer may begin. On closing, either the client or the server may request that the connection be ended with transmission of a FIN packet (denoted by F), and the other agrees to close the connection by transmitting its own FIN packet (denoted by FA). In addition, the different steps of a connection are only allowed to exist for an amount of time to free up resources that are not being used. Figure 5.4 depicts the use of the flags.

By defining the states of a finite-state machine to reflect the steps of a connection activity and using the flags as the events that bring about transitions among the states, we can model a TCP connection as an FSM. In addition, the FSM can be made to handle anomaly detection; for this, a failure state can be introduced to indicate the occurrence of a disallowed event or an attempted illegal transition. When the time-ordered flags of a TCP connection are submitted to the FSM, then the connection is flagged as anomalous if the connection enters a failure state or does not complete. The state that the connection was in and the event that led to the failure can be stored to give an indication of the reason that the failure occurred.

The resulting FSM can be used to detect some network management issues and network security events as well as a tool to study the behavior of TCP on

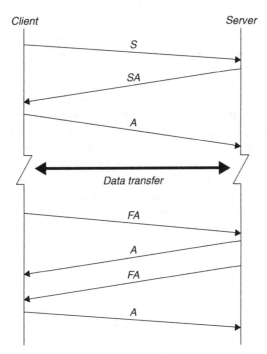

**FIGURE 5.4.** The three-step process of TCP.

the Internet. More precisely, the FSM is constructed as follows; the events are determined by flags including the following values:

- U: For urgent pointer valid, meaning that the data contained in packet is urgent)
- A: For acknowledgement number valid (acknowledge receipt)
- P: For push data (clear the buffer)
- R: For reset connection
- S: For synchronize sequence numbers (i.e. initiate connection)
- F: For no more data (i.e., finish connection)

Seven states can be defined in the FSM as follows:

- The *listen* state is the imaginary starting point for all connections.
- *Connection requested* and *connection established* are two states needed to establish the connection and complete the handshake by passing through two states.
- The *Data transfer* is a state where the connection may enter after its establishment. When the connection is in this state, data can be transmitted
- The *closing* and *closed* states are used to allow a graceful termination of the connection. If it is terminated abruptly, then it may skip *closing* and proceed directly to *closed*.
- The *failure* state represents that the connection has got lost from the protocol specification by attempting to access a state out of order or by introducing an illegal event.

Let us now describe the effect of the events. A TCP connection progresses from one state to another based on the information contained in the headers of the packets exchanged (mainly defined by the flag). It should start in a *listen* state. When the first SYN is sent, the connection moves to the *connection requested* state. When the SYN is acknowledged, the connection enters the *connection established* state. When the handshake is complete and until the closing begins, the connection is in a *data transfer* state. If the connection is terminated gracefully, the *closing* state is entered when one side has sent a FIN packet. If the connection is terminated via a RST packet or the second FIN packet, then the connection moves to the *closed* state and remains there. If an event or transition that is not specified occurs, the connection enters the *failure* state and stays there. The resulting FSM is depicted by Figure 5.5, where the *failure* state is omitted.

Twenty-two specified events can be distinguished in the above description. Table 5.1 describes these events. It can be mentioned that among these events, four events can be used for acknowledgement, seven events can be used to request a connection closure, and seven events are used to tear down a connection.

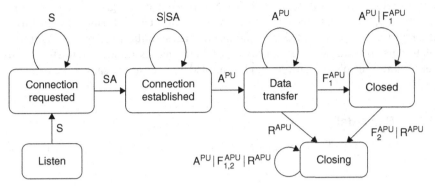

**FIGURE 5.5.** The FSM of TCP connection.

**TABLE 5.1   The FSM events**

| Event label | Flag set | Event description |
|---|---|---|
| S | {S} | Request to open connection |
| SA | {SA} | Agree to open connection. |
| $A^{PU}$ | {A, PA, AU, PAU} | Acknowledgement of receipt. |
| $F^{APU}$ | {F, FA, FP, FU, FPA, FPU, FAU, FPAU} | Request to close connection. |
| $R^{APU}$ | {R, RA, RP, RU, RPA, RPU, RAU, RPAU} | Tear down connection. |

## 5.5   PETRI NET-BASED MODELING

A Petri net is a mathematical representation of discrete distributed systems. It represents graphically the structure of a distributed system, such as a communication network, as a directed bipartite graph. Petri Nets constitute a very powerful tool for both qualitative and quantitative system analysis. Unlike queueing networks, they can easily be used to model blocking and synchronization aspects. However, they present the disadvantage that they do not provide any means for direct representation of scheduling strategies [6, 7].

The major components of a Petri net are the *places*, *transitions*, and *directed arcs*. Arcs take place between places and transitions. The places from which an arc is issued to a transition are called the input places of the transition; the places to which an arc arrives from a transition are called the output places of the transition. Places may contain any number of tokens. For this, a distribution of tokens over the places of a Petri net is used; it is referred to as a *marking*. Transitions act on the input tokens by a process called *firing*. A transition is *enabled* if it can fire, meaning that there are tokens in each of its input places. When a transition fires, it consumes a predefined number of tokens from each input place, performs some processing task, and places a specified number of tokens into each of its output place. After firing a transition, the marking of the input and the places of the transition are changed accordingly. A transition fires atomically, meaning that the firing process can be performed in one non-interruptible step, provided that the input places contain the required number of tokens. In addition, the execution of Petri nets is nondeterministic, in the sense that multiple transitions can be enabled and fire at the same time or in any order [8].

### 5.5.1   Basic-definitions

Formally, a **Petri Net** (PN) can be defined as a 5-tuple $PN = (P, T, I^{inp}, I^{out}, M_0)$, where:

- $P$ is a finite and non-empty set of places,
- $T$ is a finite and nonempty set of transitions
- $P \cap T = \Phi$.
- $I^{inp}, I^{out}: P \times T \to N$ are called backward and forward incidence functions, respectively.
- $M_0: P \to N$ is the initial marking.

The incidence functions $I^{inp}$ and $I^{+}$ specify the interconnection between places and transitions. If $I^{inp}(p; t) > 0$, then there is an arc leading from place $p$ to transition $t$ and several tokens, equal to $I^{inp}(p; t)$, are deduced from place $p$ when t is fired. If $I^{out}(p; t) > 0$, then there is an arc starting from transition $t$ and arriving to place $p$ and several tokens, equal to $I^{out}(p; t)$, are added to place $p$ when $t$ is fired. The incidence functions assign natural numbers to arcs, which are referred to as weights of the arcs. When each input place of transition $t$ contains at least as many tokens as the weight of the arc connecting it to $t$, the transition is said to be enabled.

An enabled transition $t_0$ may fire, in which case it deletes tokens from its input places and adds tokens in its output places of $t_0$, changing the marking $M$ into a new marking $M'$ as follows:

$$M'(p) = M(p) - I^{inp}(p; t_0)$$
$$M'(p) = M(p) + I^{out}(p; t_0)$$
$$M'(p) = M(p) \text{ in the other cases}$$

The initial arrangement of tokens in the net (called initial marking) is given by the function $M_0$, which specifies how many tokens are contained in each place. Figure 5.6 illustrates a basic Petri net with four places and two transitions.

**Example.** Consider the Petri depicted by Figure 5.6, where the initial marking $M_0$ is defined by $M_0(P1) = 1$, $M_0(P2) = 0$, $M_0(P3) = 2$, and $M_0(P4) = 1$. In addition, the backward and forward incidence functions $I^{inp}$ and $I^{out}$ are given by:

$$I^{inp}(P1; T1) = I^{inp}(P2; T2) = I^{inp}(P3; T2) = 1$$
$$I^{out}(P2; T1) = I^{out}(P3; T1) = I^{out}(P4; T2) = I^{out}(P2; T2) = 1$$

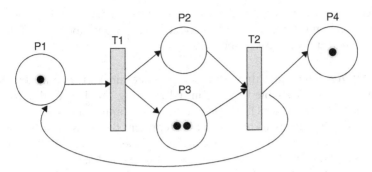

**FIGURE 5.6.** Example of a Petri net with initial marking.

At the initial state, only transition T1 is firable.

The state of a Petri net, observed at an instant $t$, is nothing but an $n$-tuple
$$S = (s_1, \ldots, s_n),$$

where $n$ is the number of places in the Petri net and $s_j$ is the number of tokens present, at the instant $t$, in $j^{th}$ place of the Petri net. A state-transition list L, $L = (S_1, t_1; \ldots; S_m, t_m)$ or simply $(t_1, \ldots, t_m)$ is called a *firing sequence* if each transition $t_j, j \leq m$, is firable on the marking $S_j$ (i.e., there are enough tokens in the input places of $t_j$ occurring in $M_j$ for transition $t_j$) and that $S_{j+1}$ is the state obtained from $S_j$ after firing $t_j$. In this case, the marking $M_n$ is called *reachable* from $M_0$ through the firing sequence. Formally, the last marking $M_n$ in the sequence L is written as $M_0[L > M_n$. The set of all firing sequences that can be reached, in the Petri net $N$, starting from the initial marking $M_0$ are noted as *Reach* $(N, M_0)$.

Finally, let us define the state transition matrices $W^-$ and $W^+$ by the number of tokens taken by each transition from each place and the number of tokens given by each transition to each place, as defined by $I^{inp}$, $I^{out}$, respectively. The sum $W = W^+ - W^-$ is involved in the following equation:

$$M_0 - M_n = W^T.\sigma$$

where $s$ is a vector defining how many times each transition is fired in the sequence. Note that the equation can be carried out if there are enough tokens for each transition to fire. This means that the satisfiability of the equation is required, but not sufficient, so that state $M_n$ can be reached from state $M_0$.

Getting back to the above example, the state transition matrices $W^-$, $W^+$, and $W$ are given by:

$$
W^I = \begin{pmatrix}
* & t_1 & t_2 \\
p_1 & 0 & 1 \\
p_2 & 1 & 0 \\
p_3 & 1 & 0 \\
p_4 & 0 & 1
\end{pmatrix}, \quad
W = \begin{pmatrix}
* & t_1 & t_2 \\
p_1 & 1 & 0 \\
p_2 & 0 & 1 \\
p_3 & 0 & 1 \\
p_4 & 0 & 0
\end{pmatrix}, \quad
W = \begin{pmatrix}
* & t_1 & t_2 \\
p_1 & -1 & 1 \\
p_2 & 1 & -1 \\
p_3 & 1 & -1 \\
p_4 & 0 & 1
\end{pmatrix}
$$

Three issues are important to the study of the dynamics of a Petri net. They are the reachability, liveness, and boundedness. We describe in the following the major features of these properties.

**Reachability.** The reachability in a Petri net aims at finding erroneous marking that are reachable from an initial marking $M_0$. It is dealt with using the reachability graph (GR), which is a directed graph whose nodes represent the Petri net states (or markings) and arcs represent the transitions between the pairs of states, if any. The graph can be built as a result of the following process: starting from the initial state ($M_0$), represented as the root of GR, all possible transitions are explored and the resulting states are added to GR. At the $i^{th}$ state, the transitions from the newest nodes states are explored and the resulting states are added to GR, if any.

As the graph may be infinitely large, reaching all markings seems impractical by the traditional methods, such as the depth-first search. Although reachability seems to be a useful tool to find erroneous states, the constructed graph usually has too many states to explore. To alleviate this problem, some techniques can be used to prove that erroneous states can be reached without a complete expansion of GR. Such tools include the definition of new classes of Petri nets that can represent generic nodes and transitions.

**Liveness.** Petri nets can be described as having four levels of liveness; $L0,\ldots,$ $L4$. A Petri net is considered $Lk$ live, $k \leq 4$, if all its transitions are $Lk$ live. A Petri net transition $t$ is:

- $L0$ live, or *dead*, if it cannot be fired; meaning that it is not in any firing sequence reachable from $M$.
- $L1$ live if it can possibly be fired. This means that $t$ may occur in a firing sequence starting from $M_0$ (or there is an achievable marking on which $t$ can be fired).
- $L2$ live if, for any positive number $k$, transition $t$ can be fired at least $k$ times in a firing sequence starting from $M_0$.
- $L3$ live if there exists a firing sequence where $t$ is fired infinitely
- $L4$ live if, in any reachable state $M$, transition $t$ is $L_1$ live

It is worth it to notice that the aforementioned liveness properties are increasingly stringent requirements; this means, for instance, that if a transition is $L_3$ live, it is automatically $L_1$ and $L_2$ live as well. The use of these properties is very important in modeling communication networks and distributed computer systems. In particular, they can be used to state that nodes in a communication network can never lock up.

**Boundedness.** A Petri net is inherently $k$-bounded if any place in any reachable state does not contain more than $k$ tokens. A Petri net is *safe* if it is 1-bounded. A Petri net is inherently bounded if all of its reachability graphs are finite. Formally, boundedness can be addressed using the function $K : S \rightarrow \mathbb{N}^+$ assigning to each place $s \in S$ some positive number $n \in \mathbb{N}^+$ defining the maximum number of tokens that can occupy that place. Boundedness is typically used to model system resources such as a switching capacity and buffer size.

Extensions of ordinary Petri Nets take into consideration different issues that need to be integrated into the net description such as the temporal aspects. In particular, colored Petri nets (CPNs) allow transitions to fire in different modes and stochastic Petri nets (SPNs) attach an exponentially distributed firing delay to each transition, which specifies the time the transition should wait after being enabled before it fires. Generalized stochastic Petri nets (GSPNs) allow two types of transitions to be used: immediate and timed. Once enabled, immediate transitions fire without waiting any time. However, if more than one immediate transition is enabled at the same time, the transition to fire is chosen based on some firing weights (or probabilities) assigned to these transitions. Timed transitions fire after a random exponentially distributed firing delay.

Let us now give a formal definition of the CPN. One can say that a Petri net $PN = (P, T, I^{inp}, I^{out}, M_0)$ is a CPN if it is equipped with color function C: $P \cup T \rightarrow ColorSet$, where $ColorSet$ is a fixed set of colors, such that the following property holds:

For each transition t, $I^{inp}$ $(p; t) > 0$ or $I^{out}$ $(p; t) > 0$ implies $C(t) = C(p)$.
For all places $p$, all the tokens in $p$ considered by $M_0(p)$ have the color $Cp$.

## 5.5.2   Queueing Petri Nets

Petri nets have the disadvantage that they do not provide any means for the direct representation of scheduling strategies. The attempts to eliminate this disadvantage have led to the emergence of the queueing petri nets (QPNs). The main idea in the creation of the QPN formalism was to add queueing and timing aspects to the places of colored Petri nets. This is done by allowing queues (or service stations) to be integrated into the places of CPNs. A place that has an integrated queue is called a queueing place and consists of two components: a finite queue and a depository for tokens that have completed their service at the queue. The behavior of the net is summarized as follows. When a transition is fired, the tokens output to an output place of the transition are inserted into the queue of the place according to the queue's scheduling strategy. Tokens in a queue of a place are not available for transitions until they finish their services. After completion of its service, a token is immediately moved to the depository, where it becomes available for output transitions of the place. The queueing place is called a timed queueing place. Figure 5.7 depicts a queueing place in a QPN.

In addition to timed queueing places, a QPN also introduces immediate queueing places, which are called untimed places. Tokens in immediate queueing places can be viewed as being served immediately. Scheduling in

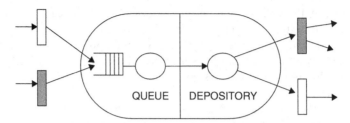

**FIGURE 5.7.** A queueing place.

such places have priority over scheduling/service in timed queueing places and firing of timed transitions. An enabled timed transition fires after an exponentially distributed delay according to a specific policy. Enabled immediate transitions fire according to relative firing frequencies and their firing has priority over that of timed transitions.

We now give a formal definition of a QPN and then present an illustrative example. A queueing Petri net is a 8-tuple QPN $= (P, T, I^{in}, I^{+}, M_0, C, Q, W)$, where:

1. The 6-tuple $(P, T, I^{out}, I^{in}, M_0, C)$ is a colored Petri net with color function $C$.
2. $Q$ is a finite vector of values, say $Q = (q_1, \ldots, q_n)$, where $n$ is the number of places in $P$ and the $j^{th}$ component $q_j$ denotes the description of the queue in $pj$, if $pi$ is a timed place, or $j =$ "U", if $pi$ is an untimed place.
3. $W$ is a finite vector of functions ($W = (w_1, \ldots, w_s)$) having $s$ components, where $s$ is the number of transactions in $T$. The $j^{th}$ component $wj$, in $W$, is defined on $C(tj)$ such that for all $c$ in $C(tj)$, $wj(c)$ is the description of a probability distribution function specifying the firing delay due to color $c$, if transition $tj$ is a timed transition. It defines the weight specifying the relative firing frequency caused by color $c$ in $C(tj)$, if transition $tj$ is an immediate transition.

**Example.** Let us consider a communication system taking data packets from several terminals and then multicasting those over three channels. A QPN model, which is depicted in Figure 5.8, gives a representation of this system. The QPN contains seven places and nine transitions. Place p2 represents several terminals, where users start jobs (modeled with tokens of color "o") after a certain thinking time.

These jobs request service at the CPU (represented by the -/C/1-PS queue, where C stands for Coxian distribution) and two disk subsystems (represented by the -/C/1-FCFS queues). To enter the system each job has to allocate a certain amount of memory. For the sake of simplicity, the amount of memory needed by each job is assumed to be the same, which is represented by a token of color "m" on place p1.

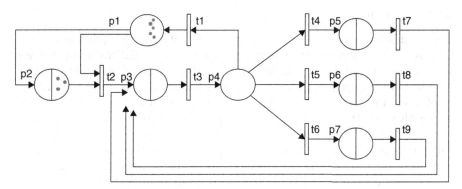

**FIGURE 5.8.** A QPN model server system.

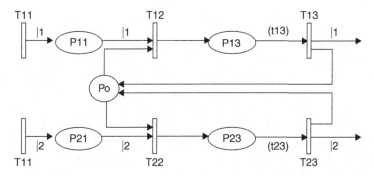

**FIGURE 5.9.** An example of a timed Petri net.

To model time using a Petri net, positive numbers greater than zero, $d(P)$ or $d(T)$, are associated to place $P$ and transition $T$, describing the occurrence of nonprimitive events. The delay may be modeled either as a deterministic or stochastic variable. However, if a stochastic model is used, then calculations consider usually the expected values. To illustrate this, let us consider the example depicted by Figure 5.9, where two types of resources are processed, $r1$ and $r2$. The method is illustrated as follows. The arrival of resource $j$, for $j = 1$, 2, is made through $Tj1$ with input flow $Ij$. After its arrival, resource $rj$ eventually waits in place $Pj1$ for a token to be in place $P0$. When this happens, starting the processing of $rj$ is enabled (and transition $Tj2$ is fired). During processing, whose duration is assumed to last a second, the related token resides in $Pj3$. Finally, at the end of processing, transition $Tj3$ fires and the resource becomes available, as marked by the return of the token to $P0$.

Two types of time computations can be performed in a timed Petri net: the time duration spent to move from marking $M$ to marking $M'$ and the total expected steady-state use $rm$ at station $m$, which is the sum of its expected usage by each class of customers.

### 5.5.3  Invariants

A general definition of an invariant considers that it is simply a predicate that is true for all markings, given an initial marking. A particular invariant that we consider in this subsection is called the *place-invariant* (or S-invariant). The S-invariant is an integer *n*-vector *v*, where *n* is with dimension equal to the number of places in the Petri net. The *i*th component of this vector, say $v_i$, corresponds to the *i*th place. It is a non-negative integer attached to the marking or token content of the *i*-th place (or weight). The invariant gives the definition for conservation in the Petri net by stating that the weighted sum of the token content of the places in the Petri net is constant for any firing sequence.

A formal definition of the S-invariant is given as follows. A non-negative integer vector *v* which is in the kernel or null space of the transpose of the incidence matrix, $C^t$. By the definition of the kernel of $C^t$, vector *v* satisfies the relation:

$$C^t.v = 0$$

The set of places whose corresponding components in an S-invariant *v* is strictly positive is called the *support* of the invariant *v* and is denoted by $<v>$. The support is said to be *minimal* if and only if it does not contain the support of another invariant but itself and the empty set. The support of an S-invariant *v* is a set of places of the Petri net. It characterizes naturally a subnetwork, denoted by [*v*] and called S-invariant net, whose set of places is $<v>$ and whose transitions are the input and output transitions of the places occurring in $<v>$. Therefore, an S-*invariant net* is a Petri net whose set of places is the support of an S-invariant.

**Example.** Consider the Petri net depicted by Figure 5.10 (a) along with the incidence matrix C.

$$C = \begin{bmatrix} 1 & -1 & 0 \\ 1 & 0 & -1 \\ -1 & 1 & 0 \\ -1 & 0 & 1 \end{bmatrix}$$

Then, an S-invariant *v* should satisfy the following equations:

$$v_1 + v_2 - v_3 - v_4 = v_2 - v_1 = v_4 - v_2 = 0$$

Solving the aforementioned equations yields $v_1 = v_3$ and $v_2 = v_4$. Thus, two minimal support S-invariants can be deduced. They are deduced by setting:

$$v_1 = 1, v_2 = 0 \text{ or } v_1 = 0, v_2 = 1$$

The corresponding S-components are shown in Figure 5.10(b).

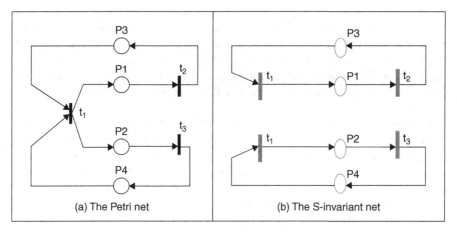

FIGURE 5.10. Example of Petri net and *S*-invariant net.

## 5.6 PROTOCOL VALIDATION

Networking protocol validation is usually done using a combination of simulation and testing techniques. These two techniques are valid approaches and complement each other to some point. In fact, simulation offers the possibility to run a large set of tests under identical circumstances and allows some parameters to be varied and their effects to be studied and analyzed. On the one hand, the goal of simulation is to debug and investigate the system design. On the other hand, live testing is often applied during protocol development. Live testing poses the difficulty of conducting several comparable tests, but if it can be done in a structured way, it may expose errors or problems that are not visible in simulation. Testing and simulation are not exhaustive methods and cannot guarantee that there are no undiscovered subtle errors or design flaws in a protocol. A third alternative allows using formal verification to cover all situations possible in a system model. The objective of formal verification is to improve the testing reliability by reasoning about the systems based on mathematical logic. In particular, a formal system model can be checked to comply fully with a given set of requirements.

Another approach to the challenge of developing correct communication systems and security protocols is to build an executable model of the system. Constructing an executable model usually leads to a more complete specification facilitating a systematic investigation of scenarios, which can considerably decrease the number of design errors. Finite-state machines [10] and colored Petri nets [11], among others, can be used to provide such executable models. They define graphical languages for constructing models of communication systems and analyzing their properties.

The preceding sections have shown that the two forms of Petri nets are ordinary Petri nets and high-level Petri nets. In the ordinary Petri nets, a system can be modeled by a graph, which has two kinds of nodes, places and transitions. In the high-level Petri nets, such as the colored Petri nets, predicated and transition nets, and numerical Petri nets, each token can hold and represent different information and data. CPNs, which can be used in a graph, have four essential elements: places, transitions, arcs, and tokens. As finite-state machines and other tools, CPNs can be used to detect protocol failures and check properties.

There are also many other useful usages of the CPNs [12, 13]. The usages are mainly based on various features, such the availability of a graphical representation, an explicit description of states and actions, and well-defined semantics, which unambiguously define the behavior. CPNs can integrate the specification of control and synchronization with the description of data manipulation, to provide a semantics that builds on true concurrency, instead of interleaving. Many formal analysis methods may be defined by which properties of CPNs can be proved.

CPNs can be simulated interactively or automatically. An interactive simulation provides a way to "walk through" a CPN model while investigating different scenarios in detail and checking whether the CPN works as expected. During the interactive simulation, the modeler is responsible for determining the next step by selecting the event between the enabled events in the current state. He can observe directly the effects of the individual steps on the representation of the CPN model. In addition, the modeler typically sets up breakpoints and stop criteria to facilitate the testing process. However, FSM verification methods are based on exhaustively simulating all the possible behaviors of a closed protocol model.

Finite-state machines and CPNs are used by many different special-purpose verification systems for the validation and verification of security protocols. Some of these systems are fully automatic and contain a theorem prover, whereas some others need user guidance and are, in some sense, proof checkers rather than proof generators. In particular, a large work has addressed, during the last decade, the representation of security and cryptographic protocols, verify cryptographic and security protocols, and compute their weaknesses using CPNs. For this, the validation of a security protocol is mainly done through the following five steps:

- Step 1: It describes the protocol in a CPNs form.
- Step 2: It defines the acceptance check steps (ACS).
- Step 3: It describes the intruder model.
- Step 4: It finds the insecure states.
- Step 5: It applies the matrix analysis steps and then solve the following equation:

$$M_n = M_0 + A \sum_{i=1}^{m} \sigma_i^t$$

where $M_n$ is the insecure state, $M_0$ is the initial marking, $A$ is the matrix description, and $\sigma_i^t$ is a transpose vector, which determines the firing states.

Let us now analyze and verify a key agreement protocol using colored Petri nets and observe how some of these steps work. The protocol is based on Diffie-Hellman-like scheme. However, it assumes that the entities $A$ and $B$ that use it have private keys to sign their message. The protocol scenario includes the exchange of three messages:

- $A \rightarrow B$: $ID_A, g_x$
- $A \leftarrow B$: $ID_B, g_y, E_k(Sig_B(g_x, g_y), k_B)$
- $A \rightarrow B$: $ID_A, E_K(Sig_A(B_x, B_y), k_A)$

where $ID_A$ is the identity of $A$, $x$ and $y$ are random values generated by $A$ and $B$, respectively, $k_B$ is the public key of entity $B$, $g_x = g^x mod\ p$, $g_y = g^y mod\ p$, $k = g^{xy} mod\ p$, $E_k$ is the encryption function using the key $k$, and $Sig_B(g_x, g_y)$ is the signature of $B$ made on $(g_x, g_y)$.

For the lack of space, we only depict the CPN that can be defined to handle all the transitions and places required by the protocol; see Figure 5.11. One can notice that the CPN contains six transitions: sign, send, receive, encrypt, decrypt, and verify, three places denoted by M1, M2 and M3 related to the three messages exchanged through the protocol; and a fourth place called "reject" that characterizes the state of the system (sender or receiver) after a message is rejected.

The process developed by the intruder, say $I$, which is a man in the middle, can be represented by a CPN using the same transitions and places. In the case of man-in-the-middle attack, we can notice that the intruder can modify the outgoing messages from the client to the server, and conversely. Hence, the intruder CPN adds three places, so that the six messages are related to the following messages:

- $M_1: ID_A, g_x$
- $M_1': ID_A, g_z$
- $M_2: g_y, E_{k2}(Sig_B(g_z, g_y), k_B)$
- $M_2': g_z, E_{k1}(Sig_B(g_z, g_x), k_B)$
- $M_3: E_{k1}(Sig_A(g_x, g_z), k_A)$
- $M_3': E_{k2}(Sig_A(g_z, g_y), k_A)$

The man-in-the-middle attack has the ability to control the negotiation between the sender (or client) and the receiver (or server). The intruder shares $k1$ with the sender and $k2$ with the receiver. The above attacks are explained as follows:

- The intruder $I$ intercepts $M_1$, stores the needed information, and sends its own data instead of $A$'s data to $B$ as in $M_1'$.

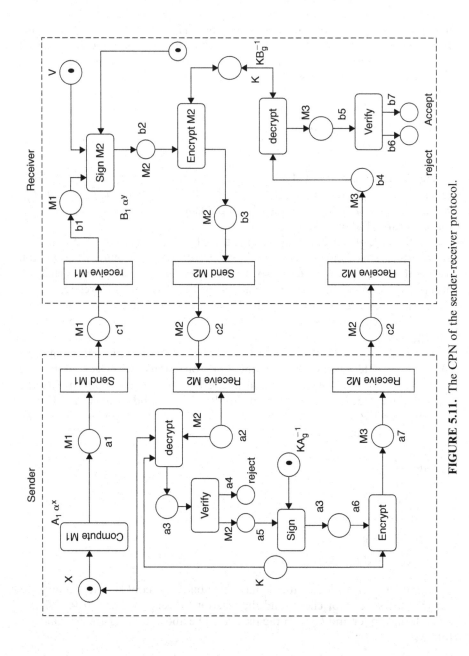

**FIGURE 5.11.** The CPN of the sender-receiver protocol.

146

- $B$ then gets the shared key $k2$ with the intruder. He then signs a message by its private key, encrypts it with the shared key, and assumes that he is sending $M_2$ to $A$.

- Intruder $I$ intercepts $M_2$ then stores $B$'s data and decrypts it to get $B$'s public key and verifies the signature. Also, $I$ signs a new message using its secret key, encrypts it with the shared key $k1$ with $A$, and sends it to $A$.

- $A$ receives the message $M$, decrypts it to get the public key from it, and validates the signature in the message for acceptance or rejection. Then, the client signs, encrypts a new message $M3$, and believes that it could be sent to the server.

- Intruder $I$ intercepts the message $M3$, decrypts it to get the public key, and validates the signature. Then, the intruder can fabricate the new message $M$ and impersonate the server by it.

- $B$ decrypts $M$ and validates the signature. Then it decides to accept or reject the negotiation.

From the analysis above, it is clear that the intruder can now eavesdrop, store, insert, modify, or delete all subsequent messages. The secure state $M$ and the insecure state $Mn$ can also be easily determined.

## 5.7  SUMMARY

When modeling and evaluating the performance of computer and communication systems, complex system components (involving networks, switches, and traffic control mechanisms) as well as complex behaviors and workloads (often a mix of constant bit rate traffic, interactive and real-time traffic, and bursty traffic) need to be taken into account to achieve trustworthy performance measures. Often, this need leads to the use of measurement-based approaches implementing high-level techniques for the performance evaluation and data representation models that can reproduce a real representation of the data processed by the system, and validation models.

Much work has been done to develop ways to check automatically that a profile does, in fact, reflect the actual execution behavior of a system. Another set of works has addressed the formal validation of communication systems. This chapter describes the most used models to provide the aforementioned needs. In particular, the finite-state machines, the Petri nets, the program profilers, and ratio gaming are described and reviewed. Several case studies have been presented to show how these models are used in modeling and validation of communication systems.

## REFERENCES

[1] T. Ball, and J. R. Larus. "Efficient Path Profiling". In proceedings of the 29th Annual International Symposium on Microarchitecture, pp. 46–57, 1996.

[2] T. Ball, and J. R. Larus, "Optimally Profiling and Tracing Programs," ACM Transactions on Programming Languages and Systems, Vol. 16, No. 4, pp. 1319 – 1360, 1994.

[3] M. O. Rabin, and D. Scott, "Finite Automata and their Decision Problems," *IBM* Journal of Research and Development, Vol. 3, No. 2, pp. 115–125, 1959.

[4] L. Vigan'o. "Automated Security Protocol Analysis with the AVISPA Tool." Electronical Notes Theoretical Computer Science, Vol. 155, pp. 61–86, 2006.

[5] J. Padhye, and S. Floyd, "On Inferring TCP Behavior." In Proceedings of the ACM SIGCOMM '01 Conference on Applications, Technologies, Architectures, and Protocols for Computer Communications, pp. 287–298, 2001.

[6] F. Bause,. "QN + PN = QPN—Combining Queueing Networks and Petri Nets." Technical report no. 461, University of Dortmund, Germany, 1993.

[7] F. Bause, and F. Kritzinger,. "Stochastic Petri Nets—An Introduction to the Theory." Vieweg Verlag, 2002.

[8] T. Murata, "Petri Nets: Properties, Analysis and Applications," Proceedings of the IEEE, Vol. 77, No. 4, pp. 541–580, 1989.

[9] J. Desel, and G. Juhás, *"What Is a Petri Net? Informal Answers for the Informed Reader,"* Hartmut Ehrig et al. (eds.), Unifying Petri Nets, LNCS 2128, pp. 1–25, 2001.

[10] G. J. Holzmann, "Design and Validation of Computer Protocols," Bell Laboratories, Prentice-Hall, Englewood Cliffs, NJ, 1991.

[11] K. Jensen, "Colored Petri Nets: Basic Concepts, Analysis Methods and Practical Us Practical Use," Vol. 3. Springer, Berlin, Germany, 1997.

[12] K. Jensen, "A Brief Introduction to Colored Petri Nets," Workshop on the Applicability of Formal Models, pp. 55–58, Aarhus, Denmark, 1998.

[13] K. Jensen, L. M. Kristensen, and L. Wells, "Coloured Petri Nets and CPN Tools for Modelling and Validation of Concurrent Systems," International Journal of Software Tools Technology Transfer , Vol. 9, pp. 213–254, 2007.

## EXERCISES

1. Two experiments were repeatedly performed on two systems S1 and S2. Each experiment is declared either passed or failed. The results collected are presented in the first two columns of Table 5.2.

   a. Compare the two systems by taking each experiment individually, depict in a single chart the results, and show in that case that system S2 performs better in both experiments.

**TABLE 5.2  Results of experiments in Exercise 1**

| S1 | | | | S2 | | | |
|---|---|---|---|---|---|---|---|
| Test | Total | Passed | %passed | Test | Total | Passed | %passed |
| 1 | 240 | 60 | 25 | 1 | 40 | 12 | 30 |
| 2 | 60 | 4 | 6.6 | 2 | 480 | 40 | 8.3 |
| | 300 | 64 | | | 520 | 48 | |

    b. Add the results of the two experiments and plot the result in a graphic chart. Can you conclude that in that case S2 performs better?

2.

    a. Define the state transition machine that represents the behavior of a "close" button on a typical window on a computer screen. The button is assumed to perform as follows:
- The button changes its appearance as soon as the mouse button pressed down with the pointer over the button. However, the window does not close immediately.
- The window only closes if the mouse button is released with the arrow still over the button.
- If the pointer is dragged away from the button, holding the mouse button down, the "close" button of the window simply changes its appearance back to the "up" position and the window remains open.

    b. Give a definition of the sets of states and transition.

    c. Check whether this machine is optimized and optimize it if that is not the case.

    d. Modify the finite-state machine to allow the window start the display of information for a few seconds after the "close" button has been pushed and before the window is closed.

    e. Consider the finite-stet machine depicted by the following figure (Figure 5.2) and representing a communication systems. Assume the system receives single input values (0 or 1) and outputs a single output value (0 or 1) for each input. A transition is labeled by an expression of the form $a/b$ where $a$ is the input and $b$ is the expected output of the system.

    f. Define the state transition table under the following form:

| Current state | Input | New state | Output |
|---|---|---|---|

    g. Define the output sequence of the system if the following sequence is submitted starting from state $S0 = 00111001000011110000$; see Figure 5.12.

3. Consider the following Petri net shown in Figure 5.13.

    a. Give the incidence matrix.

    b. Study the dynamics of the Petri net and compute all its possible markings.

4. We consider a communication node where packets are preprocessed by a machine M1, stored in a temporary buffer, and finally assembled by a second machine M2; see Figure 5.14. A single robot R moves the parts between the input line, M1, the buffer, M2 and the output line. The buffer can hold at most seven preprocessed items.

    a. Use a Petri net to describe this system

    b. Show that the obtained Petri net is live and bounded.

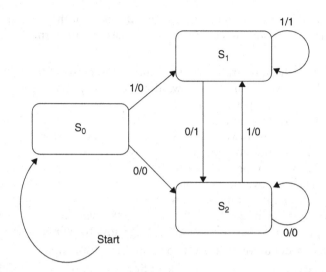

**FIGURE 5.12.**

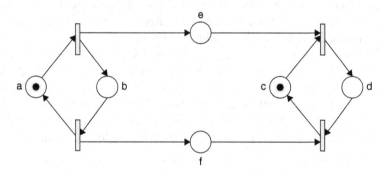

**FIGURE 5.13.**

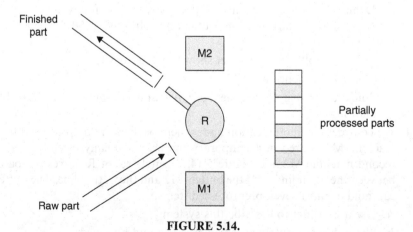

**FIGURE 5.14.**

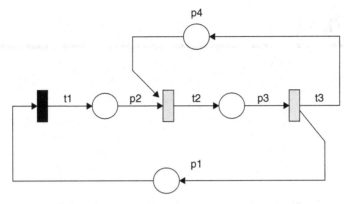

**FIGURE 5.15.**

  c. Extend the Petri net such that the output of M1 can be transferred
     directly to M2 without being stored in the buffer.

5.

  a. Determine the minimal support $S$-invariants of the Petri net shown in
     Figure 5.15.

  b. More generally, determine the minimal support S-invariants of the
     Petri net deduced from the above Petri net by adding to the middle
     line n pairs of (places, transitions).

# CHAPTER 6

# BASICS OF QUEUEING THEORY

Queueing theory typically represents a useful field of applied probability theory [1, 2]. It is known to have various applications in a large spectrum of domains, such as communication networks, computer systems, and transportation. Queueing theory has attracted a great interest and has generated a huge number of publications and tools. A large list of interesting introductory documents on queueing theory organized around some useful textbooks and some interesting courses can be found on the Internet. The subject of queueing theory can be described as follows. Consider a service system and a population of customers (or items), which at some times enter the service system to access a service (or to be provided a service). It is often the case that the service system can only serve a limited number of customers. If a new customer arrives and the service is exhausted, the customer enters a waiting line (or queue) and waits there until the service facility becomes available. Therefore, three major components constitute a service system (called also service center): the population of customers, the service facility, and the waiting queue.

## 6.1 QUEUE MODELS

### 6.1.1 Simple Queues

The scope of queueing theory includes the study of cases where several service systems are organized into a network. In such a network, a single customer

*Fundamentals of Performance Evaluation of Computer and Telecommunication Systems,*
By Mohammad S. Obaidat and Noureddine A. Boudriga
Copyright © 2010 John Wiley & Sons, Inc.

(called also a job) can walk through a specific path, visiting several service systems and accessing services [3, 4].

Several situations can show how queueing theory is useful as follows:

- In data communication, for example, standard frames called packets (or cells in specific networks) are transmitted over wireless or wired links from one switch to another. In each switch, incoming packets can be buffered when the arriving demand exceeds the switching or output link capacity. When the buffer is full, incoming packets will be lost. Estimating the packet delay at the switches, the loss rate, and the buffer occupation would help to manage the traffic efficiently in the *communication network*.

- In multiprocessor computer systems, nodes (individual computers/processors) may need to access a shared memory at the same time. In such a case, we need a service policy to decide which node can use the shared resource first and who comes next. Clearly, some nodes have to wait for their turn to use the shared resource. Queueing theory schemes can be used to estimate the mean waiting time and mean queueing time for the node in the system.

- Other examples of the use of queueing theory are in networking. Consider more complicated tasks such as the dimensioning of buffers in routers or multiplexers, determining the mean number of trunks in a central office, calculating end-to-end throughput in networks, and so on. Therefore, queueing theory tries to find performance metrics of communication networks such as: (a) the mean waiting time in the queue, (b) the mean usage of the service facility, (c) the mean system response time (waiting time in the queue plus service times), and (d) the distribution of the number of customers in the queue and the distribution of the number of customers in the system. These metrics are typically investigated in a stochastic scenario, where parameters, such as the interarrival times of the customers and the service times, are assumed to be random.

- Another set of examples can be given by call centers working on behalf of commercial enterprises (or insurance companies). The call center responds by phone to customer's questions related to the activity of the enterprise. The call center establishes work organization, where each team helps customers from a specific city (or specific subactivity) only. Using queueing theory would help in estimating how long customers have to wait until an operator becomes available, how long a communication can be authorized, or whether the number of incoming phone lines is acceptable.

- A final example of queueing theory can be given by a service center that represents an airline counter, where passengers are expected to check in before they can go on board the plane. The check-in is usually done by one or several employees. However, there are often multiple passengers. A newly arriving passenger proceeds directly to the end of the queue, if the service center is busy. This corresponds to a first-in–first-out FIFO service discipline. Queueing theory in such a case can help reducing the waiting time for customers and optimizing the number of employees needed to perform the task.

The simplest queuing system contains a server as a central component [as depicted by Figure 6.1(a)]. The server provides a given service to customers. Customers arrive at the system to be served. If the server is idle, then a customer is served immediately. Otherwise, the arriving customer joins a waiting area/queue. When the server has completed serving a customer, the customer leaves the system. If customers are waiting in the queue, then one of them is immediately scheduled for service depending on the service policy used. The server in this model can represent any entity that performs a specific function or provides a well-specified service for a given population of customers. Examples of entities include: (a) a computer/processor that provides service to other processes, (b) a transmission line that provides a transmission service to data packets, and (c) a printer that provides a printing service for job requests.

Figure 6.1(b) shows a generalization of the simple model we have been discussing for multiservers, all of which share a common queue. If an item (customer) arrives and at least one server is available, then the item is immediately sent out to that server. It is assumed that all servers are identical; thus, if more than one server is available, it makes no difference which server is chosen for the item. If all servers are busy, then a queue begins to build for the waiting customers. As soon as one server becomes free, an item is accepted from the queue using the discipline in use.

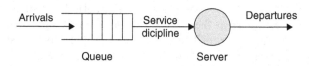

(a) Single server

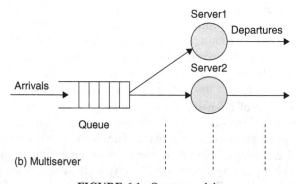

(b) Multiserver

**FIGURE 6.1.** Queue models.

## 6.1.2  Basic Models

A basic model of a service center is shown in Figure 6.2. The customers arrive to the service center in a random way. The service facility can have one or several servers; each server can serve one customer at a time. The service times needed for all customers are also modeled as random variables. Throughout this chapter and the next chapters, unless otherwise specified, we assume that the following assumptions are satisfied by the basic queueing models:

- The customer population is of infinite size, the $n$th customer $Cn$ arrives at time $\tau_n$. The interarrival time $tn$ between two customers is defined as: $t_n = \tau_n - \tau_{n-1}$. We assume that the interarrival times $tn$ are independent and identically distributed (iid) random variables, meaning that they are independent from each other and all $tn$ are drawn from the same distribution, which is denoted by distribution function $A(t) = Pr(tn > t)$. The related probability density function (generally referred to as the pdf) $a(.)$ is given by the derivative of function $A$ (i.e., $a(t) = \frac{dA}{dt}(t)$).
- The service times $xn$ for customer $Cn$ are also assumed iid random variables with the common distribution function (denoted by $B(t)$) and the respective pdf $b(t)$. Obviously, $a(t)$ and $b(t)$ are considered independent.

Queueing systems may differ not only in their distributions of the inter-arrival and service times but also in the number of servers, the size of the waiting line (infinite or finite), the service discipline, and so forth. Some common service disciplines are as follows:

- First-come, First-out (*FIFO*): A customer that finds the service center busy goes to the end of the queue. This discipline is also referred to as first-come, first-served (FCFS).
- Last-In, First-Out (LIFO): A customer that finds the service center busy proceeds immediately to the head of the queue. It will be served next, given that no more customers arrive.
- *Preemptive LIFO* (P-LIFO): After arrival to the system, a customer immediately enters service and pushes the customer in service, if any, back to the head of the queue. Customers may be pushed out of service several times before completing service and leaving.
- *Random Service*: The customers in the queue are served in random order, meaning that when completed, the next customer to enter service is randomly chosen among the customers waiting in the queue.
- *Round Robin*: Every customer gets a time slice. If its service is not completed, then it will reenter the queue.
- *Processor sharing*: Whenever $n$ customers ($n > 0$) are present in the system, the server processes all of them simultaneously, but at a uniform rate of $1/n$ each. This means that all current customers are in service.

- *Priority Disciplines*: Every customer in the queue has a (static or dynamic) priority; the server selects always the customers with the highest priority. This scheme can use the preemption discipline.
- *Shortest Job First* (SJF): When service is completed, the customer to enter service next is the customer in queue with the smallest remaining service time. If a customer arrives with a service time smaller than the customer in service, then the new customer enters service immediately, forcing the current customer to get back into the queue. As with P-LIFO, customers can enter service several times before finally completing service and departing.

It is obvious that the customer delay in the aforementioned service disciplines might change.


### 6.1.3  Kendall Notation

The Kendall Notation can be used to give a short characterization of queueing systems. In this notation, a queueing system description has the form $A/B/m/N/S$, where:

- $A$ denotes the distribution of the interarrival time (i.e., the distribution followed by the aforementioned function A).
- $B$ denotes the distribution of the service times (i.e., distribution described by the aforementioned function B).
- $m$ denotes the number of servers.
- $N$ denotes the maximum size of the waiting line in the finite case (if $N$ is infinity then this letter is omitted).
- $S$ is an optional parameter that denotes the service discipline used (FIFO, LIFO, RR, etc.).

If $S$ is omitted, then the default service discipline is FIFO. For $A$ and $B$, the following abbreviations are common:

- $M$ *(Markov)*: This distribution denotes the exponential distribution with $A(t)$CDF $= 1 - e^{-\lambda t}$ and $a(t) = $ pdf $= \lambda e^{-\lambda t}$, where $\lambda > 0$ is a parameter. The name $M$ comes from the fact that the exponential distribution is the only continuous distribution with the Markov property, meaning that it is memoryless.
- $D$ *(Deterministic)*: This is a deterministic distribution where all parameters are constant (i.e., have the same values).
- $E_k$ *(Erlang-k)*: Erlangian distribution with $k$ phases ($k \geq 1$). The $E_k$ distribution is given by:

$$A(t) = 1 - e^{-k\lambda t} \left( \frac{\sum_{0 \le j \le k-1} (k\mu t)^j}{j!} \right)$$

where $\mu > 0$ is a parameter. This distribution is used in modeling telephone call arrivals at a switch node.

- $H_k$ (Hyper-k): This defines a hyperexponential distribution with $k$ phases, where we have $A(t) = \sum_{0 \le j \le k-l} q_j(l - e^{-\mu_j t}))$, and $\mu_j > 0$; $q_j > 0$, and $i \in \{1.k\}$ are parameters. In addition, the equality $\sum_{0 \le j \le k} q_j = 1$ must hold.

- G(General): This stands for general distribution with very few parameters specified. In most cases, the set of specified parameters include at least the mean and the variance.

The simplest queueing system, the $M/M/1$ system (with FIFO service), can then be described as follows. Consider a single server, such as an infinite waiting line, in which the customer interarrival times are iid and exponentially distributed with some parameter $\lambda$, and the customer service times are also iid and exponentially distributed with some parameter $\mu$. One can be mainly interested in steady-state solutions, where the system after a certain running time tends to reach a stable state, meaning that the distribution of customers in the system does not change after that. This is well distinguished from transient solutions, where the short-term system response to different events is investigated.

A general tendency in queueing theory is presented as follows. If both interarrival times and service times are exponentially distributed, then large set service-related quantities can be estimated. If one among the two distributions is not exponentially distributed, but the other is, then the computation gets harder. Unfortunately, the computation of parameters is quasi unfeasible for the case of $G/G/1$ queues. For example, one cannot do a lot in calculating the mean waiting times.

## 6.2  QUEUE PARAMETERS

Some important parameters are generally associated with a queuing model. Their determination is important to the engineering of the real system associated with queue model. The relevant performance parameters in the queueing models are as follows:

- The distribution of the waiting time and the sojourn time of a customer. The sojourn time is the waiting time plus the service time.

- The distribution of the number of customers in the system (including or excluding the one or those in service).
- The distribution of the amount of work in the system. That is the sum of service times of the waiting customers and the residual service time of the customer in service.
- The distribution of the busy period of the server. During this time, the server is working continuously.

In particular, one may be interested in the mean (average) of performance measures, such as the mean waiting time and the mean sojourn time. Customers arrive at the system at some average rate (computed as the number of arriving customers per second) $\lambda$. At any given time, a certain number n ($n \geq 0$) of customers w'ill be waiting in the queue; the average number waiting $w$ can be estimated, and the mean time that an item must wait, $Tw$, can be determined in various situations. $Tw$ is averaged over all incoming customers, including those that do not wait at all. Figure 6.2 illustrates the structure of a queueing system and its main parameters.

The server handles incoming customers with an average service time $Ts$. This is defined by the time interval between the acceptance of a customer into the server and the departure of that customer from the server. The utilization parameter, $\rho$, is the fraction of time that the server is busy, measured over some interval of time. Two additional parameters applying to the system as a whole can be defined, as follows: the average number of customers staying in the system, including the item being served (if any), and the customers waiting; and the average time $Tr$ that a customer spends in the system, waiting and being served.

If we assume that the capacity of the queue is infinite, then no customers are ever lost from the system; they are just delayed until they can be served. Under such circumstances, the number of departures should be equals to the number of arrivals (measured may be at a different moments). As the arrival rate increases, the utilization along with congestion increases. The number of

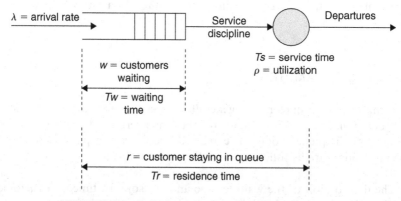

**FIGURE 6.2.** A single server queueing system structure.

waiting customers becomes higher, which increases the waiting time. When $\rho$ reaches the value 1, the server becomes saturated, working 100% of the time. Therefore, the theoretical maximum input rate that can be handled by the system is $Ts$. However, queues become large near system saturation, growing without bound when $\rho = 1$. Practical considerations, such as response time requirements or buffer sizes may limit the input rate for a single server.

To work well with a queueing model, one needs to make the following assumptions on queues, services, and customers [5]:

- *Assumption on customer population*: Population is assumed infinite, which means that the arrival rate is not altered by the drop of customers. If the population is finite, then the number of customers available for arrival is reduced by the number of customers currently waiting in the system. This would typically reduce the arrival rate.
- *Assumption on queue size*: Unless otherwise stated, we assume an infinite queue size. This allows the waiting line to grow without bound. With a finite queue, it is possible for customers to be dropped from the system. In practice, any queue is finite. Typically, this will make no noticeable difference in the model analysis.
- *Assumption on service discipline*: The discipline FIFO is what is normally implied when the term queue is used. Another possibility is LIFO, which may be encountered in practice.

For example, a packet-switching node may choose to send out packets on the basis of: (a) the shortest first, which generates the most outgoing packets or (b) the longest first, which minimizes the processing time. In addition, one can be interested, in particular, in the variability of various parameters. However, blocking can occur when some of the aforementioned assumptions are not satisfied. It puts more complexity on the system analysis. A queue may be either blocked or unblocked at any given time $t$. Typically, a queue is blocked when a packet is in transit between that queue and its downstream neighbor (which may have, in most cases, the queue occupied). A blocked queue will remain blocked as long as its downstream link is busy and the queue has at least one packet to send.

Now let us notice that, with the exception of utilization, all the parameters used in single queue analysis apply to the multiserver case. These parameters keep the same interpretation. If $N$ identical servers are used in the queueing model and $\rho$ is the utilization of each server, then we can consider $N\rho$ to be the utilization of the entire system. The term $N\rho$ is often referred to as the traffic intensity, $u$. Therefore, the theoretical maximum utilization is $N \times 100\%$ and the theoretical maximum input rate is:

$$\lambda\max = N/T_s$$

where $T_s$ is the service time.

One can say that the key characteristics typically chosen for the multiserver queue correspond to those for the single-server queue. That is, we assume an infinite population and an infinite queue size, with an infinite queue shared among all servers. Unless otherwise stated, the service discipline is FIFO. Moreover, if all servers are assumed identical, the selection of a particular server for a waiting item should have no effect on service time [6].

By way of contrast to multiserver queue, one can consider the structure of multiple single-server queues (as depicted in Figure 6.3). As we will see later, this apparently minor change in structure between multiserver queue model and the multiple single-server queue model has a significant impact on the expression of the performance parameter.

### 6.2.1  Examples of Simple Queueing Models

Several examples can be considered to explain the nature of simple queueing models. We describe in the following three queueing models.

The *Infinite-Server Queue*. This model belongs to the class of the simplest models. It allows the availability of an infinite number of servers so that no customers have to wait in a queue. After arrival at time $t_n$, the $n$th customer $C_n$ enters service immediately at any available server. It then leaves at time $t_n + S_n$. The customers should cause no congestion to each other and are not subject to collision. Let $L_\infty(t)$ denote the total number of customers in service at time $t$, and $V_\infty(t)$ denote the workload (i.e., the sum of all the remaining service times). The workload $V_\infty(t)$ is defined as the sum of all remaining service times in the system at time $t$. The computation of $L_\infty(t)$ and $V_\infty(t)$ gives:

$$L_\infty(t) = \sum_{n,\, t_n \le t} \chi\{S_n > t - t_n\}$$

$$V_\infty(t) = \sum_{n,\, t_n \le t} (S_n - min\{S_n, t - t_n\})$$

where $\chi\{S_n > t - t_n\}$ is the indicator function of the event $\{S_n > t - t_n\}$, meaning that:

$$\chi\{S_n > t - t_n\} = 1 \iff S_n > t - t_n.$$

This is true because, for $t_n = t$, the remaining service time of $C_n$ is exactly $S_n - min\{S_n, t - t_n\}$.

The *Split and Match Queue*. The split and match models are applicable to manufacturing and production systems, where customers (or jobs) are instantaneously split into components that are served at separate parallel single-server FIFO queues, after the arrival to the facility. Then, match up again when all components have finished service. The split and match queue model is composed of $c$ FIFO single-server stations placed in parallel and are jointly fed by one common arrival process.

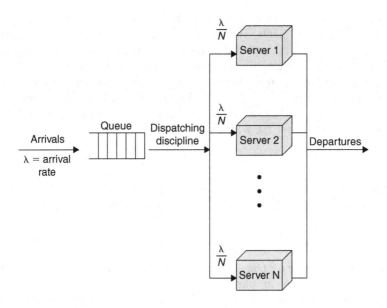

(a) Multiserver queue

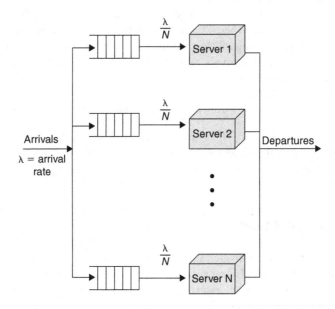

(b) Multiple single-server queues

**FIGURE 6.3.** Multiserver versus multiple single-server queues.

Assume that customer $C_n$ arrives to the system, say at time $t_n$, with a job consisting of $c$ components, and assume the $i$th component requires service at the $i$th station. Then, after arrival to the system, the job instantaneously is split into components. When all the $c$ components have finished service, the components match up again into the original job, and the customer departs as one unit. Let now $k_n = (S_{n,1}, ..., S_{n,c})$ be the vector of service times $S_{n,j}$ and define $D_n = (D_{n,1}, ..., D_{n,c})$, where $D_{n,j}$ is the work in system at the $i$th station at time $t_{n-}$ (or just before $t_n$), which satisfies the recursion:

$$D_{n+1,j} = \max(D_{n,j} + S_{n,j} - (t_{n+1} - t_n), 0)$$

It is exactly the delay in the $i$th queue of the $i$th component of the $n$th job, not including $i$th service. The sojourn time $W_n$ of $C_n$ is then given by

$$W_n = \max\{D_{n,j} + S_{n,j} | \ 1 \leq j \leq c\}$$

The FIFO *Multiserver Queue*. This is a multiserver model including $s$ servers offering their services in parallel and only one queue for the arrival of customers that will wait for service. The queue is assumed to have infinite length and the service discipline is FIFO. Like the single-server models, customer $C_n$ takes a service time $S_n$, goes to the first available server, gets served, and then departs. The workload vector, which is denoted by $X_n = (X_{n,1}, ..., X_{n,c})$, where $X_{n,j}$ is precisely how long it will take the server $j$ to complete processing all the customers currently in the queue at time $t$ (in the absence of any new arrivals and in collaboration with the other $c$ centers), is defined by the recursion:

$$X_n = Ro(X_n + S_n \cdot I_1 - (t_{n+1} - t_n) \cdot I_e), 0)$$

with $I_1 = (1,0,0,...,0)$, $I_e = (1,1,...,1)$, and $Ro$ is the reordering operator, which rewrites the coordinates of a vector in the ascending order. One can easily show that $X_{n,l}$ is exactly the delay of customer $C_n$.


## 6.3  LITTLE'S LAW

In this section, we consider some important laws in queueing systems dealing with customer arrivals and sojourn time. The most known result is referred to as Little's law [7], which asserts that the average number of customers, $L$, in a queueing system is equal to the rate at which customers arrive, $\lambda$, multiplied by the mean sojourn time of a customer, $W$. Little's law and similar other laws are based on a sample path analysis with no a priori specific stochastic assumptions are considered. Little's law is a general result that applies to all models including G/G/1-queues. Moreover, it holds for different service disciplines [8].

## 6.3.1 The Formula

Let us consider a queueing system in which customers arrive from the outside, spend some time in the system, and then leave the system. $C_n$ denotes the $n$th customer; assume that $C_n$ arrives and enters the system at time $t_n$. The process $\{ t_n : n \geq 0 \}$ is assumed to be an increasing sequence of non-negative numbers with counting process $\{N(t)\}$, where $N(t) =$ the number of arrivals during interval $(0,t]$. We also assume that after entering the system, $C_n$ spends $W_n = 0$ units of time in the system and then leaves at time $t_n^d = t_n + W_n$. Note that the departure times are not necessarily ordered. This means that we do not require that customers depart in the same order that they arrived. Finally, let us consider that $\{Nd(t)\}$ denotes the counting process for departure times. Note that:

$$N_d(t) \leq N(t), \ t \geq 0$$

The number $L(t)$ of customers in the system at time $t$, is defined explicitly by:

$$L(t) = \sum_{n:\ t_n \leq t} P\{W_n > t - t_n\}$$

The value $\lambda$ can be viewed as the long term arrival rate. Assume that the arrival rate in the system, the mean sojourn time, and mean number in the system are given by the limits (when they exist) of the following real numbers, respectively:

$$\lambda = \lim_{t \to \infty} \frac{N(t)}{t}, \quad w = \lim_{n \to \infty} \frac{1}{n} \sum_{j=1}^{n} W_j, \quad L = \lim_{t \to \infty} \frac{1}{t} \int_0^t L(s)ds$$

**Theorem.** *If $\lambda$ and $w$ exist and are finite, then $L$ exists and $L = \lambda w$.*
**Proof.** Let us first notice in order to derive the following inequalities:

$$\sum_{j:\ t_j^d 1} W_j \leq \int_0^t L(s)ds \leq \sum_{j=1}^{N(t)} W_j$$

and that the theorem is valid if we can state that:

$$\lambda w \leq \lim_{t \to \infty} \frac{1}{t} \sum_{j:\ t_j^d 1} W_j \leq L = \lim_{t \to \infty} \frac{1}{t} \int_0^t L(s)ds \leq \lim_{t \to \infty} \frac{1}{t} \sum_{j=1}^{N(t)} W_j \leq \lambda w$$

However, a rigorous computation of $\int_0^t L(s)ds$ can be conducted, as follows:

$$\int_0^t L(s)ds = \int_0^t \left\{ \sum_{j:\ t_j \leq s \leq t} P\{W_j > s - t_j\} \right\} ds$$

$$= \sum_{j:\ t_j \leq t} \int_{t_j}^t P\{W_j > s - t_j\} ds$$

$$= \sum_{j:\ t_j \leq t} \min\{W_j, t - t_j\} = \sum_{j:\ t_j + W_j \leq t} W_j + \sum_{j:\ t_j \leq t \leq t_j + W_j} (t - t_j)$$

But, because $w_j \geq t - t_j$ for all $j$ occurring in the second sum of the right term of the last expression, we obtain an upper bound of $\int_0^t L(s)ds$ by considering:

$$\sum_{j:\ t_j + W_j \leq t} W_j + \sum_{j:\ t_j \leq t \leq t_j + W_j} (t - t_j) \leq \sum_{j:\ t_j + W_j \leq t} W_j + \sum_{j:\ t_j \leq t \leq t_j + W_j} W_j = \sum_{j:\ t_j \leq t} W_j$$

$$= \sum_{j=1}^{N(t)} W_j$$

Deriving the upper bound by $t$, we get:

$$\frac{1}{t} \int_0^t L(s)ds \leq \left( \frac{N(t)}{t} \right) \frac{1}{N(t)} \sum_{j=1}^{N(t)} W_j$$

Taking the limit, as $t \to \infty$, gives:

$$\lim_{t \to \infty} \left( \frac{N(t)}{t} \right) \frac{1}{N(t)} \sum_{j=1}^{N(t)} W_j = \lambda w$$

Let us now prove that:

$$\lim_{t \to \infty} \left( \frac{1}{t} \sum_{j:\ t_j^d 1} W_j \right) \geq \lambda w.$$

For this, let us notice that an easy computation can prove that $\lim_{n \to \infty} \frac{W_n}{t_n} = 0$. Thus, for all $\varepsilon$, there is $n_0$ such that, for all $j \geq n_0$, $t_j^d = t_j + W_j \leq 1 + \varepsilon)t_j$. This means that if $t_j \leq t/(1 + \varepsilon)$ and $j \geq n_0$, then customer $C_j$ has left by time $t$. Thus, there are exactly $N(\frac{t}{1+\varepsilon}) - (n_0 - 1)$ such customers. From this, it follows that:

$$\sum_{j:\ t_j^d \leq t} W_j \geq \sum_{j=m}^{N\left( \frac{t}{(1+\varepsilon)} \right)} W_j = \sum_{j=1}^{N\left( \frac{t}{(1+\varepsilon)} \right)} W_j - \sum_{j=1}^{m-1} W_j$$

Dividing by $t$ and taking $t$ to infinity gives us:

$$\lim_{n\to\infty} \frac{1}{t} \sum_{j:\, t_j^d \le t} W_j \ge \lim_{n\to\infty} \frac{1}{t} \sum_{j=m}^{N\left(\frac{t}{(1+\varepsilon)}\right)} W_j = \lim_{n\to\infty} \frac{1}{t} \left( \sum_{j=1}^{N\left(\frac{t}{(1+\varepsilon)}\right)} W_j - \sum_{j=1}^{m-1} W_j \right)$$

$$\ge \lim_{n\to\infty} \frac{1}{t} \left( \sum_{j=1}^{N\left(\frac{t}{(1+\varepsilon)}\right)} W_j \right) = \frac{\lambda w}{1+\varepsilon}, \quad \forall \varepsilon.$$

**Example.** Assume that messages enter and leave a network via one of $D$ ports. The network contains $K$ nodes (or packet switches). At node $k$ we measure $R_k$ packets per second for a mean throughput rate. The mean flow time of a packet, waiting plus switching time, at node $k$ is given by $E(F_k)$. The mean flow time of a packet through the network is denoted by $E(F)$, whereas the total mean external arrival rate at port $j$ is denoted by $\lambda_j$, and we denote by $\lambda$ the aggregate total network throughput rate:

$$\lambda = \sum_{j=1}^{D} \lambda_j$$

From Little's law, we deduce that: $E(F) = \frac{1}{\lambda} \sum_{k=1}^{K} R_k E(F_k)$. Because packets can be switched through more than one internal switch, the packet throughput rate within the network can go above the external packet arrival and departure rate:

$$R == \sum_{k=1}^{K} R_k \ge \lambda = \sum_{j=1}^{D} \lambda_j$$

Rewriting the mean flow time $E(F)$ gives:

$$E(F) = \frac{R}{\lambda} \sum_{k=1}^{K} \frac{R_k}{R} E(F_k)$$

Because we can identify the mean number of nodes visited per packet, $N$, and the mean flow time,

$$V = \frac{R}{\lambda} \quad \text{and} \quad Z = \sum_{k=1}^{K} \frac{R_k}{R} E(F_k),$$

then we deduce that the mean time a packet spends in the network is equal the mean number of nodes visited per packet multiplied by the mean time per node.

## 6.3.2  Applications

Assume a queueing system with customer arrival times $t_n$, arrival rate $\lambda$ with counting process $N(t)$ and a continuous time quantity of interest, denoted by $H(t)$, such as queue length and workload. Let $g_n(t)$ denote the contribution by the nth customer $C_n$ at time $t$ to the quantity $H(t)$, and this contribution is nonzero only for a finite interval of time of length $l_n$ starting from arrival time $t_n$. This implies that a customer does not have an effect on the quantity $H(t)$ before its arrival. Let $G_n$ denote $C_n$'s cumulative contribution over the interval $[0, \infty]$, $H$ be the time average of $H(t)$, and $G$ the empirical average of all the $G_n$.

When $l_n = W_n$ and $g_n(t) = 1$, for $t \in (t_n, t_n + W_n)$, one can show that:

$$G_n = W_n, H(t) = L(t), \text{ and } H = L.$$

Thus, the following result holds.

**Theorem.** If $\lambda$ and $G$ exist and are finite, then $H$ exists and $H = \lambda G$, provided that $\lim\limits_{n\to\infty} l_n/n = 0$

The proof is similar to the Little's law. One can easily derive the following inequalities:

$$\sum_{j:\, t_j + l_j} G_j \leq \int_{[0,t]} H(s)ds \leq \sum_{1 \leq j \leq N(t)} G_i$$

The rest of the proof follows the same way as Little's law has been established.

Let us now compute the average workload $V(t)$ in a single-server FIFO queue. Let us recall that the delay of customer $C_n$ is the work found by $C_n$ upon its arrival at time $t_n$ (without including the service $S_n$ required by $C_n$) and that $D_n = V(t_{n-})$. Our goal is to derive an expression for average workload:

$$E(V) = \lim_{t\to\infty} \frac{1}{t} \int_0^t V(s)ds$$

using the relation $H = \lambda G$, for $H(t) = V(t)$. Because $V(t)$ is the sum of all remaining service times in the system, we can set $l_n = W_n = D_n + S_n$ and $g_n(t)$ as:

$$g_n(t) = \begin{cases} S_n, & t_n \leq t \leq t_n + D_n \\ S_n - t + (t_n + D_n), & t_n + D_n \leq t \leq t_n + D_n + S_n \\ 0, & else \end{cases}$$

The quantity denotes the remaining service time of customer $C_n$ at time $t$. After entering service at time $t_n + D_n$, the remaining service time decreases at rate 1 until completion of service at time $t_n + D_n + S_n$. Thus, $V(t)$ is given by:

$$V(t) = \sum_{n=1}^{\infty} g_n(t).$$

An easy computation of $G_n$ gives:

$$G_n(t) = \sum_{t_n}^{t_n + D_n + S_n} g_n(s)ds = S_n . D_n + S_n^2/2.$$

Now assume that $\lambda$ exists and is finite. Assume also that the following limit exists and is finite:

$$G = \frac{1}{n} \sum_{j=1}^{n} S_j . D_j + S_j^2/2.$$

Finally, assume that:

$$\lim_{n \to \infty} \frac{1}{n} W_n = 0.$$

Then we can conclude that:

$$E(V) = \lambda(E(S . D) + E(S^2)/2).$$

## 6.4  PRIORITY MANAGEMENT

Priority occurs in queueing theory when some types of customers require to be serviced before other types. More specifically, one can consider an $M/G/1$ queue with $n$ types of customers. The type $i$ customer arrives according to a Poisson stream with rate $\lambda_i$, $1 \leq i \leq n$. The service time and residual service of a type $i$ customer is denoted by $B_i$ and $R_i$, respectively. The type $i$ customer has a higher priority than type $j$ if $i < j$. Two rules can be set up to provide service to customers with priority in a queueing model: the non preemptive priority rule and the preemptive-resume priority rule [9].

The non-preemptive priority rule states that higher priority customers may not interrupt the service time of a lower priority customer, but they have to wait until the service time of the low priority customer has been completed. With the preemptive-resume priority rule, interruptions are allowed and after the interruption the service time of the lower priority customer resumes at the point where it was interrupted. In a preemptive system, the queue can stop the current entry half way through its execution to start the new one.

**Non-preemptive priority.** Let us denote the mean waiting time of a type $i$ customer by $E(W_i)$ and the number of type $i$ customers waiting in the queue by $E(L_i^q)$. In addition, let $\rho_i = \lambda_i E(B_i)$. For the highest priority customers, we have $E(W_i) = E(L_i^q)E(B_1) + \sum_{j=0}^{n} \rho_j E(R_j)$. Combining this with the Little's law, which states that $E(L_i^q) = \lambda_1 E(W_1)$, produces the following:

$$E(W_1) = \frac{\sum_{j-1}^{n} \rho_j E(r_j)}{1 - \rho_1}$$

The computation of the mean waiting time for the lower priority customers is more difficult. Consider type $i$ customers (for $i > 1$). The waiting time of a type $i$ customer can be divided in many portions $C_1, C_2, \ldots C_n, \ldots$. The first portion $C_1$ is the amount of work associated with the customer in service and all customers with the same or higher priority present in the queue at the customer's arrival. The second portion, $C_2$, is the amount of higher priority work arriving during $C_1$. The third portion $C_3$ is the amount of higher priority work arriving during $C_2$, and so on.

Therefore, for the first portion of work, an arriving type $i$ customer has to wait for the sum of the service times of all customers with the same or higher priority present in the queue plus the remaining service time of the customer in service. Thus,

$$E(C_i) = \sum_{j-1}^{i} E(L_j^q)E(B_j) + \sum_{j=1}^{n} \rho_j E(R_j).$$

To complete the determination of $E(C_k)$, let us consider the density function $f_k(x)$ and the relation between $E(C_{k+1})$ and $E(C_k)$. One can easily show that:

$$(C_{k+1}) = \int_{t=0}^{\infty} E(C_{k+1}|C_k = t)f_k(t)dt = \int_{t=0}^{\infty} (\lambda_1 t E(B_1) + \ldots + \lambda_{i-1} t E(B_{i-1}))f_k(t)dt$$

$$= \left(\sum_{j=1}^{i-1} \rho_j\right) E(C_k)$$

This finally shows that: $E(C_k) = \left(\sum_{j=1}^{i-1} \rho_j\right)^k E(C_1)$, for $k > 0$. In addition, $E(W_i)$ can be determined by:

$$E(W_i) = \frac{E(C_1)}{1 - (\rho_1 + \ldots + \rho_{i-1})} \quad \text{for } i \geq 2.$$

**Preemptive-resume priority.** For a type $i$ customer, no lower priority custo-mers exist because of the preemption rule. Thus, we can assume that $\lambda_{i+j} = 0$. for all $1 \leq j \leq n - i$. The waiting time of a type $i$ customer can again be divided into portions $\{C_i\}_{i \geq 1}$. $C_1$ is equal to the total amount of work in the system after arrival because we assumed that no lower priority customers exist. Moreover, one can recognize the total amount of work in the system does not depend on the order in which the customers are served. Therefore, at each moment, it is exactly the same as in the system where the customers are served according to the non-preemptive priority rule. Thus, $\{C_i\}_{i \geq 1}$ and $\{W_i\}_{n \geq i \geq 1}$ have the same distribution as in the system with non-preemptive priorities (assuming that $\lambda_{i+j} = 0$, for all $1 \leq j \leq n - i$).

**Conservation law.** Let us consider a single-server queue with $n$ types of customers. Type $i$ customers arrive according to a general arrival stream with rate $\lambda_i$ for all $1 \leq i \leq n$). The mean service time and mean residual service time of type $i$ customer are denoted by $E(B_i)$ and $E(R_i)$, respectively. Let us define $\rho_i = \lambda_i E(B_i)$ and assume that:

$$\sum_{j=0}^{n} \lambda_j E(R_j) < 1.$$

One can state that the server can handle the amount of work offered per unit of time. Customers enter service in an order independent of their service times, and they may not be interrupted during their service (e.g., the customers may be served according to FCFS, random or a non-preemptive priority rule). The conservation law [10, 11] for the mean waiting times states that:

$$\sum_{j=0}^{n} \rho_j E(W_j(SD)) \text{ is constant with respect to service discipline } (SD).$$

This states that a weighted sum of these mean waiting times is independent of the service discipline. This implies that an improvement in the mean waiting of one customer type because of a service discipline will always degrade the mean waiting time of another customer type. Let $E(V(SD))$ and $E(L_i^q(SD))$ denote the mean amount of work in the system and the mean number of type $i$ customers waiting in the queue, respectively, for discipline $SD$. $E(V(SD)$ is given by:

$$E(V(SD)) = \sum_{i=1}^{n} E(L_i^q(SD)E(B_i) + \sum_{i=1}^{n} \rho_i E(R_i).$$

The first term is the mean amount of work in the queue, whereas the second term is the mean amount of work at the server. Clearly, the latter does not depend on the discipline $SD$. One can make the observation that the amount of work in the system does not depend on the order in which the customers are served. The amount of work decreases with one unit per unit of time independent of the customer being served. When a new customer arrives, the amount of work is increased by the service time of the new customer. Therefore, the amount of work does not depend on $SD$. Consequently, by using the above equation and $L_i^q(SD) = \lambda_i E(W_i(SD))$, one can deduce the deviation law.

## 6.5   ANALYSIS OF M/M/1 SYSTEMS

The M/M/1-Queue has iid interarrival times, which are exponentially distributed with parameter $\lambda$ and also iid service times with exponential distribution of parameter $\mu$. The system has only a single server and uses the FIFO service discipline. The waiting line is of infinite size. It is easy to find the underlying Markov chain. As the system state, we use the number of customers in the system. The M/M/1 system is a pure birth/death system, where at any point in time, at most one event occurs, with an event either being the arrival of a new customer or the completion of a customer's service. What makes the M/M/1 system really simple is that the arrival rate and the service rate are not state dependent [12]. The state-transition-rate diagram of the underlying continuous time Markov chain (CTMC) is shown in Figure 6.4.

### 6.5.1   Steady-State Probabilities

We denote the steady-state probability that the system is in state $k$($k$ is natural integer) by $p_k$, which is defined by $p_k = lim_{t \to \infty} P_k(t)$, where $P_k(t)$ denotes the probability that $k$ customers are in the system at time $t$. We note that the steady-state probability $P_k$ is not dependent on $t$. We focus on a fixed-state $k$ and look at the flows into and out of the state. The state $k$ can be reached from state $k - 1$ and from state $k + 1$ with the respective rates $\lambda P_{k-1}(t)$ (the system is with probability $P_{k-1}(t)$ in the state $(k - 1)$ at time $t$ and goes with the rate $\lambda$ from the predecessor state $k - 1$ to state $k$) and $\mu \lambda P_{k+1}(t)$ (the same from state $k + 1$). The total flow into the state $k$ is then:

$$\lambda P_{k-1}(t) + \mu \lambda P_{k+1}(t).$$

The state $k$ is left with the rate $\lambda P_k(t)$ to the state $k + 1$ and with the rate $\mu \lambda P_k(t)$ to the state $k - 1$ (for $k = 0$ there is only a flow coming from or going to state

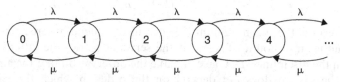

**FIGURE 6.4.** Flow diagram for the M/M/1 queue.

1). The total flow out of that state is then given by $\lambda P_k(t) + \mu\lambda P_k(t)$. The total rate of change of the flow into state $k$ is then given by the difference of the flow into that state and the flow out of that state:

$$\frac{dP_k(t)}{dt} = \lambda(P_{k-1}(t) - P_k(t)) + \mu(P_{k-1}(t) - P_k(t)).$$

However, in the limit $(t \to \infty)$, we require that $dP_k(t)/dt = 0$. So, we arrive at the following steady-state flow equations:

$$0 = \mu p_1 - \lambda p_0$$
$$= \lambda(p_{k-1} - p_k) + \mu(p_{k-1} - p_k), \quad \text{for all } k > 1$$

An easy resolution of these equations gives $p_k = \left(\frac{\lambda}{\mu}\right)^k p_0$. Furthermore, because $p_k$ are probabilities, the normalization condition: $(\sum_{0 \leq j} p_j = 1)$ can be translated into the following:

$$1 = p_0 + \sum_{0 < j} p_j = p_0 \left(\sum_{0 \leq k} \left(\frac{\lambda}{\mu}\right)^k\right) = p_0 \left(1 - \left(\frac{\lambda}{\mu}\right)\right)^{-1}$$

This gives:

$$p_0 = 1 - \frac{\lambda}{\mu} \quad \text{and} \quad p_k = \left(\frac{\lambda}{\mu}\right)^k \left(1 - \frac{\lambda}{\mu}\right).$$

Obviously, in order for $p_0$ to exist, it is required that $\lambda < \mu$; otherwise, the series will diverge. This is the stability condition for the M/M/1 system. It also makes sense intuitively; when more customers arrive than the system can serve, the queue size goes to infinity.

## 6.5.2  Estimating System Characteristics

Several characteristics can be extracted easily. These include the queue utilization, the mean number of the customers in the queue, the mean response time, and the tail probability. The utilization $u$ gives the fraction of time that the server is busy. In the M/M/1 case, this is simply the complementary event to the case where the system is empty. The utilization can be observed as the steady-state probability that the system is not empty at any time in the steady state. Therefore, we have:

$$u = 1 - p_0 = \frac{\lambda}{\mu} = \rho.$$

The mean number of customers in the system is given by:

$$E[N] = \sum_{k=0}^{\infty} k p_k = p_0 \left( \sum_{k=0}^{\infty} k \rho^k \right) = (1 - \rho) \frac{\rho}{(1 - \rho)^2} = \frac{\rho}{1 - \rho},$$

given that the equality $\sum_{0 < k} k x^k = x(1 - x)^2$ holds. Therefore, the mean number of customers in the system for varying utilizations can be analyzed. As it can be observed for instance, $E(N)$ grows to infinity as $\rho \to 1$. Thus, for higher utilizations, the system tends to become unstable.

The mean response time $T$ is the mean time a customer spends in the system, i.e., waiting in the queue and being serviced. We simply apply Little's law to find the following:

$$E(T) = \frac{E(N)}{\lambda} = \frac{\left( \frac{1}{\mu} \right)}{(1 - \rho)} = \frac{1}{(\mu - \lambda)}$$

Finally, let us show how the Tail Probabilities in an M/M/1 system can be computed in the case where the number of customers is finite. If a customer arrives at a full system, it is lost. We want to determine the size of the waiting line that is required to lose customers only with a small probability. As an example, consider a router for which the buffer space is finite and packets can be lost with probability $10^{-6}$. We assume we use an M/M/1 queue (with infinite waiting room) as an approximation. We are now interested in the probability that the system has $k$ or more customers. The probability $Pr(N > k)$ is called a *tail probability* and thus would lose a customer in reality. We have:

$$Pr[N > k] = 1 - Pr[N \leq k] = 1 - \sum_{v=0}^{k} p_v = 1 - p_0 \frac{1 - \rho^{k+1}}{1 - \rho} = \rho^{k+1}.$$

**Example.** Let A and B be two routers and assume that: (a) A sends an average of 10 packets per second to B, (b) the packet size is exponentially distributed with mean size equal to 480 bytes, and (c) the line speed is 128 kbit/s. The question is to determine how many packets are waiting in router A for transmission or being transmitted and what is the probability that this number is 16 or more.

Using the previous formulas, one can perform the following:

- The utilization $r$ of the line between A and B is $r = 12$ packet/s $\times$ 480 bytes/packet $\times$ 8 bits/byte $= 0.72$
- $E(N)$ is equal to $0.72/(1 - 0.72) = 2.57$
- The probability that the number of packets is 16 or more is:

$$Pr[N \geq 16] = (1 - \rho) \sum_{i=16}^{\infty} \rho^i = \rho^{16} = (0.72)^{16}.$$

**Example.** (Increasing arrival and service rates by the same factor): Given an M/M/1 system, suppose that we increase the arrival rate and the service rate by a factor of $k$. The impact of the factor on utilization, throughput X, mean number in the system $E[N]$, and mean time in system $E[TS]$ is determined as follows:

Given that $\lambda_{new} = k\lambda$ and $\mu_{new} = k\mu$, we have:

- The utilization is unchanged because $U = \dfrac{k\lambda}{k\mu} = \dfrac{\lambda}{\mu}$.

- The throughput is increased by a factor of $k$.
- The mean number in the system is unchanged, $E(N) = \dfrac{\rho_{new}}{1 - \rho_{new}} = \dfrac{\rho}{1 - \rho}$
- The mean time in the system is divided by $k$, $E(T_{new}) = \dfrac{1}{\mu_{new} - \lambda_{new}} = \dfrac{1}{k(\mu - \lambda)}$

### 6.5.3 Handling Priorities

In this subsection, we consider an M/M/1 system serving different types of customers. For the sake of simplicity, we assume that there are two types only, say type 1 and type 2; but, the analysis can easily be extended to situations involving more types of customers. Type 1 and type 2 customers arrive according to independent Poisson processes with rate $\mu_1$, and $\mu_2$, respectively. The service times of all customers are exponentially distributed with the same mean $1/\mu$. We assume that $\rho_1\mu_1 + \rho_2\mu_2 < 1$, where $\rho_i = \lambda_i/\mu$ is the occupation rate due to type i customers. Type 1 customers are treated with priority over type 2 jobs. In the following subsections, we will consider two priority rules, namely the preemptive-resume priority and non-preemptive priority.

**Preemptive-resume priority.** In the preemptive-resume priority rule, type 1 customers have absolute priority over type 2 jobs. Absolute priority means that when a type 2 customer is in service and a type 1 customer arrives, the type 2 service is interrupted and the server proceeds with the type 1 customer. Once there are no more type 1 customers in the system, the server resumes the service of the type 2 customer at the point where it was interrupted.

Let the random variable $Li$ denote the number of type $i$ customers in the system and $Si$ the random variable denoting the sojourn time of type $i$ customers. To determine $E(Li)$ and $E(Si)$, for $i = 1, 2$, We have:

$$E(S1) = \frac{\dfrac{1}{\mu}}{1 - \rho_1} \text{ and } E(L1) = \frac{\rho_1}{1 - \rho_1}.$$

Knowing that the service times of all customers are exponentially distributed with the same mean, the total number of customers in the system does not depend on the order in which the customers are served. So this number is the same as in the system where all customers are served in order of arrival. Therefore, we have:

$$E(L1) + E(L2) = \frac{\rho_1 + \rho_2}{1 - \rho_1 - \rho_2}$$

This allows the computation of $E(L2)$ and the deduction of $E(S2)$, using the Little's law. Therefore, we have:

$$E(L2) = \frac{\rho_1}{(1 - \rho_1)(1 - \rho_1 - \rho_2)} \text{ and } E(S2) = \frac{\frac{1}{\mu}}{(1 - \rho_1)(1 - \rho_1 - \rho_2)}.$$

**Non-preemptive priority.** We now consider the situation that type 1 customers have nearly absolute priority over type 2 customers. The difference with the previous rule is that type 1 customers are not allowed to interrupt the service of type 2 customers. This priority rule is called non-preemptive. The mean sojourn time of type 1 customers is given by:

$$E(S1) = (E(L1) + 1 + \rho_2)\frac{1}{\mu}.$$

The term $\rho_2\frac{1}{\mu}$ indicates that an arriving type 1 customer finding a type 2 customer in service has to wait until the service of the type 2 customer has been completed. Using the following property, called the PASTA property, the probability that the arriving type 1 customer finds a type 2 customer in service is equal to the fraction of time the server spends on type 2 customers, which is $\rho_2$. Then using the Little's law (i.e., $E(L1) = \lambda_1 E(S1)$), we find the following:

$$E(S1) = \frac{(1 + \rho_2)/\mu}{(1 - \rho_1)}, E(L1) = \frac{(1 + \rho_2)\rho_1}{(1 - \rho_1)} \text{ and } E(L2)$$

$$= \frac{\rho_2(1 - \rho_1(1 - \rho_1 - \rho_2))}{(1 - \rho_1)(1 - \rho_1 - \rho_2)}$$

By applying Little's law, one can deduce $E(S2)$ as:

$$E(S2) = \frac{(1 - \rho_1(1 - \rho_1 - \rho_2))/\mu}{(1 - \rho_1)(1 - \rho_1 - \rho_2)}$$

PASTA Property: Assuming arrivals to a queue form a Poisson stream, each arriving job will view the queue length distribution that is equal to the long-term steady-state queue length.

An intuitive proof of the PASTA property can be stated as follows. Let $L_t$, $t \geq 0$, be the random variable representing the number of customers in the queue. The probability of Poisson arrival during the interval of time $[t - \Delta t, t]$ is given by the probability of a Poisson event in the interval $[0, \Delta t]$, as denoted by

$Pr(N(\Delta t) \geq 1)$. Because the interval times are exponentially distributed, we deduce that:

$$
\begin{aligned}
Pr(N(\Delta t) \geq 1 \mid L_{t-\Delta t} = i) &= Pr(N(\Delta t) \geq 1) \\
&= Pr(N(\Delta t) \geq 1) \times Pr(L_{t-\Delta t} = i) \\
&= Pr(L_{t-\Delta t} = i \mid N(\Delta t) \geq 1) = Pr(L_{t-\Delta t} = i) \\
&= Pr(L_{t-\Delta t} = i).
\end{aligned}
$$

As $\Delta t$ goes to 0, we find out that the probability that a customer arriving at time $t$ will view the system in state $L_t = i$ and set the results.

### 6.5.4 Estimating the Busy Period

We can distinguish cycles in a server life. A cycle is the time that lasts between two consecutive arrivals finding an empty system. Clearly, a cycle starts with a busy period (denoted by BP) during which the server is serving customers, followed by an idle period (denoted by IdP) during which the system is idle (the queue is empty). Due to the memoryless property of the exponential distribution, an IP is exponentially distributed with mean $1/\lambda$.

In the sequel, we compute an estimation of the mean and the distribution of a BP. It is clear that the mean busy period divided by the mean cycle length is equal to the fraction of time the server is working, so one can deduce that

$$
\frac{E(\text{BP})}{E(\text{BP}) + E(\text{IdP})} = \frac{E(\text{BP})}{E(\text{BP}) + 1/\mu} = \rho.
$$

This gives the value of $E$ (BP) as $\dfrac{1/\mu}{1-\rho}$.

Let the random variable $C_n$ be the time till the system is empty again if $n$ customers are now present in the system. Clearly, $C_1$ is the length of a busy period, because a busy period starts when the first customer after an idle period arrives, and it ends when the system is empty again. The random variables $C_n$ satisfy the following recursion relation. Suppose $n$ ($> 0$) customers are in the system. Then, the next event occurs after an exponential time with parameter $\lambda + \mu$: with probability $\lambda / (\lambda + \mu)$, a new customer arrives, and with probability $\mu / (\lambda + \mu)$, service is completed and a customer leaves the system. Then, if $V$ is an exponential random variable with parameter $\lambda + \mu$, then variables $C_n$ satisfy the following, for $n - 1$:

$C_n = V + C_{n+1}$ with probability $\lambda / (\lambda + \mu)$
$C_n = V + C_{n-1}$ with probability $\mu / (\lambda + \mu)$

## 6.6  THE M/M/M QUEUE

The M/M/m-Queue ($m > 1$) has the same interarrival time and service time distributions as the M/M/1 queue (exponential interarrival times with mean $1/\lambda$); it operates $m$ servers in the system, and the waiting line is infinitely long. As in the M/M/1 case, a complete description of the system state is given by the number of customers in the system (because of the memoryless property). The state-transition-rate diagram of the underlying CTMC is shown in Figure 6.5. In the following, we will analyze the M/M/m model, where customers are served in order of arrival. The occupation rate, $\rho = \lambda/m\mu$, per server, is assumed to be smaller than one.

**Steady-state probabilities.** Using the above described technique of evaluating the flow equations together with the well-known geometric summation yields the following steady-state probabilities:

$$\lambda p_{n-1} = min\,(n,\,c)\,\mu p_n, \quad n \geq 1$$

Iterating this formula gives the following:

$$p_k = \begin{cases} p_0 \dfrac{(m\rho)^k}{k!} : k \leq m \\[2ex] p_0 \dfrac{\rho^k m^m}{m!} : k \geq m \end{cases}$$

The probability $p_0$ is deduced from normalization:

$$p_0 = \left[\sum_{k=0}^{m-1} \frac{(m\rho)^k}{k!} + \left(\frac{(m\rho)^m}{m!}\right)\frac{1}{1-\rho}\right]^{-1}$$

where $\rho = \lambda/\mu$. In addition, the probability $Pwait$ that a customer has to wait (or the *delay probability*) can be computed by:

$Pwait = \Sigma_{j>m} p_{m+j} = p_m/1 - \rho$. The mean number of customers in the system is given by:

$$E[N] = \sum_{k=0}^{\infty} k p_k = m\rho + \rho\frac{(m\rho)^m}{m!}\frac{p_0}{(1-\rho)^2} = Pwait\frac{\rho}{1-\rho}.$$

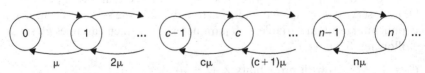

**FIGURE 6.5.** Flow diagram for the M/M/m queue.

The mean response time again can be evaluated simply using Little's formula:

$$E[S] = Pwait \frac{1}{(1 - \rho)c\mu}.$$

**Distribution of the waiting time.** To evaluate the probability that an arriving customer must enter the waiting line because of the nonavailability of servers, we compute $Pr(N > t)$ and use random variables $D_k, k \geq 1$, which determine the $k$th interdeparture time. We have:

$$Pr(N > t) = \sum_{n=0}^{\infty} (P\left(\sum_{k=1}^{n+1} D_k > t\right) p_{m+n}$$

The random variables $D_k$ are independent and exponentially distributed with mean $\frac{1}{m}\mu$. In a similar way, we find that:

$$Pr(N > t) = \sum_{n=0}^{\infty} \sum_{k=0}^{n} \frac{(mt\mu)^k}{k!} e^{-m\mu t} p_m \rho^n$$

$$Pr(N > t) = \frac{p_c}{1 - \rho} \sum_{k=0}^{\infty} \frac{(mt\rho\mu)^k}{k!} e^{-m\mu t} = Pwait \cdot e^{-m\mu(1-\rho)t}, \quad t \geq 0.$$

Let us notice that this probability is often used in communication networks. It states that the probability that a newly arriving call at a central office will get no trunk, given that the interarrival times and service times (call durations), are exponentially distributed can be calculated as follows:

$$Pr[Queueing] = \sum_{k=m}^{\infty} p_0 = \sum_{k=m}^{\infty} p_0 \frac{(m\rho)^k}{m!} \frac{1}{m^{k-m}}$$

$$= \frac{\left(\frac{(m\rho)^m}{m!}\right)\left(\frac{1}{1-\rho}\right)}{\left[\sum_{k=0}^{m-1} \frac{(m\rho)^k}{k1} + \left(\frac{(m\rho)^m}{m!}\right)\left(\frac{1}{1-\rho}\right)\right]}$$

and is often called the Erlangs C formula.

## 6.7 OTHER QUEUES

Two queue models with single servers are of interest: the $M/E_r/1$ queue and the $M/G/1$ queue.

## 6.7.1  M/E_r/1 Queue

The Erlang distribution can be used to model service times with a low coefficient of variation (less than one), but it can also arise naturally. For instance, a job has to pass, stage by stage, through a series of $r$ independent production stages, where each stage takes an exponentially distributed time. The analysis of the $M/E_r/1$ queue is similar to that of the $M/M/1$ queue shown in Figure 6.6.

We consider a single-server queue. Customers arrive according to a Poisson process with rate $\lambda$ and are processed in the order of their arrival. The service times are $E_r$ distributed with mean $r/\mu$. In addition, the occupation rate $\rho$ that is equal to $\lambda r/\mu$ is less than one. To describe the state of a nonempty system, we use a two-dimensional description, with the pair $(k, l)$: note that $k$ designates the number of customers in the system and $l$ represents the remaining number of service phases of the customer in service. An alternative way to describe the state is by counting the total number of not completed phases of work in the system, which is equal to the number $(k - 1)r + l$.

Let $p_n$ be the equilibrium probability of $n$ phases in the system comparing the flow out of state $n$ and the flow into state $n$; one can obtain the following:

$$\lambda p_0 = \mu p1$$

$$(\lambda + \mu)p_n = \mu p_1 + n \quad \text{for } 1 \leq n \leq r - 1$$

$$(\lambda + \mu)p_n = \lambda p_{n-r} + \mu p1 + n \quad \text{for } r \leq n$$

Looking for a solution under the form $p_n = x^n$, the above system of equations leads to the equation $= \lambda - (\lambda + \mu)\, x^r + \mu\, x^{r+1} = 0$. Thus, it can be demonstrated that this equation has exactly $r$ roots $x_k$ satisfying $|x_k| < 1$, whereas $x = 1$ is another root. A general solution has the form $p_n = \sum_{k=0}^{r} c_k x_k^n$. This is a linear combination of the coefficients $c_k$. An easy computation shows that:

$$c_k = \frac{1 - \rho}{\Pi_{k \neq j}\left(1 - \dfrac{x_j}{x_k}\right)}$$

Now, let $q_n$ be the probability of having $i$ customers in the system. Clearly, we have the following:

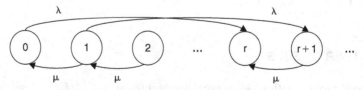

**FIGURE 6.6.**  One-dimensional flow for $M/E_r/1$.

$$q_0 = p_0$$

$$q_n = \sum_{k=1+r(i-1)}^{ir} p_k = \sum_{k=1}^{r} c_k (x_k^{1-r} + x_k^{2-r} + \dots + 1)(x_k^r)^i$$

**Example.** Consider an $M/E2/1$ queue with $\lambda = 1$ and $\mu = 4$. The equilibrium probability $p_n$ is given by

$$p_0 = 4p_1, 5p_n = 4p_{1+n} \quad \text{for } 1 \le n \le r-1 \text{ and } 5p_n = p_{n-r} + 4p_{1+n}$$

This leads to equation $4x^3 - 5x^2 + 1 = 0$, the roots of which are 1, 9/64, and $-25/64$. Setting that, for $n \ge 0$,

$$p_n = c_1 \left(\frac{9}{64}\right)^n + c_2 \left(\frac{-25}{64}\right)^n$$

where

$$c_1 = \frac{1-\rho}{1 - \dfrac{x_2}{x_1}} = \frac{27}{136} \quad \text{and} \quad c_2 = \frac{1-\rho}{1 - \dfrac{x_1}{x_2}} = \frac{75}{64}$$

We can deduce the numerical value of the equilibrium probabilities. Let us now compute the distribution of the waiting times. For this, let the random variable $L$ denote the number of phases working in the system and $Bi$ the amount of work for the $i$th phase. Thus, the random variables $Bi$ are independent and exponentially distributed with mean $1/\mu$. We have the following result for $E(L)$:

$$E(L) = \sum_{n=1}^{\infty} np_n = \sum_{n=1}^{\infty} \sum_{k=1}^{r} c_k n x_k^n = \sum_{k=1}^{\infty} \frac{c_k x_k}{(1 - x_k)^2}$$

Because the waiting time can be expressed as $W = \sum_{k=1}^{L} B_k$, the estimation of $P(W > t)$ gives the following:

$$P(W > t) = \sum_{n=1}^{\infty} P\left(\sum_{k=1}^{n} B_k > t\right) p_n$$

$$= \sum_{n=1}^{\infty} \sum_{k=0}^{n-1} \frac{(\mu t)^k}{k!} e^{-\mu t} \cdot \sum_{k=1}^{r} c_k x_k^n$$

$$= \sum_{k=1}^{r} \frac{c_k}{1 - x_k} x_k e^{-\mu(1-x_k)t}$$

## 6.7.2 M/G/1 Queues

Customers in the M/G/1 queue arrive according to a Poisson process with rate $\lambda$. They are served following a FIFO discipline [5]. In addition, the service times are iid. The state of the M/G/1 queue can be described by a pair $(n, x)$, where $n$ denotes the number of customers in the system and $x$ represents the service time already received by the customer in service. This is a two-dimensional case. The first dimension is discrete, and the second dimension is continuous. This adds some complexity to the computation of the related parameters. However, if one looks at the system just after departures, then the state description can be simplified to first dimension only, because $x = 0$ for the new customers in service.

Let $N_k^D$ be the number of customers left behind by the $k$th departing customer. The number of customers left behind by the $(k + 1)$th customer is clearly equal to the number of customers present when the $k$th customer departed minus one plus the number $A_{k+1}$ of customers that arrived during the customer's service time. Therefore, we can write

$$N_{k+1}^D = N_k^D + A_{k+1}$$

We now discuss the transition probabilities $p_{i,j} = P(N_{k+1}^D = j \mid N_k^D = i)$. Clearly, one can establish the following expression for $P_{i,j}$

$$P_{i,j} = 0 \text{ for } j < i - 1$$

In addition, for all $j \geq i - 1$, $P_{i,j}$ defines the probability that exactly $j - i + 1$ customers arrived during the service time of the $(k + 1)$th customer. This is valid for $i > 0$. In state 0, the $k$th customer leaves behind an empty system and then $P_{0,j}$ defines the probability that during the service time of the $(k + 1)$th customer, exactly $j$ customers arrived. Hence, the matrix $P$ of transition probabilities takes the following form:

$$P = \begin{pmatrix} \alpha_0 & \alpha_1 & \alpha_2 & \alpha_3 & \cdots \\ \alpha_0 & \alpha_1 & \alpha_2 & \alpha_3 & \cdots \\ 0 & \alpha_0 & \alpha_1 & \alpha_2 & \cdots \\ 0 & 0 & \alpha_0 & \alpha_1 & \cdots \\ \cdot & \cdot & \cdot & \cdot & \cdots \end{pmatrix}$$

where $\alpha_j$ is the probability that during a service time, exactly $j$ customers arrive. If the service times are independent and identically distributed with distribution function $F_B(.)$ and density function $f_b(.)$, it is easy to show that:

$$\alpha_j = \int_0^\infty \frac{(\lambda t)^j}{j!} e^{-\lambda t} f_B(t) dt.$$

The transition probability diagram is depicted in Figure 6.7.

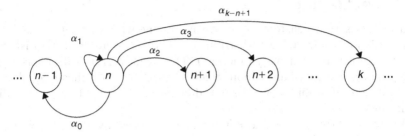

**FIGURE 6.7.** Transition probability diagram for M/G/1.

Now, let $N(t)$ be the random variable defining the number of customers at time $t$. We have also: $d_n = \lim_{k \to \infty} P(N_k^D = n)$ and $p_n = \lim_{t \to \infty} P(N(t) = n)$. Cleary we have $P_n = d_n$, for all $n \geq 0$. Because it can be deduced using $d_k$ and $\alpha_k$, for $k < n$. We can state that:

$$p_n = d_n = d_{n+1}\alpha_0 + d_n\alpha_1 + \ldots + d_1\alpha_n + d_0\alpha_n, \text{ for all } n \geq 0.$$

To solve and analyze this system, we need to compute the following generating functions $P(z)$ and $Q(z)$ and noting that $d_0 = p_0 = 1 - \rho$:

$$P(z) = \sum_{n=0}^{\infty} d_n z^n \text{ and } Q(z) = \sum_{n=0}^{\infty} \alpha_n z^n.$$

The computation of $P$ gives the following:

$$P(z) = \sum_{n=0}^{\infty} (d_{n+1}\alpha_0 + d_n\alpha_1 + \ldots + d_1\alpha_n + d_0\alpha_n)z^n$$

$$= \frac{1}{z}Q(z)(P(z) - d_0) + d_0 Q(z).$$

This shows that

$$P(z) = \frac{(1 - \rho)(1 - z)Q(z)}{P(z) - z}.$$

However the computation of $Q(z)$ gives:

$$Q(z) = \sum_{n=0}^{\infty} \left( \int_0^{\infty} \frac{(\lambda t)^n}{n!} e^{-\lambda t} f_B(t) dt \right) z^n = \int_0^{\infty} \left( \sum_{n=0}^{\infty} \frac{(\lambda t z)^n}{n!} \right) e^{-\lambda t} f_B(t) dt$$

$$= \int_0^{\infty} e^{-\lambda(1-z)t} f_B(t) dt.$$

The working out of the distribution of the sojourn time and the time spent in the system by a customer can be performed in a similar way.

### 6.7.3  G/M/1 Queues

In a G/M/1 system, customers arrive one by one with an interarrival times identically and independently distributed according to an arbitrary distribution function $F$ and a density function $f$. The mean interarrival time is equal to $\frac{1}{\lambda}$. The service times are exponentially distributed with mean equal to $\frac{1}{\mu}$. For the sake of stability, we assume that the occupation rate $\rho$ is smaller than one.

The state of the G/M/1 queue is typically described by a pair $(n, x)$ where $n$ denotes the number of customers in the system and $x$ is the elapsed time since the last arrival. It is worth to notice that, as in the M/G/1 queue, the state description is much easier at special points in time. If we look at the system on arrival instants, then the state description can be reduced to $n$ only. For this, let $a_k$ denote the number of customers in the system just before the $k$th arriving customer. In the following, we will determine the limiting distribution $\pi_n = \lim_{k \to \infty} Pr(a_k = n)$ and then compute the sojourn time in the system.

Sequence $\{a_k\}_{k \geq 0}$ defines a Markov chain with transition probabilities:

$$p_{n,m} = Pr(a_{k+1} = m | a_k = n)$$

.   Obviously, one can determine that:

- For $m \leq n + 1$, $P_{n,m}$ is equal to the probability that exactly $m + 1 - n$ customers are served during the interarrival time of the $(k + 1)$th customer
- For $m > n + 1$, $P_{n,m}$ is equal to zero
- For all $n, m, n', m'$ such that $n + 1 - m = n' + 1 - m' = i$, $P_{n,m} = \alpha_i$, because they are both equal to the probability that $i$ customers are served during the interarrival of the $(k + 1)$th customer. The determination of $\alpha_i$ is done by noticing that, given the time duration $t$ of the interarrival time, the number of customers served is Poisson distributed with parameter $\mu.t$. Therefore, one can have:

$$\alpha_i = \int_{t+0}^{\infty} \frac{(\mu t)^i}{i!} e^{-\mu t} f(t) dt.$$

The determination of transition probabilities is terminated by noticing that $p_{n,0} = 1 - \sum_{i=1}^{n} \alpha_i$. Figure 6.8 depicts the Markov chain (MC) defined by the sequence $\{a_k\}_{k \geq 0}$.

Now, it easy to deduce the relations linking the elements in the sequence $\{a_k\}_{k \geq 0}$. We can have:

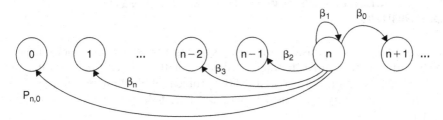

**FIGURE 6.8.** Markov model for G/M/1

$$a_0 = \sum_{i=1}^{\infty} a_i p_{i,0}, \quad a_n = \sum_{i=1}^{\infty} a_{n-1+i} \alpha_i \quad n \geq 1.$$

To solve this system of equilibrium equations, one can attempt a solution under the form $x^n$. Substituting this form into the second equation, we deduce that:

$$x = \sum_{i=1}^{\infty} \alpha_i x^i,$$

$$x = \sum_{i=1}^{\infty} x^i \int_{t+0}^{\infty} \frac{(\mu t)^i}{i!} e^{-\mu t} f(t) dt = \int_{t+0}^{\infty} \sum_{i=1}^{\infty} \frac{(x\mu t)^i}{i!} e^{-\mu t} f(t) dt, \text{ and}$$

$$x = \int_{t+0}^{\infty} e^{-\mu(1+x)t} f(t) dt.$$

The determination of $x$ is made using the Laplace-Stieljes transform, and taking $0 < x < 1$. Finally, by using the normalization condition, we obtain $a_n = (1 - x)x^n$.

An arriving customer finds $n$ customers in the system with probability $a_n$. Let $A$ be a random variable denoting the number of customers $n$, and the system is found on the arrival of a customer. The mean number of customers in system is given by:

$$E(A) = \sum_{n=0}^{\infty} na_n = \sum_{n=0}^{\infty} n(1 - x)x^n = \frac{x}{1 - x}.$$

Knowing that the mean sojourn time $E(S)$ is given by $E(S) = \frac{1}{\mu}(E(A) + 1)$ and by applying Little's theorem, we can write:

$$E(S) = \left( \frac{x}{1 - x} + 1 \right) \frac{1}{\mu} = \frac{1}{\mu(1 - x)}.$$

## 6.8 QUEUEING MODELS WITH INSENSITIVE LENGTH DISTRIBUTION

In this section, we consider queueing systems for which the queue length distribution is insensitive to the distribution of the service time, but it only depends on its mean. We also address the problem of blocking probability. For the sake of simplicity, we consider two cases: infinite length queues and the loss systems.

### 6.8.1 Infinite Queue Systems

In this model, customers arrive according to a Poisson process with rate $\lambda$. Their service times are iid with some general distribution function. The number of servers is infinite. So a server is always available for each arriving customer. Hence, the waiting time of each customer is zero, and the sojourn time is equal to the service time. Thus by Little's law, we immediately obtain that $E(L) = \lambda E(B)$, where $\lambda E(B)$ denotes the mean amount of work that arrives per unit of time. We now determine the distribution of $L$ by computing the probabilities $p_n$ that $n$ customers are in the system. To this end, we consider two models $M/M/\infty$ and $M/D/\infty$.

In the $M/M/\infty$ model, the service times are exponentially distributed with mean $1/\mu$. Figure 6.9 depicts such a model. By equating the flow between states $(n-1)$, $n$, and $(n+1)$ we obtain:

$$p_{n-1}\lambda = p_n n\mu.$$

We then deduce

$$p_n = \frac{\lambda}{n\mu}p_{n-1} = \frac{\rho}{n}p_{n-1} = \ldots = \frac{\rho^n}{n!}p_0.$$

Because the sum of the probabilities $p_n$ is equal to 1, it holds:

$$1 = \sum_{0\leq n} p_n = p_0 \sum_{0\leq n} \frac{\rho^n}{n!} = p_0 \cdot e^\rho, p_0 = e^{-\rho}, \quad \text{and} \, p_n = \frac{\rho^n}{n!}e^{-\rho}.$$

We therefore deduce that the number of customers in the system has a Poisson distribution with mean $\rho$. Let us now consider the model $M/D/\infty$ and let $b$ denote the constant service time. The probability $p_n(t)$ that exactly n customers

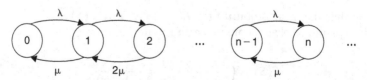

**FIGURE 6.9.** Flow diagram for M/M/8.

are in the system at time $t$ can be shown to be equal to the probability that, during the interval $[t-b, t]$, exactly $n$ customers have arrived. Because the number of customers arriving in a time interval of length $b$ is Poisson distributed with mean $\lambda b$, we deduce that:

$$p_n(t) = \frac{(\lambda b)^n}{n!} e^{-\lambda b} = \frac{\rho^n}{n!} e^{-\rho}.$$

## 6.8.2 Loss Systems

In this section, we only consider models where customers arrive according to a Poisson process with rate $\lambda$. Their service times are independent and identically distributed with some distribution function. Assume that $c$ servers are available under use and that each newly arriving customer enters immediately a service, if there is a server available; otherwise, the customer is lost. When the distribution function is general, this system is referred to as the M/G/c loss system.

Our objective now is to determine the probabilities $p_n$ of $n$ customers in the system. We also address the particular case of $p_c$, where $c$ is the number of servers. Probability $p_c$ is the so-called blocking probability, denoted by $B(c, \rho)$. For this, let us consider the queue model M/M/c/c. We also have:

$$p_{n-1}\lambda = p_n n\mu.$$

And we can deduce the following:

$$p_n = \frac{\left(\frac{\lambda}{\mu}\right)^n \frac{1}{n!}}{\sum \left(\frac{\lambda}{\mu}\right)^n \frac{1}{n!}} = \frac{\rho^n \frac{1}{n!}}{\sum\limits_{n=0}^{c} \rho^j \frac{1}{j!}}, \quad 0 \le n \le c.$$

It can be stated that, for a general service time distribution, that the probabilities $p_n$ are given by:

$$p_n = \frac{\rho^n/n!}{\sum\limits_{n=0}^{c} \rho^j/j!}, \quad \text{where } 0 \le n \le c, \quad \text{and } \rho = \lambda E(B).$$

We thus have:

$$B(c, \rho) = p_c = \frac{\rho^c/c!}{\sum\limits_{n=0}^{c} \rho^j/j!}, \quad \text{where } \rho = \lambda E(B).$$

Using the Little's law, we obtain the equality $E(L) = \rho(1 - B(c, \rho))$.

A recursive formula for the blocking probability $B(c, \rho)$ can be established as follows. Let us write it first as:

$$B(c,\rho) = \frac{\rho^c/c!}{\sum_{n=0}^{c} \rho^j/j!} = \frac{\rho^c/c!}{\sum_{n=0}^{c-1} \rho^j/j! + \rho^c/c!}$$

$$= \frac{\dfrac{\rho^c}{a.c!}}{1 + \dfrac{\rho^c}{ac!}}, \quad \text{for } a = \sum_{n=0}^{c-1} \rho^j/j!.$$

Because

$$B(c-1,\rho) = \frac{\rho^{c-1}/c!}{\sum_{n=0}^{c-1} \rho^j/j!} = \frac{\rho^{c-1}/c!}{a},$$

we can deduce the following recursion:

$$B(c,\rho) = \frac{\rho B(c-1,\rho)}{c + \rho B(c-1,\rho)}$$

$$B(0,\rho) = 1.$$

## 6.9  SUMMARY

We have considered and analyzed in this chapter the use of M/M/1, M/M/c, M/Er/1, and M/G/1 queues. We also developed the basics, formal techniques that can be used to determine various helpful functions and parameters including the distribution of the waiting time and sojourn time of a customer, distribution of the customer in the system, and distribution of the busy period of the server.

For the sake of simplicity, we have omitted the study of G/G/1 because this type of queueing system is difficult to handle and is intimately linked to the complexity of the distribution of the interarrival time. Finally, the chapter includes several examples that illustrate the concepts and models presented.

## REFERENCES

[1] A. O. Allen, "Probability, Statistics, and Queueing Theory—With Computer Science Applications, Computer Science and Applied Mathematics," Academic Press, New York, 1978.

[2] R. Nelson, "Probability, Stochastic Processes, and Queueing Theory—The Mathematics of Computer Performance Modeling," Springer Verlag, New York, 1995.

[3] W. Feller, "An Introduction to Probability Theory and Its Applications", Vol. 1, Wiley, New York, 1968.

[4] W. Feller, "An Introduction to Probability Theory and Its Applications," Vol. 2, Wiley, New York, 1968.

[5] M. Eisenberg, "Queues with Periodic Service and Changeover Time," Operations Research, Vol. 20, No. 2, pp. 440–451, 1972.

[6] G. Bolch, S. Greiner, H. de Meer, and K.S. Trivedi, "Queueing Networks and Markov Chains" 2nd edition, Wiley, New York, 1998.

[7] J. D. C. Little, "A proof of the Queueing Formula L = λW," Operational Research, Vol. 9, pp. 383–387, 1961.

[8] T. Takine, "Distributional Form of Little's Law for FIFO Queues with Multiple Markovian Arrival Streams and Its Application to Queues with Vacations," Queueing Systems, Vol. 37, Nos.1-3, pp. 31–63, 2001.

[9] J. A. Hooke, "A Priority Queue with Low-Priority Arrivals General," Operations Research Vol. 20, pp. 373–380, 1972.

[10] L. Schrage, "An Alternative Proof of a Conservation Law for the Queue G/G/1," Operational Research, Vol. 18, pp. 185–187, 1970.

[11] Kleinrock, "A Conservation Law for a Wide Class of Queueing Disciplines," Naval Research Logistic Quart, Vol. 12, pp. 181–192, 1965.

[12] L. Kleinrock, "Queueing Systems, Vol. 1: Theory", Wiley, New York, 1975.

## EXERCISES

1. In a work station, orders arrive according to a Poisson arrival process with arrival rate $\lambda$. An order consists of $N$ independent jobs. The distribution of $N$ is given by

$$P(N = k) = (1 - p)p^{k-1}, k \geq 1$$

Each job requires an exponentially distributed amount of processing time with mean $1/\mu$.

   a. Derive the distribution of the total processing time of an order.

   b. Determine the distribution of the number of orders in the system.

2. A printer is attached to the LAN of an enterprise. The printing jobs are assumed to arrive with a Poissonian rate $\lambda$, and the printing service times are assumed to obey the exponential distribution with rate $\mu$. Because the capacity of the printer has become insufficient with regard to the increased load, three alternatives can be used to improve the printing service:

   a. Replace the old printer by a new one twice as fast, i.e., with service rate $2\mu$.

   b. Add a similar printer (service rate $\mu$) and divide the users in two groups of equal size directing the printing works in each group to their own printer. The arrival rate of jobs to each printer is $\lambda/2$.

   c. Add a similar printer, constitute a single printing queue where all jobs are accepted. The job at the head of the queue is sent to whatever printer becomes free first.

   d. Compute, in each case, the mean sojourn of a job j (i.e., time in system from the arrival of $j$ until its full completion).

   e. At heavy load, compare the sojourn time in case b) and c) with respect to case a).

3. Consider two machines working in parallel having a common buffer. Assume that: a) jobs arrive according to a Poisson stream with rate $\lambda$; b) the processing times are exponentially distributed with mean $1/\mu_1$ on machine 1 and $1/\mu_2$ on machine 2; c) $\mu_1$ is bigger than $\mu_2$; and d) jobs are processed in order of arrival. Finally, we assume that $\rho = \lambda/(\mu 1 + \mu 2)$ is smaller than one and that a job arriving when both machines are idle is assigned to the faster machine.

   a. Compute the distribution of the number of jobs in the system.

   b. Determine the mean number of jobs in the system.

   c. Determine when it is better to not use the slower machine at all.

4. Consider the $M/E_2/1$ queue with an arrival rate of 8 customers per hour and a mean service time of 6 minutes.

   a. Compute the distribution of the waiting time.

   b. Determine the fraction of customers that have to wait longer than 4 minutes.

5. Customers arrive at a post office according to a Poisson process with a rate of 40 customers per hour. Half of the customers have a service time that is the sum of a fixed time of 10 and an exponentially distributed time with a mean of 12. The other half has an exponentially distributed service time with a mean of 2 min.

   Determine the mean waiting time and the mean number of customers waiting in the queue.

6. Determine the distribution of the sojourn time in case of exponentially distributed service times with mean 1 and hyperexponentially distributed interarrival times with distribution function:

$$F(t) = \frac{1}{2}(1 - e^{-t/2}) + \frac{1}{4}(1 - e^{-t/8}).$$

7. The distribution of the interarrival time in a queueing system is assumed to be given by:

$$F(t) = \frac{7}{12}(1 - e^{-2t}) + \frac{5}{12}(1 - e^{-3t}), \quad t \geq 0$$

   The service times are assumed exponentially distributed with a mean of $1/3$.

   a. Determine the distribution of the number of customers in the system just before an arrival.

   b. Determine the distribution of the waiting time.

8. A small company offering phone services has six resources available. The costs are $6 per resource per day for resource maintenance, depreciation, etc.). Customers are assumed to arrive according to a Poisson process with a rate of 5 customers per day. A customer uses a resource for an exponential time with a mean of 1.5 days. Using a resource costs $7 per day. Arriving customers for which no car is available are lost (they will go to another company).

   a. Determine the fraction of arriving customers for which no resource is available.

   b. Determine the mean profit per day.

   c. The company is considering to make available more resources. How many resources should be provided to maximize the mean profit per day?

# CHAPTER 7

# QUEUEING NETWORKS

A queueing network is a collection of interconnected queues (or service stations) that are used for representing the structure of many systems, including computer and telecommunication systems with several of resources that provide service to a collection of customers [1, 2]. The customers' competition for the resource service corresponds to queueing into the service queues. The analysis of the queueing network consists of evaluating a set of performance measures, such as resource utilization, throughput, and customer response time. The success of using queueing network models in system performance evaluation is mainly due to the possibility of reaching high accuracy in the performance results and good efficiency in the model analysis and evaluation.

In this chapter, we describe the fundamental properties of queueing networks. In particular, we present major classes of queueing networks, including the class of open networks, the class of closed networks, and the product form networks. We will also give examples on these models.

## 7.1 FUNDAMENTALS OF QUEUEING NETWORKS

In a distributed computer environment, for instance, isolated queues are unfortunately unable to perform efficient analysis of a given problem. Often, the problem to be analyzed consists of several interconnected queues. Figure 7.1 illustrates this situation.

*Fundamentals of Performance Evaluation of Computer and Telecommunication Systems,*
By Mohammad S. Obaidat and Noureddine A. Boudriga
Copyright © 2010 John Wiley & Sons, Inc.

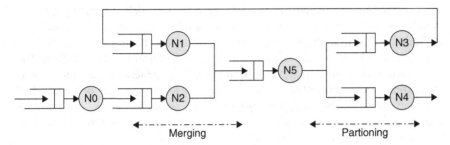

**FIGURE 7.1.** Example of a queueing network.

- The partitioning and merging of traffic, as illustrated by nodes 1 and 5, respectively.
- The existence of queues in tandem, or series, as illustrated by nodes 3 and 4.

To deal with partitioning and merging of traffic streams, we assume that traffic arrives at a queue (e.g., node N5) with a mean arrival rate of $\lambda$, and that there are two paths, A and B, by which an item (i.e., a customer) may leave (to nodes N3 and N4). When an item is serviced, it leaves via path A with probability $\pi$ and via path B with probability $(1 - \pi)$. The traffic distribution of streams A and B will differ from the incoming distribution. It is worth noticing that, if the incoming distribution is Poisson with mean rate $\lambda$, then the two departing traffic flows will also have Poisson distributions, with mean rates of $\pi\lambda$ and $(1-\pi)\lambda$. A similar situation exists for traffic merging. If, for example, two Poisson streams with mean rates of $\lambda 1$ and $\lambda 2$ are merged, the resulting stream is Poisson with a mean rate of $\lambda 1 + \lambda 2$. Both of these results can be generalized to more than two arriving streams for merging and more than two departing streams for partitioning.

Partitioning and merging are used in models of parallel and distributed computer systems. Moreover, another feature can occur in queueing networks, which does not occur in single queues. It is called *blocking*. Blocking takes place when a customer waiting for a departure from a server is unable to join the next queue because of limited waiting space, and therefore, the customer stays in server (blocking it). No exact method has been developed for analyzing general queuing problems that have such characteristics. However, if the traffic flow is Poisson and the service times are exponential, an exact solution exists.

### 7.1.1 Queueing Network Models Classification

Queueing network models, in general, are more complex than simple single-server queueing networks. The simple queueing systems have been applied to analyze congestion in computer and communication systems. Queueing network models represent such systems as a network of interacting service centers whose analysis often provides reasonably accurate prediction of their performance. Despite the assumptions of the class of queueing networks, queueing network models have been observed to be robust models. Queueing network models can be analyzed by analytical methods or by simulation. Analytical methods require that the model satisfies a set of assumptions and constraints and are based on a set of mathematical computable relationships that characterize the system behavior. Simulation is a general technique of wide application and flexibility, but its main drawback is the potential high development and computational cost to obtain accurate results.

Systems modeled by queueing networks can roughly be grouped into three categories [3]. They are as follows:

1. *Open networks*: Customers, in open networks, arrive from outside the system to be served, and then they depart. Thus, a queueing network is called open if jobs can enter the network (from outside) and jobs can get out of network. An example of an open network is given by a packet switched data network.

2. *Closed networks*: A fixed number of customers (say K) are confined inside the queueing network and circulate among the queues. An example of a closed network is the CPU job scheduling problem. Thus, the queueing network is said to be closed if jobs cannot enter or leave the network. This leaves the number of jobs within the network to be constant.

3. *Mixed networks*: Customers, in mixed networks, belong to different classes. Customers in the same class see the network the same way, open or closed. A mixed network can be any combination of the two aforementioned types.

A queueing network can also have population constraints. If the network is closed, this means that a customer (or job), can enter a queue, be served, then depart to another queue, and remain in the network. If the network is open, this means that customers arrive from outside the system if there is room in the network, are served, and then depart to another queue or leave the network (and are immediately replaced by another customer(s)). This constraint is called fixed number of customers. Another property, called limited buffer capacity, allows a bounded number of customers to enter the network.

A set of queues sharing a common service gives an example of networks with population requirements. Two other classes of queueing networks are of interest: the tandem (or cyclic) networks and product form networks [2, 4]. They will be discussed extensively in this chapter. A tandem network is a set of single-server queues organized sequentially and defining only one path to follow by the customers. In a tandem queue, the input for each queue except the first one is the output of the previous queue. Figure 7.1 gives an example of a set of single-server queues organized sequentially or in tandem (i.e., subnetwork reduced to the subset queues N0 and N2). Assume, for example, that the input to the first queue in the tandem is Poissonian. Then one can say that, if the service time of each queue is exponential and the waiting lines have infinite capacity, the output of each queue is a Poisson stream statistically identical to the input. When the output stream of a queue is fed into the next queue, the delays at the second queue are the same as if the original traffic had bypassed the first queue and had been fed directly into the second queue. Thus, the queues are independent and can be analyzed one at a time, and the mean total delay for the tandem network is equal to the sum of the mean delays observed at each queue.

On the other hand, the precise characterization of the class of product form network is not easy [4–9]). Product form queueing network characterization holds under special assumptions. The product form characterization is related to some properties of the queueing network model that are defined on the Markov process underlying the queueing model. Product form networks have the special structure such that their solutions can be obtained without generating their underlying state space. Some sufficient conditions for product form characterization based on these properties have been derived. Two important properties can be considered: the local balance property and the quasi-reversibility property [10]. Informally speaking, the quasi-reversibility of a service center states that the current state, past departures, and future arrivals are mutually independent. Examples of quasi-reversible queues are: (a) a multiclass service center with first come-first served queueing discipline and exponential service time distribution, identical for each customer class and (b) a multiclass service center with processor sharing scheduling and arbitrary phase-type service time distribution. The local balance property states that the rate at which the customers leave a single node of the network is equated to the rate at which they enter it. The local balance property is concerned with a local situation and reduced the computational effort in the determination of the system steady state. Finally, let us say that product form queueing networks have a simple closed form expression of the stationary state distribution that allows defining efficient algorithms to evaluate average performance measures.

In this chapter, we first classify the queueing networks and then present the approaches that have been developed to perform queuing analysis. We introduce product form queueing networks and their properties. We finally study the resolution of product-form networks that satisfy the local balance property and discuss special classes of queueing networks, including the Jackson networks and BCMP networks.

### 7.1.2  Queueing Network Models with Finite Capacity Queues

Queueing networks with finite capacity queues have been used to represent systems with finite capacity resources and population constraints. When a queue reaches its maximum capacity, in such systems, the flow of customers into the service center is stopped and the blocking phenomenon originates. Various blocking mechanisms have been defined and analyzed in the literature to provide various behaviors of real systems with limited resources [11].

Exact solution algorithms, for the performance analysis of queueing networks, have been proposed to evaluate parameters such as the average performance indices, queue length distribution, and passage time distribution [12]. In some special cases, queueing networks with blocking show a product form solution, under particular constraints, for various blocking types [4]. A queueing network model with blocking is formed by M nodes (or service centers) and a set of customers. For each service center, we define the number of servers $s$, the service time distribution, the queue capacity, and the service discipline.

Let $Si$ denote the state of node $i$, which includes the number of customers in node $i$, denoted by $ni$. Let $\mu i$ denote the service rate of node $i$, (meaning that $1/\mu i$ is the average service time). Let $Bi$ denote the maximum number of customers admitted at node $i$, that is, in the queue and in the servers ($Bi = c + s$), $1 \le i \le M$. Thus, the total number of jobs in node $i$ satisfies the constraint $ni = Bi$. When the queue reaches the finite capacity ($ni = Bi$), the node is said to be blocked.

Various blocking types have been defined to provide system behaviors. Three major blocking types can be distinguished. These are as follows:

- *Blocking after service* (BAS): If a job attempts to enter a full capacity queue $j$ upon completion of a service at node $i$, it is forced to wait in the server of node $i$, until the destination node $j$ releases a job. The server of source node $i$ stops processing jobs. It will be resumed as soon as a departure occurs from node $j$. At that moment, the job waiting in node $i$ immediately moves to node $j$. If more than one node is blocked by the same node $j$, a scheduling policy must be applied.

- *Blocking before service* (BBS): A job declares its destination node $j$ before it starts receiving service at node $i$. If at that time node $j$ is busy, the service at node $i$ does not start and the server is blocked. Moreover, if node $j$ becomes busy (full) while a job whose destination is $j$ is served at node $i$, node $i$ service is interrupted and the server is blocked. The service of node $i$ will be resumed as soon as a departure occurs from node $j$.

- *Repetitive service blocking* (RS): A job upon completion of service at node $i$ attempts to enter its destination, node $j$. If node $j$ is busy (full), the job is looped back into the sending queue $i$, where it receives a new service according to the service discipline. Two subclasses can be distinguished depending on whether the job, after receiving a new service, chooses a new destination node independent of the one that it had selected previously: RS-RD (Repetitive Service-Random Destination) and RS-FD (Repetitive Service-Fixed Destination).

Queueing networks with finite capacity queues and blocking can have dead-lock. Deadlock prevention or resolution techniques must be applied. Deadlock prevention for closed queueing networks with blocking types BAS, BBS, and RS-FD requires that the overall network population $N$ is less than the total buffer capacity of the nodes in each possible cycle in the network. For RS-RD blocking, it is sufficient that routing matrix $P$ is irreducible and that $N$ is less than the total buffer capacity of the nodes in the network. Deadlock prevention for open queueing networks requires the following additional population constraint for each possible cycle in the network with finite capacity queues and where each node in the cycle has a blocking mechanism different from RS-RD.

Blocking mechanisms have been used to model systems with finite capacity resources in several fields. For example, blocking mechanisms can model specific communication protocols of store-and-forward communication networks. Blocking mechanisms have been extensively applied to production and manufacturing systems.

## 7.2 MODEL INPUTS AND OUTPUTS IN QUEUEING NETWORKS

We discuss, in this section, the inputs and outputs of general networks of queues that consist of separable queueing networks. For the sake of simplicity, we first present this material in the context of models with a single customer class. Then, we discuss certain computer system characteristics that cannot be represented directly using the inputs available for separable models and certain performance measures that cannot be obtained directly from the available outputs.

The basic entities in queueing network models are service centers, which represent system resources, and customers comprising users, jobs or transactions.

*Customers*: They are represented by the workload intensity, which may be described in any of three ways:

1. *A transaction workload* has its intensity specified by a parameter A, indicating the rate at which requests (customers) arrive. A transaction workload has a population that varies over time. Customers that have completed service leave the model.
2. *A batch workload* has its intensity specified by a parameter $N$, indicating the average number of active jobs (customers); $N$ need not be an integer. A batch workload has a fixed population. Customers that have completed service can be thought of as leaving the model and as being replaced instantaneously from a backlog of waiting jobs.
3. *A terminal workload* has its intensity specified by two parameters: $N$, indicating the number of active terminals (customers>, and Z, indicating the average length of time that customers use terminals ("think") between interactions; again, $N$ does not need to be an integer.

### 7.2.1 Model Inputs

A terminal workload is similar to a batch workload in that its total population is fixed. In fact, a terminal workload with a think time of zero is in every way equivalent to a batch workload. On the other hand, a terminal workload is similar to a transaction workload in that the population of the central subsystem (the system excluding the terminals) varies, provided that the terminal workload has a nonzero think time. Note that $N$ is an upper bound on the central subsystem population of a terminal workload, whereas no upper bound exists for a transaction workload.

Often models with transaction workloads are referred to as open models, since there is an infinite stream of arriving customers. Models with batch or terminal workloads are referred to as closed models, since customers "recirculate." This distinction is made because the algorithms used to evaluate open models differ from those used for closed models. It highlights the similarity between batch and terminal workloads.

Service centers may be of two types: queueing and delay centers. Customers at a queueing center compete for the use of the server. The time spent by a customer at a queueing center has two components: time spent waiting and time spent receiving service. Queueing centers are used to represent any system resource at which users compete for service (e.g., the CPU and I/O devices). Customers at a delay center each (logically) are allocated their own server, so that there will be no competition for service. Thus, the residence time of a customer at a delay center is exactly that customer's service demand there. The most common use of a delay center is to represent the *think time* of terminal workloads.

Delay centers are useful in situations where it is necessary to impose some known average delay. For instance, a delay center could be used to represent the delay incurred by sending large amounts of data over a dedicated low-speed transmission line.

The service demand of a customer at center k, denoted by $D_k$, is the total amount of time the customer requires in service at center $k$. The set of service demands characterizes the behavior of the customer in terms of processing requirements. In a single class model, customers are indistinguishable with respect to their service demands, which can be thought of as representing the "average customer" in the actual system. $D_k$ can be computed as the measured busy time of device $k$ divided by the number of system completions $(D_k = B_k/C)$, or may be thought of as the product of the number of visits that a customer makes to center $k$ and the service requirement per visit $(D_k = V_k \times S_k)$. For simplicity and the need to reduce the number of parameters and facilitate obtaining their values, we generally will choose to parameterize models in terms of $D_k$ and define $D$ to be the total service demand of a customer at all centers.

## 7.2.2 Model Outputs

The list of the outputs obtained by evaluating a single-class queueing network model contains two types of outputs: system measures and center measures. System measures include the response time $R$, the system throughput $X(N)$ for a batch or terminal class with population size $N$ and the average queue length at center $k$ for a transaction class with arrival $\lambda$, say $Q_k(\lambda)$.

Center measures include the utilization of center $k$, the average residence time at center $k$, the throughput of center $k$, and the average queue length at center $k$.

*Utilization*: The utilization of a center may be interpreted as the proportion of time during which the device is busy, or equivalently, the average number of customers in service there.

*Residence Time*: Similar to $D_k$, the total service demand of a customer at center $k$, residence time $R_k$ is the total residence time of a customer at center $k$ (considering several visits). Thus, the average time spent per visit at center $k$ can be calculated as $R_k/V_k$. Obviously the system response time $R$ corresponds to the sum of the residence times at the various centers.

*Queue Length*: The average queue length at center $k$, $Q_k$, includes all customers at that center, whether waiting or receiving service. The number of customers waiting can be calculated as $Q_k - U_k$, since $U_k$, can be interpreted as the average number of customers receiving service at center $k$. $Q$ denotes the average number in the system. For a batch class, $Q = N$. For a transaction class, $Q = XR$ (According to Little's law [13]). For a terminal class, $Q = N - XZ$ ($Q = XR$ and $R = N/X - Z$.).

### 7.2.3 Multiple Class Models

**Inputs.** Multiple class models consist of $C$ customer classes, each of which has its own workload intensity ($\lambda_c$, $N_c$, and $Z_c$) and its own service demand at each center $k$ ($D_{c,k}$). Within each class, the customers are indistinguishable. Multiple class models that consist entirely of open (transaction) classes are referred to as open models. Models that consist entirely of closed (batch or terminal) classes are referred to as closed.

The overall workload intensity of a multiple class model is described by a vector with an entry for each class: $\lambda = (\lambda_1,\dots,\lambda_C)$ if the model is open and $N = (N_1,\dots,N_C)$ if it is closed. Similar to the case for single class models, the scheduling discipline at a queueing center does not have to be specified. Roughly, the assumption made is that the scheduling discipline is class independent. The same performance measures will result from any scheduling discipline that satisfies this assumption, along with the earlier assumption that exactly one customer is in service whenever there are customers at the center.

**Outputs.** All performance measures/metrics can be obtained on a per-class basis (e.g., $U_{c,k}$ and $X_c$) as well as on an aggregate basis (e.g., $U_k$ and $X$). For utilization, queue length, and throughput, the aggregate performance measure equals the sum of the per-class performance measures (e.g., $U_k = \sum_{c=1}^{C} U_{c,k}$. For residence time and system response time, however, the per-class measures must be weighted by relative throughput, as follows:

$$R = \sum_{c=1}^{C} \frac{R_c X_c}{X} \quad \text{and} \quad R = \sum_{c=1}^{C} \frac{R_{c,k} X_c}{X}$$

## 7.3  OPEN NETWORKS

Let us assume that the open queueing network is serving a single class of customers (or jobs). The arrival rate $\lambda_i$ of customers for node $i$ in an open network is computed by considering two types of arrivals: the arrivals from outside and the arrivals from the other nodes. The arrival rate $\lambda_i$ can be written as follows:

$$\lambda_i = \lambda_{0,i} + \sum_{j=1}^{M} \lambda_j q_{j,i}, \quad i = 1, ..., M$$

where $\lambda_{0,i}$ designates the arrival rate of customers from outside and $q_{j,i}$ is the probability that a customer is transferred to node $i$ after service completion at node $j$. A similar equation holds for the destination $D$. Since the total stream exiting the network must be equal to the stream entering to the network, we have:
$q_{0,0} = 0$ and

$$\lambda = \sum_{j=1}^{M} \lambda_{0,j} = \sum_{j=1}^{M} \lambda_j q_{j,0}$$

The last equations are called traffic equations. Solving the traffic equations would allow for determining the so-called mean number of visits to node $i$, referred to as $e_i = \frac{\lambda_i}{\sum_{j=1}^{M} \lambda_{0,j}}$. Let $p_{0,i}$ be the probability that a customer entering the network from outside first enters node $i$. The mean number of visits $e_i$ can be written as follows:

$$e_i = p_{0,i} + \sum_{j=1}^{M} e_j q_{j,i}$$

The most important performance metrics for open queueing networks are: (a) the steady-state probability $\pi(k)$ that each node $i$ contains exactly $k_i$ customers; (b) the utilization of node $i$, denoted by $\pi_i$; (c) the mean number of customers at node $i$, denoted by $E(C_i)$; (d) the mean response time at node $i$; and (e) the mean waiting time at node $i$. For this, let the network state be determined by the vector, $N = (N_1, ..., N_M)$, where $M$ is number of nodes in the queueing network and $N_i$ designates the number of customers in node $i$. Its possible values are denoted by $n = (n_1, ..., n_M)$, and the network is said to be at state $n$ if $N = n$; i.e., $N_1 = n_1$, ..., $N_M = n_M$. The steady-state probability $\pi(n) = P\{N = n\}$, which represents the probability that the system is at state $n$ is an important object in the analysis of the open queueing network because the mean value of all other performance metrics can be computed using such probabilities. The computation of these metrics can be done as follows:

- The utilization $\rho_i$ of node $i$ is given by $\rho_i = \sum\limits_{k=1}^{\infty} \pi_i(k)$, where $\pi_i(k)$ is the probability that node $i$ is at state $k$. It is worth noticing that $\pi_i(k) = \sum\limits_{k_i=k} \pi(k_1, ..., k_M)$.

- The throughput $\lambda_i$ of node $i$ represents the rate at which customers leave the node. If the service rate at node $i$ is denoted by $\mu_i$, then $\lambda_i$ is shown to be equal to $\lambda_i = \sum\limits_{k=1}^{\infty} \mu_i \pi_i(k)$.

- The mean number of customers $E(C_i)$, the mean response time $E(T_i)$, and the mean waiting time $E(W_i)$ at node $i$ can be easily computed as:
$$E(C_i) = \sum\limits_{k=1}^{\infty} k\pi_i(k), \ E(T_i) = \frac{E(C_i)}{\lambda_i}, \text{ and } E(W_i) = E(T_i) - \frac{1}{\mu_i}, \text{ respectively.}$$

Let us now consider that the queueing network is serving customers belonging to various classes. The customer classes differ in their service time and routing probabilities. Then, if the number of the $r$th class at node $i$ is denoted by $k_{r,i}$ and the state of node $i$ is $S_i = (k_{i,1}, ..., k_{i,R})$ where $R$ is the number of customer classes, the probability that the $i$th node is in state $S_i = k$ is given by:

$$\pi_i(k) = \sum\limits_{S_i=k} \pi(S_1, ..., S_M).$$

- The utilization $\rho_{i,r}$ of the $i$th node for customers in the $r$th class is given by:

$$\rho_{i,r} = \frac{1}{m_i} \sum\limits_{k,k_r>0} \pi_i(k) \frac{k_{i,r}}{k_i} \text{Min}\{m_i, k_i\}$$

where $m_i$ is the number of parallel servers at node $i$ and $k_i = \sum\limits_{r=1}^{R} k_{i,r}$.

- The throughput $\lambda_{i,r}$ of node $i$ with respect to the $r$th class is given by:

$$\lambda_{i,r} = \sum\limits_{k:\, k_r>0} \mu_i \frac{k_{i,r}}{k_i} \pi_i(k).$$

In addition, the mean number of customers, mean response time, and mean waiting time at node $i$ with respect to the $r$th class can be determined, respectively, by:

$$E(C_{i,r}) = \sum_{k:\,k_r>0} k_r \pi_i(k),\, E(T_{i,r}) = \frac{E(C_{i,r})}{\lambda_{i,r}},\, \text{ and } E(W_{i,r}) = E(T_{i,r}) - \frac{1}{\mu_{i,r}}$$

## 7.3.1 Jackson Networks

The simplest type of network is an open network called the Jackson network which has the following three assumptions: (a) It is an arbitrary network of M queues, (b) the service time of any queue $i$ is exponentially distributed with rate $\mu_i$, and (c) the arrivals from outside the network to queue $i$ represent a Poisson process with mean rate $\lambda_i$. In addition, upon departure from queue $i$, a customer chooses the next queue $j$ randomly with the probability $q_{i,j}$ or exits the network with the probability $q_{i,d}$ (this is referred to as probabilistic routing). The model can be extended to cover the case of predetermined routes. The network is open to arrivals from outside of the network (source or node $s$). From the source $s$ customers arrive as a Poisson stream with intensity $\lambda$, where a fraction $q_{s,i}$ of them enter queue $i$ (intensity $\lambda\,q_{s,i}$). Figure 7.2 depicts a Jackson network with four nodes.

The openness of the network requires that from each node there is at leastone a path to the sink 0; i.e., the probability that a customer entering the network will ultimately exit the network is 1. The conservation of flows can be stated as follows. Let $\lambda$ be the average customer flow through node $i$. Stream $\lambda_i$ is composed of the direct stream from the source and the split output streams from other nodes:

$$\lambda_i = \lambda q_{0,i} + \sum_{j=1}^{M} \lambda_j q_{j,i}, \quad i = 1, \ldots, M.$$

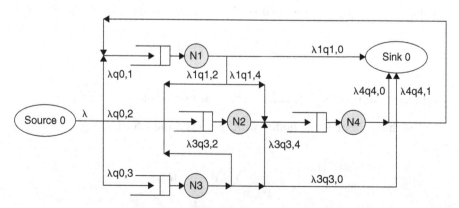

**FIGURE 7.2.** Example of a Jackson network.

The conservation laws constitute a set of $M$ linear equations from which the $\lambda_i$ can be retrieved.

Example: Assume that $M$ is equal to 1. One should have $\lambda_1 = \lambda + q\lambda_1$. This gives the following expression for $\lambda_1$:

$$\lambda_1 = \frac{\lambda}{1-q}$$

**Jacksons theorem.** *The state probability $p(k)$ of a Jackson network is given by*:

$$\pi(k) = \pi_1(k_1) \times \ldots \times \pi_M(k_M) = \prod_{i=1}^{M} \pi_i(k_i)$$

*where $k$ is the system state, $k_i$ is the number of customer at node $i$,* $\pi_i(k_i) = (1 - \rho_i)\rho_i^{k_i}$, and $\rho_i = \frac{\lambda_i}{\mu_i}$.

The theorem shows that: (a) the network behaves as if it were composed of independent $M/M/1$ queues, (b) the state probability has a product form (showing the independence), and (c) the number of customers in one node does not impact the number of customers in the other nodes.

**Proof of Jackson's Theorem**

Let $\lambda_{i,j}$ and $q_{i,j}$ be the rate at which jobs leaving queue $i$ go to queue $j$, and the probability that a job departing queue $i$ moves directly to queue $j$, respectively. During an interval of length $\Delta t$, only four possible events may occur:

1. A customer arrives from outside the network
2. A customer leaves the network to the outside world
3. A customer leaves one queue and enters another queue
4. None of the above.

These four events are integrated into the following equation:

$$\pi(k_1, k_2, \ldots, k_n | t + \Delta t) = \sum_{j=1}^{M} \pi(k_1, \ldots, k_{j-1}, k_j - 1, k_{j+1}, \ldots, k_n | t)\lambda_{0,j}\Delta t$$

$$+ \sum_{j=1}^{M} \pi(k_1, \ldots, k_{j-1}, k_j + 1, k_{j+1}, \ldots, k_n | t)\mu_j q_{j,0}\Delta t$$

$$+ \sum_{i=1}^{M}\sum_{j=1}^{M} \pi(k_1, \ldots, k_{i-1}, k_i + 1, k_{i+1}, \ldots, k_{j-1}, k_j - 1, k_{j+1}, \ldots, k_n | t)$$

$$\mu_i q_{i,j}\Delta t + \pi(k_1, \ldots, k_n | t)(1 - \Delta t\sum_{j=1}^{M}(\lambda_{0,j} + \mu_j))$$

This gives after moving $\pi(k_1,k_2,...,k_n)$ to the left-hand term, dividing all objects by $\Delta t$, and taking limits when $\Delta t$ tends to 0:

$$\frac{d}{dt}\pi(k_1,k_2,...,k_n|t)=\sum_{j=1}^{M}\pi(k_1,..,k_{j-1},k_j-1,k_{j+1},..,k_n|t)\lambda_{0,j}$$

$$+\sum_{j=1}^{M}\pi(k_1,..,k_{j-1},k_j+1,k_{j+1},..,k_n|t)\mu_j q_{j,0}$$

$$+\sum_{i=1}^{M}\sum_{j=1}^{M}\pi(k_1,..,k_{i-1},k_i+1,k_{i+1},..,k_{j-1},k_j-1,k_{j+1},..,k_n|t)\mu_i q_{i,j}$$

$$-\pi(k_1,k_2,...,k_n|t)\sum_{j=1}^{M}(\lambda_{0,j}+\mu_j).$$

Since

$$\frac{d}{dt}\pi(k_1,k_2,...,k_n|t)=0 \quad \text{for} \lambda_j<\mu_j, 1\leq j\leq M,$$

we can deduce that;

$$\pi(k_1,k_2,...,k_n|t)\sum_{j=1}^{M}(\lambda_{0,j}+\mu_j)=\sum_{j=1}^{M}\pi(k_1,..,k_{j-1},k_j-1,k_{j+1},..,k_n|t)\lambda_{0,j}$$

$$+\sum_{j=1}^{M}\pi(k_1,..,k_{j-1},k_j+1,k_{j+1},..,k_n|t)\mu_j q_{j,0}$$

$$+\sum_{i=1}^{M}\sum_{j=1}^{M}\pi(k_1,..,k_{i-1},k_i+1,k_{i+1},..,k_{j-1},k_j-1,k_{j+1},..,k_n|t)\mu_i q_{i,j}$$

Assume that $\pi(k_1,k_2,...,k_n)=\prod_{i=1}^{M}(1-\rho_i)\rho_i^{k_i}$, substituting this into Equation 7.1, one can deduce that:

$$\sum_{j=1}^{M}(\lambda_{0,j}+\mu_j)=\sum_{j=1}^{M}\frac{\lambda_{0,j}}{\rho_j}+\sum_{j=1}^{M}\rho_j\mu_j q_{j,0}+\sum_{i=1}^{M}\sum_{j=1}^{M}\frac{\rho_i}{\rho_j}\mu_i q_{i,j}.$$

Identifying each term would give:

- $\sum_{j=1}^{M}\frac{\lambda_{0,j}}{\rho_j}=\sum_{j=1}^{M}\frac{\lambda_{0,j}\mu_j}{\lambda_j}\rho_j q_{j,0}$

- $\sum_{j=1}^{M}\rho_j\mu_j q_{j,0}=\sum_{i=1}^{M}(1-\sum_{j=1}^{M}q)=\sum_{i=1}^{M}\lambda_i-\sum_{i=1}^{M}\sum_{j=1}^{M}\lambda_i q_{i,j}=\sum_{i=1}^{M}\lambda_{0,i}$

- $\sum_{i=1}^{M}\sum_{j=1}^{M}\frac{\rho_i}{\rho_j}\mu_i q_{i,j}=\sum_{j=1}^{M}(\frac{\mu_j}{\lambda_j}\sum_{i=1}^{M}\lambda_i q_{i,j})=\sum_{j=1}^{M}\frac{\mu_j}{\lambda_j}(\lambda_j-\lambda_{0,j})=\sum_{j=1}^{M}\mu_j-\sum_{j=1}^{M}\frac{\mu_j\lambda_{0,j}}{\lambda_j}$

Replacing these terms back into previous equation $(\lambda = \sum_{j=1}^{M} \lambda_{0,j} = \sum_{j=1}^{M} \lambda_j q_{j,0})$ gives the following perfect identity, which completes the proof of the theorem:

$$\sum_{j=1}^{M} \lambda_{0,j} + \sum_{j=1}^{M} \mu_j = \sum_{j=1}^{M} \frac{\mu_j \lambda_{0,j}}{\lambda_j} + \sum_{j=1}^{M} \lambda_{0,j} + \sum_{j=1}^{M} \mu_j - \sum_{j=1}^{M} \frac{\mu_j \lambda_{0,j}}{\lambda_j}$$

A particular consequence can be deduced from Jackson's theorem related to the fact that a Jackson network satisfies the local balance property:

$$\mu_i \pi(k_1, k_2, ..., k_n) = \lambda_i \pi(k_1, .., k_{i-1}, k_i + 1, k_{i+1}, .., k_n)$$

This can easily be checked using $\lambda_i = \rho_i \mu_i$ for all $1 \le i \le N$.

**Example:** Let us consider the open queueing network depicted by Figure 7.3, where two nodes are considered (representing the CPU and an I/O device)

One can deduce that $\lambda_1 = \lambda + \lambda_2$ and $\lambda_2 = q\lambda_1$. This determines $\lambda_1$ and $\lambda_2$ as given by:

$$\lambda_1 = \frac{\lambda}{1-q}, \lambda_2 = \frac{\lambda q}{1-q}.$$

Using the fact that $\rho_i = \frac{\lambda_i}{\mu_i}$, for $i = 1,2$, and $\pi(k_1, k_2) = (1 - \rho_1)\rho_1^{k_1}(1 - \rho_2)\rho_2^{k_2}$, we can determine the major performance parameters. The mean number of customers and the mean waiting time, for example, are given by:

- Mean number of customers at node $i$: $E(C_i) = \dfrac{\rho_i}{1 - \rho_i}$

- Mean waiting time at node $i$: $E(W_i) = E(T_i) - \dfrac{1}{\mu_i} = \dfrac{1}{\mu_i}\dfrac{\rho_i}{1 - \rho_i}$

Let us now consider the problem of minimizing the mean number of customers $N$ in the queueing network or, equivalently, the mean time $T$ spent by customers in the network. Assume that the capacities $\mu_i$ can be freely chosen except for the constraint (e.g., cost constraint) $\sum_{i=1}^{M} \mu_i = A$. The problem is

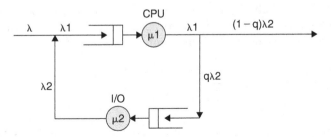

**FIGURE 7.3.** An open queueing network.

equivalent to finding a minimum of:

$$E(C) = \sum_{i=1}^{M} E(C_i) = \sum_{i=1}^{M} \frac{\lambda_i}{\mu_i - \lambda_i}.$$

This can be achieved by considering the following function:

$$f(\mu, \lambda, x) = \sum_{i=1}^{M} \frac{\lambda_i}{\mu_i - \lambda_i} + \left( \sum_{i=1}^{M} \mu_i - A \right)$$

When considering $\frac{\partial f}{\partial \mu_i} = 0$, one can deduce that $\mu_i = \lambda_i + \left(\frac{\lambda_i}{x}\right)^{1/2}$. By inserting this expression into the expression of the constraint, one can obtain:

$$\frac{1}{\sqrt{x}} = \frac{A - \sum\limits_{j=1}^{M} \lambda_j}{\sum\limits_{j=1}^{M} \sqrt{\lambda_j}}.$$

Consequently, we have:

$$\mu_i = \lambda_i + \frac{\sqrt{\lambda_i}}{\sum\limits_{j=1}^{M} \sqrt{\lambda_j}} \left(A - \sum_{j=1}^{M} \lambda_j\right).$$

## 7.4   CLOSED QUEUEING NETWORKS

A closed queueing network consists of $M$ nodes. In contrast to an open network, there is no external source or sink. A constant population of $K$ customers is in the network. Since no customer can enter or leave the network, the arrival $\lambda_i$ for node $i = 1,...,N$ of a closed network is computed using the following equations:

$$\lambda_i = \sum_{j=1}^{N} \lambda_j p_{j,i}$$

where $p_{j,i}$ is the probability that a customer leaves node $j$ to join node $i$. The mean number of visits (or visit ratio) $e_i$, at node $i = 1,...,N$, can also be computed directly using the routing probabilities $p_{i,j}$. This gives a set of $n$ equations:

$$e_i = \sum e_j p_{j,i}, \text{for} i = 1, \ldots, N.$$

The system described by above equation has only $N-1$ independent homogeneous linear equations in closed networks. The visit ratios, therefore, can only be determined up to a constant factor, for example $e_1$. These visit ratios are determined assuming that $e_1 = 1$.

The probabilities $\pi_i((k_1, ..., k_N)$ that node $i$ ( $= 1,...,N$) contains exactly $k_i$ customers, assuming that the closed network contain $K$ customers, is given by:

$$\pi_i(k) = \sum_{\substack{k_1+..+k_N=K \\ k_i=k}} \pi(k_1, .., k_N).$$

Knowing the value $\pi_i(k)$ will help the determination of the performance parameters in a way similar to that used in open queueing networks.

**Example:** Consider a closed queueing network containing two nodes (node 1 and node 2) and serving $m$ customers (as described in Figure 7.4). The system of equations to compute the steady-state probability vector says that the flow of departures from a state is equal to the flow of arrivals to that state. This conservation property, which is written as:

$$\sum_{j \in S} \pi_j(m)q_{j,i} = \pi_i(m) \sum_{j \in S} q_{i,j}$$

where $S$ is the state space and $m = (m_1, m_2)$ is a state, shows the following three cases based on the different values of $(m_1, m_2)$:

- $\pi(m, 0)\mu_1 - \pi(m-1, 1)\mu_2 = 0$ or $\pi(m, 0) = \pi(m-1, 1)$
- $-\pi(1, m-1)\mu_1 + \pi(0, m)\mu_2 = 0$ or $\pi(1, m-1) = \pi(0, m)$
- $\pi(m_1, m_2)(\mu_1 + \mu_2) - \pi(m_1 + 1, m_2 - 1)\mu_1 - \pi(m_1 - 1, m_2 + 1)\mu_2 = 0$

    $2\pi(m_1, m_2) - \pi(m_1 - 1, m_2 + 1) = \pi(m_1 + 1, m_2 - 1)$, for $m_1 \neq 0$ and $m_2 \neq 0$

In addition, a numerical resolution shows that a unique solution can be determined knowing the values of $\mu_1$ and $\mu_2$. Once the steady state is known, the other performance measures can be determined. For example, the mean number of customers, the mean response times, throughput, and utilizations are given by:

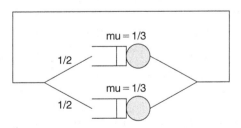

**FIGURE 7.4.** Example of a closed Jackson network.

- Mean number of customers: $E(M_1) = \sum_{j=1}^{M} j\pi_1(j)$ and $E(M_2) = \sum_{j=1}^{M} j\pi_2(j)$
- Mean response time: $E(T_1) = \frac{E(M_1)}{\lambda_1}$ and $E(T_2) = \frac{E(M_2)}{\lambda_2}$
- Throughput: $\lambda = \lambda_1 = \lambda_2 = \rho_1\mu_1 = \rho_2\mu_2$
- Utilization: $\rho_1 = 1 - \pi_1(0)$ and $\rho_2 = 1 - \pi_2(0)$

## 7.4.1 The Closed Jackson Networks

A closed queueing network is called a closed Jackson network (representing a production of $N$ workstations [9], serving one type of customers) if the following assumptions are true:

1. The probabilities of arrivals from "outside" to node $i$ and departures from node $i$ are equal to zero ($\lambda_{0,i} = 0$ and $\lambda_{i,0} = 0$).
2. Service times for each server at node $i$ are independent, exponentially distributed with mean $1/\mu_i$ and the processing order is FCFS.
3. The probability of moving from node $i$ to node $j$ (after the service at node $i$ is completed) is $P_{i,j}$ and it is state-independent.

Let us assume that there are $m$ customers moving among the $N$ nodes. The routing of customers through the network is Markovian. When the service at node $i$ is completed, the customer joins the queue in front of server $j$, $j = 1$, $2,\ldots,k$ with probability $P_{i,j}$, and $\sum_{j=1}^{N} P_{i,j} = 1$. Let $P$ denote the matrix of routing probabilities $P_{i,j}$. We assume that $P$ is irreducible, meaning that a customer can reach from each node any other node in one or more transitions.

Since the processing times are assumed to be exponential and the routing is Markovian, this network can be described by a Markov process with states $k = (k_1,..,k_N)$, where $k_i$ denotes the number of customers in workstation $i$. The possible states are the ones for which $k > 0$ and $\sum_{j=1}^{N} k_j = M$.

This means that the number of possible states is finite since it is equal to the binomial coefficients:

$$\binom{N+K-1}{N-1} = \frac{k!(N-1)!}{(N+k-1)!}$$

Let $\pi(k)$ denote the equilibrium probability of state $k$. By equating the flow out of and into state $k$, we obtain:

$$\pi(k_1, k_2, ..., k_n) \sum_{j=1}^{M} \mu_j$$

$$= \sum_{i=1}^{M} \sum_{j=1}^{M} \pi(k_1, .., k_{i-1}, k_i + 1, k_{i+1}, .., k_{j-1}, k_j - 1, k_{j+1}, .., k_n) \mu_i q_{i,j}$$

A product form solution can be found under the form:

$$\pi(k_1, k_2, ..., k_n) = C x_1^{k_1} x_2^{k_2} ... x_N^{k_N}$$

Substitution of this form into the balance equation gives that the $x_i$'s should satisfy:

$$x_i \mu_i = \sum_{j=1}^{N} x_j \mu_j P_{j,i}.$$

Setting $e_i = x_i \mu_i$ gives the following system of equations:

$$\begin{cases} e_j = \sum_{i=1}^{N} e_i P_{i,j}, \quad j = 1, .., N \\ \sum_{j=1}^{N} P_{i,j} = 1. \end{cases}$$

It is clear that $e_i$ can be interpreted as the relative visiting frequency or relative arrival rate to node $i$. The above set of equations does not have a unique solution, and therefore, we have to add a normalization equation, such as $e_1 = 1$. Thus, $e_1$ denotes the mean number of times a customer has to visit node $i$ before returning to node 1. Therefore, we will have:

$$\pi(k_1, k_2, ..., k_n) = C \left(\frac{e_1}{\mu_1}\right)^{k_1} \left(\frac{e_2}{\mu_2}\right)^{k_2} ... \left(\frac{e_N}{\mu_N}\right)^{k_N}.$$

The state description of the multiple customer-type system is more complex than the single-customer type system that we just described. The state vector $k = (k_1, ..., k_N)$, where $k_i$ denotes a subvector describing the (aggregate) situation at workstation $m$; that is, $k_i = (k_{i,1}, .., k_{i,N})$ with $k_{i,r}$ indicating the number of type $r$ customers in node $i$. It is worth noticing that the stochastic process with state $k$ is not a Markov process. To predict the future at time $t$, we actually have to know the exact order of customers at each node in addition to their number because the routing is customer-type dependent.

Let $e_{i,r}$ be the relative visiting frequency of type $r$ customers to node $i$. For each customer of type $r$, the frequencies $e_{1,r}, e_{2,r}, .., e_{N,r}$ satisfy the following set of equations:

$$e_{j,r} = \sum_{i=1}^{N} e_{i,r} P_{i,j}^r, \quad j = 1, .., N.$$

Assuming that $e_{1,r} = 1$, this system of equation has a unique solution. Therefore, it can be stated that the equilibrium equation still has a product form:

$$\pi(k_1, k_2, ..., k_n) = C\pi_1(k_1)...\pi_N(k_1)$$

where

$$\pi_i(k_i) = \frac{(\sum_{j=1}^{N} k_{i,j})!}{\prod_{j=1}^{N} (k_{i,j}!)} \prod_{j=1}^{N} (\frac{e_{i,j}}{\mu_i})^{k_{i,j}}$$

Let us write $C = 1/G(M,K)$; then $G(M,K)$ should guarantee that $\{p(n)\}$ is a valid probability distribution. This shows that:

$$G(M, K) = \sum_{n_1+..+n_M=M} \prod_{i=1}^{K} \rho^{n_i}.$$

An iterative computation of $G(M,K)$ is performed using the following steps:

1. For any $m$ and $k$ $(m = 0,..., M; k = 1,..., K)$, define:

$$G(m, k) = \sum_{n_1+..+n_M=m} \prod_{i=1}^{k} \rho_i^{n_i}$$

2. For a closed network of single-server queues, $G(M,K)$ can be computed iteratively using the following recursive relation:

$$G(m, k) = G(m, k - 1) + \rho_k G(m - 1, k)$$

For the boundary conditions, we can write:

$$G(m, 1) = \rho_1^m, \quad G(0, k) = 1, \text{ for } m = 0, 1, ..., M \text{ and } k + 1, 2, ..., K.$$

The above recursive equation can be stated easily. In fact, for $k > 0$, we can split $G(m,k)$ into two sums over disjoint sets of states corresponding to $n_k = 0$ and $n_k > 0$. This gives:

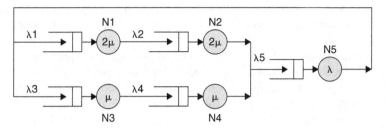

**FIGURE 7.5.** Example of a closed product form network.

$$G(m,k) = \sum_{\substack{n_1+..+n_M=m}} \prod_{i=1}^{k} \rho_i^{n_i} = \sum_{\substack{n_1+..+n_M=m \\ n_k=0}} \prod_{i=1}^{k} \rho_i^{n_i} + \sum_{\substack{n_1+..+n_M=m \\ n_k>0}} \prod_{i=1}^{k} \rho_i^{n_i}$$

$$G(m,k) = \sum_{\substack{n_1+..+n_M=m}} \prod_{i=1}^{k-1} \rho_i^{n_i} + \sum_{\substack{n_1+..+n_M=m \\ n_k>0}} \prod_{i=1}^{k} \rho_i^{n_i}$$

The first sum in the right term is obviously $G(m, k_{-1})$. Finally, observing that $n_k > 0$, one can define a new variable $n'_k$, such that $n_k = n'_k + 1$, and show the second sum is equal to $\rho_k G(m-1,k)$.

**Example:** Let us consider the queueing network depicted by Figure 7.5 where

$$\lambda_1 = \lambda_2 = \lambda_3 = \lambda_4, \quad \lambda_5 = \lambda_1 + \lambda_2, \quad \rho = \frac{\lambda}{\mu}$$

$$\rho_1 = \rho_2 = \frac{\lambda_1}{2\mu}, \quad \rho_3 = \rho_4 = \frac{\lambda_3}{\mu}, \quad \rho_5 = \frac{\lambda_3}{\lambda}$$

Letting $\lambda_1 = 2\mu$, we deduce that:

$$\rho_1 = \rho_2 = 1, \quad \rho_3 = \rho_4 = 2, \quad \rho_5 = 4/\rho.$$

The computation of $G(2,2)$, for example, based on the iterative algorithm using these values, can be performed, which gives:

$$G(m,1) = \rho_1^m, \quad G(0,k) = 1, G(1,2) = 2, G(1,3) = 4, \text{ and } G(2,2) = 3$$

## 7.5  PRODUCT FORM NETWORKS

The closed Jackson queueing networks and open Jackson networks have the particular feature that steady-state probability of these networks can be expressed as the product of the state probabilities of the individual nodes. This property is very important because it allows for determining a solution for the steady-state probability without generating the underlying state space. Queueing networks that have this property are referred to as product form networks [7, 14].

Early in the 1960s, Jackson [8, 9] introduced product form queueing network models for open exponential networks. On the other hand, Gordon and Newell [15] discussed several assumptions on the model characteristics and provided a simple closed form expression of the stationary state distribution and some average performance indices. The class of product form models was extended to include various interesting and useful characteristics to represent more complex systems. These features include different types of customers of the networks, various queueing disciplines, state-dependent service rate, state-dependent routing between the service centers, and some constraints on the population of subnetworks. One of the most important results concerning product form queueing networks was introduced by Basket, Chandy, Muntz, and Palacios (BCMP) [3], and known as BCMP theorem. It defines the well-known class of BCMP queueing networks with product form solution for open, closed, or mixed models with multiple classes of customers and various service disciplines and service time distributions.

The stationary state distribution is expressed as the product of the distributions of the single queues with appropriate parameters and, for closed networks, with normalization constant. An important property of queueing networks with product form is the arrival theorem, which states that the distribution at arrival times at a node is identical to the distribution at arbitrary times of the same network, for open networks, and of a network with one less customer for closed networks [16]. This induced the definition of a series of recurrence equations between average performance measure for closed networks from which we derived a recursive computational algorithm, the mean value analysis (MVA [17]), that avoids the direct computation of the normalization constant.

Product form queueing networks provide detailed results and operational analysis in terms of performance indices such as queue length distribution, average response time, resource utilization, and throughput. These performance indices are evaluated for each component and for the overall network. Product form network analysis is based on a set of assumptions on the system parameters that leads to a closed form expression of the stationary state distribution.

### 7.5.1  Local Balance

Numerical techniques operating on the global balance equations can derive the steady-state solution. These equations balance the rate at which customers leave a state with the rate at which they enter that state. The problem in solving numerically the global balance is that the number of equations increases tremendously with the number of states and can reach high complexity.

To reduce the computational efforts, another set of balance equations can be set up. To this end, two sets of balance properties have been defined [6]:

1. *The local balance property*: This property means that the departure rate from a state of the queueing network caused by the departure of one customer from node *i* equals the arrival rate to this state because of an arrival of a customer to that node.

2. *The station balance property*: A service discipline is said to have station-balance property if the service rates at which the customers in a position of the queue are served are proportional to the probability that a customer enters this position.

With the local balance property, one can say that the rate at which customers enter a single node of the network is equal to the rate at which they leave it. With the station balance property, one can state that the queue of a node is partitioned into positions and the rate at which a customer enters this position is equal to the rate at which the customer leaves this position. It has been shown that each of these properties can be considered as sufficient (but not necessary) conditions for the existence of a unique product - form solution of the system of global balance.

Let us consider the development made in [5] to develop a formal description of the local balance property. For this, we assume that the queueing network can be represented by a continuous Markov chain with a state space $S$. A state $n$ of the system is a vector $n = (n_1,...,n_k)$, where $n_i$ is the number of customers at node *i*. A transition from state $n$ to state $n'$ is determined by three vectors: the vector of remaining customers, say $m$; the vector of leaving customer from the state say $g$; and the set of entering customer to set $n'$, meaning that:

$$n = m + g, \text{ and } n' = m + g'.$$

We denote such a transition by $q(m,g,g')$. The transition rate from $n$ to $n'$ is then given by:

$$q(n, n') = \sum_{\substack{m+g=n \\ m+g'=n'}} q(m, g, g').$$

In addition, in a transition from $n$ to $n'$, the routing groups $g$ and $g'$ are completely determined if $m$ is fixed. Let us assume that the Markov chain is irreducible, there is a unique stationary distribution $\pi$, and $q(n)$ is uniformly bounded by a constant $C$ (i.e., $q(n) < c$, for all $n$). Based on these assumptions, the distribution is stationary if and only if for all state $m + g$, we have:

$$\pi(n) \sum_{\substack{m,g':m+g=n \\ g \neq g'}} q(m, g, g') = \sum_{\substack{m,g':m+g=n \\ g \neq g'}} \pi(m + g')q(m, g, g').$$

Distribution $\pi$ (or the related queueing network) satisfies the group local balance property if for all states the following equality is satisfied:

$$\pi(m+g)\sum_{g'\neq g}q(m,g,g') = \sum_{m,g'\neq g}\pi(m+g')q(m,g,g')$$

In addition, $\pi$ satisfies the local balance property if groups $g$ and $g'$ occurring in the preceding equality satisfy the equation:

$$\sum_{i=1}^{K}g_i = \sum_{i=1}^{K}g_i' = 1$$

Obviously, group local balance property is a generalization of local balance property. For the rest of this section, we will only focus on the local balance property. However, the product form solution that will be discussed for networks satisfying the local balance property applies to the group local balance property [5].

### 7.5.2  The BCMP Networks

The results obtained for Jacksons networks have been extended in [3] to queueing networks having several customer classes, different queueing strategies, and generally distributed service times. They are called BCMP networks and can be open, closed, or mixed. The BCMP networks fulfill the following assumptions in the case of the FIFO queueing discipline (different assumptions are stated for the three other disciplines):

- Distribution of the service times: The services times should be exponentially distributed and class independent ($\mu_{i,1} = \mu_{i,2} = \ldots = \mu_{i,R}$).
- Local-dependent service rates: The service rate of a node is only allowed to depend on the number of customers at this node.
- Arrival processes: If the network is open, the arrival process is Poisson where all customers arrive at the network from one source with an overall arrival rate $\lambda$ ($\lambda$ can depend on the number of customers in the network). The arriving process of customers of class $r$ to node $i$ is assumed to be distributed according to probability $P_{0,i,r}$ such that:

$$\sum_{i=1}^{N}\sum_{j=1}^{R}p_{0,i,r} = 1$$

For the sake of clarity, we made the choice to not describe the assumptions related to the three remaining disciplines. In addition, we have not considered the case where the arrival process consists of U Poisson flows with the FIFO queueing discipline. However, it is worth noticing that the first assumption does not apply for the three aforementioned disciplines, meaning that a node implementing one of the three disciplines can have any kind of service time discipline and the service rate for a particular class of customers can depend on the number of that class. In addition, one can state that these assumptions lead to four product form node types and the local balance property. The types are referred to as follows:

*Type-1*: -/M/m – FIFO
*Type-1*: -/G/2 – LIFO-PR
*Type-2*: -/G/3 – PS
*Type-3*: -/G/? – IS

where PR stands for PRiority queue, PS stands for Processor Sharing queue and IS stands for Infinite Server queue.
**BCMP theorem** Version 1: The steady-state probabilities of a BCMP closed network have the following product form:

$$\pi(k) = \frac{1}{G(K)} \prod_{i=1}^{N} F_i(S_i)$$

where $G$ is a normalizing constant, $N$ is the number of nodes, $S = (S_1, \ldots, S_N)$ is the global state, $S_i = (k_{i,1}, \ldots, k_{i,R})$ is the state of node $i$, $K$ is the total number of customers, and $F_i(S_i)$ is a function that depends on the type and state of each node. Functions $G(K)$ and $F_i(S_i)$ are given by

$$G(K) = \sum_{\substack{N \\ \sum_{i=1} S_i = K}} \prod_{i=1}^{N} F_i(S_i)$$

$$F_i(S_i) = \begin{cases} (k_i)! \frac{1}{\beta_i(k_i)} \cdot \left(\frac{1}{\mu_i}\right)^{k_i} \prod_{r=1}^{R} \frac{1}{(k_{i,r})!} \cdot e_{i,r}^{k_{i,r}} & \text{type 1} \\[3mm] (k_i)! \prod_{r=1}^{R} \frac{1}{(k_{i,r})!} \left(\frac{e_{i,r}}{\mu_{i,r}}\right)^{k_{i,r}} & \text{type 2, 3} \\[3mm] \prod_{r=1}^{R} \frac{1}{(k_{i,r})!} \left(\frac{e_{i,r}}{\mu_{i,r}}\right)^{k_{i,r}} & \text{type 4} \end{cases}$$

where $k_i = \sum_{r=1}^{R} k_{i,r}$ represents the total number of customers of all classes at node $i$, $e_{i,r}$ is the visit ratio, and $\beta_i(k_i)$ is given by:

$$\beta_i(k_i) = \begin{cases} k_i! & m_i \geq k_i \\ m_i! . (m_i)^{k_i - m_i} & m_i \leq k_i \\ 1 & m_i = 1 \end{cases}$$

**BCMP theorem** Version 2: The steady-state probabilities of the **BCMP** open network, under a load- independent arrival, have the following product form:

$$\pi(k_1,..,k_N) = \prod_{i=1}^{N} \pi_i(k_i)$$

where

$$k_i = \sum_{r=1}^{R} k_{i,r}$$

represents the total number of customers of all classes at node $i$ and $\pi_i(k_i)$ is given by:

$$\pi_i(k_i) = \begin{cases} (1 - \rho_i)\rho_i^{k_i} & \text{for type 1, 2, 3} \\ e^{-\rho_i}\frac{\rho_i^{k_i}}{k_i!} & \text{for type 4.} \end{cases}$$

Also, we have:

$$\rho_i = \sum_{r=1}^{R} \rho_{i,r} \text{ with}$$

$$\rho_{i,r} = \begin{cases} \lambda_r \frac{e_{i,r}}{\mu_i} & \text{type 1} \\ \lambda_r \frac{e_{i,r}}{\mu_{i,r}} & \text{type 2, 3, 4.} \end{cases}$$

**Proof of the BCMP theorem**:
The proof of this theorem is very complex. We give here the basic idea used for BCMP of type 1. A complete solution can be found in several places, including [3]. To find a solution for the steady-state probabilities $\pi(S)$, the following global balance equations have to be solved:

$$\pi(S)\begin{bmatrix} \text{State transition rate} \\ \text{from state S} \end{bmatrix} = \sum_{S'} \pi(S')\begin{bmatrix} \text{State transition rate} \\ \text{from state S' to state S} \end{bmatrix}$$

with the normalization condition:

$$\sum_{S} \pi(S) = 1.$$

Inserting the equation provided in the BCMP theorem in the above equations can lead to a system of local balance equations [17].

## 7.6  MEAN VALUE ANALYSIS

Mean value analysis (MVA) has been developed by Reiser and Lavenberg for the analysis of closed networks with product form solution [18]. The MVA is based on two laws:

- The Little's theorem [13]: This law expresses, as stated in Chapter 2, a relation among the mean number of customers, the throughput, and the mean response time of a node or the overall system.
- The Arrival theorem [19]: This theorem applies for all networks admitting a product form solution. It states, for example, that in an open network a customer entering any queue sees the same state probabilities (the probability the system is in a state just before the arrival) are the same as the equilibrium probabilities p(n).

At first we discuss the proof of arrival theorem. Consider first an open network with product form solution. Assume we have a customer transiting from queue $i$ to queue $j$. Insert between these queues a virtual queue 0 with a very high service rate $\mu_0$. In the limit $\mu \to \infty$, it is clear that the added queue has no effect on the system performance because customers transiting from queue $i$ to queue $j$ will spend an infinitesimal time in the added virtual queue. The virtual queue, however, enables "catching" the transiting customer. The transition occurs precisely in the short interval when there is a customer in queue 0, i.e., when $N_0(t) = 1$. The state distribution seen by the transiting customer is the distribution of the other queues conditioned on $N_0 = 1$.

Now make use of the fact that the extended system also is a Jackson network with a product form solution. Denote the state vector of the extended system by $n'$; i.e. $n' = (n_0, n_1, ..., n_M)$. Then, the following holds:

$$\pi(n') = \pi(N' = n') = \prod_{i=0}^{M} \pi_i(n_i)$$

The theorem is stated when showing that $\pi(N_1 = n_1, ..., N_M = n_M | N_0 = n_0) = \pi(n)$. This can be deduced from the following:

$$\pi(N_1 = n_1, ..., N_M = n_M \Big| N_0 = 1) = \frac{\pi(N_0 = 1, N_1 = n_1, ..., N_M = n_M)}{\pi(N_0 = 1)} = \pi(n)$$

Let us consider in the sequel closed Jackson networks. Then we have the following results listed under the form of propositions.

*Proposition 1.* In a closed Jackson network with $M$ customers and normalization function occurring in the product form solution denoted by $G(M)$, we have the following:

1. The probability that at steady - state, the number of customers in station $j$ greater than or equal to $m$ is:

$$P\{n_i \geq m\} = \rho_j^m \frac{G(M-m)}{G(M)}, 0 \leq m \leq M.$$

2. The probability that in steady state there are $m$ customers at station $j$ is:

$$P\{n_j = m\} = \rho_j^m \frac{G(M-m) - \rho_i G(M-m-1)}{G(M)}, 0 \leq m \leq M.$$

3. The average number of customers and the average throughput of queue $j$ are given by:

$$N_j(M) = \sum_{m=1}^{M} \rho_j^m \frac{G(M-m)}{G(M)} \quad \text{and} \quad \gamma_j(M) = \lambda_j \frac{G(M-m)}{G(M)}.$$

**Proof.** Property 1 can be deduced by computing $P\{n_j > m\}$, for $0 \leq m \leq M$. This gives:

$$P\{n_j > m\} = \sum_{\substack{n_1 + .. + n_K = M \\ n_j \geq m}} \frac{\rho_1^{n_1} .... \rho_K^{n_K}}{G(M)}$$

$$= \frac{\rho_1^{n_1}}{G(M)} \sum_{\substack{n_1 + .. + n_K = M \\ n_j \geq 0}} \rho_1^{n_1} .... \rho_K^{n_K} = \frac{\rho_1^{n_1}}{G(M)} G(M-m)$$

The second, third, and fourth properties can be deduced easily by considering that:

$$P\{n_j = m\} = P\{n_j \geq m\}\_P\{n_j \geq m+1\}$$

$$N_j(M) = E(n_j) = \sum_{m=1}^{M} P\{n_j \geq m\}$$

$$\gamma_j(M) = \mu_j P\{n_j \geq 1\}$$

**Example:** Consider the tandem network depicted in Figure 7.6 where we assume that: $\lambda_1 = ... = \lambda_K = 1$ and $\lambda_1 = \mu$. This shows that $\lambda_i = 1$ for all $i$. Then $G(M)$ and $\pi(n)$ can be computed for all states $n$.

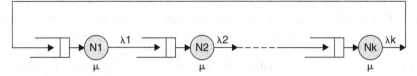

**FIGURE 7.6.** A k-station cyclic network.

$$G(M) = \sum_{n_1+..+n_K=M} \rho_1^{n_1} \cdots \rho_K^{n_K}$$

$$= \sum_{\substack{n_1+..+n_K=M \\ n_j \geq 0}} 1 = \frac{(M+K-1)!}{M!(K-1)!}$$

$$\pi(n) = \frac{1}{G(n)} \prod_{j=1}^{K} \rho_j^{n_j} = \frac{M!(K-1)!}{(M+K-1)!}.$$

For queue $j$, using Proposition 1, we can deduce the average throughput $\gamma_j(M)$, the mean number of customers $N_i(M)$, and the mean time delay $T_j(M)$. For example, we have:

$$\gamma_j(M) = \lambda_j \frac{G(M-m)}{G(M)} = \mu \frac{(M+K-2)!}{(M-1)!(K-1)!} \times \frac{M!(K-1)!}{(M+K-1)!} = \frac{M}{M+K-1}$$

Let us now consider the use of the Arrival theorem with closed Jackson networks.

***Theorem*** (Arrival theorem): In a closed Jackson network with $M$ customers, the occupancy distribution seen by a customer upon arrival at queue $j$ is the same as the occupancy distribution in a closed network with the arriving customer removed.

**Proof.** A reading of the theorem shows that in a closed network with $M$ customers, the expected number of customers found upon arrival by a customer at queue $j$ is equal to the average number of customers at queue $j$, when the total number of customers in the closed network is $M-1$. This means, for example, that an arriving customer sees the system at a state that does not include itself.

Now, let us consider the computation of performance measures in the presence of $M$ customers:

- $Nj(M)$: Average number of customers in queue $j$.
- $Tj(M)$: Average time a customer spends (per visit) in queue $j$.
- $\gamma j(M)$: Average throughput of queue $j$.

MVA allows the calculation $Nj(M)$ and $Tj(M)$ *directly*, without the need for computing $G(M)$ or deriving the stationary distribution of the network. An iterative computation can be performed to determine $Nj(M)$ and $Tj(M)$. Using the Arrival theorem, one can show that the expected number of customers that an arrival finds at queue $j$ is $Nj(m-1)$. Since the service rate for all customers at the queue is $\mu j$, we have:

$$T_j(m) = \frac{1 + N_j(m-1)}{\mu_j}, j = 1, \ldots, K, m = 1, \ldots, M$$

On the other hand, the throughput $\gamma_j(m)$ is directly derived from

$$\gamma_j(M) = \lambda_j \frac{G(M-m)}{G(M)}$$

Using Little's theorem, we can say that:

$$N_j(m) = \gamma_j(m) T_j(m) = \lambda_j \frac{G(M-m)}{G(M)} T_j(m), \ m = 1, \ldots, M$$

Knowing that $m = \sum_{i=1}^{K} N_i(m)$, gives us the following expression:

$$m = \sum_{i=1}^{K} N_i(m) = \sum_{i=1}^{K} \lambda_i \frac{G(M-m)}{G(M)} T_i(m) = \frac{G(M-m)}{G(M)} \left( \sum_{i=1}^{K} \lambda_i T_i(m) \right)$$

Then $\frac{G(M-m)}{G(M)}$ can be derived by:

$$\frac{G(M-m)}{G(M)} = \frac{m}{\sum_{i=1}^{K} \lambda_i T_i(m)}.$$

Therefore, we can deduce that the throughput of and mean number of customers at node $j$ is equal to:

$$\gamma_j(M) = \frac{m\lambda_j}{\sum_{i=1}^{K} \lambda_i T_i(m)}, N_j(m) = \frac{m\lambda_j T_j(m)}{\sum_{i=1}^{K} \lambda_i T_i(m)}$$

## 7.7    ANALYSIS USING FLOW EQUIVALENT SERVERS

The flow equivalent server (FES) method is based on the Norton's theorem that has been established for electronic circuits [20]. It represents a good tool for the exact analysis of product form closed networks and their approximation analysis. The main idea behind the FES method is the reduction of the queueing network based on the selection of a set $\Lambda$ of subnetworks that partitions the original network and combines all the nodes of each subnetwork into a flow equivalent server, while guaranteeing that the reduced network has the same behavior as the original network. The reduced queueing network is easier to analyze. Two cases are considered: (a) two subnetworks are selected ($|\Lambda| = 2$), and (b) more than two subnetworks are selected.

### 7.7.1 The Case $|\Lambda| = 2$ and One Subnetwork is Reduced to One Node

Assume that the closed network serves $K$ jobs, to determine the service rates $\mu_{c,k}$ of the FES node $c$, the selected node, say node 1, is short circuited by setting the mean service time in that node to zero. The throughput $\lambda_{1,k}^{sc}$ in the short-circuit path with job $k$, for $k \leq K$, is computed as a function of the number of jobs using one of the product-form solutions provided in the preceding sections. Then, we construct an equivalent reduced network consisting only of the selected node, node 1, and the FES node (cyclic or tandem network). The visit ratios in both nodes are set equal to the original ratio $e_1$. The load-dependent service rate of node $c$ is the throughput along the short-circuit path when there are $k$ jobs in the network Thus:

$$\mu_{c,k} = \lambda_{1,k}^{sc}, \ 1 \leq k \leq K.$$

Figure 7.7 depicts graphically the reduction of a given closed network with four nodes.

***The case*** $|\Lambda| > 1.$ The reduction of a closed product form network when more than one is selected assumes that the network is partitioned into several subnetworks. The reduction allows the analysis of the subnetworks independently from each other. A subnetwork $j$ is analyzed by short-circuiting the nodes that do not occur in that subnetwork. The computed throughputs of the short-circuited network, associated with subnetwork $j$, define the load-dependent service rates of FES node $j$.

The FES approach is achieved using a four-step procedure:

- In a first step, the original network is divided into $M$ subnetworks.
- During the second step, a short-circuited network is built and analyzed for each subnetwork. The short-circuited network associated with subnetwork

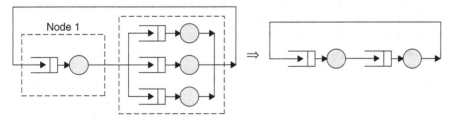

**FIGURE 7.7.** Reduction of a closed product form network.

*j* is denoted by the SC-*j* network. It is obtained by short-circuiting all nodes that do not belong to subnetwork *j*. The analysis is made using any product-form algorithm.

- In the third step, subnetwork *j* is replaced by a unique node, called FES node *j*, and an equivalent reduced network is built using the original network and the new nodes. The load service rates of the FES node *j* are set equal to the throughputs of subnetwork *j*, for $j = 1, ..., M$.
- During the forth step, the normalizing constant of the reduced network is set identical to the convolution product of the normalizing constant of the constituting networks. The performance metrics/measures of the original network are then computed.

## 7.8  SUMMARY

This chapter has dealt with using queueing networks in the analysis of computer and communication systems. The product form networks have been discussed, and the mean value analysis has been presented. The Jackson and BCMP networks are also analyzed and investigated. The analysis using (FES) also has been discussed. Various examples have been presented and explained to show the applicability of the presented theorems and concepts.

## REFERENCES

[1] L. Kleinrock, "Queueing systems, Volume I: Theory," Wiley, New York, 1975.

[2] L. Kleinrock, "Queueing systems, Volume II: Computer Applications," Wiley, New York, 1976.

[3] S. Balsamo, and V. De Nitto Personè, "A Survey of Product-Form Queueing Networks with Blocking and Their Equivalences," Annws of Operation Research Vol. 48, pp. 31–61, 1994.

[4] S. Balsamo, V. De Nitto Personè, and R. Onvural, "Analysis of Queueuing Networks with Blocking," Springer, Dordrecht, The Nether lands, 2001.

[5] R. Boucherie, and N. M. Van Dijk, "Product Forms for Queueing Networks with State-Dependent Multiple Job Transistions," Advance in Applied. Probability, Vol. 23, pp. 152–187, 1991.

[6] K. Chandy, J. Howard, and D. Towsley, "Product Form and Local Balance in Queueing Networks," Journal of the ACM, Vol. 24, No. 2, pp. 250–263, 1977.

[7] N. M. Dijk, "Queueing Networks and Product Forms," Wiley, New York, 1993.

[8] J. R. Jackson, "Networks of Waiting Lines," The Journal of Operations Research Society of America Vol. 5, pp. 518–521, 1957.

[9] J. R. Jackson, "Jobshop-Like Queueing Systems," Management Science, Vol. 10, pp. 131–142, 1963.

[10] R. D. Nelson, "The Mathematics of Product Form Queuing Networks," ACM Computing Surveys, Vol. 25, No. 3, pp. 339–369, 1993.

[11] R. O. Onvural, "Survey of Closed Queueing Networks with Blocking," ACM Computing Surveys. Vol. 22, No. 2, pp. 83–121, 1990.

[12] J. D. C. Little, "A Proof of the Queueing Formula L = W," Operational Research, Vol. 9, pp. 383–387, 1961.

[13] K. M. Chandy, and A. J. Martin, "A Characterization of Product-Form Queuing Networks," Journal of the ACM, Vol. 30, No. 2, p. 286–299, 1983.

[14] W. J. Gordon, and G. F. Newell "Cyclic Queueing Networks with Exponential Servers," Operations Research, Vol. 15, No. 2, pp. 254–265, 1967.

[15] F. Basket, K Chandy, R. Muntz, and F. Palacios, "Open, Closed, and Mixed Networks of Queues with Different Classes of Customers," Journal of the ACM, Vol. 22, No. 2, pp. 248–260, 1975

[16] K. S. Sevcik, and I. Mitrani, "The Distribution of Queueing Network States at Input and Output Instants," Journal of the ACM, Vol. 28, No. 2, pp. 358–371, 1981.

[17] M. Reiser, and S. Lavenberg, "Mean Value Analysis of Closed Multichain Queueing Networks," Journal of the ACM, Vol. 27, No. 2, pp. 313–322, 1980.

[18] K. Chandy, "The Analysis and Solutions of General Queueing Networks," Proceedings of the 6th Annual Princeton conference on Information Sciences and Systems, pp. 224–228. 1972.

[19] S. Lavenberg, and M. Reiser, "Stationary State Probabilities at Arrival Instants for Closed Queueing with Multiple Types of Customers," Journal of Applied Probability, Vol. 17, pp. 1048–1061, 1980.

[20] K. Chandy, U. Herzog, and L. Woo, "Parametric Analysis of Queueing Networks," IBM Journal of Research and Development, Vol. 19, No. 1, pp. 43–49, 1975.

## EXERCISES

1. Consider the following queueing network in Figure 7.8. Suppose the second server is replaced by one exactly twice as fast.

   a. Is there a significant improvement in the mean response time of the above network? Justify your answer.

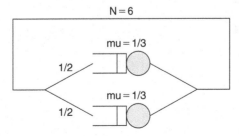

**FIGURE 7.8.** An example of a queueing network with two queues.

    b. Given the replacement has been made, is there any further modification you would propose to improve the mean response time in the closed system that does not involve spending more money? By how much would the modification improve the system performance?

    c. If the above system were an open system, would the replacement cause the mean response time to improve?

2. Consider an open network consisting of two nodes (node 1 and 2). Customers arrive to node 1 from outside with a rate r1 customers/s. Customers arrive to node 2 from outside with a rate r2 = 10 customers/s. Thirty percent of the customers completing service at node 1 will move to next queue up at node 2 (the rest leave the system). Fifty percent of the customers completing service at node 2 will next queue up at node 1 (the rest leave the system). The mean service time at node 1 is $E\{S1\} = 0.1$ sec. The mean service time at node 2 is $E\{S2\} = 0.05$ sec.

    a. In this network, how high can we make r1?

    b. When r1 is maximized, how much does the utilization of node 2 become?

3. A packet-switched Jackson network routes packets among two routers, according to the routing probabilities shown in Figure 7.9. Notice that there are two points at which packets enter the network, and two points at which they can depart.

    a. What is the maximum allowable rate for r1 that the network can tolerate?

    b. Let $r_1$-max be the maximum allowable rate. Set $r_1 = 0.9\ r_1$-max. What is the mean response time for a packet entering at the router 1 queue?

4. In all parts of this exercise assume all packets come from a single class.

    a. The system consists of a single (FCFS) server. Jobs arrive according to a Poisson process with rate $\lambda$. The service rate at the server depends on

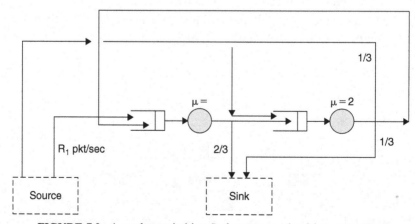

**FIGURE 7.9.** A packet-switching Jackson network with two queues.

the number of jobs in the system. When there are $n$ jobs in the system, the job in service is served with rate $\mu(n)$. This is called a "load-dependent service rate." Determine the limiting probability, $\pi_i$, of having $i$ jobs in the system.

b. Your system is now a Jackson network of load-dependent servers. The state of the network is $(n_1, n_2, \ldots, n_k)$, where $n_i$ denotes the number of jobs at server $i$. Let $\mu_i(n_i)$ denote the service rate at server i when there are $m$ jobs at server $i$.

   i. Solve for the limiting probabilities $\pi(n_1, n_2, \ldots, n_k)$ using the local balance approach. This will not be a closed form.

   ii. Prove that the limiting probabilities have a product form solution.

   iii. Check the solution by making the service rate constant at each server; i.e., $\mu_i(n_i) = \mu i$, for all $n_i$.

   iv. What is the limiting probability that there are $n_1$ jobs at server 1?

c. The system is now a Jackson network, where each server is an M/M/m m-server queue. Determine the limiting probabilities, $\pi(n_1, n_2, \ldots, n_k)$.

5. Consider a mixed queueing network depicted in Figure 7.10. Assume that four classes of customers are served. Class 1 and Class 2 are open. Class 3 and Class 4 are closed. Assume also that Node 1 is of Type -/G/1 and that node 2 is of Type -/G/1. The dashed lines represent the open traffic.

Assume the mean service times are given by

$$\frac{1}{\mu_{11}} = .4, \quad \frac{1}{\mu_{12}} = .8, \quad \frac{1}{\mu_{13}} = .3, \quad \frac{1}{\mu_{14}} = .5,$$

$$\frac{1}{\mu_{21}} = .6, \quad \frac{1}{\mu_{22}} = 1.6, \quad \frac{1}{\mu_{23}} = .5, \quad \frac{1}{\mu_{24}} = .8$$

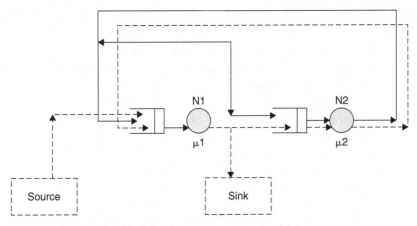

**FIGURE 7.10.** Mixed queueing network with two queues.

The routing probabilities are as follows:

$p_{0,11} = p_{0,11} = p_{21,11} = p_{22,12} = p_{23,13} = p_{24,14} = 1$, $p_{0,13} = p_{0,14} = p_{11,11}$
$= p_{12,12} = 0$,

$p_{13,13} = p_{11,21} = p_{13,23} = .5$, $p_{12,22} = p_{14,14} = .6$, $p_{14,24} = .4$

a. Compute the utilization, by Class 1 and 2, of the two nodes.
b. Using the (MVA) scheme, analyze the closed queueing network obtained by leaving out the customers of open classes.
c. Find the performance measures of the open classes (mean response time and mean number of customers).

6. Terminals are connected to a front-end processor to a computer system. Each terminal has a dedicated 300-bit-per-second line. Each operator at a terminal is repeating the same job, spending a certain amount of time reading and thinking and typing, denoted $T_{th}$, and then striking a send key. Then, the screen data are transmitted over the link to the front end processor; on the average, 400 bits of data are input. The front-end processor is connected to the computer system by a high-speed data link. Each job enters a staging queue where it waits until it can enter the computer system for processing. The computer system can hold at most five jobs at a time: If there are less than five jobs in the system, a job in the staging queue will enter the system immediately; otherwise, jobs are queued for entry in order of arrival.

   The system consists of a single processor and a single disk, and each job requires an average of $Tproc = 2$ seconds of processor time and $Ndisk = 30$ disk accesses. Each disk access requires a 50-msc access time. Once the job completes execution, it is transmitted back over the high-speed link to the front-end processor, and the terminal displays the output. On the average, each screen has 4800 bits of information for output. Assume times for signals to propagate are negligible.

   a. Show each step of processing a job, the resources required for that step, and the mean time duration of that step.
   b. What is the bottleneck resource in this system?
   c. Determine an upper bound on the mean throughput rate versus the number of active terminals.
   d. Mean response time is defined as the time interval from when the operator initiates transmission of a screen of data until the start of output on the screen. Plot a lower bound on mean response time versus the number of active terminals. Clearly label all regions and breakpoints in terms of model parameters.
   e. Suppose that the terminals' links are replaced with 56,000-bits-per-second links connected to a front end that is now connected to a space satellite earth station and that propagation time of signals between

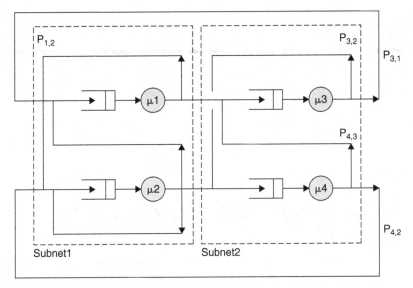

**FIGURE 7.11.** An example of a queueing network with two subetworks.

the terminals and the front end is negligible. The one-way propagation time of signals from the front end to the computer system is one fourth second. Re-answer the preceding questions.

7. In the queueing network presented in Figure 7.11, two subnetworks are considered: subnet1 and subnet2. The following values are given:

$N = 4$, $K = 2$ jobs, $\mu_1 = 1$, $\mu_2 = 2$, $\mu_3 = 3$, $\mu_4 = 1$

The routing probabilities are given by

$$p_{1,2} = p_{1,3} = 0.5; \ p_{2,1} = p_{2,2} = 0.3, \ p_{2,4} = 0.4;$$
$$p_{3,4} = p_{3,1} = 0.5; \ p_{4,2} = 0.6, \ p_{4,2} = 0.4.$$

a. Compute the visit ratios.

b. Use the MVA to compute the load-dependent throughputs and normalizing constants of the two subnetworks.

c. Determine the reduced network and compute its normalization constant.

d. Compute the mean number of jobs at each node, throughputs, and mean response times.

# CHAPTER 8

# OPERATIONAL AND MEAN VALUE ANALYSIS

In this chapter, we consider the quantitative aspects of queueing models and introduce the input parameters and performance metrics that can be obtained from the queueing network models. The notions of service times, arrival rates, service demands, usage, queue lengths, response time, throughput, and waiting time are discussed here in more precise terms. We also introduce a set of operational laws, which represent the basic quantitative relationships between performance quantities. We present first the approaches known as operational analyses [1], which are used to establish relationships among quantities based on measured or known data about the systems. Many variations and uses are presented for the Little's formula. In addition, the mean value analysis (MVA), approximate MVA, and the bounding analysis are discussed and reviewed.

## 8.1  OPERATIONAL LAWS

To address the problem of establishing relationships among quantities based on measured data, some commonly accepted operational analysis notation is required for the measured data. The following is a partial list of such measured quantities:

- $T$: The length of time during which we observed the system
- $K$: Number of resources in the system

*Fundamentals of Performance Evaluation of Computer and Telecommunication Systems,*
By Mohammad S. Obaidat and Noureddine A. Boudriga
Copyright © 2010 John Wiley & Sons, Inc.

- $B_i$: Total busy time of resource $i$ in the observation period $T$
- $A_i$: Total number of service requests (i.e., arrivals) to resource $i$ in the observation period $T$
- $A_0$: Total number of requests submitted to the system in the observation period $T$
- $C_i$: Total number of service completions from resource $i$ in the observation period $T$
- $C_0$: Total number of requests completed by the system in the observation period $T$

From these known measurable quantities, which are referred to as *operational variables*, a set of derived quantities can be obtained. A nonexhaustive list contains the following:

- $S_i$: Mean service time per completion at resource $i$; $S_i = \dfrac{B_i}{C_i}$
- $X_i$: Throughput, or the number of completions per unit time, at resource $i$; $X_i = \dfrac{C_i}{T}$
- $X_0$: System throughput; $X_0 = \dfrac{C_0}{T}$
- $U_i$: utilization of resource $i$; $U_i = \dfrac{B_i}{T}$
- $\lambda$: Arrival rate (arrivals per unit time) at resource $i$; $\lambda_i = \dfrac{A_i}{T}$
- $V_i$: Average number of visits per request to resource $i$; $V_i = \dfrac{C_i}{C_0}$

From these measurements, we can establish several relationships. We can therefore derive the first fundamental law. Algebraically, it holds:

$$U_i = \frac{B_i}{T} = \frac{C_i}{T} \times \frac{B_i}{C_i} = X_i \times S_i$$

Equation $U_i = X_i \times S_i$ is referred to as the *utilization law* of the resource $i$.

The notation presented above can be easily extended to the case where multiple classes are served by the system. The definition and relationships are simply modified by adding the class number $r$ ($r \in \{1, 2, .., R\}$) to the subscript. Therefore, the utilization law applied to class $r$ and resource $i$ is given by:

$$U_{i,r} = X_{i,r} \times S_{i,r}, \quad 1 \leq i \leq K, \ 1 \leq r \leq R.$$

To show how the operational approach might be applied, consider the following example.

**Example 1.** Assume during an observation period of 180 s that: (a) a single resource located at a node in the network is observed to be busy for 30s, (b) a total of 1200 transactions were observed to arrive to the node, and (c) the total number of observed completions is 1200 transactions (meaning that as many completions as arrivals occurred in the observation period).

Let us determine the mean service time per transaction, the utilization of the resource, and the system throughput.

To solve this in a straightforward manner using operational analysis, let us consider that the measured quantities are as follows:

$T = 180$ s, $K = 1$ resource, $B_1 = 30$ s, $A_1 = A_0 = 1200$ transactions, and $C_1 = C_0 = 1200$ transactions

Thus, the required metrics are as follows:

- The service time per transaction is $S_1 = \dfrac{B_1}{C_1} = \dfrac{30}{1200} = \dfrac{1}{40} = 0.025$ s per transaction
- The utilization of the resource is $U_1 = \dfrac{B_1}{T} = \dfrac{30}{180} = 16.66\%$
- The system throughput is $X_0 = \dfrac{C_0}{T} = \dfrac{C_0}{T} = \dfrac{1200}{180} = 6.66$ tps (transaction per second)

## 8.1.1   Service Demand Law

Service demand law is an important tool for performance modeling. The concept of service demand is tightly linked to a resource and the requests applying to use the resource. Denoted by $D_i$, it is typically defined as the total average time spent by a request of a specific class being served at resource $i$. The service demand of a request is the sum of all service times during all visits to a given resource. More precisely, when considering a set of requests using the same resource, one can compute the service demand at the resource as the average, for the whole set of requests, of the sum of the service times at that resource. It is worth noticing, however, that the service demand does not include queuing time, because it is the sum of service times. Additionally, service demands are input parameters for queueing network models.

There is an easy way to obtain service demands from resource utilizations and system throughput. By multiplying the utilization $U_i$ of resource $i$ by the observation interval $T$, one can deduce the total time during which the resource was busy. If this time is divided by the total number of completed requests, denoted previously by $C_0$, then the average amount of time that the resource was busy serving the requests can be estimated. The following defines precisely the service demand:

$$D_i = \frac{U_i}{C_0} \times T = \frac{U_i}{C_0/T} = \frac{U_i}{X_0}$$

The above relationship is referred to as the *service demand law*. It can be rewritten as follows:

$$D_i = \frac{U_i}{X_0} = V_i \times S_i, \ 1 \leq i \leq K.$$

In the case of a multiclass model, let us denote the service demand of class $r$ at resource $i$ by $D_{i,r}$. Then, one can deduce the following formula:

$$D_{i,r} = \frac{U_{i,r}}{X_0} = V_{i,r} \times S_{i,r}, \ 1 \leq i \leq K, \ 1 \leq r \leq R$$

## 8.1.2 Forced Flow Law

There is an easy way to relate the throughput of resource $i$, $X_i$, with the system throughput, $X_0$. The forced flow law describes this relationship. It states that:

$$X_i = V_i \times X_0, \ 1 \leq i \leq K$$

This can be stated as follows. Assume that every request that completes service at the database server performs an average of $V_i$ visits to resource $i$. Because $X_0$ requests are completed per second, the throughput of resource $i$ is $V_i \times X_0 (= X_i)$ visits per second. In other words, the throughput $X_i$ of resource $i$ is equal to the average number of visits ($V_i$) made to that resource multiplied by the system throughput ($X_0$).

The multiclass formula of the forced flow law is given by:

$$X_{i,r} = V_{i,r} \times X_0, \ 1 \leq i \leq K, \ 1 \leq r \leq R$$

**Example 2.** Consider a storage network with one server and $n$ nodes used to support the database server. Each node includes a local storage and database component. Assume that all database transactions have similar resource demands and that the database server S0 is under a constant load of transactions. Therefore, the storage network can be modeled using a single-class closed queueing network (as depicted in Figure 8.1). Finally, the server

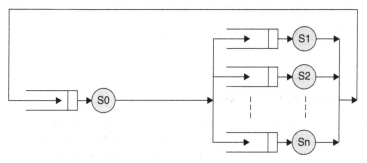

**FIGURE 8.1.** Closed queueing network storage server.

**TABLE 8.1  Measurement Data**

| Source | Number of reads/sec | Number of writes/sec | Total I/Os/s | Utilization |
|--------|--------------------|--------------------|-------------|------------|
| 1 | 32 | 10 | 42 | 0.30 |
| 2 | 32 | 11 | 43 | 0.30 |
| 3 | 32 | 12 | 44 | 0.30 |
| — | — | — | — | — |
| $n$ | 32 | $10 + n - 1$ | $32 + n - 1$ | 0.30 |

assumes that S0 is labeled as resource 1 and the database at node $Si$, $i < n$, is labeled resource $i + 1$. Measurements taken during an observation interval of 1 hour duration provide the number of transactions executed, the number of reads and writes per second on each storage and their utilization, as shown in Table 8.1. Let us determine the throughput of each resource, the average service time per request on each node, and the average number of inputs/outputs (I/Os) on each node.

The throughput of each resource $X_i$ ($i > 1$), is the total number of I/Os per second (i.e., the sum of the number of reads and writes per second). This value is depicted in the fourth column of the table. Using the utilization law, we can deduce the average service time: $S_i = \dfrac{U_i}{X_i}$. Therefore, we have

$$S_i = \frac{U_i}{X_i} = \frac{0.30}{32 + i - 1}, \quad i \geq 2$$

The throughput, $X_0$, of the database server is given by $X_0 = C_0/T$.

However, the value of $V_i$ for each disk $i$, according to the forced flow law, can be obtained as $X_i/X_0$. The database server throughput is 3.8 tps and the throughput of each disk in I/Os per second is given in the fourth column of Table 8.1. Thus,

$V_1 = X_1/X_0 = 32/3.8 = 8.4$ visits to resource 1 per database transaction
$V_2 = X_2/X_0 = 36/3.8 = 9.5$;
$V_3 = X_3/X_0 = 50/3.8 = 13.2$;
etc.

### 8.1.3  The Flow Balance Assumption

Often, it is convenient to assume that the system under analysis satisfies the so-called *Flow Balance Property*, namely, that the number of arrivals ($A$) equals the number of completions ($C$), and thus the arrival rate ($\lambda$) equals the throughput ($X$) of the system. Formally, this is written as follows:

$$A = C \implies \lambda = X$$

The flow balance assumption can be tested over any measurement interval, and it can be strictly satisfied by careful choice of the measurement interval.

## 8.2 LITTLE'S FORMULA

A system is responsible for processing $n$ jobs. All jobs are ready for processing at time $t = 0$. Let $J(t)$ be the number of jobs in the system processed at time $t$. We wish to determine the mean number of jobs in the system over the time interval starting at zero until the system becomes empty. Let $L_k$ denote the time at which the $k$th job completes its execution and leaves the system. Because there are a total of $n$ jobs and the last job leaves at $L_n$, we should have $J(0) = n$ and $J(L_n) = 0$.

The mean number of jobs in the system, denoted by $E(j)$ is easily computed over the observation interval $[0, L_n]$, as equal to:

$$E(j) = \frac{1}{L_n}(nL_1 + \sum_{i=1}^{n-1}(n-i)(L_{i+1} - L_i) = \frac{1}{L_n}\left(\sum_{i=1}^{n} L_i\right).$$

Let $F_k$ denote the total time spent in the system by job $k$. One can determine that job 1 spends $L_1$ amount of time in the system, job 2 spends $L_1 + L_2$ amount of time in the system, and job $j$ spends $\sum_{k \leq j} L_k$ amount of time in the system. Therefore, we can observe that:

$$E(j) = \frac{1}{L_n}\left(\sum_{i=1}^{n} F_i\right).$$

We now reorganize this expression, by inserting a multiplication and a division by $n$. This gives:

$$E(j) = \frac{n}{L_n}\left(\frac{1}{n}\sum_{i=1}^{n} F_i\right).$$

We recognize form the above formula the mean throughput rate, $\lambda = \frac{n}{L_n}$, and the mean time for a job to flow through the system, $E(F) = \frac{1}{n}\sum_{i=1}^{n} F_i$.

Finally, we obtain the result stating that the mean number in system equals the mean throughput rate multiplied by the mean time in system. This is called *Little's law:*

$$E(J) = \lambda \times E(F)$$

Little's law defines a relationship between three quantities: the mean number of jobs in system, the mean arrival rate, and the mean time in system [2]. If these quantities are unknown, one can try to bound each of them using the best available information. The more restrictive the information, the better the bounds.

Now, let us try to relax the assumptions that we have stated to obtain Little's law by allowing the arrivals to occur at arbitrary points in time, rather than having all jobs occurring at time zero for processing. Let $A_k$ denote the arrival time or ready time of the job $k$. The quantity $F_k \times (L_k - A_k)$, $1 \le k \le n$, denotes the flow time of the job $k$, from arrival ($A_k$) to departure ($L_k$). Then, we can compute $E(J)$ as follows:

$$E(j) = \frac{n}{L_n}\left(\frac{1}{n}\sum_{i=1}^{n} F_i \times (L_i - A_i)\right).$$

Because

$$E(F) = \frac{1}{n}\sum_{i=1}^{n} F_i \times (L_i - A_i),$$

we can also write

$$E(J) = \lambda \times E(F).$$

Now, let us notice that Little's law holds exactly when the system is initially empty (or idle) with no work, and after a period of observing its operation, we stop collecting information when the system is empty (or entirely idle). In practice, this may not be true because observations may be collected over a finite time interval, and the state at the start of observation and the state at the end of observation may not satisfy the all empty (or all idle) state assumption.

### 8.2.1   Variants of Little's Law

Under various technical conditions, Little's law may still hold. However, some weaker statements such as the *Little's Inequality* can hold. To make the latter precise, let us consider that the observation interval of a system under operation starts at $T$, which is chosen so that: (a) $n$ jobs are observed to both start and finish; (b) $L_k$ is the leaving instant of the job $k$, $k = 1,...,n$; (c) $J(.)$ denotes the total number of jobs in the system at any point in time, and (d) $F_k$, $k = 1,...,n$, denote the time in system or flow time for job $k$. From these definitions and applying the above results, we can state that:

Mean number of jobs $= E(J) = \frac{1}{L_n} \int_T^{T+L_n} J(t)dt$

Note that a job may have entered the system prior to $T$, but not yet left, entered prior to $T$ and left, or entered during the measurement time, but not yet left. This implies that:

$$E\ (J) = \text{Mean number in system} \geq \frac{n}{L_n} \times \frac{1}{n} \sum_{k=1}^{n} F_k.$$

Assuming that $n$ is large and that the end effects are negligible, which can only be checked with controlled experimentation), then we identify $\frac{1}{n} \sum_{k=1}^{n} F_k$ as the mean time in the system. This shows that $E\ (J)$ is close and bigger than $\lambda x E\ (F)$.

Finally, assume that jobs perform multiple steps and consider the following analysis. Each job has $S$ types of steps, and requires one or more resources at each step for a mean time $T_k, k = 1,\ldots,S$. *Consider the* system is observed over an interval with n job completions occurring at time instants $L_k, k = 1,\ldots,S$. We denote $J\ (t)$ the $S$-tuple $J\ (t) = (J_1\ (t),\ldots, JS(t))$ as the number of jobs in execution in each step, meaning that $J_k(t)$ denotes the number of jobs in execution in step $k$ in the system. The state space is of feasible $S$-tuples $J(t)$ and is denoted by $\Omega$. The fraction of time the system is in state $J(t)$ over the observation interval is denoted by $\pi(J)$. From Little's law and the linearity of the expectation, we can deduce that:

$$E(J_k) = \sum_{J \in \Omega} J_k \cdot pi(J) \geq \lambda \cdot \bar{T}_k$$

where the mean throughput rate is simply the total number of jobs divided by the observation time interval, $\lambda = \frac{n}{L_n}$, and $T_k$ is given by averaging it over the fraction of time the system is in each state as follows:

$$\bar{T}_k = \frac{1}{N} \sum T_k \pi(J_k)$$

**Example 1.** (Telephone Traffic): Consider that voice telephone calls are made between two locations. Assume that the data available can be characterized as follows. During a peak busy hour of the day, on average, $\lambda_{tel}$ calls are arriving per minute that are successfully completed, with a mean holding time per successful call of $T_{tel}$. A total of $C$ circuits are made available. The problem is to compute the number L of links that are actually needed, supposing that one link can handle one voice telephone.

The mean number of calls in progress during the busy hour is given by Little's law:

Mean number of calls in progress $= \lambda_{tel} \times T_{tel}$

Consider that the number of calls in progress at any instant of time $t$ is denoted by $J(t)$ $(\in \Omega)$. The system is observed over a time interval of duration $T$ and the fraction of time the system is in a given state is assumed to have stabilized at $\pi(J)$. Hence,

$$E(\min(J, C)) = \sum_{J \in \Omega} \pi(J) \min(J, C) = \lambda_{tel} \times T_{tel}.$$

Because each link can handle one call, we can deduce that we need approximately $L$ links, where $L$ is given by:

$$L = \lambda_{tel} \times T_{tel}.$$

In practice, we would put in more than $L$ links as given by Little's law because we will have fluctuations about the mean value and some calls attempts will be blocked or rejected because all links are busy. We will return to this topic later on.

When used in conjunction with the other basic laws, Little's law can help the determination of various parameters. For instance, combined with the flow balance assumption and the forced flow law, Little's law allows the calculation of the device utilizations for systems whose workload intensities are described in terms of an arrival rate. The next example discusses such an issue.

**Example 1.** Consider the queueing network model depicted in Figure 8.2, which includes three devices (a central processing unit [CPU] and two disks) and shows three types of jobs (compilation, execution, and editing sessions).

Assume the data gathered for the system is given in Table 8.2.

To calculate the utilization of a device in this system, we apply the utilization law separately to each job class, then sum the results. Let us consider, for example, the CPU utilization. We have:

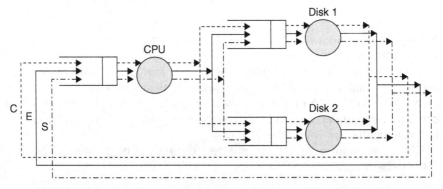

**FIGURE 8.2.** Computing utilization using Little's and flow balance laws.

**TABLE 8.2** **Data gathered from the system described in the above example**

| Job type | Arrival rate | Service demand (second/job) | | |
|---|---|---|---|---|
| | | CPU | Disk 1 | Disk 2 |
| Compilation | 360 | 4.0 | 0.8 | 0.5 |
| Execution | 180 | 8.0 | 6.0 | 5.2 |
| Editing session | 120 | 0.6 | 0.4 | 0.3 |

$$Ut(\text{CPU}) = (360 \times 4.0 + 180x \times 8.0 + 120 \times 0.6)/3600 = 0.4 + 0.4 + 0.02 = 0.82$$

Thus, the total CPU utilization must be equal to 82%. The flow balance assumption states that the throughput of the system will be the same as the arrival rate to the system.

Little's Law has been established for continuous random variables in a more general environment in a previous chapter.

## 8.2.2 Interactive Response Time Law

Consider an interactive system composed of a database server serving $M$ users each using a workstation to access the server system interactively. Users work independently and can be either in a thinking state (i.e., composing and sending requests to the server) or a waiting state (i.e., waiting for a response from the server). Let $Z$ and $R$ be the average think time and the average response time, respectively. On the one hand, the think time $Z$ of a user is defined as the time spent between the moments when the customer receives a reply to a request until a subsequent request is submitted. On the other hand, the response time is the duration of the interval of time elapsed between two successive think intervals made by the user.

Let $Th$ and $Wa$ be the average number of clients thinking and the average number of users waiting for a response, respectively. Depending on whether the users are in think state, $Th$ and $Wa$ define the average numbers of users at the workstations and at the database server, respectively. Thus, we can state clearly that:

$$Th + Wa = M.$$

By applying Little's law to the queueing subnetwork containing just the workstations, it holds:

$$M = X0 \times Z$$

This is true because the average number of requests submitted per unit time (or throughput of the set of clients) must be equal to the number of completed requests per unit time (system throughput $X_0$). Similarly, by applying Little's law to the subnetwork containing just the database server, we have:

$$N = X_0 \times R$$

where $R$ is the average response time. By adding the two equations, we obtain

$$M = X_0(Z + R).$$

Equivalently, we can deduce that:

$$R = \frac{M}{X_0} - Z.$$

This formula is known as the *interactive response time law*. The multiclass version of the interactive response time is given by:

$$R_r = \frac{M_r}{X_{0,r}} - Z_r$$

where $R_r$, $M_r$, $Z_r$, and $X_{0,r}$ represent the average response time, the number of users, the average think time, and the system throughput for class $r$, respectively.

## 8.3   BOTTLENECK ANALYSIS

A bottleneck in a system is an obstacle to movement or progress. If the forced flow assumption holds, we can show that at high loads, system performance is determined by the device with the highest utilization, which is the bottleneck. The ratio of the completion rates of any two devices, using the forced flow law is given by the ratio of their visit ratios:

$$\frac{X_i}{X_j} = \frac{V_i \times X}{V_j \times X} = \frac{V_i}{V_j}$$

Because the utilization is given by $U_i = X_i \times S_i$, we can deduce a similar relationship between the utilizations of the two given devices:

$$\frac{U_i}{U_j} = \frac{X_i \times S_i}{X_j \times S_j} = \frac{V_i \times S_i}{V_j \times S_j}$$

If the $V_i$'s are intrinsic properties of the customers and each $S_i$ is independent of the queue length at device $i$, then the system has load independent parameters. In such a case, the throughput and utilization ratios are the same for all loads on the system. This observation can be used to determine asymptotes for system throughput $X$ and response time $R$.

We say that device $i$ is saturated if its utilization approaches 1. Devices that operate near full utilization tend to have long queues; a saturated device is a bottleneck device. We will use the subscript $b$ to denote a device capable of saturating. In general, every network has at least one bottleneck device. Because the utilization ratios are fixed, the device with the largest $V_i$ . $S_i$ will be first to achieve 100% of utilization as $N$ increases. Let $U_b$ be the largest utilization. So, we have:

$$V_b \times S_b = \{V_b \times S_b | K \geq i \geq 1\}.$$

As $N$ becomes large, we have $U_b \to 1$ and

$$X_b \to \frac{1}{S_b}. \text{ Because } XV_b = X_b, \text{ we deduce that:}$$

$$X_{max} = \frac{X_b}{V_b} \to \frac{1}{V_b S_b}$$

is the maximum possible value of the throughput as $N$ increases. The total of all service required by a job while in the system is given by:

$$R_{min} = \sum_{i=1}^{K} V_i S_i.$$

This denotes the smallest possible value of mean response time. In fact, $R_{min}$ is the response time when $N = 1$. This implies that $X = \frac{1}{R_{min}}$, when $N = 1$ and that $X \leq \frac{N}{R_{min}}$, when $N > 1$.

Figure 8.3 depicts the throughput as a function of the load, $N$. The system throughput, $X$, increases monotonically from $1/R_{min}$, at $N = 1$, to the asymptote $y = \frac{1}{V_b S_b}$ and remains below the straight line $X = \frac{N}{R_{min}}$ as shown in Figure 8.3.

If we were to hypothesize that $k$ jobs (where $k \leq K$, the total number of devices in the $k$ system) always manage to avoid each other in the network so that $X = \frac{N}{R_{min}}$, we would require that:

$$\frac{k}{R_{min}} \leq \frac{1}{V_b S_b} \text{ or } k \leq N^*$$

where $N^*$ represents a load beyond which queueing is certain to exist somewhere in the network. $N^*$ is given by:

$$N^* = \frac{R_{min}}{V_b S_b} = \frac{\sum_{i=1}^{K} V_i S_i}{V_b S_b}.$$

Consider now that a customer at the terminal is in the thinking mode, that is, the system is waiting for it to do something. The think time, $Z$, is the average time a user spends between receiving a prompt and typing a command;

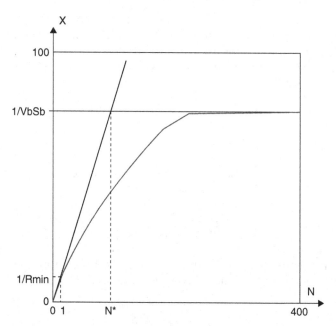

**FIGURE 8.3.** System throughput versus system load.

otherwise, a customer is somewhere inside the central subsystem either being served or waiting to be served. The aforementioned results give the values of response time for the interactive system described earlier with $M$ terminals and an average think time:

$$R = \frac{M}{X} - Z$$

When $M = 1$, we must have $R = R_{min}$. The throughput, $X$, cannot exceed the value $\frac{1}{V_b S_b}$. Thus, it holds:

$$R \geq MV_b S_b\_Z \geq MV_i S_i - Z, \quad 1 \leq i \leq K$$

where the first inequality approaches an equality for large $M$. Figure 8.4 depicts the response time asymptote and its intersection with the horizontal axis (as given by $M_b = \frac{Z}{V_b S_b}$).

The response time asymptote crosses the minimum response time $R_{min}$ at a value $M_b^*$ such that $M_b^* V_b S_b - Z = R_{min}$. Therefore, $M_b^*$ is given by:

$$M_b^* = \frac{R_{min} + Z}{V_b S_b} = N^* + M_b.$$

In the case where there are more than $M_b^*$ terminals, queueing is inevitable in the central system.

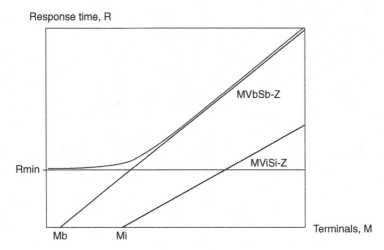

**FIGURE 8.4.** Response time Versus number of terminals.

## 8.4  STANDARD MVA

The most popular exact solution method for closed product form queuing networks is the classical Mean Value Analysis (MVA) technique [3]. The MVA is an efficient technique that allows analyzing product form queueing networks and obtaining mean values for performance metrics such as queue length, response time, and throughput. The efficiency comes with a price—MVA does not compute the joint probability distribution for queue lengths. However, in many (if not most) performance evaluation situations, the mean values are the performance metrics of interest.

### 8.4.1  Single Class Systems

We start the discussion of mean value analysis with systems serving a single job class. These systems may either be open or closed.

*Open systems*: Let $D_m$ be the total demand of a single customer for queue $m$, $V_m$ be the visit ratio for queue $m$, queue 0 be the queue representing the "outside world," and $\mu_m$ be the service rate at queue $m$. Thus, $V_m$ is the average number of visits a single customer makes to queue $m$.

In addition, one can see that $D_m = \frac{V_m}{\mu_m}$, and that the maximum throughput for the system occurs at the value of the arrival rate that saturates the queue with the largest demand. Assume that the arrival rate is equal to $\lambda$ then we have:

- Maximum throughput $= \dfrac{1}{\max\{D_m | 1 \leq m\}} = \lambda_{sat}$

- Throughput for queue $m$ *at* $\lambda < \lambda_m$ is $\lambda_m = \lambda V_m = X_m(\lambda)$.

- Utilization of queue $m$ at $\lambda < \lambda_m$ is $\rho_m = \lambda_m \frac{1}{\mu_m} = \lambda D_m$.
- Response time at queue $m$ when $\lambda < \lambda_m$ is $R_m(\lambda)$.

1. For an infinite server (IS) queue, $R_m(\lambda)$ is given by:

$$R_m(\lambda) = V_m \frac{1}{\mu_m} = D_m$$

2. For a first-come-first-served FCFS queue: $R_m(\lambda)$ is characterized by the sum of two factors, when the arrival rate is equal to $\lambda$ we have

$$R_m(\lambda) = V_m \frac{1}{\mu_m}(1 + A_m(\lambda)) = (1 + A_m(\lambda))D_m$$

where $A_m(\lambda)$ is the average number of customers at queue $m$ as observed by an arriving job.

However, the network has a product form serving a single open class. The average number of customers at queue $m$ is equal to the expectation $Q_m(\lambda)$ of the length of queue $m$ when the arrival rate is equal to $\lambda$ It holds:

$$A_m(\lambda) = Q_m(\lambda).$$

Because $Q_m(\lambda) = \lambda R_m(\lambda)$, we have:

$$R_m(\lambda) = D_m(1 + \lambda R_m(\lambda))$$

$$R_m(\lambda) = \frac{D_m}{1 - \lambda D_m} = \frac{D_m}{1 - \rho_m(\lambda)}.$$

This gives, in the cases of IS and FCFS, the following expressions:

- Queue lengths: $Q_m = \lambda R_m = \begin{cases} \rho_m(\lambda), & \text{for IS} \\ \dfrac{\rho_m(\lambda)}{1 - \rho_m(\lambda)}, & \text{for FCFS} \end{cases}$

- System response time: $R(\lambda) = \sum\limits_{m=1}^{M} R_m(\lambda)$

- Average number of customers: $Q(\lambda) = \lambda R(\lambda) = \sum\limits_{m=1}^{M} Q_m(\lambda)$.

When the queueing is closed, the three quantities of great interest are $Q$, $R$, and $X$. They are defined by the following three equations:

$$X(N) = \frac{N}{\sum_{m=1}^{M} R_m(N)}$$

$$Q_m(\lambda) = X(N) R_m(N)$$

$$R_m(N) = \begin{cases} D_m, & \text{for IS} \\ D_m(1 + A_m(N)), & \text{for FCFS} \end{cases}$$

where $R_m(N)$ is the response time at center $m$ when the total number of customers in the system is $N$. The other quantities are defined similarly. The knowledge of $A_m(N)$ would complete the computation of $R_m(N)$, $X(N)$, and $Q_m(N)$. Unfortunately, the equality $Q_m(N) = A_m(N)$ does not hold and cannot be used. However, if the network has a product form, we have the following relation [4]:

$$Q_m(N - 1) = A_m(N).$$

This gives us the following iterative system (called MVA) that can be easily solved using an algorithm of linear complexity and the fact that $Q_m(0) = 0$, for all $m$ smaller then $M$.

$$X(N) = \frac{N}{\sum_{m=1}^{M} R_m(N)}$$

$$Q_m(\lambda) = X(N) R_m(N)$$

$$R_m(N) = \begin{cases} D_m, & \text{for IS} \\ D_m(1 + Q_m(N - 1)), & \text{for FCFS} \end{cases}$$

### 8.4.2 Multiple Class Systems

In a multiple class queueing networks, each job class may have its own demand for each queue. The routing of jobs between queues and the per-visit service demand are assumed to be class dependent. The results for mean value analysis will distinguish between an open and closed system in this subsection.

*Open systems*: To develop MVA for multiple class systems, we need the following quantities:

$C$: Number of classes

$\lambda$ : Arrival rate vector $(\lambda_1, ..., \lambda_C)$, where $\lambda_j$ is the arrival rate for class $j$

$\mu_{j,m}$ : Service rate of class $j$ at queue $m$

$V_{j,m}$ : Visit ratio for class $j$ at queue $m$

$D_{j,m}$ : Average total demand of class $j$ at queue $m$

$\rho_m(\lambda)$ : Utilization of queue m by all jobs

$\rho_{j,m}$ : Utilization ratio of queue $m$ by class $j$

$R_{j,m}(\lambda)$ : Average stay time of class $j$ jobs at queue $m$

$Q_{j,m}(\lambda)$ : Average number of jobs of class $j$ at queue $m$

$X_{j,m}$ : Throughput for class $j$ at queue $m$

$A_{j,m}(\lambda)$ : Expected number of jobs of class $j$ at queue $m$ at an arrival instant

Obviously, we can have the following:

$$\rho_{j,m}(\lambda) = X_{j,m}(\lambda) \cdot \frac{1}{\mu_{j,m}} = \lambda_j D_{j,m}$$

$$\rho_m(\lambda) = \sum_{j=1}^{C} \lambda_j D_{j,m}$$

$$X_{j,m}(\lambda) = \lambda_j V_{j,m}$$

$$R_{j,m}(\lambda) = \begin{cases} D_{j,m}, & \text{for IS} \\ D_{j,m}(1 + A_{j,m}(\lambda)), & \text{for FCFS} \end{cases}$$

The computation of the above system of equations is easy in the case of IS. Let us consider the FCFS case and assume that the network has a product form. We have:

$$A_{j,m}(\lambda) = Q_m(\lambda) = \sum_{k=1}^{C} Q_{k,m}(\lambda).$$

This shows that $A_{j,m}(\lambda)$ is independent of $j$, $1 \le j \le C$. Thus, the computation of $R_{j,m}(\lambda)/R_{k,m}(\lambda)$ gives:

$$\frac{R_{j,m}(\lambda)}{R_{k,m}(\lambda)} = \frac{D_{j,m}}{D_{k,m}} \quad \text{and} \quad R_{k,m}(\lambda) = \frac{D_{k,m}}{D_{j,m}} \cdot R_{j,m}(\lambda).$$

However, because $R_{j,m}(\lambda) = D_{j,m}(1 + A_{j,m}(\lambda))$, we can deduce that:

$$R_{j,m}(\lambda) = D_{j,m}(1 + \sum_{k=1}^{C} Q_{k,m}(\lambda)).$$

This can be written as follows:

$$R_{j,m}(\lambda) = D_{j,m}\left(1 + \sum_{k=1}^{C} \lambda_k R_{k,m}(\lambda)\right).$$

Using the above formula, this implies that:

$$\frac{R_{j,m}(\lambda)}{D_{j,m}} = \left(1 + \sum_{k=1}^{C} \lambda_k \frac{D_{k,m}}{D_{j,m}} \cdot R_{j,m}(\lambda)\right)$$

$$\frac{R_{j,m}(\lambda)}{D_{j,m}} = \left(1 + \frac{R_{j,m}}{D_{j,m}} \sum_{k=1}^{C} \lambda_k D_{k,m}(\lambda)\right).$$

We then deduce that:

$$\frac{R_{j,m}(\lambda)}{D_{j,m}} = \frac{1}{(1 - \sum_{k=1}^{C} \lambda_j D_{k,m})} \quad \text{and} \quad R_{j,m}(\lambda) = \frac{D_{j,m}}{(1 - \sum_{k=1}^{C} \lambda_j D_{k,m})}.$$

Thus, we have:

$$R_{j,m}(\lambda) = \frac{D_{j,m}}{1 - \sum_{k=1}^{C} \rho_{k,m}(\lambda)} = \frac{D_{j,m}}{1 - \rho_{k,m}(\lambda)}.$$

In addition, we have:

$$X_j(N) = \frac{N_j}{\sum_{m=1}^{M} R_{j,m}(N)}, \quad 1 \le j \le C.$$

Finally, knowing the values of the quantities $D_{j,m}$, $\rho_{k,m}(\lambda)$, $X_{k,m}(\lambda)$, $V_{k,m}$, and $\lambda_{k,m}$, one can deduce the quantities $X$, $Q$, and $R$.

*Closed systems:* Consider the vector $N = (N_1, ..., N_C)$ of customers, where $N_j$ is the number of customers of class $j$ in the system. Then, similar to the case where a single class is considered in a closed system, the following equations hold:

$$X_j(N) = \frac{N_j}{\sum_{m=1}^{M} R_{j,m}(N)}$$

$$Q_{j,m}(N) = X_j(N) R_{j,m}(N)$$

$$R_{j,m}(N) = \begin{cases} D_{j,m}, & \text{for IS} \\ D_{j,m}(1 + A_{j,m}(N)), & \text{for FCFS.} \end{cases}$$

The above expression is easy to explain. Consider, for example, the case of FCFS queues and assume that all classes of customers must observe the same service time distribution. Then, we can establish that $D_{j,m} = D_{k,m}$ for all classes $j$ and $k$. Also, we assume that the distribution of the residual lifetime of an exponential random variable is identical to the original distribution, so that it does not matter how long a job has been in service at the arrival instant. Finally, assume the network has a product form solution.

Let us denote by $N - I_j$ the vector:

$$N - I_j = N_1, ..., N_{j-1}, N_j - 1, N_{j+1}, ..., N_C), \quad 1 \leq j \leq C.$$

For the closed product-form networks, we have:

$$A_{j,m}(N) = Q_{j,m}(N - I_j) \text{ for all } j \text{ and } m.$$

Thus, the following system can be easily computed using the initial state of $Q_{j,m}$ and an algorithm of time complexity:

$$C \times M \prod_{k=1}^{C} (N_j - I_j).$$

## 8.5 APPROXIMATION OF MVA

The preceding section shows that by using MVA, the first moment of sojourn times and the moment of the number of customers in each queue can be obtained based on the arrival instant distribution theorem and the Little's law. Because of the high memory requirements of the exact solution algorithms, approximation methods have been developed to compute the mean values, including the well-known self correcting approximation technique (SCAT) [5], which is simply an approximation of MVA. There are many extensions of MVA considering the type of service centers that have product form or multiple customer classes. The moment analysis (MA) [6] is a generalization of MVA that also allows the derivation of higher moments of the population at any queueing station.

Consider a closed separable queueing network with $C$ classes of customers and $K$ load-independent service centers. The customer population of the queueing network is represented by vector $N = (N_1, ..., N_C)$ where $N_k$ is the number of customers belonging to class $k$, for $k \leq C$. The total number of customers in the network is denoted by $|N| = N_1, +.. + N_C$. The mean service demand of class $c$ at center $k$ is denoted by $D_{c,k}$. Now let us recall that an exact MVA algorithm involves repeated applications of the following equations:

$$A_{c,k}(\vec{n}) = Q_k(\vec{n} - I_c)$$

$$R_{c,k}(\vec{n}) = D_{c,k} \cdot (1 + A_{c,k}(\vec{n})), \quad R_c(\vec{n}) = \sum_{k=1}^{K} R_{c,k}(\vec{n})$$

$$Q_{c,k}(\vec{n}) = R_{c,k}(\vec{n}) \cdot X_c(\vec{n}), \quad Q_k(\vec{n}) = \sum_{k=1}^{C} Q_{c,k}(\vec{n})$$

$$X_c(\vec{n}) = \frac{n_c}{Z_c + R_c(\vec{n})}$$

with initial conditions $Q_k(0) = 0$, for all $k$; where $\vec{n} = (n_1, .., n_C)$ is a population that ranges from $\vec{0}$ to $N$ and $A_{c,k}(\vec{n})$ is the average number of customers a class $c$ customer finds at center $k$ when it arrives to that center, given that the network population is $\vec{n}$.

The approximate MVA algorithms improve the time and space complexities by substituting approximations for $A_{c,k}(\vec{n})$ that are not recursive. Among all approximate algorithms for separable queueing networks, we will consider the Bard-Schweitzer proportional estimation algorithm, the Chandy-Neuse Linearizer algorithms, and the Zahorjan-Eager-Sweillam aggregate queue length algorithm [7–10].

## 8.5.1 The Bard-Schweitzer Proportional Estimation Algorithms

The Bard large customer population (LCP) is an approximate MVA algorithm [9]. Unlike other algorithms, LCP allows the knowledge of error bounds. It is based on the following approximation:

$$Q_{j,k}(\vec{n} - I_c) \approx Q_{j,k}(\vec{n}), \quad \text{for any class } j.$$

This is because when the population is large, there is not a significant change in mean queue length at any center by reducing a class population by one customer. Thus, the approximation equation of the LCP becomes:

$$A_{c,k}(\vec{n}) = Q_k(\vec{n} - I_c) = \sum_{j=1}^{C} Q_{j,k}(\vec{n} - I_c) \approx Q_k(\vec{n})$$

This can be used to solve iteratively the MVA equations. It has been demonstrated that the solutions of the LCP algorithm exist and are unique. Unfortunately, the algorithm does not provide accurate solution when the population size is small. However, the Bard-Schweitzer proportional estimation algorithm (PE) [10] requires lower execution time and reduces space requirements than the exact MVA algorithm. PE uses the LCP algorithm and defines relatively accurate solutions for product-form queueing networks with large population and small population as well. It is based on the following approximation:

$$Q_{j,k}(N - I_c) \approx \begin{cases} \frac{N_c-1}{N_c} Q_{j,k}(N), & c = j \\ Q_{j,k}(N), & c \neq j \end{cases}$$

Using this equation gives us the following approximation of the PE algorithm:

$$Q_{c,k}(N)) = Q_k(N - I_c) = \sum_{j=1}^{C} Q_{j,k}(N - I_c) \approx Q_k(N) - \frac{1}{N_c} Q_{c,k}(N)).$$

The time and space complexities of PE algorithm are of the form O (KC). In addition, it has been shown that the PE algorithm has a unique solution and that the iterations converge to that solution.

## 8.5.2   The Chandy-Neuse Linearizer Algorithms

A Chandy-Neuse Linearizer algorithm is an iterative approximate MVA algorithm. It works by deriving an algebraic expression equivalent to $Q_k(N - I_c)$. The algorithm is based on the following equation:

$$A_{c,k}(N)) = \sum_{j=1}^{C} (N_j - \theta_{j,c}) . (\frac{Q_{j,k}(N)}{N_j} + \delta_{j,c,k}(N))$$

where

$$\theta_{j,c} = \begin{cases} 1, & j = c \\ 0, & j \neq c \end{cases} \text{ and } \delta_{j,c,k}(N) = \frac{Q_{j,k}(N - I_c)}{N_j - \theta_{j,c}} - \frac{Q_{j,k}(N)}{N_j}$$

Whereas the following assumption holds:

$$\delta_{j,c,k}(N - I_c) = \delta_{j,c,k}(N)$$

The approximation used in the PE algorithm is equivalent to assuming that all the $\delta$-terms are vanishing. The Chandy-Neuse Linearizer algorithm uses iterations to determine successively better approximations for the $\delta$-terms using the following five-step procedure:

Approximate $\delta$ Procedure

   ***Initialization step***: Set $\delta_{j,c,k}(N - I_j) = \delta_{j,c,k}(N) = 0$ for $1 \leq c \leq C$, $1 \leq i \leq C$, $1 \leq j \leq C$, and $\leq k \leq K$

   **Step 1:** Solve the six equations characterizing the MVA algorithm at population N.

**Termination step**: If termination conditions are satisfied then stop.

**Step 2**: Solve the six equations characterizing the MVA algorithm at each population $N - I_i$ for All $1 \le i \le C$

**Step 3** (Updating): Update the $\delta$-terms using:

$$\delta_{j,c,k}(N) = \frac{Q_{j,k}(N - I_c)}{N_j - \theta_{j,c}} - \frac{Q_{j,k}(N)}{N_j} \quad \text{and} \quad \delta_{j,c,k}(N - I_c) = \delta_{j,c,k}(N).$$

Typically, the linearizer algorithm is used with only three iteration for the $\delta$-terms, because it is computationally expensive.

### 8.5.3 The Zahorjan-Eager-Sweillam Aggregate Queue Length Algorithm

The Zahorjan-Eager-Sweillam aggregate queue length (AQL) algorithm presents a modification of the linearizer algorithm. It is more efficient and obtains similar accuracy as the linearizer algorithm. The AQL bases its approach on the following approximation:

$$A_{c,k}(N)) = (N - 1)(\frac{Q_{j,k}(N)}{N} + \rho_{j,c,k}(N))$$

where

$$\rho_{c,k}(N) = \frac{Q_k(N - I_c)}{N - 1} - \frac{Q_k(N)}{N}.$$

In addition, the AQL algorithm uses the following approximation:

$$\rho_{c,k}(N - I_j) = \rho_{c,k}(N), \quad \text{for all } j$$

The iteration is used in AQL to determine better approximations for the $\rho$-terms. Like the linearizer algorithm, the AQL algorithm different implementation methods have been provided to implement AQL. A typical implementation is described using the following five-step procedure.

Approximate $\delta$ Procedure

**Initialization step**: Set $\rho_{c,k}(N - I_j) = \rho_{c,k}(N) = 0$ for, $1 \le c \le C$, $1 \le j \le C$, and $1 \le k \le K$.

**Step 1**: Solve the six equations characterizing the MVA algorithm at population $N$.

**Termination step**: If termination conditions are satisfied then stop.

**Step 2:** Solve the six equations characterizing the MVA algorithm at each population $N - I_i - i$ for All $1 \leq i \leq C$.

**Step 3** (Updating): Update the $\rho$-terms using:

$$\rho_{c,k}(N) = \frac{Q_k(N - I_c)}{N - 1} - \frac{Q_k(N)}{N} \text{ and } \rho_{c,k}(N - I_j) = \rho_{c,k}(N).$$

The accuracy of the AQL algorithm depends, as in the linearizer algorithm, on the termination conditions. Zahorjan et al. in [8] suggested that termination after three iterations is not sufficiently accurate.

## 8.6 BOUNDING ANALYSIS

In this section, we describe techniques to compute two classes of performance bounds: the asymptotic bounds and the balanced system bounds. Asymptotic bounds hold for a larger class of systems than do balanced system bounds [11–13]. They also are simpler to compute. The compensating advantage of the balanced system bounds is that they provide more precise information than asymptotic bounds. Several characteristics of bounding techniques make them interesting and useful. These characteristics include:

1. The development of these techniques provides important insight into the basic factors influencing the performance of communication systems. In particular, the critical influence of the system bottleneck can be highlighted and quantified.
2. The bounds can be computed rapidly. Bound analysis, therefore, is suitable as a first estimation modeling technique that can be used to remove inadequate alternatives at an early stage of the analysis.

In many cases, several alternatives can be treated together, with a single bounding analysis providing useful information about them all. In contrast to the bounding techniques discussed here, more sophisticated analysis techniques require considerably more computations, which are infeasible to perform by hand. However, bounding techniques are most useful in system-sizing studies. Such studies can be relevant to long-range planning and consequently often are based on basic estimates of system characteristics. Bounding techniques also can be used to estimate the potential performance gain of alternative upgrades to existing systems.

For the sake of clarity, we restrict our discussion of the bounding analysis to the single class of jobs. Multiple class generalizations can be established, but they are not commonly used. In addition, the bounding techniques are most constructive for capacity studies of the bottleneck problem, for which single class models are enough. Additionally, a major attraction of bounding techniques in practice is their simplicity, which would be lost if multiple classes were included in the models.

The models we consider in this section can be typically described by: (a) the number of service centers, say K; (b) largest service demand at any single center, denoted by Dmx; (c) sum of the service demands at the centers, D; (d) type of the customer class (i.e., batch, terminal, or transaction); and (e) average think time (if the class is of terminal type).

For models with transaction type workloads, the throughput bounds indicate the maximum customer arrival rate that can be processed by the system, whereas the response time bounds reflect the largest and smallest possible response times that these customers could experience as a function of the system arrival rate. For models with batch or terminal type workloads, the bounds indicate the maximum and minimum possible system throughput and response time as functions of the number of customers in the system.

We refer to throughput upper and response time lower bounds as optimistic bounds (becuase they indicate the best possible performance), and we refer to throughput lower and response time upper bounds as pessimistic bounds (because they indicate the worst possible performance). Although we treat only bounds on system throughput and response time in this section, the generalization of these methods to other performance measures, such as service center throughputs and utilizations, is easy to perform.

## 8.6.1 Asymptotic Bounds

Asymptotic bounding analysis provides bounds on system throughput and response time in single class queueing networks [1]. Asymptotic bounds are derived by considering the (asymptotically) extreme conditions of light and heavy loads. The validity of the bounds depends on the following assumption: The service demand of a customer at a center does not depend on how many other customers currently are in the system or at which service centers they are located.

**Transaction workloads.** For transaction workloads, the throughput bound indicates the maximum possible arrival rate of customers that the system can process successfully. If the arrival rate exceeds this bound, then an accumulation of unprocessed jobs (or customers) grows continually as jobs arrive. Thus, in the long run, an arriving job has to wait an indefinitely long time (because it can find any number of jobs already waiting in queue when it arrives). This is what is often called a saturated system case. The throughput bound thus should be the arrival rate that separates feasible saturation from processing.

The main tool to determining the throughput bound is the utilization law, $U_k = X_k.S_k$, $1 \leq k \leq K$,, for each center $k$. If $\lambda$ denotes the arrival rate to the system, then $X_k$ can be determined as $X_k = \lambda.V_k$. Thus, the utilization law can be rewritten as: $U_k = \lambda.D_k$, where $D_k$ is the service demand at center $k$. To compute the throughput bound, we can note that as long as all centers have utilizations less than 1, an increased arrival rate can be accommodated.

However, when a center reaches a utilization equal to 1 (i.e., getting saturated), the entire system becomes saturated because no increase in the arrival rate of customers can be handled successfully. Therefore, we define the throughput bound as the smallest arrival rate, denoted by $\lambda_{sat}$, at which a center in the system saturates. Let $k_0$ be the index of the bottleneck center. Then:

$$U_{k_0}(\lambda) = \lambda D_{k_0} \leq 1 \text{ and } \lambda = 1/D_{k_0},$$

Therefore, the system can process arrival rates less than $1/D_{k_0}$; but, it saturates for arrival rates greater than or equal to $1/D_{k_0}$.

**Batch and terminal workloads.** To derive the bounds on the throughput, one can consider the heavy load situation. As the number $n$ of customers in the system becomes large, the utilizations of all centers grow, but clearly no utilization can exceed one. From the utilization law, we have for each center $k$:

$$U_k(n) = X(n)D_k \leq 1$$

Because the bottleneck center (i.e., center $k_0$) is the first to saturate, it restricts system throughput most severely. We conclude that:

$$X(n) = 1/D_{k_0}.$$

This is easy to state, because if each customer requires on average $D_{k_0}$ time units of service at the bottleneck center, then in the long run jobs cannot be completed any faster than one every $D_{k_0}$ time units. Now, consider the light load case. At the extreme, a single customer alone in the system gets a throughput of $1/D + Z$, because each interaction consists of a period of service of average length $D = \sum_{k=1}^{K} D_k$ and a think time of average length Z. As more customers are added to the system, there are two bounding situations as follows:

- The smallest achievable throughput occurs when each additional customer is queued and served after all the customers are already in the system. In such a situation, $(n-1)/D$ time units are spent queued behind other customers, $D$ time units are spent in service, and $Z$ time units are spent thinking. Thus, the throughput of each customer is $1/(nD + Z)$ and the system throughput is $n/(nD + Z)$.
- The largest achievable throughput occurs when the additional customers are not delayed by the customers in the system. In this case, no time is observed in queueing, $D$ time units are spent in service, and $Z$ time units are spent thinking. Thus, the throughput of each customer is $1/(D + Z)$, and system throughput is $n/(D + Z)$.

The aforementioned observations can be summarized as the asymptotic bounds on the system throughput:

$$\frac{n}{nD + Z} \leq X(n) \leq \min(1/D_{k_0}, \frac{n}{D + Z}).$$

Figure 8.5 depicts the general form of the asymptotic bounds on throughput.

Bounds on the response time $R(n)$ can be deduced by transforming the throughput bounds using Little's law. Replacing $X(n)$ and inverting the three components in the previous inequalities gives the following:

$$\max(D_{k_0}, \frac{D + Z}{n}) \leq \frac{R(n) + Z}{n} \leq \frac{nD + Z}{n}.$$

This implies that:

$$\max(D, nD_{k_0} - Z) \leq R(n) \leq nD$$

## 8.6.2  Balanced Systems Bounds

With little additional amount of computation compared with what is required for asymptotic bounds, tighter bounds can be obtained. These bounds are called balanced system bounds because they are based on systems that are *balanced*, in the sense that the service demand at every center is the same (i.e., $D_1 = D_2 = ... = D_K$). To perform this, we first set up some particular properties of balanced systems [14]. Then, we give details on how these properties can be used to determine bounds that complement the asymptotic

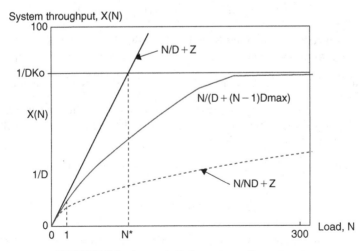

**FIGURE 8.5.** Asymptotic bounds on throughput.

bounds. However, the analysis of balanced systems requires that various assumptions be made about the system being modeled. This is in contrast to asymptotic bounds, which require only that the service demand of a customer at a center does not depend on how many other customers are currently in the system or at which centers they are located.

Intuitively, one can see that the utilization of center $k$ is given by: $U_k(n) = n/(n + K - 1)$. Using the utilization law, the system throughput is given by:

$$X(n) = \frac{U_k}{D_k} = \frac{n}{n + K - 1} \times \frac{1}{D_k}$$

where $D_k$ is the the service demand at center $k$.

Let $D_{k_0}, D_{k_1}$, and $D_{k_2}$ denote the maximum, average, and minimum service demands at the centers of the model that we wish to evaluate. We bound the throughput of that system by the throughputs of two related balanced systems: one with service demand $D_{k_2}$ at every center, and the other with service demand $D_{k_0}$ at every center:

$$\frac{n}{n + K - 1} \times \frac{1}{D_{k_0}} \leq X(n) \leq \frac{n}{n + K - 1} \times \frac{1}{D_{k_2}}.$$

These inequalities hold because of all systems with $K$ centers, $n$ customers, and maximum service demand $D_{k_0}$, the one with the lowest throughput is the balanced system with demand $D_{k_0}$ at each center. Similarly, of all systems with $K$ centers, $n$ customers, and minimum demand $D_{k_2}$, the one with the highest throughput is the balanced system with demand $D_{k_2}$ at each center. Corresponding bounds on average response times are given by:

$$(n + K - 1)D_{k_2} \leq R(n) \leq (n + K - 1)D_{k_0}$$

Tighter balanced system bounds can be obtained by constraining the total demand, $D$, or equivalently, the average demand $D_{k_1}$. Among all systems having a given total service demand $D = \sum_{k=1}^{K} D_k$, the system with the highest throughput (and the lowest average response time) is the one in which all service demands are equal (i.e., $sD_k = D/K$, $k \geq 1$). Thus, the following (optimistic bounds) are given by:

$$X(n) \leq \frac{n}{n + K - 1} \times \frac{1}{D_{k_1}} = \frac{n}{D + (n - 1)D_{k_1}}$$

$$R(n) \geq D + (n - 1)D_{k_1}.$$

Similarly, of all systems with total demand $D$ and maximum demand $D_{k_0}$, the one with the lowest throughput has $D/D_{k0}$ centers with demand $D_{k_0}$ and zero demand at the remaining centers. Therefore, "pessimistic" bounds can be deduced as follows:

$$\frac{n}{n + \frac{D}{D_{k_0}} - 1} \times \frac{1}{D_{k_0}} = \frac{n}{D + (n-1)D_{k_0}} \leq X(n)$$

$$D + (n-1)D_{k_0} \geq R(n).$$

The throughput curve for the bottleneck and the balanced bounds are depicted in Figure 8.6. The lower balanced system bound asymptotically approaches the bottleneck upper bound at high loads. This means that:

$$\lim_{N \to \infty} \left( \frac{N}{D + (N-1)D_{\max}} \right) = \frac{1}{D_{\max}}$$

The asymptotic bottleneck bound $\frac{1}{D_{\max}}$ and the optimistic balanced bound intersect at $N^+$ such that

$$\frac{1}{D_{\max}} = \frac{N^+}{D + (N-1)D_{av}}$$

### 8.6.3 Illustrative Example

A company has $m$ geographically distributed sites where three types of systems need to be deployed. A modeling study was initiated to determine those sites at

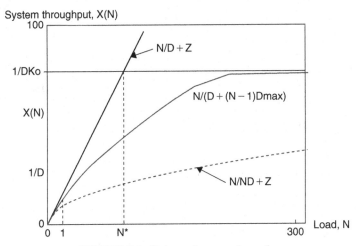

**FIGURE 8.6.** Balanced system bounds.

which the less expensive system would be placed. A bounding model was used to assess the performance to be expected from each of the three systems. Figure 8.7 depicts the queueing network. The parameters used in this model are the following: the number $K$ of service centers is equal to 2; the type of customer class is terminal; and parameters $D$, $D$ max, and think time are described by Table 8.3.

Applying the model of each of the three systems leads to the computation of the optimistic asymptotic bounds. The pessimistic bounds are easy to perform. These bounds reveal the following:

- At heavy load conditions, performance of system 2 will be inferior to that of the system 1. This is a consequence of the fact that the CPU is slower, which is the bottleneck device.
- Rather than a performance gain of 1.5 to 2, a performance degradation could be expected in moving from systems 1 to systems 2 whenever the number of active terminals exceeded some threshold.
- A performance gain can be obtained when moving from systems 1 to systems 3 although not the expected factor of two or more.

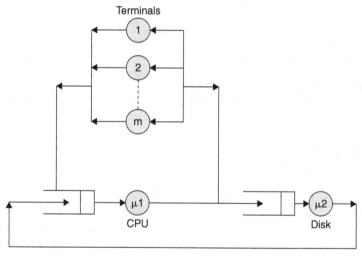

**FIGURE 8.7.** A queueing model for the case study.

**TABLE 8.3  Data about system described in Figure 8.7**

|            | System 1 | System 2 | System 3 |
|------------|----------|----------|----------|
| Dmax       | 4.6 s    | 5.1 s    | 3.1 s    |
| D          | 8.6      | 7.0      | 5.0      |
| Think time | 60 min   | 60 min   | 60 min   |

- The performance gain of system 2 over system 1 at lighter loads is negligible.

Consequently, there is no performance reason to invest in systems for any sites. Eventually, the company can decide to install system 3. Without the simple modeling study, the company might have ordered system 2 without doing the needed benchmark tests on it, which could lead to disappointing results.

## 8.7  CASE STUDY: A CIRCUIT SWITCHING SYSTEM

On arrival, each call in a switching network must find a path through the switching network to an idle receiver; if no path is available, then a decision is made concerning more call processing. Each call requires temporarily a receiver for messages and call handling services; if no receiver is available, then the system decides what subsequent action is required for that call.

We assume that, in switching networks, each call on arrival must be assigned to one of $S$ channels (or paths or links); if no channel is available, then the call is blocked or cleared from the system, and presumably it will retry later. If a call is accepted, then it holds a link and then requires a receiver; if no receiver is available, then calls queue until a receiver is available. $R$ receivers are present in the system.

We propose in this case study to determine the capacity of the switching system, which is the joint choice of number of links and receivers that allow the largest possible mean completion rate of calls while still meeting call setup delay goals. We also show that the number of links and the number of receivers are coupled. In fact, we show that it is possible to choose jointly the number of links and receivers to achieve capacity superior to that when each is chosen separately.

The state of the system at any instant of time is given by a pair $(i, j)$, where $i$ denotes the number of calls in the setup phase and $j$ represents the number of calls in the talking phase. The space of states $\Omega$ is given by:

$$\Omega = \{(i,j) \mid 0 \le i + j \le S, \ 0 \le i, j \le S\}.$$

The space W is organized as $\Omega = \bigcup_{k=0}^{S} \Omega_k$, where $\Omega_k$ denotes the set of states where there are only $k$ calls in setup and talking phase:

$$\Omega_k = \{(i,j) \mid 0 \le i, j \le S, \ i + j = k\}.$$

The arrival statistics of calls are assumed to be Poissonian, meaning that the sequence of interarrival times of calls is independent exponentially distributed random variable, with mean arrival rate $\lambda$. The first step of call setup involves holding a link and a receiver for a mean time interval denoted by $T_{ctr}$. The second step of talking involves holding a link for a mean time interval denoted by $T_{tlk}$.

*Mean value analysis.* At any time $t$, the mean number of receivers busy with call setup and the number of links or trunks busy with call setup or talking are given by:

$$\lambda T_{ctr} = E(\min(R, i)), \lambda(T_{ctr} + T_{tlk}) = E(\min(S, j))$$

The mean throughput rate is upper bounded by:

$$\lambda \le \min(\frac{S}{T_{ctr} + T_{tlk}}, \frac{R}{T_{ctr}}).$$

Thus, two bottlenecks can occur here, as follows:

- If links are bottleneck, then one can conclude that $\dfrac{S}{T_{ctr} + T_{tlk}}$.
- If receivers are bottleneck, then one can deduce that $\dfrac{R}{T_{ctr}}$.

*Jackson analysis.* Given these assumptions made previously, one can state that the system is a Jackson network. The fraction of time the system is in state $(i, j)$, averaged over a suitably long time interval, denoted by $\pi(i, j)$, is given by:

$$\pi(i,j) = \frac{1}{G} \prod_{k=0}^{i} \frac{\lambda T_{ctr}}{f_{rec}(k)} \prod_{k=0}^{j} \frac{\lambda T_{tlk}}{f_{trk}(k)}$$

where $f_{rec}(k)$ and $f_{trk}(m)$ are given by:

$$f_{rec}(k) = \begin{cases} 1, & k = 0 \\ \min(R, k), & k > 0 \end{cases}, \quad f_{rec}(k) = \begin{cases} 1, & k = 0 \\ \min(S, k), & k > 0. \end{cases}$$

*Blocking analysis.* The fraction of time that an arriving call finds the $S$ links busy and is cleared or blocked from entering the system is called the blocking probability, denoted by $B$. The approach used to compute blocking probability involves calculating the fraction of time the system has all $S$ links occupied. It holds that:

$$B = \sum_{(i,j)\in\Omega_k} \pi(i,j) = \frac{G_S}{G}, \quad G = \sum_{k=0}^{S} G_k$$

$$G_k = \sum_{(i,j)\in\Omega_k} \prod_{m=0}^{i} \frac{\lambda T_{ctl}}{f_{rec}(m)} \cdot \prod_{n=0}^{j} \frac{\lambda T_{tlk}}{f_{trk}(n)}, \quad 0 \le k \le S.$$

*Waiting Time Distribution.* Let $\pi_{acc}(i,j)$ denote the fraction of time that the system is in state *(i,j)* and an arriving call is accepted. This can be easily computed by:

$$\pi_{acc}(i,j) = \frac{\pi(i,j)}{1-B}$$

$$= \frac{1}{(1-B)G_*} \cdot \prod_{m=0}^{i} \frac{\lambda T_{ctl}}{f_{rec}(m)} \cdot \prod_{n=0}^{j} \frac{\lambda T_{tlk}}{f_{trk}(n)}, \quad (i,j) \in \Omega_a = \bigcup_{k=0}^{S-1} \Omega_k$$

where

$$G_* = \sum_{(i,j)\in\Omega_*} \prod_{m=0}^{i} \frac{\lambda T_{ctl}}{f_{rec}(m)} \cdot \prod_{n=0}^{j} \frac{\lambda T_{tlk}}{f_{trk}(n)}$$

Let now $\pi(i)$ be the marginal distribution of $\pi_{acc}(i,j)$, meaning that:

$$\pi(i) = \sum_{j=0}^{S-i-1} \pi_{acc}(i,j).$$

Let $X$ be the random variable denoting the time interval from when an accepted call arrives until it is first assigned a receiver. Recall that calls are processed in order of arrival. If $(R-1)$ or fewer receivers are busy, the accepted call does not wait at all. Thus the probability $P(X=0)$ that an accepted call does not wait is determined by:

$$P(X=0) = \begin{cases} \sum_{0\le i\le R-1} \pi(i), & R<S \\ 0, & R=S \end{cases}.$$

The probability that an accepted call waits greater than $n > 0$ to start receive processing is computed by:

$$P(X > n) = \begin{cases} \sum_{i=0}^{R-1} \pi(i) + \sum_{i=R}^{S-1} \pi(i) \cdot \left(\frac{R}{R+zT_{rec}}\right)^{i-R+1}, & R < S \\ 1, & R = S \end{cases}$$

The total call setup delay, denoted by $T_{set}$, is the sum of the waiting time $X$ plus the receiver processing time $Y$, $T_{set} = X + Y$. Using Little's law, we obtain:

$$E(T_{set}) = \frac{1}{\lambda(1-B)} \sum_{i=0}^{S} \sum_{j=0}^{S-1} i\pi(i,j).$$

*Asymptotic behavior.* Now, assume given $R$ receivers and $S$ links, with mean setup time $T_{rec}$ and mean call talking time $T_{tlk}$, we consider the problem of finding the largest mean arrival rate $\lambda$ such that the blocking $B$ is lower than some threshold $\delta$, and the fraction of time a call waits in setup before it starts processing is acceptable; meaning that probability $P(X > n)$ is lower than a small threshold $\varepsilon$. Thus,

$$B < \delta, \quad P(X > n > 0) < \varepsilon.$$

As $\lambda$ grows to infinity, we observe that the long term time averaged distribution becomes concentrated in the states where all $S$ links are always busy (i.e., as soon as a call completes, another is ready to take the link). We have:

$$\lim_{\lambda \to \infty} \pi(i,j) = \begin{cases} \frac{1}{G} \prod_{m=0}^{i} \frac{\lambda T_{rec}}{f_{rec}(m)} \cdot \prod_{n=0}^{j} \frac{\lambda T_{tlk}}{f_{trk}(n)} & (i,j) \in \Omega_S \\ 0, & i+j < S. \end{cases}$$

As the arrival rate becomes infinite, the blocking approaches one. In fact, we have:

$$B = 1 - \frac{\lambda_{\max}}{\lambda} + \ldots, \lambda \to \infty$$

The mean throughput rate is given by:

Mean call throughput rate $= \lim_{\lambda \to \infty} (\lambda(1-B)) = \lambda_{\max} = \min(\frac{R}{T_{rec}}, \frac{S}{T_{tlk}+T_{rec}})$.
In particular when R = S, we have:

$$\lambda_{\max} = \frac{S}{T_{tlk}} \cdot \frac{1}{\frac{1}{T_{rec}} + \frac{1}{T_{tlk}}} \cdot$$

In fact, it is also possible for the interaction between links and receivers to limit the maximum mean call completion rate below either of these upper bounds. Because the network or links are used for two purposes, control or call setup and talking or data transfer, it is possible for $\lambda_{\max}$ to be less than $S/T_{tlk}$, which would be the limit because of links being a bottleneck.

## 8.8 SUMMARY

Performance metrics that can be obtained from the queueing network models are discussed in this chapter. In particular, the notions of service time, arrival rate, service demand, utilization, queue length, response time, throughput, waiting time, and response time are analyzed here in more precise terms and their computation (or estimation) is developed for the systems. A particular interest has been given, in this chapter, to the standard MVA, the approximation of MVA, and the bounding analysis. We also presented several examples to illustrate the applications of these algorithms and laws.

## REFERENCES

[1] P. J. Denning, and J. P. Buzen, "The Operational Analysis of Queueing Network Models," Computing Surveys, Vol. 10, No. 3, pp. 225–261, 1978.

[2] J. D. C. Little, "A Proof of the Queueing Formula L = $\lambda$.W," European Journal of Operations Research, Vol. 9, pp. 383–387, 1961.

[3] M. Reiser, and S. S. Lavenberg, "Mean Value Analysis of Closed Multichain Queueing Networks," Journal of the ACM, Vol. 27, No. 2, pp. 313–322, 1980.

[4] S. S. Lavenberg, and M. Reiser, "Stationary State Probabilities at Arrival Instants for Closed Queueing Networks with Multiple Types of Customers," Journal of Applied probability, Vol. 17, No. 4, pp. 1048–1061, 1981.

[5] D. Neuse, and K. M. Chandy, "SCAT: A Heuristic Algorithm for Queueing Network Models of Computing Systems," ACM Sigmetrics Performance Evaluation Review, Vol. 10, No. 3, pp. 59–79, 1981.

[6] J.C. Strelen, "A Generalization of Mean Value Analysis to Higher Moments Moment Analysis," ACM Sigmetrics Performance Evaluation Review, Vol. 14, No. 1, pp. 129–140, 1986.

[7] K.M. Chandy, and D. Neuse, "Linearizer: A Heuristic Algorithm for Queueing Network Models of Computing Systems," Communications of the ACM, Vol. 25, No. 2 pp. 126–134, 1982.

[8] J. Zahorjan, D. L. Eager, and H. M. Sweillam, "Accuracy, Speed, and Convergence of Approximate Mean Value Analysis," Performance Evaluation, Vol. 8, No. 4, pp. 255–270, 1988.

[9] Y. Bard, "Some Extensions to Multiclass Queueing Network Analysis," in Performance of Computer Systems, M. Arato, A. Butrimenko, and E. Gelenbe (eds.), North-Holland, the Amsterdam, The Netherlands, 1979.

[10] P. J. Schweitzer, "Approximate Analysis of Multiclass Closed Networks of Queues," Proceedings of the International Conference on Stochastic Control and Optimization, pp. 25–29, Amsterdam, The Netherlands, 1979.

[11] L. Guan, M. E. Woodward, and I. U. Awan, "Bounding Delay through a Buffer using Dynamic Queue Thresholds," 20th International Conference on Advanced Information Networking and Applications Vol. 1 (AINA'06), pp.623–628, 2006.

[12] H. Kobayashi and B.L. Mark, "System Modeling and Analysis," Prentice Hall, Upper Saddle River, NJ, 2008.

[13] J. C. S. Lui, R. R. Muntz, and D. Towsley, "Bounding the Mean Response Time of a Minimum Expected Delay Routing System: An Algorithmic Approach," IEEE Transactions on Computes, Vol. 44, No. 12, pp. 1371–1382, 1995.

[14] J. Zahorjan, K. C. Sevcik, D. L. Eager, and B. I. Galler. "Balanced Job Bound Analysis of Queueing Networks," Communications of ACM, Vol. 25, No. 2, pp. 134–141, 1982.

## EXERCISES

1. The average delay experienced by a packet when traversing a computer network is 100 ms. The average number of packets that cross the network per second is 128 packets/s. What is the average number of concurrent packets in transit in the network at any time?

2. A computer system has one CPU and two disks: disk 1 and disk 2. The system is monitored for 1h and the utilization of the CPU and disk 1 are measured to be 32% and 60%, respectively. Each transaction makes five I/O requests to disk 1 and eight to disk 2. The average service time at disk 1 is 30 ms and at disk 2 is 25 ms.

   a. Find the system throughput.

   b. Find the utilization of disk 2.

   c. Find the average service demands at the CPU, disk 1, and disk 2.

   d. Find the system throughput, response time, and average queue length at the CPU and the disks. when the degree of multiprogramming is n, for $1 \leq n \leq 4$.

   e. Based on the above results, define a good approximation for the average degree of multiprogramming during the measurement interval.

3. Consider an interactive system with a CPU and two disks. The following measurement data were gathered by observing the system during an interval of 1 hour:

| | |
|---|---|
| Active terminals = 30, | Think time = 12 s |
| Completed transactions = 1,600 | Disk1 accesses = 48,000 |
| Disk2 accesses = 24,000 | CPU busy = 720 s |
| Disk1 busy = 480 s | Disk2 busy = 640 s |

   a. Determine the visit counts ($V_k$), service times per visit ($S_k$), and service demands ($D_k$) at each center.
   b. Give optimistic and pessimistic asymptotic bounds on throughput and response time for 5, 10, 20, and 40 active terminals.

4. Consider the interactive system shown in Figure 8.8. The visit counts and average service times have been measured as presented in Table 8.4 and assume that $Z = 20$ s.
   a. Discuss whether an 8-s response time is feasible with 30 users logged on. If this is not the case, then propose the changes required to achieve it.
   b. Discuss whether a 10-s response time is feasible when 50 users are logged on the system. If not, compute how much CPU speedup is required.

5. A communication system contains $N = 12$ identical nodes organized into a ring. We assume that each node transmits to only one other node, each node receives from only one other node, and all nodes are connected by identical one way transmission links with transmission rate $C = 10^6$ bits/s. All packets are routed around the ring in one direction. Packets can arrive at any node and are transmitted to any other remaining node, and then they leave the system. All packets have a fixed size B. The fraction of the total network packet load entering at node I and departing at a node that is J nodes away is denoted by $F_{I, I+J}$, where $I$ and $J$ are considered as elements of $Z/12$ (i.e., integers modulo 12). The total mean packet arrival rate to the system is denoted by $\lambda$.

TABLE 8.4  Data about the system described in Exercise 4

| Number | Device | $S_2$ | $V_1$ | $D_I = V_I S_I$ |
|---|---|---|---|---|
| 1 | CPU | 0.05 | 20 | 1.00 |
| 2 | Disk | 0.08 | 11 | 0.88 |
| 3 | Fast disk | 0.04 | 8 | 0.32 |
| | | | $R_{min}$ | 2.20 |

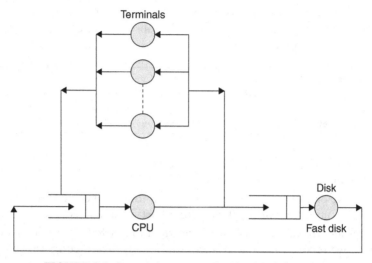

**FIGURE 8.8.** Interactive system described in Exercise 4.

Finally, assume that:

    a. All nodes are statistically identical, meaning that the value of $F_{I,I+J}$ is independent of I.

    b. No node can send packets to itself (i.e., $F_{I,I} = 0$, $I \in \{0, 1, .., 11\}$.

    c. Any packet in the network has a unique source and a unique destination; meaning that:

$$\sum_{I=0}^{11} \sum_{J=1}^{11} F_{I,I+J} = 1.$$

    i. Assume that $F_{I,I+J} = \frac{1}{N(N-1)}$ ($= 120$), then find an upper bound on the maximum mean packet switching rate for this system.

    ii. Determine the value(s) of $F_{I,I+J}$, $0 < I,J, < N-1$, that provide the largest mean packet switching rate.

    iii. Determine the value(s) of $F_{I,I+J}$, $0 < I,J, < N-1$, that provide the smallest mean packet switching rate.

6. A variable bandwidth circuit switch consists of two input links, each capable of handling two time slots per frame; two output links, each capable of handling two time slots per frame; and a central switch, capable of switching four time slots per frame. Assume that two types of calls are switched: one requiring one slot per frame and the other two slots per frame. The arrival process for each call type is assumed to be a simple Poisson. The sequence of call holding times for each call type is assumed to be independent and identically distributed random variables.

Finally, assume that each call type is equally likely to go from any input link to any output link.

a. Determine the blocking for each call type versus the fraction of arrivals that are low bandwidth assuming:

   i. The two call types have identical call holding times of one frame.

   ii. The low-bandwidth call has a holding time of 10 frames, and the high bandwidth call has a holding time of 1 frame.

   iii. The high-bandwidth call has a holding time of 10 frames, and the low bandwidth call has a holding time of 1 frame.

b. Assume all the high-bandwidth calls arrive on 1 input link and are destined for one output link. Assume the low-bandwidth calls arrive on the other input link and are all destined for the other output link. Repeat all the above.

c. Repeat all the above if the switch capacity is increased to eight slots per frame.

7. The queueing network model in Figure 8.9 has three job classes 1, 2, and 3. We assume the followings:

   • Class 1 is an open class, whereas 2 and 3 are closed classes.

   • Class 2 has two jobs, whereas class 3 has only one job.

   • Class 1 arrival rate is $\lambda_1 = 1$. Class 1 jobs leaving queue 1 go to queue 2 with probability 0.2 or to queue 3 with probability 0.8. Class 1 jobs leaving queues 2 and 3 always leave the system.

   • Class 2 jobs departing queue 1 are routed to queue 2 or queue 3 with equal probability.

   • Class 3 jobs departing queue 1 always go to queue 2.

   • The queueing network has a product form, and the mean service times are given by:

$$\frac{1}{\mu_{1,1}} = 0.2, \ \frac{1}{\mu_{1,2}} = 1, \ \frac{1}{\mu_{1,3}} = 0.5; \ \frac{1}{\mu_{2,1}} = 0.05, \ \frac{1}{\mu_{2,2}} = 0.1,$$

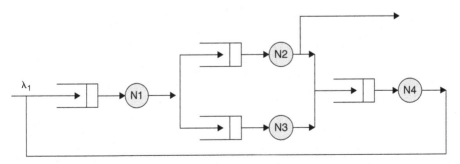

**FIGURE 8.9.** The queueing network model of Exercise 7.

$$\frac{1}{\mu_{2,3}} = \frac{1}{\mu_{2,4}} = 0.04; \quad \frac{1}{\mu_{3,1}} = 0.1, \quad \frac{1}{\mu_{3,2}} = 0.4, \quad \frac{1}{\mu_{3,4}} = 0.2$$

a. Find the queue utilizations by class 1 jobs.
b. Find the visit ratios $V_{j,m}$ and the demands $D_{j,m}$, for $j = 1,2,3$ and $m = 1,...,4$.
c. Find the response times for open class 1.
d. Compute the total queue utilizations.

# CHAPTER 9

# INTRODUCTION TO SIMULATION TECHNIQUE

In general, simulation is the process of designing a model (replica) of a real system to study its behavior using experiments that are run under different operating conditions and environments. The goal is to understand the behavior of the system under study or investigate the performance using various operating strategies, designs, and settings depending on whether the system or a prototype of it exists in reality or is just a design on paper. It is important to note that simulation measures the performance of the model of the system, not the real system. In *Webster's Collegiate Dictionary*, simulation is defined as an assemblage of objects united by some form of regular interaction or interdependence.

The act of simulating anything usually corresponds to certain important characteristics or behaviors of a chosen physical or abstracted system. This chapter introduces the fundamental concepts of simulation as a performance evaluation technique for computer and telecommunication systems. Principles and basics of simulation techniques, simulation terminology; and random-number-generation techniques, which include linear congruential generators, Tausworthe generators, mixed generators, and extended Fibonacci generators are reviewed. The chapter also sheds some light on the commonly used random-number generators, seed selections, and various tests for testing random-number generators. Finally, the chapter concludes by discussing the concepts related to the popular pseudorandom-variate-generation techniques, including the inverse transformation, rejection, characterization, convolution, and composition.

*Fundamentals of Performance Evaluation of Computer and Telecommunication Systems,*
By Mohammad S. Obaidat and Noureddine A. Boudriga
Copyright © 2010 John Wiley & Sons, Inc.

## 9.1   INTRODUCTION

Simulation analysis is considered an important performance-evaluation technique. It is more accurate than the analytic modeling and less accurate than the measurment technique. However, it is not as expensive as the measurement scheme. Simulation is generally used before altering an existing system or before building a new system to minimize the failure chances to meet requirements and remove unanticipated bottlenecks, to avoid underuse or overuse of resources, and to increase the system performance. With the help of simulation, one can answer queries, such as follows: For a new telecommunication network or computer system, what is the best possible design available? What should be the necessary resource requirements? Does a new design or topology provide better performance than existing ones? In case of traffic load raises by 50%, what will be the performance of the system or network? To increase the performance of system, which type of protocol should be used? In case of link failure, what will be the impact?

Simulation is a general term that is used in many disciplines, including performance evaluation of computer and telecommunications systems. It is the procedure of designing a model of a real system and conducting experiments with this model for the purpose of understanding its behavior, or of evaluating various strategies and scenarios of its operation. Others defined simulation as the process of experimenting with a model of the system under study using computer programming. It measures a model of the system rather than the system itself [1–14].

In this context, a model is a description of a system by symbolic language or theory to be deserved as a system with which the world of objects can be expressed. Hence, a model is a system interpretation or implementation of a theory that is true. Shannon defined a model as, "the process of designing a computerized model of a system and conducting experiments with this model for the purpose either of understanding the behavior of the system or of evaluating various strategies for the operation of the system [1–35]".

According to the above definition of a model, we can redefine simulation as the use of a model, which may be represented using various ways, such as a flowchart, pseudocode, block diagram, or as schematic diagram, before coding it into a computer program often called a "simulator" to conduct experiments that, by deduction, communicate an understanding of the behavior of the system under study. Simulation experiments or runs are essential in any simulation study because they help to: (a) ascertain something unknown or test an assumption and (b) aid to find candidate's solutions and (c) offer a mean for assessing them.

The simulation of any system including computer and telecommunication systems involve three types of entities: (a) a real system, (b) a model, and (c) a simulator (simulation program). These entities are to be understood in their interrelation to one another as they are related and dependent on each other in one way or another. Keep in mind that the real system is a source of raw data, whereas the model is a set of instructions for data gathering. The simulator is a tool for carrying out model instructions. We need to validate any simulation model to make sure that the assumptions, distributions, inputs, outputs, results, and conclusions are correct. We also have to verify the simulator to make sure that the model assumptions have been implemented by the simulationist properly and that the simulator has been debugged from all programming errors [1–35].

The simulation of a particular system can be defined as an operation to be performed on a model of that system. Reconfiguration with the model can be done. However, it is impossible, expensive, and impractical when using the real system. Operations that are related to the model can be easily studied, so the properties that are concerned with the performance of the genuine system can be assumed. To estimate the performance of the already available or yet to be proposed systems under various conditions or configurations, one can consider simulation as the best possible tool. Simulation is generally used before altering an existing system or before building a whole new system to reduce the failure possibilities to meet requirements and to remove unforeseen bottlenecks; it is also used to avoid less or over access of resources and to enhance the system is performance. With the help of simulation, one can answer queries like: For a new telecommunications network, what is the best possible topology design available? What should be the necessary resource requirements? In case of traffic load raises by 50%, what will be the performance of the telecommunications network? To increase the performance of a network, which type of routing protocol should be used? In case of link failure, what and how will be the impact? Whereas on the other side, weather simulators and flight simulators that are continuous simulators will always try to enumerate the changes related to system constantly as a part of response towards controls. When compared with continuous simulation, discrete simulation is less featured and its implementation part is much simpler, so that is why discrete simulation is extensively used in a variety of situations, especially the simulation of computer and telecommunication systems.

Systems in general can be divided into deterministic and stochastic types [1–10]:

- In deterministic systems, the new state of the system is completely established by the preceding state and by the activity or input.
- In stochastic systems, the system encloses a certain amount of uncertainty or randomness in its movement from one state to another. A stochastic system can enter more than one possible state after a state in response to an input or activity. Obviously, a stochastic system is nondeterministic from the point of view that the next state cannot be explicitly forecasted if the current and the stimulus are known.

Simulation analysis is an attractive tool to predict the performance of any systems for the following reasons [1–20]:

1. Simulation can be rewarding in terms of time and efforts.
2. Simulation encourages full solutions.
3. Simulation conveys skill, information, and knowledge together.
4. Simulation can promote innovative attitude for trying new concepts or ideas. Various organizations have under used resources and systems, which if fully used, can result in notable improvements in quality and efficiency. Simulation can be worthwhile tool to communicate, experiment with, and assess such proposed solutions, scenarios, schemes, designs, or plans.
5. Simulation can forecast results for possible courses of action in a speedy manner.
6. Simulation can justify the effect of variances occurring in a node, element, or a system. It is essential to note that performance computations based mainly on mean values neglect the effect of variances, which may lead to incorrect conclusions.

To perform a methodical and successful simulation study and analysis, the following steps should be followed [1–5, 10]. Figure 9.1 summarizes these major phases.

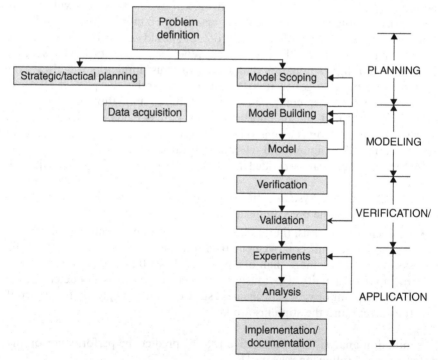

**FIGURE 9.1.** Overview of the simulation methodology.

**I. Planning Phase.** In the planning phase, the following tasks have to be identified:

1. Problem outlining: If a problem statement is being developed by the analyst, it is important that policy makers comprehend and concur with the formulation. Keep in mind that a problem well defined is half solved. So, it is important to establish the problem statement and aims of the simulation task ahead of time.

2. Resource assessment: An approximate of the resources required to gather data and analyze the system under study should be performed. Resources including time, money, personnel, and equipment must be planned for and thought of. It is better to amend objectives of the simulation study at early phase than to fall short because of a lack of vital resources.

3. System and data analysis: This step includes a thorough investigation in the literature of previous schemes, techniques, and algorithms for the same problem. Many projects have not succeeded because of misinterpretation of the problem at hand. Identification of factors, variables, initial conditions, and performance metrics is made in this phase. In addition, the level of detail of the model must be agreed on.

**II. Modeling Phase.** Here, the simulationist constructs a system model, which is an imitation of the real system understudy or a representation of some aspects of the system to be analyzed.

- Model construction: This task consists of abstraction of the system into mathematical relationship with the problem formulation.
- Data acquirement: This task entails identification, description, and gathering of data.
- Model transformation: This task involves preparation and troubleshooting of the model for computer processing.

Models can be classified into the following types: (a) descriptive models, (b) physical models such as the ones used in aircrafts and buildings, (c) mathematical models such as Newton's law of motion, (d) flowcharts, (e) schematics, and (f) computer pseudocode.

The chief phases in model building consist of: (a) preliminary simulation model diagram; (b) building of flow diagrams; (c) assessment of model diagram with a team; (d) launching of data gathering; (e) adjusting the top-down design; testing; and validation for the required degree of granularity; (f) total data collection; (g) iteration through steps above (e) and (g) until the required degree of granularity has been achieved; and (h) ultimate system diagram, transformation; and verification.

It is necessary to mention the following two important concepts in this context [1–11]:

- **Model scooping:** This refers to the method of finding out what process, entity, function, device, and so on, within the system should be taken into account in the simulation model, and at what granularity.
- **Level of details:** This is established based on the element's effect on the steadiness of the analysis. The proper level of details will differ depending on the modeling and simulation aims.
- **Subsystem modeling.** When the system to be evaluated is large, a subsystem modeling is carried out. All subsystem models are later tied properly. To characterize subsystems, there are three common methods, as follows:
  - **Flow scheme:** This technique has been employed to study systems that are characterized by the flow of physical or information entries through the system such as pipeline computer systems.
  - **Functional scheme:** This scheme is valuable when no directly visible flowing entities are in the system, such as manufacturing processes that do not use assembly lines.
  - **State-Change scheme:** This is helpful in systems that are described by a large number of interdependent relationships and that must be tested at regular intervals to identify state changes.
- **Variable and parameter assessment.** This is performed normally by gathering data over some period of time and then figuring out a frequency distribution for the needed variables. This kind of analysis may aid the modeler to come across a well-known variate/distribution that can characterize the activities of the system or subsystem.
- **Selection of a programming language/simulation software package.** The simulationist should choose whether to use: (a) a general-purpose programming language such as Java, C++, or C; (b) a simulation language such as SIMSCRIPT III, MODSIM III, CSIM, or JavaSim; or (c) a simulation package such as Opnet, NS2, NS3, Network III, Comnet III, QualNet, and GloMoSim. In general, using a simulation package may save money and time; however, it may not be flexible and effective to use simulation packages as they may not contain capabilities to do the task such as modules to simulate some protocols or some features of the network or system under study.

**III. Verification and Validation (V&V).** Verification is the procedure of noting whether the model realizes the assumptions considered accurately or not. Others consider it basically the process of troubleshooting the simulation program (simulator), which implements the model of the system under study. It is possible to have a verified simulator that actually represents an invalid model. Also, it is possible to have a valid model that represents an unverified simulator.

The validation procedure refers to making sure that assumptions considered in the model are realistic in that, if properly realized, the model would generate outcomes close to these obtained in real systems. Model validation is basically aimed at validating the assumptions, input parameters and distributions, and output values and conclusions. Validation can be carried out by one of the following schemes: (a) relating the results of the simulation with results previously obtained by the real system working under the same environments, (b) expert insight (intuition), (c) analytic results via queueing theory or other mathematical schemes, (d) another simulation model, and (e) artificial intelligence and expert systems.

**IV. Applications and Experimentation.** Following the verification and validation of the model, the simulator has to be run under different operating conditions and environments to reveal the behavior of the system under study. Keep in mind that any simulation study that does not include experimentation with the simulation model is not useful. It is through testing and experimentation the analyst can appreciate the system and make recommendations about its design and most favorable operational modes. The level of experiments relies mainly on the cost to approximate performance measures, sensitivity of performance metrics to particular variables, and the correlation among control variables [1–5, 10, 11].

The realization of simulation results into practice is an essential task that is performed after testing and experimentation. Documentation is crucial and should contain a full record of the whole project activity, not just a user's manual.

Factors which should be given special attention in simulation analysis include: (a) pseudo random number generators (RNGs), (b) random variates (RVs) or observations, or observations (c) programming errors, (d) specification errors, (e) duration of simulation, (f) sensitivity to parameters, (g) data gathering, (h) optimization parameter errors, (i) incorrect design, and (j) influence of seed values or initial conditions.

The chief advantages of the simulation technique include [1–5, 10–12]:

- Flexibility: Simulation permits controlled experiments free of risk. Some important experiments cannot be conducted on the real physical system due to inconvenience, risk, and cost.
- Speed: It permits time compression operation of a system operation over extensive period of time. The results of conducting experiments can be obtained much faster than real-time experiments on the real physical system.
- Simulation modeling allows sensitivity analysis by manipulating input variables to find the design parameters that are critical to the operation of the system under study and that influence its operation notably.

- It is a good training tool: In any simulation study, the simulation group consists of experts in programming, mathematics, statistics, system science, and analysis, as well as in technical documentation. The communication between the team members provides tremendous training opportunity.
- It does not disturb the real system; simulation analysis can be performed on the system without the need to disturb the physical system under study. This is critical as running tests on the real system may be pricey and also can be catastrophic. In addition, in some cases the physical system does not exist physically and it is only design on paper.

The major disadvantages of simulation are as follows [1–11]:

- Simulation may become costly in terms of time, money, and manpower.
- In simulation modeling, we usually make a hypothesis about input variables and parameters, and distributions and if these assumptions are inaccurate, then the obtained outcomes may not be credible.
- It is not easy to select initial conditions, and not doing so may influence the reliability of the model.

Figure 9.2 represents a simplified illustration of the simulation process. The nature of the process involved here is iterative. All simulation experiments and

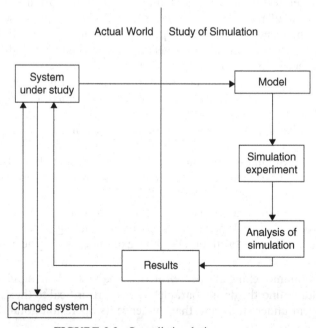

**FIGURE 9.2.** Overall simulation process.

changes do not incur cost in hardware parts, and any change can be made in the simulation model easily and risk free. Almost all simulation software tools have this efficient feature. To achieve success in simulation analysis, well-qualified problem formulators, simulation modelers, and analysts are much needed and crucial.

The process of producing a model is called modeling. With the help of the model, the analyst can easily predict the impact of changes on the system. The model should always be a close representation of the actual system, and most of its significant features should be included. In the same way, the model should not be too compound to understand and to experiment with. Practitioners who practice simulation always advocate the increase in the complication of the model iteratively. Model validity is an important issue in modeling.

In most simulation studies, the models that generally used are mathematical models. Various classifications are involved in mathematical modeling, which include deterministic, in which both the input variables and output variables are fixed, or stochastic; in this case either, input or output variables is probabilistic. Classifications also include static or dynamic. Generally, simulation models of computer systems and networks are classified as dynamic and stochastic.

Many stages are involved in simulation modeling process, which include the following [1]:

1. Defining the project and identifying its goals
2. Providing Model abstraction
3. Representing the model in digital form
4. Performing experiments with the model and generating the entire documentation of the project

This process represents an iterative method until a level of granularity is reached. Scientific disciplines, such as software engineering, artificial intelligence (AI), math, statistics, and databases, are applying foremost influence on the simulation modeling process (SMP) because of the advances in their respective fields that can help to provide a credible model and simulator. As shown in Figure 9.3, the simulation task is a data-concentrated process.

A study related to a system begins in the following cases:

1. When a problem persists with the present surviving system
2. When experimenting with the real (actual) system is not possible, or when the system is under construction

The modeler should always choose a combination of assumptions, which are appropriate, realistic, and adequate. After devising a conceptual model, it should be changed into a digital model. However, the digital model reliability is affected directly by the accuracy of verification and validation phases. After acquiring a

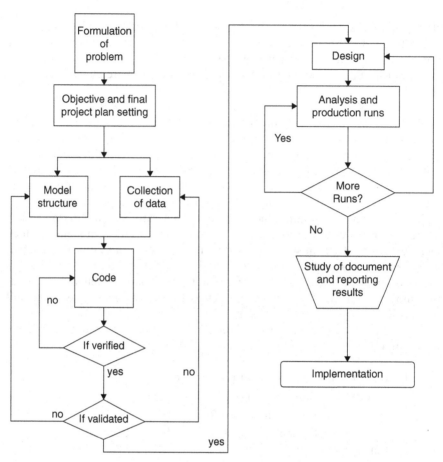

**FIGURE 9.3.** The simulation modeling process.

precise and reliable digital model, the simulation modeler proceeds toward the experimental stage. To meet the goals of the study, statistical tests are designed. Monitoring a model under a single combination of experimental condition gives inappropriate information. That is why always within a framework, various combinations of experimental conditions should be considered.

Now, we will take up the issue of randomness in simulation. Few simulations accept inputs only in the form of nonrandom and fixed values, which typically correspond to factors that illustrate the model and the particular alternative that we are going to evaluate. If the system that is to be simulated is like the above, then one can achieve a simulation model that is deterministic. The one thing good about this deterministic simulation model is that because the input has no randomness, there will no randomness in size and the interarrival times that exist between consecutively incoming parts in batches. Deterministic values for the input are represented by the big dots, and the big dots that are on the outputs also stand for the performance of the output

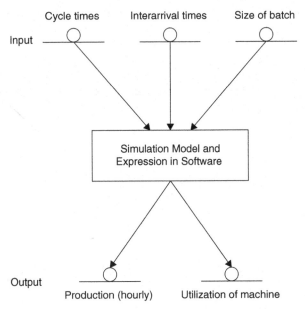

**FIGURE 9.4.** DIDO simulation.

(deterministic), which is achieved by converting the input into output by means of simulation's logic. Figure 9.4 illustrates a deterministic-in–deterministic-out (DIDO) simulation paradigm. Several different runs are to be made to evaluate the unlike input-parameter combinations before dealing with the tentative output. Most systems have some type of randomness or uncertain input, so that is why the simulation models that are practical should also offer for such variable input; such models are called stochastic simulation models. Actually, if the randomness in the input is ignored, then it may cause errors in the output of simulation model. A random-in–random-out (RIRO) simulation paradigm is illustrated by Figure 9.5.

## 9.2 TYPES OF SIMULATION

Usually, simulation models can be grouped into three different categories [3]: (a) static versus dynamic simulation model, where a static model is an illustration of a system at a specific time or one that may be used to characterize a system in which time plays no role such as Monte Carlo models, whereas a dynamic simulation model characterizes a system as it advances over time; (b) deterministic versus stochastic models where a deterministic model does not include any probabilistic elements whereas stochastic model has as a minimum some random input elements; and (c) continuous versus discrete simulation models where a discrete-event simulation is related to modeling of a system as it changes over time by illustration in which the state variables vary straight away

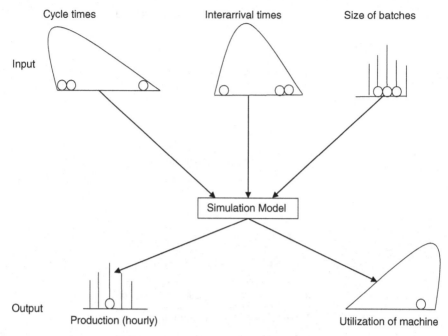

**FIGURE 9.5.** RIRO simulation paradigm.

at separate points in the time frequently called events. However, continuous simulation deals with modeling of a system by an illustration in which the state variables change continuously with respect to time.

To keep track with the up-to-date value of simulation time during any simulation study, we require a mechanism to move forward simulation time from one value to another. The variable that provides the current value of simulation time is called simulation clock. The means that can be employed to move forward simulation clock are [1–3]: (a) fixed-increment time advance scheme and (b) next-event time advance, which is used most often.

- **Fixed-Increment Time Advance:** In this scheme, the simulation clock is moved forward in fixed treads. After each update of the clock, a test is made to discover whether any events should have taken place during the previous fixed period (step). If some events were listed to have occurred during this period/interval, then they are viewed as if they have occurred at the end of the interval, and the system state is updated to reflect this.

- **Next-Event Time Advance:** In this case, the initial value of simulation clock is set to zero, and the times of occurrences of future events are found out. Then, the simulation clock is progressed to the time of occurrence of the most pending event in the future event list, after that the state of the system is updated consequently. Additional future events are found out in a similar

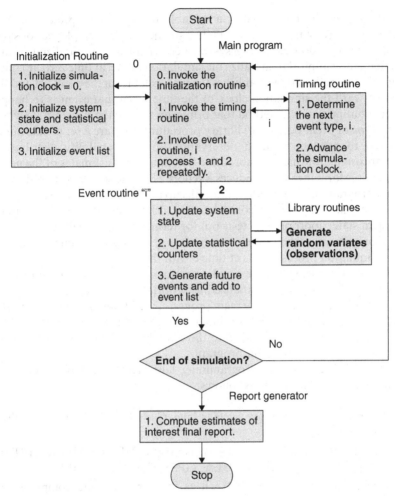

**FIGURE 9.6.** Summary of the next-event-time advance scheme.

way. This technique is reiterated until the stopping condition/criterion is satisfied. Figure 9.6 summarizes the next-event time advance scheme.

Note that the fixed-increment time advance technique is not exploited in discrete-event simulation because of the following disadvantages: (a) it is difficult to establish which event to process first when events that are not simultaneous in actuality are treated as such in this method and (b) mistakes are presented because events are handled at the end of the step/interval in which they occur, which is inaccurate.

The key components that are instituted in most discrete-event simulation models via the next-event time advance scheme are as follows [1–15]: (a) system state that is the set of state variables required to explain the system at a specific time, (b) simulation clock that is a variable that gives the present value of simulated time, (c) statistical counters that are the variables employed for saving statistical information regarding system performance, (d) initializing routine that is a method applied to initialize the simulation model at time zero, (e) timing routine that is method that establishes the next event from the event list and then moves forward the simulation clock to the time when that event is to happen, (f) event routine that is a method that brings up to date the system state when a specific type of event occurs, (g) library procedures that are a set of subroutines employed to produce random observations from probability distributions, (h) report originator that is a subroutine that figures out estimates of the needed metrics of performance and produces a report when the simulation finishes, and (i) main program that is a method that calls up the timing routine to find out the next event and then moves control to the related event routine to update the system state, appropriately tests out for termination and calls on the report originator/generator when the circumstances for ending the simulation are met.

The simulation process starts at time 0 with the main program calling on the initialization routine, where the simulation clock is set to zero, the system state and statistical counters are initialized appropriately as well as the event list. Once control comes again to the main program, it will call on the timing routine to determine the most eminent routine. If event $i$ is the most eminent one, then simulation clock is moved forward to the time that this event will happen and control is returned to the main program.

In general, the available programming languages/packages for computer and networks simulation are as follows:

- General purpose languages such as Java, C++, C, C#, Fortran, and Visual Basic.
- Special Simulation Languages such as SIMSCRIPT III, SIMSCRIPT II.5, MOSIM III, SLAM II, SIMULA, GPSS, GASP IV, CSIM.
- Special Simulation Packages such as the computer and computer communication-based packages; examples include NS3, NS2, OPNET, QualNet, GloMoSim, COMNET III, and Network II.5.

Classification in simulation is performed based on the system type it studies, which means simulation can be either continuous or discrete. In discrete-event-driven simulation, the modeler has to think in event terms that can change the systems condition. However, the systems status is delineated by the set of variables like queue number, server condition, number of servers it works on, and so on. The system that varies its state instantly at certain discrete time points employs discrete event simulation (DES). Computer and telecommunication systems are usually modeled using discrete event simulation. Discrete event simulation has three major stages: construction of the model, testing design, and execution of experiments. To accomplish distributed discrete event simulation, one has to think about what type of simulation is used for it.

The following gives a brief description on the execution of discrete event simulation on a uniprocessor system and the results that are anticipated from it. Changes in the state of the system being represented are described by discrete events. Many future events are created and scheduled by these jobs. In the process of executing simulation trial, discrete event system events are accumulated in an event-list prearranged based on simulation time at which they take place. In the event list, first the event with lowest simulation-time is eliminated, and this removed event is first executed and then necessary updates are made in the simulation state and probably other events are scheduled. This process of execution proceeds until all the other events are executed or if any other stopping criterion is met. The simulation-time advance rate (STAR) rely on both the simulator hardware and the simulation software. Under experimental operating circumstances, the discrete event system model's characteristics are described by discrete system event trials statistics, which include resource uses and response times. To demonstrate variability clearly, confidence levels are needed, as here the statistics may fluctuate from one simulation trim to other simulation trim. More and more estimation methods in confidence interval are introduced, which include independent replications, batch means, regeneration, and estimations regarding spectral and automatic regression schemes. The autoregressive method is highly recommended as it is more accurate and convenient although it is not extensively used. To acquire any confidence intervals more quickly, the design part of the experiment has to be applied with techniques that are a set of transforms like variance reduction schemes. Techniques such as alteration of event probabilities are also used. It is worth mentioning that these discrete event system statistical techniques are also valid for distributed discrete event systems. They are hardly ever mentioned as variance reduction techniques; they are only a part of experimental design, and the essentials of the distributed discrete event system algorithm are complicated by confidence interval generation. They slow down the simulation-time advance rate. Generally, if the events are not assured to happen at normal intervals and if there is no good grip on the time step, which means the time should not be too small as it makes the simulation run longer than that it should. Moreover, the time should not be too large as it makes the events out of control, in such a case an event-driven simulation is preferred [1–20].

## 9.3 SOME TERMINOLOGY

Each and every simulation model corresponds to a system of some sort of form. However, in general, a system can be a network comprising computers, a multiprocessor computer system, an assembly line, a facility providing service, or a health care system. When compared with each other, all these systems are completely different, but when comparison is made in terms of components, they are not that dissimilar. Dynamic entities and resources are the general system components. Objects that move along the system and that ask for services that are provided by resources of system are called dynamic entities. An entity has attributes through which it describes its characteristics. If an event occurs inside the system, then it is called as an endogenous event, and if it occurs outside the system then it is called an exogenous event.

Services to an entity are provided be means of resources. However, these resources are again categorized depending on the service type they provide, which include servers that can be machines or can be persons. Resources are connected to activities; these activities can be time periods of particular length. The system's state is a set of variables that are required to illustrate the performance of the system. With the help of the simulation clock, which is an internal one, sampling occurs from a random number stream, and over time, the system's random behavior can be modeled by simulation. Each and every time when a function is called up, new numbers are generated. This series of numbers is also called random number stream or sequence. Computers cannot generate true random numbers. However, only pseudorandom numbers are generated by computers, and these numbers are arithmetically random so they can be used in simulation modeling.

## 9.4 RANDOM-NUMBER-GENERATION TECHNIQUES

Random Number Generators (RNGs) are considered as a major building block in any simulation model. Most programming languages have built-in procedures/subroutines that can generate pseudorandom numbers according to one generation algorithm or another. From these random sequences, we can generate random variates using various algorithms. The generator function that is used to produce random number sequences should have desired characteristics that include the following [1, 10, 11, 31]:

1. The period should be large, as a small period may cause the generated sequence to recycle, which limits the useful length of simulation runs and ends up producing incorrect results.
2. It should not be computational expensive. The generation of random numbers should not take too much time, as simulation analysis requires thousands of random numbers per run.
3. Correlation between consecutive generated numbers should be small. In addition to the requirement of having independent successive values, these values should be uniformly distributed.

The third requirement is not easy to establish. That is why several techniques have been devised to test for this requirement. It is found that when generating random numbers, certain departures from ideal randomness may occur. Among these the following:

1. The variance of produced numbers may be high or low.
2. The average of the produced numbers may be high or low.
3. The generated numbers may not follow the uniform distribution.
4. It is possible to have cyclic variation. Examples on this problem include: (a) autocorrelation between numbers and (b) some numbers above the average followed by some below average.

Special tests are used to test RNGs. If some generation schemes fail any of the tests, then such schemes should be dropped in favor of others that pass all possible tests. Careful thoughtfulness and checking should be considered when generating random numbers (RNs), including: (a) the procedure should be portable to different platforms and computer systems, (b) the procedure must be fast, (c) the period of the generated sequence should be long, (d) produced Random Numbers (RNs) must have ideal statistical uniformity and independence characteristics, and (e) the generated RNs should be reproducible under same initial conditions (seed value).

Below is a description of the commonly used techniques to generate pseudorandom numbers.

**Linear Congruential Generators (LCGs)** LCGs are the most popular RNGs. Lehmer discovered in 1951 that the remainders of consecutive powers of a number have good randomness characteristics. Basically, he got the $n$th number in the string by dividing the $n$th power of an integer "$a$" by another integer "$m$" and then taking the remainder:

$$Xn = a_n \bmod m$$

Another way to compute $Xn$ relies in knowing $X_{n-1}$:

$$Xn = aX_{n-1} \bmod m$$

The parameter "$a$" is called the multiplier, and "$m$" is the modulus. Lehmer has chosen $a = 23$, $m = 10^8 + 1$ and such values were implemented on the eight-digit decimal early computer, the electronic numerical integrator and computer (ENIAC). The latter was designed by John Mauchly and J. Presper Eckert of the University of Pennsylvania and is considered the first electronic computer.

Most of today's RNGs are based on Lehmer's scheme and generally follow the following expression:

$$Xn = aX_{n-1} + b \bmod m$$

where $Xn$ values are integers between 0 and $(m-1)$, whereas "$a$" and "$b$" are non-negative constants.

The LCGs are widely accepted because they can be studied without difficulty and definite assurance can be made about their characteristics employing the theory of congruence. In the literature, the name linear congrunetial generators is often used as a short name for mixed linear congruential generators. The word "mixed" refers to the fact the multiplication and addition operators are used to generate such random numbers. Many researchers have investigated these generators, and the following observations have been found:

1. The period cannot exceed $m$ because $X$ values should be between 0 and $(m - 1)$. Clearly the modulus m should be large to have good randomness characteristics.
2. If the value of b is nonzero, the maximum value of m is obtained if and only if:
    a. Each prime number that is a factor of m is also a factor of $(a - 1)$.
    b. The integers "$m$" and "$b$" have no shared factors other than 1.
    c. The value of $(a - 1)$ is a multiple of 4, if the integer m is a multiple of 4.
3. The value of the modulus $m$ should be a power of 2 so as to have efficient computation of $m$.

LCGs takes the following forms: (a) multiplicative LCGs $m = 2^k$, and (b) multiplicative with $m \neq 2^k$. When $m = 2^k$, we obtain a full period. The highest value of the period of the multiplicative LCG with $m = 2^k$ is only one fourth the full period, which is achieved only when the multiplier is of the form $a = 8i \pm 3$ and the seed value is an odd integer.

In the field of simulation and Monte Carlo calculations, the most widely used generator that generates random numbers are the LCGs because they maintain nominal state space when compared with other generators. Moreover, their use in the environment related to parallel computing is much more attractive. To generate streams of pseudorandom numbers, LCGs are a good choice. Because LCGs are associated with a combination of least state space and rapid generation speed, they can be rapidly used with Monte Carlo simulation. Moreover, LCGs are also popular for distributed and parallel simulation.

To generate many pseudorandom number streams of high quality, two ways exist to use congruential random number generators. One approach is to divide the sequence arriving from single congruential random number generator into many possible small subsequences. The other scheme is to give a separate generator for each and every stream.

We define the splitting method by providing dissimilar initial points on a single congruential random-number generator for each and every substream, which means we have here:

$$X_{i,n+1} = bX_{i,n} + c \pmod{m}$$

Because $U_{i,n} = X_{i,n}/m$, many different initial values $X_{i,0}$ in the interval [0, 1] are achieved. An exclusive set of numbers is allocated to each and every substream from the initial point along the congruential random number generator sequence to the subsequent starting point. Overlapping is also permitted. The behavior of $(U_n, U_{n+1} \ldots U_{n+s-1})$ is examined via special tests such as the standard spectral test by means of locating parallel hyper planes, which are the most extensively spaced system and cover all $s$-tuples.

**Combined Linear Congruential Generators.** Recent advances in computer and communication technology have helped greatly to speed up simulators; however, applications of modeling and simulation have also increased. Many systems such as communication networks, aerospace systems, airplanes, aerospace shuttles, weather forecasting, and environment monitoring and protection have become more and more complex; therefore, it is essential to develop simulation models and study them in a speedy manner to choose the optimum design and operational mode. When dealing with complex and large simulation models, it important to rely on RNGs that have longer periods and other good randomness characteristics. One good scheme to address this is to combine two or more multiplication congruential RNGs in a way to get a new RNG that has excellent statistical characteristics as well as longer period [1–35].

**Tausworthe Generators (TGs).** For applications such as cryptography, random number streams of long period are required to get good encryption characteristics. To increase the length of the period and to enhance the generators statistical properties, the best way is the combination approach. However, there will be no assurance for improvement if the combinations are blind. Understanding the resulting generator structure is important. Combined multiple recursive generator and Tausworthe or generalized feedback shift registers are the generators that are effectively analyzed among the combined generators class.

The general form for Tausworthe is:

$$b_n = c_{q-1}b_{n-1} \oplus c_{q-2}b_{n-2} \oplus \ldots \oplus c_0 b_{n-q}$$

$$c_i \text{ and } b_i \text{ are binary variables}$$

The $\oplus$ symbol stands for the exclusive or (XOR) logic operation. The generator uses the last $q$ bits of the sequence. Tausworthe generators can be implemented by hardware using the linear feedback shift registers (LFSRs) concept. The period of Tausworthe generator depends on the characteristic polynomial. The period is the smallest positive integer n for which $(X^n - 1)$ is divisible by the characteristic polynomial. The maximum possible period is with a poly of order $(q = 2^q - 1)$. Such polynomials are called primitive polynomials [1, 10, 23].

**Example 1.** We can use the polynomial: $X^7 + X^3 + 1$ to produce a random sequence of length 127 as shown below.

We start by having:

$$b0 = b1 = b2 = b3 = b4 = b5 = b6 = 1$$

By using the XOR operation in place of addition mod 2, we get

$$b_{n+7} \oplus b_{n+3} \oplus b_n = 0$$

or we can rewrite this as follows:

$$b_n = b_{n-4} \oplus b_{n-7}$$

Based on the above expression, we obtain the following results:

$b7 = b3 \oplus b0 = 1 \oplus 1 = 0$
$b8 = 0, b9 = 0, b10 = 0, b11 = 1, b12 = 1, b13 = 1, b14 = 0,$
$b15 = 1, b16 = 1, b17 = 1, b18 = 1, b19 = 0, b20 = 0,$ and so on.
The final results are
Seed = 1111111
0000111
0111100
1011001
0010000
0010001
0011000
1011101
0110110
0000110
0110101
0011100
1111011

The period of this generator is 127 bits, which is equal to $2^7 - 1$. Clearly, the above polynomial is a primitive one.

The drawbacks of Tausworthe Generators are as follows [1, 10, 22]:

1. TGs have no reasonable local behavior even though their series generate reasonable test results in a full cycle.
2. In case of runs up and down test, their performance is disappointing.
3. Even though the sequential correlation is zero, it is believed that some prime polynomials might offer reduced correlations of high order.
4. Only few primal polynomials are good enough.

It is worth noting here that LFSRs have been used to generate random element stereogram (numbers) to generate visual patterns that can be used to test whether infants or noncommunicative people perceive depth in seeing objects or not. For more details on this application, see references [36–39].

**Midsquare Generator.** In this technique, the random number seed is used to generate the next random number, which in turn is transformed into the new seed value. The algorithm was proposed by John von Neumann and Metroopolis in the 1940s. It can be summarized as follows:

- Start with an intial 4-digit positive integer seed, X0
- Square it to get an integer with up to eight digits
- Take the middle four digits as the next four-digit number, X1
- Place a decimal point at the left of X1 and repeat the process

This method is straightforward to implement; however, it has the following drawbacks:

1. Short repeatability periods.
2. Numbers may not bypass randomness test.
3. When a 0 is produced, all next generated numbers will be 0. This may bring about trouble in simulation.

**Example:**

Let $X0 = 5497$
$(5497)^2 = 30217009$, thus $X1 = 2170$ and $R1 = 0.2170$
$(2170)^2 = 04708900$, thus $X2 = 7089$ and $R2 = 0.7089$
$(7089)^2 = 50253921$, thus $X3 = 2539$ and $R3 = 0.2539$ and so on.

**Extended (Additive) Fibonacci Generators.** Fibonacci sequences are generated using the relationship below:

$$X_n = X_{n-1} + X_{n-2}$$

Another method to generate such sequences is to employ the following expression:

$$X_n = X_{n-1} + X_{n-2} \bmod m$$

The latter expression produces sequences with disfavored randomness characteristics, particularly its high serial correlation characteristic. Others have expanded the latter approach by absorption the 5th and 17th recent values as shown next:

$$X_n = X_{n-5} + X_{n-17} \bmod 2^k$$

This last generator has been shown to pass many statistical examinations.

**Blum Blum Shub (BBS) Technique.** This scheme was suggested in 1986 by Lenore Blum, Manuel Blum, and Michael Shub [40]. The BBS has the general form shown below:

$$x_{n+1} = (x_n)^2 \bmod M$$

In the above expression, $M = pq$ and it is the product of two considerable primes $p$ and $q$. On every step of the algorithm, some output is produced from $x_n$. The output is typically either the bit parity of $x_n$ or one or more of the least significant bits of $x_n$.

The two prime numbers, $p$ and $q$, must both be congruent to 3 (mod 4) so as to guarantee that each quadratic residue has one square root that is also a quadratic residue and the greatest common divisor, $\gcd(f(p-1), f(q-1))$ should be small in order to have the cycle length large.

Any random value, $x_i$, can be computed directly from the expression:

$$x_i = \left(x_0^{2^i \bmod (p-1)(q-1)}\right) \bmod M$$

The BBS generator is not appropriate for use in simulations; its chief application is in cryptography because it is not very fast.

**Mersenne Twister Algorithm.** This pseudorandom number generator was devised in 1997 by Makoto Matsumoto and Takuji Nishimura [36]. It is based on a matrix linear recurrence over a finite binary field. It can produce high-quality pseudorandom numbers. The name of this generator is originated from the fact its period length is chosen to be a Mersenne prime. When $2^n - 1$ is prime it is said to be a Mersenne prime. It is worth mentioning that as of August 2007, only 44 Mersenne primes are known; the largest know prime number, $(2^{32,582,657} - 1)$, is a Mersenne prime. For the last many years, it has been found that the largest known prime has nearly always been a Mersenne prime.

The prevalent and regularly used variant of the algorithm is the Mersenne Twister MT19937, with 32-bit word length. There is another alternative with a 64-word length, MT19937-64, which produces a different sequence. Inherently, this method is not good for cryptography application [1–35].

For many other applications, however, the Mersenne twister is becoming the pseudorandom number generator of choice. Given that the library is portable, freely available, and generates good quality pseudorandom numbers quickly, it is rarely a bad choice.

The Mersenne twister is designed with Monte Carlo simulations and other statistical simulations in mind. The often used variant of Mersenne Twister, MT19937, has the following major characteristics [1, 24, 30, 35, 40]:

1. It is deemed to be a fast scheme.
2. It was intended to have a period of $2^{19937} - 1$. In general, there is no reason to use larger ones, as the bulk of applications do not necessitate $2^{19937}$ unique combinations, where the latter quantity equals $4.315425 \times 10^{6001}$ in decimal.
3. There is negligible serial correlation between successive generated values, which provide good randomness characteristics.

4. It was found to pass almost all available randomness tests.

The Mersenne Twister algorithm is basically a twisted generalized feedback shift register (TGFSR). It is describe by the following parameters:

$w$: word size

$n$: degree of recurrence

$m$: middle word, or the number of parallel sequences, $1 = m = n$

$r$: separation point of one word, or the number of bits of the lower bitmask, $0 = r = w - 1$

$a$: coefficients of the rational normal form twist matrix

$b, c$: TGFSR(R) tempering bitmasks

$s, t$: TGFSR(R) tempering bit shifts

$u, l$: additional Mersenne Twister tempering bit shifts with the constraint that $2^{nw-r} - 1$ is a Mersenne prime. Such a preference simplifies the primitivity check and $k$-distribution test that are needed in the parameter search.

For a word $x$ that is $w$ bits wide, we can write:

$$x_{k+n} := x_{k+m} \oplus \left(x_k^u | x_{k+1}^l\right) A \quad k = 0, 1, \ldots$$

with $|$ as the bitwise $OR$ and $\oplus$ as the bitwise XOR function. In addition, $x^u$, $x^l$ are the upper and lower bitmasks applied.

Here, the twist transformation $A$ is defined in a rational, normal way:

$$A = R = \begin{pmatrix} 0 & I_{w-1} \\ a_{w-1} & \left(a_{w-2,\ldots a_0}\right) \end{pmatrix}$$

where, $I_{n-1}$ is the $(n-1) \times (n-1)$ identity matrix. The rational normal form has the advantage that it can be efficiently written as:

$$xA = \begin{cases} x \gg 1 & x_0 = 0 \\ (x \gg 1) \oplus a & x_0 = 1 \end{cases}$$

where

$$x := \left(x_k^u | x_{k+1}^l\right) \quad k = 0, 1, \ldots$$

For the sake of achieving the $2^{nw-r} - 1$ theoretical superior limit of the period, $f_B(t)$ should be a primitive polynomial. Having $f_B(t)$ a characteristic polynomial of:

$$B = \begin{pmatrix} 0 & I_w & \cdots & 0 & 0 \\ \vdots & & & & \\ I_w & \vdots & \ddots & \vdots & \vdots \\ \vdots & & & & \\ 0 & 0 & \cdots & I_w & 0 \\ 0 & 0 & \cdots & 0 & I_{w-r} \\ S & 0 & \cdots & 0 & 0 \end{pmatrix} \quad \leftarrow m\text{th row}$$

$$S = \begin{pmatrix} 0 & I_r \\ I_{w-r} & 0 \end{pmatrix} A$$

The twist procedure can enhance the classical GFSR with the following major characteristics:

1. The period can accomplish the theoretical upper limit of $2^{nw-r} - 1$, not including if the seed value is 0.
2. The likelihood of having equidistribution in $n$ dimensions; the LCGs at best can manage with realistic distributions in five dimensions.

**Parallel Random Number Generation Issues.** Sequential random number generators should always have efficient randomness properties and possess constant generation time for each random number. By indicating the starting state, which is also known as "seed," a random number generator is started. Parallel random number generation is needed for several simulation applications, especially in the area of computational science and engineering. For some applications such as Monte Carlo simulations, it is vital that the random number generator has good randomness properties. In large-scale simulations on parallel computers, we use enormous quantities of random numbers and necessitate parallel algorithms for random number generation. Therefore, making sure that such random number sequences have good randomness characteristics is essential to have proper and credible simulation analysis [25, 29, 30, 33].

Different parallel random number generators have been proposed in the literature. However, most of them use the same basic idea, which is to parallelize a sequential generator by taking the elements of the sequence of pseudorandom numbers it generates and distributing them among the processors of the parallel system using one way or another. Among these schemes a scheme that relies on dividing the sequence into nonoverlapping adjacent parts, each of which is produced by a different processor. Clearly, this approach permits an arbitrary element of the sequence to be computed. Of course, it is possible to divide the period of the generator by the number of processors/ nodes of the parallel system and hop ahead in the sequence by this quantity for every node. Otherwise, the length of each part of numbers could be selected much larger than could be used by any node.

Below is a list of the requirements for a parallel random number generator:

1. Efficient randomness must be exhibited by each sequence produced on each processor of the parallel computer system.
2. Any sequence that is generated on any processor pair must not have any mutual correlations.
3. For a random number of processors, the generator must work.
4. The application output should always be regenerated, without showing impact on the number of processors on which the application runs.
5. Every processor on its own must generate a sequence that must not be reliant on the other processors.
6. The memory required for each processor should be predetermined and must not vary.

The limited number of efficient sequential generators prevents the opportunity of using a separate generator for each processor. Hence, the random number sequence produced by the sequential generator must be split into different parallel processors. The same generator and dissimilar seed for each processor cannot be used. This may result in the considerable overlie in the generated sequences depending on the starting seeds choice. Thus, it is imperative to assign subsequences that are disjoint of the real sequence to other processors. The subsequence selection must be such that each subsequence can be produced proficiently. Two major accepted policies are used to perform such allocations: the contiguous subsequence and leapfrog techniques. A brief description of each is given below.

1. **Contiguous Subsequence Technique.** The only way to assign subsequences of the original sequence to the processors is to allow each subsequence to be adjacent to the original subsequence. If $T$ is the subsequence length assigned to each processor, processor $j$ here must produce:

$$x_j T, x_j T + 1, x_j T + 2, \ldots, x_{(j+1)} T + i$$

Because the starting element as required is given, each processor should calculate its subsequence without depending on the other processors. Here, the $T$ value must be greater than the number of random numbers for each processor as needed by the application. Or else, the two subsequences produced on the other processors will overlap [25, 29, 30, 33].

Using the contiguous subsequence technique for parallelizing a generator, one need to find an efficient way of producing the seeds as needed for the parallel generator extracting from the sequential generator seed. Once the above procedure is completed, every processor can produce its own subsequence without depending on the other processors. This can be considered as the primary advantage in this contiguous subsequence technique. However, it also posses many disadvantages. It might not be achievable to calculate the random numbers needed on every processor. In this case, the $T$ value must be large so that the application is definite in not using more than $T$ numbers on other processor. This means that the random numbers that are used always depend on the processors on which the application runs. It is not possible to write code so that the application result is not reliant on the processors on which it runs.

Consider an example to parallelize a generator using the above technique. A linear congruential generator is considered

$$y_r = (by_{r-1} + c) \bmod n$$

By recursion for the above equation, it can be observed that $y_r = (B_k y_{r-k} + C_k) \bmod n$, where $B_k = b^k \bmod n$ and $C^k = c(b^k - 1) / b - 1 \bmod n$. Using this, we can calculate: $y_{jT}$ as $(B_{jT} y_0 + C_{jT})$.

2. **Leapfrog Technique.** This scheme depends on dividing the original sequence to protect the reproducibility and properties of randomness. Let $y_0, y_1, y_2, \ldots$ be a random number sequence produced by a sequential generator. In this technique, processor $j$ produces all $L^{\text{th}}$ numbers in the random number series starting at $y_i$, where $L$ is the number of processors. Here the $j$ processor produces $y_j, y_{j+L}, y_{j+2L}$. In this technique, as each processor leaps over the original sequence $L$ numbers, it is called the leapfrog technique. Multiple streams produced here are nonoverlapping and jointly produce successive terms of the original sequence. This allows the user to make a code that makes the results identical with implementation of the single processor and it is not dependent on the number of processors which are already used [25, 29, 30, 33].

It is not simple to execute a parallel random number generator with the leapfrog technique and protect all the conditions stated earlier. As an example, consider a linear congruential generator given by

$$y_r = (by_{r-1} + c) \bmod n$$

Here, $y_j$ is the seed and $y_r$ is the $r^{\text{th}}$ random number. When considering an $L$ processor system, the processor calculates $y_r$ and has to wait for the calculation of $y_{r-1}$, which again has to remain for the calculation of $y_{r-z}$ and so on. To satisfy the requirement for noncommunication, a method for calculating $y_r$ by means of only $y_{r-nL}$ need to be established and for the generation of $y_r$, only a stable number of operations must be used. As the random-number generator is described as an equation recitation of the calculation of the $r^{th}$ random number $y_r$, the same equation recursive application must be calculated for describing all the best possible ways for calculating $y_r$ from earlier numbers. If a method of calculating $y_r$ is achievable using several operations, which are constant and earlier produced random numbers on the same processor, these can be employed to parallelize the generator with the leapfrog technique. Considering the linear congruential generator, this is specified by an equation of the following form:

$$y_r = (by_{r-1} + c) \bmod n$$

By using the recursive application of the above equation, we get $y_r = (B_k$ $y_{r-k} + C_k) \bmod n$; here $B_k = b^k \bmod n$. By selecting $k = L$, the above equation permits for computing the next number on every processor by using the earlier number on the similar processor. After the calculations of the seeds for every processor and $B_L$ and $C_N$ are calculated, a parallel stream is produced at the sequential generator rate [1, 3, 16–30].

## 9.5 SURVEY OF COMMONLY USED RANDOM NUMBER GENERATORS

a. Currently, the most widely accepted multiplicative linear congruential generator is

$$y_m = 7^5 y_{m-1} \bmod (2^{31} - 1)$$

In the above equation $(2^{31} - 1)$ is referred to as a prime number where its primitive root is $7^5$. This generator has the full period of $2^{31} - 2$.

This Multiplicative Linear Congruential Generator is extensively used in the systems listed below [1, 10, 24, 25, 30–32, 35]:

1. SIMPL/I systems also referred to as IBM 1972.
2. IBM's APL system.
3. IMSL Scientific library.
4. PRIMOS Operating System.

b. After a thorough search by Fishman and Moore of all full period multiplicative RNGs with modulus $2^{31} - 1$, it was found that the following two RNGs were the best form the point view of randomness characteristics and efficiency of implementation [5, 26]:

$$y_m = 48,271 y_{m-1} \mathrm{Mod}\left(2^{31} - 1\right)$$
$$y_m = 69,621 y_{m-1} \mathrm{Mod}\left(2^{31} - 1\right)$$

Currently, the most preferred way to generate random numbers is by using multiplicative congruential random number generator.

c. The most popular IBM's randomizer, which was devised in the 1960, is RANDU IBM's RANDU is a kind of the linear multiplicative congruential randomizer. To achieve uncomplicated computation, RANDU's modulus and multiplier are selected to be primes. Its expression is given by:

$$y_m = (2^{16} + 3) y_{m-1} \bmod 2^{31} = 65539\, y_{m-1} \bmod 2^{31}$$

By using shift and add instructions, the multiplication by $2^{16} + 3 = 65,538$ can be achieved effortlessly. There is no scope for complete period in IBM's RANDU, and it is shown as erroneous in many aspects. It lacks properties related to efficient randomness. Just like all other linear congruential generators, the bits with low order possess a small period. The generator is no longer used. Because it fails spectral test badly for dimensions greater than 2 and other reasons, many simulation results that relied on using it as a RNG in the 1970s are considered doubtful.

d. SIMULA language, which is a process-oriented language based on discrete simulation, uses the following generator:

$$y_m = 5^{13} y_{m-1} \bmod 2^{35}$$

where $2^{33}$ is the maximum available possible period and the disadvantage with the SIMULA RNG is that it lacks efficient randomness properties.

e. The Unix Operating system uses the following generator:

$$y_m = (1,103,514,245 y_{m-1} + 12,345) \bmod 2^{32}$$

Like all other linear congruential generators with modulus equal $2^k$, the binary version of the produced $y_m$ values has a recurring bit form.

## 9.6 SEED SELECTION

The seed of a RNG is pretty much like a key of a cipher. In fact, some ciphers such as RC4 use a RNG on the inside, seeded by the key, to combine pseudorandom output with plain text to produce cipher text. The invention of a RNG's seed is like the finding of a cipher's key. One should guard the

RNG seed from illegal release. The simulationist should select the RNG seed in such a way that it is not easily guessed.

A seed can be described as a number that has the ability to determine whether the random number generator creates a new random number set or replicates the exact series of random numbers. The seed value that we use to initialize a random number generator should be such that it should not affect the simulation results. Conversely, an incorrect grouping of a seed and a random generator results in invalid and wrong conclusions. When simulating simple systems where we have only one variable, the seed value can take any value. When simulating more complex systems where random number sequences are needed to generate several variables, seed selection should be chosen with caution. This simulation type is known as multistream simulations and most simulations are of multistream type [1, 10, 24, 25, 30–32, 35].

The key recommended rules to select the seed for a RNG are listed below [1, 10, 30–32]:

1. **Stay away from using zero.** Using zero as a seed may be fine for some generators; however, it may not work for others. To be in the safe side, do not use zero as a seed. For instance, in mixed linear congruential generators, the seed value can be zero. Nevertheless, a zero seed makes the multiplicative linear congruential generator and Tausworthe generator stay at zero. This may cause serious and confusing problems in the simulation results.

2. **A random number stream should not be subdivided.** A common error committed by some simulationists is to use a single stream for all the variates. With the help of single seed, say $v_0$, the sequence ($v_1, v_2, v_3 \ldots \ldots$) is generated. Here the analyst can use $v_1$ to produce random interarrival times, $v_2$ to produce random service times, and so on. This might lead to a strong correlation between the two generated random variates. It is essential to make sure that streams selected are not overlapping. Each stream should possess a separate seed. Otherwise, we will get wrong simulation results, which leads to erroneous results and confusing conclusions.

3. **Seeds have to be used in consecutive replications.** When experiments related to simulation are repeated many times, the random-number stream should not be reinitialized; instead, the seeds that are left over from the earlier run can be used. It is imperative that the analyst does not use a random seed.

4. **Select an odd value for the seed.** Even though an even number may work in some cases, it does not work for others. Therefore, it highly recommended avoiding choosing an even value for the seed.

## 9.7   RANDOM VARIATE GENERATION

Random variate generation (RVG) is a vital part of the domain of any discrete event simulation study. It comes into play whenever there is a need to simulate the uncertainty in the conduct of an entity in the system under study. When the sample of randomness of the entity to be analyzed is identified, the operation of entity is said to follow a particular stochastic distribution. Otherwise, the behavior is simulated using empirical approaches.

Any random process is described by: (a) gathering of data on the random phenomenon, (b) approximating the acquired data to a known probability distribution, and (c) inference of parameters of the probability distribution.

Simulation of the random process begins when the random phenomenon has been identified. For instance, if the random operation is arrival of packets to a server system, then the interarrival times of packets to the system can be characterized to follow an exponential distribution with a known mean. To simulate this stochastic process, we will need random values for interarrival times of packets sampled from an exponential distribution with the same mean.

In general, a random variable is a real-valued function that maps a sample space into the real one. For instance, the interarrival times of packets to a server system can be represented by random variable. In general, the term random variate refers to a particular value of a random variable. The process of random variate generation refers to the generation of random variates for a given random variable. The method that is responsible for generating random variates is called a RVG. For instance, a random variate generator for the Poisson distribution generates random variates that satisfy the Poisson probability distribution. It is important to mention here that random variate generators are of two types: univariate and multivariate. The former involves the generation of a single variate at a time, whereas the latter involves the generation of a vector of variates at a time, which do not show mutual independence.

A variable that is taken from an identical distribution of pseudorandom numbers is called a random variate. Stochastic models, while simulating are often referred to by random variates. Random variates may possess uniform distributions or nonuniform distributions. The term random deviate is used for nonuniform random variates. The major techniques that are often used to generate random variates are explained below [1, 10, 24, 25, 30–32, 35].

### 9.7.1   Inverse-Transform Method

This technique is considered the easiest route to generate a sample. The general form of the inverse transform scheme is obtained by computing the probability density function (pdf) of $X = g(x)$ for some function $g$, and then trying to find a function $g$ such that the required pdf is obtained.

Let us assume that $X$ is a random variable with CDF $F_X(x)$. Because $F_X(x)$ is a nondecreasing function, the inverse function $F_X^{-1}(y)$ may be defined for any value of $y$ between 0 and 1 as shown below:

$$F_X^{-1}(y) = \text{in } f\{x: F_X(x) > = y\} \quad 0 < = y < = 1$$
$$F_X^{-1}(y) \text{ here is the value } x \text{ for which } F(x) = y.$$

Let $U$ be uniformly distributed over the interval $(0, 1)$, then we can write

$$X = F_X^{-1}(U) \text{ has the CDF } F_X(x).$$

To prove this, we write

$$P(X < = x) = P(F_X^{-1}(U) < = x) = P(U < = F_X(x)) = F_X(x).$$

To obtain a value, such as $x$, of a random variable $X$, get a value, say $u$, of a random variable $U$, then compute the inverse function, $F_X^{-1}(U)$, and put it equal to $x$.

**Algorithm for the** Inverse -Transform Method:

1. Produce $U$ from $U(0, 1)$,
2. Return $X = F^{-1}(U)$.

**Example.** Produce a random variable from the uniform distribution given by $U(a, b)$:

$$f_x(x) = \frac{1}{(b-a)}; \quad a \le x \le b$$

$$f_x = 0; \quad \text{otherwise}$$

For this pdf, the CDF is given by:

$$F(x) = \int f(x) \cdot d(x)$$

Therefore, we get

$$F(x) = \begin{pmatrix} 0 & x < a \\ \frac{x-a}{b-1} & a \le x \le b \\ 1 & x > b \end{pmatrix}$$

And $U$ is given by

$$U = \frac{x-a}{b-a}$$

$$X = F^{-1}x(U) = a + (b-a)U.$$

**Example.** Produce a random variable with the pdf given below:

$$f_X(x) = \begin{pmatrix} 2x & 0 \le x \le 1 \\ 0 & \text{otherwise} \end{pmatrix}$$

From the given pdf, we can easily obtain the cumulative distribution function (CDF), $F(x)$:

$$F(x) = \begin{cases} 0 & ; \quad x < 0 \\ \int\limits_0^1 2x.dx = x^2 & ; \quad 0 \le x \le 1 \\ 1 & ; \quad x > 1 \end{cases}$$

$$U = X^2$$

Thus, the random variate can be generated using: $X = F^{-1}x\,(U) = (U)^{1/2}$

The algorithm to generate discrete distributions using the inverse transforms method can be summarized as follows:

1. Generate $D \sim d_j\,(0, 1)$.
2. Locate the least possible integer, which is positive $m$, such that $D \le G$ $(X_{ck})$ and return

$$X_c = x_{ck}$$

In step 2, many numbers of comparisons are being made, which means much execution time is vested in step 2 itself. However, with the help of proficient search techniques, the execution time can be minimized.

The algorithm to generate empirical distribution using the inverse transform method can be summarized as follows:

1. Generate $D \sim d_j\,(0, 1)$
2. Locate the least possible integer, which is positive $m$ $(0 \le m \le n - 1)$ such that $D \le G(x_m)$, and return the value:

$$X_c = G^-(D) = b_m + [D - G(b_m)](b_{m+1} - b_m)/[G(b_{k+1}) - G(b_m)].$$

Usually, when applying the inverse transform method to empirical distribution, we need the fundamental cumulative distribution function $G(x_c)$, which should be there in some form so that its related inverse function $G^-(x_c)$ can be found algorithmically or analytically. Exponential and uniform are some applicable distributions. However, for many probability distributions, finding the inverse transform is either very hard or impossible.

The inverse transformation scheme is a popular and powerful random variate generation scheme. This technique can be used to generate the following random variates: exponential, geometric, logistic, and Weibull. It cannot be used to generate normal random variates, as CDF is not available in a closed form for the Normal distribution.

## 9.7.2 Acceptance—Rejection Method

Both the inverse-transform method and the composition method deal directly with the CDF of the variate that is to be produced. Because of their direct dealing, these techniques are direct techniques whereas the acceptance-rejection method (ARM) is an indirect method. In cases where the direct schemes, such as the inverse transform and the composition methods fail or if they are inefficient, the acceptance-rejection method can then be used. The latter method then specifies a function $Ø$, which majors the original probability density function, $g(x)$.

To carry out the acceptance-rejection method let $g(x)$ be given by:

$$g(x) = C.i(x)h(x)$$

The probability density function, $g(x)$ is majorized by $Ø(x) = C.i(x)$, which means that the value of $Ci(x) \geq g(x)$ for all the values of $x$. We also have:

$$0 < h(x) = g(x) \, Ø(x) \leq 1.$$

Now using the above criteria, two variates are to be generated, $D$ from $d_j$ (0, 1) and $Y$ from $i(y)$ and the inequality $D \leq h(Y)$ has to be tested. We recognize from $g(x)$, that $Y$ has a requisite variate if the inequality holds; otherwise, the pair $(D, Y)$ is rejected and we try until it is successful. See Figure 9.8.

Formally, we can summarize the accept-reject algorithm for the generation of random variate as follows:

1. Generate $D$ from $d_j$ (0, 1).
2. Generate $Y$ from $i(y)$, independent of $D$.
3. If $D = g(Y)$, return $X_c = Y$. Otherwise, go to step number 1.

**Example.** Generate a random variate from the probability distribution function:

$$g(y) = 2y; 0 \leq y \leq 1; \text{ otherwise, it is 0.}$$

using the acceptance-rejection method.

For ease, take the value of $i(y)$ as 1, $y$ value ranges from (0, 1) i.e., $0 \leq y \leq 1$. Take the value of $C$ as 2.

In this situation, $h(x) = \frac{1}{2} g(x) = x$; with this criterion the above algorithm can summarized as follows:

1. Generate $D$ from $d_j$ (0, 1).
2. Generate $Y$ from $d_j$ (0, 1); independent of $D$.
3. If $D \leq Y$, return $X_c = Y$. Otherwise, go to step number 1.

The efficiency of this scheme depends mainly on being able to decrease the number of rejections.

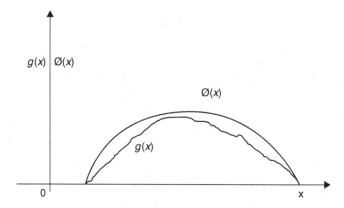

**FIGURE 9.8.** The acceptance-rejection method.

### 9.7.3   Characterization Method

The characterization method depends on several particular features of some other distributions. Such features allow variates to be produced using the algorithms modified for them.

For instance, if the random interarrival times are distributed exponentially with a mean value of $1/\lambda$, then m, which is the number of arrivals during a specified period $T$, has a Poisson distribution with parameter $\lambda T$. By continuously producing exponential variates up to the sum value surpass $T$, a Poison variate can be achieved easily and will return back the number of variates produced as Poisson variates.

### 9.7.4   Convolution Method

In this scheme, the desired random variate $X$ can be expressed as a sum of other random variates that are independent and identically distributed (iid) and can be generated more easily than direct generation of $X$. Thus, the convolution method is basically based on summing two or more random independent variables to obtain a newly random variable with the desired distribution. Binomial and Erlang variates can be realized using this convolution method. In case of the convolution technique, the cumulative distributive frequency of the required distribution is not significant, but what matters is the relation to other variates that are simply generated.

The convolution algorithm can be summarized as follows:

1. Generate $Y1$, $Y2$, ..., $Yn$ independently from their distributions
2. Return: $X = Y1 + Y2 + \ldots + Yn$
3. The pdf of $X$ can be obtained mathematically by the convolution of the pdf's of $Y1$, $Y2$, ...and $Yn$. The name of this scheme "Convolution" came

from here, although no mathematical convolution process is needed in this case.

This needs at least $n$ uniforms. Examples of random variables that can be expressed as sums like this include the Erlang, hypoexponential, triangle, and binomial distributions.

Following are some examples of the applications of this scheme [1, 3, 10]:

1. The chi-square distribution with $V$ degrees of freedom is a sum of squares of $v$ unit normal variates $N (0, 1)$.
2. The summation of $m$ geometric variates is a distribution described as the Pascal distribution.
3. The summation of $k$ exponential variates is an Erlang-$K$ variate. This means that we can produce an Erlang variate by generating $k$ exponential variates and then adding them.
4. We can produce normal variaes by relying on the property that the sum of a large number of variates from any distribution has a normal distribution.
5. The triangle variate can be produced by relying on the property that the sum of two uniform variates is a triangle distribution [1, 10, 28, 0, 31, 35].

## 9.7.5  Composition Method

In this method the CDF, $F(x)$ is given in terms of a weighted sum of other CDFs as shown below:

$$F(x) = \sum_{j=1}^{n} p_j F_j(x)$$

In the above expression, $pj = 0$ and $\sum_{j=1} Pj^n = $ Number of functions, $n$, which is selected on the basis of best fit and effort to produce $F(x)$.

## 9.8  TESTING OF RANDOM NUMBER SEQUENCES

The testing of pseudorandom sequences entails comparison of the sequence with what would be supposed from the uniform distribution. This is because a true random sequence should follow a uniform distribution. The general method for testing a random number sequence can be summarized as follows:

1. Devise a null assumption $H_0$ about the single chance experiment, which was replicated $N$ times to produce a sequence of $N$ values. To check a sequence of apparently random numbers, our null hypothesis $H_0$ is that each result of the chance experiment is evenly likely, and that each test of the probability experiment is autonomous of all preceding trials.

2. Set up a real valued function $g$, which by some means tests the null hypothesis $H_0$. To check a sequence of allegedly random numbers, our function $g$ may be one that tallies the number of events of a particular outcome.

3. Define mathematically a sequence of $N$ random variables:

$$(X1, X2, ..., Xn)$$

and relate the function $g$ to the sequence of $N$ random variables producing a new random variable $y$:

$$y = g(X1, X2, ..., Xn)$$

Next, find out the pdf of $y$ either by mathematical computation or by obtaining a table of the specific probability density function that is of interest.

4. Take the particular sequence of values supposedly acquired by conducting a probability experiment $N$ times:

$$(x1, x2, ..., xn)$$

and apply the function $g$ to obtain a particular value $y$:

$$y = g(x1, x2, ..., xn)$$

5. Decide from the pdf of $y$ how possible or unsure we are to get our value of $y$ assuming our null hypothesis $H_0$ is true. If the probability is little, then we may discard our hypothesis $H_0$ as being most probably inaccurate.

The major desirable properties of random numbers are consistency and autonomy. Many tests have been applied to ensure that the wanted properties are achieved. These tests aim at providing a quantitative measure that embeds desired randomness characteristics, including long period and little or no correlation between produced numbers.

The major techniques that are used to test random sequences are described below.

### 9.8.1   Frequency Analysis or Chi-Square Test

Basically, a frequency test or chi-square ($\chi^2$) test examines whether the frequency of different random numbers is consistent with the subsequences that would be produced by a uniform distribution. This test is broad and can be employed for any distribution. It can be used to test random numbers that are (iid) uniformly between 0 and 1, as well as for testing random variate generators. The Chi-square scheme checks the assumption that the probability distribution for a given outcome experiment is as specified. For the die tossing experiment, it tests the probability that each possible outcome is equally likely with a probability of 1/6.

Among the examples of chi-squared tests where the chi-square distribution is only approximately valid, we can mention the following:

1. Probability-ratio tests, which are employed for testing if there is indication of the necessity to shift from a straightforward model to a more complex one.
2. Pearson's chi-square test, which is also called the chi-square goodness-of-fit test or chi-square test for independence.
3. The portmanteau test in time-series analysis, which tests for the existence of autocorrelation. It basically tests whether any of a group of auto-correlations of a time series is not zero. Examples on portmanteau tests include the Ljung-Box test and the Box-Pierce test.

The steps for Chi-square test are summarized below:

1. Create a histogram of the observed data (random numbers). The numbers are grouped into cells (tiers or classes).
2. Evaluate observed frequencies with those obtained from the specific density function. For $K$ classes, let $O_i$ be the observed frequencies and $E_i$ be the expected frequencies. The difference, $D$, is given by

$$D = \sum (O_i - E_i)^2 / E_i$$

This is done for $i = 1$ to $K$.

3. For a precise match (fit) between the observed frequencies and expected frequencies, $D$ should be equal to zero, but because of randomness characteristics, $D$ usually is not equal to zero.
4. The disparity or difference ($D$) can be proved to have a chi-square distribution with $(K - 1)$ degree of freedom, where $K$ is the number of cells.
5. Finally, use significance level, $a$, for not rejecting or confidence level $(1 - \alpha)$ depending on the requirements. The null assumption (hypothesis) that the observations are from the particular distribution cannot be rejected at the specified $\alpha$ value if the calculated difference, $D$, value is smaller than the critical value found from the chi-square tables using the entry $\chi^2_{[(k-1),\,(1-a)]}$; see Table 9.1.

It is worth mentioning that not only are excessively large values of chi-square regarded as highly impossible but also are excessively small values of chi-square.

**TABLE 9.1** Chi-Square table.

| Degrees of Freedom | 0.01 | 0.025 | 0.05 | 0.10 | 0.25 | 0.50 | 0.75 | 0.90 | 0.95 | 0.975 | 0.990 |
|---|---|---|---|---|---|---|---|---|---|---|---|
| 1 | 0.000 | 0.0009 | 0.004 | 0.158 | 0.102 | 0.455 | 1.32 | 2.71 | 3.84 | 5.02 | 6.63 |
| 2 | 0.20 | .051 | 0.103 | 0.211 | 0.575 | 1.386 | 2.773 | 4.605 | 5.991 | 7.378 | 9.210 |
| 3 | 0.115 | 0.216 | 0.352 | 0.584 | 1.213 | 2.366 | 4.108 | 6.251 | 7.815 | 9.348 | 11.344 |
| 4 | 0.297 | 0.484 | 0.711 | 1.064 | 1.923 | 3.357 | 5.385 | 7.779 | 9.488 | 11.143 | 13.277 |
| 5 | 0.554 | 0.831 | 1.145 | 1.610 | 2.675 | 4.351 | 6.626 | 9.236 | 11.070 | 12.832 | 15.086 |
| 6 | 0.872 | 1.237 | 1.635 | 2.204 | 3.455 | 5.348 | 7.841 | 10.645 | 12.592 | 14.449 | 16.812 |
| 7 | 1.239 | 1.690 | 2.167 | 2.833 | 4.255 | 6.346 | 9.037 | 12.017 | 14.067 | 16.013 | 18.475 |
| 8 | 1.646 | 2.180 | 2.733 | 3.490 | 5.071 | 7.344 | 10.219 | 13.362 | 15.507 | 17.535 | 20.090 |
| 9 | 2.088 | 2.700 | 3.325 | 4.168 | 5.899 | 8.343 | 11.389 | 14.684 | 16.919 | 19.023 | 21.666 |
| 10 | 2.558 | 3.247 | 3.940 | 4.865 | 6.737 | 9.342 | 12.549 | 15.987 | 18.307 | 20.483 | 23.209 |
| 11 | 3.053 | 3.816 | 4.575 | 5.578 | 7.584 | 10.341 | 13.701 | 17.275 | 19.675 | 21.920 | 24.725 |
| 12 | 3.571 | 4.404 | 5.226 | 6.304 | 8.438 | 11.340 | 14.845 | 18.549 | 21.026 | 23.337 | 26.217 |
| 13 | 4.107 | 5.009 | 5.892 | 7.042 | 9.299 | 12.340 | 15.984 | 19.812 | 22.362 | 24.736 | 27.688 |
| 14 | 4.660 | 5.629 | 6.571 | 7.790 | 10.165 | 13.339 | 17.117 | 21.064 | 23.685 | 26.119 | 29.141 |
| 15 | 5.229 | 6.262 | 7.261 | 8.547 | 11.037 | 14.339 | 18.245 | 22.307 | 24.996 | 27.488 | 30.578 |
| 16 | 5.812 | 6.908 | 7.962 | 9.312 | 11.912 | 15.339 | 19.369 | 23.542 | 26.296 | 28.845 | 32.000 |

$1 - \alpha$

| df | | | | | | | | | | |
|---|---|---|---|---|---|---|---|---|---|---|
| 17 | 6.408 | 7.564 | 8.672 | 10.085 | 12.792 | 16.338 | 20.489 | 24.769 | 27.587 | 30.191 | 33.409 |
| 18 | 7.015 | 8.231 | 9.390 | 10.865 | 13.675 | 17.338 | 21.605 | 25.989 | 28.869 | 31.526 | 34.805 |
| 19 | 7.633 | 8.907 | 10.117 | 11.651 | 14.562 | 18.338 | 22.718 | 27.204 | 30.144 | 32.852 | 36.191 |
| 20 | 8.260 | 9.591 | 10.851 | 12.443 | 15.452 | 19.337 | 23.828 | 28.412 | 31.410 | 34.170 | 37.566 |
| 21 | 8.897 | 10.283 | 11.591 | 13.240 | 16.344 | 20.337 | 24.935 | 29.615 | 32.671 | 35.479 | 38.932 |
| 22 | 9.542 | 10.982 | 12.338 | 14.041 | 17.240 | 21.337 | 26.039 | 30.813 | 33.924 | 36.781 | 40.289 |
| 23 | 10.196 | 11.689 | 13.091 | 14.848 | 18.137 | 22.337 | 27.141 | 32.007 | 35.172 | 38.076 | 41.638 |
| 24 | 10.856 | 12.401 | 13.848 | 15.659 | 19.037 | 23.337 | 28.241 | 33.196 | 36.415 | 39.364 | 42.980 |
| 25 | 11.524 | 13.120 | 14.611 | 16.473 | 19.939 | 24.337 | 29.339 | 34.382 | 37.652 | 40.646 | 44.314 |
| 26 | 12.198 | 13.844 | 15.379 | 17.292 | 20.843 | 25.336 | 30.435 | 35.563 | 38.885 | 41.923 | 45.642 |
| 27 | 12.879 | 14.573 | 16.151 | 18.114 | 21.749 | 26.336 | 31.528 | 36.741 | 40.113 | 43.194 | 46.963 |
| 28 | 13.565 | 15.308 | 16.928 | 18.939 | 22.657 | 27.336 | 32.620 | 37.916 | 41.337 | 44.461 | 48.278 |
| 29 | 14.256 | 16.047 | 17.708 | 19.768 | 23.567 | 28.336 | 33.711 | 39.087 | 42.557 | 45.722 | 49.588 |
| 30 | 14.953 | 16.791 | 18.493 | 20.599 | 24.478 | 29.336 | 34.800 | 40.256 | 43.773 | 46.979 | 50.892 |
| 40 | 22.164 | 24.433 | 26.509 | 29.051 | 33.660 | 39.335 | 45.616 | 51.805 | 55.758 | 59.342 | 63.691 |
| 50 | 29.707 | 32.357 | 34.764 | 37.689 | 42.942 | 49.335 | 56.334 | 63.167 | 67.505 | 71.420 | 76.154 |
| 60 | 37.485 | 40.482 | 43.188 | 46.459 | 52.294 | 59.335 | 66.981 | 74.397 | 79.082 | 83.298 | 88.379 |
| 70 | 45.442 | 48.757 | 51.739 | 55.329 | 61.698 | 69.334 | 77.577 | 85.527 | 90.531 | 95.023 | 100.425 |
| 80 | 53.540 | 57.153 | 60.391 | 64.278 | 71.144 | 79.334 | 88.130 | 96.578 | 101.880 | 106.629 | 112.329 |
| 90 | 61.754 | 65.647 | 69.126 | 73.291 | 80.625 | 89.334 | 98.650 | 107.565 | 113.145 | 118.136 | 124.116 |
| 100 | 70.065 | 74.222 | 77.929 | 82.358 | 90.133 | 99.334 | 109.141 | 118.498 | 124.342 | 129.561 | 135.807 |

[a]Chi-square values in the following table are shown in 'degree of freedom' values and $(1 - \alpha)$ values. The $\alpha$ value depends on the chosen significance level. For example, in case of 10% significance level, $\alpha = 0.1$ and the $(1 - \alpha)$ value will be 0.90.

Another note about the chi-square distribution, most tables of the chi-square distribution go up to 30 degrees of freedom (DF). Over this limit, the distribution comes close to the normal distribution. If the probability experiment has more than 30 degrees of freedom, which is equal to (number of possible outcomes − 1), then the chi-square distribution for DF > 30 is converted into the normal distribution with mean = 0 and variance = 1.

One difficulty with chi-square test is the correct selection of cell boundaries. The cell sizes influence the overall conclusions; however, there are no concrete procedures for choosing the right sizes. This suggests that a chi-square test is always inexact, whereas the kolmogorov-smirnov (K-S) test to be covered next is exact as long as all factors of the expected distributions are identified. A final note about chi-square test is that it is used for discrete distributions when sample sizes are large. However, if it is used for continuous distributions, then the test is considered only an approximation.

### 9.8.2 Kolmogorov-Smirnov (K-S) Test

The major drawbacks of the chi-square test are the choice of the number and size of the intervals, as well as the fact that it is designed for discrete distribution, which means if it is used for continuous distributions, then the result is only an approximation. K-S test is intended to resolve these problems. Given the assumed distribution function $F$, this test compares $F$ with the observed distribution function, $F'$, of the samples.

The K-S test statistic $D$ is the biggest total departure between $F(x)$ and $F'(x)$ over the range of the random variable:

$$D = \text{Max} \ \{F'(x) - F(x)\}$$

where $F'(x)$ is defined as:

$$F'(x) = [\text{number of samples} = x]/N$$

In the above expression, $N$ is the number of samples. To test against a uniform distribution, we should follow the following steps:

1. Normalize the produced numbers between 0 and 1.
2. Sort the samples in an ascending order:

   $$U_1 = U_2 = \ldots U_n \text{ where } 0 \leq U_i \leq 1$$

3. Calculate $K+$ and $K-$, which are defined as the maximum observed deviation above and below the expected CDF in a sample size $n$, respectively. These valves are given as

   $$K+ = \sqrt{n} \ \text{Max} \ [F_o(x) - Fe(x)]$$
   $$K- = \sqrt{n} \ \text{Max} \ [Fe(x) - F_o(x)]$$

**TABLE 9.2  Standard table for K-S Test.**

| Sample Size ($N$) | Level of Significance for D = MAXIMUM $[F_0(X) - S_n(X)]$ | | | | |
|---|---|---|---|---|---|
| | 0.20 | 0.15 | 0.10 | 0.05 | 0.01 |
| 1 | 0.900 | 0.925 | 0.950 | 0.975 | 0.995 |
| 2 | 0.684 | 0.726 | 0.776 | 0.842 | 0.929 |
| 3 | 0.565 | 0.597 | 0.642 | 0.708 | 0.828 |
| 4 | 0.494 | 0.525 | 0.564 | 0.624 | 0.733 |
| 5 | 0.446 | 0.474 | 0.510 | 0.565 | 0.669 |
| 6 | 0.410 | 0.436 | 0.470 | 0.521 | 0.618 |
| 7 | 0.381 | 0.405 | 0.438 | 0.486 | 0.577 |
| 8 | 0.358 | 0.381 | 0.411 | 0.457 | 0.543 |
| 9 | 0.339 | 0.360 | 0.388 | 0.432 | 0.514 |
| 10 | 0.322 | 0.342 | 0.368 | 0.410 | 0.490 |
| 11 | 0.307 | 0.326 | 0.352 | 0.391 | 0.468 |
| 12 | 0.295 | 0.313 | 0.338 | 0.375 | 0.450 |
| 13 | 0.284 | 0.302 | 0.325 | 0.361 | 0.433 |
| 14 | 0.274 | 0.292 | 0.314 | 0.349 | 0.418 |
| 15 | 0.266 | 0.283 | 0.304 | 0.338 | 0.404 |
| 16 | 0.258 | 0.274 | 0.295 | 0.328 | 0.392 |
| 17 | 0.250 | 0.266 | 0.286 | 0.318 | 0.381 |
| 18 | 0.244 | 0.259 | 0.278 | 0.309 | 0.371 |
| 19 | 0.237 | 0.252 | 0.272 | 0.301 | 0.363 |
| 20 | 0.231 | 0.246 | 0.264 | 0.294 | 0.356 |
| 25 | 0.210 | 0.220 | 0.240 | 0.270 | 0.320 |
| 30 | 0.190 | 0.200 | 0.220 | 0.240 | 0.290 |
| 35 | 0.180 | 0.190 | 0.210 | 0.230 | 0.270 |
| Over 35 | $1.07/N$ | $1.14/N$ | $1.22/N$ | $1.36/N$ | $1.63/N$ |

Keep in mind that the K-S test is based on the observation that the difference between observed CDF, $F_o(x)$, and expected CDF, $Fe(x)$, should be small.

4. A check is made to determine whether the values of K+ and K− are smaller than the critical value picked up from the K-S Table, $K_{[n,(1-\alpha)]}$; see Table (9.2, where $\alpha$ is the significance level. The observations are said to come from the specified distribution at the level of significance, $\alpha$ or the confidence level $(1-\alpha)$. The value $n$ signifies the number of random numbers. Again, by comparing the computed K+ and K− with the values listed in the above mentioned K-S table, we can determine whether the numbers under test or observations are uniformly distributed.

One final note, because the K-S-test does not group samples into cells, it is more susceptible to outliers. Therefore, the K-S test makes better use of each sample and is considered to be more accurate than the chi-square test. Both the K-S test and the chi-square test are suitable for testing the consistency of a sample statistics, provided that sample size is high. However, basically the K-S test is the dominant among the two tests. Moreover, the K-S test can be applied to small sample sizes, whereas the chi-square is used only for large values, say a minimum of 50 or so [1, 10, 20–35].

### 9.8.3 Serial Test

This test basically measures the extent of randomness between consecutive numbers in a sequence. The steps for this test can be summarized as shown below [1, 4, 5, 10]:

a. Produce a sequence of $M$ successive sets of $N$ random numbers each.
b. Divide the number range into $k$ periods.
c. For each group, build an array of size $k \times k$. The arrays are initialized to 0. Check the string of numbers from left to right pairwise. Make sure not to check any number twice. If you find the left member of the pair is in interval $i$ while the right member is in interval $j$, then increase the $(i, j)$ element of the array by 1.
d. Although an array has been built for each cluster, compare the outcomes of the $M$ group with everyone and with the likely value using the chi-square scheme.

### 9.8.4 Runs Test

The runs test is exploited to check the randomness of oscillation of numbers in the string. The steps for this test are summarized below [1, 3, 5, 10]:

a. Make sure that you have or that you produced $N$ random numbers.
b. Construct a binary string such that for any two successive numbers, such as $x_i$ and $x_{i+1}$ of the stream, the $i$th bit is 0 if $x_{i+1} > x_i$ and 1 if not.
c. Put into a table the occurrence of happening of runs, i.e., successive 1s or 0s of each length. Contrast the tabulated occurrences with the expected values. It is not feasible to use the chi-square method directly because successive runs are not autonomous.

### 9.8.5 Serial Correlation Test

Let us have a string of random numbers; therefore, we can calculate the covariance between numbers that are $k$ values spaced out, that is to say, between $x_n$ and $x_{n+k}$. This is also called autocovariance at a lag of $k$ and is often represented by $R_k$, which is given by the following expression:

$$R_k = 1/(n - k) \sum (U_n - 0.5)(U_{n+k} - 0.5)$$

In the above expression, for large values of $n$, $R_k$ is normally distributed with an average zero and a variance of $1/\{144\,(n-k)\}$. The $100(1-a)$ % confidence interval for the autocovariance is given by

$$R_k \pm Z_{1-\alpha/2}/12\,(n-k)^{0.5}$$

Here, the value of $\alpha$ is called the significance level and k = 1. Now, if this range does not contain a zero, then we can say that the string has a large correlation.

## 9.8.6 Spectral Test

This test is employed to verify for a flat spectrum by examining the observed estimated spectral density function with the K-S test. Cleary, it tests the autonomy of adjacent sets of numbers. Basically, this test determines the maximum distance between neighboring hyper planes; the bigger the distance, the more inferior the generator [1, 3, 4, 5, 10].

## 9.9 SUMMARY

Simulation modeling is an important technique that can help to predict and evaluate effectively and economically the performance evaluation of computer and telecommunication systems. Because of the availability of abundant computation power and high-speed communication networks and systems, this scheme is becoming more and more widely accepted and used. In this chapter, we introduced and explained the basic concepts and foundations of the simulation technique of performance evaluation.

We investigated various phases that are needed to construct a simulation model, simulate experimental design, and perform simulation analysis. The simulation modeling process and various stages involved in simulation analysis were also discussed. Simulation types have been reviewed with particular attention to discrete event simulation. Various random-number-generation techniques like linear congruential generators, Tausworthe generators, combined generators, and extended Fibonacci generators were discussed along with their properties. A survey on commonly used random-number generators was also given.

Various random-variate generation techniques are also discussed, which include inverse transformation method, acceptance-rejection method, characterization method, convolution method, and composition method. Finally, various techniques involved in testing random number sequences are discussed, which include the K-S test and Chi-square test.

## REFERENCES

[1] M. S. Obaidat and G. I. Papadimitriou (eds.), "Applied System Simulation: Methodologies and Applications," Kluwer, Dordrecht, The Netherlands,

[2] H. Kobayashi, and B. L. Mark, "System Modeling and Analysis," Pearson Education, Upper Saddle River, NJ, 2008.

[3] A. M. Law, and W. D. Kelton, "Simulation Modeling and Analysis," 4th Edition", McGraw-Hill, New York, 2007.

[4] J. Banks, J. S. Carson, B. L. Nelson, and D. M. Nicol, "Discrete-Event System Simulation", 4th Edition, Prentice-Hall, Upper Saddle River, 2005.

[5] G. S. Fishman, "Discrete-Event Simulation: Modeling, Programming, and Analysis," Springer-Verlag, New York, 2001.

[6] T. Altiok, and B. Melamed, "Simulation Modeling and Analysis with ARENA," Elsevier, New York, 2007.

[7] S. M. Ross, "Simulation, 4th edition, Academic Press, New York, 2006.

[8] U. Pooch, and J. Wall, "Discrete Event Simulation-A Practical Approach," CRC Press, Boca Raton, FL, 1993.

[9] B. P. Zeigler, H. Praehofer and T. G. Kim, "Theory of Modeling and Simulation," 2nd Edition, Academic Press, New York, 2000.

[10] R. Jain, "The Art of Computer Systems Performance Evaluation," Wiley New York, 1991.

[11] M. S. Obaidat, "Simulation of Queueing Models in Computer Systems," in S. Ozekici (ed.), Queueing Theory and Applications, Taylor and Francis, London, UK, 1990.

[12] D. Kelton, "Statistical Issues in Simulation," Proceedings of the 1996 Winter Simulation Conference, pp. 47–54, 1996.

[13] G. Gordon, "System Simulation, 2nd edition", Prentice Hall, Upper Saddle River, NJ, 1978.

[14] B. J. T. Morgan, "Elements of Simulation," Chapman & Hall, London, UK, 1984.

[15] W. Biles, "Statistical Considerations in Simulation on a Network of Microcomputers", Proceedings of the 1985 Winter Simulation Conference, pp. 388–393, 1985.

[16] B. Schmidt, "Determination of Confidence Intervals in the Simulation of Stochastic Discrete Events," Summer Computer Simulation Conference, pp. 241–27, 1982.

[17] G. Marsaglia, "Random Numbers Fall Mainly in the Planes," Proceedings of National Academy of Sciences, pp 25–28, 1968.

[18] P. L'Ecuyer, F. Panneton "A New Class of Linear Feedback Shift Register Generators," Proceedings of the 2000 Winter Simulation Conference, pp. 690–696, 2000.

[19] M. Sakamoto, and S. Morito, "Combination of Multiplicative Congruential Random Number Generators with safe Prime Modulus," Proceedings of the 1995 Winter Simulation Conference, pp. 309–315, 1995.

[20] P. L'Ecuyer, "Uniform Random Number Generators: A Review," Proceedings of the 1997 Winter Simulation Conference, pp. 127–134, 1997.

[21] M. J. Durst, "Using Linear Congruential Generator for Parallel Random Number Generation," Proceedings of the 1989 Winter Simulation Conference, pp. 462–466, 1989.

[22] S. K. Park, and K. W. Miller, "Random Number Generators: Good Ones Are Hard to Find", Communications of the ACM, pp. 1192–1201, 1988.

[23] P. L'Ecuyer, "Maximally Equidistributed Combined Tausworthe Generators," Mathematics of Computations, Vol. 65, No. 213, pp. 203–213, 1996.

[24] P. L'Ecuyer, "Efficient and Portable Combined Random Number Generators," ACM Transactions on Modeling and Computer Simulation (TOMACS), Vol. 1, pp. 99–112, 1991.

[25] S. Aluru, "Parallel Additive Lagged Additive Fibonacci Random Number Generators," Proceedings of the 10th International Conference on Super Computing, pp. 102–108, 1996.

[26] G. S. Fishman, and L. R. Moore, "An Exhaustive Search for Optimal Multipliers," Proceedings of the 1984 Winter Simulation Conference, pp. 198–200, 1984.

[27] J. R. Koza, "Evolving a Computer Program to Generate Random Numbers Using the Genetic Programming Paradigm," Proceedings of the Fourth International Conference on Genetic Algorithms, San Diego, CA, pp. 37–44, 1991.

[28] J. Soto, "Statistical Testing of Random Number Generators," Proceedings of the 22nd National Information Systems Security Conference, Crystal City, VA, 1999.

[29] M. Mascagni, "Parallel Linear Congruential Generators with Prime Module," Communications of the ACM, Vol. 24, No. 5–6, pp. 923–936, 1998.

[30] R. Y. Rubinstein, B. Melamed, "Random Numbers, Variates, and Stochastic Process Generation," in Modern Simulation and Modeling, Wiley, London, UK, 1998.

[31] S. Tezuka, P. L'Ecuyer, "Efficient and Portable Combined Tausworthe Random Number Generators," in ACM Transactions on Modeling and Computer Simulation, pp. 99–112, 1991.

[32] M. Pidd, "An Introduction to Computer Simulation," in Proceedings of the 1994 Winter Simulation Conference, Orlando, Fl, pp. 7–14, 1994.

[33] P. D. Hortensius, and R. D. Mcleod, "Parallel Random Number Generation for VLSI systems Using Cellular Automata," IEEE Transactions on Computers, Vol. 38, No. 10, pp. 1466–1473, 1989.

[34] R. G. Sargent, "Verifications and Validations of Simulation Models," Proceedings of the 2003 Winter Simulation Conference, Washington, D.C., pp. 121–130, 2003.

[35] P. L'Ecuyer, "Testing Random Number Generators," Proceedings of the 24th conference on Winter simulation, pp. 305–313, 1992.

[36] M. Matsumoto and T. Nishimura, "Mersenne Twister: A 623-Dimensionally Equidistributed Uniform Pseudo-Random Number Generator," ACM Transactions on Modeling and Computer Simulation (TOMACS), Vol. 8, No. 1, pp. 31–30, 1998.

[37] M. S. Obaidat, and L. E. Leguire, "A Dynamic and Static Microcomputer-based Stereogram Generator," IEEE Transactions on Systems, Man and Cybernetics, Vol. 21, No. 01, pp. 228-2231, 1991.

[38] M.S. Obaidat, and D. S. Abu-Saymeh, "A Microcomputer-based Video Pattern Generator for Binocular Vision Test," IEEE Transactions on Instrumentation and Measurement, Vol. 43, No. 1, pp. 89–93, 1994.

[39] M. S. Obaidat, and D. S. Abu-Saymeh, "A Real-time Video Pattern Generator for Use in Ophthalmology," Journal of Medical Engineering & Technology, Vol. 23, No. 4, pp. 127–143, 1999.

[40] L. Blum, M. Blum, and M. Shub, "A simple Unpredictable Pseudo Random Number Generator," SIAM Journal of Computing, Vol. 2, 1986.

## EXERCISES

1. Describe what do you think would be the most effective way to study each of the following systems:

    a. A wireless local area network that consists of 100 nodes.

    b. A 1000-procesor massively parallel computer system.

    c. The performance of an Asynchronous Transfer Mode (ATM) based local area network LAN system.

    d. The operation of a simple bank branch in a town.

2. For each of the systems in problem 1, assume that it has been decided to make a study via a simulation model. Discuss whether the simulation should be static or dynamic, deterministic or stochastic, and continuous or discrete.

3. The technique for producing an exponential random variate with mean interarrival time of $1/\lambda$ uses the formula, $-1/\lambda \ \mathrm{Ln} \ U$, where $U$ is a uniformly distributed random variate between 0 and 1, $U$ (0, 1). This approach could correctly be modified to return $-1/\lambda \ \mathrm{Ln} \ (1-U)$. Explain why this is possible.

4. Which type of simulation would you use for the following problems:

    a. To model traffic in a wireless cell network given that the traffic is bursty.

    b. To model scheduling in a multiprocessor computer system given that the request arrivals have a geometric distribution.

    c. To verify the value of $\pi$, which is defined as the ratio of a circle's circumference to its diameter; C/D.

5. Using the multiplicative congruential method, find the period of the generator for $a = 17$, $m = 2^6$, and $X_0 = 1, 2, 3$, and 4. Comment on the produced numbers and resulting periods.

6. Generate five 6-bit numbers using the Tauseworthe method for the following characteristic polynomial starting with a seed of
    $X_0 = (0.111111)_2$
    $X^6 + X + 1$.

7. Generate 15,000 numbers using a seed of $X_0 = 3$ in the following generator:

   $Xn = 7^5 X_{n-1} \bmod (2^{31} - 1)$.

   Group the numbers into 20 equal-size cells and test for uniformity using the chi-square test at 90% confidence. Show all of your work.

8. Generate 15 numbers using a seed of $X_0 = 7$ in the following generator:

   $X_n = (5X_{n-1} + 1) \bmod 16$.

   Perform a K-S test and check whether the sequence passes the test at 95% confidence level.

9. Given a random variate that has the following pdf.

   $f(x) = \min (X, 2 - X) \quad 0 = X = 2$.

   Develop algorithms to generate this variate using each of the following methods:

   a. Inverse transformation.

   b. Rejection.

   c. Composition

10. Write a computer program to generate an exponentially distributed random variate. Generate 3000 values.

11. Write a computer program to generate a Poisson distributed random variate. Generate 5000 values.

# CHAPTER 10

# COMMONLY USED DISTRIBUTIONS IN SIMULATION AND THEIR APPLICATIONS

When the random variable takes values in the set of real numbers, the probability distribution can be specified by the cumulative distribution function (CDF). The value taken by a CDF at a real $x$ is the probability that the random variable is smaller than or equal to $x$. The concept of the probability distribution and the random variables that they describe underlies the disciplines of simulation and probability. Probability distributions are often a more appropriate way to describe real quantities because there is variability in almost any value that can be measured in a population or a system. In addition, almost all measurements are made with some intrinsic error.

A probability distribution is called *discrete* if its cumulative distribution function only increases in jumps. It is called *continuous* if its cumulative distribution function is continuous. Various probability distributions have been used in various different applications. Examples on the most important ones are the exponential distribution, normal distribution, Poisson distribution, geometric distribution, and binomial distribution. We present in the following the description and the properties of the probability distributions, which are widely used in the simulation of computer and telecommunication systems.

Probability distributions are used on both theoretical and practical levels. Among the most practical uses of the probability distributions are the following:

*Fundamentals of Performance Evaluation of Computer and Telecommunication Systems,*
By Mohammad S. Obaidat and Noureddine A. Boudriga
Copyright © 2010 John Wiley & Sons, Inc.

- To compute confidence intervals for parameters and define critical regions for hypothesis tests.
- To determine a reasonable distributional model for the data or phenomenon.
- To allow simulation studies with random numbers generated from a specific probability distribution.

## 10.1 EXPONENTIAL DISTRIBUTION

### 10.1.1 Definition

The exponential distribution constitutes a specific important class of continuous probability distribution [1]. It is being used to model many systems. The probability density function (pdf) of an exponential distribution has the following form:

$$f(t, \lambda) = \begin{cases} \lambda e^{-\lambda t}, & t \geq 0 \\ 0, & t \leq 0 \end{cases}$$

where $\lambda > 0$ is a parameter of the distribution, often called the *rate parameter*. The distribution is supported on the interval $[0, \infty]$. If a random variable $X$ has this distribution, the CDF is the integration of pdf and is given by:

$$F(x, \lambda) = \begin{cases} 1 - \lambda e^{-\lambda t}, & x \geq 0 \\ 0, & x \leq 0 \end{cases}$$

Figure 10.1 depicts the probability density function and the cumulative distribution function for the exponential distribution for different values of $\lambda$.

Exponential distributions are often used to model the time between independent events that happen at a constant average rate. The exponential distribution is used to model systems where a component, initially in state $s_0$, changes to state $s$, at time $t$, with constant probability per unit time $\lambda$. Therefore, the integral from 0 to $t$ of the exponential distribution function is the probability that the system is in state $s$ at time $t$. In real-world scenarios, the assumption that $\lambda$ is constant is rarely satisfied; but in different situations, $\lambda$ can be assumed constant during an interval of time. For example, the rate of incoming phone calls differs according to the time of day. But if we focus on a time interval during which the rate is roughly constant, such as around a rush hour, the exponential distribution can be used as a good approximate model for the time until the next phone call arrives.

Exponential variables that can also be used to model the interarrival times (i.e., the times between customers entering the system) are often modeled as

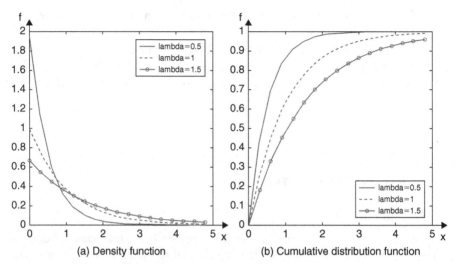

(a) Density function    (b) Cumulative distribution function

**FIGURE 10.1.** Probability density function and cumulative distribution function of the exponential distribution.

exponentially distributed variables. However, the length of a process that can be thought of as a sequence of several independent tasks is better modeled by a variable following the sum of several independent exponentially distributed variables. Reliability theory also makes use of the exponential distribution, because of the memoryless property of this distribution. It is also convenient because it is so easy to add failure rates in a reliability model. The exponential distribution is however not appropriate to model the overall lifetime of systems or technical devices, because the "failure rates" here are not constant. In fact, more failures are likely to occur in the beginning and end of the life cycle of a system.

### 10.1.2  Properties of Exponential Distributed Variables

**Mean and variance.** The expected value and variance of an exponentially distributed random variable $X$ with rate parameter $\lambda$ are given by:

$$E(X) = \int_0^\infty e^{-yt} dt = \frac{1}{\lambda}, \text{ and}$$

$$V(X) = \sigma^2(X) = \int_0^\infty (e^{-yt} - \frac{1}{\lambda})^2 dt = \frac{1}{\lambda^2}.$$

**Example.** If one is expecting to receive phone calls at an average rate of two per unit interval, then one can expect to wait half of the unit interval every call.

**Memorylessness.** A major feature of the exponential distribution is its memorylessness. Memorylessness completely characterizes the exponential distribution, i.e., the only probability distribution that enjoys (continuous) memorylessness is the exponential distribution. This states that if a random variable $X$ is exponentially distributed, then its conditional probability obeys the following relation:

$$P(X > s + t \mid X > s) = P(X > t), \quad \text{for all } s, t \geq 0$$

Here, $X$ measures the time to wait until the first arrival of a packet in a computer system or telecommunication network, and $s$ and $t$ represent real numbers.

**Quartiles.** The inverse cumulative distribution function (or quantile function) for the exponential distribution with parameter $\lambda$ is given by:

$$F^{-1}(p, \lambda) = \frac{-\ln(1-p)}{\lambda}, \quad \text{for} \in [0, 1].$$

**Estimation of the rate parameter $\lambda$.** Assume we know that a given variable $X$ is exponentially distributed, the likelihood function for $\lambda$, given an independent and identically distributed sample $x = (x_1, \ldots, x_n)$ drawn from variable $X$, is given by:

$$L(\lambda) = \prod_{j=1}^{n} \lambda e^{-\lambda x_j} = \lambda^n e^{-\lambda(x_1 + \ldots + x_n)} = \lambda^n e^{-\lambda n \bar{x}}$$

where $\bar{x}$ is the sample mean given by $\bar{x} = \frac{1}{n} \sum_{1 \leq j \leq n} x_j$.

## 10.2 POISSON DISTRIBUTION

### 10.2.1 Definition

The Poisson distribution is a discrete probability distribution. It expresses the probability of a number of events occurring in a fixed period of time if these events occur with a known average rate and are independent of the time since the last event. The Poisson distribution was first defined by S.D. Poisson (in 1837) when approximating formulas for the binomial distribution, knowing that the number of trials is large and the probability of success is small.

The Poisson distribution is a one parameter discrete distribution that takes non-negative integer values [2]. The probability that there are exactly $k$ occurrences ($k$ being a non-negative integer, $k \in N$) is given by the so-called Poisson probability distribution function:

$$f(k, \lambda) = \frac{\lambda^k e^{-\lambda}}{k!}$$

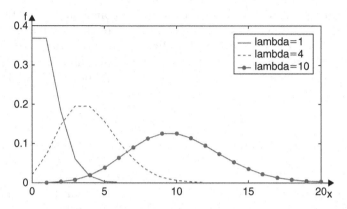

**FIGURE 10.2.** Poisson distribution function.

where $\lambda$ is a positive real number to the expected number of occurrences that occur during the given interval. Figure 10.2 depicts the Poisson distribution function for different values of $\lambda$. The horizontal axis and the connecting lines, in the figure, represent the index $k$ and guide to indicate the three functions). The expectation value of $X$ is given by:

$$E(X) = \sum_{k=0}^{\infty} \lambda \frac{\lambda^k e^{-\lambda}}{k!} = \lambda e^{-\lambda} \sum_{k=0}^{\infty} \frac{\lambda^k}{k!} = \lambda e^{-\lambda} e^{\lambda} = \lambda$$

In addition, the parameter $\lambda$ is not only the mean number of occurrences of events but also its variance. Thus, the number of observed occurrences fluctuates about its mean $\lambda$ with a standard deviation of $\sqrt{\lambda}$. These fluctuations are referred to as *Poisson noise*. Therefore, as the size of the numbers in a particular sample of Poisson random numbers gets larger, so does the variability of the numbers.

The Poisson distribution is appropriate for applications that involve counting the number of times a random event occurs in a given interval of time, area, or distance or similar parameter. It applies to various phenomena of discrete nature, whenever the probability of the phenomenon happening is constant in time or space. Sample applications that involve Poisson distributions include: (a) the number of phone calls at a call center per minute, (b) the number of viruses that can infect a systems connected to a given network during a unit of time, (c) the number of packets entering a communication switch in a unit of time, (d) the number of times a Web server is accessed per minute, and e) the number of flaws per 100 meters of video tape. Other examples include various events occurring in different domains such as: (a) the number of Geiger counter clicks per second, (b) the number of spelling mistakes one makes while typing a single page, and (c) number of animals killed found per unit length of a road.

We will show in the following that the Poisson distribution is related to the exponential distribution and the binomial distribution. Particularly, we will show that: (a) if the number of counts follows the Poisson distribution, then the interval between individual counts follows the exponential distribution; and (b) the Poisson distribution is the limiting case of a binomial distribution where $n$ approaches infinity and $p$ goes to zero while $np = \lambda$.

If $\lambda$ is observed to be the average number of occurrences per unit time, let $N_t$ be the number of occurrences before time $t$ then we have:

$$P(N_t = k) = f(k, \lambda t) = \frac{(\lambda t)^k e^{-\lambda t}}{k!}.$$

The waiting time $X$ until the first occurrence is a *continuous* random variable with an exponential distribution (with parameter $\lambda$). The probability distribution for $X$ can therefore be derived as

$$P(X > t) = P(N_t = 0) = e^{-\lambda t}$$

### 10.2.2 Properties of Poisson Distribution

**Sums of Poisson-distributed random variables.** If random variables $X_i$, $i = 1 \ldots n$ follow a Poisson distribution with parameter $\lambda_i$ and $X_i$ are independent, then the sum $S = \sum_{i=1}^{n} X_i$ also follows a Poisson distribution whose parameter is the sum: $\lambda = \sum_{i=1}^{n} \lambda_i$.

**The moment-generating function.** The moment generating function of the Poisson distribution with expected value $\lambda$ is given by:

$$E(e^{tX}) = \sum_{k=0}^{\infty} e^{tX} f(k, \lambda) = \sum_{k=1}^{\infty} e^{tk} \frac{\lambda^k e^{-\lambda}}{k!} = e^{\lambda(e^t - 1)}$$

**Maximum likelihood.** Given a sample of $n$ measured values $k_i$, to estimate the value of the parameter $\lambda$ of the Poisson population from which the sample was drawn, one can form the log-likelihood function defined by:

$$L(\lambda) = \log(\prod_{i=1}^{n} f(k_i, \lambda))$$

$$= \sum_{i=1}^{n} \log(f(k_i, \lambda)) = \sum_{i=1}^{n} \log(\frac{e^{-\lambda} \lambda^{k_i}}{k_i!})$$

$$= -n\lambda + (\log \lambda)(\sum_{i=1}^{n} k_i) - \sum_{i=1}^{n} \log(k_i!)$$

To compute a maximum, we can determine the derivative of function $L$, with respect to $\lambda$, and equate it to zero. This gives

$$\frac{dL(\lambda)}{d\lambda} = -n + \frac{1}{\lambda} \sum_{i=1}^{n} k_i = 0$$

Solving for $\lambda$ yields the maximum-likelihood $\hat{\lambda}$ estimate of $\lambda$ using

$$\hat{\lambda} = \frac{1}{n} \sum_{i=1}^{n} k_i$$

.

## 10.3   UNIFORM DISTRIBUTION

### 10.3.1   Basics on the Uniform Distribution

The uniform distribution is a discrete distribution that has a constant probability distribution function between two parameters, called the minimum (denoted by $a$) and the maximum (denoted by $b$). The uniform distribution appears in probability theory as an exact distribution in some problems and as a limit in others. The concept of a uniform distribution on $[a, b]$ corresponds to the representation of a random choice of a point from the interval.

The standard uniform distribution is a special case of the beta distribution, obtained by setting both of its parameters to 0 and 1, respectively. The cumulative uniform distribution function of the Uniform distribution is given by:

$$F(x, a, b) = \frac{x - a}{b - a} \chi_{[a,b]}(x)$$

where $\chi_{[a,b]}$ is the function defined by: $\chi_{[a,b]}(x) = 1 \Leftrightarrow x \in [a, b]$.

A discrete uniform distribution can be characterized by the following property: If a random variable has $n$ possible values $k_i, \dots k_n$ that are equally probable, then it has a discrete uniform distribution. Therefore, the probability of any outcome $k_i$ is $1/n$. The cumulative distribution function of a discrete uniform distribution is given by

$$F(x, n) = \frac{1}{n} \chi_{\{k_1 \dots k_n\}}(x)$$

where $\chi_{\{k_1 \dots k_n\}}$ is the function defined by: $\chi_{\{k_1 \dots k_n\}}(x) = 1 \Leftrightarrow x \in \{k_1, k_2, \dots, k_{n-1}, k_n\}$. Figure 10.3 depicts an example of CDF, $F$, with 10 values given by $\{k_1 = 0, k_2 = 1, k_9 = 8, k_{10} = 9\}$. For this example, $F$ is given by

$$F(x, 10) = \frac{i}{10}, \quad x \in [i - 1, i]$$

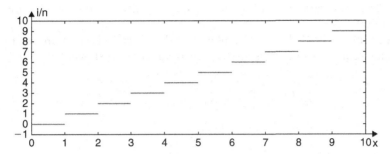

**FIGURE 10.3.** Cumulative distribution function for a discrete uniform distribution.

**Example.** A simple example of the discrete uniform distribution is throwing a fair die. The possible values of $k$ are 1, 2, 3, 4, 5, and 6. Each time the die is thrown, the probability of a given score is 1/6.

The discrete uniform distribution can be used to represent random occurrence with several possible outcomes.

The continuous uniform distribution is one of the simplest distributions to use. It is commonly used if a random variable is bounded and no additional information is available, for example:

a. Distance between source and destination of message on a computer network.
b. Seek time on a disk of a computer system.

## 10.4  NORMAL DISTRIBUTION

### 10.4.1  Definition

The normal distribution is a two-parameter family of curves. The first parameter, denoted by $\mu$, is the mean, and the second parameter, denoted by $\sigma$, is the standard deviation. The pdf of normal distribution is given below [3]:

$$f(x, \mu, \lambda) = \frac{1}{\sqrt{2\pi}\sigma} e^{-(x-\mu)^2/2\sigma^2}$$

The Gaussian function $\varphi(x) = \frac{1}{\sqrt{2\pi}} e^{-x^2/2}$ is the density function of the "standard" normal distribution, i.e., the normal distribution with parameters $\mu = 0$ and $s = 1$. The first use of the normal distribution has been as a continuous approximation to the binomial through the central limit theorem, which states that the sum of independent samples from any distribution with finite mean and variance converges to the normal distribution as the sample size goes to infinity.

The CDF evaluated at real number $x$ of the normal distribution, see Figure 10.4, and computed in terms of the density function as shown below:

$$F(x, \mu, \sigma) = \frac{1}{\sqrt{2\pi}\sigma} \int_{-\infty}^{x} e^{-(t-\mu)^2/2\sigma^2} \, dt$$

$$= \Phi\left(\frac{x-\mu}{2\sigma}\right)$$

where $\Phi(x)$ is the cumulative distribution function of the standard normal distribution (or $F(x,0,1)$).

$$F(x, 0, 1) = \frac{1}{\sqrt{2\pi}} \int_{-\infty}^{x} e^{-t^2/2} \, dt.$$

The standard normal cumulative distribution function can be expressed in terms of the so-called Gaussian error function (Ger):

$$\Phi(x) = \frac{1}{2}\left(1 + Ger\left(\frac{x}{\sqrt{2}}\right)\right)$$

where $Ger(-)$ is defined by:

$$Ger(x) = \frac{2}{\sqrt{\pi}} \int_{0}^{\infty} e^{-t^2} \, dt.$$

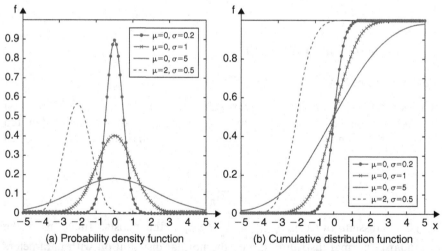

(a) Probability density function       (b) Cumulative distribution function

**FIGURE 10.4.** Probability density function and cumulative distribution function of the normal distribution.

The expression of *Ger(x)* cannot be evaluated in closed form in terms of elementary functions [4]. However, it can be expanded in a Taylor series as follows:

$$Ger(x) = \frac{2}{\sqrt{\pi}} \sum_{n=0}^{\infty} \frac{(-1)^n}{2n+1} \cdot \frac{x^{2n+1}}{n!}$$

The Tailor series converges for every real number $x$. In addition to approximation based on Taylor series, the values of $F(x)$ may be approximated by a variety of methods, such as numerical integration, asymptotic series, and continued fractions.

Finally, let us notice that the normal distribution has various applications in different domains including modeling errors of any type.

## 10.4.2 Properties

**Quantile function.** The inverse standard normal cumulative distribution function, or quantile function, can be expressed in terms of the inverse Gaussian error function by $\Phi^{-1}(y) = \sqrt{2} Ger^{-1}(2y - 1)$. More generally, the inverse cumulative distribution function can be expressed as:

$$F^{-1}(y, \mu, \sigma) = \mu + \sigma\sqrt{2} Ger^{-1}(2y - 1)$$

**Moment generation function:** The moment generating function is defined as the expected value of $e^{tx}$, wherever this expectation exists. The moment-generating function generates the moments of the probability distribution. It can be determined for a normal distribution whose moment-generating function is given by:

$$E(e^{tx}) = \int_{-\infty}^{\infty} \frac{1}{\sqrt{2\pi}\sigma} e^{-(x-\mu)^2/2\sigma^2} e^{tx} dx = e^{\mu t + (\sigma t)^2/2}$$

Because the moment-generating function exists in an interval around $t = 0$, and $E(e^{tx}) = 1 + \sum_{j=1}^{\infty} t^j m_j$ then the $n$th moment is given by:

$$\frac{d^{(n)} E(e^{tx})}{dt^n}\Big|_{t=0}$$

**Parameter estimation for the normal distribution.** To use statistical parameters such as mean and standard deviation reliably, it is important to have a good estimator for them. The maximum likelihood estimates (MLEs) provide one such estimator. However, an MLE might be biased, meaning that the expected value of the parameter under estimation might not be equal to this parameter. An unbiased estimator that is commonly used to estimate the parameters of the normal distribution is the minimum variance unbiased estimator (MVUE). The MVUEs of parameters $\mu$ and $\sigma^2$ for the normal distribution are the sample average and variance.

*a) Maximum likelihood estimation of parameters:* Suppose $X_1, \ldots, X_n$ are independent and normally distributed random variables with mean value $\mu$ and variance $\sigma^2$. The observed values of these random variables make up a sample from a normally distributed population. It is used to estimate the population mean $\mu$ and the population standard deviation $\sigma$. The joint probability density function of $X_1, \ldots, X_n$ is:

$$f(x_1, \ldots, x_n; \mu, \sigma) = \frac{a}{\sigma^n} \prod_{i=1}^{n} e^{-(x_i - \mu)^2 / 2\sigma^2}$$

As a function of $\mu$ and $s$, the likelihood function $L(\mu, \sigma)$ is proportional to:

$$\sigma^{-n} e^{-\sum_{i=1}^{n} (x_i - \mu)^2 / 2\sigma^2}$$

In the method of maximum likelihood, the values of $\mu$ and $\sigma$ that maximize the likelihood function are taken to be estimates of the population parameters. Obviously, the likelihood function is an increasing function when the sum $\sum_{i=1}^{n} (x_i - \bar{x})^2$ decreases. Therefore, the maximum likelihood is minimal when this sum is minimal. Let $\bar{x}$ be defined by:

$$\bar{x} = \frac{1}{n} \sum_{i=1}^{n} x_i$$

which is the sample mean.

Therefore, the sum $\sum_{i=1}^{n} (x_i - \bar{x})^2$ is minimized by $\mu = \bar{x}$, that is, the max-imum-likelihood estimate of $\mu$. Then, we substitute $\bar{x}$ in the likelihood function. The value of $\sigma$ that maximizes the resulting expression is obtained using the logarithm of the likelihood function, and we have:

$$l(\sigma) = \log(L(\bar{x}, \sigma) = cte - n \log \sigma - (\sum_{j=1}^{n} (x_i - \bar{x})^2) / 2\sigma^2$$

Applying the derivative to $l(\sigma)$, we obtain:

$$\frac{dl(\sigma)}{d\sigma} = \frac{-n}{\sigma} + \frac{1}{\sigma^3} \sum_{j=1}^{n} (x_i - \bar{x})^2 = \frac{-n}{\sigma^3} (\sigma^2 - \frac{1}{n} \sum_{j=1}^{n} (x_i - \bar{x})^2).$$

Obviously, it is maximized when $\sigma^2 = \frac{1}{n} \sum_{j=1}^{n} (x_i - \bar{x})^2$. Consequently, the computed value is maximum-likelihood estimate of $s^2$, and its square root is the maximum-likelihood estimate of $s$. This estimator is biased because, if

$$\sigma^2 = \frac{1}{n} \sum_{i=1}^{n} (X_i - \overline{X})^2, \text{ where } \overline{X} = \frac{1}{n} \sum_{i=1}^{n} X_i.$$

Then:

$$E(S^2) = \frac{n-1}{n} \sigma^2.$$

*b) Unbiased estimation of parameters:* Because the maximum likelihood estimator of the population mean $\mu$ from a sample is an unbiased estimator of the mean, the following estimator is used. It is an unbiased estimator of the variance $s^2$. It can be given by:

$$S^2 = \frac{1}{n-1} \sum_{i=1}^{n} (X_i - \overline{X})^2.$$

This equation is the MVUE associated with $\sigma^2$.

### 10.4.3 Multinomial Distribution

The binomial distribution with parameters $n$, $p$, and $k$ is the distribution of the random variable $X$, which counts the number of events that occur when $n$ successive packets are received (or a coin is tossed $n$ times), assuming that for any packet, the probability that the packet contains an error (or a head occurs in the case of coin tossing) is $p$. The distribution function is given by the formula:

$$P(X = k) = b(n, p, k) = \binom{n}{k} p^k (1 - p)^{n-k}$$

A straightforward computation shows that the expectation and variance of X are equal to $np$ and $np(1 - p)$.

Binomial distribution arises as a special case of multinomial distribution defined as follows. The multinomial distribution is the probability distribution of the number of "successes" in $n$ independent Bernoulli trials, each trial resulting in one of some fixed finite number $k$ of possible outcomes occurring with probabilities $p_1,...,p_k$, and there are $n$ independent trials. We can use a random variable $X_i$ to indicate the number of times outcome number $i$ was observed over the $n$ trials. Then, the multinomial distribution $X$ can be defined as the distribution of the vector $(X_1,..., X_n)$ [5]. The probabilities are given by:

$$P(X = (k_1,...,k_n)) = P(X_1 = k_1,..., X_n = k_n))$$

$$= \begin{cases} \frac{n!}{k_1!\dots k_n!} \prod_{j=1}^{n} p_j^{k_j}, & \text{if } \sum_{j=1}^{n} k_j = n \\ 0 & , \quad \text{otherwise} \end{cases}$$

Each component $X_j$, $j \in \{1,\dots,n\}$ of random variable $X$ separately has a binomial distribution with parameters $n$ and $p_j$, and has an expected value equal to $np_j$ and a variance equal to $np_j(1 - p_j)$.

It seems that, because of the constraint that the sum of the components is $n$, then variables are correlated. The covariance matrix $\{Cov_{i,j}\}_{i,j \leq n}$ is characterized by:

- The off diagonal values that are given by $Cov_{i,j} = \text{cov}(X_i, X_j) = -np_ip_j$, $i \neq j$
- The elements of the diagonal that are given by $Cov_{i,i} = \text{var}(X_i) = -np_i(1 - p_j)$.

It is well known that the Poisson distribution can be used as an approximation to the binomial distribution when the parameter $n$ is large and $p$ is small. For this, let us consider a random variable $X$ having a binomial distribution with parameters $n$ and $p$. Assume that $X$ counts the occurrences of an event in a given interval and that there we can observe $\lambda t$ occurrences of an event in a time interval of length $t$. If this time interval is divided into $n$ small intervals, then we should have $\lambda t = np$ Thus, we have:

$$p = \frac{\lambda t}{n}$$

When computing $P(X = k)$, one can state the following:

- $P(X = 0) = b(n,p,0) = (1 - p)^n = \left(1 - \frac{\lambda}{n}\right)^n$
- $\dfrac{b(n,p,k)}{b(n,p,k-1)} = \dfrac{\lambda - (k-1)p}{k(1-p)} \cong \dfrac{\lambda}{k}$, for large $n$ (and, therefore, small $p$)
- $P(X = 1) \approx \lambda e^{-\lambda}$ and $P(X = k) \approx \dfrac{\lambda^k}{k!} e^{-\lambda}$, for large $n$.

Thus, one can deduce that when $n$ is large, the distribution of $X$ is the Poisson distribution.

**Example.** A network transmits, on the average, one erroneous packet per $10^6$ packets. Assume that it is sending a message of 100 packets. Let $X$ be the number of erroneous packets for the message. Then the exact probability distribution for $X$ would be obtained by considering a binomial distribution with $p = 10^{-6}$. The expected value of $X$ is $\lambda = 100(1/10^6) = 10^{-4}$. The exact probability that $X = 10$ is $b(100; 10^{-6}; 10)$, and the Poisson approximation shows that this probability is equal to:

$$P(X = 10) \approx \frac{10^{-40}}{10!} e^{-10^{-4}}.$$

### 10.4.4 Log Normal

A random variable $X$ has a log-normal distribution if, and only if, its logarithm is normally distributed. Thus, if $X$ is a random variable with a normal distribution, then the random variable $e^X$ has a log-normal distribution. The definition is coherent because $\log_a X$ is normally distributed if and only if $\log_b X$ is normally distributed.

The log-normal distribution has the following probability density function (pdf):

$$f(x, \mu, \sigma) = \frac{1}{\sigma \sqrt{2\pi x}} e^{-(\log x - \mu)^2 / 2\sigma^2}, \ x > 0$$

where $\mu$ and $\sigma$ are the median and standard deviation of $\log(X)$. The expected value and the standard deviation of $X$ are given by:

$$E(X) = e^{\mu + \sigma^2/2} \text{ and } \sigma^2(X) = (e^{\sigma^2} - 1)e^{2\mu + \sigma^2}$$

More generally, the $k$th moment, $k \geq 2$, is given by:

$$m_k(X) = e^{k\mu + k^2\sigma^2/2}$$

To provide the maximum likelihood estimators of the log-normal distribution parameters $\mu$ and $\sigma$, one can use the approach applied to the normal distribution. Otherwise, one can notice that the density function $f_L$ of the log-normal distribution and the normal distribution, $f_N$, are linked by the formula:

$$f_L(x, \mu, \sigma) = \frac{1}{x} f_N(\log x, \mu, \sigma)$$

We can write the log-likelihood function $l_L(\mu, \sigma)$ using the log-likelihood function $l_N(\mu, \sigma)$ as:

$$l_L(\mu, \sigma) = \sum_{k \leq n} \log(x_k) + l_N(\mu, \sigma)$$

Because the first term in the right side of the equation is constant with respect to $\mu$ and $\sigma$, the logarithmic likelihood functions $l_L(\mu, \sigma)$ and $l_N(\mu, \sigma)$ reach their maximum with the same values of parameters $\mu$ and $s$. Therefore, the formulas for the normal distribution maximum likelihood parameter estimators, which we have previously established, can be used to deduce that

$$\hat{\mu} = \frac{1}{n} \sum_{k \leq n} \log(x_k) \quad \text{and} \quad \hat{\sigma}^2 = \frac{1}{n} \sum_{k \leq n} (\log(x_k) - \hat{\mu}).$$

## 10.5 WEIBULL DISTRIBUTION

The Weibull distribution is one among the most popular statistical models for life data. It is also used in many other applications, such as weather forecasting and fitting data of all kinds. It may be employed for traffic engineering analysis with smaller sample sizes. The Weibull distribution is a continuous probability distribution with the pdf:

$$f(x, k, \lambda) = \begin{cases} \frac{k}{\lambda} \left(\frac{x}{\lambda}\right)^{k-1} e^{-(x/\lambda)^k}, & x \geq 0, k > 0 \\ 0 & , x < 0 \end{cases}$$

where $k > 0$ is called the shape parameter and $\lambda > 0$ is called the scale parameter of the distribution [6]. The CDF for the Weibull distribution is given by:

$$F(x, k, \lambda) = \begin{cases} 1 - e^{-(x/\lambda)^k}, & x \geq 0, k > 0 \\ 0 & , x < 0 \end{cases}.$$

It is worth noting that when $k = 1$, the Weibull distribution becomes exponential. This means that the exponential distribution is a special case of the Weibull distribution. Figure 10.5 depicts the aforementioned functions for different values of $k$ and $\lambda$.

An important quantity called the hazard rate or failure rate in the Weibull distribution is defined by $\frac{kx^{k-1}}{\lambda^k}$. The following three situations can occur: (a) if $k < 1$ the hazard rate decreases over time; (b) if $k = 1$ the hazard rate is constant over time and the distribution becomes exponential distribution; and (c) If $k > 1$ the hazard rate increases over time. To see why this definition is made, let us recall that, if $f(t)$ and $F(t)$ are a pdf and its CDF, then the hazard rate is given by:

$$h(f)(t) = \frac{f(t)}{1 - F(t)}.$$

Substituting pdf and CDF, the exponential distribution for $f(t)$ and $F(t)$ above yields exactly $\frac{kx^{k-1}}{\lambda^k}$.

The Weibull distribution is often used to mimic the behavior of other statistical distributions such as the normal and the exponential. Current applications also include reliability and lifetime modeling. The Weibull distribution is more flexible than the exponential for these purposes.

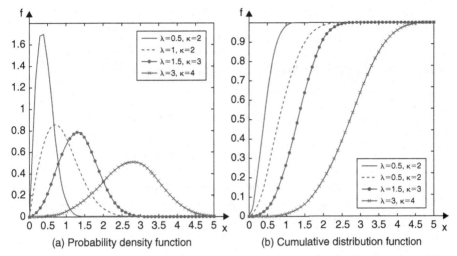

**FIGURE 10.5.** Probability density function and cumulative distribution function of the Weibull distribution.

The Weibull distributions also can be used: (a) for fading channel modeling, because the Weibull fading model seems to exhibit good fit to experimental fading channel measurements; (b) to model the dispersion of the received signals level produced in radar systems; (c) to produce statistical model in reliability engineering and failure analysis; (d) to represent manufacturing and delivery times in industrial engineering problems; and (e) to describe wind speed distributions and weather forecasting models.

The Weibull distribution is closely related the Gamma function. One can observe, for example, that the expected value, nth moment, and standard deviation of random variable $X$ having a Weibull distribution are given respectively by:

$$E(X) = \lambda \cdot \Gamma\left(1 + \frac{1}{k}\right), \sigma^2(X) = \lambda^2 \cdot \Gamma\left(1 + \frac{2}{k}\right) \text{ and } m_n = \lambda^n \cdot \Gamma\left(1 + \frac{n}{k}\right)$$

## 10.6 PARETO DISTRIBUTION

### 10.6.1 Definition

If $X$ is a random variable, we say it has a Pareto distribution if there are a positive parameter "$k$" and a positive real value "$a$" such that the probability that $X$ is greater than some number $x$ is given by:

$$P(X > x) = \left(\frac{a}{x}\right)^k, \quad x \geq a$$

It follows that the probability density function is given by:

$$f(x, k, a) = k\frac{a^k}{x^{k+1}}, \quad x \geq a, k > 0.$$

The Pareto distribution is a probability distribution that applies to social, scientific, and geographic situation. It can be applied to many situations in communication [7]. Pareto distribution is a continuous distribution (Figure 10.6.) The expected value and standard deviation (if $k < 1$) of a random variable $X$ following a Pareto distribution are given as follows:

$$E(X) = \frac{ka}{k-1}, \quad \text{and } \sigma^2(X) = \frac{k}{k-2}\left(\frac{a}{k-1}\right)^2, k < 1$$

In addition, the nth moment of a Pareto random variate, $X$, is given by:

$$m_n(X) = \frac{ka^n}{k-n}.$$

The moments are only defined for $k > n$. This means that the moment generating function, which is just a Taylor series, is not defined.

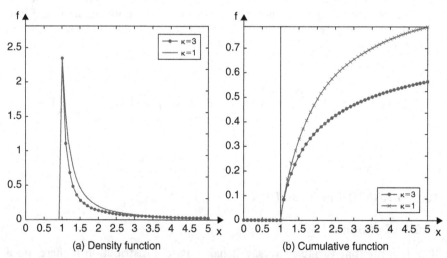

(a) Density function          (b) Cumulative function

**FIGURE 10.6.** Pareto probability density function and its cumulative distribution function.

This distribution is not limited to describing wealth or financial income, but it can also be applied to many situations in which equilibrium can be found using the distribution. The following examples represent typical examples sometimes observed as approximately Pareto-distributed: Frequencies of words in longer texts, the file size distribution of communication traffic (using, for example, the TCP protocol), and the standardized price returns on individual stocks.

### 10.6.2 Properties of Pareto Distribution

**Parameter estimators.** Given a sample $x = (x_1, \ldots, x_n)$ of a Pareto distribution, the likelihood function $L(k, a)$ for parameters $k$ and $a$ is given by:

$$L(k, a) = \prod_{i=1}^{n} k \frac{a^k}{x_i^k} = k^n a^{kn} \prod_{i=1}^{n} \frac{1}{x_i^{k+1}}.$$

Applying the logarithm function to $L(k, a)$, the logarithmic likelihood function is:

$$l(k, a) = \log(L(k, a)) = n \log(k) + nk \log(a) - (k + 1) \sum_{i=1}^{n} \log(x_i).$$

It can be observed that the function $\log(L(k, a))$ is monotonically increasing with respect to the parameter $a$. *Because* $x_i \in [a, \infty]$ for every $1 \leq i \leq n$, we can conclude that the least $xi$ gives an estimation of parameter a (i.e., $\hat{a} = \min_i x_i$). To find the estimator for $k$, we compute the partial derivative with respect to $k$ and equate it to zero as follows:

$$\frac{\partial l(k, a)}{\partial k} = \frac{1}{k} + n \log(a) - \sum_{i=1}^{n} \log(x_i) = 0$$

Thus, the maximum likelihood estimator for $k$ is given by:

$$\hat{k} = 1 / \log(a) - \sum_{i=1}^{n} \log(x_i)$$

**Generalized Pareto distribution.** The generalized Pareto distribution allows a continuous range of possible shapes that include the exponential and Pareto distributions. The probability density function for the generalized Pareto distribution has three parameters, called the shape parameter $k$, the location parameter $\mu$, and the scale parameter $\sigma$. It is given by:

$$f(x, k, \mu, \sigma) = \frac{1}{\sigma}\left(1 + k\frac{x - \mu}{\sigma}\right)^{(-1 - \frac{1}{k})}$$

The related cumulative distribution function is:

$$F(x, k, \mu, \sigma) = 1 - (1 + k\frac{x - \mu}{\sigma})^{(-\frac{1}{k})}, \quad \text{for } x \geq \mu \text{ and } x \leq \mu - \frac{\sigma}{k}(\text{if } k < 0).$$

When $k$ approaches 0, the probability density function is equivalent to:

$$g(x, \mu, \sigma) = \frac{1}{\sigma}e^{-\frac{x - \mu}{\sigma}}.$$

In this case, the generalized Pareto distribution is equivalent to the exponential distribution.

## 10.7   GEOMETRIC DISTRIBUTION

The geometric distribution is a discrete distribution, defined on the non-negative integers. It is useful for modeling the runs of consecutive successes (or failures) in repeated independent trials of a system. The geometric distribution models the number of successes before one failure in an independent succession of tests where each test results in success or failure.

The geometric distribution pdf, is given by:

$$f(k, p) = p(1 - p)^k.$$

The expected value of a geometrically distributed random variable $X$ is $1/p$ and the standard deviation is $\sigma^2(X) = \frac{1-p}{p}$. The CDF, is given by:

$$F(k, p) = P(X > k) = 1 - (1 - p)^k$$

For the geometric distribution, the parameter $p$ can be estimated by equating the expected value with the sample mean. Specifically, let $k_1, \ldots, k_n$ be a sample such that $k_i > 1$, $i \geq 1$. Then $p$ can be estimated by:

$$\hat{p} = (\frac{1}{n}\sum_{i=1}^{n}k_i)^{-1}$$

**Example.** The use of geometric distribution is important in the theory of waiting queues. Let us assume that a queue of packets is waiting for service at a switching node. It is often assumed that, in each small time slot, either 0 or 1 new packet arrives to the switch. The probability that a packet (or a customer) arrives is $p$ and that no customer arrives is $q = 1 - p$. Then the time $X$ until the next arrival has a geometric distribution. The probability that no customer arrives in the next $n$ time slots, denoted by $P(X>n)$, can be computed as follows:

$$p(x>n) = \sum_{j=n-1}^{x} pq^{j-1} = q^n p \sum_{j\geq 0} q^j = q^n$$

Like the exponential distribution, the geometric distribution is memoryless. This means that if an experiment is repeated until the first success, then, given that the first success has not yet occurred, the conditional probability distribution of the number of additional trials does not depend on how many failures have been observed. For example, a die that one throws does not have a "memory" of the failures observed. Formally, the memoryless property in this context states that:

$$P(X > i+j \,|\, X > i) = \frac{P(\{X > i+j\} \cap \{X > i\})}{P(X > i)} = \frac{P(X > i+j)}{P(X > i)}$$

$$= \frac{(1-p)^{i+j}}{(1-p)^i} = (1-p)^j = P(X > j).$$

One can notice that the geometric distribution $Y$ is a special case of the negative binomial distribution with $r = 1$. More specifically, if $X_1 \ldots X_n$ are independent geometrically distributed random variables with parameter $p$, then the random variable $Y = \sum_{j=1}^{n} X_j$ follows a negative binomial distribution with parameters $r$ and $p$.

However, let us consider $r$ and $k$ such that $0<r<1$, and $0<k \leq n$, then the random variable $X_k$ has a Poisson distribution with expected value $r^k/k$. The finite sum: $Y = \sum_{j=1}^{n} jX_j$ has a geometric distribution taking values in the set of natural integers, $N$, with expected value $r/(1-r)$.

## 10.8  GAMMA DISTRIBUTION

### 10.8.1  Definition

The gamma distribution is a family of continuous probability distributions characterized by two parameters that represent the sum of $k$ exponentially distributed random variables, each of which has a mean $\mu$[8]. The pdf of the gamma distribution can be expressed using the gamma function $\Gamma$:

$$f(x, a, b) = \frac{1}{b^a \Gamma(a)} x^{a-1} e^{-\frac{x}{b}}, \ x > 0, \ a > 0, \ b > 0$$

where $a$ is called the *shape* parameter and $b$ is called the *scale* parameter of the gamma distribution (see Figure 10.7). The gamma function is defined by:

$$\Gamma(a) = \int_0^{\infty} t^{a-1} e^{-t} dt.$$

Alternatively, another parameterization of the gamma distribution can be used in terms of the shape parameter and a parameter $\beta$, called the rate parameter, defined by $\beta = 1/b$. Both parameterizations are commonly used. Their use is dependent on the nature of the problem to be modeled.

The CDF of the gamma distribution can be expressed in terms of the gamma function $\Gamma$:

$$F(x, a, b) = \int_0^x f(t, a, b) dt = \frac{\gamma\left(a, \frac{x}{b}\right)}{\Gamma(a)}$$

where the incomplete gamma function $\gamma$ [9] is defined by:

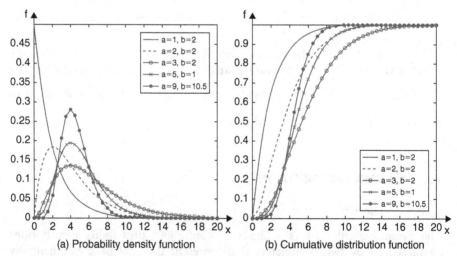

(a) Probability density function    (b) Cumulative distribution function

**FIGURE 10.7.** Probability density function and cumulative distribution function of the gamma distribution.

$$\gamma(a, x) = \int_0^x t^{a-1} e^{-t} dt$$

Notice that $\Gamma(a) = \gamma(a, x) + \int_x^\infty t^{a-1} e^{-t} dt$, $x > 0$. Figure 10.7 shows the pdf anf CDF of the gamma distribution.

### 10.8.2  Properties of Gamma Random Variate

Parameter estimation: Let $N$ be independent and identically distributed random observations $(x_1, \ldots, x_n)$. The likelihood function associated with these observations is given by:

$$L(a, b) = \prod_{i=1}^N f(x_i, a, b).$$

Computing the logarithm of $L(a, b)$, we obtain the log-likelihood function $l(a, b)$ as:

$$l(a, b) = \log(L(a, b))$$

$$= (a - 1) \sum_{i=1}^N \log(x_i) - \sum_{i=1}^N \frac{x_i}{b} - N(a \log(b) - \log(\Gamma(a))).$$

By taking the partial derivative of $l(a,b)$, with respect to $b$, and equating it to zero, we can find the maximum likelihood estimate of the $b$ parameter. A direct computation shows:

$$\hat{b} = \frac{1}{aN} \sum_{i=1}^N x_i.$$

After substitution into the log-likelihood function, we get:

$$l(a, \hat{b}) = (a - 1) \sum_{i=1}^N \log(x_i) - \sum_{i=1}^N \frac{x_i}{b} - N\left(a - a \log\left(\frac{\sum_{i=1}^N x_i}{an}\right) - \log(\Gamma(a))\right).$$

The maximum of $l(a, \hat{b})$ with respect to $a$ is obtained by taking the derivative and setting it equal to zero. This gives:

$$\log(a) - \frac{\Gamma'(a)}{\Gamma(a)} = \log\left(\frac{1}{n} \sum_{i=1}^N x_i\right) - \frac{1}{n} \sum_{i=1}^N \log(x_i).$$

This equation does not have a closed-form solution as a function of $a$. A numerical solution can be determined, using for example the Newton's method and starting with an initial value for $a$, which can be obtained using the approximation:

$$\log(a) - \frac{\Gamma'(a)}{\Gamma(a)} \approx \frac{1}{2k} + \frac{1}{12k + 2}$$

Thus, $a$ can be approximated by:

$$a \approx \frac{3 - \bar{s} + \sqrt{(\bar{s} - 3)^2 + 24\bar{s}}}{12\bar{s}}, \quad \text{where } \bar{s} = \log\left(\frac{1}{n}\sum_{i=1}^{N}x_i\right) - \frac{1}{n}\sum_{i=1}^{N}\log(x_i).$$

**Inverse gamma distribution.** This is a two-parameter family of a continuous probability distribution that represents the multiplicative inverse of the gamma distribution. The inverse gamma distribution's probability density is defined over the subset of positive real numbers by:

$$g(x, a, b) = \frac{b^a}{\Gamma(a)}x^{-a-1}e^{-\frac{b}{x}}, \quad x > 0, a > 0, b > 0$$

where $a$ and $b$ are called the shape parameter and the scale parameter, respectively. However, the CDF is given by:

$$G(x, a, b) = \frac{\Gamma(a, \frac{x}{b})}{\Gamma(a)}, \quad \text{where } \Gamma\left(a, \frac{x}{b}\right) = \int_{x/b}^{\infty} t^{a-1}e^{-t}dt$$

where $\Gamma(a, \frac{x}{b})$ is the upper incomplete gamma function.

**Example.** Consider the problem of testing computer memory chips and collecting data on their lifetimes. Assume that these lifetimes follow a gamma distribution. Assume that we want to know how long we can expect the average computer memory chip to last. Parameter estimation is the process needed for determining the parameters of the gamma distribution that is suitable, in some sense, for the situation. Sample values (or observations $(x_1, \ldots, x_n)$) are needed. The observations are the fixed constants. The variables $a, b$ to be determined are the unknown parameters. MLE involves calculating the values of the parameters that give the highest likelihood given the particular set of data as previously explained. The 95% confidence interval can be decided for $a$ and $b$ to give a range of likely values.

## 10.9   ERLANG DISTRIBUTION

The Erlang distribution is a continuous distribution that was developed by Agner Krarup Erlang, a Danish engineer and mathematician who invented queueing theory and traffic engineering disciplines, to study the number of telephone calls that might be made at the same time to the operators of the switching stations. It was more generally used in communication traffic engineering and has been developed to consider waiting times in queueing systems. The Erlang distribution is characterized by two parameters: an integer $k$, called the shape, and a real number $\lambda$, called the rate [10].

The probability density function $f(2)$ of the Erlang distribution is given by:

$$f(x, k, \lambda) = \frac{\lambda^k x^{k-1} e^{-\lambda}}{(k-1)!}, \quad x > 0.$$

An alternative parameterization can be made by substituting in the above expression $\lambda$ by $1/\theta$, where $\theta$ is referred to as the scale parameter. The expression shows that the Erlang distribution is only defined when the parameter $k$ is a positive integer.

The Erlang distribution is a special case of the gamma distribution where the shape parameter $k$ is an integer. When the shape parameter $k$ equals 1, the distribution simplifies to the exponential distribution.

The cumulative distribution function of the Erlang distribution can be shown to be equal to:

$$F(x, k, \lambda) = \frac{\gamma(k, \lambda x)}{(k-1)!}$$

where $\gamma()$ is the lower incomplete gamma function defined in the previous section. Figure 10.8 depicts the probability density function and cumulative distribution function of the Erlang distribution.

The Erlang distribution, which measures the time between incoming calls, can be used in conjunction with the expected duration of incoming calls to produce information about the traffic load measured in *Erlang units*. Typically, if the mean arrival rate of new calls is $\lambda$ per unit time and the mean call holding time is $h$, then the traffic, in Erlangs $A$ is $\lambda h$. This can be

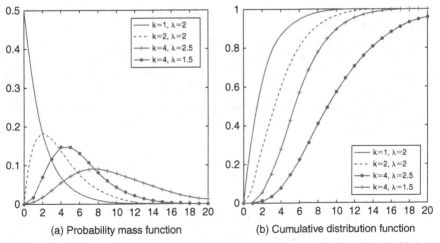

(a) Probability mass function      (b) Cumulative distribution function

**FIGURE 10.8.** Probability mass function and cumulative distribution function of Erlang distribution.

performed to determine the probability of packet loss or delay, according to various assumptions made about whether blocked calls are aborted (as given by the Erlang B formula) or queued until served (as given by the Erlang C formula).

The Erlang B formula assumes an infinite population of sources (e.g., telephone subscribers), which jointly offer traffic to $N$ servers. The rate of arrival of new calls is assumed to be equal to a constant value $\lambda$. The rate of call departure is equal to the number of calls in progress divided by the mean call holding time, say $h$. Erlang B formula determines the blocking probability in a loss system, where a request for resources should be aborted if it is not served immediately. This means that such systems do not queue requests, and blocking occurs when a new request arrives from a source and finds all the servers already busy. The Erlang B formula computes the probability of call loss as follows:

$$P(N, \lambda h) = \frac{(\lambda h)^N}{N!} \left( \sum_{i=0}^{n} \frac{(\lambda h)^i}{i!} \right)^{-1}.$$

To compute the Erlang formula, tables are built based on the following recursive relations:

$$P(0, \lambda h) = 1$$

$$P(N, \lambda h) = \frac{\lambda h P(N - 1, \lambda h)}{N + \lambda h P(N - 1, \lambda h)}$$

where $N$ is the number of resources under request and $\lambda h$ is the total amount of traffic offered in Erlangs.

Similarly, the Erlang C formula assumes an infinite population of sources, which jointly offer traffic of $\lambda h$ Erlangs to $N$ servers. Additionally, a request arriving will be queued if the all the servers are found busy. Moreover, an unlimited number of requests might be held in the queue. Erlang C formula determines the probability of queueing offered traffic, assuming that blocked calls stay in the system until they are served:

$$P(W) = \frac{a^n}{n!} \cdot \frac{n}{n - a} \left( \sum_{i=0}^{<n} \frac{a^i}{i!} + \frac{a^n}{n!} \cdot \frac{n}{n - a} \right)^{-1}, \quad a = \lambda h$$

where $a$ is the total traffic offered in units of Erlangs, $n$ is the number of servers, and $P(W)$ is the probability that a customer has to wait for service. Note that the Erlang unit is a dimenionless unit used generally in telephone networks as a statistical measure of the volume of telecommunication traffic.

## 10.10  BETA DISTRIBUTION

Beta distributions have two free parameters, which are labeled according to one of two notational conventions. The beta probability density function is given by:

$$f(x, \alpha, \beta) = \frac{1}{B(\alpha, \beta)} x^{\alpha-1}(1-x)^{\beta-1}, \quad B(\alpha, \beta) = \int t^{\alpha-1}(1-t)^{\beta-1} dt$$

$$f(x, \alpha, \beta) = \frac{\Gamma(\alpha+\beta)}{\Gamma(\alpha)\Gamma(\beta)} x^{\alpha-1}(1-x)^{\beta-1}$$

where $\Gamma$ is the gamma function [11]. The expected value and variance of a beta random variate $X$ with parameters $\alpha$ and $\beta$ are given by the expressions:

$$E(X) = \frac{\alpha}{\alpha + \beta}$$

$$\sigma^2(X) = \frac{\alpha\beta}{(\alpha+\beta)^2(\alpha+\beta+1)}$$

The cumulative distribution function is given by:

$$F(x, \alpha, \beta) = \frac{\gamma(x, \alpha, \beta)}{\Gamma(\alpha, \beta)}$$

where $\gamma(x, \alpha, \beta)$ is the incomplete beta function.

Let us have n observations $(x_1, \ldots, x_n)$ and let $\bar{x}$ and $\sigma$ be the sample mean and sample standard deviation, respectively:

$$\bar{x} = \frac{1}{n}\sum_{i=1}^{N} x_i, \quad \sigma^2 = \frac{1}{n}\sum_{i=1}^{N}(x_i - \bar{x})^2$$

The method of moments estimates the parameters as follows:

$$\alpha = \bar{x}\left(\frac{\bar{x}(1-\bar{x})}{\sigma^2} - 1\right)$$

$$\beta = (1-\bar{x})\left(\frac{\bar{x}(1-\bar{x})}{\sigma^2} - 1\right)$$

Several generalizations have been proposed to the beta distribution [12]. Examples of generalizations include two random variables as defined by the following two probability density functions:

- $$g_1(x, a, b, p, q) = \frac{|a|}{b^{ap} B(p, q)} x^{ap-1} (1 - (\tfrac{x}{b})^a)^{q-1}, \quad \text{for } 0 < x^a < b^a, a > 0,$$
$$p > 0, q > 0$$

- $$g_2(x, a, b, p, q) = \frac{|a| x^{ap-1}}{b^{ap} B(p, q)(1 + (\tfrac{x}{b})^a)^{p-q}}, \quad \text{for } 0 < x < \infty, a > 0, p > 0,$$
$$q > 0$$

The generalized beta variables of first kind, $g_1$, include Pareto and gamma and some other distributions. For example, the Pareto case is deduced by Pareto$(x, b, p) = g_1(x, -1, b, p, -1)$ and the gamma distribution can be deduced from $\lim_{a \to 0} g$. In addition, the generalized beta of second kind, $g_2$, nests many important distributions as special cases (or limiting cases), including the gamma, the exponential, the Weibull, the lognormal, and some other distributions.

Finally, let us mention that the beta distribution and its generalized distributions have been shown to be highly useful in the study of family income, daily stock returns, and the estimation of the slope of regression models (Figure 10.9). In addition, it can be used as a rough model in the absence of data distribution of a random proportion such as the proportion of

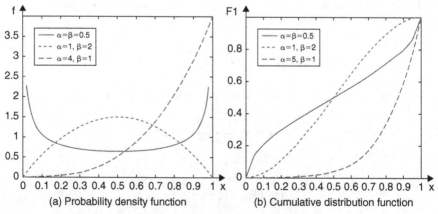

(a) Probability density function          (b) Cumulative distribution function

**FIGURE 10.9.** Beta probability density function and cumulative distribution function.

defective items in a sample, portion of frames/packets that need to be retransmitted, and part of remote procedure calls (RPCs) taking more than a particular time.

## 10.11 BINOMIAL DISTRIBUTION

### 10.11.1 Definition

The binomial distribution is the discrete distribution that is known to be associated with the problem that studies number of 1 in a sequence of $n$ independent $\{0,1\}$ experiments, where the result yields success with a given probability $p$. Such a success/failure experiment is also called a Bernoulli trial. This means that, when $n = 1$, then the binomial distribution *is* the Bernoulli distribution (Figure 10.9). Therefore, the binomial distribution models the total number of successes in repeated trials from an infinite population under the following conditions:

- Only two outcomes are possible on each of $n$ trials.
- The probability of success for each trial is constant.
- All trials are independent of each other.

A random variable $X$ following the binomial distribution with parameters $n$ and $p$ (e.g., number of successes in $n$ independent success/failure experiment) would have a probability of getting exactly $k$ successes given by the probability mass function (pmf), $f$, defined by:

$$f(k,n,p) = \binom{n}{k} p^k (1-p)^{n-k}$$

for all $k = 0, 1, 2, \ldots, n$

where $\binom{n}{k}$ is the binomial coefficient is read as "$n$ choose $k$," also denoted as $C(n, k)$, $_nC_k$, or $^nC_k$. The formula can be stated as follows. Because $k$ successes can occur anywhere in a sequence of $n$ events, provided that $k \le n$, the probability of $k$ successes knowing their location is given by $p^k(1-p)^{n-k}$. The formula follows from the fact that the number of possible locations of $k$ successes within a sequence of $n$ events is equal to $\binom{n}{k}$.

Because the probability of computing the probability of $n - k$ successes, knowing that the probability of a success is equal to $1 - p$, is nothing but the probability of having $n$ successes, knowing that the probability of a success is equal to $p$, one can deduce that the pmf, $f(-)$, satisfies the following relation:

$$f(k,n,p) = f(n-k,n,1-p).$$

Reference tables for binomial distribution probability computation are set up. The cumulative distribution function can be defined as follows:

$$F(k,n,p) = P(X \le k) = \sum_{j=0}^{k} \binom{n}{j} p^j (1-p)^{n-j}$$

provided $k$ is an integer and $0 = k = n$. Figure 10.10 shows the pmf and CDF for the Bionomial distribution.

Let us finally notice that Bernoulli has derived the binomial distribution in early times (about 1713), and Pascal had considered the special case where $p = \frac{1}{2}$ earlier than he did.

### 10.11.2  Properties

**Mean and deviation.** Let $X$ be a binomial distributed random variable (denoted by $X \approx B(n,p)$), and the expected value and standard deviation of $X$ are given by:

$$E(X) = \sum_{k=0}^{n} kP(X = k) = \sum_{k=0}^{n} k \binom{n}{k} p^k (1-p)^{n-k}$$

$$= \sum_{k=1}^{n} np \binom{n-1}{k-1} p^{k-1} (1-p)^{n-1-(k-1)} = np \sum_{j=0}^{n-1} \binom{n-1}{j} p^j (1-p)^{n-1-j} = np$$

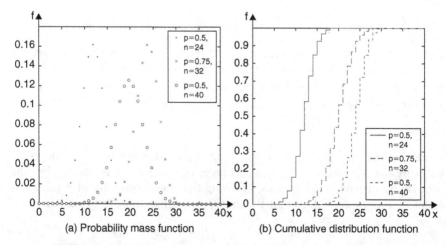

(a) Probability mass function    (b) Cumulative distribution function

**FIGURE 10.10.** Binomial pmf and cumulative distribution function.

$$\sigma^2(X) = E((X - np)^2) = np(1 - p).$$

The variance can be computed directly or by using the following remarks:

- For $n = 1$, it is easily proven that:

$$\sigma_1^2 = (1 - p)^2 p + (O - p)^2 (1 - p) = p(1 - p)$$

- Now suppose that $n$ is general. Because the trials are independent, we may add the variances for each trial, assuming that $X$ is the sum of $n$ independent Bernoulli variables. The following holds:

$$\sigma^2 = \sum_{k=1}^{n} \sigma_1^2 = np(1 - p)$$

**Approximation.** Assume that if the parameter is large enough (e.g., in some sense such as $n\,(p - 1) < 10$), the binomial distribution $B(n, p)$ can be approximated by the normal distribution $N\,(np,\,np(1 - p))$. In addition, the binomial distribution converges to the Poisson distribution as the number of trials $n$ grows to infinity, whereas the product $np$ remains fixed. This means that either $p$ is assumed nonconstant or $p$ is taken sufficiently small. Therefore, the Poisson distribution with parameter $\lambda = np$ can be used as an approximation to B$(n, p)$.

Practical experimentations show that we can obtain good approximations in the following cases:

- If $n > 20$ and $np > 10$, then $N(np, np(1 - p)) \approx B(n, p)$
- If $n > 20$ and $p < 0.05$, then $Exp(np) \approx B(n, p)$
- If $n > 100$ and $np < 10$, then $Exp(np) \approx B(n, p)$.

**Parameter Estimation for the Binomial Distribution.** Parameter estimation is the process of determining the parameter, $p$, of the binomial distribution that suits well a given set of experiments of a binomial distributed random variable $X$. Let us have $n$ observations $(x_1, \ldots, x_n)$, then p can be approximated by:

$$\hat{p} = \frac{1}{n} \sum_{i=1}^{N} x_i.$$

### 10.11.3  Negative Binomial Distribution

In its simplest form, the negative binomial distribution models the number of successes before a specified number of failures are reached in an independent series of repeated identical trials. Its parameters are the probability of success in a single trial $p$ and the number of failures, which is denoted by $r$. A special case of the negative binomial distribution, when $r = 1$, is the geometric distribution, which models the number of successes before the first failure as explained in a previous section. Typically, parameter $r$ can take on noninteger values. The negative binomial has no interpretation in terms of repeated trials; but, it is suitable in modeling count data.

When the $r$ parameter is an integer, the negative binomial probability distribution function is given by:

$$f(k, r, p) = \binom{r + k - 1}{k} p^r (1 - p)^k$$

When $r$ is not an integer, the binomial coefficient in the definition of the probability mass function is replaced by an equivalent expression using $\Gamma$ function. This gives:

$$f(k, r, p) = \frac{\Gamma(r + k)}{\Gamma(r)\Gamma(k + 1)} p^r (1 - p)^k.$$

## 10.12   CHI-SQUARE DISTRIBUTION

### 10.12.1   Definition and Properties

The chi-square distribution (also referred to as $\chi^2$ distribution) is one of the most widely used distributions in statistical significance tests [13]. It is useful because under reasonable assumptions, easily computed quantities can be proven to have distributions that can be approximated by $\chi^2$ distribution if the null hypothesis is correct [15, 16]. The $\chi^2$ distribution has one parameter, denoted by $k$, which is a positive integer that specifies the number of degrees of freedom as follows:

Consider $k$ random variables $X_i$, $i \leq k$, which are independent and normally distributed with expected value zero and standard deviation 1, then the random variable $X$ defined by:

$$X = \sum_{k=1}^{n} X_k$$

is a $\chi^2$ distributed random variable. (This can be written as $X \approx \chi_k^2$). The $\chi^2$ distribution is a special case of the gamma distribution. The pdf of the $\chi^2$ distribution $f(\text{-},\text{-})$ is defined by:

$$f(x, k) = \begin{cases} \dfrac{1}{2^{k/2}\Gamma(x/2)} x^{-1+k/2} e^{-x/2}, & x \geq 0 \\ 0, & x < 0 \end{cases}$$

where $\Gamma$ denotes the gamma function.

The cumulative distribution function of the $\chi^2$ distribution $X$ is:

$$F(x,k) = P(X \leq x) = \int_0^x \frac{1}{2^{k/2}\Gamma(t/2)} t^{-1+k/2} e^{-t/2} dt$$

$$= P(X \leq x) = \frac{\gamma(k/2, x/2)}{\Gamma(k/2)}$$

where $\gamma(\text{-},\text{-})$ is the lower incomplete gamma function. In addition, the expected value of a random variable having chi-square distribution with $k$ degrees of freedom is $k$ and the standard deviation is $\sqrt{2k}$.

Let now $X$ be a $\chi^2$ distributed random variable of $k$ degrees of freedom. When $k$ goes to infinity, the distribution of $X$ goes to the normal distribution. In fact, it has been shown that $\sqrt{2X}$ is approximately normally distributed with an expected value equal to $\sqrt{2k-1}$ and a standard deviation equal to 1.

It is worth noting that tables of the $\chi^2$ distribution are widely available and that the function is included in many spreadsheets and statistical packages. The distribution was first derived by Karl Pearson in 1900. In Pearson's original paper, he used the character $\chi^2$ for the sum. Ever since, statisticians and molders have started to refer to this distribution as the chi-square distribution. The $\chi^2$ distribution is used whenever a sum of squares of normal variables is involved, for instance, to model sample variances. Figure 10.11 shows the pdf and CDF of the chi-square distribution.

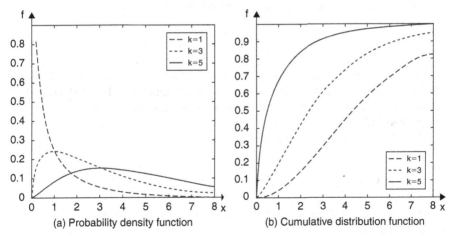

(a) Probability density function    (b) Cumulative distribution function

**FIGURE 10.11.** Chi-square probability density function and cumulative distribution function.

## 10.12.2 Related Distributions

**Inverse-chi-square distribution.** The inverse-$\chi^2$ distribution is the distribution of a continuous random variable whose inverse has a $\chi^2$ distribution. Its pdf is defined by:

$$f(x,k) = \frac{1}{2^{k/2}\Gamma(k/2)} x^{-1-k/2} e^{-1/2x}, \; x > 0.$$

**Chi distribution.** The $\chi$ distribution has only one parameter, denoted by $k$, which specifies the number of degrees of freedom (i.e., the number of $X_i$) involved in the definition of the related variable. The probability density function and the cumulative distribution function of a $\chi$ distributed function are expressed as follows that:

$$f(x,k) = \frac{2^{1-k/2}}{\Gamma(k/2)} x^{k-1} e^{-x^2/2} \text{ and } F(x,k) = g(k/2, x^2/2)$$

where $g$ $(k, x)$ is called the regularized gamma function. The following expressions can be easily computed for the expected value and variance:

$$\mu = \sqrt{2}\frac{\Gamma((k+1)/2)}{\Gamma(k/2)}, \sigma^2 = k - \mu^2$$

This distribution comes when a $k$-dimensional vector's orthogonal components are independent and each follows a standard normal distribution. The length of such a vector will then have a $\chi$ distribution.

**F-distribution.** The F-distribution is a continuous probability distribution, also called the Fisher-Snedecor distribution. It is defined using two $\chi^2$ distributed variables, $X_1$ and $X_2$, as follows:

Let $X$ be the random variable defined below:

$$X = \frac{k_2 X_1}{k_1 X_2}$$

Then $X$ has an F distribution if $X_1$ or $X_2$ has a $\chi^2$ distribution with $k_1$ or $k_2$, respectively. In addition, $X_1$ and $X_2$ should be independent. The F-distribution arises frequently as the null distribution of a test statistic, and most notably in the analysis of variance.

The pdf of an F-distributed random variable $X(X \approx F(k_1, k_2))$ is given by:

$$f(x, k_1, k_2) = \frac{1}{xB(k_1/2, k_2/2)} \left(\frac{k_1 x}{k_1 x + k_2}\right)^{k_1/2} \left(\frac{k_2}{k_1 x + k_2}\right)^{k_2/2}$$

where $x$ is a non-negative real value, $d_1$ and $d_2$ are the degrees of freedom, and B is the beta function.

It is useful in hypothesis testing and can be applied to model the ratio of sample variates, for example, in the F-test for regression analysis of variances.

## 10.13   STUDENT'S *T* DISTRIBUTION

The *t*-distribution (or Student's *t*-distribution) is a probability distribution that is used in the problem of estimating the mean of a normally distributed population when the sample size is small. It was discovered by William V. Gosset, [14–16] through his work at the Guinness brewery. The *t*-distribution is a family of curves depending on a single parameter (the degrees of freedom). As the degree of freedom I½ goes to infinity, the *t*-distribution converges to the standard normal distribution. Suppose that $n$ independent random variables $X_1,...,X_n$ that are normally distributed with expected value $\mu$ and standard deviation $s$ and let $\bar{X}_n$ and $S_n$ be the their sample mean and sample standard deviation:

$$\bar{X}_n = \frac{1}{n}\sum_{k=1}^{n} X_k, S_n = \frac{1}{n-1}\sum_{k=1}^{n}(X_k - \bar{X}_n)^2$$

It can be easily shown that the variable $Z$ can be defined by:

$$Z = \frac{\sqrt{n}}{\sigma}(\bar{X}_n - \mu)$$

and is normally distributed with mean 0 and variance 1, because the sample mean $\bar{X}_n$ is normally distributed with mean $\mu$ and standard deviation $\frac{\sigma}{\sqrt{n}}$. The variable $T$ defined by:

$$T = \frac{\sqrt{n}}{S_n}(\bar{X}_n - \mu)$$

is shown [14] to have the following probability density function:

$$f(x) = \frac{\Gamma(n/2)}{\sqrt{(n-1)\pi}\Gamma((n-1)/2)}(1 + x^2/(n-1))^{-n/2}$$

The distribution of $T$ is called the *t*-distribution and parameter $(n-1)$ is called the number of degrees of freedom. It can be observed that the distribution depends only on v and not $\mu$ or $s$. This feature makes the *t*-distribution special in theory and practice. For a *t*-distribution with $n$ degrees of freedom, the expected value is 0, and its variance is $(n-1)$ $(n-3)$ if $n > 3$.

The *t*-distribution is related to the F-distribution in the following way. The square of a *t*-distributed random variable with $n-1$ degrees of freedom is an F distribution with $n-1$ degrees of freedom.

Confidence intervals based on *t*-distribution: Suppose the number $\alpha$ is chosen such that:

$$P(-\alpha < T < \alpha) = \beta$$

where $T$ is $t$-distributed with $n-1$ degrees of freedom. This inequality is equivalent to

$$P(\bar{X}_n - \frac{S_n}{\sqrt{n}}\alpha < \mu < \bar{X}_n + \frac{S_n}{\sqrt{n}}\alpha) = \beta$$

Therefore, we can conclude that the interval $[\bar{X}_n - \frac{S_n}{\sqrt{n}}\alpha, \ \bar{X}_n + \frac{S_n}{\sqrt{n}}\alpha]$ is a $\beta$-percent confidence interval for $\mu$. There are special tables available for $t$-distribution for different degrees of freedom values [14]; See Appendix.

## 10.14   EXAMPLES OF APPLICATIONS

Noise plays an important role in telecommunication systems and networks. In theory, it determines the theoretical capacity of the communication channel, whereas in practice it estimates the number of errors occurring in a digital communication system using the channel. We will consider in this section how the noise determines the error rates. Two subsections will be used for this. In the first subsection we provide a description of noise. In the second subsection, we investigate how digital communication allows high fidelity. The Binary Phase-Shift-Keying (BPSK) system, which is a digital modulation scheme, will be considered as an illustrative example. Finally, we describe how the bandwidth of the channel carrier may be altered.

### 10.14.1   Noise Description

Noise is a random signal in the sense that we cannot predict its value and can only make statements about the probability of it taking a particular value, or range of values. The probability density function $f(x)$ of a random signal, or random variable/variate $x$ is defined to be the probability that the random variable $\mathbf{x}$ takes a value between $x_0$ and $x_0 + dx$. We write this probability as $f(x) = P(x_0 < x < x_0 + dx)$. The probability that the random variable will take a value between $u$ and $v$ is then defined as the integral of the probability density function $f$ over the interval $[u, v]$:

$$P(u < x < v) = \int_u^v f(t)dt$$

If we want to know the probability of, say the noise signal $N(t)$ having the value $\pm v$, we would evaluate:

$$P(-v < x < v) = \int_{-v}^v N(t)dt$$

Many naturally occurring noise sources can be described by a normal or Gaussian random variable as zero-mean, e.g., white noise. The statement that noise is zero-mean says that on average the noise signal takes the value zero.

Assuming that the noise is zero mean, we compute the probability $P(-v<x<v)$ using the following expression:

$$P(-v<x<v) = \frac{1}{\sqrt{\pi}} \int_{-v}^{v} e^{-t^2} dt = crf(v)$$

where $erf(x) = \frac{2}{\sqrt{\pi}} \int_0^x e^{-t^2} dt$ is called the error function. The integral is difficult to evaluate and is approximated by use of tables that exist for various value of **x**.

The signal-to-noise ratio (SNR) is an important quantity in determining the performance of a communication channel. The noise power referred to in the definition of SNR (or S/N) is the mean noise power. It can therefore be rewritten as:

$$SNR = 10\log_{10}(S/\sigma^2) \ dB$$

where $S$ is the mean signal power.

## 10.14.2 Error Estimation

In the absence of noise, the signal, $V$, from a BPSK system can take one of two values $\pm v$. In the ideal case, if the signal is greater than 0, then the value that is read is assigned a 1. If the signal is less than 0, then the value is read as 0. When noise is present, this distinction becomes blurred. There is a finite probability of the signal dropping below 0, and thus being assigned 0, even though a 1 was transmitted. When this happens, we say that a bit-error has occurred. The probability that a bit-error will occur in a given time is referred to as the bit-error rate (BER). In actuality, we may decide that our threshold of deciding whether the signal is interpreted as a 0 or a 1 is set at v/2, such that any signal detected between a 0 (is read if $-v <V <0$) and a 1 is $v <V <0$.

We assume (without loss) that the signal $V$, has the signal levels $\pm v$ noise $N$ of variance. The probability that an error will occur in the transmission of a 1 is:

$$P(N + v<0) = P(N< -v)$$

$$= \frac{2}{\sqrt{\pi}} \int_{-\infty}^{-v} e^{-t^2} dt = \frac{1}{2}(1 - crf(v)) = \frac{1}{2}crf(v).$$

Similarly, the probability that an error will occur in transmission of a 0 is given by:

$$P(N - v > 0) = P(N<v)$$

$$= \frac{2}{\sqrt{\pi}} \int_{v}^{\infty} e^{-t^2} dt = \frac{1}{2}crf(v).$$

This result guarantees the expression for the probability of error without reference to which value (1 or 0) is transmitted. It is usual to write these expressions in terms of the ratio of (energy per bit/ (noise power per unit Hz), $E_n$. The power **S** in the signal is on average $v^2$, and the total energy in the signaling period $T$ is $v^2 T$. The average energy per bit is, therefore,

$$E = (v^2 T + v^2 T)/2 = v^2 T$$

For BPSK, the signaling period is half of the reciprocal of the bandwidth $B$ ($B = 1/2T$). Therefore, we have:

$$P(\text{error}) = \frac{1}{2} crfc\left(\sqrt{\frac{E}{E_n}}\right).$$

Similarly, other digital modulation techniques can be addressed. For example, it can be shown that Quadrature Phase-Shift Keying (QPSK) has twice the error probability of reflecting the fact that with a QPSK, there are more ways an error can occur. It can also be stated that the narrow-band Frequency-Shift Keying (FSK) has an error probability rather worse than QPSK.

Incoherent demodulation schemes always have a higher probability of error than coherent schemes. Incoherent schemes produce an output proportional to the *square* of the input. Power detection always decreases the SNR. To see this, suppose the input, $X$, is of the form $X = V + N$. The input $SNR_{in}$ is:

$$SNR_{in} = \frac{V^2}{N^2}$$

Considering the square of the input signal $V$, the output is $X^2 = (V + N)^2$. Assume the SNR is large, with respect to $N^2$, and the SNR of the output is determined by:

$$\text{SNR}_{\text{out}} = \frac{V^4}{(2VN)^2} = \frac{V^2}{(2N)^2} = \frac{SNR_{in}}{4}.$$

This decrease in the signal-to-noise ratio induces an increase in the error probability. The detailed analysis is beyond the scope of the section. Although poorer, however, their performance is good this. This explains the widespread use of incoherent FSK.

Error rates are usually quoted as BERs. The conversion from error probability to BER is numerically simple. However, the conversion assumes that the probabilities of errors from bit to bit are independent. This may be considered a reasonable assumption. In particular, a loss of timing can cause multiple bit failures that can increase the BER. When signals travel along the channel, they are attenuated. As the signal is losing power, the BER increases with the length of the channel. Regenerators, when placed at regular intervals, can consistently reduce the error rate over long channels. To determine the BER of the channel with g regenerators, it is simple to calculate first the probability of no error. This probability is the probability of having no error over one regenerator, raised to the $gh$ power:

$$P(\text{No error over } g \text{ regenerators}) = (1 - P(\text{error}))^g.$$

Assuming the regenerators are regularly spaced and the probabilities are independent. The BER is then determined simply by:

$P(\text{error over } g \text{ regenerators}) = 1 - P(\text{No error over } g \text{ generators}).$

## 10.15 SUMMARY

In this chapter, we have reviewed the aspects of the commonly used distributions in modeling and simulation of computer and telecommunication systems. Some of these distributions are continuous whereas the others are discrete. Among the major probability distributions that are used to model computer and telecommunication systems, we have investigated the exponential, Poisson distribution, uniform, normal, Weibull, Pareto, geometric, beta, binomial, gamma, Erlang, chi-Square, chi-distribution, inverse chi-distribution, F, and Student's $t$-distribution. Case studies and applications of such stochastic distributions have been presented. In particular, case studies have been given to show how these distributions can be used to determine the error estimation and the noise description on a communication link.

## REFERENCES

[1] N. Balakrishnan, and A. P. Basu, "The Exponential Distribution: Theory, Methods, and Applications," Gordon and Breach, New York, 1996.

[2] J. H. Ahrens, and U. Deiter, "Computer methods for sampling from Gamma, Beta, Poisson and Binomial Distributions," Computing, Vol. 12, pp. 223–246, 1974.

[3] Wlodzimierz B. "Normal Distribution: Characterizations with Applications," Lecture Notes in Statistics, Vol. 100, 1995.

[4] M. Abramowitz, and I. A. Stegun, (eds.) "Handbook of Mathematical Functions with Formulas, graphs, and mathematical tables," Dover, New York, 1962.

[5] N. L. Johnson, "An Approximation to the Multinomial Distribution: Some Properties and Applications", Biometrika, Vol. 47, pp. 93–103, 1960.

[6] W. Weibull, "A Statistical Distribution Function of Wide Applicability" Journal of Applied Mechanics Vol. 18, pp. 293–297, 1951.

[7] H. J. Malik, "Estimation of the Parameters of Pareto Distribution," Metrika, Vol 15, pp. 126 – 132, 1970.

[8] A. C. Atkinson, and M. C. Pearce, "The Computer Generation of Beta, Gamma and Normal Random Variables," Journal of the Royal Statistical Society, A, Vol. 139, pp. 431–461, 1976.

[9] G. Arfken, and H. Weber, "Mathematical methods for physicists," Harcourt/ Academic Press, 2000.

[10] A. K. Erlang, "Solution of Some Problems in the Theory of Probabilities of Significance in Automatic Telephone Exchanges", The Port Office Electrical Engineers Journal, Vol. 10, pp. 189–197, 1917.

[11] M. Evans, N. Hastings, and B. Peacock, "*Beta Distribution.*" In "Statistical Distributions, 3rd edition", pp. 34–42, Wiley, New York, 2000.

[12] J. B. McDonald, and Y. J. Xu, "A generalization of the beta distribution with applications", Journal of Econometrics, Vol. 66, Nos. 1 pp. 133–152, 1995,

[13] E. B. Wilson, and M. M. Hilferty, "The Distribution of Chi-Square," Proceedings. of the National. Academy of Sciences USA, Vol. 17, pp. 688–689, 1931.

[14] W.S. Gosset, "The Probable Error of a Mean," Biometrika, Vol.6, No. 1, pp. 1–25, 1908.

[15] M. S. Obaidat, and G. I. Papadimitriou, "Applied System Simulation: Methodologies and Applications", Springer, New York, 2003.

[16] G. I. Papadimitriou, B. Sadoun, and C. Papazoglou, "*Fundamentals of System Simulation,*" in "Applied System Simulation: Methodologies and Applications," (M. S. Obaidat and G. I. Papadimitriou, Eds.), Springer, New York, 2003.

## EXERCISES

1. The hazard rate function $r(-)$ (or failure rate function) is defined as follows. Let $X$ be a continuous random variable with probability density function $f(t)$ and cumulative distribution function $F(t) = P(X < t)$. Then $r(t)$ is formally defined by $r(t) = f(t)/F(t)$.

   a. Consider the probability that a $t$-year old item will fail during the next $dt$ seconds. Show that $P(X \in [t, t + dt | X > t) = r(t)dt$

   b. Assume that $r(t)$ is constant; show that $f(t)$ is the exponential probability distribution function.

   c. Assume that $X$ is exponentially distributed $(X \approx Exp(\lambda)$, compute $E(X|X>t)$.

2. Let $X$ be a discrete random variable with the geometric distribution with $p = 1/3$.

   a. Compute the probability $P(X>n)$.

   b. Show that $E(X > n + k | X > n) = P(X > k)$

3. Consider a random variable $X$ that represents the number of trials until the first success. Assume that each trial is a success with probability $p$. $X$ is distributed geometrically. Assume also that a trial occurs every $d$ steps (instead of every step). Let $Y$ be the time until the first success.

   a. Determine the distribution of $Y$.

   b. Show that $P(Y>t) = e^{-pt}$.

4. Assume that given two exponentially distributed independent random variables $X_1$ and $X_2$ such that $X_1 \approx Exp(\lambda_1)$ and $X_2 \approx Exp(\lambda_2)$.

a. Show that $P(X_1 < X_2) = \frac{\lambda_1}{\lambda_1 + \lambda_2}$.

b. Let $X = \min(X_1, X_2)$; show that $X_1 \approx Exp(\lambda_1 + \lambda_2)$.

5. Consider two Poisson processes $X_1$ and $X_2$ having rates $\lambda_1$ and $\lambda_2$, respectively. Define the merge process $X$ as the process studying the arrival of all events related to $X_1$ and $X_2$.

a. Show that $X$ is a Poisson process with rate $\lambda_1 + \lambda_2$.

b. Reversely, let $X$ be a Poisson process with rate $\lambda$. Assume the each event related to $X$ is classified as type 1 with probability $p$ and as type 2 with probability $(1 - p)$. Then show that type $i$ events constitutes a Poisson with rate $\lambda_i$. Show that $\lambda_i = \lambda p$ and $\lambda_i = (1 - p)$.

c. Let $N_1(t)$ for $i = 1, 2$, be the number of type $i$ events. Compute the joint probability $P(N_1(t) = n_1, N_2(t) = n_2)$ that there are $n_i$ events of type $i$, by time $t$, for all $i$.

d. Consider now that time interval $[0, t]$ is subdivided into interval of length $d$. Show that the probability $P$(more than 2 type 1 arrivals in any interval) tends to 0 as d tends to 0.

6. Consider a stream of packets arriving according to a Poisson process with rate $\lambda$ per second. Suppose each packet is of type 1 with probability 5% and of type 2 with probability 95%. Given that 100 type 1 packets arrived during the previous second:

a. What is the expected number of type 2 packets which arrived during the previous second?

b. What is the probability that 2000 type 2 packets arrived during the previous second?

c. Assume now that the type 1 packets arrive according to a Poisson Process with rate $\lambda 1 = 30$ packets/s, type 2 packets arrive according to a Poisson Process with rate $\lambda 2 = 10$ packets/s, and the streams are statistically multiplexed into one stream. Suppose we are told that 60 packets arrived during the second. What is the probability that exactly 40 of those were type 1?

7. Suppose packets arrive according to a Poisson Process with rate $\lambda$ and that by time 30 s 100 packets have arrived. What is the probability that 20 packets arrived during the first 10 s?

8. The number of packets per unit time arriving at a node in a communication network is a Poisson random variable $X$ with rate having an exponential distribution ($X \approx Exp(\lambda)$). Find the minimum mean square error estimation of the rate $\lambda$ given the observation $X$.

9. Consider an additive noise channel with input signal represented by a random variable $X$ having a uniform distribution ($X \approx U(0, 1)$) and output signal $Y = X + Z$, where $Z$ is a Gaussian noise with variance proportional to the signal, i.e., $X \approx U(0, 1) Z|\{X = x\} \approx N(0, \alpha x)Z|\{X = x\}$ for some constant $\alpha > 0$. Find the minimum mean square estimation of $X$ given $Y$.

10. Let $X$ be a discrete random variable ($rv$) whose range is equal to the set of all integers 0, 1, 2, 3,...
    a. Show that $E(X) = \sum_{n=1}^{\infty} P(X > n)$.
    b. Show that, for all integer $r$, we have $E(X^r) = \sum_{n=1}^{\infty} rn^{r-1} P(X > n)$.

11. Suppose that the time between requests to a Web server (computed in seconds) is exponentially distributed with rate parameter 2.5
    a. Give the mean and standard deviation of the time between requests.
    b. Find the probability that the time between requests is less that 1.
    c. Find the median, the first quartile, and the interquartile range of the time between requests.

12. Suppose that a random variable $X$ has the gamma distribution with shape parameter $k$.
    a. Show that $E(X) = k$ and $V(X) = k$.
    b. More generally, show that the moments can be computed using the gamma function $\Gamma$ by:
    $E(X^n) = \Gamma(n + k)/\Gamma(k)$, for $n > 0$; and

    $E(X^n) = k(k = 1)...(k + n - 1)$ if $n$ is a positive integer.
    c. Assume now that $k = 3$ and that the random variable $X$ represents the lifetime of a device (in 100- h units). Find the probability that the device will last more than 300 h.

13. Assume that the life of a communication device follows a Weibull distribution with parameters $k = 2$ and $\lambda = 10,000$ h.
    a. Determine the probability that the device lasts at least 5000 h.
    b. Determine the mean time until failure of a device.

14. Let $F(x) = 1 - 1/x^a$ for $x \geq 1$ where $a > 0$ is a parameter. Show that $F$ is a distribution function. In particular,
    a. Say whether the related density function $f$ is given by $f(x) = a/x^{a+1}$ for $x \geq 1$.
    b. Show that $E(X^n) = a / (a - n)$ if $n < a$ and $E(X^n) = \infty$ if $n \geq a$.
    c. Show that the expectation and variance are given by: $E(X) = a/(a - 1)$ if $a > 1$ and $V(X) = a / [(a - 1)^2(a - 2)]$ if $a > 2$.

# CHAPTER 11

# ANALYSIS OF SIMULATION RESULTS

The process of analyzing simulation outputs is a vital one, as without such an analysis, we will not be sure that the simulator is valid and verified (V&V). Whenever a model needs to be implemented for a real-time purpose, we need to verify and validate the model to test whether the functionality of the model fulfills our requirements and meets the desired aim. This chapter provides a close look at the various techniques used for verifying and validating a simulation model. It deals with both the functional and structural verification processes. Major schemes in verification and validation are investigated and discussed along with examples. We also will shed some light on various techniques that are used in transient removal, as transient results may affect the credibility of simulation results if they are not removed. In addition, we will review the approaches that are employed for terminating simulation along with the stop criteria.

## 11.1  INTRODUCTION

Typically, whenever a concept, strategy, or new system needs to be implemented in real time, it is first simulated using a simulation model. These models are largely used for predicting the behavior of the system given a set of experiments, operational scenarios, and conditions, as well as for solving problems. Furthermore, the results obtained from these simulation models are used in making decisions, which affect the individuals, the organizations, and their

*Fundamentals of Performance Evaluation of Computer and Telecommunication Systems,*
By Mohammad S. Obaidat and Noureddine A. Boudriga
Copyright © 2010 John Wiley & Sons, Inc.

infrastructures. Hence, the correctness of these models and their results are of vital importance and need to be addressed. The process that deals with the above concern is termed as verification and validation and is often referred to in the literature using the abbreviation V&V [1–5]. Verification, on the one hand, is, the process of testing the computer program that simulates the system under study (usually called the "simulator") to make sure that it is doing what it is supposed to do. In other words, it is basically troubleshooting the simulation program (simulator). It tests to make sure that the model has been implemented in software correctly.

Validation on the other hand is the process of checking to make sure that the assumptions, inputs, distributions used, results, outputs, and conclusions are valid. In other words, it is the process of making sure that the model is a credible representation of the system or subsystem under simulation study.

It is possible that we obtain a simulation model that is

1. Valid and verified
2. Valid but unverified
3. Invalid but verified
4. Invalid and unverified

It is worth noting that in defense simulation we have also a process called accreditation. The latter refers to the decision about the appropriateness of a simulation for a particular application, and hence, it is about the simulator's credibility. Accreditation can be considered a stamp of approval from a specialized authority [1–5].

In other words, verification deals with determining whether the implemented model addresses the customer's specifications, i.e., it makes sure that the program of the model and its implementation are correct [2–5]. Validation determines to what level the model represents the real world truthfully to the intended application of the model. Apart from verifying and validating the simulation models, one more thing needs to be taken into consideration: the model accreditation. Model accreditation deals with the certification of the model so that it is acceptable to use for a specific purpose. Usually, models are developed for a specific purpose, and therefore the validity of the model should be checked so that it meets the needed aim. If the purpose of the model is to perform several tasks, then its validity must be tested with respect to each defined task that it should perform. Usually, various experiments are carried out to check for the applicability of the model. The model may work perfectly fine for some set of inputs, but not for another. Hence, a model is considered valid for a set of inputs if the accuracy of the output falls within the acceptable range. This accuracy needs to be defined before the development process begins. Figure 11.1 summarizes the relationship between validation and verification.

V&V are considered to be a part of the development process of the model. A major issue associated with the simulator is finding out the accuracy of the

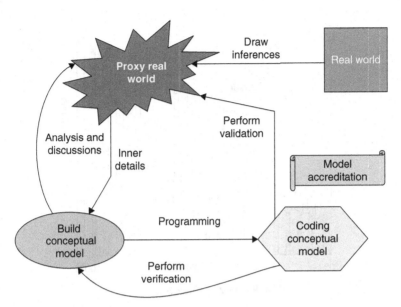

**FIGURE 11.1.** Verification and validation relationships.

simulation model with the representation of the system being studied. The process of validating a model for its complete domain is costly, and furthermore, it is time consuming. To avoid such a setting, tests are conducted to the point that confidence is gained over the model such that it is regarded to be valid for a specific application [2–6]. If the experiment of the model for any test input determines that the model does not support the needed accuracy, then in such a case the model is considered to be invalid or improper. However, if the model is truthful for the given set of experimental conditions, then it does not mean that the model works 100% or is valid for the complete domain to which the application is relevant. The relationship between the cost of performing the process of model validation with respect to the value of the model to the user is represented as model confidence, which is shown in Figure 11.2. This is important in cases where high model confidence is required [1–4].

Verification and validation methods vary on matters like the phase of the development life cycle, the degree of risks, abstraction degree, size, complexity, and the availability of the resources. Many techniques exist for the verification and validation process. Nevertheless, V&V process is still considered a challenge to the simulationist.

## 11.2  FUNDAMENTAL APPROACHES

Several methods are used for deciding the validity of the simulation model. Of these, let us discuss the major four of these fundamental approaches. One approach that is frequently used relies on the model development group to come

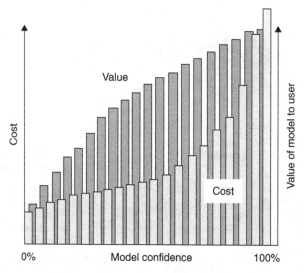

**FIGURE 11.2.** Model confidence.

to a decision on whether a simulation model is valid. The simulation team/group typically consists of a programmer, a system engineer, a mathematicians/ statistician, and a technical writer. A subjective assessment is made only on the basis of the various results achieved, which are conducted as a part of the development process [1–4]. Nevertheless, if the size of the simulation team is small, then a better approach is to have the users of the system or model help in determining the validity of the simulation model. This also gives an idea of how credible the model is. Another methodology, which is termed as independent verification and validation, uses a third party for finding out the validity of the simulation model. This approach is mostly used when the simulation models are of a huge size. The third party should have complete information about the planned use of the simulation model to perform independent verification and validation. This can be conducted in one the following two ways: (a) during the development stage of the simulation model or (b) after finalizing the development of the simulation model. In the first case, the development team gets the required input from independent verification and validation team and tests for the validity of the model as it is developed [1–5]. The development of the model should not move to the next stage pending all the requirements specified for the validity test are achieved at the current degree. In the second case, the entire set of simulation inputs is applied by the verification and validation team on the simulation model to test the validity of the model over its application area. The latter scheme, which can be used for finding out the validity of model, employs a scoring model. Scores are established in a subjective way when performing various stages of the validation process, and these are combined together to create the category scores and the final score for the simulation model. A simulation model is deemed to be valid if the final and the category scores are greater than the passing score for the model. This method is used infrequently in practice because of several reasons, which include: (a) a model could get a passing score; however, it has a flaw that needs to be addressed or corrected; (b) this scheme tends to be more objective than subjective and thus cannot be relied upon; (c) the scores may also guide to overconfidence in the model; and (d) the scores can also be employed to compare models and choose one over another.

This section shows how the verification and validation processes are related to the model development process [1–5]. This correlation can be viewed in the following two different ways: (a) a straightforward view and (b) a complex view. Let us consider the simple vision of the model development procedure. The problem entity refers to the system that needs to be modeled. The analysis and the modeling stage leads to the development of the conceptual model, where as the programming and completion phase leads to the development of the computerized model.

The conceptual model validation is defined as the process of checking whether the theories and assumptions based on which the conceptual model is made are accurate. However, the computerized model verification deals with assuring that the implementation of the conceptual model in programming is correct. Now, if the models output performance is truthful with the models domain, then it is known as operational validation. Data validity guarantees that the experimental data employed for constructing the model as well as evaluating, testing, and experimenting with the model are adequate and convincing. Figure 11.3 shows this in the context of the overall modeling process.

Figure 11.3 illustrates the method used to design a valid simulation model. During this process, several versions of the model are developed before getting the final version. To validate the model, several validation methods are used. The connection between the verification and validation process as related to the simulation model development is shown in Figure 11.4.

The model comprises two world, namely a real world and a simulation world. The actual world consists of a problem entity. The actions of the system are described by the system theory, which is achieved by monitoring the system and by hypothesizing from the system data and outcomes. Basically, theory validation compares the theories along with the system data and the results over an appropriate field. This process necessitates various experiments to be conducted on the real system.

The simulation world is the compound element of this model. The conceptual model signifies a logical model of the system for a set of particular aims. The simulation model specification deals with the written constraints of the programming implementation of the conceptual model. The conceptual model, which executes on a computer system, can be used to perform a set of predefined experiments. Simulation model data and outcomes represent the experimental data used over the simulation model to get the results [2–5].

Conceptual model validation can be defined as a process that helps in finding out whether the principal theories and assumptions employed for modeling the system serve the intended objectives.

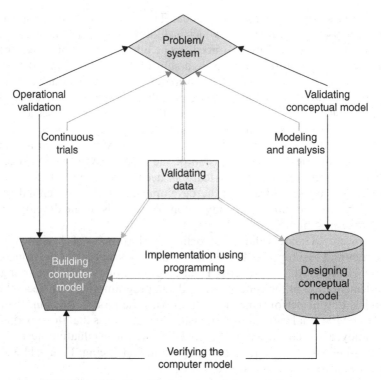

**FIGURE 11.3.** Simplified version of the modeling process.

Specification verification guarantees that the software design and the programming specification, as well as implementation specifications to build up the conceptual model, are accurate. Implementation verification guarantees that the realization of the simulation model has taken place according to the specifications of the model. Operational validation helps in determining whether the output obtained from the simulation model meets the required level of accuracy and whether it functions as per the essential aims of the system. Figure 11.4 shows how system theories and simulation models can be developed in an iterative manner. In each iteration, the verification and validation processes are carried out. This procedure is repeated until a valid accepted system theory is obtained.

## 11.3 VERIFICATION TECHNIQUES

This section gives a description of the various verification techniques used for verifying simulation models. Following is a brief description of the main often used schemes.

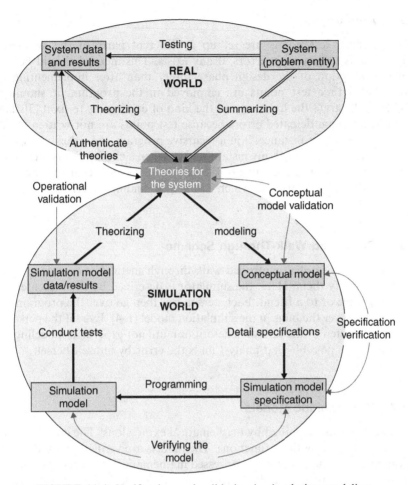

**FIGURE 11.4.** Verification and validation in simulation modeling.

## 11.3.1  Top-Down Modular Design

In this approach, the model is prearranged as a group of modules such as procedures, subroutines, and so on. These modules cooperate with each other with the help of interfaces that are well defined. The interface for each module consists basically of several input and output variables or the data structures that hold them. On specifying the module function and interface, the module can be developed, debugged, and maintained autonomously; i.e., the model can be divided into smaller components and each component can subsequently be verified independently [1–4]. Every module that is divided has a dissimilar functionality. These modules can be divided even more into submodules and so on. This process goes on until the modules are small enough so that the errors can be easily identified and fixed.

### 11.3.2 Antibugging

In this scheme, test points are set up at different parts of the simulation program so as to recognize errors, if any exists. This method should be used from the inception of the design phase rather than after implementing the model. Every time test points are employed in the program, it should be possible to illustrate the location and the kind of error so as to fix it [3]. They should handle unanticipated errors because test points are not written for the whole test space. For instance, if in a recursive program, the value of a specific variable needs to be even at any instant of time, then a checkpoint is introduced in the program to show the value of the variable for every recursion. For each recursion, the value is printed, which can help in finding an error.

### 11.3.3 Controlled Walk-Through Scheme

The major purpose of a controlled-walk-through method is to recognize the errors and rectify them. Here, the simulator is described by the presenter to a group of people or to a friend. Each person can then go over the program step by step to discover the bugs in the simulation model [1–4]. Even if the person or persons who listen to the analyst's description are not experts in modeling and simulation, it is possible that analyst finds the error by himself/herself.

### 11.3.4 Deterministic Models

Here, the events are signified by mathematical expressions. The conduct of the model is expressed by these functions. The models are verified by randomizing the variables. Because events are expressed mathematically, it is possible simply to find out what would be the outcome for a specific input. By running the simulation program, we can easily troubleshoot it if any variation different from what is expected at the output is found.

### 11.3.5 Run Unique Case Studies

Here, the analyst runs various case studies including boundary conditions to observe how the model behaves. In such cases, the input can be a single variate, single compute node, single router, or single user. Under such test, the outcome value of the simulation model is documented. These results are then contrasted with these from analytical results under similar operating conditions and environments and are then analyzed. It is worth mentioning that a model that works fine for simple special cases may not work for more complex case studies. So this test is necessary, however, passing it is insufficient to say that the model is verified 100%.

## 11.3.6 Tracing Technique

In general, a trace is a series of events that are appropriately ordered alongside with their individual variables. The output produced from the trace can be used in rectifying bugs in the model. The main drawback of the tracing technique is that it causes an extra processing overhead. Traces can be offered at a variety of levels of detail, including events, procedures, and variables [1–4]. Consequently, the user must be permitted to select the granularity of detail in the trace and be permitted to trace some chosen events, selected procedures as well as special variables.

## 11.3.7 Graphic Displays

Normally, running a simulation program takes a long period of time. Graphical displays can aid in monitoring the status of the execution of the simulation model at any instant of time. Such a method helps the analyst to get more insight into the simulation model. If the model departs from the regular behavior, it indicates the presence of a bug, thus helping the user to troubleshoot the model. Instead of trying to locate errors in the program, a graphic display can easily find such errors. It is worth mentioning here that simulation packages that have graphical tools and animation for verification purposes are appealing to the potential customers; the graphic features make the package salable.

## 11.3.8 Test for Continuity

In this technique, the simulation program is run for several times under different inputs. For each variate, a minor change in input must only produce a small change in the output. However, if produced change is extreme or huge, then it shows the existence of an error in the simulator that has to be resolved [1–5].

## 11.3.9 Degeneracy Tests

Here, the simulation program is checked under different intense or boundary conditions. Testing for such conditions can aid in finding errors that would not have been identified otherwise. In addition, this scheme helps the user to test whether the input parameter is within the permitted limits as dictated by the system's specifications.

## 11.3.10 Test for Consistency

In this approach, the behavior of the simulation model is checked for input parameters that should produce similar results. For example, two nodes that each send at 20 Mbps should load the network similar to four nodes that each send at a rate 10 Mbps.

### 11.3.11 Seed Independence

Here, the simulation program should generate same results for different seed values. In other words, the seed values should not affect the final conclusions. Any deviation from this will signal some problems in the model.

## 11.4 VALIDATION TECHNIQUES

In this section, we will introduce the commonly used validation techniques that are often used to validate simulation models [1–4]. It is highly recommended to use more than one scheme as this gives better validity to the simulation model.

Below is a description of the major techniques used in the validation of any simulation model.

### 11.4.1 Professional Perception

This scheme is perhaps the most widely used in the validation of simulation models. The results from the simulation program are inspected by a professional expert who is knowledgeable of the behavior, operation, and design of the system or subsystem under study. Such a skilled person can tell by just looking at the values of performance metrics and related performance evaluation plots under different operating conditions and input values whether the results make sense or not. Moreover, this authority/expert can check to determine whether the logic of the model is acceptable and whether the relationship between the input and output is reasonable.

For example, if the mean speedup in a multiprocessor computer system decreases with the increase in the number of processors/nodes in the system, then something must be wrong in the model, which can be either caused by a validation or verification problem. From our experience, we found this problem occurs more often because of validation problems.

### 11.4.2 Analytic Results

This scheme relies on developing an analytic model of the system under study using queueing theory, linear algebra, and so on. In some cases, a ready-to-go analytic model can be found and can be easily applied to the system being analyzed. In other cases, the analyst needs to develop the model from scratch, which could be a challenge as a closed form expression for the required performance metric as a function of design and input parameters is not easy to derive.

The validation of the simulation model is performed by comparing the performance results between the analytic (theoretical) and simulation results under same conditions or close by. It is important to note that the validation of a simulation model by an analytic one should be considered closely, as both are approximate. Nevertheless, it is a useful approach and definitely much better than no validation at all, especially if the results of simulation make sense to an expert.

### 11.4.3 Testing Results or Real-System Measurements

In this technique, we use real-time measurements on the system itself or on a prototype version of the system under development. This is the most credible technique to validate a simulation model; however, in many cases, the system may not exist physically except as a design on paper. One more thing to be added is that measurement results may have some inaccuracies because of the setting of measurement devices and other possible measurement errors; nevertheless, this approach is the most accurate approach to validate simulation models.

### 11.4.4 Comparing with Other Simulation Models

In this technique, we compare the results of the simulation model with these obtained from other valid simulation models performed by independent groups. It worth mentioning that the two models may not address the same scenarios, but at least we may find some common case studies or even close settings. The analyst should be careful not to compare the simulation model with an invalid model, as this may lead to mistakes.

### 11.4.5 Degenerate Check

Here, the model's degeneracy behavior is tested by selecting the proper input values.

For example, we can conduct a test to determine whether the mean number in the queue of a single-server model keeps on increasing with respect to time when the arriving rate is greater than the service rate.

### 11.4.6 Validity of the Events

In this method, occurrences of events in the simulation model are compared with these for the real system to observe their similarity. Examples include testing the exit rate of packets being serviced by an asynchronous transfer mode (ATM) switch or a router.

### 11.4.7 Extreme Condition Tests

The outcomes of the simulation model should be reasonable for any extreme cases of the operation of the system under study. For example, if the number of nodes in a multiprocessor computer system is zero, then the throughput of the system should be zero, and the average mean delay of a packet or a message should be zero as well.

### 11.4.8 Validation Using Historical Data

If a comparable type of system is being constructed, then part of the historical data of the current system can be used to test whether the simulation model acts as required.

### 11.4.9 Historical Schemes

Three major techniques of validation are rationalism, empiricism, and positive economics schemes. In the first scheme, we assume that all the basic hypotheses are true, and everybody concurs with it. Inferences are extracted, which are used to construct a valid simulation model. In the case of empiricism, each hypothesis along with its effect must be experimentally validated. As for the third technique, positive economics, it necessitates that the model should forecast the future and is not concerned about the assumptions.

### 11.4.10 Internal Validity

Numerous copies of the stochastic models are employed to determine the degree of stochastic variability in the simulation model. If a large amount of variability is found, then this indicates that the model is inconsistent.

### 11.4.11 Multistage Validation

Here, the historical methods are combined to perform a multistage validation. The method can be divided into the following three steps: (a) the assumptions for the simulation model are based on monitoring, theory, and common understanding; (b) models hypotheses are validated by checking them empirically; and (c) the last step deals with contrasting the relationship between input and output with that of a real-world system.

### 11.4.12 Sensitivity Analysis of Parameter Variability

Here, the values of inputs parameters of the model are varied continuously and the output is logged. This output behavior should match that of the output of a real system for the same parameters and conditions.

### 11.4.13 Predictive Validation

In this technique, the conduct of the model is forecasted ahead of time for a set of inputs. As the model is run with these inputs, the results are logged and the behavior of the model is compared with the forecasted one to test whether they are similar.

## 11.5 VERIFICATION AND VALIDATION IN DISTRIBUTED ENVIRONMENTS

To verify simulation models in distributed environments, we need to pay attention to the following four areas: compliance, compatibility, correctness, and credibility. Compliance suggests that the specific simulations, which are used for the simulating the distributed environment, must be able to suit the protocols and constraints for that environment. In case of defense simulation, distributed interactive simulation (DIS) protocols are employed, here, we use a special method for validating the distributed simulation [1–5]. One more issue is compatibility, which tests whether individual simulations have the potential to work collectively in a well-organized manner. The difficulty here is the necessity to get interoperability, where the accuracy of simulations working collectively in a distributed simulation environment has to be monitored. In some cases, it would be needed to substitute some individual simulations in the distributed simulation so as to accomplish the required goals [3–6]. The surge of data in distributed simulation is also significant as it guarantees the validity of the simulation model. Credibility deals with the level of confidence with which one can guarantee that the simulation model works correctly by generating the results. Others refer to it as accreditation.

Validating the data that are used as input to the simulation model is vital [6–8] because the conceptual model is based on such data. Input data are used to validate the model and conduct the required experiments with the validated model. A conceptual model can be built only when we have sufficient data so that the theories can be extended to the problem entity that is used as a foundation for building the model. In addition, it is used for establishing the rational relationships among various blocks of the model [2–4, 6].

Behavioral data are used for operational validity to test whether the model works in the proper way. Good model confidence can be achieved only if behavioral data exists, as it helps to accomplish satisfactory operational validity. The main concern with data is that we need to have it accurate, appropriate, and sufficient, if any modifications are performed on the data, then these transformations should be done properly and accurately. It is important to mention that some good methods need to be devised for gathering and retaining the efficient data. Proper testing of collected data has to be performed using efficient techniques, such as internal steadiness checks, to make sure that the available data are accurate and valid [2–8].

The validity of the conceptual model is based on the certainty that: (a) the theories and the deductions that are used for constructing a conceptual model are accurate and (b) the makeup of the model, its logical demonstration, and the relationships between the entities are realistic and serves the intended intention, which the model needs to reveal. The fundamentals and assumptions that are employed for devising the model should be checked either by analytical analysis or statistical techniques. In addition, an assessment of the theories should be performed to ensure that they were applied properly. For instance, if the theory asserts the use of a Markov chain, then we have to determine whether the system or the model exhibits Markov property and whether all the states and their transitions are proper [4–10].

The next procedure comprises assessing all the individual submodels and compeleting one to determine whether they are realistic and meet the intended aim of the analysis. The assessment process of the model requires us to check if the model and the components are represented in the proper detail: fine grain, medium grain, or coarse grain. Moreover, it requires ensuring that the logical and mathematical relationships have been employed for the model's intended purpose [8–12]. Face validation and traces are considered the prime validation schemes that are used for the evaluation end. The former helps to test whether the conceptual model is accurate and reasonable. This method uses flowcharts, graphical models, or model of mathematical expressions. The use of traces validation scheme helps to discover for each submodel and model whether the common sense used is realistic and whether the required accuracy is maintained. Subsequent to conducting the validation if any mistakes are found in the model, the conceptual model has to be revised and the process of validation has to be conducted all over again [8–15].

Computerized model verification is a procedure that is applied to ensure that the implementation of the conceptual model is accurate. Verification is influenced by the programming language that is used for implementing the conceptual model. Implementation of the model can be done using: (a) standard general purpose programming languages, such as Java, C++, C#, and C; (b) simulation languages, such as MODSIM III, SIMSCRIPT III, SLAM II, and GPSS; and (c) special simulation packages that are optimized for a certain application area, such as GloMoSim, OPNET, NS2, NS3, QualNet, NETWORK II.5, and COMNET III.

The key advantage of using a simulation language is that it is flexible and makes the process of building the simulation model easy; it shortens the time of programming development when compared with standard general purpose programming languages. In addition, most simulation languages have built-in features that facilitate the simulation process, such as dynamic-storage allocation, random-variate-generation procedures, and garbage-collection routines, among others.

Simulation packages are much easier to use and learn. However, they are not flexible, and sometimes the analyst may not find the needed model available in them that will lead him or her to build the required model from scratch using either a general purpose or a simulation language.

Structured walk through and traces are the popular schemes, which are used to test whether the simulation model has been programmed properly. If the model is coded using a general purpose programming language, then the design, development, and implementation must be done using the usual software engineering techniques, such as object-oriented design as well as structured and modularity programming. Verification in such a case is conducted by determining that the simulation functions such as time flow mechanism, pseudorandom variate generator, and random-variate generator are working properly.

Static testing and dynamic testing are the two techniques that are applied to test the simulation model. If static examination is used, then in such a case, the analysis of the simulation program is performed to check whether it is reasonable to use the scheme. If dynamic testing is used, then the simulation program is run under different operating environments and conditions, and the results collected from the execution are used to check the correctness of programming and its implementation. Among the techniques used are traces and inspecting the relationship between input output using various validation methods, among others. If we have numerous variables, then these can be combined in a way so that the number of tests performed can be decreased [11–18].

Operational validation is defined as procedure that is used to check the output of the model to discover whether it has the required accuracy for the projected aim of the simulation model behavior over the field of the model's application. The schemes can be employed in a subjective or in an objective way [13–16], see Table 11.1.

A high level of model confidence can be achieved by comparing the model's input and output under different conditions and environments [15–22]. We can achieve this by using the following three different techniques: (a) using graphs, which represent the model and system behavior that can be employed to make a subjective assessment; (b) using confidence intervals; and (c) using a method called hypothesis tests. With these different techniques, it is often desired to use confidence intervals and hypothesis tests for comparisons because they permit for objective decisions. However, the issue is that these two techniques cannot be used regularly because of the following reasons: (a) statistical suppositions that are made here cannot be fulfilled, and if fulfilled, it is not easy to realize them and (b) usually there is a lack of availability of data from the system under

TABLE 11.1 Operational validity categorization

|  | Observable System | Nonobservable System |
|---|---|---|
| Subjective Method | • Contrast using graphical displays | • Investigate simulation model behavior |
|  | • Investigate simulation model behavior | • Contrast with other simulation models |
| Objective Method | • Contrast using graphical displays | • Contrast with other simulation models using statistical tests |

study, and therefore, statistical results acquired from the existing data seem to be pointless. Because of these issues, graphs are normally employed for the operational validation. Next, let us explain these schemes.

In the graphical evaluation of the data-based scheme, the system and model behavior can be characterized in the form of graphs under the set of different operating conditions and experimental settings to determine whether the behavior of the model meets the required accuracy. These graphs can be characterized by three ways: histograms, box plots, and scatter plots.

An example on a scatter plot graph is described next. The key aspect that we would like to look on while validating a model is the parameter on which we will base the validity of the model; see Figure 11.5.

Confidence intervals are meant to be obtained for the differences in the averages, variances, and distributions of the simulation model and system output variables for various operating conditions. It is desired to find the range of correctness of the models. We can identify this with the help of confidence intervals, joint confidence regions, and simultaneous confidence intervals. The statistical schemes employed to deal with the accuracy can be divided into two approaches: (a) univariate statistical scheme that uses Bonferroni inequality to find the confidence interval and (b) multivariate statistical scheme that can be employed to develop simultaneous confidence intervals and joint confidence regions.

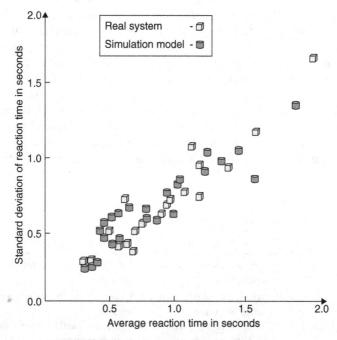

**FIGURE 11.5.** Example of a scatter graph.

We can identify two states for hypotheses:

- $H_0$: This shows that for the different operating conditions, the model satisfies the needed range of the accuracy; hence, the model is considered to be valid.
- $H_1$: This shows that for different operating conditions, the model does not satisfy the needed range of accuracy; hence, the model is considered to be invalid.

When testing the hypotheses, we can find two possible types of errors: rejecting a valid model and accepting the invalid model as a valid model. The first error type is called the model builder's risk and is denoted by $\alpha$. The second error type is called the model user's risk and is signified by $\beta$. At all times, the second type of error, $\beta$, should be kept small. The degree of similarity between the system and the model is known as the validity measure and is usually represented by $\lambda$; see Figure 11.6.

## 11.6 TRANSIENT ELIMINATION

In almost all simulation types, we are interested in the performance of the simulation model at a steady state. This means that we need to remove

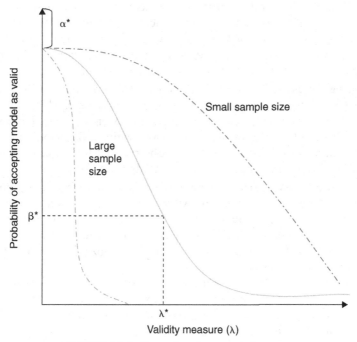

**FIGURE 11.6.** Operating characteristic curves.

the initial part of results from the final results to have accurate conclusions. This initial fraction is usually called the transient part/state. Identifying the ending of a transient state is called as transient state removal. The chief issue about transient state is that it is not easy to define the duration of the transient state and where it actually finishes. Next, we list the main heuristic techniques that are usually applied for transient elimination [3–9].

1. **Long-run approach.** In this method, the simulation program is run for a long length to the extent that the presence of initial conditions will be negligible or will not affect the result. This technique seems to be easy, nevertheless, it wastes the computation resources. Moreover, it is not easy to decide the length of the simulation run that can diminish the affect of initial results [2–9].

2. **Batch means approach.** In this scheme, the simulation is executed for a long time and then it is divided into several equal durations. Each part of the division is termed as a batch. The mean observation in each batch is termed as a batch mean. That is why this technique is called after batch means. Let us divide a long run of $N$ observations into $m$ batches each of size $n$. Assume that $xij$ signifies the $j^{th}$ observation in the $i^{th}$ batch. Then, the method can be summarized as follows [2–5]:

   (a) A batch average is computed for each batch.

   (b) The overall average is then computed.

   (c) Finally, the variance of the batch means is then calculated.

   The above steps (a) and (c) are replicated by varying the size of each batch $n$. A graph is then plotted with variance for a range of batch sizes $n$. When the variance starts decreasing, the corresponding value of $n$ is defined as the length of the transient interval [1–4].

3. **Truncation technique.** In this technique, we assume that the variability in the transient state is higher than that in the steady state, which is usually a valid assumption. This scheme measures the extent of the variability, such as the highest and lowest number of observations. By mapping out these observations on a graph, we can to observe that the trajectory becomes stables as the simulation gets to the steady state [3–8].

4. **Initial data deletion.** Here, some initial observations from the sample are removed after overall analysis. All through the steady state, the average does not vary even though the observations are removed. However, the average can change even during a steady state because of unpredictability of the observations. This outcome can be minimized by averaging across several replications [1–10].

   Assume that we have $m$ replication each of size $n$ and let $xij$ denote the $j^{th}$ observation in the $i^{th}$ iteration where $j$ varies from 1 to $n$ along the time axis, and $i$ varies from 1 to $m$ along the replications axis. Then, the approach can be summarized by the following steps:

   (a) By averaging across the replications, a mean trajectory is obtained.

(b) Then the overall (general) mean is obtained.

(c) We assume that the length of the transient state is l. The whole (overall) mean is found by deleting the first l observations, from the mean path or trajectory.

(d) The relative change in the whole mean is computed.

(e) We then reiterate the steps by varying the values of l from 1 to $(n - 1)$. The graphs of the general average and relative modification is plotted to see that after a specific value of l, the relative change plot calms down. This point is called the knee, which basically gives the length of the transient interval or marks the end of the transient state [3–10].

5. **Good initialization.** In this approach, the simulation program is started in a state that is close to the expected steady state, which is usually nonzero. Here, the length of the transient period is reduced, thereby having a small effect on the overall performance results. For example, the typical queue length in the input or output buffer of an ATM switch model is not zero, so in simulation, we initialize the queue with a typical value that is found from historical data.

6. **Moving mean of autonomous replications.** This approach is similar to that of the initial data deletion technique, except that the mean in this scheme is determined over a moving time interval window rather than by calculating the overall mean. Let us assume that we have $m$ replications each of size $n$. Now, let $xij$ denote the $j^{\text{th}}$ observation in the $i^{\text{th}}$ iteration, where $j$ varies from 1 to $n$ across the time axis and $i$ varies from 1 to $m$ across the replications axis. The steps below summarize the method:

(a) The mean trajectory is obtained by averaging the replications.

(b) We then plot a path or trajectory for the moving average of the successive $2k + 1$ values, where $k$ represents the moving time interval window.

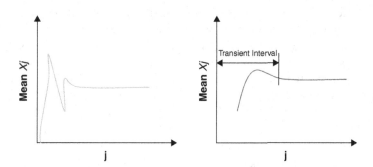

**FIGURE 11.7.** Moving average of autonomous replications.

(c) Repeat step (b) for different values of $k = 2, 3,....$, and so on until a smooth plot is obtained.

(d) The length of the transient interval is obtained by finding the knee on this plot.

Figure. 11.7 shows two different trajectories of moving averages. The plot of the second trajectory is smooth; hence, identifying the knee is easy.

## 11.7 STOPPING PRINCIPLES FOR SIMULATIONS

In simulation modeling, it is vital to simulate the system under study for a sufficient length of time. If the simulation time is short, then the accuracy and credibility of the results are in doubt. However, if the simulation time is too long, then we basically waste the computation power and involved resources. Three main approaches enable the simulation to run until the confidence interval is reached: autonomous replications, rebirth, and batch means schemes.

1. **Autonomous replications.** Here, simulation is repeated with different seed values to obtain different replications. If we have $m$ replications that are conducted of size $n + n'$, where $n'$ represents the transient interval length, then we discard the first $n0$ observations and use the following steps [2–9]:

   (a) For each replication, the average is calculated.

   (b) The whole mean is then calculated for all replications.

   (c) The variance of these replicate means is then calculated.

   (d) The confidence interval is obtained by the summation of the overall mean and the variance as shown below: Overall mean $\pm$ $Z_{1-a}$ Var $(x') = x'' \pm Z_{1-a}$ Var $(x')$, where $Z_{1-a}$ is found from special tables, such as the quantile unit normal variate table.

   The width of the confidence interval is inversely proportional to the square root of $mn$. This means that we can get a narrower confidence interval by either increasing $m$ or $n$.

2. **Rebirth technique.** A rebirth or regeneration point is described as the moment at which the system comes into the independent stage. The interval between two such points is called the rebirth or generation cycle. Assume that we have a regenerative simulation that contains $m$ phases whose sizes are $N1, N2, N3...Nm$. The confidence interval can be found by performing the following steps:

   (a) The cycle sums are computed, and the general mean is found.

   (b) The differences between expected and noticeable/observable cycle sums are computed.

(c) The variance for these differences is also calculated along with the mean cycle length.

The confidence interval is determined by using the overall average, variance, and average cycle length. We can notice that the rebirth technique does not necessitate the transient interval to be eliminated. This scheme has a few drawbacks, which include: (a) the length of cycles is changeable, (b) most of the variance reduction techniques cannot be employed as the length of the cycles is variable and cannot be predicted, (c) the expected values for means and variances are not equal to the quantity that is being estimated, and (d) it is not easy to find the rebirth points [1–5].

3. **Batch averages.** In this approach, the whole length of the simulation length is partitioned into $m$ batches of similar size $n$ by getting rid of the transient interval period. The long run of $(n + n')$, is partitioned into $m$ batches by removing the transient interval where $n'$ signifies the transient interval length and the following steps can be followed for this technique:

(a) For each batch, the average is determined.

(b) After finding the average for all batches, the general average is then calculated.

(c) The variance of the batch means is then determined.

The confidence interval is then found as the summation of the entire mean and the variance. The size of the confidence interval is conversely proportional to square root of $mn$. Therefore, a thinner confidence interval can be achieved by either increasing $n$ or $m$ values [1–10].

## 11.8 ACCREDITATION

Accreditation is the process of management or organizational judgment that decides whether a simulation is acceptable for a specific application. It is basically a stamp of endorsement. Others used the term certification or confirmation to mean the same thing [1–10].

In some cases, accreditation choice for simulation entails an official process and is usually based on V&V information developed primarily to sustain such a choice. In other instances, the choice is casual.

In defense modeling and simulation, there are procedures that categorize who has the power to accredit simulation models for different applications. Related professional societies have developed policies for V&V and accreditation as well as standards. The assessment for accreditation is typically performed by a third independent party. It often contains not only verification and validation but also matters such as documentation and the degree of ease of use of the simulation. The short form VV&A is often used for verification, validation, and accreditation. These days, it is common to have a track or session in a conference as well as a section in a simulation journal called VV&A.

## 11.9 SUMMARY

Analyzing simulation results and data in general is a vital process for any modeling and simulation project. The V&V processes of simulation models are considered the major processes in analyzing any simulation model. The key role of verification and validation is to lower the risk of improper simulation use. V&V offer information that permit the risk of unsuitable use of a simulation to be known or to affirm the state positively.

Regrettably, no set of definite tests can easily be applied to find out the "accuracy" of the model. In addition, no available algorithm can be used to determine which techniques to use [20–27]. In recent days, especially in defense modeling and simulation, the process of accreditation has become more important and verification, validation, and accreditation operations are now grouped together and called VV&A.

## REFERENCES

[1] M. S. Obaidat, and G. I. Papadimitriou, (Eds.), "Applied System Simulation: Methodologies and Applications," Kluwer Academic Publisher, Dordrecnt, The Netherlands, 2003.

[2] D. K. Pace, "Verification, Validation and Accreditation of Simulation Models," "in M.S. Obaidat and G.I. Papadimitriou, (Eds.). Applied System Simulation: Methodologies and Applications, Springer, New York, 2003.

[3] R. Jain, "The Art of Computer Systems Performance Evaluation", Wiley, New York, 1991.

[4] L. Alawneh, M. Debbabi, F. Hassaine, Y. Jarraya, and A. Soeanu, "A Unified Approach for Verification and Validation of Systems and Software Engineering Models," Proceedings of the 13th Annual IEEE International Symposium and Workshop on Engineering of Computer Based Systems, pp. 409–418, March 2006.

[5] R.G. Seargent, "Verification and Validation of Simulation Models," Proceedings of the 37th Winter Simulation Conference, pp. 130–143, December 2005.

[6] T. F. Brady, and E. Yellig, "Simulation Data Mining: A New Form of Computer Simulation Output," Proceedings of the 2005 Winter Simulation Conference, pp. 285–289, December 2005.

[7] A.M. Law, and W.D. Kelton, "Simulation Modeling and Analysis", 4th Edition, Mc-Graw Hill, New York, 2007.

[8] H. Reub, and L. de Moura, "From Simulation to Verification (and Back)," Proceedings of the 2003 Winter Simulation Conference, pp. 888–896, December 2003.

[9] N. Robertsen, and T. Perera, "Automated Data Collection for Simulation," Simulation Modeling: Practice and Theory, pp. 349–364, 2002.

[10] S. Narayanan, and S. A. Mcllraith, "Simulation, Verification and Automated Composition of Web Services," Proceedings of the 11th International Conference on World Wide Web, pp. 77–88, May 2002.

[11] S. M. Ross, "Simulation, 55th Edition," Academic Press, New York, 2006.

[12] B. P. Zeigler, H. Praehofer, and T.G. Kim, "Theory of Modeling and Simulation, 2nd Edition" Academic Press, New York, 2000.

[13] S. Robinson, "A Steady State Output Analysis," Proceedings of the 37th Winter Simulation Conference, pp. 763–770, December 2005.

[14] J. M. Paul, A. J. Suppe, and D. E. Thomas, "Modeling and Simulation of Steady State and Transient Behaviors for Emergent SOCS," Proceedings of the 14th International Symposium on System Synthesis, pp. 262–267, September 2001.

[15] P. W. Glynn, "Initial Transient Problem for Steady State Output Analysis," Proceedings of the 2005 Winter Simulation Conference, pp. 739–740, December 2005.

[16] L. Chwif, R. J. Paul, M. Ribeiro, and P. Barretto, "Discrete Event Simulation Model Reduction: A Casual Approach," Simulation Modeling: Practice and Theory, pp. 930–944, 2006.

[17] D. Kelton, "Statistical Analysis of Simulation Output," Proceedings of the 2003 Winter Simulation Conference, pp. 23–30, December 2003.

[18] U. Pooch, and J. Wall, "Discrete Event Simulation—A Practical Approach," CRC Press, Boca Raton, FL, 1993.

[19] R. Y. Rubinstein, and B. Melamed, "Modern Simulation and Modeling", Wiley, New York, 1998.

[20] J. Banks, J. S. Carson, II and B. L. Nelson, "Discrete Event System Simulation", 2nd Edition, Prentice Hall, Upper Saddle River, NS, 2004.

[21] O. Balci, "Verification, Validation, and Testing," The Handbook of Simulation, Wiley, New York, 1998.

[22] M. S. Obaidat, "Performance Evaluation of Computer and Telecommunications Systems," SIMULATION Journal, Vol. 72, No. 5, pp. 295–303, 1999.

[23] M. S. Obaidat, "Performance Evaluation of High Performance Computing/ Computers," Journal of Computer and Electrical Engineering., Vol. 26, No. 3–4, pp. 181–185, 2000.

[24] M. S. Obaidat, "Performance Evaluation of Telecommunication Systems: Models, Issues and Applications," Computer Communications Journal, Vol. 34, No. 9, pp. 753–756, 2001.

[25] M. Ould-Khaoua, H. Sarbazi-Azad, and M.S. Obaidat, "Performance Modeling and Evaluation of High-performance Parallel and Distributed Systems," Performance Evaluation Journal, Vol. 60, Nos. 1–4, pp. 1–4, 2005.

[26] M. S. Obaidat, "Performance Evaluation of Wireless and Communications Systems," Computer Communications Journal, Vol. 29, pp. 923–925, 2006.

[27] M. S. Obaidat, "Advances in Performance Evaluation of Computer and Telecommunication Systems," Simulation: Transactions of the Society for Modeling and Simulation Journal, Vol. 83, No. 2, pp. 135–137, 2007.

## EXERCISES

1. Compare and contrast verification, validation, and accreditation.

2. For the following sequence of observations, find the length of transient interval. Show all of your work using a plot of the value versus

observation number. 2, 4, 6, 8, 10, 12, 14, 16, 18, 20, 22, 20, 18, 20, 22, 20, 18, 20, 22, 20, 18,...

3. What are the disadvantages of the rebirth technique as a stopping criterio of simulation?

4. Compare and contrast various techniques that can be used for transient elimination.

5. Locate several examples of real simulation problems or projects reported in the literature where the validation issue is discussed. Evaluate whether the used validation technique is adequate or not.

6. Survey the literature and find out the methods used to verify some reported simulation models for computer systems or communication networks. Comment on the adequacy of each approach used.

7. Accreditation of simulation models is an important issue in defense modeling and simulation. Write a report explaining how this is performed and show state-of-the art techniques in this area.

# CHAPTER 12

# SIMULATION SOFTWARE AND CASE STUDIES

Simulation software is essential for building simulation models, as selecting the right software affects the time needed to develop the simulator and the flexibility in running simulation experiments under different operating and load conditions. Simulation models can be designed using regular general-purpose programming languages, simulation languages, or simulation packages. Designing the simulation models with regular programming languages requires much effort, as each and every task needs to be specified by the programmer. Sometimes it is difficult to implement several scenarios, as the languages do not have the necessary built-in features to do so. To overcome this problem, object-oriented languages have been used more often as they are more efficient in designing real-world entities with the modular approach as compared with traditional structured programming languages.

The underlying concepts of these languages help the modeler to design every possible scenario, but everything needs to be programmed from scratch. The more the programming, the higher is the probability of errors in the simulation program. Simulation languages have been developed to shorten the time required to develop the simulation model. However, they are not usually as flexible as general-purpose programming languages and are considered slower. Simulation packages are developed for a certain application and require little programming efforts, if not none. However, they are the least flexible, and

*Fundamentals of Performance Evaluation of Computer and Telecommunication Systems,*
By Mohammad S. Obaidat and Noureddine A. Boudriga
Copyright © 2010 John Wiley & Sons, Inc.

sometimes, you will not find the needed software module for the specific task/protocol built into the package.

This chapter discusses the alternatives for selecting software to develop simulation models. A comparison of the simulation languages with the general-purpose programming languages is provided to evaluate which languages are better suited for simulation and what makes one better than the other. A survey of commonly used simulation packages for modeling computer and telecommunication systems is given. Finally, the chapter discusses several case studies where some tools described have been used for simulating several network-related protocols, topologies, and policies.

## 12.1  INTRODUCTION

After the conceptual model is devised in detail by showing the event flows, the next main task ahead is the coding of the model using a selected programming language or a simulation package. These languages can be general-purpose, high-level languages like C + +, C#, and Java, dedicated simulation languages, such as MODSIM III and SLAM II, or special simulation packages, such as OPNET, NS2, NS3, GloMoSim, QualNet, OMNeT + +, or Network III. It is essential to make a clever decision as to which programming tool/language should be used for developing the simulation model based on the existing constraints, if any [1–44].

Several aspects can affect the choice of the language/tool to be used for developing the simulator, including the programmer's ease of learning or familiarity with the language, software available on the site where simulation needs to be conducted, the complexity of the model, requirement for graphical analysis, and time limitations. In the next sections, we will shed some light on the different characteristics that simulation software should have. Moreover, a brief description of how a model can be realized in the chosen simulation language/tool or general-purpose language will be presented.

## 12.2  SELECTION OF SIMULATION SOFTWARE

When selecting software tools for simulating a model, we have to consider the following issues:

- The attention should not be just on the simplicity of using the software. Instead, we should also think about the accuracy of the software and the level of granularity to which we can program the model. Moreover, we need to investigate how the software can be applied to the considered application [1–6].
- An essential principle when selecting simulation software is its executing speed. Developing a model accurately relies on the speed of execution

[1-10]. This is because when a programmer starts debugging, he may need to wait for the simulation to run up to a specific point where there is an error.

- We need to check what features the simulation package provides, for instance, whether it is possible to add/drop an entity.
- In addition, we need to discover whether the simulation software can be used to link to the external code, which is written in some high-level programming language, such as C + +, Java, C#, or C. This is a vital characteristic, as we may want to use procedures, which are developed in some other language and that match the intended application criteria.
- We must take into consideration how does the simulation software output the results, whether it produces a report, displays the execution in a graphical way, or offers animation attributes of the execution with respect to real time [2–12]. Moreover, we have to test whether the software tool offers any support for troubleshooting.

## 12.3 GENERAL-PURPOSE PROGRAMMING LANGUAGES

Most simulation analysts and programmers prefer general-purpose programming languages such as C, C + +, C#, and JAVA for coding their simulators. General purpose programming languages can be divided into the following main categories:

1. **Assembly languages**. These languages use low-level mnemonics to model the underlying hardware and represent computations. Assembler code is a first-level construct of the hardware. Although assembly languages are fast when executed; however, each processor has basically its own syntax, addressing modes and instruction set, which make the transportability of the code from one platform to another a major concern. In general, assembly languages are not often used for general simulation problems.

2. **Procedural programming languages**. In general, a procedural programming language gives a list of procedures that the program should finish to arrive at the required state. Here, a program is represented like a cookbook recipe. Every program has an initial state, a list of actions to complete, and an end point. This scheme is called the imperative programming. Integral to the concept of procedural programming is the notion of a procedure call. Procedures, which are also called subroutines' or methods, are small parts of code that do a specific function. A subroutine or a procedure is basically a list of computations to be done. Through dividing the programming task into small sections, procedural programming permits a section of code to be reused in the program without the need to make multiple copies. This approach makes it easier for programmers to comprehend and maintain program

organization. Examples on this category of programming languages include Fortran and Basic.

3. **Structured programming languages**. These languages are a special kind of procedural programming. They offer additional tools to handle the problems that larger programs were introducing. Here, the program is broken into small sections of code that are simple to comprehend. The program uses variables local to each subroutine. Moreover, structured languages do not permit the use of the GOTO statement. The top-down paradigm is employed in designing such programs. Successive design iterations then put in increasing facet to the sections until the design is done. Examples of such programming languages include C and Pascal.

Time management is an essential issue when running the simulation program. Organizing time is simple in the case of procedural-oriented programming languages. Typically, we have a countervariable termed CLOCK that is set to 0 when the simulation is begun. If the simulation model is centered on a cyclic scan, then a predetermined value is increased for each time the clock requires to move ahead. If the simulation is based on the event scan (also called the next-event) approach, then the increase is added to the CLOCK based on the number of imminent events.

All of these high-level languages have good procedural or subprogram means for simulating the execution of events. Typically, a procedure or subroutine is defined for every event. As an example, let us consider simulating the execution of a one-way queuing model, such as the arrival of a customer for a specific service, the end of service, exit of a customer from the queue, and what would occur when the queue is filled when a new customer arrives [1–6]. Now each event is programmed using a subroutine, which represents the variation of the system state based on the occurrence of the events.

It is worth noting here that managing queues in C and Pascal is more efficient when contrasted with that of old languages such as Fortran. Although Fortran is not used often in simulation these days, we point out here that it is inefficient in processing of lists. Furthermore, pointer management is ineffective in Fortran because pointers are used as an inner part of any multidimensional array. Therefore, it is not easy to access a particular pointer and consumes a lot of time. This results in slowing the execution speed [3–8].

One essential aspect that should be considered is that the programmer must also code for printing the formatted results. Simulation software packages have a built-in code for showing the outputs, whereas general-purpose programming languages do not have such a feature. In addition, routines for diagnosing programming errors should be designed by the programmer. These should detect errors such as syntax errors, and undefined variables [4–12]. To detect logical errors, the programmer should be familiar with the results that the model produces. Simulation models that are developed using general-purpose programming languages are usually less expensive to run. Because each feature of the model has to be dealt with, the programmer should be familiar with the fine details of the model.

4. **Object-oriented programming (OOP) languages**. This type of programming is relatively new and is considered effective. In this paradigm, the designer identifies both the data structures and the types of operations that can be applied to these structures. The blend of a quantity of data with the actions that can be carried on it is called an object. Hence, a program is made up of a set of collaborating objects, instead of a list of instructions. An object can save state information and cooperate with other objects; however, usually each object has a separate and restricted task. In OOP, a class is defined as a template from which objects are formed. Thus, it basically portrays a set of variables and methods. These methods can be available to all other classes or can have limited access. Fresh classes can be obtained from a parent class. The derived ones inherit the traits and behavior of the parent. This is called inheritance. However, they can also be expanded using new structures and methods. Additional classes can be added, which use the interfaces of the available classes. The message passing scheme is used to facilitate communication among objects.

Encapsulation is an important feature of any object-oriented language. It refers to how the implementation specifications of a class are concealed from all objects outside that class. Programmers can detail what information in an object can be shared with others. Moreover, OOP has an important attribute called polymorphism. The latter denotes that objects of diverse types can get the same message and react in special ways. The various objects should only have the same interface. The client or the calling object does not need to be familiar with precisely what kind of object it is calling; only that it has a method of a particular name with described arguments. Typically, polymorphism is often applied to derived classes that substitute methods of the parent class with special behaviors. It is worth noting here that together inheritance and polymorphism make OOP adaptable and simple to extend. OOP programs are simple to develop and maintain. This approach is widely accepted in larger software projects because objects can be divided between teams and developed concurrently. Examples on object-oriented languages include Java, Visual Basic, C#, and C + + .

## 12.4  SIMULATION LANGUAGES

Simulation languages are special programming languages that are optimized for simulation applications. In this regard, we indentify two categories of simulation languages: object-oriented simulation languages and traditional simulation languages.

1. **Object-Oriented Simulation Languages:** Object-oriented simulation languages offer basically the same advantages as that of the normal object-oriented languages. Among the major advantages here is that because the language is used primarily for simulating different situations, the language offers the system analyst a library that includes a set of modules that are used to characterize the entities in the real setting. Essentially, all the modeler needs to do is to reuse these modules in building the model. The simulationist has to adjust the modules with the needed factors to produce the required report. This is possible as such languages have built-in routines for report generation. Furthermore, such languages permit the modeler to develop his or her own suite of modules to satisfy model conditions. Examples include MODSIM III, SIMSCRIPT III, and Modelica.

2. **Traditional Simulation Languages:** These languages are mainly designed for coding and executing the simulation applications. They have built-in features and routines that make the task of the simulationist easy. Examples on such languages include General-Purpose Simulation System (GPSS), General Activity Simulation Program (GASP), SIMSCRIPT II.5, and Simulation Language for Alternative Modeling (SLAM) II. In the next section, we review the main aspects of commonly known simulation languages.

### 12.4.1 Examples on Simulation Languages

This section reviews examples of popular simulation languages and reviews their main aspects and features.

**General-Purpose Simulation System Language.** In 1961, Gordon introduced the GPSS simulation language. Severral modifications have been made to GPSS since then, and currently we have version 5 of GPSS. Here, the system is described as a group of blocks. Any activity in the system under study is represented with the aid of a block, and each line in the block shows a path to the subsequent activity [5–15]. GPSS provides some preidentified blocks, and the analysts are limited to program only with these particular blocks. Transactions in GPSS are defined as a set of entities that bypass all the way through the system. For example, a transaction is defined for the arrival of jobs to a server in a client-server system. Every entity in the simulation model has several attributes that are characterized as parameters. Part of these attributes is employed in creating logical assessments for the blocks. Other symbols or numbers are related with each block. To process this data, every block gets an amount of time for the operation.

Transactions in GPSS use a GENERATE block to come into the system. The information used for representing the GENERATE block is shown in Figure 12.1.

As shown in the Figure, letters A, B, C, D, E, F, and G are the operands of the block. The average interarrival time is given by the operand A, whereas B represents the average modifier. When the first arrival generation occurs, the time for it is given by C. The total number of arrivals to be generated is given by D whereas E gives the priority rank for every transaction and F represents the number of factors/parameters for every transaction. G shows the kind of the parameter in terms of whether it is full word or half word [5–20]. In the case where no values are given for a parameter, default values are set. Transactions in GPSS use a TERMINATE block to depart the system. Figure 12.2 depicts the notation used to represent the TERMINATE block. In general, the TERMINATE block has an operand A, which indicates how much the termination counter is incremented.

The arrangement of the transactions is performed on a priority basis [5–28]. Priority levels can be in the range of 0–127. The transaction that has the top priority is run first. When we experience two transactions with the same priority, the transactions are progressed based on the order of their generation or in a first-in, first-out (FIFO) manner. The execution of the transaction in the system can be delayed based on two reasons [6–30]:

1. The transaction might go through an ADVANCE block that is depicted by the notation shown in Figure 12.3. The ADVANCE block shows some activity that takes some time such as dealing with the job by the computer machine.

2. One more reason for which a transaction may be stopped is that a transaction tries to enter a block if it is currently occupied by another

**FIGURE 12.1.** GENERATE block.

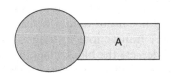

**FIGURE 12.2.** TERMINATE block.

**FIGURE 12.3.** ADVANCE block.

**FIGURE 12.4.** TRANSFER block.

transaction. Blocks execute transactions in a sequential manner until the transaction comes on a TRANSFER block. The notation for this block is shown in Figure 12.4.

The operand S is the selection factor that basically finds out the path that the transaction must take. GPSS supports eight random-number generators (RNGs), which are represented as RN1-RN8. Every RNG is a resource for uniform random numbers and variates. The inverse transformation technique is used to generate many types of nonuniform random variates, such as the exponential variate.

The simulation clock in GPSS is maintained by the control program. The progress of transactions is monitored by the following two lists: (a) the present events sequence/chain and (b) the future events sequence/chain. Every transaction includes an attribute called block departure time (BDT), which basically specifies the time at which the transaction should depart from the current block. Moreover, the current events chain includes the list of all transactions whose block departure time is not as much as or equal to that of the current clock time. All transactions whose block departure time is greater than that of the present simulation time are saved in the future events chain list. Every time a transaction in future events chain list has a block departure time that is equal to that of the simulation time, the transaction is shifted to the current events chain list. If a transaction in the current events chain list finds an ADVANCE block, then it is moved to the future events chain list [5–9].

GPSS offers two kinds of resources for which the transactions contend: facilities and storages. In general, a facility is a resource that may be used by only one transaction at any instant of time, whereas a storage is a source that may be distributed by many transactions as long as the limit of the storage is not exceeded. Figure 12.5 depicts the block diagrams for facility and storage.

In Figure 12.5, A stands for the facility or the number of storage. The SIEZE and RELEASE blocks are used for keeping a facility, whereas the ENTER and

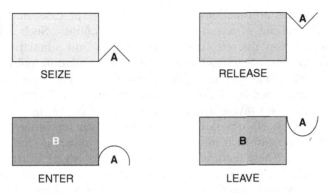

**FIGURE 12.5.** Block diagrams for storage and facility.

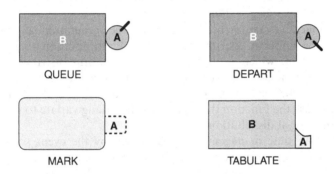

**FIGURE 12.6.** Block diagrams for gathering data.

LEAVE blocks are employed for keeping the storage. The operand B in the ENTER and LEAVE block describes the storage capacity [5–12].

To gather the statistical data on the result of performance evaluation of the system under study, we use four control blocks to collect the required data; see Figure 12.6. The details for these block diagrams are briefly described next. The QUEUE block is used to enlarge the size of the queue for the transactions that are waiting in the queue. The length of the queue is reduced whenever a transaction departs the queue.

The MARK and TABULATE blocks are employed to find out the transit time between two points of the model for a transaction [6–9].

The subroutines that are used to generate output in the GPSS are precoded and formatted; therefore, the modeler does not have to worry about showing the output. One major drawback of GPSS is that its simulation models run slower, and therefore, they take more time to run when compared with the models written in other high-level languages, such as C++. Nevertheless, GPSS is considered a flexible language [6–14].

**General Activity Simulation Program.** The GASP simulation language was introduced by A. Pritsker and N. Hurst. The recent version of GASP is GASP

IV. The fundamental functions of the simulation in case of GASP are performed via the aid of a suite of Fortran subroutines. Such subroutines are used to develop discrete, continuous, and hybrid simulation models. Actually, GASP has integrated the discrete event simulation and the continuous event simulation under a common structure [7–19]. The main categories of the functions performed by GASP are: (a) management of the events, (b) state variables updating, (c) saving and getting back the data, (d) initialization, (e) gathering the data, (f) observing the programs, (g) reporting the events, (h) calculating the statistical information, and (i) producing reports and the random variables. These features of GASP are sustained by Fortran subroutines. In addition to these subprograms, the GASP simulation language offers an interface for the user-described subprograms [4–12]. Subprograms described by the users are employed to simulate the events, report the errors with messages, and produce outcomes in the required format. The user-described modules are called stubs or dummy programs.

The multiplicative congruential random-number generation scheme is used to generate the uniform distributions in GASP. In addition to the normal DRAND function, which is used to generate uniform distribution, GASP employs other functions to generate other random variates, such as the triangular, normal, lognormal, Erlang, beta, gamma, and Poisson distributions. We can use the function that generates the Erlang variate to generate the popular exponential distribution.

In GASP IV, time management is performed by the event scan method. A subroutine is used to move on the simulation clock and to scan the future events list. This method is used for discrete systems. Because GASP supports discrete, continuous, and hybrid simulations modeling, the above scheme is customized to go with both the continuous and hybrid simulation systems [4–11]. Events that occur at a specific instant of time are often called "time events," and these events that occur when the system arrives at a specific state are called "state events."

The EVNTS subroutine handles all events of GASP; it has a GOTO statement that calls on the necessary routines. Because GASP has been developed with the aid of Fortran subroutines, administrating the queues is inefficient because Fortran does not have the dynamic functionality to enlarge and reduce the length of the queue. As an alternative, the size of the queue must be defined ahead of time.

The processes of collecting data as well as computing and generating the reports are efficient in GASP. In addition to the normal output that the GASP produces, it also offers flexibility for the user to produce the output when needed. The only thing the user needs to do is to program the logic for producing the output in user-described subroutines.

GASP can be installed on any computer that has a Fortran compiler, which is a nice feature. Furthermore, programmers who are familiar with Fortran programming language can easily write simulation programs using the GASP. In GASP, a subroutine called ERROR is used for debugging the model. If there is an illogical situation, the ERROR subroutine is invoked. When executed, the ERROR subroutine identifies the error that caused the system to depart from its usual behavior. Moreover, it offers a sample of the system state when the error takes place. If the user desires to spot the errors aside from the ones that are recognized by the ERROR subroutine, he may take in the information in a user described subroutine called UERR.

The key benefit of using GASP is that the language provides many subroutines that do the required functions. This means that less programming effort is needed from the modeler/simulationist.

**SLAM Language.** The SLAM is the first simulation language that permitted a modeler to devise a system explanation via any combination of three schemes (world views). Such an incorporated construction allows the SLAM II user to benefit from the simplicity of the process-oriented technique and expand a model with discrete event constructs should the process-oriented method become too limited.

SLAM is a simulation language that is written in ANSI Fortran. It is used to model both discrete event systems and continuous systems. The recent version of SLAM is SLAM II. As a simulation language, SLAM can use either an event orientation or a process orientation approach for modeling the discrete event system, whereas it uses differential or difference equations for modeling continuous systems. The hybrid or discrete continuous systems can be modeled by integrating the continuous oriented scheme with event or process-based approach. In the case of the process-oriented approach, the structure of the network is characterized by using some symbols termed nodes and branches. Nodes are employed to model the entities, and the activities or the events associated with the entity are represented by the branch [9–16]. The flow of entities is managed by five nodes: CREATE, COLCT, ACCUMULATE, TERM, and ASSIGN. A QUEUE node is used to characterize a machine or a set of machines along with its queue. Routing entities to different queues is done by the SELECT node. At any time, an entity matches up with a particular criterion, the stream of the entities is ended by MATCH node. An AWAIT node is employed to allocate a resource to an entity. As soon as the entity is done using the resource, it bypasses via a FREE node to free the resource. When we want to seize a resource from an entity of lower priority and assign it to the higher priority entity, then this process is conducted by the PREEMPT node [9–25]. The form of the resource or the availability of the number of the resources can be modified with the help of ALTER node.

SLAM offers a suite of standard subprograms that conducts the functions like scheduling of the events, manipulation of files, gathering of statistics, and producing the random samples. Figure 12.7 shows SLAM organization for discrete-event modeling. The starting condition for simulation is decided by the user in a subroutine called INTLC. The EVENT subroutine describes what would happen to the state of the system when a specific type of event occurs. User-specified output reports can be produced by using the subroutine OUTPUT; this is in addition to the standard reports that are provided by

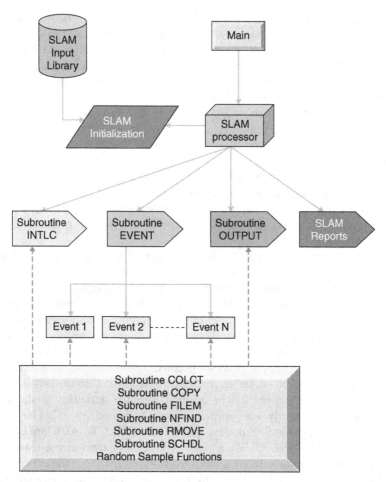

**FIGURE 12.7.** Organization of SLAM for discrete-event modeling.

the SLAM [14]. The subroutine COLCT is employed for generating the statistics. Subroutines like COPY, NFIND, RMOVE, and FILEM are used to conduct file management. The scheduling of different events is performed using the subroutine SCHDL. Random sample distributions are produced using the random sample functions. In addition to this, SLAM has subroutines that perform functions like retrieving entity attributes, connecting and disconnecting various entities from files, producing reports, producing histograms and graphs, tracing the entity, clearing the statistics, and reporting if they occur; see Figure 12.7.

SLAM uses differential equations for implementing simulation programs for a continuous model. Such equations illustrate the manners of the state variables. Usually, the coding of these equations is performed in Fortran by

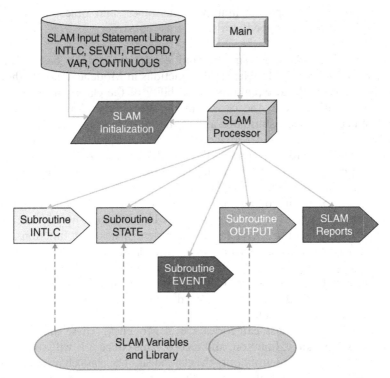

**FIGURE 12.8.** Overall organization of SLAM for continuous modeling.

using the SLAM specified arrays. Figure 12.8 shows the overall organization of SLAM for continuous simulation modeling.

The subroutine STATE is used to code the differential equations. The INTLC subroutine is employed to describe the starting values of these variables. As for difference equations, a fixed step size (time) is employed. For differential equations, variable step size is used with the help of Runge-Kutta-Fehlberg Numerical Integration scheme [14]. RECORD and VAR are used to draw the input variables over time.

**Modelica Language.** Modelica is an object-oriented simulation language that is used for hierarchical modeling of the physical systems. The chief properties of Modelica when compared with other object oriented languages are as follows:

1. Modeling in Modelica is noncasual and is based on algebraic and differential equations.
2. Modeling capability is expanded to multidomain; i.e., we can combine many characteristics, such as mechanical, thermal, and electrical in a single application model.

3. The ideas of templates, multiple inheritance, and object oriented are combined and described in a single-class construct.

Variables, local-class description, and equations are the basic building ingredients of a class in Modelica [15]. Functions in Modelica may be thought of as local class without equations. Reusability of the classes in Modelica is more when contrasted to the classes in the customary object-oriented languages. When a class is instantiated and connected, the class adjusts itself to the data-flow context. Connectors in Modelica are also normal classes. Graphical editor is employed for developing the simulation charts. To set up a link between different objects that are instantiated from other classes, we only have to draw a line between them [15–20].

A Modelica program consists of only classes. Such classes hold variables or parameters that are used to signify the data. A key difference here is that we use equations to explain the manners of the system instead of functions. Such equations may be taken over from other base classes or they can be written down unambiguously for the specific class. The Connect statement may be used to describe equations. Connect (V1, V2) stand for the fact that variables V1 and V2 are tied. Such variables are termed connectors, and the objects are considered connected objects.

Seven constrained class categories are in Modelica. These are type, connector, model, package, function, and record. This concept is valuable because the programmer has to identify only the class ideas. The class characteristics, its syntax, and semantics are all alike for these seven classes [15]. Translating an object from one kind to another is fairly simple because all that is needed is to modify the kind of the class.

We may come across some scenarios where it would be simpler to show the manners of the system by writing procedures instead of using equations. In such cases, we can carry out the computations in a procedural manner. An example on this is computing the polynomial value as the degree of the polynomial is unknown exactly and is bound to vary continuously. To run such scenarios, Modelica offers a special class called function that has public inputs, public outputs, and an algorithm section wherever the procedures are realized and no equations.

The key feature of any simulation model is the quantity of time it requires to run the simulation model. Consequently, we have to maintain a variable that keeps track of the time during the execution stage [15–20]. Modelica offers a predefined system variable called time, which moves ahead through the simulation run.

**MODSIM III Language.** MODSIM III is an object-oriented, modular, and block-structured simulation language that is robustly typed. It has been developed by CACI. MODSIM III partitions the simulation program into several modules. Every module is saved in a unique file. The benefit of this technique is that every module can be compiled independently. Furthermore, a module may be used in many programs. Because MODSIM III is robustly typed, each task, expression, and data type is verified for steadiness during compilation [17]. The simulation method supported by MODSIM III is a process-oriented scheme. MODSIM III is chiefly employed for discrete system simulation.

In MODSIM III, objects are divided in two separate blocks. The definition block describes the type of object by specifying the variables and methods that operate on these variables. In the realization block, the object actions are described with the help of methods. Generally, each object has ASK and TELL methods. Executing an ASK method is like executing a procedure call. When the ASK statement is executed, it points to the object to invoke the method. Then, it waits until the method ends its execution. Once execution is done, it moves to the next statement after ASK. The ASK method may be an appropriate method or it could act as a function that returns the value. ASK methods are not permitted to pass the simulation time.

Another name for the TELL method is the deferred or delayed method call. This call is asynchronous. When the TELL statement is executed, it points to the object to invoke the method [17, 18]. As soon as the method is invoked, the calling code executes the next statement without waiting for the method to finish its execution. TELL methods are permitted to bypass the simulation time and they act only as a proper method and do not return any value.

One more method, known as WAITFOR, exhibits both the characteristics of the ASK method and TELL method. In case of WAITFOR methods, the simulation time is passed with the assistance of the WAIT statement.

MODSIM III has a prebuilt Resource object in its library, which assists in forming the resource objects as and when required. The use of inheritance attribute helps to get new objects from the presented objects, which are employed as general interface that offers additional potential.

MODSIM III includes a graphical interface that explains the scenarios of the system on the screen as an animation operation. Moreover, plots are developed when the simulation is executing, which can be used to examine the behavior of the system [17]. In addition to displaying the results, it also proposes various alternatives that can be realized to enhance the efficiency. Thus, this aids the modeler to comprehend and evaluate the system in a better way. Such a scheme helps the modeler to recognize the errors in a speedy manner. This technique reduces the overall time needed to execute the simulation model. Furthermore, the graphical editor makes it easy to describe a scenario by just dragging and dropping the icons in the editor. Such icons are then linked to explain the interrelationships between themselves.

The development setting in MODSIM III is made of the following components: compilation manager, the object manager, and the debugging manager. These three means together help in modeling the advanced systems proficiently.

The compilation manager tool is used to find out repeatedly the modules that have been edited or modified since the previous compilation. It recognizes such modules and recompiles only these modules and the modules that depend on the edited ones.

The object manager component aids the modeler to surf the object, its variables, and the procedures associated with it. The object manager offers an abstract outlook of the compound objects beside their attributes, and procedures, along with the inheritance charts for the objects. The inheritance characteristics comprise all the capabilities that objects hold after extending from another class.

Whenever we stopover an object, this information is recorded, which assists the modeler to return to the preceding object. The browsing feature explains which ancestor object described the method and which object actually realized it.

The debugging manager tool provides great features. When a runtime error occurs during the execution of the model, the MODSIM III goes into a debugging mode, thus permitting the modeler to find out where the error took place and then helps him to check the variables. Because a trace of the execution is kept, the modeler can always go back and forth and examine the order of execution of the modules and procedures at the time of error.

**SIMSCRIPT III Language.** SIMSCRIPT III is an object oriented language that is supported by CACI. It has a modular design that is an extension to the features of SIMSCRIPT II.5. The object-oriented features of the SIMSCRIPT III like these occur in many object-oriented languages like Java, C + +, and so on.

The program organization in SIMSCRIPT III is made up of a preamble, which is a block of declarations and is followed by a number of procedures [18]. All declarations that are made in the preamble are global, which means they can be used by whichever routine in the main program.

The essential data types in SIMSCRIPT III are called modes. These include real, double, integer, alpha, text, and pointer. Integer is a signed 32-bit value. Real and double are floating point values. Alpha resembles a character that is enclosed within double quotations. Text symbolizes a string of characters and pointer is a reference to a 32-bit address in the system.

Variables are described with the given data types. A possible kind of variable declaration is "define fin as a real variable." If this declaration is made in the preamble, then the variable is termed a global variable. If it is defined inside a routine, then it is called a local variable. Arrays are also declared in the same format as variables.

SIMSCRIPT III can support both arithmetic and logical expressions. A single line in the SIMSCRIPT program can contain many statements. The read statement is used to read the formatted input, and the write statement is used to show the formatted output. Moreover, print performs the same functionality as that of write [18]. The "if" statement tests whether the condition is satisfied, and if yes, it executes the statement below, and if the condition is not satisfied, the statements following the else are executed. The select statement works like that of a case statement in C++. SIMSCRIPT III supports various kinds of looping structures such as *while loop*, *for loop* and *do while loop*. The *Leave* statement is used for ending the loop. A *Find* statement can also be used to terminate the loop. But *Find* can be used to terminate only for the first iteration of the loop.

Functions and subroutines are both procedures except for the fact that function returns a value whereas the subroutine does not. Functions are pronounced with the help of a define statement. Whenever we want to invoke these functions, we invoke them using a *Call* statement.

The declaration for the classes starts with the begin class block. Classes in SIMSCRIPT III have three elements, i.e., variables, methods and sets. An object is an instance of class. Objects are generated by executing the *Create* statement. Once created, all the object variables are initialized to zero, and the object reference is assigned to a reference variable. Whenever we want to remove an object, we use *Destroy* statement, which deallocates the memory assigned to the object and eliminates its reference.

Attributes in the class are described with the help of *Define* statement. The declaration is similar to defining variables. Methods in classes are declared with the aid of *Every* statement. The arguments are declared using a *Define* statement. If there is no *Define* statement, then the method is supposed to be a subroutine. Sets are doubly linked lists that are used to hold the objects [18]. The file statement conducts the act of inserting an object into the set. To eliminate the object from the set, we use the *Remove* statement.

In order to generate, Uniform Pseudo Random sequences in SIMSCRIPT III, the linear congruential generators (LCGs) are used. An array termed SEED.V contains 10 seed values. These values are chosen by using a stream number. Several distributions such as Poisson, exponential, Erlang, Binomial, Gamma, Triangular, and lognormal can be produced with the help of the linear congruential generator.

Process methods in SIMSCRIPT III are subroutines that can be executed either by issuing a *Call* statement or a *Schedule* statement. The Call statement is used to execute the process method right away. If we want to execute the process method at some simulation time, then we can do so by using the *Schedule* statement. The *Interrupt* statement can then be used to remove the routine from the future events list. The put on hold routines can be resumed by issuing the *Resume* statement. Statistics in SIMSCRIPT III are computed using the Accumulate or *Tally* statement [18].

**Yet Another Network Simulation Language (YANSL).** The YANSL is primarily designed for network simulation via the object-oriented methodology. This language has the key facets sustained by GPSS, SLAM, SIMAN, and INSIGHT. The classes for the YANSL package are selected from the available modeling frameworks. YANSL is created by gathering all of these classes. Such characteristics can be used to design more sophisticated structures [17–22]. The simulation classes that are used here are for statistics gathering, variate production, and administrating simulation time. Figure 12.9 depicts the hierarchy of the nodes in YANSL. As observed in Figure 12.9, the higher level nodes are used directly by the modeler. These comprise: the assign node, activity node, queue node, source node, and sink node. Nodes that are described at the lower level are abstract and less explicit. As an example, the QueueNodeBase class does not contain characteristics such as producing statistics. Sink and queue nodes are destination nodes because they can have the transactions split whereas the source node is called a departure node. Every action in a network has some kind of necessities for the resource [17–29]. In YANSL, the nodes permit the transaction to be generated at the source node, stay at queue node and obtain the jobs at the assignment node. The delay is initiated by the activity nodes and the transaction departs the network via the sink nodes.

Activity nodes supply resources to the transactions. The structure for the resources in YANSL permits the resources to be recognized as individuals, teams, or a member in other groups.

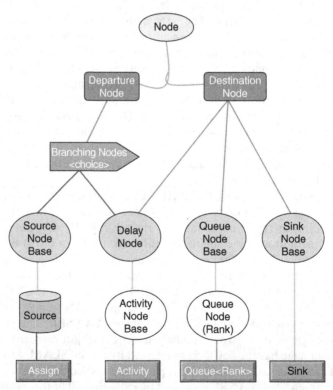

**FIGURE 12.9.** Hierarchy of node in YANSL.

The Resource choice scheme is used when there is a selection for the resource service. Such options offer a greater flexibility for in making function decisions, without using a separate class for each function Figure 12.10.

YANSL classes are made up of the choice classes within themselves. The choice consists of various schemes, which help the resources to make a decision on what to choose and what to do next, as well as categorizing the choices for several transactions at the queue [17].

**SIMULA Language.** Simula is an object oriented simulation language, which encapsulates the idea of objects. Actually, there are two versions of Simula: Simula I and Simula 67. They were developed by the Norwegian Computing Center and were influenced heavily by the Algol 60 programming language [21].

The data types supported by the simula language are integer, real, and Boolean. This language consists mainly of two main concepts: the class and the reference variables. Doubly linked lists in Simula are employed with the help of routines that are described in the class called Simset. Discrete-event simulation programs are written using the simulation class that contains the procedures, routines, and concepts. Below is the simple definition of the class in Simula [21]:

*Begin class C1;*
*Begin Outtext ("This is program in Simula");*
*End;*
*Reference (C1) test;*
*test:- new C1;*
*End;*

Whenever a procedure is called, all the statements in the body of the procedure are executed, and it returns the information by some of its

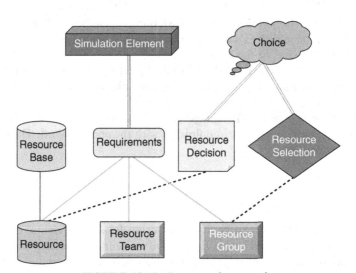

**FIGURE 12.10.** Resource framework.

parameters [21]. However, the class is called with the help of the new operator that then instantiates the object. The attributes of the class are accessed using the dot notation. Whenever we instantiate several objects, we have to manage these objects well. Such information about the objects is sustained with the aid of a reference variable that may be of type real or an integer.

The syntax for defining the reference variable is given by:

*Ref(classname) ReferenceVariable;*

Classes can be described in the hierarchy block structure, which is achieved by the help of prefixed classes.

Doubly linked lists that are also called sets are administered by the routines that are described in the class called SIMSET. At least one member exists in the set, and the first object in the set is called HEAD. The subclass to SIMSET is HEAD. LINK is one more member, which is a subclass to SIMSET [21–24]. The reference variables for HEAD and LINK are termed as SUC and PRED, respectively. Here, SUC denotes successor and PRED means predecessor. The sets are managed by the procedures that are explained in HEAD and LINK. Several procedures defined in the HEAD are FIRST, LAST, and EMPTY. The reference to the former member and last member of the set are given by the FIRST and LAST procedures, respectively. If the set is empty, then the EMPTY procedure when executed on the set returns true.

SIMULATION is considered a subclass of SIMSET. It consists of several processes that are prefixed by the PROCESS. The PROCESS object may be in any one of the three possible states: active, passive, and suspended. In addition, there is one more state called terminated, which means that the running of the object is done.

The event list in Simula can be managed with the help of the three key procedures: HOLD, PASSIVATE and ACTIVATE. If there is an object on which we execute the statement HOLD (8), then, this indicates that the object is rescheduled to be active as soon as the simulation time advances by 8. Until then, the object is put in the event list.

Each time we execute the PASSIVATE procedure on any object it puts the active object in the passive status by moving the object from the event list. This will start the next object in the list to be active [21].

**Hierarchical Simulation Language (HSL).** In HSL, the program module starts with the model keyword and finishes with the end keyword. The syntax is given as below:

*model test*

    ....

    ...

*End test;*

Global variables in HSL can be described using four fundamental data types: integer, Boolean, real, and string. Every time we define a variable, we can either give a value to the variable or just pronounce it without giving the value for it.

If not specified, the variable is set with a default value. Arrays are declared in the following format [22]:

*<data type> arrayname [ ];*

Constant values in HSL are defined using a constant keyword. Statistics for every variable may be acquired by declaring the required variable with *stat* keyword. Furthermore, there exists a data structure called *queue* that is employed for seizing the entities. Resources used in the simulation model are confirmed using the *resource* keyword.

Type casting of the objects in HSL can be performed using the entity *class* [22]. The entity class is also useful for declaring the abstract attributes. Syntax for entity class declaration is as shown below:

*Entity <declared name>*
*Abstract data types and definitions*
*End <declared name>*

The hierarchy of the entities is set up by using the object-oriented characteristics of inheritance. The entities that are described in the model may be allocated with priorities. The *setPriority* keyword is employed to give a priority for the entity that is employed in the system. Hierarchical simulation modeling may be used for process-oriented modeling as well. The *start* declaration in the program states the set of processes that will be run when the simulation is executed. To end these processes for the period of the simulation, conditions for ending are specified with the aid of a *stop* statement. The *clock* keyword follows the simulation clock by moving the time based on the criteria put by the modeler. The *trace* of simulation can be generated via the keyword called *trace* which is described in the program where the analyst senses to know about the state of the system at that point of time.

The *report* keyword is used for producing the reports whilst running the simulation. All the statistical data such as the use of resources, queues, entities, and processes are presented in the report.

The process *definition* in HSL is made up of the name of the process, the listing of parameters allocated to the process, entity parameter, and statement sequence [22]. The passing forms for parameter might be in, out, or inout. The designation for function in case HSL consists of the name of the function, its kind, and the string of statements. When a *return* statement is executed, only the function *run* ends.

Some HSL statements are essential for programming in simulation as they modify the running time of the simulation run. The process can be postponed for a specific duration of time by running the *delay* statement. If we want to delay the process for an endless duration of time, then it can be performed by executing the *suspend* statement. Now, if we desire to continue running the process, then it may be done by executing the *awaken* statement.

If an entity desires a particular type of resource to perform an activity, it can obtain the resource by executing the *request* statement. Following the completion of the activity, the resource can be given away by executing the *release* statement.

In HSL, the random variates are produced using the *rand01* function. The initial values for random-number generators are produced using the *setseed* function. The *Uniform* function generates uniform distributions or variates. Moreover, the *Expo* function and *Erlang* function produce exponential and Erlang variates, respectively. Statistical data about the simulation run are produced using the *stat* function [22].

## 12.5 SIMULATION SOFTWARE PACKAGES

Simulation packages are becoming popular in academia and industry because of their ease of use for developing quick models and teaching. They help in designing simulation models using graphical user interface without knowing the fundamental details of the simulation languages. Normally, these packages are application specific and can deal with the modeling aspects for a specific domain. Because using simulation packages will entail little coding by the modeler, there are few chances of syntactic errors. Nearly all the functionalities are predefined and are saved in the simulation libraries. Some of these packages are available free of charge as an open resource; however, some of them are not. Nevertheless, some simulation package companies offer a free site license for academic institutions after signing on a special contract.

Below, we describe briefly main software simulation packages that are used for computer and telecommunication systems.

**Network Simulator 2 (NS 2).** Network simulator 2 is a simulation package, which was developed for computer networks simulation. This simulation package supports several network protocols. Many network protocols such as Transmission Control Protocol (TCP), User Datagram Protocol (UDP), Hypertext Transfer Protocol (HTTP), and Dynamic Host Configuration Protocol (DHCP) can be modeled using this package [26]. In addition to this, several kinds of network traffic types, such as constant bit rate (CBR), available bit rate (ABR), and variable bit rate (VBR), can be generated easily using this package. It is a popular simulation tool for modeling several network topologies.

Moreover, NS 2 models use the object-oriented approach. It supports two kinds of nodes: the unicast node and multicast node. The unicast node carries out unicast routing, whereas the multicast node deals with multicast routing. The default nodes are the unicast nodes.

Connections between the nodes are created using the compound objects. *Queue* objects and *snoop* queue objects are employed for monitoring the queues in the network simulator package. The *AtEvent* handler used by the simulator is employed for scheduling the events in the model.

NS 2 has been developed by using C + + programming language and OTcl [26–28]. OTcl is a relatively new language that uses object oriented aspects. It was developed at Massachusetts Institute of Technology (MIT) as an object-oriented extension of Tool command language (Tcl). Figure 12.11 illustrates class hierarchy in NS 2.

The tracing in the NS 2 package is made with the help of trace-all and nam-trace-all commands.

To view the animation of the model, we use the NAM tool, which is the network animator. The graphical user interface depicts the traces of the network under various topologies. Packet level animation can also be demonstrated by NS 2.

The network animator is invoked by running the NAM command. Figure 12.12 shows the network animator interface [26–29].

TCL scripts are employed to describe the models in NS 2. In order to design a model using NS 2, one must have a deep perceptive of the TCL language. Agents in the NS 2 are generated using the set command. The agent is run by executing the start command on the agent name. The *recv* and *timeout* are the main methods that should be described in the agent class. Packets are generated by using the packet class in the package [26–28].

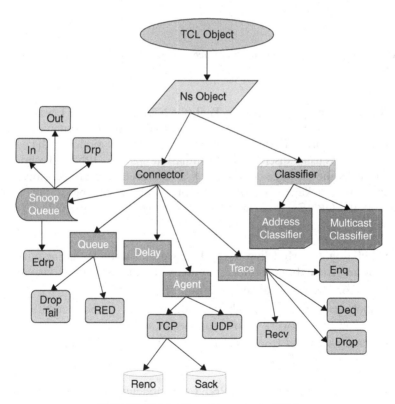

**FIGURE 12.11.** Class hierarchy in NS 2.

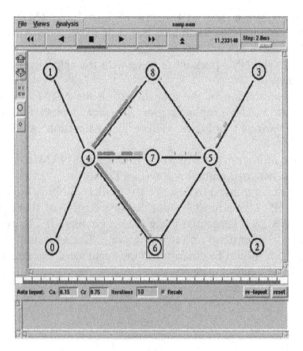

**FIGURE 12.12.** Network animator interface showing the topology of nodes and packet traversal in NS 2.

**Optimized Network Engineering Tool (OPNET).** The OPNET was basically designed by OPNET Technologies, Inc. to analyze the performance of communication networks. The performance is predicted by modeling the communication systems using discrete event simulation [32, 44]. OPNET Technologies Inc. improves the package continuously and every few years develops a new version of the package. The latest version as of the writing of this book is known as the OPNET Modeler 10.5. The key features of the OPNET are as follows:

- Simulation and Modeling Cycle: It has powerful tools that help in model building, simulation running, and analyzing the simulation outputs.
- It supports hierarchical configuration of modeling.
- It includes a rich set of library modules that support communication protocols and network-related topologies and mechanisms.
- It contains a good troubleshooting facility and the model can be readily compiled and easily run.

The three types of editors in OPNET for modeling three types of networks are as follows:

- Network topology models are modeled using the Network editor.
- Data flow models are designed using the Node Editor.
- Control flow models are expressed by using the Process Editor.

Furthermore, the simulation can be run by using the simulation tool or debugging tool. The simulation tool is used for executing the model in a normal manner; however, if we want to interact while executing the simulation, then it is preferred to run it using the debugging tool [32].

Many available tools can be used for analyzing the simulation results. The *probe* editor is used for collecting the data. The statistical results are acquired by employing the analysis tool. Data processing is performed with the aid of the *filter* tool. The dynamic actions of the model can be observed using the *animation* viewer.

Entities in the network model are represented as nodes, and interaction between the entities is facilitated with the help of a link. To broadcast data from one entity to all others, we employ bus link and radio link for mobile communication. To decrease complexity, networks are abstracted as subnetworks. Figure 12.13 illustrates the interface of an optical network engineering tool showing connection of nodes in the Network Editor [32–36, 44].

Interrupts can be used to facilitate the communication among the processes. The *probe* editor in the OPNET contains various kinds of probes for collecting output data. The statistic *probe* is used to acquire statistics

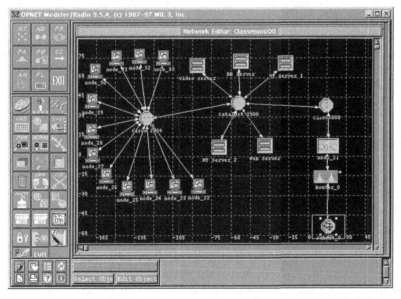

**FIGURE 12.13.** Interface of optical network engineering tool in OPNET showing connection of nodes in the Network Editor.

like the bit-error rate and throughput performance metrics. To produce the animation effect, sequences in the simulation automatic animation *probe* are used. The custom animation probe can be used to collect the animation characteristics for process and link models. The statistic *probe* gathers the data; however, it does not produce the output results. To produce the statistical output data, *statistic probe* is used. The analysis tool in OPNET is used to show the information in terms of graphs. Analysis panels are used to present these graphs. Filter models in OPNET are described as block diagrams that are linked together using the filter elements. Filter models are represented in the hierarchical order; the functions on the vectors that are discrete. The input vectors may be described as the vectors that are supplied to the filter. The resulting vector that is produced after processing the filter is called the output vector [44].

**OMNeT + + simulation package.** OMNeT++ is an open-source discrete-event simulation package that is used for simulating the computer communication networks and distributed computer systems. The programming feature in OMNeT++ follows a modular approach. This package supports three kinds of modules: simple, complex, and system modules. Components in the model communicate with each other using message passing [27]. Modules that are active are called active modules. Complex modules are structured by assembling the simple modules. Messages are transmitted using the gates in case of simple modules. The input interface and the output interface are termed "gates." Links are used to connect the input and output gates.

Functionalities in the modules can be coroutine based and event processing based. In the coroutine-based programming, the code in the module runs on its own by producing a thread that is managed by the kernel, which bypasses the events.

In event-processing function-based approach, the task is called by the kernel that passes the message as an argument. This message is handled by the function and is sent back.

The network topology can be altered dynamically. Moreover, there is flexibility to include and remove modules when the simulation is running. Links in the model can be reorganized during the run of the simulation model.

OMNeT++ simulation package offers a standard library that described some standard modules that can be employed during the modeling process of the system under study [27]. Modules for troubleshooting, tracing, and animating are efficient in this package. Figure 12.14 shows an example of an OMNeT++ graphical interface between routers and nodes in a model for a network [27]. The library contains the message classes, container classes, routing classes, random-number generator classes and statistical classes. Statistical classes are used for gathering the data when the simulation is on the run to assess the performance of the simulated system. Message classes are employed to offer message packets for different sorts of networks. Container classes offer different storing services, such as queues, and stacks, and these services maintain the general actions on these classes. Routing classes offer the

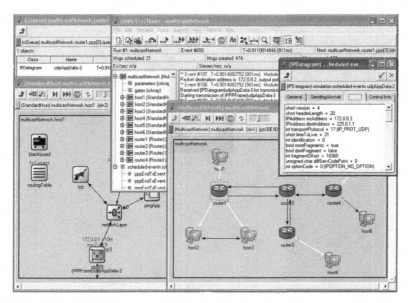

**FIGURE 12.14.** OMNeT++ graphical interface showing the interconnection between nodes and routers in a network model.

foundation for using a variety of routing schemes for moving the message packets in the network. Tracing and simple debugging are considered the key features of OMNeT++ package [27]. To trace the behavior of the system, OMNeT++ employs three methods: automatic animation, module output windows, and object inspectors. Figure 12.15 shows a snapshot of a debugging and trace interface example in OMNeT++ [27–29].

In OMNeT++ model animation, the model is executed and the behavior is tested to determine whether it is correct. Every time we model, we may produce textually some data as a checkpoint for troubleshooting. The kind of data that are used for debugging is exhibited in the module output window [27]. The status of the object at any point of time may be shown using object monitors.

**GloMoSim Simulation Package.** GloMoSim is a simulation package that is primarily used for simulating wireless network systems. It is being designed using the parallel discrete-event simulation capability provided by PARSEC. The name GloMoSim has been derived from the words: global mobile system simulator. The GloMoSim library consists of a set of modules in which each module simulates a particular wireless protocol.

Figure 12.16 depicts the main parts of the GloMoSim software package. There are two options of GloMoSim: one for simulating the models in a shared memory setting and the other one for simulating the models in a distributed memory environment.

Parallel Simulation Environment for Complex Systems PARSEC is a parallel simulation language[1] that is coded in C. PARSEC has been developed

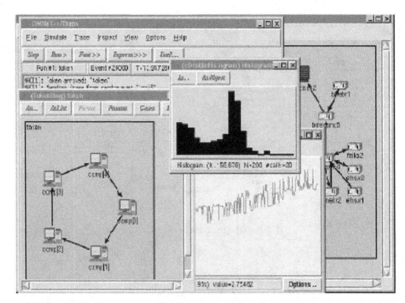

**FIGURE 12.15.** Screenshot of debugging and trace interface in OMNeT++.

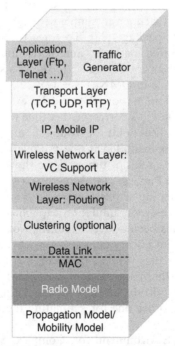

·**FIGURE 12.16.** Architecture of GloMoSim package.

by the Parallel Computing Laboratory at UCLA, for sequential and parallel execution of discrete-event simulation models. It can also be used as a parallel programming language. PARSEC can be used to describe the library in GloMoSim [40]. Rather than coding each and every component, a graphical environment called PAVE is provided, which can be used to develop the simulation models. PARSEC defines each node as an entity.

This method has some drawbacks, as each node needs extra memory for running the process, and also the simulation time is enhanced as overhead of context switching exists among the entities. This will affect the overall simulation performance negatively. To overpower these problems, GloMoSim launched a new scheme called node aggregation. This method helps GloMoSim to simulate several nodes in a network by only using a single entity. In an entity, the status of every node is shown by a data structure. For sequential simulation, a single entity is enough, as there is only one processor. However, for parallel simulation, the number of entities that must be described is equal to the number of processors on which the simulation operation is executed.

The overall design of GloMoSim is based on a layered approach where layers interact with each other via different application programming interfaces (APIs). Thus, the entity in each layer is represented differently. By increasing the number of layers, the number of entities increases in the simulation. The dilemma that occurs here is that at some point of time during the simulation, entities at various layers might require to get into a common variable. This is not doable as the entities exist in various layers. Such a situation can be overcome by announcing the variable as global ones.

GloMoSim maintains three kinds of routing algorithms: Ad hoc On-Demand Distance Vector Routing Algorithm (AODV), Fisheye State Routing protocol (FSR), and Wireless Routing Protocol (WRP). In addition to the protocols present in GloMoSim, it also offers the capability of adding new protocols to the library. The graphical setting requires the Java environment to be installed on the system. Figure 12.17 shows an interface of GloMoSim in a metropolitan ad hoc network simulation [40].

**QualNet Developer Simulation Package.** QualNet is a simulation software package that was initially developed as a command line simulation tool, but afterward it was improved using a graphical user interface. QualNet is basically developed using the main aspects of GloMoSim. The graphical user interface in QualNet is built using Java programming language. Every network-related protocol has been coded using the C programming language. Program design in QualNet follows a modular oriented style [34]. QualNet is primarily used for discrete-event modeling. QualNet can be applied to simulate all kinds of networks including Metropolitan and Hoc Network Simulation MANET, fixed, and wireless networks, which include cellular wireless networks, data wireless networks, and satellite networks. The key benefits in using the QualNet developer are: (a) modularity of the program design, (b) flexibility in terms of scalability, (c) support of the automatic creation of objects using rapid prototyping, (d) availability of graphical user interface for modeling the

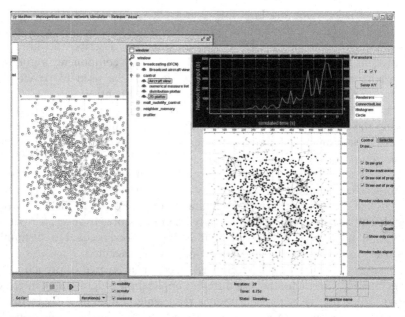

**FIGURE 12.17.** Interface of GloMoSim showing Metropolitan Ad hoc Network simulation.

protocols, and (e) the ability to measure the performance characteristics of the protocol at each layer. Figure 12.18 illustrates a QualNet interface showing the connection of nodes using TCP [34].

The structure of QualNet pursues a layered approach that is similar to that of physical networks. Layers used in QualNet are the application layer, transport layer, network Layer, Internet Protocol (IP) layer, Medium Access Control (MAC) layer, and physical Layer. The layers communicate with each other using messages that are encoded in the structure of packets. The QualNet simulation package consists of several tools and components that aid the modeler to simulate and analyze the model powerfully, see Figure 12.19.

The main components of QualNet are QualNet animator, QualNet designer, QualNet analyzer, and QualNet tracer. The animator is the means that aids the analyst to set up the experimental and picture the running of the simulation visually. QualNet designer is used to model the protocols where the prototyping is founded on the finite-state machine (FSM) paradigm. The analyzer is used for gathering the statistical data when the simulation is on the run and the statistical information is depicted graphically. The QualNet tracer is employed to display the execution trace at the packet level. Models can be built either by using the command line interface or by using the graphical user interface [34]. When designing using command line, we can use the config text files. If the model is built using the graphical user interface then we may use the animator. After executing the simulation program, statistical data can be collected. The

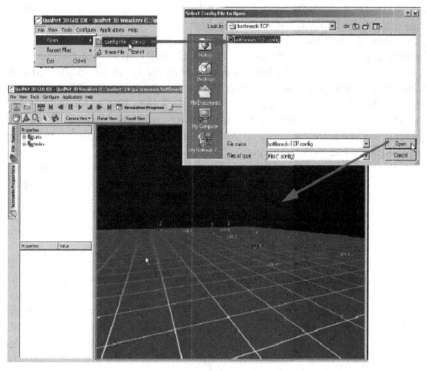

**FIGURE 12.18.** A QualNet interface showing the linking of nodes using TCP.

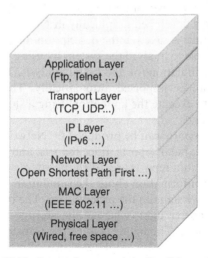

**FIGURE 12.19.** Layered approach in QualNet architecture.

packet traces of the network model can be taken from the trace file, and the trace dump can be found at trace.dmp files.

**Network II.5 Simulation Package.** Network II.5 is an object-oriented simulation package that is based on the SIMSCRIPT II.5 simulation language. It is supported by CACI. Network II.5 consists of three major hardware elements and four software elements. These hardware and software elements are considered the data structures of the package. The hardware elements consist of the storage device, transfer device, and the processing element, whereas the software elements consist of instructions, messages, semaphores, and modules. The processing elements in Network II.5 can carry out one or more instructions and can dispatch many messages over transfer devices to storage devices and other processing elements. The transfer device element in Network II.5 can run several protocols such as ALOHA, Token ring, and Ethernet. A set of instructions that can execute one or more processing elements is called as a module. Messages in Network II.5 have a specific name and a predetermined length [35].

The main functions of Network II.5 are system definition, simulating the system, and analyzing the system functions. The form-based interface and graphical layout of the hardware elements define the piece features and manage the system definition. The graphical user interface is employed for building the simulation model. Fundamentally, no programming is needed when using Network II.5. Thus, a lot of time is saved when using it to simulate a network or a computer system. The simulation and the event traces are produced when the simulation is run [35].

Network II.5 offers several tools for investigating the simulation outcomes. Animation is considered a major tools. The animation interface can aid in seeing the working simulation model. The package can plot graphs based on the information collected during the simulation run. Such graphs are useful for the analysis of the network performance [35].

The structure that is developed graphically in Network II.5 using the form-based graphical interface is saved in the description data file in textual format. In addition to being able to analyze the system by using traces, we also can use the snapshots of the simulation for additional analysis. The topology information of a network can be imported automatically. The animation interface permits the modeler to execute the animation using a step by step manner or a run continuously manner.

Different kinds of reports can be produced by Network II.5, which include, the graphical reports, tabular reports, trace reports, and snapshot reports. The trace reports, and snapshot reports are called the interactive reports. Moreover, the trace report offers information about the simulation trace step by step. The processing element block handles the process data. The transfer device building block handles the transfer data, whereas the storage device building block processes the stored data. The major task of the transfer device is to link the processing elements and the storage devices. Every storage device (memory) that is described in Network II.5 has a limited size that is given in bits. If an

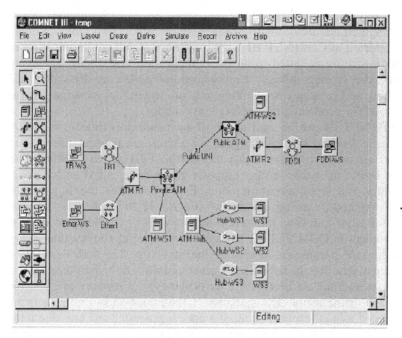

**FIGURE 12.20.** Interface in COMNET III showing the ATM topology.

action occurs, such as reading a file, then the instruction confirms the availability of the file on the memory/storage device. If we have a write operation, then it checks whether there is enough space to perform the requested operation. A storage device can function as a multiported memory; therefore, a single storage device can be used to provide service to multiple processing elements [35].

**COMNET III Simulation Package.** COMNET III is a simulation package supported by CACI and is meant to be used for the performance analysis and evaluation of communication networks. It is developed using the object-oriented approach. The analyst does not need to do any kind of programming; rather, he needs to use the elements and libraries to simulate a given communication network. The modeler can adjust the components by programming them using an object-oriented language environment called MODSIM II. The latter is a popular object-oriented simulation language supported also by CACI. In addition to the standard objects that exist in the library the analyst can describe his own objects in the library [39]. An incorporated graphical environment is offered by COMNET III that is used for generating, executing, and analyzing the model of the communication network under study. Moreover, the analyst can communicate with the model during the execution.

Aside from simulating the computer communication networks, COMNET III can also be used to simulate application scheduling and storage resources scheduling. Subnetworks are described hierarchically in a COMNET III model.

Nodes and links are employed to characterize the network topology. These can be configured hierarchically to produce subnetworks. Two kinds of nodes can be supported in COMNET III: application nodes and communication nodes. Applications are executed using these application nodes [39]. They can also include the storage devices. Communication nodes are basically used for switching and routing when linking to a subnetwork. A message generator is employed for producing the messages at a node.

COMNET III can be used to model a synchronous transfer mode (ATM) systems and networks. It is designed for discrete-event simulations. The communication nodes in object library of COMNET III can be classified into four node objects: the router node, computer group node, ATM switch node, and computer and communication node. Every node has the functionality of producing and receiving the traffic. Figure 12.20 depicts an interface in COMNET III showing the ATM topology [39]. The integrated graphical environment in COMNET III has a simulation set of choices that is used for providing the parameters to execute the simulator. The nodes and links that are used to describe the network are generated with the help of the create menu. The node and link attributes for a particular type of network are described by using the define menu. The statistics of the nodes, links or the network are introduced using the report menu. If a node is generated and any characteristics for the node are not given then the default values are assigned to the node using the archive menu. The Integrated Development Environment (IDE) of COMNET III offers a different kind of reports such as node reports, link reports, application reports, message and response reports, session reports, transport and command reports [39].

The analyst needs to verify the model by executing the verify command before running the simulation model. Then the parameters for running the simulation program are set by using run parameters from simulate menu. In order to see the simulation execution, the animate option should be used. This shows the model to work at the packet level. As soon as the parameters are set, we can execute the simulation model by running the start simulation command from the simulate menu. Then, after running the simulation model, the reports are produced in the text file. Such reports may be used for additional analysis of the system under study [39]. In addition to these reports, COMNET III can offer snapshots of the system at various points of time to know the behavior of the system under analysis. When a model is produced in COMNET III, it should be saved for running the simulation as many times as needed under different operating conditions and environments.

**OptSim simulation software.** OptSim is a simulation software package that offers the environment for designing and simulating optical networks. It is basically used for evaluating the performance of optical communication network systems. Optical networks, such as the ones based on Dense Wave Division Multiplexing (DWDM), and Time Domain Multiplexing (OTDM), Optical LANs, and others, can be modeled and simulated uisng OptSim simulation environment [37].

The communication system in OptSim is modeled as a collection of blocks or icons that are linked to each other. A system function is represented with the help of an icon. The flow of data is modeled from one icon to the other as they are hooked up. For instance, if we have two icons representing laser diode and optical fiber, then it means the optical transmission of laser goes into the fiber [37]. The performance of the communication network can be predicted with the ability with which the different types of tools offer. Moreover, OptSim can aid in optimizing the design and operation of the present optical communication network.

The factors for each of the elements can be represented as functions that involve statistical values and the variables. Based on the impact that these values make on the system's performance, these factors or parameters may be optimized in accordance with the on hand design to increase the performance.

Simulation modeling of the optical network can be performed using the graphical user interface offered by the OptSim simulation environment. Models designed using OptSim are usually accurate and can minimize the overall cost when designing complex systems. The outcome of the simulation model is demonstrated on the screens using the OptSim environment. Figure 12.21 gives an example of an OptSim interface.

There are about 400 element/component models that are included in the library of the OptSim. These components are categorically divided. Among these are signal generators, light emitting devices and Lasers, different types of

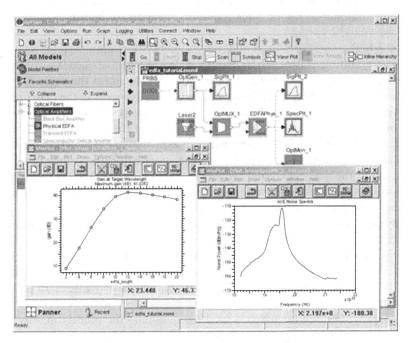

**FIGURE 12.21.** Interface of OptSim.

optical amplifiers, optical fiber, filters, and decision devices. In addition, users can specify their own component models using C++ and can integrate them easily into the simulation framework [36, 37].

The outcomes acquired can be shown in the form of graphs, plots, waveforms, spectrums, scattering diagrams, and polarization plots. The graphical interface is user interactive, and thus the analyst can modify the parameters to change the plot without rerunning the simulation for analysis purpose; see Figure 12.21. The results generated by OptSim can be analyzed using third-party tools. The performance analysis can be conducted at the component level based on the test function and the current factors or parameters provided by the component.

**Queuing Network Analysis Tool (QNAT).** The QNAT is a simulation package that is used for modeling and analyzing queuing networks. It is designed for windows platforms. The calculations required for the model are performed using Mathematica, which is a computational software tool. The computational processes carried on are unseen by the user. The information about the design of the network is advanced to Mathematica with the help of an ASCII file, which is an internal element of the package [42]. It is hard for the graphical user interface when the network is large to forward the information, and hence, the changes can be made directly in the text file in order to inform about the configuration of the network.

The logical organization of QNAT is shown in Figure 12.22. At first, the classification is based on the availability of the nodes, i.e., whether there is finite or infinite number of nodes. Such a feature is important because the methods used for analysis vary a lot.

If the buffer size for all the nodes in the network is infinite, then fork join nodes and multiple classes can be employed. When we have queues with infinite buffer size, then the following parameters are considered for the analysis of the network: (a) availability of different classes of the customers in the network; (b) the type of network that can be nonblocking or the blocking network; (c) if the network is open, closed, or mixed; (d) availability of the nodes in the network; and (e) total number of customers who are available in every closed class.

In addition to these examples, some other information about the availability of servers in the queue, external arrivals for the node, and time for servicing at the node for each class of customers are needed. In case of fork join nodes, the number of sibling queues and synchronizing queues also has to be defined [42].

**Anylogic 5.0.1 Tool.** This simulation tool is used for many strategic applications that are at an operational level, such as logistics, transport systems, and telecommunication networks. It integrates the behaviors of both the discrete and continuous systems. In Anylogic, the design of simulation models is carried out with the help of comprehensive features of Unified Modeling Language (UML).

Java programming language is used for designing the models in Anylogic; hence, it facilitates the execution of the simulation models on any platform [23]. Nevertheless, the package is developed to run only on the windows operating

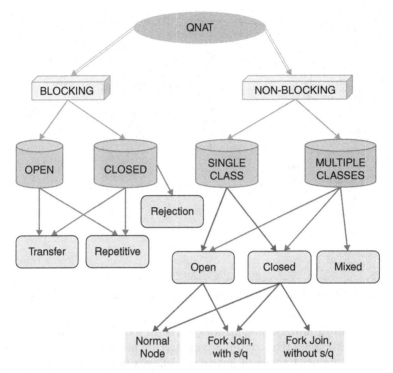

**FIGURE 12.22.** QNAT logical structure.

system environment. Figure 12.23 depicts the interface of the Anylogic simulation model.

Given that the models in Anylogic are designed using Java programming language, the architecture of these models is very much tending to the structure of Java. This indicates that the package library in anylogic maintains attributes such as polymorphism, inheritance, classes, and objects.

The modeling language in Anylogic is centered on the UML Active objects are the basic building blocks in the Anylogic package, as they describe the makeup of entities beside their behavior. Because of the characteristic of inheritance, active objects also encapsulate other objects to a required depth. Active objects use boundary objects to cooperate with the environment.

Discrete modeling employs message passing means for interacting with other objects. Ports are used for transmitting and getting the messages. If an object desires to send a message, then the message is sent out to all the ports. When a message is delivered at the port, it will either be saved in the queue or advanced to the object directly [23]. State charts can be used by Anylogic to define the states, events, and conditions. Anylogic can support static and dynamic timers.

In Anylogic, continuous modeling employs differential equations and algebraic equations, and it also uses the blend of both differential and algebraic

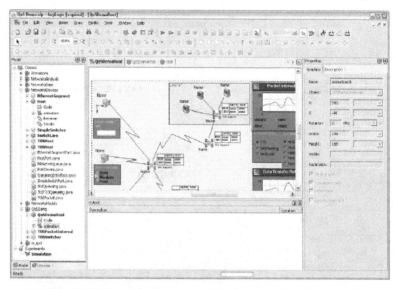

**FIGURE 12.23.** Example interface of the Anylogic simulation package.

equations with variables changing always. As for hybrid modeling in Anylogic, the name itself implies that continuous models are modeled using discrete-event methods. An essential aspect of hybrid modeling is the hybrid state charts that map equations to the events. Anylogic can use only two dimensional (2-D) animations that are performed using Java [23].

**MetroWAND Package.** This simulation software package is used to model communication networks, and it helps the vendors to streamline several function-alities, streamline such as modeling the network and planning for the network services. MetroWAND is mainly used for modeling networks such as Synchronous Optical Networks (SONET), Wave Division Multiplexing (WDM)-based networks, and Synchronous Digital Hierarchy (SDH)-based networks. In such networks, the package can be used for simulating the routing methods, failure scenarios, analyzing the various types of traffic types, and analyzing system performance in terms of throughput, capacity allocation, and system usage [36].

The recent version of MetroWAND available is MetroWAND 3.3. Metro-WAND simulation package has an Extensible Markup Language (XML)-based graphical user interface. It is available in two tool packages known as MetroWAND Ring and MetroWAND Mesh packages. MetroWAND includes an equipment library that is highly valuable when designing network models. This library aids in creating a bill of materials (BOM), which is useful for providing an efficient solution. This aspect helps the library to follow changes that occur when designing a network model. In addition of being able to design the network, it also can find out the cost of building the network and maintenance cost. The Network Management System (NMS) of the Metro-WAND is employed in designing bandwidth capacity allocation [36–37].

The SONET, SDH, and WDM ring networks can be modeled using the MetroWAND Ring tool. Optimization of the number of rings, rings placement, and traffic routing in various ring technologies is facilitated by MetroWAND Ring. It also facilitates interconnection of the single-or-dual ring topologies. Figure 12.24 depicts the main architectural blocks of the package.

MetroWAND tool helps the modeler simply to determine whether there are any links or nodes dead for various settings and configurations of the network [37]. Moreover, it helps in building a mesh network over a ring network. Figure 12.25 depicts an example on an interface of MetroWAND [37].

**NetRule 7.1 Tool.** This network modeling software tool is used for modeling local area networks (LANs) and wide area networks (WANs). The cost and performance of the network is found out before hand by using analytic analysis on the simulation operation [45]. Good accuracy is obtained by using the analytical analysis. In addition to designing new models, existing network topologies may be brought in. We can optimize already existing networks using this tool. The simulation model is run faster when compared with other simulation packages. The NetRule needs a Java environment that supports graphical user interfaces for running the simulation models. NetRule's library specifies protocols and entities that are used for simulating the network model.

The objects in the library are stored in the form of .net (extension) text files. The on-hand library can be changed to satisfy the requirements of the network model to be realized.

When the simulation model is run, the results obtained from the analytical calculations are given in the form of tables. Many tabular formats are supported by the NetRule interface, which can be used to display the tables in the reports. Several parameters are predefined for all of the objects, and the results are gathered only for these predefined parameters. In addition to showing the results in tabular columns, the package also offers the animation features that can be used to observe the flow of entities in the networks. The key drawback is that the parameters for gathering the results are predefined, and

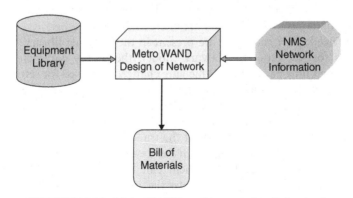

**FIGURE 12.24.** MetroWAND architecture for design tool.

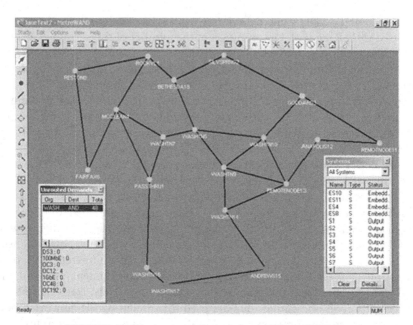

**FIGURE 12.25.** An example interface of MetroWAND.

thus the user cannot specify his parameters for the analysis purpose. Objects that are represented in the network topology can be traversed using the NetRule graphical user interface [45].

The package can be used to compare the performance of various network configurations under different scenarios. Instead of removing or adding the entities used in the model, the package enables the entity if it is required in the network topology or disables it if not required. The major benefits of simulating the network model using this package is that the execution of the model is fast, as mathematical calculations are used for determining the simulation performance. Subnet objects are employed for hierarchical modeling in NetRule. A subnet can be thought of as a set of nodes that are interconnected together.

Objects needed for modeling are present in the NetRule library. To match the objects for the required network model, the object parameters can be modified. Most time parameters, which are changed, are used for setting out the metrics at lower layers such as the physical or data link layer. The Transport layer is the highest layer that can be configured by altering the parameters [45]. Moreover, the library includes the modules that support the queuing and flow control means for diverse protocols at the transport layer. Because NetRule is based on the object-oriented approach for developing the simulation models, the modules used for developing them can be reused. In addition to the standard library, the package also allows the analyst to specify his on her own user libraries. Animation results can be displayed only at the network level and not at the node level. In addition to displaying the results in tabular format, they can also be shown as diagrams and plots [45].

## 12.6 COMPARING SIMULATION TOOLS AND LANGUAGES

The most essential decision to be made when developing a simulation model is selecting the simulation tool whether it is a general purpose programming language, a simulation language, or a simulation package. The flexibility of the software and its easiness of use determine in a way the degree of flawlessness of the model.

Simulation languages are usually optimized for the simulation task. These can be object-oriented or structured-based simulation languages. Examples include MODIM III, SIMSCRIPT III, JavaSim, GPSS, and SLAM II. The main advantages of using simulation languages when coding the simulation program are summarized below:

1. Simulation languages decrease the amount of programming time.
2. They have basic building blocks that are akin to Simulation.
3. They have better error detection.
4. They are flexible.
5. Some simulation languages provide dynamic storage allocation during execution, which is a nice feature that helps to avoid running out of memory when running the simulation program.

Simulation languages in general have built-in mechanisms/functions that help to shorten the development time of the simulation program. The major ones are: (a) generation of random variates, (b) managing simulation time, (c) handling routines to simulate event executions, (d) managing queues, (e) data collection, (f) data analysis, and (g) formulating output results.

On the negative side, simulation languages have some disadvantages. The major drawbacks of simulation languages are: (a) the modeler needs to learn a special language, (b) the user will find himself using an unusual compiler, (c) there might be a portability problem, and (d) simulation languages, in general, have some processing inefficiencies. Simulation languages differ from each other in various aspects. Among these include: (a) initialization requirements, (b) time management, (c) mode and nature of data entry, (d) methods for random number and variate generation, (e) base code language, (f) data collection and analysis methods, (g) output format, (h) ease to learn and use, and (i) proper documentation and technical support [1–40].

When evaluation one simulation language against another, we look basically at the following aspects:

1. Flexibility: Degree of supporting various concepts.
2. Portability: Availability of language/compiler.

3. Debugging capabilities.
4. Ease of learning.
5. Run-time consideration: The interest here is the run time and computational speed.
6. Programming facilities: Ease of programming, availability of simulation constructs, dynamic storage management, standard report facilities, and compiling requirements.

General-purpose programming languages do not offer any capability directly optimized for simulation purposes. This means that the modeler has to program all details of the event scheduling, time advance scheme, statistics collecting capability, generation of random variates from the required distributions, and report generation procedure. The good thing about general-purpose programming languages in this context is that they are more flexible than simulation languages or simulation packages. However, for large models, the models become complex and difficult to debug. Also, such complex models are slow when they are run unless a carefully organized approach and efficient list processing techniques are used [1–4].

Currently, numerous simulation packages are designed to model and simulate computer systems and networks. Some are less expensive than the others, although you can find free good simulation packages such as NS 2. Some package are generic and can be used for not only modeling and simulation of computer systems and/or networks, whereas others are optimized for simulation of only computer systems or computer networks and telecommunication systems. Of course, you will find some of these packages powerful and flexible, while the others are basic and inflexible. In general, simulation packages are excellent solutions for teaching purposes, but for advanced research they may not flexible enough [1–20].

## 12.7   CASE STUDIES ON SIMULATION OF COMPUTER AND TELECOMMUNICATION SYSTEMS

In this section, we will present examples of the simulation of computer and telecommunication systems using various tools.

### 12.7.1   Case Study 1: Simulation of an IEEE 802.11 Wireless Networks Using NS 2

In this example, simulation is used to evaluate the performance of wireless LANs under different configurations and operating conditions. In general, wireless networks have high bit-error rate (BER). The major reasons for high BER are atmospheric noise, multi path propagation, and interference.

In wireless networks, signal decay is higher than in wired networks. Thus, diverse transmission results can be detected for different transmission rates because of radio propagation characteristics. Such a propagation environment guides to phenomena including the hidden terminal problem. In this case study, we used NS2, which is simulation a package, to model the wireless LAN under study. NS 2 is basically an extension of Object Tool command language (OTCL); therefore, it looks more like a scripting language that can output some trace files. Nevertheless, a companion component called NAM (for Network Animator) permits the user to have a graphical output.

Here, we present the simulation results of IEEE 802.11 standard/Direct Sequence (DS) with transmission rates of 2, 5 and 11 Mbps. The model used is an optimized model for the IEEE 802.11 MAC scheme. We varied the number of nodes using 2, 5, 10, 15, and 20 nodes in the WLAN system. Traffic is assumed to be generated with large packets of size 150 bytes and the network was simulated for different load conditions ranging from 10% to 100% of the channel capacity. The model allows us to determine the maximum channel capacity of the IEEE 802.11 standard. The obtained results are shown in Figures 12.26-12.28 [1, 8].

As shown in Figures 12.26-12.28, the normalized channel throughput decreases as the number of nodes increases. Basically, this is a general result of the Carrier Sense Multiple Access (CSMA) protocol. As shown in Figure 12.29, we also analyzed the broadcast mode of operation and found that the collision rate is more than 10% for a load larger than 50% of the channel capacity. This low performance for broadcast traffic is a familiar matter in IEEE 802.11 WLAN standard [1].

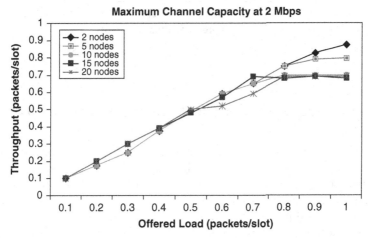

**FIGURE 12.26.** Throughput versus offered load for a 2-Mbps WLAN.

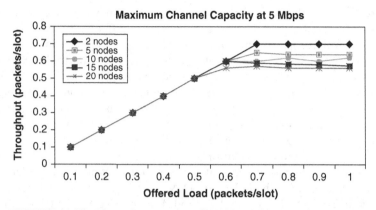

**FIGURE 12.27.** Throughput versus offered load for a 5-Mbps WLAN.

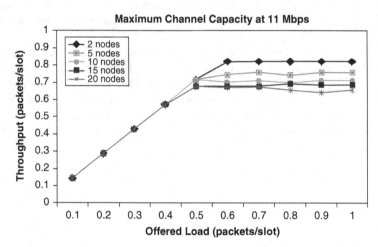

**FIGURE 12.28.** Throughput versus offered load for a 11-Mbps WLAN.

### 12.7.2  Case Study 2: Simulation of Adaptive ABR Voice Over ATM Networks

In this example, we analyze the performance of voice quality when sent over the ABR service in ATM networks using simulation. Sources can adjust the rate at which they send traffic to the network based on the feedback provided by the Resource Management (RM) cells. As the conflict to network resources increases, bandwidth in this case, sources begin reducing the rate at which they send traffic. The effectiveness of the scheme under various scheduling/drop policies and other operating conditions is assessed using simulation analysis. In addition, sensitivity analysis is applied to various key parameters, such as

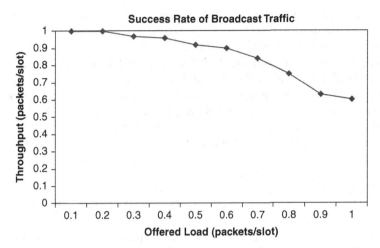

**FIGURE 12.29.** Throughput versus offered load in the broadcast mode of operation with 10 stations.

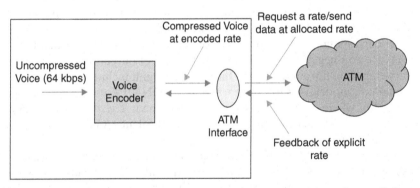

**FIGURE 12.30.** General framework for ABR voice over ATM (an explicit rate environment).

queue size, and average interval length, to investigate their effect on the performance metrics.

Figure 12.30 shows the framework under which we investigated the efficiency of adapting compressed voice sources in a rate-controlled network. Uncompressed voice (64 kbps) is fed to an encoder that decreases the number of bits required to represent the voice signal. We assumed that the encoder can support coding voice to match a target size (in bits).

It is worth noting that the number of bits used to encode voice influences the quality of the compressed voice. The output bit stream from the encoder is inserted into the network. This rate relies on the feedback sent by the explicit-rate ABR congestion-control scheme, in which a source first demands a rate from the network and the network reacts with an allowed rate, based on the contention for the network bandwidth [12, 13].

Voice is transmitted over the ATM Adaptation Layer type 2 (AAL2). The latter is used for bandwidth efficient transmission of low-rate, short, and variable length packets in delay susceptible applications, such as packetized voice and video where a timing relationship is required between the source and the destination [46, 47]. This adaptation layer exploits bandwidth use by multiplexing multiple low-rate connections (logical channels) in a single Virtual Circuit (VC). Because carriers charge is based on the number of open VCs, this multiplexing results in savings in bandwidth and overall costs.

Network switches run the Explicit Rate Indication for Congestion Avoidance (ERICA) Algorithm. The full explanation of the ERICA switch algorithm and the Pseudo-code can be found in Ref. [48], and based on that Pseudo-code, the pertinent parts of the ABR service were realized in the simulations.

Modeling of voice traffic has been studied widely in the literature. Normally, these models characterize speech as a Markov chain with various number of states. The more the number of states in the model, the more complex it is. A Markov chain is a mathematical model that captures the behavior of a closed system. The probabilities of a Markov chain are typically inserted into a transition matrix that represents which state follows which other state. Usually, a Markov chain is characterized by a weighted directed graph in which the weights correspond to the probability of that evolution. This means that the weights are non-negative and that the total weight of outgoing edges is positive. If the weights are normalized, then the overall weight, including self-loops, is 1. The common model used for voice traffic is the ON-OFF model first proposed in Ref. [49], where a two-state sequence is assumed. The two states relate to the talk spurt and silence phases; A Talking, B Silent (ATBS) and A Silent, B Taking (ASBT).

Figure 12.31 depicts the model and an example of its event sequence [12, 46–49]. As shown in Figure 12.32, the activities are special, which means that while A is talking, B is silent, and vice versa. A similar thing applies to the silence state. This means that the model does not consider double talk and mutual silence. Therefore, it does not model two-way conversations exactly. Here, we consider the holding time in the talk state and the silence state time are exponentially distributed with average times of 352 ms and 650 ms, respectively [23].

Figure 12.33 depicts the network model used in our simulation modeling. This model has $N$ ABR sources, which send voice traffic to switch1, where the link capability between the sources and this switch is 64 Kbps. The link between the two switches, Link, has a rate of T1 (1.544 Mbps). It is assumed the source and destination are placed at the east and west coasts of the United States with about 4800 km.

As a cell moves from the source to the destination, it experiences the following delay components:

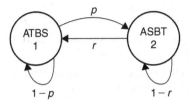

**FIGURE 12.31.** A two-state Markov chain representing ON-OFF voice.

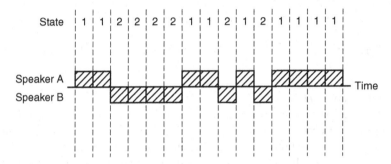

**FIGURE 12.32.** The event sequence in the ON-OFF voice model.

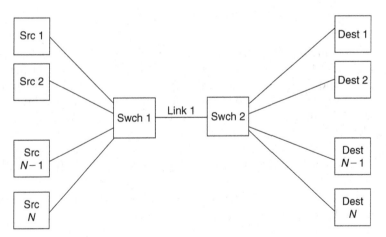

**FIGURE 12.33.** The $N$ ABR source configuration.

1. End-to-End Propagation Delay: The time needed for the cell to go from the source to the destination. This is the electromagnetic delay, and in our simulation model, the end-to-end propagation delay is set to 25 ms.

2. Packetization/Depacketization Delays: This is the time required to fill up an ATM cell payload at the voice encoding rate: 5.5 ms + 5.5 ms = 11 ms (for plain PCM), assuming AAL2 is used. If the voice is compressed, packetization will need more time.

3. Queuing Delay: This is the time cells must to wait in the switch buffer until they get time to be served. It depends on the buffer size, and the existing load.

4. Switching Delay: This is the time needed to set up a path and time needed for propagation through the switch. We neglected in our simulation model.

5. Serialization Delay: The time required to clock out the cell from the output buffer to the link (0.275 ms to clock out at the 1.544 Mbps T1 rate).
   Serialization delay = frame size (bits) / link bandwidth (bps).

Given the above, the total delay is:
Total Delay = $D_{prop} + D_{pack/depack} + D_{queuing} + D_{serialization} + D_{switching}$
In the context of this problem, the target delay is the delay bound beyond which quality is considered underprivileged. In the simulation model, the target delay is 125 ms, assuming echo chancellors are employed. If we allow an average of five switches (see Figure 12.34), the delay deviation introduced by every switch is as follows:

$$\frac{125 - 25 - 5.5 - 5.5}{5} = 12.8 \text{ ms}$$

To support high-quality voice, we consider delay-variation bounds of 10 ms and 20 ms, and thus, we have two types of voice traffic based on the delay variation bound: one that can afford a 35 ms end-to-end delay and an other that can afford 45 ms. This does not include the Packetization delay nor the additional delay incurred by compression. The main assumptions considered in the model are:

1. It is assumed that the switches support only Available Bit Rate (ABR) traffic.

2. Sources can send traffic from the beginning of the simulation until the end, following the two-state Markov model.

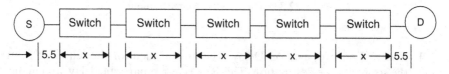

**FIGURE 12.34.** Delay components encountered from the source to the destination.

3. The link data rate is fixed at T1 rate of 1.544 Mbps.
4. Packetization delay is restricted to 5.5 ms, and in case of encoding at a rate less than 64 Kbps, cells are sent partially filled.
5. The per-VC queuing scheme is used.
6. Switching delay is equal to the time taken by the switch fabrics to setup the path plus the propagation time in the switch. We have assumed this is negligible (in other words, if there is no queuing, the throughput is 100% and equal to the link capacity).
7. Service time is assumed to be constant.
8. Since it is assumed the only traffic serviced by the switch is voice, no weighted queuing is necessary [46–50].

The Quality of Service (QoS) metrics that have been considered are as follows:

1. Mean cell transfer delay (CTD), which is a function of the propagation delay, queuing delay, and packetization/depacketization delay.
2. Cell loss ratio (CLR), which is the number of cells lost divided by the total number of transmitted cells.
3. Cell delay variation, (CDV), which is not a major concern here because ATM has a low CDV, and because this can be taken care of by the playout buffer [1–10, 46–50].

In addition, another performance metric that has been introduced by the authors in references [12–13] and called the degradation of voice quality (DVQ), which is defined as:

$$DVQ = \frac{\text{Number of cells lost} + \text{Number of cells above the delay threshold}}{\text{Total number of cells}}.$$

Scheduling is important to guarantee fairness between users; several scheduling policies have been investigated to determine how they affect the overall voice quality without taking into account the fairness of each algorithm or the computational cost: (a) earliest deadline first (EDF), (b) longest queue first (LQF), and (c) round robin (RR).

A drop policy is required so that when a specific threshold is reached, cells can be dropped. The drop policies considered are as follows:

1. Tail-drop: Cells are dropped if there is no buffer to include them in.
2. Selective discard: If a particular threshold is reached, cells from sources that are used more from the buffer are dropped, and hence fairness can be achieved.

The simulation model was implemented using C++. The model includes two classes, a *Switch* class, and a *Node* class. The *Switch* class implements all the functions performed by an ATM switch, namely, receiving cells from sources, scheduling, switching, and running the ERICA congestion avoidance algorithm. The class is driven by the following two events: (a) arrival of a new connection and (b) arrival of a new cell.

The Node class essentially simulates nodes whether sources or destinations. This class simulates all what sources and destinations do such as sending data and forward resource management (FRM) cells, handling arriving backward resource management (BRM) cells, and computing the demand. The class is driven by the next departure time. At the beginning, the module tests if any awaiting BRM cells have arrived before this departure. If yes, it calls the *serve BRM cell* module. Then the algorithm checks whether the cell can be produced within the current talk spurt; if not, then the time for the silence state is determined, and the current time is moved forward by this amount. This means that no cells are produced during this quiet (silence) state.

To determine whether to send a data cell or an FRM cell, the number of cells sent so far is checked to determine whether it is divisible by 32. If yes, then a FRM cell is sent; otherwise, a data cell is sent. The current time is moved forward by the time needed to generate a cell, which depends on the current source rate.

When a BRM cell arrives to the source, it has to adjust its current rate if it is more than what the network can accommodate. The source compares the explicit rate value in the BRM cell with its current rate; if the ER value is less, then; the source has to decrease its rate to that amount and alters the time needed to generate a cell. The simulator was run under various conditions and operating environments.

Figure 12.35 depicts how sources modify their rate as a result of more conflict on the bandwidth. As can be observed, the higher the number of sources, the lower the rate at which sources can send. This can be used by the operator to offer a variety of levels of service based on the customer or application requirements.

Figure 12.36. depicts DVQ for a delay threshold of 35 ms. As shown in Figure 12.35, the higher the number of sources the worse the quality of voice. This can be explained as follows. The higher the number of sources, the higher the traffic load on the system and, hence, the greater the probability of cells being dropped and/or delayed in the switches.

Figure 12.37 shows the consequence of increasing the number of sources on cells lost and cells delayed.

As observed in Figure 12.38, the voice quality has been degraded for different queue sizes. The results can better be construed if we look at Figure 12.39 where the CLR starts to decline as the queue size increases. Furthermore, as the queue size grows up, the number of cells delayed will increase because more cells are delayed rather than go down by the switch. This means that the

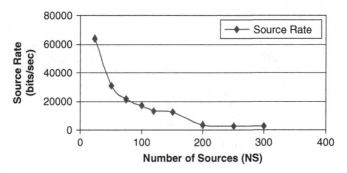

**FIGURE 12.35.** Source rate versus number of sources.

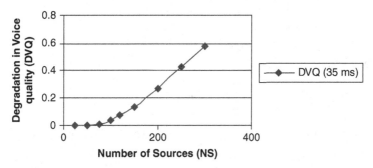

**FIGURE 12.36.** DVQ versus number of sources (35 ms threshold).

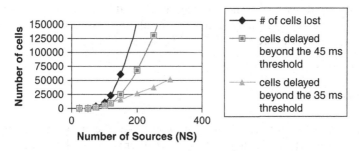

**FIGURE 12.37.** Number of cells lost versus number of sources.

shorter the queue size, the better the quality of service and usage of the bandwidth.

The consequence of drop policies on the voice quality was analyzed, and Figure 12.40 shows this effect. As depicted in Figure 12.40, the buffer size is 200

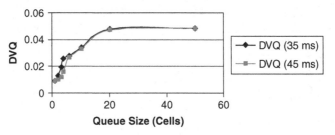

**FIGURE 12.38.** DVQ versus queue size.

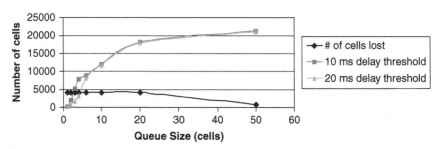

**FIGURE 12.39.** Number of cells lost/delayed versus queue size.

cells, and the threshold is 80% occupancy level. Under low load conditions, both drop policies offer about similar results. While the load grows, selective discard scheme gives better voice quality.

Analytic analysis has been employed to validate the results of simulation. Figure 12.41 depicts the analytic and the simulation results for the source rate. As shown, the results are close.

## 12.8  SUMMARY

Computer and telecommunication system models can be simulated using general-purpose programming languages whether structured or object-oriented languages, simulation languages, or simulation software packages. When developing simulation models using general-programming languages, the modeler will need to exert more efforts and time into the development of the simulation model, thereby increasing the time and efforts of the simulation task. Furthermore, the more the programming, the higher is the probability of the errors in the code. There might be some problems that cannot be modeled easily using traditional general-purpose programming languages, as they lack the necessary features to simulate the model smoothly. Object-oriented

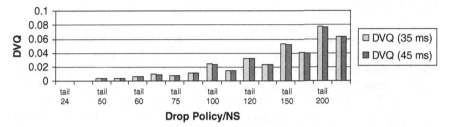

**FIGURE 12.40.** DVQ versus drop policy.

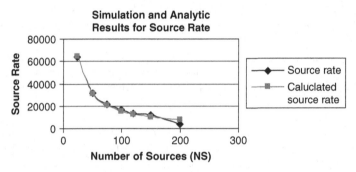

**FIGURE 12.41.** Analytic and simulation results for the average source rate.

languages can overcome the shortfalls of the general languages as they use the object concept. These are helpful in realizing the real-world scenarios. However, still, everything has to be developed from the scratch. Therefore, the cost of development increases. To reduce the programming time, simulation languages are used. These have built-in features that make the simulation task easier. These modules from the library can be reused, and the user can define their own modules to create the simulation model. In this case, the modeler needs to have knowledge of the simulation language. Simulation packages offer a graphical user interface to develop the simulation models. Such models can be executed using the animation interface that demonstrates the execution of the simulation on the run. Statistics are gathered during the execution and reports are produced automatically by the report tool provided by almost all state-of-the-art simulation packages. The only disadvantage associated with the use of simulation packages is that the execution of the simulation takes longer, and most packages are developed for particular applications. In addition, such packages are inflexible. We concluded the chapter by presenting two detailed case studies on the use of modeling and simulation to predict the performance of telecommunication systems: an IEEE 802.11 wireless LAN and adaptive ABR voice over ATM networks.

## REFERENCES

[1] M. S. Obaidat, and G. I. Papadimitriou (Eds.), "Applied System Simulation: Methodologies and Applications," Springer, Norwell, MA, 2003.

[2] G. I. Papadimitriou, B. Sadoun, and C. Papazoglou, *"Fundamentals of Systems Simulation,"* in M. S. Obaidat, and G. I. Papadimitriou, (Eds.), "Applied System Simulation: Methodologies and Applications," Springer, Norwell, MA, 2003.

[3] A. M. Law, "Simulation Modeling & Analysis, 4th Edition," McGraw Hill, New York, pp. 187–213 1999.

[4] R. Jain, "The Art of Computer System Performance Analysis," 2nd edition," Wiley New York, 1991.

[5] J. Banks, J. S. Carson II, and B. L. Nelson, "Discrete Event System Simulation," 4th edition," Pearson Prentice Hall, Upper Soddle River, NJ, 2005.

[6] U. Pooch, and J. Wall, "Discrete Event Simulation," CRC Press, Boca Raton, FL, 1993.

[7] M. S. Obaidat, and N. Boudriga, *"Modeling and Simulation of ATM Systems and Networks*, M. S. Obaidat, and G. I. Papadimitriou," in Applied System Simulation: Methodologies and Applications," Kluwer Academic Publis, Norwell, MA, 2003.

[8] M. S. Obaidat, and D. B. Green, *"Simulation of Wireless Networks,"* in M. S. Obaidat, and G. I. Papadimitriou, (Eds.) "Applied System Simulation: Methodologies and Applications," Kluwer Academic Publishers, Norwell, MA, 2003.

[9] T. J Schriber, "Perspectives on Simulation Using GPSS," Proceedings of 1995 Winter Simulation Conference, pp. 451–456, 1995.

[10] R. C. Crain, J. O. Henriksen, "Simulation Using GPSS/H," Proceedings of 1999 Winter Simulation Conference, pp. 182–187, 1999.

[11] D. K. Pace, *"Verification, Validation, and Accreditation of Simulation Models,"* in M. S. Obaidat, and G. I. Papadimitriou, (Eds.), "Applied System Simulation: Methodologies and Applications," Springer, Norwell, MA, 2003.

[12] M. S. Obaidat, and S. Obeidat, "Modeling and Simulation of Adaptive ABR Voice Over ATM Networks," Simulation: Transactions of the Society for Modeling and Simulation International, Vol. 78, No. 3, pp. 139–149, 2002.

[13] S. Obeidat, and M. S. Obaidat, "Performance Evaluation of Adaptive ABR Voice over ATM Networks," Proceedings of the 2002 International Symposium on Performance of Computer and Telecommunication Systems, pp. 422–429, San Diego, CA, 2002.

[14] D. K. Carter, and A. D. Baker, "Considerations in Developing a Formally Based Visual Programming Language Reference Manual: A Case Study on SLAM II Language," ACM SIGPLAN, Vol. 32, No 6, pp. 34–39, 1997.

[15] M. Otter, and H. Emquivst, "Modelica—Language, Libraries, and Tools Conferences, Modelica Association, pp. 1–12, April 2002.

[16] P. Fritzson, and V. Engelson, "Modelica—A Unified Object-Oriented Language for System Modeling and Simulation, ECCOP-Modelica, pp. 67–90, 1998.

[17] J. Goble, "MODSIM III—A Tutorial," Proceedings of the 1997 Winter Simulation Conference, pp. 601–605, 1997.

[18] S. V. Rice, A. Marjanski, H. Markowitz, and S. M. Bailey, "The SIMSCRIPT III Programming Language for Modular Object-Oriented Simulation," Proceedings of the 2005 Winter Simulation Conference, pp. 621–630, 2005.

[19] J. A. Joines, and S. D. Roberts, "Design of Object Oriented Simulations in C++,"Proceedings of the 1996 Winter Simulation Conference, pp. 65–72, 1996.

[20] http://staff.um.edu.mt/jskl1/talk.html.

[21] http://www.answers.com/topic/simula-1.

[22] D.P. Sanderson, R. Sharma, R. Rozin, and S. Treu, "The Hierarchical Simulation Language HSL: A Versatile Tool for Process-Oriented Simulation," ACM Transactions on Modeling and Computer Simulation, Vol. 1, No 2, pp. 113–153, 1991.

[23] "Agent Based Modeling Tutorial," Available at: http://www.xjtek.com/files/docs/en/AgentBasedModelingTutorial.pdf.

[24] http://web1.rsoftdesign.com/products/network_modeling/Artifex/pdfs/artifex.pdf.

[25] http://www.isi.edu/nsnam/ns/.

[26] S. Chung, and M. Clay Pool, "NS by Example," Available at: http://nile.wpi.edu/NS/.

[27] A. Varga, "The OMNET++ Discrete Event Simulation System," ACM Transactions on Modeling and Computer Simulation, pp. 212–218, 2001.

[28] www.omnetpp.org

[29] http://trace.eas.asu.edu/tools/index.html.

[30] http://poisson.ecse.rpi.edu/~hema/qnat/.

[31] "Viptos—Visual interface Between Ptolemy and Tiny OS," Available at: http://ptolemy.eecs.berkeley.edu/viptos/.

[32] X. Chang, "Network Simulations with OPNET," Proceedings of the 1999 Winter Simulation Conference, pp. 307–314, 1999.

[33] jimjansen.tripod.com/.../colis99/colis99.html

[34] http://www.tel.unomaha.edu

[35] http://www.caciasl.com/pdf/N25.pdf

[36] http://www.rsoftdesign.com

[37] "Opt Slim Provides Physical Layer Design Br FTTH/FTTP Access Networks" Available at: http://www.rsoftdesign.co.jp/pdfs/rsoft_review_vol4_no1.pdf.

[38] http://www.etse.urv.es/DEI/informacio/simuladors/comnet/ATM.pdf

[39] J. Jones, "COMNET III: Object Oriented Network Performance Prediction," Proceedings of 1995 Winter Simulation Conference, pp. 545–547, 1995.

[40] "Glomosim A Library for parake Simulation of Large Scale Wireless Networks" Available at: http://www.scalable-networks.com/pdf/glomosim.pdf

[41] W. D. Kelton, R. P. Sadowski, and D. T. Sturrock, "Simulation with Arena," 3rd Edition," McGraw-Hill, New York, 2003.

[42] H. Kaur, D. Manjunath, and S. K. Bose, "The Queuing Network Analysis Tool," Proceedings of the 8th International Symposium on Modeling and Simulation of Computer and Telecommunication Systems, pp. 162–167, 2000.

[43] D. Xu, G. F. Riley, M. Ammar, and R. Fujimoto, "Split Protocol Stack Network Simulations Using the Dynamic Simulation Backplane," Proceedings of the 9th International Symposium on Modeling, Analysis and Simulation of Computer and Telecommunication Systems, pp. 325–332, 2001.

[44] X. Chang, "Network Simulations with OPNET," Proceedings of the 1999 Winter Simulation Conference, pp. 307–314, 1999.

[45] http://www.analyticalengines.com/

[46] M. McLoughlin, J. O'Neil, "Adapting Voice For ATM Networks An AAL2 Tutorial," General DataComm Available at: http://www.gdc.com/, 1997.

[47] U. Black, "ATM: Foundation for Broadband Networks," Volume 1, 2nd Edition Prentice Hall Upper Saddle River, NJ, 1999.

[48] R. Jain, S. Kalyanaraman, R. Goyal, S. Fahmy, and R. Viswanathan, "ERICA Switch Algorithm: A Complete Description," ATM Forum/96-1172, 1996.

[49] P. T. Brady, "A Model for Generating ON-OFF Speech Patterns in Two-Way Conversations," Bell System Technology Journal, Vol. 48, pp 2445–2472, 1969.

[50] S. Deng, "Traffic Characteristics of Packet Voice," IEEE International Conference on Communications, Vol. 3, pp. 1369–1374, 1995.

## EXERCISES

1. What are the main drawbacks of simulation packages?

2. Give examples of open-source simulation packages that are optimized for modeling and simulation of network and telecommunication systems and compare them.

3. Compare and contract object-oriented simulation languages and structured simulation languages. Give examples.

4. State the main differences between general-purpose programming languages and simulation languages. Explain when each category is used in simulation.

5. Consider a time-shared computer system that contains a single central processing unit/processor and $n$ terminals; see Figure 12.42 below. The user of each terminal "thinks" for a quantity of time that is exponentially distributed with a mean of 15 S and then sends a job to CPU with a service time that is exponentially distributed with a mean of 0.50 second. Jobs arrive in a single queue in front of the Central Processing Unit (CPU), however, they are served in a round robin rather than in a FIFO fashion. In other words, the CPU allocates to each job a maximum quantum of length $q = 0.2$ second (s). If the (remaining) service time of a job, $s$, is less than or equal to $q$, then the CPU spends time $s$ plus a fixed overhead $\tau = 0.01$ s processing the job, and the job returns to the terminal. If $s$ is greater than $q$, then the CPU spends time $q$ plus $\tau$ processing the job, the job joins the end of the queue, and its outstanding service time $s$ decremented by $q$ seconds. This method is recurred until the job's service is finally completed, at which point the job goes back to its terminal and another think time starts. The round robin scheduling scheme permits the computer to process jobs with a small service faster than jobs with a large service time without knowing the service time of each job in advance.

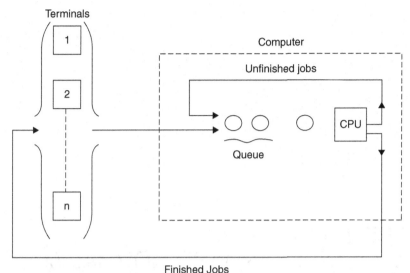

Terminals

Computer

Unfinished jobs

Queue

CPU

Finished Jobs

**FIGURE 12.42.** The time-shared computer system of problem 5.

Define the response time of a job to be the time spent between the instances the job departs its terminal and the instance that it is finished being processed at the CPU. For each of these cases $n = 30, 35 \ldots 100$, where $n$ is the number of terminals, simulate the system for 1000, 5000, 10,000, and 15,000 job completions and collect statistics on the mean and maximum response time, the time-average number of jobs waiting in the queue, and the usage of the CPU. It is required to find out how many terminals are needed on the system and still can provide users with a mean response time of 25.

a. Write the required program using a general-purpose programming language, run simulation experiments and show all your work.

b. Repeat (a) using a simulation language.

c. Comment on the efforts and results in parts (a) and (b).

6. Simulate an 802.3 Ethernet LAN system using the language or package you prefer. Assume that the interarrival times of frames follow the exponential distribution. Vary the number of nodes in the network from 0 to 100 in steps of 10. Plot the throughput versus the number of nodes in the system. Also, plot the average frame delay versus the number of nodes. Then, plot the latency and throughput relation for different number of nodes. Show all your assumptions and results.

# APPENDIX A
# TABLE OF STANDARD NORMAL (Z) DISTRIBUTION

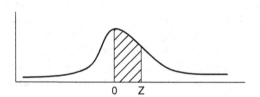

| Z | 0 | 0.01 | 0.02 | 0.03 | 0.04 | 0.05 | 0.06 | 0.07 | 0.08 | 0.09 |
|---|---|------|------|------|------|------|------|------|------|------|
| 0 | 0 | 0.004 | 0.008 | 0.012 | 0.016 | 0.0199 | 0.0239 | 0.0279 | 0.0319 | 0.0359 |
| 0.1 | 0.0398 | 0.0438 | 0.0478 | 0.0517 | 0.0557 | 0.0596 | 0.0636 | 0.0675 | 0.0714 | 0.0753 |
| 0.2 | 0.0793 | 0.0832 | 0.0871 | 0.0910 | 0.0948 | 0.0987 | 0.1026 | 0.1064 | 0.1103 | 0.1141 |
| 0.3 | 0.1179 | 0.1217 | 0.1255 | 0.1293 | 0.1331 | 0.1368 | 0.1406 | 0.1443 | 0.1480 | 0.1517 |
| 0.4 | 0.1554 | 0.1591 | 0.1628 | 0.1664 | 0.1700 | 0.1736 | 0.1772 | 0.1808 | 0.1844 | 0.1879 |
| 0.5 | 0.1915 | 0.1950 | 0.1985 | 0.2019 | 0.2054 | 0.2088 | 0.2123 | 0.2157 | 0.2190 | 0.2224 |
| 0.6 | 0.2257 | 0.2291 | 0.2324 | 0.2357 | 0.2389 | 0.2422 | 0.2454 | 0.2486 | 0.2517 | 0.2549 |
| 0.7 | 0.2580 | 0.2611 | 0.2642 | 0.2673 | 0.2704 | 0.2734 | 0.2764 | 0.2794 | 0.2823 | 0.2852 |

*(Continued)*

*Fundamentals of Performance Evaluation of Computer and Telecommunication Systems,*
By Mohammad S. Obaidat and Noureddine A. Boudriga
Copyright © 2010 John Wiley & Sons, Inc.

| Z | 0 | 0.01 | 0.02 | 0.03 | 0.04 | 0.05 | 0.06 | 0.07 | 0.08 | 0.09 |
|-----|--------|--------|--------|--------|--------|--------|--------|--------|--------|--------|
| **0.8** | 0.2881 | 0.2910 | 0.2939 | 0.2967 | 0.2995 | 0.3023 | 0.3051 | 0.3078 | 0.3106 | 0.3133 |
| **0.9** | 0.3159 | 0.3186 | 0.3212 | 0.3238 | 0.3264 | 0.3289 | 0.3315 | 0.3340 | 0.3365 | 0.3389 |
| **1** | 0.3413 | 0.3438 | 0.3461 | 0.3485 | 0.3508 | 0.3531 | 0.3554 | 0.3577 | 0.3599 | 0.3621 |
| **1.1** | 0.3643 | 0.3665 | 0.3686 | 0.3708 | 0.3729 | 0.3749 | 0.3770 | 0.3790 | 0.3810 | 0.3830 |
| **1.2** | 0.3849 | 0.3869 | 0.3888 | 0.3907 | 0.3925 | 0.3944 | 0.3962 | 0.3980 | 0.3997 | 0.4015 |
| **1.3** | 0.4032 | 0.4049 | 0.4066 | 0.4082 | 0.4099 | 0.4115 | 0.4131 | 0.4147 | 0.4162 | 0.4177 |
| **1.4** | 0.4192 | 0.4207 | 0.4222 | 0.4236 | 0.4251 | 0.4265 | 0.4279 | 0.4292 | 0.4306 | 0.4319 |
| **1.5** | 0.4332 | 0.4345 | 0.4357 | 0.4370 | 0.4382 | 0.4394 | 0.4406 | 0.4418 | 0.4429 | 0.4441 |
| **1.6** | 0.4452 | 0.4463 | 0.4474 | 0.4484 | 0.4495 | 0.4505 | 0.4515 | 0.4525 | 0.4535 | 0.4545 |
| **1.7** | 0.4554 | 0.4564 | 0.4573 | 0.4582 | 0.4591 | 0.4599 | 0.4608 | 0.4616 | 0.4625 | 0.4633 |
| **1.8** | 0.4641 | 0.4649 | 0.4656 | 0.4664 | 0.4671 | 0.4678 | 0.4686 | 0.4693 | 0.4699 | 0.4706 |
| **1.9** | 0.4713 | 0.4719 | 0.4726 | 0.4732 | 0.4738 | 0.4744 | 0.475 | 0.4756 | 0.4761 | 0.4767 |
| **2** | 0.4772 | 0.4778 | 0.4783 | 0.4788 | 0.4793 | 0.4798 | 0.4803 | 0.4808 | 0.4812 | 0.4817 |
| **2.1** | 0.4821 | 0.4826 | 0.4830 | 0.4834 | 0.4838 | 0.4842 | 0.4846 | 0.4850 | 0.4854 | 0.4857 |
| **2.2** | 0.4861 | 0.4864 | 0.4868 | 0.4871 | 0.4875 | 0.4878 | 0.4881 | 0.4884 | 0.4887 | 0.4890 |
| **2.3** | 0.4893 | 0.4896 | 0.4898 | 0.4901 | 0.4904 | 0.4906 | 0.4909 | 0.4911 | 0.4913 | 0.4916 |
| **2.4** | 0.4918 | 0.4920 | 0.4922 | 0.4925 | 0.4927 | 0.4929 | 0.4931 | 0.4932 | 0.4934 | 0.4936 |
| **2.5** | 0.4938 | 0.4940 | 0.4941 | 0.4943 | 0.4945 | 0.4946 | 0.4948 | 0.4949 | 0.4951 | 0.4952 |
| **2.6** | 0.4953 | 0.4955 | 0.4956 | 0.4957 | 0.4959 | 0.4960 | 0.4961 | 0.4962 | 0.4963 | 0.4964 |
| **2.7** | 0.4965 | 0.4966 | 0.4967 | 0.4968 | 0.4969 | 0.4970 | 0.4971 | 0.4972 | 0.4973 | 0.4974 |
| **2.8** | 0.4974 | 0.4975 | 0.4976 | 0.4977 | 0.4977 | 0.4978 | 0.4979 | 0.4979 | 0.4980 | 0.4981 |
| **2.9** | 0.4981 | 0.4982 | 0.4982 | 0.4983 | 0.4984 | 0.4984 | 0.4985 | 0.4985 | 0.4986 | 0.4986 |
| **3** | 0.4987 | 0.4987 | 0.4987 | 0.4988 | 0.4988 | 0.4989 | 0.4989 | 0.4989 | 0.4990 | 0.4990 |

# APPENDIX B
# COMMONLY USED NORMAL QUANTILES

The list contains the commonly used normal quantiles. The confidence levels shown in the first column are for the two-sided confidence intervals. For instance, for a two-sided confidence interval at 90%, $\alpha = 0.1$, $\alpha/2 = 0.05$ and $Z_{0.95} = 1.645$.

| Confidence Level (%) | $\alpha$ | $\alpha/2$ | $Z_{1-\alpha/2}$ |
|---|---|---|---|
| 20 | 0.8 | 0.4 | 0.253 |
| 40 | 0.6 | 0.3 | 0.524 |
| 60 | 0.4 | 0.2 | 0.842 |
| 68.26 | 0.3174 | 0.1587 | 1.000 |
| 80 | 0.2 | 0.1 | 1.282 |
| 90 | 0.1 | 0.05 | 1.645 |
| 95 | 0.05 | 0.025 | 1.960 |
| 95.46 | 0.0454 | 0.0228 | 2.000 |
| 98.0 | 0.02 | 0.01 | 2.326 |
| 99 | 0.01 | 0.005 | 2.576 |
| 99.74 | 0.0026 | 0.0013 | 3.000 |
| 99.8 | 0.002 | 0.001 | 3.090 |
| 99.9 | 0.001 | 0.0005 | 3.29 |
| 99.98 | 0.0002 | 0.0001 | 3.72 |

*Fundamentals of Performance Evaluation of Computer and Telecommunication Systems,*
By Mohammad S. Obaidat and Noureddine A. Boudriga
Copyright © 2010 John Wiley & Sons, Inc.

# APPENDIX C
# QUANTILES OF UNIT NORMAL DISTRIBUTION

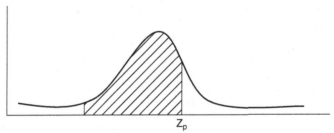

$Z_p$

The table records $Z_p$ for a given p. For instance, for a two-sided confidence interval at 95%, $\alpha = 0.04$ and $p = 1 - \alpha/2 = 0.98$. The entry in the row labeled 0.98 and column labeled 0.000 provides $Z_p = 2.054$.

| p | 0.00 | 0.01 | 0.02 | 0.03 | 0.04 | 0.05 | 0.06 | 0.07 | 0.08 | 0.09 |
|---|------|------|------|------|------|------|------|------|------|------|
| 0.5 | 0.000 | 0.025 | 0.050 | 0.075 | 0.100 | 0.126 | 0.151 | 0.176 | 0.202 | 0.228 |
| 0.6 | 0.253 | 0.279 | 0.305 | 0.332 | 0.358 | 0.385 | 0.412 | 0.440 | 0.468 | 0.496 |
| 0.7 | 0.524 | 0.553 | 0.583 | 0.613 | 0.643 | 0.674 | 0.706 | 0.739 | 0.772 | 0.806 |
| 0.8 | 0.842 | 0.878 | 0.915 | 0.954 | 0.994 | 1.036 | 1.080 | 1.126 | 1.175 | 1.227 |

*(Continued)*

*Fundamentals of Performance Evaluation of Computer and Telecommunication Systems,*
By Mohammad S. Obaidat and Noureddine A. Boudriga
Copyright © 2010 John Wiley & Sons, Inc.

| p | 0.000 | 0.001 | 0.002 | 0.003 | 0.004 | 0.005 | 0.006 | 0.007 | 0.008 | 0.009 |
|---|-------|-------|-------|-------|-------|-------|-------|-------|-------|-------|
| 0.90 | 1.282 | 1.287 | 1.293 | 1.299 | 1.305 | 1.311 | 1.317 | 1.323 | 1.329 | 1.335 |
| 0.91 | 1.341 | 1.347 | 1353 | 1.359 | *0.366* | 1.372 | 1.379 | 1.385 | 1.392 | 1.398 |
| 0.92 | 1.405 | 1.412 | 1.419 | 1.426 | 1.433 | 1.440 | 1.447 | 1.454 | 1.461 | 1.468 |
| 0.93 | 1.476 | 1.483 | 1.491 | 1.499 | 1.506 | 1.514 | 1.522 | 1.530 | 1.538 | 1.546 |
| 0.94 | *1.555* | 1.563 | 1.572 | 1.580 | 1.589 | *1.598* | 1.607 | 1616 | 1.626 | 1.635 |
| 0.95 | 1.645 | 1.655 | 1.665 | 1.675 | 1.685 | 1.695 | 1.706 | 1.717 | 1.728 | 1.739 |
| 0.96 | 1.751 | 1.762 | 1.774 | 1.787 | 1.799 | 1.812 | 1.825 | 1.838 | 1.852 | 1.866 |
| 0.97 | 1.881 | 1.896 | 1.911 | 1.927 | 1.943 | *1.960* | 1.977 | *1.995* | 2.014 | 2.034 |
| 0.98 | 2.054 | 2.075 | 2.097 | 2.210 | 2.144 | 2.170 | 2.197 | 2.226 | 2.257 | 2.290 |

| p | 0.000 | 0.001 | 0.002 | 0.003 | 0.004 | 0.005 | 0.006 | 0.007 | 0.008 | 0.009 |
|---|-------|-------|-------|-------|-------|-------|-------|-------|-------|-------|
| *0.990* | 2.326 | 2.330 | 2.334 | 2.338 | 2.342 | 2.346 | 2.349 | 2.353 | 2.357 | 2.362 |
| 0.991 | 2.366 | 2.370 | 2.374 | 2.378 | 2.382 | 2.387 | 2.391 | *2.395* | 2.400 | 2.404 |
| *0.992* | 2.409 | 2.414 | 2.418 | 2.423 | 2.428 | 2.432 | 2.437 | 2.442 | 2.447 | 2.452 |
| 0.993 | 2.457 | 2.462 | 2.468 | 2.473 | 2.478 | 2.484 | 2.489 | 2.495 | 2.501 | 2.506 |
| 0.994 | 2.512 | 2.518 | 2.524 | 2.530 | 2.536 | 2.543 | 2.549 | 2.556 | 2.562 | 2.569 |
| 0.995 | 2.576 | 2.583 | 2.590 | 2.597 | 2.605 | 2.612 | 2.620 | 2.628 | 2.636 | 2.644 |
| 0.996 | *2.652* | 2.661 | 2.669 | 2.678 | 2.687 | 2.697 | 2.706 | 2.716 | 2.727 | 2.737 |
| 0.997 | 2.748 | *2.759* | 2.770 | 2.782 | 2.794 | 2.807 | 2.82 | 2.834 | 2.848 | 2.863 |
| 0.998 | 2.878 | 2.894 | 2.911 | 2.929 | 2.948 | 2.968 | 2.989 | 3.011 | 3.036 | 3.062 |
| *0.999* | 3.090 | 3.121 | 3.156 | 3.195 | 3.239 | 3.291 | 3.353 | 3.432 | 3.540 | 3.719 |

# APPENDIX D
# QUANTILES OF STUDENT'S T-DISTRIBUTION WITH $V$ DEGREES OF FREEDOM

$t_{v,\alpha}$ where $P(Z \leq t_{v,\alpha}) = \alpha$ for a random variable $Z \sim t(v)$

| $v$ | 0.9000 | 0.9500 | 0.9750 | 0.9900 | 0.9950 | 0.9990 | 0.9995 |
|---|---|---|---|---|---|---|---|
| 1 | 3.078 | 6.314 | 12.706 | 31.821 | 63.657 | 318.31 | 636.619 |
| 2 | 1.886 | 2.920 | 4.303 | 6.965 | 9.925 | 22.326 | 31.599 |
| 3 | 1.638 | 2.353 | 3.182 | 4.541 | 5.841 | 10.213 | 12.924 |
| 4 | 1.533 | 2.132 | 2.776 | 3.747 | 4.604 | 7.173 | 8.610 |
| 5 | 1.476 | 2.015 | 2.571 | 3.365 | 4.032 | 5.893 | 6.869 |
| 6 | 1.440 | 1.943 | 2.447 | 3.143 | 3.707 | 5.208 | 5.959 |
| 7 | 1.415 | 1.895 | 2.365 | 2.998 | 3.499 | 4.785 | 5.408 |
| 8 | 1.397 | 1.860 | 2.306 | 2.896 | 3.355 | 4.501 | 5.041 |
| 9 | 1.383 | 1.833 | 2.262 | 2.821 | 3.250 | 4.297 | 4.781 |
| 10 | 1.372 | 1.812 | 2.228 | 2.764 | 3.169 | 4.144 | 4.587 |
| 11 | 1.363 | 1.796 | 2.201 | 2.718 | 3.106 | 4.925 | 4.437 |
| 12 | 1.356 | 1.782 | 2.179 | 2.681 | 3.055 | 3.930 | 4.318 |

(*Continued*)

*Fundamentals of Performance Evaluation of Computer and Telecommunication Systems,*
By Mohammad S. Obaidat and Noureddine A. Boudriga
Copyright © 2010 John Wiley & Sons, Inc.

| $v$ | 0.9000 | 0.9500 | 0.9750 | 0.9900 | 0.9950 | 0.9990 | 0.9995 |
|---|---|---|---|---|---|---|---|
| 13 | 1.350 | 1.771 | 2.160 | 2.650 | 3.012 | 3.852 | 4.221 |
| 14 | 1.345 | 1.761 | 2.145 | 2.624 | 2.977 | 3.787 | 4.140 |
| 15 | 1.341 | 1.753 | 2.131 | 2.602 | 2.947 | 3.733 | 4.073 |
| 16 | 1.337 | 1.746 | 2.120 | 2.583 | 2.921 | 3.686 | 4.015 |
| 17 | 1.333 | 1.740 | 2.110 | 2.567 | 2.898 | 3.646 | 3.965 |
| 18 | 1.330 | 1.734 | 2.101 | 2.552 | 2.878 | 3.610 | 3.922 |
| 19 | 1.328 | 1.729 | 2.093 | 2.539 | 2.861 | 3.579 | 3.883 |
| 20 | 1.325 | 1.725 | 2.086 | 2.528 | 2.845 | 3.552 | 3.850 |
| 21 | 1.323 | 1.721 | 2.080 | 2.518 | 2.831 | 3.527 | 3.819 |
| 22 | 1.321 | 1.717 | 2.074 | 2.508 | 2.819 | 3.505 | 3.792 |
| 23 | 1.319 | 1.714 | 2.069 | 2.50 | 2.807 | 3.485 | 3.768 |
| 24 | 1.318 | 1.711 | 2.064 | 2.492 | 2.797 | 3.467 | 3.745 |
| 25 | 1.316 | 1.708 | 2.060 | 2.485 | 2.787 | 3.450 | 3.725 |
| 26 | 1.315 | 1.706 | 2.056 | 2.479 | 2.779 | 3.435 | 3.707 |
| 27 | 1.314 | 1.703 | 2.052 | 2.473 | 2.771 | 3.421 | 3.690 |
| 28 | 1.313 | 1.701 | 2.048 | 2.467 | 2.763 | 3.408 | 3.674 |
| 29 | 1.311 | 1.699 | 2.045 | 2.462 | 2.756 | 3.396 | 3.659 |
| 30 | 1.31 | 1.697 | 2.042 | 2.457 | 2.750 | 3.385 | 3.646 |
| 60 | 1.296 | 1.671 | 2.000 | 2.423 | 2.660 | 3.307 | 3.460 |
| 90 | 1.291 | 1.662 | 1.987 | 2.390 | 2.632 | 3.232 | 3.402 |
| 120 | 1.289 | 1.658 | 1.980 | 2.358 | 2.617 | 3.160 | 3.373 |
| ∞ | 1.282 | 1.645 | 1.960 | 2.326 | 2.576 | 3.090 | 3.291 |

For $v \geq 30$ the quantiles of the standard normal distribution are good approximations.

# INDEX

*Fundamentals of Performance Evaluation of Computer and Telecommunication Systems,*
By Mohammad S. Obaidat and Noureddine A. Boudriga
Copyright © 2010 John Wiley & Sons, Inc.

Printed in the United States
By Bookmasters